P9-CRU-503

THE CULTURE FACTORY

THE URBAN LIFE IN AMERICA SERIES
RICHARD C. WADE, GENERAL EDITOR

LETITIA WOODS BROWN
FREE NEGROES IN THE DISTRICT OF COLUMBIA, 1790-1846
STANLEY BUDER
PULLMAN: An Experiment in Industrial Order and
Community Planning, 1880-1930
HOWARD P. CHUDACOFF
MOBILE AMERICANS: Residential and Social Mobility
in Omaha, 1880-1920
ALLEN F. DAVIS
SPEARHEADS FOR REFORM: The Social Settlements and
the Progressive Movement, 1890-1914
LYLE W. DORSETT
THE PENDERGAST MACHINE
JOSEPH M. HAWES
SOCIETY AGAINST ITS CHILDREN: Juvenile Delinquency
in Nineteenth-Century America
MELVIN G. HOLLI
REFORM IN DETROIT: Hazen S. Pingree and Urban Politics
KENNETH T. JACKSON
THE KU KLUX KLAN IN THE CITY, 1915-1930
PETER R. KNIGHTS
THE PLAIN PEOPLE OF BOSTON, 1830-1860: A Study in City Growth
ZANE L. MILLER
BOSS COX'S CINCINNATI: Urban Politics in the Progressive Era
RAYMOND A. MOHL
POVERTY IN NEW YORK, 1783-1825
HUMBERT S. NELLI
ITALIANS IN CHICAGO, 1890-1930: A Study in Ethnic Mobility
JAMES F. RICHARDSON
THE NEW YORK POLICE: Colonial Times to 1901
PETER SCHMITT
BACK TO NATURE: The Arcadian Myth in Urban America
STANLEY K. SCHULTZ
THE CULTURE FACTORY: Boston Public Schools, 1789-1860

THE CULTURE FACTORY

Boston Public Schools, 1789-1860

STANLEY K. SCHULTZ

NEW YORK
OXFORD UNIVERSITY PRESS
1973

For George M. Curtis III

Foreword

Americans have always placed immense importance on public education. More than the family or religion the school ultimately became the special repository of the values parents wanted their children to adopt and cherish. In a diverse society, particularly, education carried the shared attitudes and beliefs of many groups. Through the school doors passed the young, untrained, and uninformed; at the graduation exercises society put its ensignia on the student now ready to take his place in the democratic and competitive world before him. In the years between, young people learned not only reading, writing, and arithmetic, but also respect for the nation's past and its present culture, as well as the habits of promptness, orderliness, and self-discipline. *"The Common School,"* Horace Mann asserted with customary enthusiasm, "is the greatest discovery ever made by man. . . . Other social organizations are curative and remedial; this is a preventive and antidote." In short, education produced a future mother or father, a good citizen, and a dedicated American.

The ideal lay deep in the Republic's past, but it was put to a continuing test by the rapid urbanization of the country in the nineteenth century. Suddenly, with little warning, America's cities burst out of their historic confinement. The four decades after 1820 witnessed the fastest rate of urban growth the country had known or would ever see. The population spilled out over the old boundaries, and new areas were added to the old ones. Newcomers jammed into the historic heart of town. Every public facility was overwhelmed. The population quickly outstripped the available housing, and new construction lagged; water supplies and sewers were hopelessly inadequate; streets could no longer handle the traffic; remaining open space was filled by commercial, industrial, and residential buildings. Antebellum Americans felt the shock of the nation's first "urban explosion."

The impact on public education was particularly severe. The system was only in its infancy and in no condition to be inundated with new pupils and new responsibilities. Yet child populations mounted, requiring more teachers, more construction, and more money. In addition, educational leaders, concerned about the number of children out of school, tended to widen the category of students—emphasizing the post primary grades and experimenting with infant schools. More disturbing still, in Northern cities the problem was complicated by the rising proportion of immigrant children who came from families who were unfamiliar with American institutions and even with the language. Though educators looked abroad, especially to England and Germany, for guidance, the hard fact was that there was no foreign analogue for the nineteenth-century American city and its particular problems. Leaders here would have to devise their own system of mass public education in an urban setting.

This volume is a case study of that general problem—and a particularly important one. After all, Boston had pioneered in public education as early as the seventeenth century. In the first decades of the Republic, it prided itself on the extent and quality of its programs. As early as 1789, then redoubtable old Tory Fisher Ames could assert that "The New England people are better taught than any other and Boston better than any other city. I do not believe that any country has such judicious experiments for repelling barbarism, supporting government, and extending felicity." By 1820 opportunities were open to children from four to sixteen years in schools sustained by public taxation. Though attendance hovered around one-quarter of those eligible, the Massachusetts capital boasted the most extensive effort in the country.

Bostonians had already confronted a broad range of problems in achieving this result. But these successes were quickly dwarfed by the challenge of the next decades. The city's population jumped from 43,000 in 1820 to 178,000 in 1860. As a consequence the number of school-age children multiplied dramatically. In the primary grades alone, enrollment rose from 1,600 to over 12,000. Grammar school attendance increased proportionately. On the eve of the Civil War, total attendance passed the 25,000 mark.

The statistics, however, concealed the tough problems found by the School Committee. The most obvious was overcrowding. New construction could not keep up with the influx; makeshift quarters in stores, basements, and public buildings were fixed for classrooms. In 1833 a space investigation found that the average schoolroom measured nineteen feet by twenty-six feet and contained sixty-two students and one teacher.

Moreover, many were located in the densest and most rundown part of town where neighboring uses compromised educational objectives.

The problem was further complicated by the changing nature of the school population. The great Irish immigration dominated the Boston scene, especially in the last two ante-bellum decades. The foreign-born residents jumped from 5,000 to 64,000 and comprised one-third of the total in 1860. Those newcomers had no tradition of public education; most were illiterate and poor. Incorporating their children into Boston's system became the central task of the city. "It is a delicate point," one observer said warily, "to preserve the unity, continuity, and the predominance of the native interests."

If the School Committee's handling of immigrant children was gingerly, its approach to the black community was ambivalent. The numbers were small but the question large. The Negro population rose modestly during the four ante-bellum decades, but comprised only a fraction of the total. Yet policy had to be made in the context of the national debate over the institution of slavery. There was no doubt that black children should be taught, but was it to be separately or together with whites?

The other persistent problem was what to do with the growing number of children of the poor. It was well and good to have legislation proclaiming free education for all, but it was another thing to get families to send their young to schools with any regularity. There were always fees, parental resistance, and, of course, truancy which limited the number of poor children in classrooms. In addition, in a system which included youngsters from four to sixteen years old, only the most tenacious and fortunate could make it to final graduation.

In this volume Stanley Schultz describes and analyzes how one city met its obligations and ideals. Boston had always had a strong public tradition, but its great expansion in the nineteenth century placed an urgency on education that the town had not known before. The city fathers became increasingly apprehensive as the population grew and the number of idle and vagrant children multiplied. The fear of crime, violence, and disorder became a dominant concern of authorities. More and more, the author points out, education became a form of social insurance which protected society from serious consequences. Indeed, one contemporary described the effort "as a policy of insurance for our republican and protestant institutions. . . . Open, free, universal, these schools draw in the children of alien parentage with others, and assimilate them to the native born." They thus "grew up with the state by the state and for the state."

Constructing a comprehensive system in a city of high mobility was not easy, and there were few educational guidelines. Hence the authorities modeled their structure on the new factory system. The School Committee became the Board of Trustees: administrators the management, and the children the workers. The grade system, uniform texts, and a common curriculum were, so to speak, the interchangeable parts of this new arrangement. Gradually a bureaucracy emerged which gave permanence and stability—and, some said, boredom—to the entire enterprise.

In the process of establishing the system, the School Committee had to come to grips with perennial problems centralization or decentralization, neighborhood control or unitary decision-making, elected or appointed leadership. Mr. Schultz wisely refrains from drawing any cosmic conclusions from Boston's early struggle with these issues, but the irony does not escape him. Almost every issue now part of the contemporary educational "crisis" was found at the very beginnings of the nation's urban school system. Race, taxes, goals, religion, recruitment, and criticism were on the committee's daily agenda. There were even advocates of no schools at all who spoke the language of the despair of our own times. Indeed, the author ends his story with the Hub City on the eve of not only a Civil War but formidable educational problems.

Mr. Schultz's choice of Boston for a detailed investigation of the origins of a modern urban school system is a happy one. As an important colonial city, it pioneered in free public education; as an intellectual center, it early committed money and manpower to its educational effort; as a port city, it felt the first waves of Irish immigration; as a manufacturing town, it helped develop new factory and management practices; as a growing metropolis, it experienced the growing pains of the first "urban explosion." Moreover, its archives are rich in the materials needed to tell the story. The author exploits these advantages with skill and lucidity and in doing so illumines some of the present by his analysis of the past.

RICHARD C. WADE

New York, N.Y.   GENERAL EDITOR

December 1972   URBAN LIFE IN AMERICA SERIES

Preface

Public education in nineteenth-century America grew with the nation's cities. Rather than being a stepchild of European Enlightenment theory, or the offspring of domestic democratic trends in the age of the so-called "common man," the public school movement in the United States matured in response to what contemporaries viewed as an urban crisis. Rising crime rates, increasing pauperism, and spiraling juvenile delinquency signaled a moral dislocation in cities undergoing commercial and industrial transformation. Swarms of foreign immigrants challenged their capacity to accommodate and assimilate newcomers, as did the influx of white and black native migrants from the countryside and small towns. Everywhere the orderly patterns of existence appeared interrupted; the cities seemed to be overwhelmed by the rush of social change. Cities lacking institutionalized systems of orderly government—police departments, fire departments, centralized governmental bureaucracies—had to forge new tools to hammer out an urban discipline. A growing and increasingly diverse population; new industrial demands on the time and energy of citizens; cities bursting at the seams of their former boundaries; and social institutions like the family and the church dissolving in the heat of economic progress—all these disparate elements of urban life had to be adjusted and accommodated to each other. Between 1800 and 1860 those seeking a new urban discipline created as one of their most useful tools a system of public education. City leaders championed education to secure social order in a disorderly age.

During the four decades before the Civil War, Boston was the center of educational reform, occupying as it did the leading position in intellectual affairs and social reform efforts among antebellum cities. Over the years dominated by the reign of Horace Mann as the first Secretary of the State Board of Education (1837-48), Massachusetts in general and Boston in particular played the roles of midwife and governess to a system of public instruction that would find a home in other cities and towns of America. Both in formulating goals for the social reach of public education and in gradually erecting a bureaucratic structure to accomplish those goals, Boston leaders demonstrated to the rest of the nation the problems and promises of schooling urban Americans.

During the first two-thirds of the nineteenth century Boston spokesman for public schools designed an administrative structure to further their educational and social goals, to ensure unified control of the schools by themselves as an urban elite, and to process generations of children stamped out of the same mold, prepared, indeed conditioned, for life in the new urban America. They sought to create a hierarchy of schools for children of all ages, a structure that might truly be called a "system" in the comprehensive meaning of the word. Fortunately, they had close at hand a successful model of organizational skill. The enormous success of the factory system, under the direction of Francis Cabot Lowell and his "Boston Associates," kindled the imaginations of Boston educators and civic leaders. What, for shorthand purposes, might be labelled the "factory mentality" sparked the common school movement in the city and throughout New England. In the new methods of industrial organization the schoolmen saw the perfect model for retooling the schools to cope with such urban problems as population density, residential mobility, and the increasing numbers of rural native Americans and foreign immigrants whose arrival required innovative methods of assimilation to the routines of urban life. Boston leaders fashioned a system of schools and an educational bureaucracy in the hopes of imposing on the public a form of educational institution that I think can fairly be called "the culture factory."

Initially, I had hoped to write a comparative history of institutional change in the social orders of three nineteenth-century cities—Boston, Chicago, and St. Louis. Each was a major regional center; each experienced sudden alterations in population size and economic fortunes; each was a city of foreign immigrants as much as of "native" Americans. Further, since I had settled on public education as the most suitable "handle" by which to grasp the nature of institutional change in response to urban growth, the three cities provided a perfect opportunity; at different times each was the vanguard of educational reform during the nineteenth century. Having completed the research for Boston and Chicago, and having begun to gather material on St. Louis, I was struck with the paucity of respectable and useful historical writing on the establishment and growth of even one urban school system. Also, I was impressed by striking similarities between social and educational problems of our own times and those of the mid-nineteenth century. Issues of neighborhood schools and local control, racial and ethnic imbalance in student populations, redistribution of students among various schools in the city, burgeoning and unresponsive bureaucratic administration—these and other similarities belied our comfortable and comforting notions about one hundred years of educational progress. I became increasingly annoyed by present-day pontifications about public education as the principal weapon in the "war on poverty," for I had read too many similar statements by Bostonians in the 1830's and Chicagoans in the 1880's about schooling as the panacea for all social ills. I knew that the urban society of the nineteenth century differed fundamentally from that of the twentieth in many respects, but I also knew that then as now too many citizens seemed to place most of their hopes for social order in the basket of public education. And, one basket is not big enough to hold all of our social problems. In light of these findings and reflections, I abandoned the comparative study and chose instead to attempt a more thorough study of Boston as a model for analyzing the social role of public education in American cities. Perhaps this study will help us to understand where we have been, and how far we have to go if we are to use properly the public school as a means to social change.

Finally, a few words about the extent and limits of this study may prove useful. I have not included any lengthy discussion of the development of the high school during the period. Not that it was unimportant. Both Thomas Newman Barry, in his "Origin and Development of the American Public High School in the Nineteenth Century" (unpublished Ph.D. dissertation, Stanford University, 1962), and Michael Katz, in his more recent *The Irony of Early School Reform: Educational Innovation in Mid-Nineteenth Century Massachusetts* (Cambridge, Mass., 1968), have made helpful beginnings at showing us the significance of early efforts toward high school education. Still, the social reach of the high school was quite short. Few children attended such schools, and those who did were principally of the middle class. Since I was interested in telling the story of a social institution that attempted to touch the lives of most urban children, especially those of the poorer classes, I did not devote much attention to high school education.

Nor have I tried explicitly to evaluate the role of public schools in encouraging or discouraging social mobility, although suggestions on this subject in a book like Stephan Thernstrom's *Poverty and Progress: Social Mobility in a Nineteenth Century City* (Cambridge, Mass., 1964), demonstrate the value of that effort. Certainly educators repeatedly emphasized the role of the school in fostering social mobility. To the extent that schools succeeded in teaching lower-class native and immigrant children to read and write and to prize the "success ethic," they opened opportunities for social advancement. But I have not undertaken the task of "career-line" analysis which would illuminate the question of social mobility because I conceived my investigation as different in scope.

I have tried to show the development of public education as a social institution competing for attention, skills, and money with other urban social institutions. I hope I have imparted something of what it was like to be a child in school in the city during the first two-thirds of the nineteenth century. I have also attempted to relate the extension of formal schooling to contemporary thought about the nature of urban society and to a philosophy of individual moral behavior that appealed to men who were certain that the pace of city growth and population increase was outracing their best efforts to control it. Primarily this is a study in opinion and decision-making, an investigation of what men believed to be true, as much as one of what actually was true. I am convinced that when educational reformers advertised public schools as the best response to what they perceived as an "urban crisis," they believed their own rhetoric. But we must also remember that Horace Mann, George B. Emerson, Samuel Gridley Howe, and others were master propagandists who were not above exaggerating the extent of the "crisis" to further their cause. They knew, as a shrewd writer in 1846 observed, that "in our country the success of every moral enterprise must depend upon the favor of public opinion. If this can be secured, the cause, whatever it is, must triumph. It is to be expected, therefore, that the principal measures of reformers will be directed to the conciliation of this great and overbearing power." The public is willing to believe, the writer concluded, and too often reformers are willing to deceive, to distort the truth to gain their desired ends (*Christian Review*, XI, October 1846, 431).

I have tried to avoid imposing my own twentieth-century notions on the schoolmen of the nineteenth century—although occasionally I have slipped-up. They acted out of certain assumptions about the role of public education in challenging the problems of urban society that I cannot fully share, assumptions that Americans have begun only recently to question. I hope that my questioning of those assumptions has not shaded the telling of their story. I hope that I have done them justice or, if not, as little injustice as possible. The American faith in the saving social virtues of public education has been too strongly held to take lightly, or to render unfairly. For better, or perhaps for worse, the growth of mass public education over the past 150 years has absorbed much of our energy, imagination, and resources as a people. We might question the former, but never the latter influence on American society in Mark Twain's observation that "soap and education are not as sudden as a massacre, but they are more deadly in the long run."

For their cooperation in my research I owe special thanks to: Miss Helen Smith, in 1966 in charge of Inter-Library Loan Services, University of Chicago (where this study began as a doctoral dissertation); Mr. William J. Cunningham, Associate Superintendent of the Boston School Committee in 1966-67, for allowing me use of materials in the Boston School Committee Library; the staffs of the State Historical Society of Wisconsin, the Massachusetts Historical Society, Widener Library at Harvard University, and the Massachusetts State Archives—all of whom considerably eased the problems of research; and the Department of History, University of Chicago, the Center for Urban Studies, University of Chicago, and the Research Committee of the Graduate School of the University of Wisconsin for their financial support at various times over the past few years. For reading and criticizing portions or all of the manuscript I am grateful to: Professors Kenneth T. Jackson of Columbia University; William L. O'Neill of Rutgers University; Neil Harris and Arthur Mann of the University of Chicago; and Carl F. Kaestle of the University of Wisconsin. For many hours of stimulating conversation about the subject I wish especially to thank Steven Schlossman, currently a Ph.D. candidate at Columbia University. To four individuals I am most indebted: Professor Clifford S. Griffin of the University of Kansas who tried to teach me the meaning of the word "historian"; Professor Richard C. Wade of the City University of New York (formerly of the University of Chicago) who tried to teach me the meanings of the word "city," who first suggested looking into educational reform, and whose wisdom and patience have been a mainstay; Daniel J. Boorstin (formerly of the University of Chicago), Director of the Museum of History and Technology, Smithsonian Institution, who taught me the meanings of the verb "to think" and whose creativity, profundity, and wit as a scholar and a friend have challenged me at every turn; and last, but certainly far from least, my wife, Dorothea, whose editorial suggestions have immeasurably improved this book and whose patience with her plodding husband has been Sisyphean. Finally, I thank my sons, Christopher and Benjamin, who one day may learn what they have taught their father about childhood, family, and education.

Providence, R.I.   S.K.S.
December 1972

Contents

I. ORIGINS OF URBAN SCHOOLS

1. PIETY, PATRIOTISM, AND PUBLIC ORDER   3
   The Colonial Tradition   4
   The Conservative Persuasion   8
   The First Urban School System   14

2. THE SECULARIZATION OF PIETY, 1789-1820   22
   Charity Schools and Sunday Schools   25
   Public Rights and Primary Schools   30
   The Choice Depositories of a Free People   38

II. SOCIETY AND SCHOOLS

3. SOCIAL STABILITY AND PUBLIC SCHOOLS   47
   The Discovery of the Child   48
   The Decline of the Family   55
   The Crumbling Foundations of Christian Order   60
   The Ark of Safety   66

4. SCHOOLHOUSES AND SCHOLARS   69
   Expectations and Realities   72
   From Country to City   79
   Health, Ill Health, and the Rural Ideal   92

III. THE MACHINERY OF PUBLIC EDUCATION

5. NEIGHBORHOODS AND GRADED SCHOOLS   103
   A Standardized Product   105
   Patterns of Population   109
   The Neighborhood School and Local Control   114
   Graded Schools for the City   125

6. A WANT OF SYMMETRY: THE BEGINNINGS OF BUREAUCRACY   132
   An Administrative Oligarchy   133
   In Search of Reform: The Election Battle of 1845   138
   The Promise of Professionalism   141
   Beginning a Bureaucracy   145

IV. SEGREGATION AND INTEGRATION:
BLACKS IN PUBLIC SCHOOLS
   7. BLACK SCHOOLS IN WHITE BOSTON   157
      Segregation by Choice   159
      From Private to Public Segregation   162
      Integration by Demand: The Beginnings of Protest   168
   8. SEPARATE-BUT-EQUAL SCHOOLS?
      WHITE ABOLITIONISTS AND BLACK EDUCATION   176
      Abolitionists Join the Black Cause   178
      The Cause Accelerates   184
      The School Committee Stands Its Ground   195
      Separate-But-Equal Schools: The Roberts Case   200
      The Cause Triumphs   203

V. POVERTY, IMMIGRATION, AND PUBLIC MORALITY
   9. POVERTY AND THE URBAN CRISIS   209
      Fear of the Stranger   210
      Who Are the Poor?   214
      The Permanence of Urban Poverty   224
      The Immigrant Poor and Community Order   231
      The Immigrant Poor and Urban Disorder   237
      A Child's Garden of Vices   242
   10. EDUCATION FOR THE LOWER CLASSES   252
      Education as Social Insurance   253
      Public Schools for the Urban Poor   261
      Monitorial Schools for the Poor   263
      Separate Schools for Vagrant Children   268
      The Abortive Kindergarten   271
      Preventing Innovation: The Textbook War   274
   11. THE PITFALLS OF COERCION:
      THE STATE VERSUS THE CHILDREN OF POVERTY   278
      Patterns of Immigrant Attendance   279
      The Trials of Truancy   291
      Who Owns the Child?   302

List of Abbreviations   311

Notes   311

Index   385

Maps

1. Social Geography of Boston, 1845-1850   112
2. Location of Boston Grammar Schools, 1837   124
3. Distribution of Negroes and Location of Segregated Schools, 1850   188
4. Core and Periphery Wards of Boston, with Central Business District, 1830-1850   218
5. Distribution of Foreign Children, Ages 5-15   285
6. Location of Boston Grammar Schools, By Ward, 1850   287

Figures

1. The Principles of Piety   17
2. Deciding Upon the People's Education!!!   77
3. A Ragged Beggar Sleeping   78
4. A Civilized Place   84
5. Classrooms and Other Rooms   87
6. A Very Commodious Building   89
7. The Uncovered Schoolroom   95
8. Pure Air for Pure Minds   97
9. A Model Plan   98
10. For Endless Improvement   170
11. A Natural Setting   222
12. A Perfect Hive of Human Beings   223

Tables

1. Boston Expenditures on Schools as Per Cent of City Budget, 1820-1865   80
2. Enrollment and Expenses of Boston Schools, 1840-1860   81
3. Distribution of Boston Youth by Ages, 1810-1855   110
4. Sexual Segregation and Redistribution of Students, 1837   121
5. Negro Population of Boston, 1800-1860   189
6. Population of Boston and Its Annexes   211
7. Per Cent Gain in Native and Foreign Population, 1820-1860   213
8. Native and Foreign Population of Boston by Percentage, 1840-1855 (Per Cent)   215
9. Nativity of Bostonians, 1850-1855   215
10. Population Distribution in Core and Periphery Wards of Natives and Foreigners, 1825-1850   219
11. Daily Schedule for Children in House of Reformation, 1838   244
12. Children in the Boston House of Reformation, 1826-1847   247
13. Sentences of Children in the House of Reformation, 1846-1850   249
14. Enrollment in Boston Public Primary and Grammar Schools, 1840-1860   280
15. Boston Children by Wards, 1850   282
16. Vagrant and Truant Children in Boston, 1849   299

I

ORIGINS OF URBAN SCHOOLS

1

Piety, Patriotism, and Public Order

. . . The New England people are better taught than any other, and Boston better than any other city. . . . I do not believe that any country has such judicious expedients for repelling barbarism, supporting government, and extending felicity.

Fisher Ames (1789)[1]

Shortly before the outbreak of the American Civil War, the Massachusetts Board of Education convened to review the progress of schools and society over the past two centuries. Meeting in a time when a clash of two cultures (the North and the South) threatened national unity and when repeated outbreaks of violence within cities promised perpetual social disorder, the educators wistfully recalled the spirit of social cooperation that had marked the early founding of public schools. "For nearly two hundred years," claimed the Board, "our system of free schools was sustained directly by the people, without special care or direct aid from the government. . . . The people were then homogeneous; the sentiment in favor of education was universal; deficiencies in the schools, when they existed, were often supplied by instruction in the family." The system was not complete, the Board conceded, "yet the results are worthy of all praise." But recent events had brought to a close the golden age of social harmony. The most dramatic and dangerous challenge to social unity, warned the Board, lay in the rapid growth of industrial cities. Over the past three decades or so: the population of cities had increased substantially; immigrants from alien cultures had streamed into the country; manufacturing enterprises had created new labor markets that attracted outsiders into the cities; children unfortunately had become valuable as laborers; prosperity had concentrated wealth for the few and compounded poverty for the many. As a result, "the public schools were losing their efficiency, and the system itself its vitality." With the decline of public schools came an inevitable rise in community conflict, for, like educators elsewhere in the nation the Massachusetts schoolmen revered public edu-

3

cation as a vital institution for maintaining group harmony and social discipline. "Patriotic and good men" had become alarmed about the direction in which society was headed and had organized a Board of Education to foster a revival of public schools. To restore piety, patriotism, and public order these good men called for a return to that golden past when all classes of citizens had supported schools as founts of learning and social harmony. They wished to restore education to "that place and interest which it must have among a free people, if their institutions are to be either enjoyed or perpetuated."[2]

But, like most men who discover in the past the salvation of the present and the hope of the future, educators in mid-nineteenth-century Boston had embellished the historical truth. Municipal governments had long devoted "special care" to educational provisions; urban populations had never been "homogeneous"; deficiencies in schools were not unusual. The organization of public schools in American cities was less the result of a vague "universal sentiment" about the glories of piety and learning than an expression of pragmatic means for meeting the needs of an ever-expanding urban society. From the founding of Boston in 1630 through the late years of the eighteenth century, political leaders and educators tried to create a system of public schools. Their motives often varied, as did their methods, but one fact remained certain: all agreed that public schools were essential agencies for securing social stability and order.

THE COLONIAL TRADITION

Early Boston settlers brought with them attitudes, laws, customs, traditions, and government which typified middle-class English gentry. They came in an age devoted to education. Early seventeenth-century England was the beneficiary of a Tudor educational revolution that had sparked the founding of schools in shire and city alike. Private schools were many, sponsored by monasteries, cathedrals, and guilds. Private benevolence contributed huge sums for the founding of independent schools. In addition, Elizabethan government often forced towns to set aside lands or to collect taxes for school maintenance. To supplement town funds, parents of scholars donated fees and tuition. This mixture of clerical influence, private philanthropy, and the civil government in the support of education carried over into the young Puritan colony and wherever else Englishmen settled in the New World.[3]

More than a decade before the General Court of Massachusetts passed the famous "ould deluder Satan" law (1647) requiring town support of public education, a number of "richer inhabitants" of Boston donated funds toward the maintenance of a free school in the community. As early as 1635 Boston leaders hired the town's first schoolmaster for the "nurturing of children with us," although the man's brand of piety soon came into question when he chose the wrong side in the Antinomian Controversy and in 1638 left the community. Undaunted by their theological miscue, the members of the Town Meeting chose another teacher to carry on the noble experiment. By 1645 Bostonians deemed necessary a formal schoolhouse, as well as a house for the master. The town supplied both through special levies on merchants. To provide a permanent endowment, the Town Meeting voted land-grant support to education. By the mid-1640's tax support for public schooling had become one of the town's largest expenditures. Boston's experience exemplified that of other communities throughout New England, for other towns—including Dorchester, Roxbury, Ipswich, Dedham, Salem, and Charlestown—had followed essentially the same evolution of financial support from private subscription, tuition, rents, and grants of land to a more formal settlement of town rates.[4]

Once determined, the commitment to public education kept pace with the town's growth. By the close of the seventeenth century Boston leaders had founded two writing schools, modeled after the English petty schools, which taught basic reading and writing. During the early years of the eighteenth century the city fathers established another writing school and a public grammar school (traditionally for instruction in Latin, Greek, and Hebrew) in the populous North End. By 1720 the city contained five public schools, one in each principal section of the city. To be sure, far more private schools and academies served the city and enterprising private teachers, like their counterparts in New York City, Philadelphia, and London, offered a multiplicity of subjects ranging from surveying and navigation to dancing and needlework. Yet, at a time when private schoolmasters peddling their wares largely controlled formal education in Philadelphia and New York City, in Boston the promoters of public education had a firm foundation upon which to build. In colonial urban America, Boston led the way in public schooling.[5]

Initially the terms "public school" and "free school" referred to a Latin grammar school modeled after those in England. But during the early years of the eighteenth century a "free school" came to mean a publicly supported institution offering instruction in the basics of reading, penmanship, and arithmetic, and open to every child. In actual practice throughout New England, however, "free schools" were not always free. In Salem schools were free only to poor children, in Roxbury free to the subscribers' youth, in Dedham free to all children. Boston, traditionally suspicious of strangers, gave the word its own specific meaning. While

non-residents of the city had to pay tuition fees to enter their children
in the public schools, the city expected but did not require a small pay-
ment for "entrance and fire money" (for winter fuel) from residents with
children. Tax funds supported these "free" writing schools as well as the
Latin grammar school. The city thus hoped to ensure that no child would
be denied schooling because of poverty. Children of the "inferior" and
"middling" classes could attend free public schools. They rarely enrolled
in the grammar school which remained the province of children of
wealthier citizens, and required a tuition fee to supplement tax funds.[6]

The attention devoted to public education in Boston went beyond financial support. The city fathers accepted responsibility for maintaining educational institutions and for preserving their quality. Until 1710 the
Selectmen (akin to city councilmen) inspected and governed the schools.
After that year, however, Boston leaders, demonstrating an early recognition that public education required specialized administration, appointed
a committee of five leading citizens to visit and report periodically on the
condition of the schools. The most prominent members of the committee
usually were ministers. Clerical appointments underscored the intimate
connection between piety and learning perceived by eighteenth-century
New Englanders and attested the social importance and prestige enjoyed
by churchmen in the Puritan commonwealth. Of equal importance to residents of an urban outpost in the wilderness, clergymen generally were
the best-educated citizens and the most capable administrators.[7]

The efforts of Boston leaders to ensure educational quality reflected the
high value which they, and other colonial Americans, placed upon formal
education. Certainly, as historians have observed, the colonists did not
underestimate the educational roles played by family and church. Contemporary accounts left us by such luminaries as minister Cotton Mather,
merchant Samuel Sewall, and planter William Byrd, as well as formal
treaties like the Reverend Samuel Haven's *Preaching Christ the Great
Business of the Gospel-Ministry* (1760), stressed the importance of family
and church in instructing the young in piety and learning. Nonetheless,
to make certain that children became literate, eighteenth-century colonists in port cities and interior towns alike undertook numerous projects to
provide formal instruction. The frontier town of Kent, Connecticut, for
example, no less than cosmopolitan New York or Philadelphia, organized
within three years of its founding in 1739 a formal school in which all the
children of the community received an English education. In Boston the
commitment to formal schooling was so strongly held that even self-
serving politicians had to bow in its direction. In the seventeen-teens
young Elisha Cooke, Jr., organizer of the Boston Caucus, a proto-political
party, proposed to found a private bank of credit in the city. To help gain

public approval for the new venture, Cooke and his associates promised to contribute a portion of their profits to a charity school in the city, to Harvard College, to a scholarship fund for the sons of ministers, and to grammar schools throughout the province. Literacy training through formal education was so prized in the book-mart of the colonies that John Usher, the city's leading bookseller, often divided his orders to London between religious books and schoolbooks. In what certainly must have been one of the earliest evidences of a "correspondence course" in the country, Caleb Phillips, a private teacher in Boston in the 1720's, advertised that "Any persons in the Country desirous to Learn this Art [Short Hand], may by having the several Lessons sent Weekly to them, be as perfectly instructed as those that live in Boston."[8]

The excellence of Boston's schools derived from the public's vital interest in education. Puritanism demanded an educated clergy and a literate citizenry, able to read and interpret the Scriptures; a growing commercial center required men who could keep and understand ledgers and inventories. Throughout much of the eighteenth century, therefore, the Town Meeting voted an average of 16 per cent of its total expenses for support of schools. Rarely did residents begrudge the cost. In 1751, in response to the one serious complaint by some citizens about the sizable expenditures, a select committee reaffirmed the commitment of the town to public education. The town could and must afford the cost for "the Education of Children is of the greatest Importance to the Community."[9]

For the decade and a half immediately preceding the American Revolution the superiority of the Boston public schools remained unchallenged in spite of the city's loss in population and a period of economic recession. Between 1760 and 1766, the five public schools annually trained more than nine hundred boys, a number which was nearly 6 per cent of the entire population.[10] Parents throughout New England sent their children for instruction in the Boston public schools and in the numerous private academies and boarding schools of the city.

With the coming of the Revolution, however, matters changed. Like that of other New Englanders, the concern of Bostonians for public education gave way to the mounting needs of war preparation. The schools closed. Recalling his youth, for example, Harrison Gray Otis, later a mayor of Boston and a prominent Federalist, reported that he entered the old Latin School in Boston in July 1773 at the age of seven years and nine months. "I attended school from that time until April, 1775 (the day of the Lexington battle). . . ."[11] With the city under siege Otis and other children had an uncommon excuse for not attending school. During the years of the war public schools in Boston and throughout Massachusetts shut down as schoolmasters entered the army and as battle destroyed schoolhouses. Not until 1779 could Otis and most other children return to formal education.[12]

Following the Revolution, communities throughout the commonwealth abandoned earlier attempts at maintaining public schools. A dispersed population, one of the many results of the Revolution, made an educational system difficult to reinstate. Taxpayers were reluctant to vote money for schools when other needs—rebuilding the towns and reinvigorating commerce—appeared more pressing. Many towns discontinued all public support of Latin grammar schools and of general rudimentary education. Most towns failed to comply with the long-standing Law of 1647 requiring such support, and the Commonwealth failed to enforce the law.[13]

Still, state leaders remained convinced that schooling was a necessary public responsibility. The new Massachusetts state constitution, ratified in 1780, stressed the importance of education in attempting "to countenance and inculcate the principles of humanity and general benevolence, public and private charity, industry and frugality, honesty and punctuality, . . . sincerity, good humor, and all social affections, and generous sentiments, among the people." These virtues, of course, were important to a people living in the afterglow of seventeenth-century Puritanism. Indeed, these sentiments were strikingly similar to the depiction of a "Christian Calling" given by the Massachusetts divine John Cotton in his widely read *The Way of Life* (1641). But the social role ascribed to education by the Constitution of 1780 was more than a mere reflection of past Puritan principles. The document tacitly acknowledged the necessity of schooling to promote social order in a society becoming increasingly urban.[14]

THE CONSERVATIVE PERSUASION

The chief architect of that constitution, and its accompanying Bill of Rights, was John Adams. For some years prior to 1780 Adams had promoted state-supported public education. Like other men of the Revolutionary generation, Adams believed that the chief purpose of education was to produce young men devoted to America and to its political, moral, and religious institutions.[15] Accomplishing this task was especially important in Boston and other towns of the commonwealth. There, mob riots showed most clearly the forces of social disorder; there, as his wife Abigail lamented in a letter to him, "the poorer sort of children are wholly neglected, and left to range the Streets without Schools, without Business, given up to all Evil."[16] Employing Boston as a yardstick for measuring social change in Massachusetts, Adams noted that the simplicity of life in his youth was no more. Walking through the city streets, he complained, "my Eyes are so diverted with Chimney Sweeps, Carriers of Wood, Merchants, Ladies, Priests, Carts, Horses, Oxen, Coaches, Market men and Women, Soldiers, Sailors, and my Ears with the Rattle Gabble of them all that I cant think long enough in the Street upon any one Thing to start and pursue a Thought. I cant raise my mind above this mob Croud of Men, Women, Beasts and Carriages, to think steadily." Worse still, he observed on another occasion, were the numerous public houses and taverns which were the centers of political corruption and the breeding grounds of "Violations of the Peace and order of society. . . . Quarrells, Boxing, Duels, oaths, Curses, affrays and Riots, are daily hatching from Eggs and Spawns, deposited in the same Nests." To combat these evils of urban life Adams proposed public schools, together with churches and the militia, to form "the Virtues and Talents of the People."[17]

When Adams drafted the constitution of 1780, therefore, he emphasized the duty of the state to provide public education to inculcate all citizens with principles necessary for the maintenance of public order. "Public and private charity," "industry and frugality," "honesty and punctuality" were all virtuous principles when viewed as abstractions; they were necessary traits of character for citizens living in a commercial city with a diverse social structure. In addition, the Bill of Rights in the Massachusetts constitution required towns and cities to provide financially for "the public worship of God and the support and maintenance of public Protestant teachers of piety, religion, and morality," in schools.[18] For Adams and others disturbed by the evidences of social disorder the school and the church were the guardians of social order.

Many Bostonians shared this view of education. They believed that general schooling was vitally important in maintaining a moral, productive, God-fearing society. In 1784 a town committee report emphasized the role which many citizens believed the schools should play:

> Our free schools seem to have been interested for the Benefit of the Poor and the Rich; that the Children of all, partaking of equal Advantages and being placed upon an equal Footing, no Distinction might be made among them in the Schools on account of the different Circumstances of their Parents, but that the Capacity & natural Genius of each might be cultivated & improved for the future Benefit of the whole Community.

A willingness to spend money for schools underscored their commitment, for many other matters demanded attention. During the 1780's the return of old inhabitants and an influx of newcomers contributed to a boomtown atmosphere in the city. Financial difficulties clouded the air of expansion and progress. A need for economy therefore curtailed public spending to only the indispensable items. Among these necessities citizens voted the largest sums to highways, poor relief, and public education. There were few other places in Massachusetts, or in the rest of the new nation, where public education was as highly regarded.[19]

In 1789, when the New England states entered the new Union, various spokesmen for education were calling for an extension of public schooling on both the local and national levels. The famed Northwest Ordinance of 1787 had incorporated the New England view that "religion, morality, and knowledge being necessary to good government and the happiness of mankind, schools and the means of education shall forever be encouraged," and, following the Land Ordinance of 1785, had reserved one lot in every township for public education. Six other states, in their new constitutions, followed the lead of Massachusetts in providing for public education. Prominent citizens in New England and throughout the young nation joined in celebrating the conservative influence that public education could have in subduing the vices and encouraging the virtues of individuals living under a republican form of government.[20]

The most cogent statement of this viewpoint came from Noah Webster, the lexicographer, teacher, and author of successful school textbooks. In his essay "On the Education of Youth in America" (1787-88) Webster stressed that the education of youth underlay the moral characters of individuals, who in turn united to compose the general character of a nation. For the new nation, he wrote, "our national character is not yet formed." The opportunity should be grasped to mold that character and to organize a correct system of schools so that we "may implant in the minds of the American youth the principles of virtue and of liberty and inspire them with just and liberal ideas of government and with an inviolable attachment to their own country." If youthful minds could be kept untainted, Webster asserted, the moral character of adults would be unblemished.

That he believed a proper system of education was especially important in the growing cities was evident in Webster's remark that "large cities are always scenes of dissipation and amusement, which have a tendency to corrupt the hearts of youth and divert their minds from their literary pursuits." Curricula, he suggested, should be designed to train youth in cities for the "mercantile line" so that children could mature as moral and useful citizens. Webster maintained that those evils which threatened the tranquility of republican society—crime, drunkenness, and debauchery—could be expunged through education. Schooling could operate as an engine of social discipline. "The only practicable method to reform mankind is to begin with children," Webster claimed. If children were taught to love their country, obedience would be the result. If they

were taught to reverence law, prisons would be unnecessary. If they were
taught the proper principles of morality, they could resist "secret corruption and brazen libertinism." "Education," Webster thus urged, "should
be the first care of a legislature."[21] Over the next half-century his sentiments would be repeated until they became the foundation of an educational liturgy.

Agreeing with those sentiments, Massachusetts lawmakers enacted
in 1789 the first comprehensive state school law in the new nation.
The law required every town to support an elementary school for six
months out of twelve. Larger towns having one hundred families or more
had to maintain at least one school the year around. Grammar schools
had to be provided in communities containing two hundred families or
more. Elementary teachers had to be certified as educationally prepared
and morally fit. Towns with dispersed populations, particularly those in
the most rural areas, received aid through the authorization of a district
school system, with financial support for the districts coming from public
funds dispensed through the Town Meetings.[22]

The new law only confirmed the established practices of half a century. Still, conservative leaders took pride in their accomplishment.
Daniel Cony, a Boston Federalist, happily reported to George Thatcher,
the eminent Massachusetts congressman and jurist, that "the two houses
have newly agreed on a 'School Bill' which I believe embraces one of the
greatest and most important objects, that belongs to the business of
legislators."[23]

Some months after the enactment of the statewide law, Boston passed
a new school law, which remained unaltered for almost forty years. Its
provisions governed public education in the city during the formative
years of the nation, and during years of quickening population growth and
expansion of the city's physical boundaries. Throughout the decades of
bustling change, the schools of Boston struggled to keep pace with the
population, always laboring under the weight of a law which became
more outmoded with each passing year. Yet, when first introduced, the
Education Act of 1789 promised to order the chaotic mixture of public
and private schools then competing for students. It also offered a tool for
fashioning social harmony and a sense of community among the various
classes of citizens. Still, the Act did not pass uncontested.

In 1789 there were men of a conservative persuasion in the city who
questioned whether any alterations in the present scheme of education
were necessary. Fisher Ames, publicist and celebrated leader of the
Boston Federalists, for example, believed that "the New England people
are better taught than any other, and Boston better than any other
city. . . . I do not believe," he stated in 1789, "that any country has

such judicious expedients for repelling barbarism, supporting government, and extending felicity." Federalists like Ames and John Adams, among others, feared that too much tinkering with established social institutions might undermine the respect necessary for authority in society and government. One of the bulwarks of the authority of the dominant classes in Massachusetts—that "cordial union between the clergy, the magistracy, the bench and bar, and respectable society throughout the State" as historian Henry Adams later described it—had long been the educational system.[24]

Despite his urgings for state-supported public education, John Adams maintained that the vast majority of mankind was doomed to intellectual and moral inferiority. Schooling, he implied, would train men of good birth, wealth, and talent for their appropriately dominant role in government and society. On other men education could impose a respect for order, obedience, and subordination. "The increase and dissemination of knowledge," Adams asserted, "instead of rendering unnecessary the checks of emulation and the balances of rivalry in the orders of society and constitution of government, augment the necessity of both. It becomes the more indispensable that every man should know his place, and be made to keep it." Education alone, Adams cautioned, was not the panacea for all social problems. Those who wished to interfere with established institutions and to innovate a new social order were victims of their own illusions. "The modern improvers of society,—ameliorators of the condition of mankind, instructors of the human species,—have assumed too much," Adams proclaimed. "They have . . . undertaken to build a new universe."

The implications for educational reform were clear. A frontal attack on the current method of organizing schools was an indirect foray on the products of those schools, the members of the ruling classes in the city and throughout the state. Federalists like Adams and Ames believed that schooling should be provided for all classes in society, but they also believed that control of the schools had to remain among men like themselves. Only then would educational institutions serve the purpose for which they had been created—the inculcation of proper social behavior. To turn the governing of the schools over to the people themselves, to alter in the name of democracy the established procedures, would be to invite catastrophe. "Remember," John Adams once warned in another context, "democracy never lasts long. It soon wastes, exhausts, and murders itself."[25]

But it was precisely a more democratic control of the public schools that proponents of a new scheme of education in the city were demanding. Leading the fight was the old warhorse of the Revolution, Sam

Adams. For some years prior to 1789, Adams had campaigned actively for a new organization of the schools. Adams himself was a product of Boston schools, having attended the Latin School. In his old age, however, he worried that such an elite institution, along with the numerous private academies that abounded in the city, would subvert the general value of the common school and would foster invidious distinctions between the poor and the rich. Like his distant cousin John, Sam Adams believed that the state should provide education for its citizens and that schooling was vital to the process of training free men to be responsible supporters of republican government. The two men differed only on the question of who should direct educational enterprises in the city. Consistent with his past career, Sam Adams wanted to broaden the scope of public participation in what he conceived a public activity. He sought the election of overseers of the schools by popular vote.

In September 1789 the Town Meeting appointed a committee of one man from each ward to draft a new system for the organization and supervision of the schools. Owing to advertisements for himself, Sam Adams was among the twelve leading citizens serving on the committee. His presence portended an equalitarian outcome to the committee's deliberations; it ensured a controversial atmosphere for the committee's debates. Adams was not, as his bitter Loyalist enemy Peter Oliver described him, "so thorough a Machiavellian that he devested himself of every worthy principle," but he was a shrewd enough politician to attempt to muster support privately for his viewpoints. Perhaps it was to Adams that Fisher Ames referred when he wrote his friend George Richards Minot: "the subject [of school politics] is important, and merits a more manly independency of conduct than you have described. These sneaking fellows are their own commentators. . . . Public clamor is employed as a means of effecting the removal of that resistance which the unpopular man makes to their will."[26]

Whether Adams was directly responsible for stimulating debate, certainly a "public clamor" attended the deliberations of the appointed committee. Townsmen appeared determined to lobby the committee, to exert more direct control over the operation of the schools, and to ensure a particular kind of training for all children. Typical of letters to the newspapers supporting a reorganization of the schools was one signed "Cato." The writer cautioned against relying solely on intellectual learning as the chief objective of education; memorized facts (which then passed for "intellectual learning") would not guarantee good citizenship. The habits of children must be trained, stressed the writer, so that as adults they habitually would exercise "patriotism, economy, prudence and manly pursuits." Education was "to elevate the minds of the people to objects worthy of the pursuit and attention of a creature as rational and dignified as man."

Citizens of Boston shared, for their children, the same educational hopes that such men as Webster and John Adams entertained for the nation. To preserve a new nation the virtues of patriotism, economy, and prudence were vital. They were no less important for the expanding population of the city. Education was today's bulwark against the vagaries of tomorrow.[27]

Sam Adams and his committee reported to the Town Meeting in September 1789. After brief discussion, the suggested bill was passed.

THE FIRST URBAN SCHOOL SYSTEM

With the Education Act of 1789, Boston laid the foundation of the first comprehensive system of public schools in any American city. In reorganizing the loose system of schools already existing, the Act of 1789 dealt with male and female schooling; the types of schools to be provided; revisions in the curricula; the uniformity of instruction throughout the city; and the formation of a permanent school committee.[28]

One innovation of the Act was the first formal provision in the city's history for the schooling of girls at public expense. During the colonial period many women were literate, but they had received their education in private schools. More often than not, girls and boys did not attend the same private school together. During the years immediately preceding the Act of 1789, however, agitation for coeducational schools had begun. Bostonians were quite familiar with the widely distributed essay *Thoughts upon Female Education*, published in 1787 by the Philadelphia physician and reformer Benjamin Rush. He had argued that girls should be educated at public expense. According to Rush, women had to become the stewards and guardians of their husbands' property in a day when men had to engage in several occupations to advance their fortunes. Moreover, because of a lack of decent servants in America, women had to attend to the private affairs of their families more than was the case in Great Britain. Finally, because the principal share of the instruction of children devolved upon women, they had to be educated so that they in turn could instruct their sons in the principles of liberty and government.[29]

Bostonians agreed with these sentiments in letters to newspapers in the months before passage of the Education Act of 1789. Correspondents emphasized the need for public schooling for girls, stating that some day those girls would exert the major influences upon the men of the Republic. To the reasons advanced by Rush, Bostonians added one more.

Not only should girls be educated at the taxpayers' expense, but they should attend school with boys. It was more democratic to educate both sexes together.[30]

The Act of 1789, therefore, provided that girls were to go to school with boys and to study the same subjects. Yet, girls were required to be in school fewer hours per day—and only from April to October—while boys were to attend year around, except for a brief vacation. Despite the rhetoric about the moral role of motherhood and wifely responsibilities, clearly it was still a man's world.

The Act also attempted to establish a system of schools, each school having its own function. Continuing the tradition of a classical education, the Act provided for at least one school to teach Greek and Latin. This was to "fully qualify" pupils for the universities. Separate reading and writing schools were to be located at the south, the center and the north end of the town. These were to offer instruction in English grammar, spelling, writing, and arithmetic, including "vulgar and decimal fractions." Within the vague educational hierarchy of the times, these could be called secondary schools. No provisions existed for primary schools. Students entered the grammar schools at the age of seven and could remain until fourteen. Children under the age of seven either attended a private "dames' school," received training as apprentices to a master, or learned from their parents at home. The formulators of the Act saw little reason to interfere with these arrangements.

The Act required students to be at least ten years old and to have received prior instruction in English grammar before entering the Latin School. Most children who attended the Latin School came from the upper ranks of Boston society. Usually they attended private institutions before enrolling in the Latin School. They might have learned the rudiments of English grammar in the private schools, but, because of the incompetency of many private masters, apparently few did. Before the legislation of 1789, masters teaching in the various public schools customarily gave outside private instruction in grammar and penmanship to supplement the poor training in many private schools. Students entering the Latin School thus had acquired the necessary skills in grammar without attending public schools. But the Act (and subsequent legislation) expressly forbad the practice of private tutoring. Students entering the Latin School could attend the public schools for two hours a day, either in the morning or afternoon, to make up their deficiencies. Those few children who took advantage of this "privilege" often had to neglect one school to attend the other.[31]

By requiring training in grammar, the authors of the Act hoped to encourage the public school attendance of those children who otherwise would have enrolled only in private schools. In effect, students entering the Latin School had to spend time with other children of their neighborhoods in public schools. Since the physical boundaries of the town remained closely knit there was little residential separation of social classes. Children of various backgrounds therefore tended to mingle together in the schools.[32]

The Act of 1789 established not only a hierarchical structure of schools, it attempted as well to impose a uniform system of instruction throughout Boston. Schools were open all year. Class hours, between April and October, were 7:30 a.m. to 11 a.m., lunch recess until 2 p.m., then class again until 5 p.m.; during the winter months classes began an hour later in the morning and concluded one-half hour earlier in the afternoon. In alternate months students attended reading schools during the morning and writing schools during the afternoon. Instruction in grammar, composition, reading, spelling, and arithmetic was common to all the schools. Central to the curriculum were the principles of piety and deference to the social order.

Since the 1690's in Boston the teaching of reading and religion had united in *The New England Primer*. A primer originally was a book of private devotions, but as used in the schools *The New England Primer* was a public sermon. Combining the alphabet, secular and religious jingles, and priggish short stories on the "nature of true virtue," the *Primer* inculcated principles of piety in generations of young New Englanders. Following the Revolution it gradually dropped out of use in the cities, but as late as 1806 remained the standard text in Boston's dames' schools for young children.[33] For children who attended the public schools, the Act of 1789 required readers other than the *Primer*—readers which nevertheless presented in more sophisticated terms such spurs to industriousness as the *Primer*'s "the idle Fool Is whipt at School," and acceptance of authority as "Job feels the Rod, Yet blesses God."

Among the readers chosen for spelling, grammar, and composition, were the *Child's Companion* (a slightly modified *Primer*), *Beauties of the Bible*, *American Preceptor* by Caleb Bingham, and *An American Selection*, the third part of Noah Webster's larger work, *Grammatical Institute*. Each of these attempted to instill in students a sense of piety and obedience to established authority. In addition to selections from the Bible and noted Puritan sermons, Bingham's *American Preceptor* presented patriotic homilies by writers of "American genius." Bingham did not include any romantic fiction, being "convinced of the impropriety of inftilling falfe notions into the minds of children. . . . The compiler pledges himfelf, that this book contains neither a word nor a fentiment which would 'raife a blufh on the cheek of modefty.'" Students who used Webster's reader were constantly reminded that religion and patriotism were the chief pillars of American society. "How little of our peace and security," read one passage, "depends on REASON and how much on *religion and government.*"[34]

Let Children who would fear the LORD,
Hear what their Teachers fay,
With rev'rence meet their Parents' word,
And with delight obey.

A — In Adam's Fall
We finned all.

B — Thy Life to mend,
God's Book attend.

C — The Cat doth play,
And after flay.

D — A Dog will bite
A Thief at Night.

E — The Eagle's Flight
Is out of Sight.

F — The idle Fool
Is whipt at School.

Figure 1 "THE PRINCIPLES OF PIETY"

These two illustrations from the *Boston Primer,* nineteenth-century successor to the *New England Primer,* exemplify the mixture of religious and secular materials in children's schoolbooks; they reveal a fascinating blend of realism (the cat) and idealism (children's duties).

SOURCE: *The Boston Primer* (1808) in Houghton Library; used by permission of Harvard University Libraries.

The authors of the Act intended the public schools to foster private and public morality. The choice of reading matter underscored this role; so did the performance expected of the teacher. The master was to begin each day by leading the class in prayer, and then he would read from a portion of Scripture. Shortly after the passage of the Act, a set of resolutions for teachers approved by the Town Meeting emphasized this duty. On December 14, 1789, the Meeting voted "that it be the indispensable duty of the several Schoolmasters, daily to commence the duties of their office by prayer and reading a portion of the Sacred Scripture, at the hour assigned for opening the School, in the morning; and close the same in the evening with prayer." Although the resolutions were not part of the Act, newspapers reflected a belief that these were an appendix to the law and teachers carried out the responsibility. While encouraging private and public morality through carefully selected readings in the schools, the Act supplemented these readings with selections from Boston newspapers.[35] The ability to read and write—for communication and for the keeping of accurate records—had long been vital to the livelihood of commercial cities.[36] But a commercial city, dominated by a rising business class, also needed young men trained in the mysteries of arithmetic, profit-and-loss sheets, and balanced account books.

The Act adopted a uniform system of instruction in arithmetic in all the schools. Young boys not only learned addition, subtraction, multiplication, and division, but they struggled as well with compound addition, reduction, interest rates, exchange rates, and, as a finishing course, vulgar and decimal fractions. Training began at age eleven and lasted until age fourteen, if children even of the "middling classes" could afford to remain that long in school.

Arithmetic had not been a required subject in Boston grammar schools before 1789. Despite its introduction into the required curriculum, attempts at achieving uniformity of instruction did not fare well. Neither textbooks nor teachers were adequate.

Reacting against all things English and hoping to encourage a sense of pride in American letters, Boston educators were eager to use native-hewn textbooks. Except for *A New and Complete System of Arithmetick, Composed for the Use of the Citizens of the United States* (1788) by Nicholas Pike of Newburyport, no American arithmetics were available. Pike was the first native mathematician to gain popularity by writing textbooks. His work enjoyed quick acceptance at universities such as Yale, Harvard, and Dartmouth, but was unsuitable for grammar school use until abridged several years later.

In the absence of any printed text, arithmetic instruction was left to the schoolmasters whose knowledge and abilities varied widely. At best the training in mathematics involved tedious memorization of rules; at worst, it entailed little more than copying the simplest problems of addition. Not until some twenty years later, when Walsh's *Mercantile Arithmetic* (1807) was used in the schools, was there any uniform mathematical preparation for young men entering the business world of mercantile Boston.

Local businessmen protested the lack of appropriate training in arithmetic. In the spring of 1792 schoolmasters, School Committee members, and representatives of the business community met to consider the problem. The businessmen believed that prevailing methods hampered young men destined for a business career, and requested that teachers devote more time and effort to mathematics. Miffed at any questioning of their abilities, the schoolmasters responded that sufficient time was spent on arithmetic to qualify any youth for the ordinary business of the counting-houses.[37] There matters stood for some years. Still, even the act of requiring some mathematical instruction in the grammar schools revealed that Boston educators understood the necessity of adapting the public school curriculum to the changing business needs of the city.

Although experiencing mixed success, those responsible for the Education Act of 1789 had tried faithfully to create a uniform system of public education throughout the city. Certainly they had attempted to follow the letter and spirit of the Massachusetts law recently enacted by the General Court. This law had instructed public schoolmen "to impress on the minds of children and youth committed to their care and instruction, the principles of piety, justice and a sacred regard to truth, love to their country, humanity and universal benevolence, sobriety, industry, frugality, chastity, moderation and temperance, and those other virtues which are the ornament of human society and the basis upon which the republican Constitution is structured."[38] With the new curriculum of reading and arithmetic, the reorganizers of public education in 1789 had tried to plot a scheme of instruction designed to meet the requirements of a moralistic, commercially minded community. As a New England farmer sending his boys to Boston public schools at the turn of the century put it: "The Bible and figgers is all I want my boys to know."[39]

Perhaps following the lead of public educators, private citizens also made efforts to inculcate morality and public responsibility through schooling. In 1797, for instance, a group of Congregational Church members formed a school in Federal Street, governed by a joint stock company. The declared purpose of the school was, through the most rational and congenial means, "to impress the sentiments of morality, and induce those habits of thinking and acting. correctly, which form an essential part of early education; and upon which the success of Instruction most emphatically depends." Accordingly, instruction in the school included reading, writing, speaking, singing, arithmetic, evidence of natural and revealed religion, the principles of "Republican Government, and the Rights and Duties of a Citizen."[40]

If Boston's educators seemed idealistic in their provisions for instruction, the most important result of the Act of 1789 was pragmatic—the establishment of a permanent School Committee to oversee the administration of public education. Taking over the duties often perfunctorily performed in the past by the Selectmen or their appointees, the new Committee was to prove far more responsive to public interests. Elected annually, the Committee included one member from each of the city's twelve wards. This election distinguished the administration of schools

from those of other urban facilities and thereby demonstrated the unique
importance of public education to the citizens of Boston.[41] In effect, the
new School Committee was equated with the Board of Selectmen and
the Overseers of the Poor. In 1736 Boston first had been divided into
wards to provide more direct relief to indigents; each ward elected one
member of the Overseers of the Poor.[42] From then until the Education
Act of 1789, only the Overseers and the Selectmen were elected at large
to represent citywide interests.

Formation of the new Committee reflected two fundamental facts of
Boston life. First, political and social leaders had begun to assert the
primacy of public over private interests in urban affairs. They believed
that education was so important to the future economic fortunes and
social morality of the community it no longer could be left in private
hands alone. An educational division of labor between public and private
schools would continue for many years, but Boston leaders had taken initial steps toward achieving public control.

Second, Boston citizens had begun to recognize a need for specialized
leadership in handling urban problems. An increase in population and a
growing conviction about public responsibility for that population gradually impaired the capacity of part-time merchant politicians to administer
all the operations of government. Together with provisions for sanitation
facilities, control of fires, and police protection, the expansion of public
education called for knowledgeable administrators who could devote
much of their time to governing the schools.

Members of the first School Committee were not professional educators; indeed, some years would pass before professionals controlled
the schools. But they were men required by law to attend more to the
needs of public education than had been customary in the past. The first
overseers of the schools set the tone for future years. All were men of
position and authority in the community. They were men who had lived
through and taken part in the Revolution. Though they professed to have
the interests of the entire population in mind, they could not help but
reflect the philosophical, political, and moral interests of their own social
group. They considered themselves patriots and affirmed their educational
duty to inculcate patriotism, a love of republican institutions, and a sense
of moral responsibility among the children of Boston. These formulators
of educational policy came from various honored professions; no individual from the lower or working classes sat with the august group.

Typical of the political leaders chosen to administer the schools was
Thomas Dawes. During a long career, Dawes served as an elector of
three presidents, a member of the first Massachusetts State Constitutional
Convention, a deacon of the Old South Church, and a judge of the Mu-

nicipal Court for twenty years. George R. Minot, another committeeman, also served as a Municipal Court judge, as president of the Massachusetts Charitable Society, and was one of the earliest and most accomplished of New England historians. Also included on the Committee were the Reverend Samuel West, Dr. John Lathrop, and Dr. James Freeman—all highly respected clergymen. John Coffin Jones was a successful merchant and state senator. Other ministers, doctors, and lawyers made up the rest of the Committee. The famous architect Charles Bulfinch, as chairman of the Board of Selectmen between 1791 and 1871 remained the *ex officio* chairman of the School Committee for eighteen years.[43]

Citizens of Boston had elected men whose integrity and devotion to public service appeared unquestionable. That residents believed these respectable men would serve community interests was evident in references to "their committeemen" and "their schools."[44] The Education Act of 1789 had created a closer sense of cooperation between voters and their elected representatives on public school matters than was true of most other urban services.

Under the organization of 1789, Boston enjoyed the only public school system in the young nation open to the children of all residents, and administered by popularly elected officials. In its composition, the new School Committee provided a continuing influence of conservative, financially successful, professional men who could be counted upon to reflect the interests of the better citizens of the city. As elected officials they were subject to public whims about educational issues. But the principle had been established that in an increasingly complex urban society public education would perform a vital function in securing morality and social order.

2

The Secularization of Piety, 1789-1820

Oh no! it is not to the Sabbath-day preacher that only or principally belongs the work of making the youth realize that he is studying for eternity. It is the duty of his daily instructors.
Warren Burton (1834)[1]

In the Education Act of 1789 Boston officials believed they had created an instrument for fashioning public morality. Public schools would instill in youth the principles of piety, sobriety, frugality, and industry. Schools would inculcate deference to established authority. By requiring teachers to open and close the school day with scriptural readings and prayer, educators foreshadowed a later emphasis on the teacher as a surrogate minister. While teachers, as moral guardians of the young, were to help the church prepare children for eternity, they also were to train children for the present. Through instruction in reading, writing, and arithmetic, youth would be readied to meet the commercial needs of mercantile Boston. Officials linked public morality and peaceful commercial expansion as inseparable goals. They affirmed that only educated youth could be moral and useful citizens. Whereas once Bostonians had considered religion the primary molder of responsible citizens, they now proposed to supplement the work of the church with public schools. Whether consciously or not, educators encouraged a secularization of piety.

To fuse pious virtues with practical knowledge, educators required a comprehensive system of schools. At the turn of the nineteenth century, public education at the grammar school level was already well established. Children between the ages of seven and fourteen could enter schools where, free of any tuition charge, they received a rudimentary education. For those children who demonstrated an aptitude for scholarship and whose parents could afford to send them on to college, a Latin Grammar School provided training in the classics during a four-year preparatory course. The various schools employed fourteen masters, including the venerable John Tileston, who became the city's first official pensioner upon leaving public service. For the masters' salaries and other school expenses the Town Meeting voted over one-fifth of the public tax money.[2]

Bostonians congratulated themselves on their system of public education. The eighteen prominent citizens who sat on the School Committee basked in approval generously bestowed by their fellow townsmen. On occasions of the annual visitation of the schools by members of the School Committee, expressions of satisfaction and praise filled newspaper reports. Each year the size of the visiting committees increased. Individuals other than School Committee members wanted to see for themselves the vaunted accomplishments, and perhaps also wished to take some of the credit for Boston's dedication to education. In 1806, there was an unusually large delegation. Besides members of the School Committee, the Selectmen, the senators of Suffolk County, the sheriff and judges of the several courts, clergymen, firewardens, members of the Board of Health, town visitors, and the Overseers of the Poor all visited the schools.[3] This was a luxury possible only in a city that was still compact. In later years when population growth had brought residential expansion, fewer citizens of Boston would make the circuit on visiting days. More and more, residents would come to rely upon the School Committee to oversee the schools. But at the turn of the new century, all citizens who wished could see for themselves the results of their taxation for education.

Although citizens reveled in their support of public education, the "public" being educated was small. Of the school-age population (ages four to fifteen) only slightly more than 12 per cent attended the public grammar and writing schools. These were mostly children of the middle class. The offspring of wealthier parents enrolled in the many private schools that dotted the city. Some 500 students, slightly less than 7 per cent of all school-age children, went to private institutions. An additional 2.1 per cent, generally children of well-to-do parents, attended the Latin School. All told, the school population of Boston numbered just over 1500 students, little more than 20.6 per cent of the total school-age population.[4] The remaining children of the city either received instruction at home in the time-honored way, learned to read and write while apprenticed to a tradesman, or continued illiterate.[5]

Some parents preferred to educate their children privately; others could not afford to send them to public school. Although the public schools in principle were open to all children seven years of age or older, in practice they remained selective. The Education Act of 1789 had required that all children admitted to the schools be able to read and write; this excluded a considerable number. The authors of the Act had assumed that before entering the grammar schools children would have received the instruction "usual at the women's schools," and thus know the rudiments of reading and writing. These private dames' schools for early instruction were common enough that the Act had required the instructresses to be licensed. Women held the elementary classes in a room in their homes. Parents paid a sum fixed by the teacher for their children's instruction. In addition, other private schools prepared children either to enter the public grammar schools at age seven or the Latin School at nine or ten.[6] The requirement that children read and write before entering the grammar schools thus effectively made private schooling in one form or another an adjunct to public education.

By the early years of the nineteenth century some Bostonians had begun to grow anxious about those children barred from public instruction. Middle- and upper-class Bostonians knew that the schools could not accomplish their social tasks if children of the lower classes failed to attend. Although they were unsure of exactly who the lower classes were and referred to them vaguely as "the poor," respectable, longtime residents of the city knew that the inferior sort were a thorn in the body politic and had been so since colonial days.[7] The good citizens also knew, though probably very few could rattle off statistics to support their perceptions, that the lower classes were increasing in number. Every indicator—employment figures, available housing, the charity rolls—revealed that the size and character of the old Puritan city's population were changing.

Between the turn of the century and the early 1820's, when the town officially became a chartered city, new commercial and manufacturing endeavors brought an upsurge of population from both rural New England and abroad. The population grew from 24,937 in 1800 to 43,298 by 1820, an increase of over 40 per cent. Almost 12 per cent of the newcomers were foreigners. The city became more crowded. Residential congestion—the number of people living together under one roof, either from choice or necessity—jumped to its highest rate in over eighty years.[8] The bare increase in numbers meant a proportionate increase in the ranks of the poor. While poverty and pauperism were not yet the enormous problems they would become in later years, heavy demands were placed upon the charitable impulse and institutions of the community. To accommodate the growing numbers needing public relief, the Overseers of the Poor opened a new almshouse. Recognizing the poor as a public burden, the Overseers yearly increased expenditures. In 1818, the first year for which accurate figures were available, the Overseers spent on relief about $12,500, approximately 11 per cent of the town's total expenditures, and only slightly less than one-half the amount for such vital necessities as new streets and sewers.[9]

Whether contemptuous or alarmed, Boston citizens realized that the expanding lower classes posed financial and moral problems for the present and future security and prosperity of the city. To maintain public order and to ensure public morality, the lower classes had to be contained. During the first two decades of the nineteenth century, an increasing number of influential Bostonians would argue that the most practical container was not the almshouse or the workhouse, but the public school. Both as a humanitarian effort and as a social expedient, public education was to be provided for children of the lower classes.

CHARITY SCHOOLS AND SUNDAY SCHOOLS

Boston had not completely ignored the education of its lower-class poor. In the city, as throughout the state, individuals and philanthropic groups had provided charity schools in which children of the poor could receive elementary instruction. Some of these schools were coeducational, but most accepted only girls on the theory that boys could be apprenticed at an earlier age and thus learn to read and write. For many poor children the charity schools offered the only available means of instruction. In Boston, as in other cities, the only children who could attend these schools were those whose parents had been declared paupers. While the number of impoverished families increased, those willing to have their children considered objects fit only for charity did not. If such children did not belong to a religious society (a customary agency for instruction) they were unlikely to experience any formal training in reading and writing.[10] One attempt to create a successful charity school revealed the difficulties of reaching the poor through such institutions.

In 1814, a group of ladies who were members of the Old South Church decided to open a charity school. After renting a room in a building nearby the location of the church at Washington and Milk streets, the ladies hired a teacher and awaited the expected rush of poor children into the school. But the group soon discovered that few poor families were eager to take advantage of their charitable impulse. Some families appeared hostile to any efforts made by their social betters. Others seemed indifferent to opportunities for betterment. Still others refused to take the loss of family income that would result from sending their children to school. "The children are taken from a class of people," complained the ladies, "who usually employ them in begging from house to house, and it has been only by personal applications to the parents of these children that they have been induced to permit them to attend the School."[11] In trying to prepare the youth for entry into the public schools, the women learned that charity was not always accepted as graciously as it was offered.

The charity schools were too few and too poorly equipped to satisfy the educational needs of the poorer part of the population. Bearing the stigma of pauperism, the schools attracted few lower-class children. Certainly charity schools were not a solution to the problem of preparing more children for the public schools. As some Bostonians would discover, a better solution could be found in cooperation between secular agencies and religious bodies. With that cooperation came a reversal of historical roles. Where once the main purpose of education in New England had been to prepare men for service in the church, now the church would prepare the young for formal, secular education. The medium of the new alliance was the Sunday school.

From inception, the Sunday school movement had combined worldly and other-worldly aims. The schools were to give instruction in literacy as well as liturgy. The movement began in England in the 1780's when Robert Raikes, proprietor of the influential *Gloucester Journal,* first promoted the idea. He hoped that such schools would take children of the poor off the streets for at least one day a week and bring them into an environment where they might be instructed in literacy and morality. In 1785, at Raikes' urging, interested citizens formed the national Sunday School Society. By the close of the century English cities had over a thousand Sunday schools with an enrollment of some 69,000 students.[12]

American clergymen and other civil leaders followed the example of the British urban missionaries. The first recorded Sunday school in an American city appeared in Philadelphia in 1791 under the patronage of physician Benjamin Rush, economist Mathew Carey, and others. Paid instructors taught reading, writing, and arithmetic to those poor children who desired admission, and who, because of their employment, could not attend regular schools during the week. This First Day or Sunday School Society of Philadelphia named the Bible the basic textbook and stressed that children should be taught the Christian virtues of truthfulness, honesty, and temperance.[13]

In that same year Boston experimented with a Sunday school. This school gave instruction in religion and in the three R's. The success of this and several other similar schools prompted some citizens to suggest that the city should incorporate Sunday schools into the public school system, particularly for the sake of poor and working-class children. But during the 1790's there was considerable opposition to appropriating public money for a quasi-charitable effort.[14]

Further efforts to provide publicly supported Sunday schools came over the next few years. But most were abortive. Boston churches showed little interest in founding Sunday schools, either for children of their own congregations, or for outsiders. By 1816, however, some Protestant groups in Boston believed the time was right to extend their ministry toward the poorer classes. A group of prominent citizens—including William Thurston, a wealthy lawyer; Pliny Cutler, merchant and manufacturer; Samuel Armstrong, printer, publisher, and bookseller; Charles Cleveland, a businessman specializing in brokerage and exchange services; and Henry Homes, son of one of the leading members of the Old South Congregational Church—met to consider ways of reaching the children of the poor with instruction in literacy and morality. Out of the meeting came the organization of the Boston Society for the Moral and Religious Instruction of the Poor.[15]

At their first meeting, the men discovered they were confused about exactly who the poor were and about the extent of existing efforts in the city to provide for their spiritual and physical care. They decided to "examine into the state of the poor and the destitute, ascertain facts and adjust such a plan for their instruction and relief, as may be thought expedient." When they met again a few days later, the gentlemen were better informed—and disturbed by their discoveries. Collectively they had visited some five hundred homes. In at least a fourth, there was no Bible; there were children who never had been to school and were illiterate; and there were people young and old who knew nothing of the Christian faith.[16] Christian Boston apparently had done little for the families of the poor.

Living in crowded quarters, playing in the crooked streets and narrow alleys, working in stores and small manufacturing establishments or idling away their days in destructive mischief, far too many children grew up neglected by their parents. Parents who worked twelve to sixteen hours a day, six days a week, spent far more of their leisure hours in local saloons, gambling houses, and brothels than in disciplining or instructing their children. Both children and parents seemed destined to lives which would eventually lead to personal degradation and disruption of the social order —or so members of the Society charged. In 1817, the Reverend James Davis reported to the Boston Female Society for Missionary Purposes on the potential danger of the poorer classes in Boston's West End, north of the Commons:

> Without impropriety it may be said, *there* is the place where Satan's seat is. There awful impieties prevail; and all conceivable abominations are practiced; *there* the depravity of the human heart is acted out; and from this sink of sin, the seeds of corruption are carried into every part of town. Five and twenty or thirty shops are opened on Lord's days from morning to evening

and ardent spirits are retailed without restraint. . . . Here in
one compact section of the town, it is confidently affirmed and
fully believed, there are *three hundred* females wholly devoid of
shame and modesty.

While the section included many of Boston's colored citizens, it also
housed a large number of rural migrants and some aliens who had recently arrived in the city.[17] Whatever its composition, the poor population threatened public stability and Christian morality.

Members of the new Society for the Poor did not solely blame children
for what they called their vicious habits: "Placed in situations where they
had nothing to check but everything to quicken the growth of viscious
[sic] habits, they were advancing as rapidly as the enemy of righteousness could desire, in preparation for his wretched service, of which the
wages is death." But whether inherited sin or environmental conditions
were to blame, the fact remained that for the sake of the poor and of
the better classes of the town alike, something had to be done. Members
of the Society thus joined other civic leaders in affirming their duty to
change the lives of the poor.[18] An initial step in reclaiming future generations was educating the young. At the very least, the evils of self-perpetuating illiteracy and the economic disadvantages of the lower classes
could be mitigated. First Sunday schools and then public schools became
spearheads in the cause.

The Society opened its first Sunday school on May 11, 1817. A second
followed a month later. By the middle of 1818, the number of schools
had risen to five. Children gained admission whenever they wished. Members of the Society personally recruited many of the first pupils. Most of
the children were five years of age or older. Despite a large turnover,
school attendance averaged about 500, with over 2,000 children enrolled.

In public school rooms, rented halls, or in church buildings, the schools
met throughout the day on Sunday, with a brief break at noontime. Most
of the instruction came from readings in the Bible and in various catechisms, prayers, and hymns. Younger children used only a spelling book
so that they might learn to read better. One such book which replaced
the traditional *New England Primer* was an English work, *The Childs
First Book*. All of its reading exercises were religious in character. As in
the public schools, learning was by rote. Progress was measured by the
quantity of material ingested. In 1819, the Society's annual report proudly
asserted that in one school during the past year "there have been committed to memory . . . 158 prayers, 54,561 verses of scripture, 6212
verses of hymns and 6387 answers in the Catechisms." Members of the
Society believed that they had succeeded in blending secular and religious instruction into a palatable morsel which, when taken weekly, fed

the inner needs of the poorer children of the city. The Society had set an example which it hoped the town would emulate in "carrying the comforts of industry, peace and virtue to every fireside."[19]

The organization of Sunday schools by the Boston Society for the Moral and Religious Instruction of the Poor had both indirect and direct effects on the system of public schools. Indirectly, the Sunday schools advertised the situation of the poor to concerned citizens. Reports of the Society demonstrated the shabby lives of ignorance and impiety led by the poor. Many middle- and upper-class Bostonians, who would have otherwise remained blissfully unaware of the plight of poverty in their midst, had their curiosity first aroused by the Society's discussions of Sunday schools.

The more direct effect of Sunday schools on the public school system came from the early establishment of one such school. In May 1817 the Society petitioned the Board of Selectmen for use of the town's grammar school house in Mason Street for a Sunday school. The area, bordering the southeast side of the Common, contained Negro, foreign, and native-born working-class families.[20] "Our objects in attending to Sunday schools," a spokesman for the Society wrote to the Board, "are, to reclaim the vicious, to instruct the ignorant, to secure the observance of the Sabbath, to induce the children to attend public worship, and to raise the standard of morals among the lower classes of society." These were high hopes for a once-a-week school, but Society members were optimistic. They would reach not only children who might otherwise receive no formal training; parents, too, would benefit. This was a crucial point in later arguments favoring public schools.

A later generation of educators and social reformers in Boston would affirm that society could change the behavior of parents through attempting to mold their children. When the immigrant and poor population of the city had risen greatly in the 1840's and 1850's, a common argument employed by educators emphasized the parental effect of a "good moral tone" to the child's nature. If moral and religious teaching was powerful enough in the public schools, the force of the child's example might reclaim the parent. Immigrant parents themselves recognized this motive behind the promotion of public schools, and complained that schools only encouraged disobedience on the part of children by introducing conflicting standards of authority.[21]

For Society members in 1817 it was perhaps a moot point as to which group they hoped to reach most, the children or the parents. One point was certain. The Society lent its influence to support the notion that education could change the lives of both poor children and their parents. "We believe in this way," stated the Society spokesman to the Board of

Selectmen when petitioning for the school room, "we strike at the foundation of the evils incidental to society, and with greater prospect of success than to reform the hardened offenders,—and yet through the children, not infrequently the parent is reclaimed."[22] Later educators could reason that if once-a-week Sunday schools had such a beneficial effect, how much more might children and parents be affected through the moral force of regularly attended public schools.

Once the Mason Street School had begun operations the Society experienced a rude awakening. It had planned to devote the bulk of the Sunday school day to moral and religious instruction. Only a portion of the time was to be devoted to instructing children in reading and writing, although the Society anticipated having to offer some basic instruction. Society members were dismayed therefore to discover that most of the children whom they induced to enter the school could neither read nor write. Such ignorance could be expected of very young children, but not of children old enough to be in the public grammar schools. The Society had not taken into account the fact that most of the children it served were unable to enter the public schools because of the provision requiring skills in reading and writing. Now they discovered that "of 336 children admitted into the Mason Street Sunday School, none of whom were under five years of age, not one quarter could read words of one syllable, and most of them did not know their letters."[23]

The revelation about the illiteracy of most poor children shocked Society members. They had not fully realized the inadequacies of the city's provisions for education. Fearful that too little time would remain for moral instruction if they had to spend most of their one-day-a-week teaching the basic skills of reading and writing, Society members looked elsewhere for help in instructing the poor. They began urging the city fathers to undertake the public education of such children. The Sunday school movement thus contributed to a growing concern among Bostonians about the illiteracy and immorality of the poor. In November 1817 the yearly report of the Boston Society for the Moral and Religious Instruction of the Poor added impetus to other efforts in the city to establish schools for children between the ages of four and seven.

PUBLIC RIGHTS AND PRIMARY SCHOOLS

Between 1817 and 1820 the struggle to establish public schools for children under the age of seven centered on conflicting interpretations of private responsibility and public duty. This was not unusual in an America which had not yet clearly distinguished between private and public spheres of social responsibility, or even begun to debate the question in earnest. Or, put another way, the lines between public (government) authority and private (individual citizen) accountability were drawn so vaguely, and movement back and forth across those lines was so frequent, that almost any decision about where social responsibility lay could be made and defended as legitimate. Who should provide urban services was a fundamental issue in the struggles over public versus private enterprise that characterized nineteenth-century municipal governments. Efforts to establish and expand a system of publicly supported schools in Boston and in other cities contributed to debates on public versus private investment in social programs and helped to clarify at least some of the questions at issue. To assert the social importance of formal education was one thing; to believe that schools were important enough to make them a public responsibility, funded by tax dollars, was quite another. Those Bostonians who argued against the founding of public primary schools pointed out that charity schools, philanthropic agencies, and the apprenticeship labor system had met the educational needs of the lower classes in the past. In their eyes those private arrangements still appeared adequate. But other citizens responded that changes in the size and character of the population had rendered private endeavors inadequate to the educational needs of the city. Society, they asserted, had a duty to itself and to its lower-class citizens to provide public instruction for all children.

On May 1, 1817, a number of citizens presented to the town meeting a petition dealing with the subject of public schools. "It appears to us important," they stated, "that Schools should be provided at the expense of the Town for the instruction of children under the age of seven years." They requested that a meeting be held to discuss the subject and to take appropriate action.[24] The signers of the petition were not completely benevolent in motive. They were concerned as much with their private tranquility as with public duty. Those children attended no schools of any sort and thus were free to roam the streets as noisy, thieving, public nuisances. That signers of the petition viewed the children in this light stemmed from the changing character of their residential area.

Most of the signers lived in the old North End of the city. Interlaced by three main thoroughfares—Ann Street from the wharves inland, Hanover Street, and Salem Street—the North End had been one of the earliest areas of settlement in the city. Successful merchants had created a network of wharves and homes in the North End during the eighteenth century. Once the center of the most expensive and fashionable houses of the town, much of the area had undergone dramatic changes during and following the Revolution. Many of the leading commercial families of Boston had moved elsewhere to the south and the west. Those who remained had

to share the area with an increasing number of small merchants, tradesmen, and artisans. Brick warehouses and small manufactories now edged
streets once lined with trees. Numerous houses showed decay from years
of inattention. In addition, many of the earliest Irish immigrants in the
nineteenth century settled in the North End. Ann Street had become a
synonym for vice and intemperance. Even the church had lost its influence in this section of Puritan Boston. Contemporaries complained that
young men of the area who married wives in other parts of town "found
it difficult to persuade them to become so ungenteel as to attend worship
in the North End."[25] The North End was a residential and commercial
zone in transition. And residents of that zone saw in the expansion of educational facilities a means of holding the line against change or, at least,
of rendering change less annoying.[26]

On May 26, a town meeting in Faneuil Hall acted upon the petition
of North End residents. The meeting referred it to the School Committee,
which was to be enlarged by adding one person from each of the twelve
wards, for purposes of acting upon the request. On May 29, the Selectmen picked a committee from a list submitted by the petitioners and from
a few men nominated by the Board. This group met with the School Committee on June 18; jointly they decided that a census should be taken in
each ward.

In a limited sense, this investigation was one of the earliest "social surveys" of an urban population. The committee wished to discover not only
the population of each ward, but something about the private circumstances of the citizens as well. It wished to determine: the number of
children not attending any school; the number of dames' schools and their
enrollment; and the number of deaf, dumb, and blind persons in each
ward who either required or were receiving assistance.

When the statistics had been gathered, a sub-committee composed of
the noted architect Charles Bulfinch; lawyer, former town advocate, and
director of the Boston Athenaeum Peter O. Thatcher; and one Henry J.
Oliver arranged the returns and presented a summary report to the School
Committee. On October 30, the School Committee accepted the recommendations of the sub-committee against the present "expediency" of establishing public primary schools. On November 3, following the advice
of the School Committee, the report became public knowledge.[27]

In a city which prided itself on its educational facilities the report of
the committee should have discouraged and disillusioned many people.
The survey showed that the town supported eight public schools, including the Latin School, an African School for Negro children, and a school
in the Almshouse for the children of paupers. Total enrollment of the
eight schools was 2,365 pupils. This was approximately 16 per cent of the

school-age population. All of these children were above the age of seven, except for a few in the Almshouse. The report also took stock of private and charity schools. These figures illustrated the predominance of private over public education. Scattered throughout the city were 154 private schools for both girls and boys, enrolling a total of 3,767 students. There were 8 "charity free schools" with a total of 365 pupils. All told, over 4,000 students between the ages of four and fourteen attended private schools of one sort or another, at a total cost to their parents of almost $50,000. Bostonians thus were educating privately nearly twice as many students as were attending public schools.[28]

Even more revealing than the extent of private instruction were the numbers of children who received no instruction at all. These were the young people who so concerned the Boston Society for the Moral and Religious Instruction of the Poor and about whom the petitioners to the Selectmen were most disturbed. The report of the sub-committee showed that 283 children between the ages of four and seven, and 243 children over seven, attended no private or public schools.[29] Considering the residential transiency of the poor and the resulting difficulty of getting accurate figures, these numbers probably were gross underestimates. Whatever the real numbers involved, the justifications by the sub-committee for recommending that these children not be educated at public expense demonstrated the current attitudes of some citizens toward the role of public education and the tradition of privatism in the city.

Charles Bulfinch chaired the sub-committee and wrote the report. Bulfinch was one of Boston's luminaries. As an architect he had designed homes for prominent Federalists like Harrison Gray Otis, and public buildings such as the monumental Boston State House. At the age of twenty-seven, his eminence had led to his election to the Board of Selectmen. Serving as the chairman of that body for eighteen years, by 1817 Bulfinch had presided over vast physical expansion of the city, contributing many of the designs for wharves, warehouses, and public structures himself. He solidly represented the established order of the Boston ruling class.[30] In his report, Bulfinch admitted that the city should provide public instruction, but he also saw a limit to public responsibility. "The duty of the town to provide the means of instruction for all the children," he wrote, "is both a civil and religious obligation upon the citizens; but it is a reasonable duty, and has its limits." The limits became unreasonable when further appropriations had to be made to care for a small number of children after most were already provided for. "Considering the population of the town, which now amounts to about forty thousand inhabitants," Bulfinch observed of the reported 283 children aged seven and under who attended no schools, "together with the influx of foreigners and strangers, who are ignorant of our institutions, or who have not learned to value them, this is deemed to be a very small number." He added, further, that the Overseers of the Poor annually distributed, on the average, $550 in each ward to enable these children to go to private neighborhood schools. Bulfinch blamed the non-attendance of the reported 243 children above the age of seven on the inattention of parents, indifference to education, or inability, for various reasons, to go to either public or private schools. In theory, he was correct. These children could be accommodated within the existing school structure. Yet Bulfinch failed to mention one of the chief complaints registered by those who wanted more children in the schools. The requirement that no child of seven years or more could enter the schools without being able to read and write made it impossible for many of those not attending to go to school.[31]

If the reported figures of non-attendance were correct, then Bulfinch was right in minimizing the importance of so few children. Their accuracy, however, was questionable. If true, then approximately 97 per cent of all children under the age of fifteen attended some school, a percentage subsequently unmatched in American history.[32] But it was not in his interest for Bulfinch to question the accuracy of his statistics. He was not concerned with expanding the system of public education.

Bulfinch agreed that "it is to be deeply lamented, that any child should be suffered to grow up in ignorance." Next to actively teaching their children habits of vice, the worst disservice any parents could render a child was the neglect of his education. When the city provided educational facilities, parents had a duty to the entire community to send their children to school. Of course, Bulfinch noted, no legal compulsion should be brought to bear on parents who neglected their duty. Rather it was perhaps best that "its performance should be left to the influence of feeling and conscience." Or, he implied, a sort of generational accounting system might be the best solution. Although the current generation of children would grow up in ignorance, when they found themselves hampered as adults by their lack of education, they would become indignant with their parents and would resolve that their own children should have better advantages. By a curious twist of logic, Bulfinch argued that the next generation would be more responsible in their obligations to their offspring and to society, precisely because they had grown up in an irresponsible home atmosphere. It was an expression either of faith or of foolishness.

Bulfinch stressed that no matter how complete a system of public education might be, some people would always find fault. He correctly claimed that nowhere could a more liberal system of free schools be found than in Boston. Following their school years, Boston students were fitted well for life in the city. Presumably they had learned the principles of the English language, writing, arithmetic, and geography. In a city dedicated to commerce and Christianity little more could be asked or expected. "They become qualified to engage in mercantile and mechanical professions, are disciplined in the principles of moral and religious truth, and are formed to make valuable members of the community." Since most children apparently underwent this process of molding mercantile and moral habits, the fact that a small number did not appeared unimportant. In numbers, there was safety.

To these arguments against the formation of a primary school system, Bulfinch added the factor of cost. To be of any use, primary schools for all the children of Boston between the ages of four and seven would have to be numerous. If there were only a few, parents would not send their children, "for it would be inconvenient and dangerous to send small children to schools distant from their homes, and to allow them to assemble together in multitudes."[33] The public expense of establishing such a widespread system of neighborhood schools would be prohibitive. Bulfinch justifiably could have argued that present financial conditions made such attempts impossible. Boston still labored under a temporary debt of $70,000 contracted during the War of 1812. Taxes for all purposes were higher between 1812 and 1822 than they would be during the first decade of city government after 1822. For the five-year period following 1815 the booming manufacturing enterprises of the city slumped badly. During the same years, Boston underwent a serious currency crisis, although not as severe as that experienced by many other cities. The ice trade, which was to become a major source of revenue for Boston capitalists in future years, had just begun in 1817. Trade in general was not to advance steadily until after 1820.[34] As former chairman of the town's Committee of Finance between 1800 and 1815, Bulfinch well knew the state of the Boston economy.

Although objecting to the additional public expense, Bulfinch did not make economy the crucial point of his arguments; instead, he emphasized morality. Perhaps he honestly imagined the moral issue as the most significant matter at stake; or perhaps he believed that Bostonians would more readily accept a proposal couched in such terms. Whichever, he claimed that primary schools were unnecessary because most parents who sent their children to private tuition schools did not look upon the expense as a burden; they paid the cost cheerfully out of love and a sense of duty. This in turn made them better parents. They were more likely to devote their attention to the business of education "where a small weekly stipend is paid by them for this object, than where the whole expense is defrayed by the public treasury." Bulfinch thus effectively argued for private responsibility rather than for public duty. In so doing, he almost completely ignored the poor population of the city.

Bulfinch further implied that moral degeneration would result if public taxes usurped the province of private responsibilities. Family solidarity might break down if government assumed the cost of what rightfully belonged to the private sphere. "It ought never to be forgotten," he piously intoned, "that the office of instruction belongs to parents, and that to the schoolmaster is delegated a portion only of the parental character and rights."[35] A later generation of Bostonians, faced by broader challenges, would reach different conclusions on the relationship of the child to the family, to the school, and to the state. But in 1817, the opinion of Charles Bulfinch and other members of the committee on schools reflected a satisfaction with the status quo and a reluctance to initiate change.

The report of the Bulfinch committee did not speak for everyone, although the committee itself believed its action to be final.[36] The need for primary schools seemed imperative to a number of other Boston citizens. When the results of the sub-committee were printed by the School Committee, a new attempt began to obtain free public schooling for younger children. Newspapers published letters from various citizens demanding some provisions for primary school education. Schemes and plans outlining the steps to be taken appeared regularly. Many citizens called for new schools on the grounds both of religious and moral benevolence and of public expediency. On February 25, 1818, a letter to the editor of the *Boston Columbian Centinel* summarized the demands and enumerated the various suggestions. The writer of the letter affirmed that he spoke for a number of respectable gentlemen. The gentlemen believed that their scheme would prevent the causes and largely perfect the cure of pauperism in Boston. Unlike Charles Bulfinch and his associates, these citizens inferred that urban conditions demanded a merging of individual responsibility and social duty. The several races, nationalities, social and economic classes of the city had to find some means of adjusting to each other and to society at large. Public accommodations had to supplant purely private interests. The author of the letter stressed that primary schools would serve a utilitarian function in the life of the city.

All the children of the town between the ages of four and seven were to be educated at public expense. The existing system of Sunday schools was to be encouraged and expanded. In each ward three men were to be appointed whose duties would involve the poor and the schools. These men, of course, were to be Christians—men of discreet, judicious, prudent, industrious, and pious characters. While thirty-six men from the city's twelve wards would be a large group, their number would be small in comparison to the task outlined for them. In effect, these Christian men, aided by public schools, were to oversee and to guide every activity of the poor families in their wards. They were "to inquire into the state and circumstances of each poor family several times in the course of the year and note them down, and at the same time, encourage them to industry, cleanliness, and good morals; and by their advice and friendship, to assist them in contriving ways and means by which to gain a comfortable subsistence for themselves and children." The committee was to persuade the poor to send their children to both public schools and Sunday schools.

To carry out these responsibilities, the committee members were to conduct a periodic survey of their wards. They were to determine the number of the poor—both male and female—where they lived, where they were born, and to what church or parish, if any, they belonged. If they were not church members, they were to be encouraged to attend, and the appropriate minister would be directed to visit them to stress the advantages of attendance. Further, the letter recommended that the Board of Overseers of the Poor cease giving any financial aid in the wards unless the committee of thirty-six men suggested and approved individuals as suitable persons for charity. Finally, the letter recommended that the thirty-six be formed into a Public Board of Primary Schools for the purpose of putting the plan into operation. Only the Sunday schools were to remain privately conducted operations.

To concoct a more paternal scheme would have been difficult. Had the plan been adopted, all of the poorer families of Boston would have been under the surveillance and control of a presumably benevolent oligarchy. But the correspondent preferred to stress only positive results: the town would gain a knowledge of who its poor were and where they lived; the problems of the poor might better be understood; the town might be better protected against violence, crime, disease, and general civic unrest among native and immigrant poor. Those who did not accept the actions of the committee or who appeared beyond redemption might be accommodated under the plan's provision that the Committee "take up all vagrants and street beggars, and deliver them to the Overseers of the Poor, to be committed to the Work-House or Alms-House as the case may be."

The plan was never adopted precisely as stated. But it revealed the feelings of one leading group in the town toward the role to be played by public schools. Free public education, according to some, was to be a charity movement ministering to the poor. As the citizens who would compose the governing board of the charity were to be appointed by the Town Meeting, control of the poor effectively would remain in the hands of the better class of Bostonians. It was the duty of those citizens to care for the poor. It was also to their own advantage and protection.

THE CHOICE DEPOSITORIES OF A FREE PEOPLE

While some citizens asserted their Christian duty to provide means of educating the poor, others claimed the rights of the poor to an equal education with the rich. Equalitarian arguments became almost daily fare in the press. Most eloquent among these appeals was a statement signed "Many" which appeared in the *Boston Daily Advertiser* on April 21, 1818.

"Many" was the pseudonym of James Savage, a Boston lawyer.[37] Savage had already demonstrated his sense of public responsibility in a variety of offices. After a visit to England where he had learned about a London savings bank, he had attempted to provide a similar institution for Boston. In 1816, primarily through his efforts, the Massachusetts Legislature had incorporated the Provident Institution for Savings, one of the first savings banks incorporated in the United States. The institution was designed, in part, to encourage savings among the poor. As to education, Savage remarked in a discussion on the subject that the common schools were the children of religion and must serve their mother.[38] Now, regarding the founding of primary schools, he stressed the right of the poor to education.

"All should be taught to read," Savage began, "the poor and the rich should have an equal chance to understand the nature and principles of our republican government." Noting that many Boston parents sent their children to private tuition schools, he claimed that others, unable to meet the cost, were obliged to let their children "traverse the streets, or shut them up at home. Of this class there are hundreds among us already growing up to all kinds of iniquity." Referring to the Bulfinch report on the number of children who did not attend any school, Savage asked, "What are those children doing? Who has charge of them? Where do they live? Why are they not at school? The committee have not informed us." Savage emphasized the inherent rights of Americans to equal treatment. The children in question had a right to a "good bringing up and to a common school education." They had a right to "a common share of the friendship of the community." If parents could not or would not provide schooling, then the town had a duty to supply it. If the town failed in its duty, then the state legislature should enact laws to save these dependents. The Bulfinch report asserted that the schools were open to receive all children. But Savage protested that many parents were not financially able to qualify their children for admittance to the schools, either before or after the age of seven. If there was theoretical equality of opportunity, there were such actual inequities that "these children are as much deprived of the benefits of our schools as they would be of running after their legs were broken, or their eyes put out." Savage overstated his case, yet his statements showed the emotional peak that the issue of primary schools had reached during the early months of 1818.

As a result of the newspaper campaign and meetings by concerned citizens, a new petition on primary schools was presented to the Town Meeting on May 25, 1818. James Savage and Elisha Ticknor were the authors, although it was signed by almost two hundred of the town's leading citizens.[39]

Ticknor was a former master of the Boston public schools, a Federalist, and a devout Calvinist. Author of a reading exercise book which contained homilies such as "the people are foolish," Ticknor believed that public schools should inculcate orthodox values of church and state. His own political, spiritual, and social respectability added luster to his notions about public primary schools. Included among the other signers were William Ellery Channing, Thomas Dawes, Samuel T. Armstrong, William Ladd, Asa Whitney, and Samuel May, all men who were active in social reform efforts. The signers paid homage to the town's institutions and laws, and complained that too many children were growing up without having instilled in them a respect for law and order. They called for a system of primary schools to prepare young people for entrance into the public schools at the age of seven. To relieve the present School Committee of any added burdens, they proposed a new committee of three men in each ward to be appointed annually by the Overseers of the Poor. The cost would not be exorbitant: the schools could be taught in rented rooms throughout the town, by women who accepted low wages. However organized, the proposed schools must receive serious consideration. The "public good" required nothing less.[40]

The Town Meeting referred the petition to a committee composed of James Savage, Elisha Ticknor, Thomas L. Winthrop, Redford Webster, James Prince, Samuel May, John D. Williams, Benjamin West, and Thomas Jackson. As each of these men, with the exception of Jackson, had signed the petition, the result was a foregone conclusion. On June 3, 1818, the committee repeated the earlier figures of the number of children who did not attend any school, but also questioned their accuracy, stating that many parents were unwilling to admit they did not send their children to school. Most of the towns in the commonwealth—particularly Salem, Newburyport, and Portland—provided schools for children four years of age or older. The committee believed that Boston should do the same. Charity schools were unequipped and too few for the task. The committee urged the formation of primary schools as "highly expedient and necessary."

The committee also voted that three men from each ward should be appointed annually by the School Committee to oversee the primary schools, and that the town treasurer should appropriate an initial $5,000 for beginning the schools. When the committee presented its report on June 3, the Town Meeting postponed action until June 11. At that time, strong opposition emerged. With few exceptions, the Selectmen and the School Committee were hostile to the proposals.[41] This was to be expected after the ready acceptance by the School Committee of the Bulfinch report the previous October. The School Committee induced the popular Harrison Gray Otis to represent their interests at the Town Meeting. Otis had been educated in the Boston public schools in the immediate years before the Revolution. He had become a Federalist spokesman in Massachusetts, had served in a variety of state offices, and had established himself as the public champion of the ill-fated Hartford Convention. Elected United States senator in 1817, Otis enjoyed a reputation as an accomplished orator, the most polished Boston public speaker in the generation between Samuel Adams and Daniel Webster.[42] The School Committee confidently entrusted their case to this popular figure.

As James Savage recalled, Otis and Judge Peter O. Thatcher, also a graduate of the early Boston public schools, opposed the formation of primary schools solely on the grounds of expense. Yet, undoubtedly, Otis, Thatcher, and others in opposition believed that the current system of schools was adequate to the task of educating leaders. Their personal experience confirmed that belief. And some years later, speaking of education, Otis reiterated the Federalist principle that the few should lead and the many should follow. "It is of incomparably less moment," he said at a Harvard celebration in 1836, "that a few persons should wear the gown of the scholar, than that the great body of the community should be clad in the costume of fixed principles." A limited number of citizens, he continued, must be educated in universities so that the wants of the legislatures, the pulpits, the courts, and the schools might be supplied. The old ways of education were adequate. Innovation was unnecessary and perhaps dangerous. Otis urged that people "not trust to the promises of the conductors on the modern intellectual railroad, to grade and level the hills of science, and to take us along at rates that will turn our heads and break our bones. Let us eschew the vagaries and notions of the new schools."[43]

In 1818, both on grounds of expense and of the current adequacy of the school system, Otis opposed the formation of primary schools. But his oratorical brilliance was not sufficient, perhaps because, as statesman Charles Francis Adams later observed, "his manner of speaking is agreeable but not very affecting. He has an easy graceful manner of saying things which please, but not those which convince."[44] More likely, Otis and his fellow conservatives failed because an aroused public demanded action. Savage, Ticknor, Lewis Tappan, subsequently a leading abolitionist, and Thomas B. Wait, a journeyman printer representing the interests of his fellow working-class men, spoke in favor of the proposal. The Town Meeting accepted the report and its recommendations. Having carried the issue from the confines of the School Committee into the political arena, Savage and his companions had won a major victory. On June 16, the School Committee organized a Primary School Board, and appointed three men from each ward to serve on it.

The new Board hardly represented a cross-section of the community: it included Savage, Ticknor, Wait, and a number of ministers, lawyers, physicians, and merchants. Its composition faithfully mirrored that of its parent, about whom a Boston newspaper editor could observe: "We understand it was a long established usage to elect on this important committee three gentlemen from each of the learned professions, and the other three from gentlemen in other employments." Direction of school affairs obviously was to remain committed to the godly and well-to-do who could be depended upon to uphold the financial and moral interests of their class. Both the followers of Bulfinch, then, and the Savage crew were cultural conservatives who agreed on the social ends of formal education while disagreeing on the necessary means to achieve those ends. Though the public had forced the School Committee to expand the educational system, the Committee, through its appointive power, retained ultimate control over educational affairs in the city. If the initiation of primary schools resulted from a democratic vote, the future direction of those schools would remain in the hands of an appointed few. The governing of a civic institution in a growing city was consolidated in a centralized administration.[45]

On June 22, 1818, the new committeemen met for the first time. They chose Thomas L. Winthrop, descendant of John Winthrop and one-time lieutenant governor of the state as chairman, and James Savage as secretary of the new Primary School Board. Responsibility for organizing the new schools throughout the city devolved upon local ward committees. The new Board ordered that each ward committee begin schools in its area, consulting with the committeemen of adjacent wards if necessary. The separate committees were to engage female teachers for the schools, visit the schools at least once a month, and report quarterly to the Board on progress. Teachers, in turn, were required to keep close account of school attendance, and to make sure of the child's cleanliness and neatness. If absences occurred, the ward committeemen were to visit parents and to secure regular attendance if possible.

To allocate the funds properly required explicit knowledge of how many children in each ward were of school age and whether their parents would send them to the newly created schools. The Board therefore had requested the ward committees to survey the families in their wards. The results were perplexing, although not surprising. Excluding part of Ward Seven, from which the committee inexplicably made no return, the total number of children between ages four and seven was 2,843. Of these, 532 attended no school at all. The parents of an additional 798 children wanted their children to attend the new schools. To meet the needs of over 1,300 pupils, the Board decided to open twenty schools throughout the city. It succinctly stated the case for neighborhood schools: students should not have to go far from home. The number in each school should not exceed forty-five if they were to receive the necessary personal attention. From the sum of $5,000 allocated by the town treasury, the Board apportioned sums to the individual wards for rent, fuel, and teachers' salaries. Depending on the size of the ward and its number of residents, these sums varied from $240 to $720.[46] The Committee estimated an average of $250 for each school.

Although $5,000 seemed a paltry sum to divide among twenty schools, it was adequate. In some parts of town, teachers who had taught private schools opened their doors to all the children of the neighborhood. To cover the costs of fuel and instructional materials, the Board provided a specified sum to each of these teachers. As the schools met in private residences for the most part, costs were not high. While the Board estimated that perhaps half of the citizens of Boston preferred to pay private teachers of their own selection, it soon developed that far more parents than anticipated were eager to send their children to public schools. The first annual report of the Board noted that in every instance the new schools were filled beyond the prescribed limits.[47]

In the beginning, one-third of the children who entered the schools could not read at all; in some sections of the city the number was one-half. But by the end of the first year, the schools had begun to accomplish their goal of imparting morality through instruction in reading. Many of those children who had been illiterate, the Board boasted, could now read from the New Testament. In one school, a model pupil had memorized 438 verses in the Bible, nobly surpassing the class average of 267.[48]

The schools also were instructing poor children in an early version of manual training. To survive economically in the changing city, the acquisition of manual skills would prove crucial to the poor. In most of the schools, therefore, girls were taught to knit or sew as well as to read. During a three-month period twenty-six young girls in one school had turned out "30 shirts, 12 pair of sheets, 6 pair of pillow cases, 26 pocket handkerchiefs, 8 cravats, 10 infant's frocks, 5 coarse bags, 4 dozen towels, 4 pairs of socks, 3 pairs of mittens, and a number of small pieces of work." Emphasis on this kind of instruction would increase in later years with an influx of poor and foreign immigrants. Citizens would extol manual training over "paper knowledge," declaring that "many of our young vagrants would be kept out of the streets and sit quietly at home promoting the comfort of their families, if they knew how to sew, instead of roaming abroad, exposed to the vicious influences of a large city."[49] The founders of primary schools had recognized quite early the importance of manual instruction.

The most important accomplishment of the new schools was their apparent success in rescuing young children of the poor from the temptations of city streets and from a life doomed to ignorance. In November 1819, for example, the final report of the managers of the "School of Industry," a charitable organization privately supported for the previous seven years, stated that the Association had outlived its usefulness. Founded to take children of the poor off the streets and to teach them diligence, industry, and rudimentary knowledge, the Association had done a good job. But now the number of children in attendance was too small to warrant continuing. They now sent most of the children "to the Primary Schools, lately provided by the town, which prevents in a degree, our longer continuance to our own satisfaction."[50] In this case at least, public action supplanted private enterprise.

Once the children entered the schools, the godly men of Boston saw to it that Christian moral teachings reached those most in need of direction. Incorporated in the "Rules and Regulations" of the Primary School Committee was a provision that "in order to impress on the minds of our youth the importance of religious duties, and their entire dependence on their Maker the instructors are desired to open their schools in the morning with a short prayer, and close with the same service in the afternoon." Also, throughout the school system, the basic text for the first class (the highest class) was the New Testament.[51] The hopes of those men who a few years earlier had started Sunday schools for the children of the poor were now realized through a system of public primary schools.

By 1820, Boston's school system was flourishing. There were thirty-four primary schools scattered throughout the city. Over 1,600 students reaped the advantages of primary instruction. Almost 350 students that year passed the necessary requirements and entered the grammar schools from the primary schools. The upper schools themselves reported a total enrollment of 2,203, an increase of 223 students over the previous term. This number was approximately 22 per cent of the school-age population (ages seven to fifteen) of the community.[52] Boston now maintained, through public taxation, a system of schools which in one way or another offered instruction to all children between the ages of four and fifteen. Certainly not all children of the city attended the schools, but opportunities were open for all to learn the rudiments of formal education. For those who controlled the curricula and operation of the schools it was now possible to instill in many of the children of Boston, rich and poor alike, the moral, religious, and civic values which they believed vital in an urban and Christian society.

In his first inaugural address Josiah Quincy—the most vigorous and far-seeing mayor of Boston during the nineteenth century and the most prominent and capable urban statesman of his day—voiced his opinion of the public schools and echoed the sentiments of a number of his fellow citizens. Quincy exhorted each Bostonian to recognize that

> Above all, its schools, these choice depositories of the hope of a free people, should engage his utmost solicitude and unremitting superintendence. Justly are these institutions the pride and the boast of the inhabitants of this city. For these, Boston has, at all times, stood preeminent. Let there exist, elsewhere, a greater population, a richer commerce, wider streets, more splendid avenues, statlier palaces. Be it the endeavor of this metropolis to educate better men, happier citizens, more enlightened statesmen; to elevate a people, thoroughly instructed in their social rights, deeply imbued with a sense of their moral duties; mild, flexible to every breadth of legitimate authority; unyielding as fate to unconstitutional impositions.[53]

At the end of the second decade of the nineteenth century, Bostonians generally congratulated themselves on their benevolence and wisdom in building a system of public schools. They believed they had laid a solid foundation for the future stability of their city. Future events would confirm their optimism, but confound their methods.

II

SOCIETY AND SCHOOLS

3

Social Stability and Public Schools

*Our schools are our hope—we look to them, and their effects
upon the intelligence of our citizens, as the Ark of Safety to
our Institutions.*

Boston School Committee (1847)[1]

To place a child in public school in the early nineteenth century meant for
many parents a radical departure from tradition. In England and colonial
America most children had been reared and taught the responsibilities of
adulthood, not through formal schools, but through such established institutions as the family, the church, and the apprenticeship system of
labor. On the European continent the systematic education of children
by agencies designed for that purpose did not become prevalent until the
mid-seventeenth century, and then not for most of the young. In England,
as late as the 1820's, insistent popular demands for schooling came not
on behalf of children, but for adult tradesmen, factory hands, and mechanics. Not until the 1840's did English educators and social reformers
develop a comprehensive argument in favor of public schooling for children of the working classes.[2]

Yet, by the 1820's in New England, a clamor had arisen for new methods of raising children and for new agencies to provide formal instruction. The practice of apprenticeship had become outmoded and neglected.
Rapid growth in manufacturing and commercial activities had made the
time-consuming process of apprenticeship obsolete for training large numbers of children. According to many social critics, the institution of the
close-knit family appeared to be dissolving in the heat of economic progress. The economic, ecclesiastical, and political roles once filled by the
Puritan family in society no longer seemed applicable in the nineteenth-
century city. The Protestant Church, never unified, appeared to be splin-
tering further because of denominationalism and a rising Roman Catholicism. The decline of church discipline and social influence made it an
unreliable institution for instructing children in their social obligations.[3]

Wherever men looked, the rate of change threatened to overwhelm

47

established social relationships and institutions. And nowhere was the rate of change more visibly accelerated than in the cities. To ensure future generations against the vagaries of the present, many people demanded new means of raising youth to responsible adulthood. In Boston, and throughout urban New England, social reformers and educators urged the extension of formal education through publicly supported schools. Both in the use of permanent schools as centers of child training, and in the public nature of those schools, Bostonians helped to fashion a new social tool in America. When, by the 1820's, educators insisted on public schools for rich and poor, native and foreign, all children alike, they did so because of changes in their environment, in their own social philosophy, and in their conceptions of childhood.

THE DISCOVERY OF THE CHILD

In Boston and throughout Puritan New England during the early nineteenth century, theological reconsiderations of sin and salvation brought reassessment of the nature of children. The beliefs of two centuries began to loose their hold on some men's imaginations. The Puritans of the seventeenth century rarely had permitted youth the innocence of childhood. Theological conceptions had overridden any notion about the uniqueness of childhood as a stage of human development. The Puritans tended to consider children as adults—damned creatures requiring above all the salvation of their eternal souls. As one divine expressed, the hearts of children "are a meer nest, root, fountain of Sin, and wickedness. . . . Indeed, as sharers in the guilt of *Adam's* first sin, they're *Children of Wrath* by Nature, liable to eternal Vengeance, the Unquenchable Flames of Hell."[4] Or, as the famed *New England Primer* taught generations of children, "In Adam's Fall, We sinned All."

But, following the American Revolution, patterns of religious dissent, traced in denominationalism and the "French infidelity" (deism), forced liberal changes in Protestant dogma. Among the new attitudes about the nature of sin was a re-evaluation of the tenet of infant damnation.

Evidence of the new viewpoint surfaced as early as 1809 in Boston. Severe criticism of the doctrine of original sin came from the recently emerging Unitarian Church. In the vanguard of this left-wing Protestantism was the young minister, William Ellery Channing, who effectively set forth "The Moral Argument Against Calvinism." Channing exhorted his fellow New Englanders to adopt a more generous view of the nature of God and His benevolence, and thus a new view of man and his sinfulness. Even orthodox Congregational periodicals reflected a changing outlook on the notion of original sin and infant damnation. In 1814 a "Dissertation on the Sinfulness of Infants" asked: "if children were demons, fit for hell, would God have given them that attractive sweetness, that mild beauty, which renders them the most interesting objects on earth, and which compels us to shrink with horror from the thought of their everlasting ruin?" So effective were such challenges by the new theology that even Lyman Beecher, the champion of Puritan orthodoxy in Boston and elsewhere, eventually protested that Calvinists no longer taught infant damnation.[5]

Not all clergymen agreed with this liberal approach. Many religious conservatives throughout the pre-Civil War years continued to stress the doctrine of original sin. Theodore Dwight, a New England educator who introduced important reforms into New York City schools, asserted that "no child has ever been known since the earliest period of the world, destitute of an evil disposition—however sweet it appears." In 1840 the Reverend Heman Humphrey, a noted Orthodox minister who served both as president of Amherst College and a member of the Massachusetts Board of Education, warned that "however it might have been with our children, had sin never entered the world, we know how it is now. 'They are prone to evil, as the sparks fly upward.' " "We can leave the twig without a touch in the *right* direction," Humphrey observed, "but, if we do, we cannot hinder its being bent the *wrong* way."[6]

Despite the liberal and conservative clashes (perhaps because of them), many New England ministers and educators took a fresh look at the concept of original sin and found new reasons for focusing attention on the nature of the child. In 1847, with the publication of *Christian Nurture*, Horace Bushnell, a Congregational theologian, summarized the conflicting sentiments. At the same time he revealed the extent to which changing notions of childhood had entered the mainstream of religious thought.

Bushnell questioned the traditional assumption that children were born into sin, led lives tinged with evil until an age of consent when they could decide their own future course, and then, it was hoped, underwent a conversion experience to righteousness. He admitted that scripture and the laws of physiology compelled the belief that a child's nature was "somewhat depraved," but argued that this was not the important point. Rather, he asserted, from the moment of birth a child could be directed toward a life of righteousness or sin. Depravity did not stem from a predetermined evil nature. "The nurture of the soul and the character is to begin just when the nurture of the body begins." Assume any degree of depravity you choose, Bushnell offered, "there is yet nothing in it to forbid the possibility that a child should be led, in his first moral act, to cleave unto what is good and right, any more than in the first of his twentieth year." He condemned alike the orthodox view of raising the child as a sinner waiting for salvation, and the liberal view of no training at all, which supposed a total faith in human nature. Bushnell insisted that with the proper nurture, a child could grow up as a Christian, and never know himself as being otherwise.[7]

The implications of Bushnell's *Christian Nurture* were evident; in their religious and moral natures young people differed from adults. Nurture, not simply nature, was the primary emphasis. Rather than worry over the theological niceties of original sin and infant damnation, the important concern was raising the child. Bushnell agreed with such educators as Horace Mann about various stages of human growth—infancy, childhood, and youth—before an individual reached adulthood. Recognizing these separate stages of development, adults could provide the appropriate nurture that would ensure a moral life when children reached maturity.

The chief point made by Bushnell and others was that in the enlightened climate of nineteenth-century opinion, children no longer were considered as miniature adults.[8] Some critics might still caution, as did one writer in 1846, "remember that children are men in miniature; and though they are childish, and should be allowed to act as children, still our dealings with them should be manly, though not morose."[9] But most ministers, educators, physicians, and writers in the popular press advertised a new view of childhood as a separate biological and psychological stage of human life with problems and promises of its own.[10] Although some social theorists of the late seventeenth century had begun to discuss the uniqueness of childhood, it was not until the first half of the nineteenth century that Americans took up the debate in earnest, and adopted a new view toward the nature of the child.[11]

New Englanders showed their courtship of the child in various ways. A host of new magazines sprang up, aimed at appealing to women partly on the strength of the changing opinions about children. *Parent's Magazine*, the *Mother's Assistant*, the *Ladies' Magazine*, and *Godey's Lady's Book*, among others, portrayed the child in a new light. Fashion plates attested the change in attitude from earlier days. Children appeared with their parents, still dressed in overblown imitations of adult clothing styles, but, for the first time, also surrounded by the toys and playthings of childhood.[12] Rather than catechisms and a *New England Primer* children now held in their hands dolls and hoops.

The articles in these magazines usually emphasized the moral problems and potentials of childhood. Parents were urged to raise properly *"Citizens of enlarged benevolence"* and *"Missionaries of the Cross."* This emphasis was not surprising for many of the publications, such as the *Happy Home and Parlor Magazine* printed in Boston, had as their editors and major contributors both obscure and well-known clergymen. Together with literary-minded ladies, the ministers sought to awaken an expanding reading public to the potentials of childhood. The lessons of knowledge and virtue, they urged, must be taught the "unconscious child" who might well be "some future Washington or Franklin." That the nation needed more men like the Founding Fathers was an unquestioned assumption.[13]

Between 1830 and 1860 Boston and New England presses poured forth a rising tide of books and pamphlets on children and child-rearing. Like the magazine articles, much of the literature was moralistic and sentimental, seeking, as one author proposed, to set forth "a series of delightful instances of the success of pious maternal influence." The growing volume of "delightful" literature aroused some criticism from educators who found it too light-hearted for serious consideration about rearing children. In 1835, for example, John Hall, author of *On the Education of Children*, complained about the "current of popular treatises on this subject that almost daily issues from the press." But other writers welcomed the literature, stating that "little has been done to help mothers in the training of the young. The books are inadequate."[14] Some of the new books were important contributions to domestic reform and to what became known as "Domestic Science" and much later as "Home Economics." Among the most significant writings were those of Catherine Beecher.

A woman of forceful character and personal charm, Catherine Beecher was a member of New England's most illustrious Calvinist family. The same moral intensity that characterized her father Lyman Beecher, her two brothers Edward and Henry, and her sister Harriet, stirred Catherine as well. Despite the fact that she never married and had little practical experience with children, she devoted much of her life to piously instructing others on the correct methods of child-rearing. In 1841 she published her *Treatise on Domestic Economy*, one of the most successful books of the new genre. To the wives and mothers of New England, she offered useful suggestions on the care of infants, health, food, clothing, and related matters. If mothers were to raise their children properly, Miss Beecher insisted that they learn the *"principles* of that perfect and wonderful piece of mechanism." She believed that "the mother forms the character of the future man," and thus the future of the nation.[15]

While many writers, both the sentimental and the sensible, produced for parents a growing literature on child rearing, other authors began writing for children themselves. Throughout the first half of the nineteenth century, educators and popular writers devoted time and energy to stockpiling a mountainous collection of juvenile literature. Recognizing that children were not miniature adults and therefore required special training, the writers drew upon the experience of a prolific group of English authors for guidance in creating an American literature for children.[16]

In 1826 Lydia Maria Francis (later Child), a Boston novelist and teacher, founded the first successful children's magazine in America, *Juvenile Miscellany*. In 1827 Nathaniel William, a Boston journalist and nationally known poet, launched *The Youth's Companion*, one of the most successful and probably the most influential juvenile periodical during the nineteenth century. Several prominent educators hastened to cultivate the new field. Josiah Holbrook, Samuel R. Hall, Lyman Cobb, William A. Alcott, and Joseph Alden wrote profusely for children's magazines and also produced didactic novels and moral guidebooks.[17] Most prolific and widely read of the new writers was Samuel G. Goodrich.

Goodrich, son of a Congregational minister, settled in Boston in 1826 and began an astonishingly successful career as an author and publisher of literature for children. Writing under the pen name of "Peter Parley," Goodrich first published in 1827 *The Tales of Peter Parley about America*. He followed this volume with more than one hundred other "Parley" books which ultimately sold in the millions. Considering nonsense rhymes like "Hey Diddle Diddle" and imaginative stories like *Red Riding Hood* as unchristian and unfit for young minds, Goodrich instead had his character, a kindly old gentleman addressing groups of children, continually emphasize the virtues of life in America and the values of enterprise, thrift, and honesty.[18]

By the 1840's the new literature for children had begun to replace catechisms and Scriptures. Some conservative social observers feared the process had gone too far. Heman Humphrey, for example, vigorously protested the "baby literature upon our book-seller's counters, . . . flying abroad, like the locusts, glittering in the sun, in their septennial transmigrations."[19] But stories and books kept tumbling forth. The discovery of childhood had led to the recognition that children needed a literature of their own. If the new writings appeared too secular to some, most of the books and stories revealed grave concern about the morality of American youth. The theology of the *New England Primer* had given way to a secular morality. Christian moral principles still challenged young readers, but now in the sugar-coated guise of fiction. Like Horace Bushnell, children's authors sought the proper Christian nurture of their readers.

The discovery of childhood also led to an interest in children's hygiene and physical fitness. Every aspect of a child's physical life received detailed analysis. A flow of writings appeared on proper and improper diets, the advantages and disadvantages of nursing in infancy, the use and misuse of alcohol and drugs, early as opposed to late toilet-training, masturbation, mental health, and other problems. Interest in the health of children led to demands by doctors, health faddists, and educators for systematic training in physical exercise as a vital part of improving human beings through education. As early as 1826, a committee of Bostonians—including George Ticknor, a Harvard instructor, Josiah Quincy, Jr., son of the mayor, and other leading citizens—recommended the subscription of $5,000 for a gymnasium school to be constructed on city-donated land. The committee hoped that once the beneficial effects of physical education and exercise had proved themselves, either the city or philanthropic individuals would underwrite further expenses. At the same time, the *American Journal of Education* began a crusade for gymnasiums and school playgrounds as necessary centers of physical activity in the allegedly debilitating environment of the city where exercise and fresh air were at a premium.[20] This emphasis on exercise and fresh air continued strong throughout the antebellum years.

Like the literature on child-rearing, the discussions of hygiene and physical fitness highlighted their moral potential. The works of the leading pseudo-scientists of the day—the phrenologists—most clearly illustrated the moralistic attitudes. Phrenology asserted that the mind consisted of independent faculties or character traits that were revealed through external bumps on the skull. The Scottish practitioner George Combe introduced Americans to the new "science" on several visits to Boston and other cities between 1838 and 1840. Enthusiasm for phrenology coincided with and lent support to the new views on childhood. Orson S. Fowler, the most widely read American phrenologist, stated in his book *Education and Self-Improvement* (1844) that "virtue, *moral* perfection, *holiness, goodness*—depend considerably more upon the *health*, and are *produced* by it—by a sound and vigorous *physiology*—than most good people suppose; while depravity, sinfulness, . . . and all the vices that degrade men . . . are *caused* by—are the *legitimate, necessary products of physical derangement*—more than of all other causes combined."[21] In Boston and in other cities educators accepted many of the phrenological tenets to support their own urgings for moral improvement through physical fitness.

Horace Mann, throughout his *Sixth Annual Report* (1842), emphasized phrenological principles as the basis of physical health, and physical health in turn as the foundation of moral improvement. The understanding of physiological principles, according to Mann, was especially necessary to educate children living in crowded cities, for they had half the "bodily energy, the vital force, the stamina of constitution" enjoyed by rural youth. Another leading Boston educator, William B. Fowle, observed in 1841 that discussion by visionaries of human nature as it ought to be, was useless. "Phrenology alone, of all the systems of mental philosophy," he claimed, "lays its foundations in general facts, and not in particular experience; in human nature, and not in the specific nature of any philosopher."[22] Like Mann, Fowle believed that phrenological precepts offered a practical basis for education and moral betterment.

To urban educators, the new emphases on the nature of childhood pointed to one conclusion: the minds of children were not shadow-boxes of adulthood in which flickered all the passions and prejudices of mature life. Children, they agreed, were born with minds uncluttered and habits unformed.

"Children," declared Gideon F. Thayer, a Boston teacher and renowned educational theorist, "are brought into life plastic, and, for a time, passive beings; ready to receive . . . mouldings and impressions." Bronson Alcott, school teacher and transcendentalist mystic, stressed that infants at birth already possessed moral faculties and abilities required for instruction; Alcott added that nonetheless infants were malleable to either good or evil. The conscience of the child must be cultivated, he wrote, at an early, impressionable age. Shortly after accepting the post of Secretary of the Massachusetts Board of Education, Horace Mann explained that "I have abandoned jurisprudence, and betaken myself to the larger sphere of mind and morals. Having found the present generation composed of materials almost unmalleable, I am about transferring my efforts to the next." Mann believed that "men are cast-iron; but children are wax. Strength expended upon the latter may be effectual, which would make no impression upon the former."[23]

The plasticity of the child's nature had become such a commonly held assumption by the late 1850's that John D. Philbrick, superintendent of Boston Public Schools, could state that " 'the child is the father of the man.' Every educator should ponder this great truth. The child who has been carefully trained in the right way, for three or four years, can be kept in the right path afterwards with comparative ease."[24] The only question that many educators and reformers pondered was the best means of keeping children in the right path.

The discovery of childhood brought with it concern for the future—the future of both the child and the nation. Although Americans had always regarded their youth as the promise of the future, more than ever during the three antebellum decades they promoted the present generation as either the salvation or the destruction of the nation. Rebellious youth in the cities caused great alarm. As one popular magazine writer pointed out to readers in a story about a criminal being tried in Massachusetts courts, insubordination had characterized the villain's life "from his childhood upwards." "His whole course has been marked by self-will, breaking through all the common restraints of the family, of the school-room, of the counting-house, of social life, and of the law of God." Parents, warned the writer, should tremble. In his *Eighth Annual Report* (1844), Horace Mann stated the case in even more somber tones. Taking a cataclysmic view of social order and of the nation's future, Mann prophesied that "if we do not prepare children to become good citizens;—if we do not develop their capacities, if we do not enrich their minds with knowledge, imbue their hearts with the love of truth and duty, and a reverence for all things sacred and holy, then our republic must go down to destruction, as others have gone before it; and mankind must sweep through another vast cycle of sin and suffering."[25]

Worried over the future, Mann and other educational reformers increasingly focused attention on the present. Assuming the malleability of children's characters, they turned to debates about the proper environments for shaping the child. Surroundings, they believed, were of great importance for developing character. A motive for proper behavior, Mann wrote Elizabeth Peabody in 1836, "depends upon innate propensity," but it also resulted from "education, association, external condition, and a thousand other things."[26] In questioning the influence of environment, Mann and others found themselves re-evaluating the fundamental institutions of American society. Foremost among those affecting the rearing of youth were the family and the church.

THE DECLINE OF THE FAMILY

During the colonial years the Puritans saw the family as vital to the ordering of society. Religiously and economically the family was the lynchpin of the Puritan social structure. Whether the family unit was nuclear (husband, wife, and children living together, independent of relatives), extended (relatives such as cousins, nieces, nephews, grandparents, parents, sisters and brothers, traced by the male line, all living together in a single household), or of a modified kinship nature (two or more generations living together in the same community with children retaining dependence on parents even after they no longer shared the same roof), colonial New Englanders prized family stability as the core of social stability.[27] That evaluation of the family's importance carried over into the early years of the nineteenth century.

Americans during the first half of the nineteenth century often sentimentalized familial relationships. (This was hardly surprising for a generation that idealized the "common man" without knowing or caring who he was; that crusaded for a nation of cold water drinkers; that wept over slavery for causing the death of "Little Eva"; that found health-quack Sylvester Graham holding out a cracker to cure all social ills; and that admired novelist Mrs. Eden Southworth, a purveyor of pulp, as one of its most popular writers.) A lonely Horace Mann, bereft of wife and children, wrote to a friend returned from a visit that "I suppose you are . . .

once more in that most sacred of all places upon earth—*home;* and a member of that most divine institution in the world, family." Like many others, Mann delighted in the novel *Home* (1835) by Catherine Sedgwick. *Home* was an immensely popular book, running through twelve printings in two years. This moralistic tale of the Barclay family, living in and facing the wiles of the large city, romanticized the relationships between children and parents. Miss Sedgwick clearly outlined the moral duties of both to each other, emphasizing the importance of religious guidance and tender kindness by parents and unquestioning obedience to parental authority by children. Mann sent a copy of the novel to his sister for her children to read. "What a different world this would be," he ventured, "if our habits were formed upon the principles it contains and our life directed by them."[28]

Behind the romanticizing of the family lay a strong faith in the moral importance of family solidarity. In 1819 Noah Webster wrote to Governor John Brooks of Massachusetts, affirming that the public character of a nation derived from its families and schools. "Families, those elementary associations of man springing from the divine institution of marriage," Webster noted, "are the germs of all human society." Throughout the 1820's and the 1830's, popular magazines glorified the family while also offering helpful homemaking hints. Educators in Boston and throughout New England deified the family as "God's primary school, . . . the centre-post of social order."[29]

But the extensive public relations campaign bore the earmarks of a cover-up; the sacred institution was in trouble. Lecturers before the American Institute of Instruction, an association of educators, writers, and social reformers, often reflected contemporary hopes and fears about the social role of the family. In 1841, for instance, one E. W. Robinson stressed that "with faithful and early moral culture, *families* will be nurseries of piety. . . . This is the institution divinely designed for the primary work of education, physical and intellectual, but especially moral." Robinson emphasized that if the familial relationships could be improved, they would become the core of human happiness, but if perverted would become the source of corruption throughout society.[30] Robinson's fears about the possible consequences to social order that perverse changes in the nature of the family would entail revealed skepticism about the lasting strength of the institution. He was not alone in his fears. Despite the praise and romantic allusions to family harmony, there was growing concern about the stability of family relationships. Changing attitudes about the nature of children brought a re-examination of the nature of the family.

The reappraisal of family life between the 1830's and the 1860's became a favorite pastime of many social commentators. Harsh judgments on the instability of family life were a stock item of foreign inventories of America. Articles in domestic popular magazines attested to growing doubts about the social worth of the family as the molder of virtuous youth. By the late 1830's Boston men of wealth and prestige were complaining that "the influence of family is entirely lost. Our young ladies, for instance, do not value birth and good breeding half so much as money."[31] Cultural conservatives, of course, have always alleged a loss of breeding and gentility in their own generation as compared to that of their fathers; still, an especially poignant sense of loss pervaded the sentimental generation of the 1830's and 1840's, as evidenced in a lengthy *Boston Transcript* editorial of June 30, 1836:

> We have no old men now. No old mansions now. All are young. All are new. We are all young men now. Nobody wears a wig, nor a cocked hat, nor powder, nor small-clothes and silk stockings and buckles, nor white-topped boots, nor a queue, nor a gold-headed cane. We have changed all that. The "Gentlemen of the Old School," those patterns of manly elegance, are fast passing away. Habits, customs, marriage, men, all have changed. A bustling multitude supplies the place of a social family; and what was once a town, needing no annual director, is now a miniature world, a mighty city, where we have to ask, "who is my neighbor?"

To conservatives, indeed to men of various social persuasions, the family, as the rock of social order, appeared to be crumbling and breaking away from its historical moorings. Even the fact that the Federal Census of 1850 was the first to use the individual, not the family, as its basic unit of measurement and information, implied recognition of the decline of family solidarity.

One of the explanations for changes in family life offered by educators and social observers pointed to residential location. Writers asserted that in the country, on farms, and in small, rural towns family stability was undisturbed by any wide separation among the places of work, recreation, and dwelling. Fathers remained close to home, worked side by side with their children in the fields, read to them and aided in their lessons when district school was in session. Family harmony and security in small towns was not disrupted by hurried commercial activity, or by children at work in factories, or by the temptations of European fashions of dress and recreation that were common in the city.[32]

But in the cities, family life appeared less certain to survive. As the Reverend Edwin H. Chapin, Boston and New York City Universalist minister, phrased it: "the City especially reveals the *moral qualities* of our nature. . . . Here, more than anywhere else, the human heart is turned inside out, and its secret avenues are re-cast in the streets and bye-places." Here, Chapin charged, men worshiped at the "shrine of mammon" and preferred temporal good "to the eternal Right." In 1834 the conservative Whig spokesman Caleb Cushing warned his listeners at the annual meeting of the American Institute of Instruction that "there is, in the heart of even our purest cities, a crusade preaching against the very existence of social order, a war waged on all we most value in our national institutions, of religious, moral, social, and political." Middle-class men pursuing business success, Cushing stated, "such men, with their families cannot fail to be among the first victims of any great social convulsion."[33] Although Cushing was decrying the leveling spirit of Jacksonian democracy, his warning was clear: the activities of workingmen's parties, the demands for women's "rights," the expansion of the suffrage —all made life more tenuous in cities where any social upheaval tended to disrupt the precarious balance of family life dependent on a breadwinner whose livelihood was at the mercy of economic vagaries.

The absence of the father from the home on business purposes resulted directly from living in the city, charged various popular writers, and surely was destructive of family stability. Paternal neglect, protested the Reverend John S. C. Abbott, popular author and educator, "is at the present time one of the most abundant sources of domestic sorrow." The father, "eager in the pursuit of business, toils early and late," finding little time to discharge his duties toward his children. Journalists urged even the fathers who worked from sunrise to sunset away from home to spend at least an hour a day to keep their children from falling into a life of viciousness and crime. This children's hour was particularly important to the health of the family because the absence of the father from the home was matched by an increasing independence of girls and women at work in New England mills and factories. Rising divorce rates appeared to reflect that independence and certainly threatened the future of the family as a reliable social institution.[34]

But more than urban economic pursuits undermined order and harmony in the family. The very nature of life in the cities seemed to preclude the proper nurture of children within the family. Crowded living conditions and inadequate sanitation facilities injured health and character alike. William B. Fowle observed that only the children of farmers, fresh from the country, were active and intelligent in cities like Boston; cities debilitated their long-time residents.[35] "There is evil enough to try the child's character at home, in the country," stated a popular magazine writer, "without sending him to the city." In cities parents and children alike were exposed "to the torrents of corruption which flow through the streets, and to the exhalations of vice which arise from crowded shops and manufactories or the still more infectious atmosphere of . . . wretched habitations."[36] Bostonians and other New Englanders feared that youth in the city often learned their standards of behavior and morality in streets and alleys rather than in their homes. Children were hapless victims of the "moral jungles" of city streets. All of these difficulties of urban life pointed to an inevitable decline of family stability and authority. In his private journal Horace Mann confided that the rise of a complex, urban society promised to destroy the abilities of families to raise and educate their children properly.[37]

Friends of education and prophets of social doom alike bewailed an alleged decline in family authority. In 1842 Boston's most distinguished educator, George B. Emerson, then president of the American Institute of Instruction, spoke at its annual convention. Dwelling on the need for moral instruction to mold the conscience of the child, Emerson noted that most parents were either disinclined or unqualified by their own ignorance or their business enterprises "to give suitable instruction in social duties." On another occasion he stated that "when your homes are all what they should be," only then could moral training be left to the family. In 1843 a writer in the *Christian Watchman,* a Boston Baptist periodical, declared that parents had surrendered their responsibilities for moral education. Their laxity could destroy the nation. Soon after, Horace Mann commented on the lack of family discipline and cautioned that "the parent who would train up a child in the way he should go, must go in the way he would train up the child."[38]

In 1847, in an early example of the public opinion survey, Mann circulated among other educators a questionnaire on the efficacy of public education. In his circular Mann alleged that "pernicious family and social influences" undermined the proper training of children and asked if others agreed. Approving replies came from many leading educational reformers. That same year the Reverend Nathaniel Colver, a Baptist minister of such renown that he was considered a tourist attraction in Boston, charged that recently there had been a vast, alarming multiplication of vile and profligate young men. There was no doubt, he thought, that cities had become thronged with "enlightened and accomplished pickpockets, debauchees, house-burners, and robbers," because of the "almost universal prostration of family government and the almost entire absence of parental restraint." Indulgence appeared to be the order of the day.[39]

Social critics saw the family as society writ small, "a government or kingdom in miniature." Believing in the organic nature of society, educators and reformers asserted that the lack of parental discipline within the family caused a failure of order and authority throughout society. Without the discipline of a stable family, as one writer put it, there was "a want of CONSCIENCE in the community." In 1844, masters of the Boston school, answering charges of ineptitude laid against them by Horace Mann, explained that the fault was not theirs, but that of the family and society. The masters complained sarcastically that "it is quite offensive now-a-days to ears polite, to talk of authority, and command and injunction." Now, "we must persuade and invite, and win." William B. Fowle, Mann's associate, argued that there was little doubt "that the human race is off the track of progress, and is much more likely to be destroyed, than to attain to that perfection for which we are commanded to strive." Even Bronson Alcott, who viewed the child and the family with transcendental optimism, admitted that community affairs were social, as well as individual, concerns. But, he stated, "the State is stabbed at the hearth-side and here liberty and honor are first sold. It is injured by family neglect."[40]

The family, as a "kingdom in miniature," reflected the larger problems of society. The errors of parents were not solitary errors, an educator told his fellow teachers in 1849. Rather they were part of the cardinal and universal error of the age—the breakdown of the traditional institutions of society. The failure of the family was only the chief example of the crisis of authority in modern society.[41] Benjamin Labaree, president of a Vermont college, summarized the opinions of many educators in 1849 when he posed the rhetorical question: "are we not becoming, as a people, more and more bold, restless and impatient of restraint? Shall we not find abundant proof in the family, in the school and in society at large, that there is an increasing disrespect for law and authority?"[42]

Clearly, as far as many social critics were concerned, society had to look elsewhere than the family for a source of stability in unstable times. Traditionally, the Christian church had anchored men in periods of social stress. But just as they questioned the strength of the family, antebellum educators and reformers also doubted the institutional might of the church in urban society.

THE CRUMBLING FOUNDATIONS OF CHRISTIAN ORDER

Part of the American intellectual heritage from Europe was a belief in the social necessity of an established church. Both in the relationship of men to God and to each other, the church shouldered the responsibility of maintaining order and a sense of purpose in society. In colonial Boston and New England, men had a covenant with God, and the state in turn had a covenant with men to support God's church on earth.[43]

By the time of the American Revolution, the "Holy Commonwealth" of the Puritan fathers appeared in danger of collapsing before the onrush of libertarian demands. Timothy Dwight, grandson of Jonathan Edwards and later president of Yale College, complained that the War "unhinged the principles, the morality, and the religion of this country more than could have been done by a peace of forty years," and charged that a rising spirit of "free-thinking" threatened the state-supported church. Determined clergymen and their supporters, however, hoped to check anti-clerical hostility and to maintain state support of religion. Both in the Massachusetts Constitutional Convention of 1780 and that of 1820, Boston clergymen and laymen fought off attempts to terminate public financial support of religion, which largely meant tax support of the Congregational Church.[44] Even those reformers who demanded that no denomination should be "established" by state financial support agreed with the orthodox that the state should somehow guarantee Christianity and a legal system of public worship. For its own defense, civil government depended on public piety and morality.[45]

While liberals and conservatives alike concurred on the importance of religion to moral order and civil stability, challenges to an established church continued. Beginning in 1815 in Boston, the rapid growth of Unitarianism threatened the tradition of state support. By the early 1820's the new, dynamic Unitarian Church was solidly entrenched in the city. Public acceptance of what came to be known as the "Boston religion" alarmed many orthodox leaders of the older Congregational churches. In 1820, in the Dedham decision, the state Supreme Court opened the doors to a liberal take-over of much church property. The court upheld the plea of church members in Dedham that they had the right to elect their own minister, in this case a Unitarian, and still retain the property of the church in the face of secession by orthodox parishioners. Over the next decade at least thirty Congregational churches and their property were lost to the liberals, or as some Boston ministers claimed, were stolen by the Unitarians.[46] In 1823 conservatives in the city gained a small triumph in helping to defeat Harrison Gray Otis, the Unitarian-backed candidate for governor. In that same year Lyman Beecher, the most staunch defender of orthodoxy in New England, settled in Boston, determined to restore Calvinism, "the dethroned royal family, wandering like a permitted mendicant in the city where once it had held court, and [where] Unitarians reigned in its stead."[47]

In Unitarianism and attempts at disestablishment, Beecher saw only disaster. "These innovations in church order," he later recalled, "though resisted by many . . . became at length almost universal throughout New England." Religious experience no longer was the subject of sermons, church discipline was lax, candidates for the clergy declined, and "laxity of belief and morals prevailed."[48]

But even Beecher could not stem the tide battering the principle of an established church. By 1831 Unitarianism permeated the religious climate of the city. Bostonians and foreign observers alike heralded William Ellery Channing, the major Unitarian spokesman, as the most celebrated preacher and author of his time. Orthodox ministers felt themselves so on the defensive that they attacked Unitarianism as the "state religion," an awkward position for Boston Congregationalists to take. In 1831 the Reverend Parsons Cooke appealed to the "injured community" to prevent "the climax of abuses" from being headed "by an act of uniformity." Citizens, he implored, must stand "on the side of religious freedom and equal rights." In 1833 the Commonwealth abandoned specific legal provisions tending to guarantee the established position of Congregationalism. Yet even this "climax of abuses" underscored a tenacious belief in the social role of religion. Full equality of all denominations became law with citizens no longer required to support churches financially. But again the legislature asserted that public worship and instruction in piety "promote the happiness and property of a people and the security of a republican government."[49]

If the Congregational Church was disestablished, religion itself was not. Religious enthusiasm, in fact, quickened. Scores of quarterly reviews and weekly newspapers devoted to religious discussions of contemporary issues sprang up, with several of the most influential centered in Boston. Newer denominations, notably the Baptists and the Methodists, numerically outdistanced the older Presbyterian and Congregational churches. Evangelical preachers such as Charles G. Finney stumped the eastern seaboard, fostering revivals in Boston and elsewhere. Religion was popular, but its very vitality demonstrated its weakened position as an institutional force in society. Evangelicalism appealed to the individual and the possibility of his personal perfection, not to the organized churches acting as an institutional balance among individuals, God, and the State. The organized church as a social institution was no longer a dynamic force but had become merely a convenient and perhaps enjoyable association of individuals.[50]

A host of voluntary religious organizations attempted to perform all the social tasks once considered the province of the established church. In Boston, voluntary societies sprang up at the drop of a philanthropist's good wishes. During the first three decades of the nineteenth century hardly a year passed without a new organization entering the field of benevolence. So many groups competed with one another in elevating the poor, treating the sick, sheltering unwed mothers, and redeeming the sinful that in 1835 delegates from most of the societies•met to form a clearing-house association "in order that all relief which a pure and enlarged benevolence dictates may be freely bestowed." Harriet Martineau, the often critical English writer, could justly observe of Boston in the 1830's, that "I know of no large city where there is so much mutual helpfulness, so little neglect and ignorance of the concerns of other classes."[51]

But voluntary societies alone could not take up the slack in the moral guidance of society left by a weakening, organized Christian church. Active as they were, the associations reached only a small number of citizens. The societies functioned merely as curative agencies, attempting to salvage the moral wreckage of long-standing evils. Protestant leaders of all denominations in Boston agreed that Christianity had to go beyond the treatment of existing ills and act as a preventive force in molding a moral society. Whether Unitarian or Congregational, liberal or orthodox, Boston leaders in the 1830's and 1840's called for a revitalized Protestantism. They hoped to maintain the moral authority of religion despite social changes in the institutional structure of Christianity. As Francis Grund, a naturalized citizen who had settled in Boston, observed of his fellow townsmen, "they look upon religion as a promoter of civil and political liberty; and have, therefore, transferred to it a large portion of the affection which they cherish for the institutions of their country. . . . They see in a breach of morals a direct violation of religion: and in this, an attempt to subvert the political institutions of the country."[52] By the 1830's, many concerned Protestant leaders distrusted the religious course of events in Boston and feared what those events meant for the moral stability of society.

Catholicism and agnosticism in the city heightened the distrust of the orthodox. Catholics had increased from some 2,000 in 1820 to over 20,000 by 1835. Protestant Bostonians failed to share the enthusiasm of Bishop Fenwick, head of the Boston diocese, who reported in 1835 that "the faith is constantly spreading, and its progress has been so rapid, especially in the city of Boston, that all who have witnessed it are astonished." Many of the new parishioners were Irish, bringing with them not only a strange religion but also the political despotisms of the old world. The growth of Catholicism posed yet another problem to beleaguered Protestants and worried republicans in the city.[53]

Orthodox leaders also saw cause for alarm in a rising agnosticism, symbolized in the case of Abner Kneeland. By profession, Kneeland was a Universalist clergyman, by practice, an agnostic. In 1831 he settled in Boston and founded the *Boston Investigator*, a weekly journal devoted to religious skepticism, attacks on Calvinism, and veneration of Andrew Jackson. His diatribes against religion soon incurred the wrath of the orthodox. Samuel Gridley Howe, an influential educator and close friend of Horace Mann, denounced Kneeland as "the hoary-headed apostle of

Satan." For his derisions of property rights, of the sacredness of marriage and of God, as well as for his articles on sex education, Kneeland was indicted in January 1834 on charges of having published a "scandalous, impious, obscene, blasphemous and profane libel of and concerning God." The trial went through several convictions and appeals. Finally, in 1838, he received sentence, becoming the last man to be jailed in Massachusetts for blasphemy.[54]

To the orthodox, the *cause celebre* gave added proof of the decline of Protestant morality and of their own loss of social influence. The fact that Kneeland's case aroused the sympathies and support of religious liberals and social radicals such as William Ellery Channing, Theodore Parker, Bronson Alcott, Ralph Waldo Emerson, and William Lloyd Garrison only confirmed the view of the orthodox. Traditional Protestantism, they feared, no longer stood as the guidepost of life in Boston. Some educators who worked to extend the common schools agreed, often linking together as inseparable public education, the preservation of social order, and Protestant Christianity. In a report of the Standing Committee of the Boston Primary School Board in 1829, for example, Chairman John P. Bigelow reminded other committee members and the public that "the cause in which we are engaged is a *good*, and it may almost be said to be a *holy* one." We have the "unerring conviction," he concluded, "that in advancing the cause of education, we are promoting, by the surest methods, the greatest and best interests of our country and our religion." In 1843, Horace Mann rejoiced that the school system, in part, was designed to "quicken the vision of conscience, . . . and to inculcate the perfect morality of the Gospel." This combination was the best protection for society. In 1849 two featured speakers before the annual meeting of the American Institute of Instruction put the matter plainly. Benjamin Labaree emphasized that "the most important interests of individual and of society, the stability and the permanency of our institutions, *imperiously demand* that our children and youth be thoroughly instructed in the principles of moral and religious obligation." Charles Brooks, a close friend of Mann, was even more direct. He noted that character could be manufactured through early moral training, that morality underlay the peace and happiness of the state, and that "Christianity, enthroned in the heart of any people, is the cheapest police that any government can maintain."[55]

But, these educators asserted, a loss of authority in the churches confounded the social role of Christianity. Churches, observed Mann, had once been institutions into which children were born and morally raised. But churches no longer served that function. None of the social reforms of the day, he continued, could reach a people who had not experienced an awakening of moral sentiments in childhood. "Clergymen may about as well preach to the tenants of the churchyard as to those of the church itself." Other commentators charged that the best evidence of the lack of religious authority was the decline of family piety. A vicious cycle of indifference to religious principles had set in. Parents had surrendered the responsibilities of moral education and religious training almost entirely to teachers in Sunday schools, but Sunday schools attracted few children. A decline of teaching from the pulpit, a lack of authority in the church, and a loss of parental training had occurred which could destroy the nation. Even if the churches remained potent agencies in community life, argued George B. Emerson, "there are many children whom the instructions of the pulpit never reach; and some pulpits from which instructions adapted to little children seldom come." A reliance on the church might have sufficed when all families regularly attended, Emerson declared, and when parents daily gave religious and moral instruction at home. "But that time has passed." The loss of family piety and the declining importance of the church now threatened the stability of society.[56]

The structure of the church, like the structure of family life, had broken down in the face of urban change. "We are a busy people," George B. Emerson noted. "We live in the midst of a most active community," in which the cares of business and daily life caused persons to set aside their duties to their children. "Nothing is more important than the character of children," he continued, "but we do little to assure the proper molding of that character." People "talk much about the education of circumstances,—the church, the press, the institutions of the country, fashion, amusements, business, public opinion, the world. To these they seem willing to entrust the formation of the character of their children." But none of these was the answer to the problems of the day.[57]

Emerson, his fellow educators, and other Boston reformers interpreted the crisis of their times in light of their understanding of the structure of American society. They might, and did, express their concern about the moral nature of the individual. They assumed that a good society ultimately depended upon good individuals and often argued that by molding better individuals men might create a more perfect social order. But they seldom discussed the individual apart from his social context. They were not strict environmentalists, claiming that the institutions of society inevitably determined the nature of man. Neither personal experience nor their Christian beliefs had prepared them to adopt such a position wholly. Rather, as Horace Mann explained, they believed that all men had a potential for good or evil, only "circumstances have caused the diversities among them. Those orders and conditions of life amongst us, now stamped with inferiority are capable of rising to the common level; and of ascending if that level ascends."[58] Educators thus always were conscious of the interplay between individuals and social institutions. If circumstances and the order of social relationships alone did not determine individual character, neither could the individual exist apart from society, nor escape the weight of social institutions.

But time and again, Mann and others expressed their lack of faith in the present social institutions. They often prophesied that social instability was opening "the gates of pandemonium," letting out upon the land the "exhalations of death."[59] Their jeremiads often overstated the case. Contemporaries who sloughed off the dire warnings might dismiss them as empty rhetoric. But one conclusion was inescapable. A growing number of authors, ministers, and educators had come to believe that the structure of urban society could no longer respond to the challenges of the present or provide for the future.

Sharing with others in the discovery of the child, educators insisted that "above all others, must the children of a Republic be fitted for society as well as for themselves." They doubted the ability of the family and the church to serve as the traditional institutions of child-rearing. The rapid growth of cities, the increased pace of economic activity, and the extension of religious diversity made change itself appear to be the only constant force in society. "The stream of time is changing its direction," Mann asserted. "We must prepare ourselves to move with safety through the new realms we are now entering."[60] But if the family, the church, the state itself, were no longer reliable agencies of social stability, were there any havens of safety?

THE ARK OF SAFETY

"The Common School," proclaimed Horace Mann, *"is the greatest discovery ever made by man. . . .* Other social organizations are curative and remedial; this is a preventive and an antidote." Other educators conceded that "the pulpit, the press, the Sunday-school, the healthful discipline of the family" might continue to prove useful, but asserted that the people had selected schools in "preference to all others as the instrument best calculated to be used by them . . . to carry on the great and important work of qualifying every individual to add strength and beauty to the temple of republicanism in which they dwell." By 1840, leading educators agreed that God had established two schools—the family and the church—but added that public schools must supplement, if not completely replace, these institutions. "I would as soon give up the family or the church—almost so,—as the Common School," observed one schoolman. Schools had to become the "nurseries of the good, old, homely, substantial virtues," declared another educator, or we are doomed. In 1847 a re-

port of the Boston School Committee put the matter succinctly: "Our schools are our hope—we look to them, and their effects upon the intelligence of our citizens, as the Ark of Safety to our Institutions."[61]

Time and again during the three decades before the Civil War, Boston and New England educators affirmed that public schools had to replace the family as the chief institution for raising children to responsible adulthood. This affirmation implied that the role of the teacher in society equaled, if not exceeded, that of the parent. As a writer in the *Common School Journal* explained, in the present conditions of urban society "a vast majority of parents are unable, either on account of their own deficient education, or from want of time, to attend, in person, to the discharge of their duty." "Thus the teacher becomes their agent, supplying their place, and doing their duty." The Boston School Committee admitted that it felt the burdensome task of preparing youth "in the morning of their lives for the hours of noonday toil," and stated that "we call upon the schoolmaster to aid us; we tell him to stand in the place of the parent; we put in his hands a large part of our authority; we lay upon his shoulders a heavy portion of our responsibility."[62]

Some parents agreed with educators that the teacher had to don the mantle of parental authority. In 1836 a committee of Boston citizens informed the School Committee of their belief that schools were not intended simply as means of conveying intellectual knowledge from one brain to another. Rather, schools were to be families away from home, and "as the master stands in place of the parent; he should perform the duty of a parent; and examine closely the characters, morals and habits of each pupil." In the vast outpouring of educational literature on the role of the teacher, writers repeated the parental definition of the teacher's responsibility. This attitude had become so commonplace by the mid-1840's that Horace Mann could write that "the maxim embodied in the law of the land, and sustained by the good sense of all communities, that the teacher stands *in loco parentis,* that is, in the parent's place or stead, has been a thousand times repeated."[63]

If the public school was to replace the family in rearing children, educators believed it also had to supplant the church in the moral instruction of youth. If instructions in moral and social duties still came from the pulpits, George B. Emerson noted, to insist upon such lessons in schools would be superfluous. "But this is far from the case." Schools, therefore, were the only recourse. In daily instruction, teachers had to bring the child "to a regard for the laws of justice, integrity, truth, and reverence, so that he shall grow up mindful of the rights of others, a good neighbor, a good citizen, and an honest man." Schools had to replace the pulpit. Horace Mann affirmed that as long as society remained as unstable as it was, "every teacher has a sort of parochial duty to perform. . . . Now, and for a long time to come, . . . the teacher must be a school missionary." The Boston School Committee drew an analogy between the duties of the schoolmaster and those of ministers. As churchmen used to do, the teacher had to become a friend to students, show affectionate interest in their welfare, sympathize with them, and regard pupils on the basis of Christian love. Since authority in the church and in society at large was "avoided, disliked, unpopular," declared the Reverend John D. Hopkins before the American Institute of Instruction in 1850, "is it too much to ask that the teachers . . . use their best *influence* in favor of religion?" The schoolhouse and the church, asserted other educators, were the engines of progress, and clearly the schoolhouse had to lead the way. There, proclaimed a writer in the *Common School Journal,* "let them . . . be made good, whether they be made wise or not."[64]

Educators and reformers in Boston and throughout New England had come to agree by the 1840's that the social role of the public school was to assure social stability in a time of change. The school took precedence over the family, the church, and other social institutions because, as Horace Mann explained, "it is the only reliance of the vast majority of children." Only public education could prepare youth for the responsibilities of adulthood. Education could "adjust society to the new relations it is to fill, to remove the old, and to substitute a new social edifice, without overwhelming the present occupants in ruin." "Momentous thought!" exclaimed members of the Boston School Committee in 1850. "Thirty thousand of our fellow beings in so short a period, are to pass through and from the institution we now control, to be started on their journey, temporal and eternal, with habits formed through our counsel or by our sufferance—habits of industry or indolence—order or confusion—neatness or negligence—virtue or vice."[65]

To a generation of men whose social thought centered on the institutions which organized human relationships, it was natural that they sought to meet the challenges of the day with yet another social institution. During the years between 1820 and 1860, Boston educators and social leaders increasingly came to rely upon public schools as the best institutions for maintaining social stability.

4

Schoolhouses and Scholars

Children were huddled together in small, close, unventilated apartments, regardless of health and comfort. Every school that I attended was in a noisy neighborhood, and looked out upon crowded thoroughfares.

Henry K. Oliver (1876)[1]

Between 1820 and 1860 Boston and New England educators increasingly came to view the common school as a "community in miniature." There, the child could mature in an environment created especially for him, in surroundings tailored to fit his needs as separate from those of the adult community. There, the teacher could stand in place of the parent, examining the character, morals, and habits of each child, and exercising the moral authority that had once belonged exclusively to the family. There, also, the schoolmaster could impart the moral instruction that had once come from the pulpit, an agency whose orthodoxy and social prestige appeared ever more questionable.[2] The public school was to be a classroom, a family room, a church house—all things to all children. The school was to nurture the child to adulthood, equip him with necessary skills of a livelihood, and familiarize him with the rigors and dangers of life in the city. In short, the school was to be the social incubator of responsible citizens.

While the goal was ambitious, the optimism of Bostonians appeared equal to the task. By the mid-1820's enthusiastic citizens had erected a year-round system of primary schools, and had done so in spite of determined opposition from conservatives. Boston leaders had expanded grammar school instruction throughout the city. They had also provided a Latin High School for boys, an English High School for boys and a similar experimental school for girls (schools with less emphasis on the classics than in Latin schools), two classrooms in the House of Industry (the city poorhouse), and two separate schools for Negro children. Although total private contributions for private education still surpassed city taxes for public schools, expenditures for public education averaged nearly

69

$60,000 over the decade, or more than 16 per cent of total public expenditures.[3]

Boston seemed to deserve the praises bestowed by visitor and native alike. "The means of education are the same to all," marveled Mrs. Anne Royall, a usually cantankerous and cynical widow who supported herself by writing travelogues of American towns and cities. "There are not less than an hundred schools in Boston and vicinity, free to all, many of them without money and without price. . . . Never were the means so ample as in Boston; the whole state is one seminary of education; no excuse for ignorance; the poor are taught gratis." Educational critic James G. Carter testified that Boston alone had spent nearly as much for schooling as had the rest of the state combined. And referring to Carter's evaluation of Massachusetts' public schools, Harvard scholar George Ticknor, then a member of the Primary School Board, commented that the best proof of Boston's educational excellence was that wealthy citizens could find no better schools anywhere for their children. Indeed, by 1826, members of the City Council were suggesting that the city had built too well. Other New Englanders, they warned, heard of the superior public schools and moved to Boston to reap the advantages of free education. Yet even this criticism was a backhanded compliment, an indication of the pride that Bostonians had in their schools.[4]

Beneath the pride and optimism, however, lurked doubt. If the schools were as good as everyone said, why weren't they even better? If Boston was so dedicated to the principle of free public education, why weren't all of the children attending the public schools? During the late 1820's approximately 45 per cent of the city's school-age population attended the primary and grammar schools, a commendable number but not enough, according to the critics. Clearly, remarked some citizens, educational problems were far from solution. The City Council, wary of large expenditures in the face of a mounting public debt, refused to allocate funds for new schools. The Council was willing to build onto existing schools to provide rooms for ward political meetings, thereby satisfying two city needs with one sum. But it balked at other additions or repairs. In 1826, for example, expenditures for all public obligations exceeded income. Councilmen pointed to generous allotments to schools as partially responsible for the fiscal crisis. It was to be nearly a decade before the Council would grant funds for construction of the city's first primary school building.[5]

Although the Primary School Board and the School Committee often trumpeted their successes, they also bemoaned the failure of the general public and the city to give more support to schools. As early as 1820 the School Committee had observed that "though the present system of public education, and the munificence with which it is supported, are highly beneficial and honorable to the town," yet it could be perfected. The ominous facts, charged the Primary School Board in 1824, "that in this city a considerable number of youth should be suffered to grow up destitute of the advantages secured to the children generally, and be abandoned to idleness, vagrancy, ignorance, and crime, reflects no honor on the citizens or on our institutions, and demands prompt attention."[6]

Such comments characterized the curious mixture of praise and condemnation that filled the rhetoric of the common school movement in Boston and elsewhere. The very educators and reformers who advertised the need for common schools were the first to decry current school conditions. To be sure, their carpings were partly promotional devices. The public hardly would have voted higher taxes for new schools, equipment, and more highly paid teachers if it believed all was well. To shatter public complacency about school conditions was an educator's self-imposed duty. The criticisms of educators and reformers also were signs of healthful self-criticism. James G. Carter illustrated this tendency in noting that "the success of the free school system is just cause of congratulation; but . . . their influence has not been the greatest and best which the *same means,* under better management, might produce."[7]

Neither promotionalism nor self-criticism, however, explained the exuberance for public education on the one hand, and, on the other, the ever-present sense of dismay and defeat. However attractive a picture they painted, school authorities and educational reformers rarely failed to edge it with darker hues. "The public schools, in this city of Boston, are, we believe now, and have long been, comparatively in a prosperous state," commented Stephen Farley, a speaker before the 1834 meeting of the American Institute of Instruction. "We believe" and "comparatively"— these were words tinged with doubt. Boston schools, Farley concluded, tended toward *"what they ought to be;* and what all schools should be throughout the country." In 1845 the Boston School Committee reversed Farley's judgment. The annual report, written by Horace Mann's close friend and follower Samuel Gridley Howe, reluctantly charged that "the Grammar Schools of Boston have not the excellence and usefulness they should possess. We cannot but believe, for we see, that the other Schools [of the state] are better than most of ours." The report for the following year, prepared by Committee members less interested in reform, refuted Howe's declaration. In a metaphor that was to be oft-repeated the report asserted that "the common-school system of New England is its pride and strength; and the public schools of Boston are the richest jewel in its crown." Yet even this report dimmed its own lustrous praise of schools by exhorting citizens to "let us make them what they should be."[8]

Arguments for improving the schools invariably were accompanied by complaints about their present state. A comparison of the "is" and the "ought-to-be" was the reformers' stock-in-trade. As school systems expanded and as larger public funds for schools became available, the criticisms became more strident. Rising expectations of what an adequate system of public education could accomplish made present realities appear shoddy by comparison.

By 1855, for example, stateman Edward Everett could maintain that Boston schools had improved over the past fifty years "beyond what any one will readily conceive" who had not witnessed the changes for himself. But less than two years later, the celebrated Harvard philosopher Francis Bowen, whose chief experience had been with Boston schools, could observe of the entire New England school system: "any hovel would answer for a school-house, any primer would do for a textbook, any farmer's apprentice was competent to 'teach school.' " Boston schoolmen had been hurling the same invectives against their own schools for many years. A gulf existed between what educators and reformers believed the schools could become, and what they observed the schools to be. This disparity between expectations and realities gave rise to the educational jeremiad, that peculiar blend of praise and vilification that permeated school board reports and the pronouncements of reformers throughout the antebellum years.[9]

Educators and reformers had to adjust their conceptions of the ideal public school to fit the physical realities of an urban environment. Many persisted in measuring the city schools by a rural standard, as, indeed, they often measured the quality of urban life itself by a pastoral ideal. Since the public school was to be a model miniature community, educators stressed that the physical settings of classroom and school buildings inevitably would influence the quality of education. The school, they argued, could not be parent and clergyman unless it provided for the complete needs of the child—and these were physical as well as intellectual and moral. Much of the idealistic debate, therefore, about the social role of common schools centered around mundane matters such as the best location for the schoolhouse, the proper size of classrooms, and the need for playgrounds. In discussing the daily functioning of the public schools, educators and reformers revealed their idealistic conceptions of the perfect school for perfecting the child.

EXPECTATIONS AND REALITIES

Educators and school reformers—as college graduates, lawyers, physicians, and men in various other professions—could not help but breathe the intellectual atmosphere of their times. Whatever else was true, during the years of the common school movement a pastoral imagery suffused the intellectual horizons of America. Though the forty-year period from 1820 to 1860 saw proportionately the largest increase in urban population in the nation's history (with the peak urbanization of New England occurring in the 1840's),[10] many American intellectuals rejected that present in favor of the idyllic past. Novelists and essayists like Nathaniel Hawthorne, Herman Melville, James Fenimore Cooper, Henry David Thoreau, and Ralph Waldo Emerson perceived the nation in transition from an agrarian to an industrial society. Reacting against a prophesied age of the machine (most often symbolized by the railroad engine) these and other writers looked romantically over their shoulders to the alleged simplicity of by-gone days. In Nature—an abstract metaphor for simplicity and order —they found virtue and innocence; in the City or the Machine—verbal shorthand for complexity and disorder—they beheld decadence and artificiality.

Thus the political symbols of the period became Andrew Jackson—historian George Bancroft's "unlettered man of the West," the "nursling of the wilds"—and the log cabin. Thus the humor was wrapped in homespun and personified by riverboatman Mike Fink, backwoodsman Davy Crockett, and Yankee Colonel Jack Downing. Thus the Christian church became the Church Evangelical, crusading with its rural revivalism into the heart of even the great cities. Thus the characteristic philosophy of the period was Transcendentalism—a blend of two parts Nature and one part Mysticism—served up at the side of a pond by a man who had failed as a teacher in urban schools.[11]

Even city-born and bred Bostonians expressed this vague longing for a simplified, rural, or village past. In his *The Companion to Spelling Books*, a widely used textbook in Boston grammar schools, William Bentley Fowle wrote of innocence versus artificiality, "the town for manners, the country for morals." Ralph Waldo Emerson, who wished to demonstrate that one man could be a counterpoise to the city, still had to admit: "I wish to have rural strength and religion for my children, and I wish city facility and polish. I find with chagrin that I cannot have both." And, by the mid-1840's, the Brahmin educator and author George Ticknor could sadly recount that the Boston of his youth at the turn of the century was gone forever. Then "we . . . felt involved in each other's welfare and fate as it is impossible we should now, when our numbers are trebled, and our affairs complicated and extended till their circumference is too wide to be embraced by any one mind, and till the interests of each individual are grown too separate and intense to be bound in by any general sympathy with the whole." Ticknor could only grieve for the days when "we were then a more compact, united, and kindly community than we have ever been since, or ever can be again."[12]

Undoubtedly these pastoral longings, so pervasive in the intellectual climate of the period, influenced the attitudes of educators about the conditions of Boston schools. Who could admire the congested urban classroom when comparing it to the literary commonplace of the day, Ichabod Crane's schoolhouse in Sleepy Hollow? There "the schoolhouse stood just at the foot of a woody hill, with a brook running close by. From hence the low murmur of his pupils' voices conning their lessons might be heard in a drowsy summer's day, like the hum of a bee-hive." Indeed, who could admire the city itself when even the textbooks used by children in rural and urban schools alike painted it as artificial and corrupt when compared with the virtuous, idyllic life of the countryside? Certainly the most familiar building in all of American folklore was the "Little Red Schoolhouse," the traditional symbol of American education. Educational reformers found it far more pleasant to imagine a little red schoolhouse in the country, bordered by vines and flowers, standing sentinel near a wooded hill, than to conjure up a rather dirty, wooden or stone, one or two story building on a crowded street, surrounded by tailors' shops, wagon depots, saloons, and other sights and sounds of the city. That many Boston and New England educators fancied the image of the rural school and rejected the urban school as educationally unworthy was not surprising.[13]

Occasionally someone might rise to the defense of the urban classroom. Stephen Farley, calling for improvement, nonetheless praised the schools of Boston, New Haven, and other New England cities, regretting only that their examples did not reach and reform the country schools. In 1848, commenting on the recent annual report of the Boston schools, a writer in the *North American Review* observed that "in some respects, the city schools have advantages over those of the country. The city is the centre of intelligence, as well as of wealth. Ideas, no less than money, circulate with greater rapidity there. Books are more abundant and accessible, and the national powers are more speedily brought into activity. Talent of all kinds naturally concentrates in the city." Yet even this admirer felt compelled to warn that the activity of the city intellect might be superficial or showy.[14]

But for every admirer, there were many more detractors. Leading the chorus of jeremiads were such men as Warren Colburn, James G. Carter, William A. Alcott, George B. Emerson, Samuel G. Goodrich, and Horace Mann—each a major figure of the day. Colburn was a founder of the American Institute of Instruction, a Boston schoolteacher, for a brief pe-

riod a member of the Boston School Committee, and the author of *Colburn's First Lessons, Intellectual Arithmetic upon the Inductive Method
of Instruction* (1826), the standard mathematics textbook in Boston, and
throughout much of the nation as well. Carter, through his *Essays upon
Popular Education* (1826), and his activities as chairman of the state
House Committee on Education that created the Board of Education in
1837, fostered much of the debate on the common school movement in
New England. Alcott was a tireless writer in educational campaigns, a
former teacher in district schools, editor of the *Annals of Education* in
Boston during the 1830's, and one òf the most influential propagandists
in the discovery of the childhood movement. Emerson, second only to
Mann in public esteem as an educational missionary, served on both the
Primary School Board and the School Committee in Boston. In addition,
he was a co-author of *The School and the Schoolmaster* (1842), the leading manual for schoolteachers and administrators during the period. Goodrich was the author and publisher of the famous "Peter Parley" series—
collections of didactic stories and moral aphorisms—as well as the compiler
of numerous school textbooks.[15]

Each of these men had been born, raised, and educated in small town,
rural surroundings. Each had attended a New England district school.
Their childhood experiences led them to be sharply critical of urban
schools. A realization that education in the city posed more difficult problems than existed in the countryside kindled their enthusiasm for reform.
Although in numerous ways they measured the physical realities of urban
schools by pastoral expectations, paradoxically these reformers did not
urge a return to the rural, district school. They knew it too well.

The early training of Horace Mann was typical. Born in the small town
of Franklin, Massachusetts, in 1796, he was one of five children whose
father meagerly supported the family by cultivating a small farm. Mann's
early education was limited to a district school that belonged to the smallest district, had the poorest schoolhouse, and employed the cheapest
teachers in a town that itself was small and poor. Among his first teachers
was an itinerant master named Samuel Barrett, a gentleman learned in
languages who would teach for six months, then lose his post because of
a prolonged drunken binge. In later life Mann regretted his unhappy
childhood, the "continual privations," the few and miserable books for
children, the very poor teachers, and the fact that "until the age of fifteen
I had never been to school more than eight or ten weeks in a year."[16]

To outsiders the district schools appeared praiseworthy. The usually
critical Harriet Martineau, for example, on her visit through rural New
England in the mid-1830's, marveled that "the provision of schools is so

adequate, that any citizen who sees a child at play during school-hours may ask 'Why are you not at school?' and, unless a good reason be given, may take him to the schoolhouse of the district."[17] But those who had been trained in such schools could only criticize.

"Two principal causes have operated from the first establishment of the free schools," explained James G. Carter of the district schools, "to impair and pervert their influence. 1st, Incompetent instructors; 2d, Bad school books." Carter could not overemphasize the shabby quality of teaching in the district schools. Teachers were usually very young; they were constantly changing their employment in search of higher wages or more interesting work; worst of all, they rarely had undergone any direct training for their work. Other reformers joined in raising a familiar lament: "shall those who despair of success in any employment, be allowed to take up school-keeping as an ultimate resource?" It was not uncommon for school boards throughout New England to complain of applicants, as did one board in 1847, that "he thinks of turning peddler, or of working at shoemaking. But the one will expose him to storms, the other he fears will injure his chest. . . . He will nevertheless teach school for a meagre compensation." As was often the case, Horace Mann came closest to explaining the reasons for inadequate teaching. He noted: "we pay best,—1st, those who destroy us,—generals; 2nd, those who cheat us,—politicians and quacks; 3rd, those who amuse us,—singers and dancers; and last of all those who instruct us,—teachers."[18]

While rural teachers were incompetent, smalltown and district schoolhouses were even more inadequate. "The site for a schoolhouse," wrote Samuel G. Goodrich in 1838, "is generally in the most neglected, because the cheapest, spot in town. . . . For the sheepfold and the cow-house, sheltered situations are carefully selected; but a bleak hill-top, swept by the winter blast, or a sandy plain, scorched by the dog-day sun, will do for a schoolhouse, especially if it is so useless for everything else as to be given gratis to the district."[19] Goodrich did not exaggerate. Down through the 1840's small, wood-frame, one-room schoolhouses were common in most districts. Built usually at the juncture of several roads the schools rarely had any enclosures or trees nearby. They were centers of noise and potential danger from passing vehicles when located in populous areas; or simply dirty, sun-baked and snow-swept, ramshackle huts when built in more isolated surroundings. If the structure was fortunate enough to have windows, the glass usually was broken, giving the building the appearance from the outside of an eyeless derelict. Inside, the one room was generally no larger than thirty feet square. Next to the entrance was a fireplace and the master's desk. Against the three remaining walls, in tiers from the oldest children next to the walls to younger children nearer the center of the room, were narrow, backless benches on which the youth sat for six or more hours a day.

Such schools often accommodated over one hundred children, crammed together on benches. Neither inside nor outside were there any sanitation facilities. Ventilation was so inadequate that during the twenty-week summer term, beginning about the first of May, students broiled, while dur-

Figure 2   "DECIDING UPON THE PEOPLES EDUCATION!!!"
This cynical commentary on the ambitions and motivations of prospective school teachers in the 1830's represented the common complaints of educators about the lack of training required for the profession of teaching.
SOURCE: *Common School Assistant,* IV, No. 10 (October 1839), 73.

ing the twelve-to-sixteen-week winter term, starting about the first of December, they chilled. Discipline was harsh, with instructors brandishing and using rattan ferules (rulers). In one Massachusetts school there was even a five-foot whipping post in the center of the room. The level of education was no better than the physical surroundings, and the physical surroundings were such that an 1838 Massachusetts report on district schoolhouses accused that "there is no other class of buildings within our limits, erected for the permanent or temporary residence of our native population, so inconvenient, so uncomfortable, so dangerous to health by their construction within, or without, abandoned to cheerlessness and dilapidation." Horace Mann exaggerated only slightly when he wrote a friend that "I have no hesitation in repeating what I have so often publicly declared, that, from the bad construction of our schoolhouses, there is more physical suffering endured by our children in them, than by prisoners in our jails and prisons."[20]

Figure 3   "A RAGGED BEGGAR SLEEPING"
This example of a one-room New England district schoolhouse of the 1830's, typical of those in which the "education" of countless country children took place, appears to be in better repair than contemporaries credited to most such buildings.
SOURCE: Clifton Johnson, *Old-Time Schools and School-books* (New York: The Macmillan Co., 1904), p. 103.

If the rural schoolhouse was a symbol of pastoral virtue to some, to others it was at best a tarnished symbol. It gleamed, in unsullied splendor, only to those who never had been confined within its walls. For those who had, perhaps a popular poem by John Greenleaf Whittier best recalled "In School-Days":

> Still sits the school-house by the road,
> A ragged beggar sleeping;
> Around it still the sumachs grow,
> And blackberry-vines are creeping.[21]

FROM COUNTRY TO CITY

While rural district schools were inadequate, educators and reformers had greater expectations for urban classrooms. Country schools usually suffered from lack of funds and public apathy, but urban schools generally enjoyed more tax support and public enthusiasm. Boston especially commanded the financial resources necessary to build a first-rate system of schools. And, over the years, city fathers proved reasonably generous in allocating funds for public education.

By the mid-nineteenth century, Bostonians could boast of a longer tradition of tax support for public education than any other community in America. Within a decade after settlement public expenditures for schooling had become one of the young community's major expenses. Although the amounts spent fluctuated widely during succeeding years, as did the general state of the city's economy, the principle of taxation for education remained firm. Individuals might occasionally question the need for dramatically increasing the allotted funds, but few, if any, attacked the principle.

Throughout the years of educational reform efforts within the city, the Commonwealth, and in New England, Boston citizens showed an uncommon willingness to see their tax monies spent on education. Over the period between 1820 and 1865 the city's tax expenditures on public education (including teachers' salaries, new construction, and maintenance) averaged slightly more than 18 per cent, or nearly one-fifth of public expenditures in an arena of competing municipal interests. Even the drop after 1845 in education's share of the total city budget did not reflect a declining enthusiasm for public schools. Rather, a reallocation of resources signalled recognition by city officials that other municipal needs—including professional police and fire departments, acceptance of responsibility for a public water works, expansion of sewers, more paved streets, and a burst of expenditures on welfare institutions—required public support at least equal to that given education. Between 1845 and 1865 education's share of the total budget averaged 16.5 per cent while per-pupil expenditures gradually rose over the period. In September 1846 Horace Mann compared Boston's per-pupil expenditure with those of Providence, Rhode Island, and Philadelphia, both communities known for their support of public schools. Providence averaged $5.57 per pupil, Philadelphia $5.67,

TABLE 1
BOSTON EXPENDITURES ON SCHOOLS AS PER CENT
OF CITY BUDGET, 1820-1865

Year	Total City Expenditures	Total Spent on Schools	School Expenses Per Cent of Total	Receipts from State School Fund*	School Fund Per Cent Total Receipts
1820	$157,180.69	$44,241.43	28.14		
1825	375,214.43	76,154.38	20.29		
1830	362,334.69	55,329.65	15.27		
1835	701,611.22	120,244.38	17.13	$1,523.24	.026
1840	632,984.28	119,455.70	18.87	2,428.39	.035
1845	974,102.14	225,739.48	23.17	3,055.64	.027
1850	2,395,382.62	325,913.72	13.60	4,962.39	.028
1855	2,795,483.63	442,670.96	15.83	5,392.16	.019
1860	3,582,791.99	632,385.01	17.65	5,926.35	.017
1865	6,389,821.84	776,375.22	12.15	8,082.08	.010

* The first year of the State School Fund was 1836, although the first figure given here is listed as 1835.

SOURCES: Derived and compiled from Boston Committee of Finance, *Auditor's Reports, 1815-1867*; and, Charles Phillips Huse, *The Financial History of Boston: From May 1, 1822, to January 31, 1909*, vol. XV, *Harvard Economic Studies* (Cambridge, Mass.: Harvard University Press, 1916), Appendices I and II, pp. 348-51, 364-65, 368-71.

and Boston about $13.00. By 1860 Boston was spending $20.50 per pupil (see Table 1 and Table 2).

Boston maintained its generally high level of public support for schools without significant state aid. Despite the prophecy of reformer James G. Carter in 1826 that public schools would become extinct in the city and throughout the commonwealth if the legislature failed to shoulder some of the fiscal burdens of education, Boston's school system grew in size. Even when the state did establish a common School Fund in 1834, Boston's annual share was a pittance, averaging between 1836 and 1865 only some 2 per cent of the city's total receipts. The state law required each town or city to raise by taxation a certain amount for the education of each child (no less than $1.50 for each person between the ages of five and fifteen), and Boston always exceeded that minimum by a wide margin. The city's mayors repeatedly praised their constituents for generous support of public schools and the School Committee echoed that praise.[22] "In no city in the world," asserted committeemen in 1845 in typical

TABLE 2

ENROLLMENT AND EXPENSES OF BOSTON SCHOOLS,
1840-1860

Year	Total No. of Students Enrolled	Per Pupil Cost	Total Expenditures on Education[a]	Educational Per Cent of Total Urban Expenditure
1841	12,401	$12.43	$154,160.53	22.39
1843	15,073	13.15	198,249.32	27.02
1845	17,110	13.33	228,143.16	23.42
1847	18,896	12.81	330,149.57	10.11
1849	20,589	15.40	317,078.33	12.75
1851	21,951	13.56	297,666.80	13.53
1853[b]	22,339	12.19	272,300.25	12.15
1855	23,768	18.62	442,670.96	15.83
1857	24,988	17.47	346,622.99	9.26
1859	25,315	20.50	519,031.73	14.50

[a] This includes, as does the Total No. of Students Enrolled column, both primary and grammar schools' expenditures for teachers' salaries, cost of materials,
incidental expenses, erection and alteration of school houses.

[b] figures available for school year 1852-53, rather than 1853-54

SOURCES: Derived from Nathan Bishop, *First Semi-Annual Report of the Super-
intendent of Public Schools of the City of Boston* (Boston, 1852), pp. 45-48;
Bishop, *Third Annual Report . . . 1853*, pp. 78-79; John D. Philbrick, *Second
Semi-Annual Report of the Superintendent of Public Schools of the City of
Boston* (Boston, 1861), pp. 17-20.

booster fashion, "has there been one-half so much pecuniary liberality for
the maintenance of Common Schools, as in the city of Boston." The Committee bolstered its claim with figures "proving" the "extraordinary fact"
that appropriations for popular education in Boston alone were far larger
than those for all of England, ignoring the fact that in early Victorian
England public educational facilities largely received support from voluntary philanthropic agencies.[23] Regardless of booster exaggerations, one
claim was certain: Boston did commit a substantial amount of public tax
monies to the support of schools. If the quality of public schools could be
measured solely or even principally by monetary standards, Boston citizens evidently were willing to pay handsomely for public education.

   But the educational critics who held high expectations for the superiority of urban classrooms over rural district schools did not judge by such
standards. Educational reformers and school authorities leveled more
damning charges against the Boston schools than even against the poor

district schools of their youth. Because the city was rich, because it could provide generously for education, Boston schools should have surpassed the rural schools in every respect. Yet, according to the critics, they had not. Nor would more money alone solve the problems of the schools, although the reformers and schoolmen usually requested more funds with each passing year. As the critics saw them, the problems were not primarily monetary, but moral; not fiscal but locational; the worst one could say about city schools was that they were located in the city.

Most of the critics doubted whether schools in the city could ever provide a proper climate for the nurture of moral virtues and citizen responsibility in a republican government. They "knew" that Boston schools did not offer that climate. They based their "knowledge" on certain environmental assumptions about the ideal physical setting for a school and the distance between that ideal and the reality of city schools.

Evaluating the physical facilities of common schools in the city proved a difficult task for the critics. While the district schools of their experience tended to be much alike, schoolrooms and schoolhouses in the city varied greatly. Periodic bursts of population growth necessitated make-shift provisions. Rising land costs often brought the destruction and relocation of schoolhouses to make way for new commercial activities. The annexations of South and East Boston, of portions of Chelsea, Cambridge, and Roxbury, and landfill operations to form the West End demanded new school construction to keep up with residential shifts in neighborhoods. Not until 1845 were residential areas at all well fixed, nor would they long remain so with the rush of immigration during the late 1840's and early 1850's and a beginning suburban trend by middle-class citizens.[24] Schoolhouses and schoolrooms therefore rarely were uniform in size or style. The critics, nonetheless, were able to make several telling generalizations about school locations, the uses of school buildings for other than educational purposes, and the quality of school construction.

Schools often were located in undesirable areas. Compared with relatively isolated rural schoolhouses, urban schools usually were squeezed onto narrow lots on busy streets, surrounded by buildings that served numerous and varied functions. Throughout most of the antebellum years, except for the suburban areas, undifferentiated land usage was as common in Boston as in other cities. Places of residence, business, and entertainment on the same block often sided with one another. Churches and schools stood hard fast warehouses, business offices, and private dwellings.[25]

A typical example of undifferentiated land usage was School Street, a short street that cornered with the major thoroughfare of Tremont Street, just off The Common, in the heart of the city. In 1830, at the corner of

Tremont and School stood the mansion of a famous Boston physician. Next door, down School Street, was a stable belonging to a three-story brick public house, the Boylston Hotel. Next to the hotel was the most celebrated of all the city's schools, the Boston Latin School. Between the stable and the hotel ran a passageway to the rear of the Tremont Theater, a walkway in which the Latin School boys often lingered "at the risk of being late at morning prayers" to see famous actors on their way to rehearsals. Adjoining the schoolhouse was Cook Court, an area about twenty feet wide, which contained private residences. Beyond Cook Court was the home of another physician who maintained a pasture with sheep who were the constant targets of coal and wood chips thrown by the boys from the windows of the school. Continuing down the street a visitor would find small shops, the Second Universalist Church—pastorate of the abolitionist and communitarian reformer Hosea Bellow—a Five Cents Savings Bank, grocery stores, a well-known saddle and harness store, a book bindery, a boarding house, artists' studios, lawyers' offices, and a volunteer firemen's engine house.[26] These various businesses and residences occupied an area of less than two city blocks.

The Latin School was small but impressive. Originally it had only one room, but boasted an imposing granite façade, and a bell-towered cupola. By the 1830's, when the later popular writer Edward Everett Hale began attending at the age of nine, the school contained a number of small rooms on three stories. This most exclusive of Boston's schools had only one playground—a yard some thirty feet square—behind the school. Recesses during the day were short since only the children in the ground-floor rooms could conveniently use the playground. And, as Hale recalled, the masters did not want the rest of the children out in the street. On the whole, Hale testified, "school life of itself had little to relieve it of its awful monotony."[27]

The Latin School catered to a small number of children, and, despite its surroundings, was in a more favorable location than many of the grammar schools and most of the primary schools of the city. The lower schools especially did not fare well. Established to train those children whose "mass of mind," according to educators, was to exert the strongest influence on the commonwealth in coming years, these schools demonstrated the triumph of necessity over desirability.[28]

From their founding in 1818, primary schools had occupied whatever quarters could be found in the city, desirable or not. The Primary School Board had attempted initially to open classrooms in every area of the city's twelve wards so that young pupils would not have to travel far from home. But the city made no provisions for schoolrooms or schoolhouses, and the Board had insufficient funds to build needed structures. The early

Figure 4   "A CIVILIZED PLACE"

The Latin School, erected on School Street (named for the institution) in 1812, was the most famous of Boston's public schools. This building served the children usually of the wealthier classes and was replaced by a more modern structure in 1844.

SOURCE: Arthur Wellington Brayley, *Schools and Schoolboys of Old Boston* (Boston: Louis P. Hager, 1894), p. 43.

method, therefore, of establishing schools was to require the women teachers to find suitable locations. After obtaining a classroom, the teacher herself had to pay the annual rent from a salary which, during the 1820's, averaged $250 a year. Annual rents in different parts of the city varied from $40 to $80 for a single, small room. Teachers who had to support themselves on such meager salaries naturally tried to find the cheapest locations for schoolrooms. In some cases women who owned their own homes used one room for school. More often, they located class-rooms in buildings that had available space and disregarded the building's function.[29]

Primary schools met in unlikely locations. Stores and the basements of public buildings often housed schoolrooms. Teachers held classes in church vestries, on the upper floors of warehouses with noisy mechanics' shops above and below, and in rooms adjoining the shops of blacksmiths. Two critics—physicians John D. Fisher, a member of the Primary School Board, and William C. Woodbridge, editor of the *Annals of Education*—investigated the schools during the early 1830's and reported that "we often found the entrance to the room through the filthy back-yard of a house, or in the neighborhood of a stable, or a blacksmith's shop, or a carriage manufactory house, where the children could scarcely pass in safety. . . . Several rooms are in the second or third stories, with steep and narrow stair cases, entirely unsafe for children." Referring to those upper-story rooms, another critic observed that "the school-room is in an old shell of a house, and is small, badly ventilated, and unpleasant. The floor seems ready to fall through into the room below, and the windows rattle in their casements, most ominously." Fisher and Woodbridge were shocked to discover that "in one case . . . we were assured the houses in the narrow passage to the school, were the resorts of licentiousness!" Because of the physical locations of many schools, parents were reluctant to send their children. At one school, for instance, located on the busy thoroughfare of Washington Street, attendance dropped by almost one-half during the winter because parents and teachers were afraid to let young children cross the streets owing to sleigh racing by "youngbloods" of the area. Other parents understandably refused to send their young-sters to backroom and basement schools located in some of the city's worst areas.[30]

The Primary School Board worked long and hard throughout the ante-bellum years to improve school facilities. But a growing urban population and intransigent City Fathers, preoccupied with a host of problems con-cerning the welfare of citizens, often defeated their best efforts.

In 1828 a Primary School Board committee composed of merchant Moses Grant, lawyer Thomas Wells, and the Reverend Joseph Tucker-man, the official "minister to the poor" of the Unitarian Church, presented a memorial to the City Council describing the "serious evils and bad consequences" of the lack of suitable rooms for schools. The Council agreed that changes were called for, and suggested a way to improve the situation while saving the city money at the same time. The School Com-mitee, after consulting with the Primary Board, was to rent a suitable number of rooms for a period not longer than ten years, drawing the money from the city appropriation for primary schools. The total, how-ever, was not to exceed $2,700. This limited sum meant an average of only $48 for each room. Considering the disparity of rents in the city, many rooms which could be obtained for that annual sum necessarily would not be much better than those currently occupied. But the City Council was interested in money. The Council argued that since it was providing funds for rent, teachers' salaries no longer had to provide for classrooms, and therefore could be reduced by $50 a year. The Primary Board had little choice but to accept the action of the Council. The city was willing to spend comparatively large amounts on the grammar schools, but relatively nothing on primary schools. All the talk about the necessity of primary schools for the lower classes was silenced by eco-nomics. The new provisions lessened the responsibilities and incomes of the teachers, while they also failed to ensure better schoolrooms for the students.[31]

Again in 1829 the Primary Board petitioned the city to purchase or build decent schools; again it failed. Over the ensuing five years the Board sought better rooms from the city, eventually obtaining space in grammar schoolhouses, gun-houses, engine-rooms, ward rooms, and church vestries. Finally in 1834 the City Council appropriated sufficient funds to erect Boston's first publicly owned primary school house. The building was of wood and brick, two stories high, and contained two separate schools. In the following two years the city built four more schools. The Board members felt proud of their achievements, limited though they were. To numerous critics the Board responded "that the rooms occupied by *our* Primary Schools have at all times been equal to, and will now compare advantageously, with those used by any city in the United States." The Board may have been engaging in hyperbole, or it may have been correct. Either way there was little cause for com-placency. Throughout the 1830's most children who attended the pri-mary schools spent their days in classrooms like those of the previous decade.

The building program of the city did not keep pace with the need for classrooms. By 1842 there were 7,403 pupils attending 104 primary schools scattered throughout Boston. The city still rented 42 school-houses, of which 41 were primary schools. Since most schoolhouses con-tained at least two separate schools under different masters, possibly more than 80 of the 104 schools still rented were in undesirable locations. Nor did matters measurably change during the remaining years before the Civil War.[32]

Throughout the antebellum years grammar schools generally fared bet-ter in location than did the more numerous primary schools. The city had founded them long before it had created the lower schools and even after introducing primary education in 1818, the city fathers continued the practices of the past in lavashing more attention and funds on the grammar schools. Despite the better physical surroundings, however, the grammar schools faced many of the same problems as the primary schools. Despite the rhetoric about the value of public education and the need for more satisfactory physical plants, school buildings and locations

Figure 5   "CLASSROOMS AND OTHER ROOMS"
The new Johnson School for girls, built on Tremont Street in 1835 on the former site of a soap factory, was to meet the needs of Boston's growing South End. Perhaps, like the old school building, the new structure contained classrooms, a constables' watch-house, and a volunteer fire company.
SOURCE: Brayley, *Schools and Schoolboys,* p. 104.

usually remained secondary to the city's requirements for other public facilities such as water reservoirs and transportation lines.[33] And, when the city did authorize new school construction, the Council often designated the buildings to serve the public in several capacities at once.

Schools often served more than one purpose. While educational reformers condemned the undesirable locations of many city schools, they likewise denounced the practice of using school buildings for other than educational purposes. School buildings serving more than one public function were common. The Johnson School, located on bustling Tremont Street near The Common, for example, served as a public meeting house, a watch house for police, and as a fire station—as well as providing classrooms. In 1837 a group of parents complained to the City Council about the presence of the fire engine, claiming that it disrupted the process of education. The Council agreed, and moved the engine to a small station house—one built on the same lot, in back of the Johnson School. Other school buildings were also used for more than schooling. The basement of the Hancock School, on Hanover Street in the northeast section of the city, housed a Sunday school class, while a sub-cellar served a local merchant as a warehouse for his casks of molasses. Throughout the city, schoolhouses provided the wardrooms for neighborhood political meetings.[34]

The history of one school was typical of the multiple uses to which school buildings were put. In 1790 the town fathers provided for the construction of the Franklin School on Common Street, in the south-central area of Boston. For convenient access, the school was located just off the major artery of Washington Street. Unlike its namesake, Benjamin Franklin, the school did not serve community needs long. In 1819, due to population pressures in the area, the School Committee established a second school on the top floor of the two-story wooden building. The basement housed an old hand-engine which students often helped pull to the scene of a fire. By 1826 increased enrollment required larger quarters, and the classes moved to another location. The city made certain that the old building was well occupied, using it for primary schools, ward meeting, police and fire stations, religious services, and as a distribution center for medical supplies during a cholera epidemic in 1832. The new Franklin School was located further south on Washington Street, near Dover Street, then the extreme limits of the city. The city experienced difficulty in obtaining the land for the school, due to the demands for space by local businessmen. Once acquired, the land was hardly ideal for school purposes. It fronted the mud-flats and open marshes of the Back Bay, a swampland that many citizens considered an unsightly, stinking nuisance. The mud-flats offered an exciting, but dangerous, playground for adventuresome youth.

Like the old building and like many other schools throughout Boston, the new schoolhouse was constructed of wood. In a city plagued by fires, this type of construction threatened the existence of the building. In 1833 the threat became reality. The school had just been remodeled inside and was back in session during the fall when a fire destroyed most of the building. While repairs were being made, children shuffled back and forth to attend school in the old building on Common Street and in the vestry of the Pine Street Church. The City rebuilt Franklin School on the site of the fire only to see it again consumed in 1844. Once again rebuilding took place. But by then Franklin School was too small

Figure 6 "A VERY COMMODIOUS BUILDING"
The new Hancock School (est. 1822) built in 1847 was one of the city's most imposing, roomy, and expensive public school buildings; nonetheless, it also housed a Sunday school and a cellar warehouse for a local merchant.
SOURCE: Brayley, *Schools and Schoolboys*, p. 101.

to accommodate the neighborhood population. The city therefore erected another new schoolhouse, back on Common Street, adjacent to the original location of the first Franklin School.

The School Committee considered this new Brimmer School building a model school. Constructed of brick, the building was safer than its predecessors, and roomier as well. On the first story was a ward room, and two primary and intermediate schools. On the two floors above were two large halls, with smaller adjacent recitation rooms. But neither this, nor the new Otis School—another model school built at the same time—

served solely educational purposes. Nor were the model schools built in the most desirable locations as the School Committee attested in 1848 of the Otis School: "during the late examination, the noise and smoke from the neighboring work shops were excessively annoying."[35]

The story of the Franklin School—and its adjuncts, the Brimmer and Otis schools—illustrated the larger problems faced by all grammar schools in the city. School buildings could not be used for educational purposes alone. The needs for space to carry on the daily activities of the city were too pressing.

Schools suffered from inadequate construction. The third generalization that educational reformers offered about Boston schools was that most were unsafe and unhealthy. The charge was true that most schools built before 1840 were firetraps. Modeled after the district schools of the countryside, many primary and grammar school buildings were constructed of wood and contained only one large room. By 1829 the Primary School Board had to report that of the fifty-seven schools in the city, twenty-eight met in "rather commodious rooms" (though only one-third of these could be called "large"), while the remaining twenty-nine rooms were inadequate for classes of forty and fifty pupils. The Board considered such schoolrooms "too small, badly ventilated, crowded and, in consequence, unhealthy and unpropitious for discipline."[36]

If the Board itself was dissatisfied, critics were even more disdainful. The extensive investigation of the primary schools by Dr. John Fisher and William C. Woodbridge in 1833 reflected the disparagement of educational reformers. Fisher and Woodbridge reported their findings to the Primary School Board, and, in the hope of arousing public opinion, published them in the *American Annals of Education.* The two rejoiced that the Board itself found the schools inadequately constructed, and deplored the fact that such a statement had to be presented to the world about Boston schools. They declared their concern for the schools had been piqued by the remark of a gentleman "familiar with our prisons, that *the children of the city of Boston were,* in many cases, confined for the day, in rooms so unsuitable and unhealthy, that they would not be assigned *to the convicts of our penitentiaries.*"[37] That statement strikingly presaged Horace Mann's depiction of the rural district schools.

The report of Fisher and Woodbridge clearly demonstrated the problems of founding and maintaining decently constructed schools in a city growing in population and hard-pressed for usable space. The authors discovered that the average schoolroom measured nineteen feet in width, twenty-six feet in length, and eight to nine feet in height. The average number of students occupying those cramped quarters was sixty-two. Judged against even the minimum standards for adequate classrooms established by a widely accepted *Essay on the Construction of School-houses* in 1832 by William A. Alcott, the construction of Boston schools was shoddy. Fisher and Woodbridge charged that the schools having the most influence on the health and morals of the city's children failed, in most instances, to allow even one-half the smallest amount of space considered safe.[38]

Their report, and others similar in tone, prompted the Primary School Board to deny the "gross and false attack upon the character" of the schools. The Board pointed out that it had done all it could to build better schools. Still, the schools remained poorly constructed. In 1837 a respected Boston physician, one Dr. Perry, visited a primary school of sixty children and voiced the opinion that no child could remain in the school six hours a day for two years without risking consumption. Heating in the winter was either non-existent or dangerously hot. Ventilation was equally inadequate. In 1838 William A. Alcott visited the primary schools and found that the good doctor had not exaggerated. "There was hardly a healthy face to be seen," Alcott reported. Whether health could be judged by appearance alone was debatable. But Alcott's statistics for one school, in which over a third of the students were absent for 136 days during the year, due to ill health, suggested the dimensions of the problem.[39]

Even when the city built new and presumably better schools during the late 1830's and early 1840's, construction was often less than desirable. The greatest fault, declared the Primary School Board, lay in not providing adequate ventilation. For without a proper flow of fresh air, "the foetid air, produced by the respiration and the exhalation from the persons and clothing of fifty or sixty children, whose poverty may prevent the necessary change for cleanliness, will, in a short time, render the odor and atmosphere of the room intolerable." Despite repeated discussion about the best means of ventilating the schools, the Primary Board members and other concerned individuals found it difficult to convince the City Council to make changes. Council members, jealous of their prerogatives, often reacted hostilely to the suggestions of the educators. In 1846, for example, the Council's chairman of the Committee of Public Buildings reportedly asked what schoolmen could possibly know about construction. They may know how to care for children, he said, but not how to build, "while the Committee . . . is composed of *practical* men, who know all about the matter." There was no record of the chairman's probable chagrin when, in one new schoolhouse under his direction, the schoolmen discovered that the ventilating flues extending to the rooftop had been covered by stone coping, while in several others the flues terminated in attics which had no outlet to fresh air.[40]

By the 1840's the educational reformers had established a solid case against the adequacy of urban schools. The schools were badly located, served other than educational purposes, and were poorly constructed. For all three reasons the schools were unhealthy for their youthful occupants. And, schoolmen reasoned, if schools were unhealthy, they were also immoral. Seeing an intimate connection between the physical nature of the schools and the moral and social goals they were to serve, educators believed that urban schools were no more adequate than their rural counterparts.

HEALTH, ILL-HEALTH, AND THE RURAL IDEAL

The difficulties of educating children in the city were manifold. The economics of providing buildings and teachers for large numbers of children often confounded the city fathers. Working-class parents, competing in a race for daily bread, often refused to send to school children whose pitiful earnings helped to sustain the family. To the children themselves, of all social and economic classes, the city presented many temptations to lure them into truancy. A walk on the wharves, where the goods of the world funneled into the city daily; a trip through narrow alleys and dark passageways in which some new adventure lurked at every corner; a noontime frolic on The Common—these and other enticements were cause enough for youth to avoid crowded classrooms. Boston educators recognized all of these factors as contributions to the city's educational difficulties. But they also viewed crowded classrooms as symbolic of the city itself, of its lack of adequate space for various activities, of its unhealthy environment.

In his 1839 inaugural address Mayor Samuel A. Elliot praised the reputation of public education in Boston, but criticized the practice. "The school system of Boston," he noted, "has done more than anything else to produce the character by which the City has long been distinguished; and as the population increases, it becomes of more and more importance that the system should be adhered to and improved." But, he continued, our schoolhouses have not been constructed to meet the needs of city children. Seating was uncomfortable, destructive of good posture, and thus unhealthy. Further, the atmosphere of crowded, unventilated rooms had a pernicious effect on the health and morals of youth.

Commenting approvingly on the mayor's address, Horace Mann seized the occasion for a lengthy discussion on the health of city children. Urban youth, he asserted, suffered greatly from a lack of fresh air, summer and winter. Housing density in the city kept winds from stirring up clean air. Buildings presented double the surface for radiating heat than was found in the country. While rural children varied their activities, city youth attended school the year round, confined in "debilitating surroundings." These circumstances, Mann wryly observed, were not without an educational effect. By relating words to their environment, urban children certainly could learn the meanings of words like "warm, hot, parch, singe, scorch, crisp, burn, fry, roast, simmer, bubble, melt, oven, boiler, furnace."[41]

Mann harped repeatedly on the theme of the disadvantages of city life and the difficulty of trying to educate sound minds in sound bodies under such conditions.

> The two most grievious misfortunes of a city life are the privations of pure air and of sufficient room and accomodation for bodily exercise. In the country, every man may have, for his own, a column of air. . . . But in the city, go where one will, there are three of four persons constantly breathing into his face; even second-hand air is at a premium, and it is the height of aerial epicurism to get a few whiffs of air that the country people have used and discarded.
> In regard to the means of bodily exercise, the condition of a city resident is no better. . . . There are but few places where a man can even give a good jump, without striking against a brick wall or a granite post, or knocking somebody over. The narrow sidewalks, in addition to being encumbered with boxes and bales of goods, are crowded by throngs of men and women, interspersed here and there with a wheelbarrow, a porter's omnibus, or a baby-basket. . . . To walk through the streets of a city, without striking or being struck, is an act for which one needs to be as limber as an eel, a rope-dancer, or a party politician.[42]

Mann admitted that the treatment of children in Boston schools had improved over former years. Schoolhouses showed better construction than had been true in the early 1830's. But further improvement was vital. All available evidence indicated, in his view, that city children still attended cramped schoolrooms in which twice-breathed air destroyed their health. Mann fully accepted the current medical theory that contaminated air—"foetid vapors"—was responsible for many diseases. And he believed that it was the duty of the city to provide school buildings in which there was a flow of whatever fresh air the environment could offer. The pure air of the countryside must somehow be introduced into urban schools. One way of doing this was to relocate the schools. Schoolhouses in the city, like those in the country, should be built on spacious grounds in airy sites. Ignoring his own (and others') criticisms of the rural district school and its miserable conditions, Mann envisioned an ideal country schoolhouse in pastoral surroundings. Urban schools, at least in their physical settings, should emulate the rural ideal. Mann clinched his argument with the aphorism that "learning will never circulate, where the air is stagnant."[43]

He, of course, was not alone in his views. A host of self-styled authorities on schoolhouse construction, popular writers of children's literature, and newspaper editors joined in a romanticization of nature, stressing the physical, mental, and moral purity that derived only from "natural" settings. In a Rousseau-like back-to-nature vein, newspaper editorials urged that "instead of seeing infants confined to inaction in crowded school-rooms, with saddened looks, moist eyes, and aching heads, we should meet them in gardens and lawns, groves and pleasure grounds, wholesome air."[44]

For those who believed in bringing the country into the city, a favorite example of a rural school setting had long been the Boylston School on Fort Hill, a section in the eastern end of the city. Fort Hill overlooked the harbor and had much of its expanse covered by a shady, tree-lined park in which many of the leading families of the city had congregated in the early years of the century. In 1819 the city had constructed on Fort Hill the two-story Boylston School. Spacious for its time, the building was surrounded by a picket fence which enclosed a grassy schoolyard. This yard, and the Fort Hill park, provided ample playground space for youngsters attending the school. Even by the 1830's, when the residential character of the area had worsened, Bostonians considered the grassy areas around the school a model playground, "such a one as every school ought to have access to." Complaints about the lack of similarly spacious, grass-covered playgrounds near city schools came from many educators and interested citizens.[45]

The crush of population and demands for more commercial space in the Fort Hill district, however, brought an end to the pleasant surroundings. To meet the demands for room, the city, during the late 1830's and early 1840's, excavated many portions of the Hill. The shady park gave way to sheds and shanties of the poor, to business establishments and warehouses. Wealthier citizens moved away. The Boylston School became overcrowded as the attendance of the native and immigrant poor mounted. Like other schools in the city, Boylston could no longer boast of adequate recreational facilities.[46] To maintain an ideal physical setting for schools, a setting patterned after the romanticized conditions of the countryside, became increasingly difficult in the expanding city.

If idylic surroundings were not possible in the city, then, at least, educators argued, the rural advantages of fresh air could be incorporated into Boston schools. Proper ventilation in the schools would ensure the better health of children, and therefore of the community at large. To be sure, as Mann had emphasized, fresh air was not one of the city's most abundant commodities. While Boston had long tried to cope with the problems of disease, the city could not avoid the consequences of rapid growth. Despite sanitation efforts, during most of the antebellum period dirt and mud clogged city streets; private privies overflowed into public

Figure 7   "THE UNCOVERED SCHOOLROOM"

This drawing of an ideal playground for an infant or primary school, to be located especially in the "infected districts" of the cities, advertised the importance of shrubbery and shade trees to physical and moral education—a schoolgarden in the heart of the city.

SOURCE: Henry Barnard, *Practical Illustrations of the Principles of School Architecture* (2nd ed.; New York: C. B. Norton, 1854), p. 15.

thoroughfares; garbage that had been swept into lanes and alleys rotted and contaminated the air. The threat of cholera remained ever present, especially in the dwelling places of the poor. Dysentery, tuberculosis, diarrhea, and pneumonia raised the incidence of infant mortality year after year. Animals, including rabid dogs, roamed the streets and terrorized many residents. As late as 1850 methods of dealing with such animals remained so disorganized that the mayor and the City Council had to enlist citizens in a citywide dog slaughter, "and boys were found truanting from school in all parts of the city, with clubs in hand, to help in the bloody business. . . . Fifty-five dogs were killed the first day!"[47] Even though the city atmosphere, then, was not as pure as that in the country (or, perhaps because of this fact), educators declared a crusade against ill-ventilated schoolrooms.

Changes in schoolhouse construction for better ventilation had long been a topic of discussion among educators in Boston and throughout the rest of New England. But the campaign got actively under way in 1838 when Mann submitted a "Report on School-houses" as a supplement to his *First Annual Report* as secretary of the Board of Education. Printed as a pamphlet and reprinted in various educational periodicals, the report gained wide circulation. In 1842 George B. Emerson re-emphasized Mann's comments on the health of children and proper ventilation in a chapter entitled "The School-house" in his influential *School and School-master*.[48] In Boston, the subject aroused sufficient concern so that in February 1846 the School Committee appointed a special Committee on Ventilation to investigate and make recommendations.

This committee consisted of a well-known local physician, Dr. Henry G. Clark, a long-standing member of the School Committee, Edmund G. Loring, and a Unitarian minister, the Reverend Charles Brooks. Of these, Brooks was best known in educational circles. He had traveled in Europe during the early 1830's and had returned with definite opinions about the physical and intellectual superiority of the state-controlled Prussian schools over those in Boston and in Massachusetts. Subsequently he had aided in the establishment of the State Board of Education, had become a close friend of Horace Mann, and at Mann's request had toured the state in a whirlwind propaganda campaign for public education. To this new committee the School Committee gave full authority, even to the extent of allowing it to ventilate any three schoolhouses as an experiment. The committee's report confirmed the worst fears of those disturbed about the healthfulness of the schools.

Dr. Clark, author of the report, began with a technical discussion of the process of respiration and of the conversion of oxygen into carbonic acid. Applying the experimental data of other researchers of Boston schools, Clark concluded that during each half-day school session attended by an average of 250 pupils in one large room (he referred to grammar schools), the required amount of fresh air was 450,000 cubic feet. But the actual amount in Boston schoolrooms of that size was only 22,500 cubic feet. Within ten to fifteen minutes after the start of a class, that limited air supply became tainted. In some schools the air was so bad that Clark reported he and the other committee members noticed the foulness before reaching the rooms, while they were standing in the open entries to the schools. Clark alleged that children, as they entered such schools, had their clothes and hair impregnated with the "foetid poison." Confined in such an atmosphere, youth soon "acquire the sallow and depressed countenances which might reasonably be expected in over-worked factory operatives, or the tenants of apartments unvisited

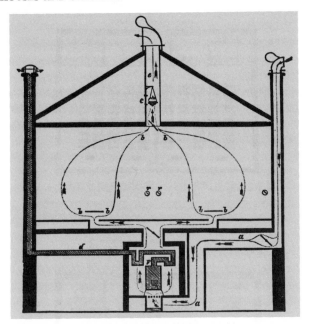

a. a. Cold-air channel, three feet in diameter, opening underneath the Furnace.

F. Furnace, three feet in diameter in a brick chamber ten feet square. The walls twelve inches thick.

d. Smoke flue, surmounted with Mr. Tredgold's chimney top.

b. b. b. b. Currents of warmed air, passing from the furnace, through a main flue of four feet in diameter, which supplies two branch flues. From these the air is diffused into all parts of the room, by means of the tablets which are placed over the mouths of the registers.

e. The ventilating shaft, two and a half feet in diameter, into which the foul gasses are collected, and from which they are finally discharged into the open air.

c. An Argand Lamp, to be lighted from the attic.

r. r. r. Registers, by means of which the whole circulation is controlled.

Figure 8   "PURE AIR FOR PURE MINDS"

This plan illustrated the ideal method of ventilating urban classrooms advanced by Dr. Henry G. Clark in 1846. Clark and others were certain that only an "agreeable and salubrious" atmosphere could make schoolrooms fit places for proper education.

SOURCE: Barnard, *Practical Illustrations*, p. 148.

by the sun or air." Conditions like these, Clark argued, affected not only the health of present and future generations in the city, but also made it impossible for the school to accomplish its goals of intellectually and morally educating children. As the annual report of the School Committee for 1846 stated, commenting on Clark's report, the bad ventilation "has driven many children from school, and many teachers from their duties and fields of usefulness."[49]

During the winter months of 1846 the Committee on Ventilation ex-

PLAN OF FIRST AND SECOND FLOOR.

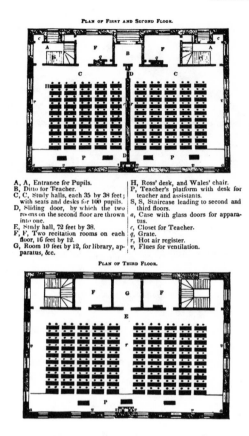

A, A, Entrance for Pupils.
B, Ditto for Teacher.
C, C, Study halls, each 35 by 38 feet ;
    with seats and desks for 100 pupils.
D, Sliding door, by which the two
    rooms on the second floor are thrown
    into one.
E, Study hall, 72 feet by 38.
F, F, Two recitation rooms on each
    floor, 16 feet by 12.
G, Room 10 feet by 12, for library, ap-
    paratus, &c.

H, Ross' desk, and Wales' chair.
P, Teacher's platform with desk for
    teacher and assistants.
S, S, Staircase leading to second and
    third floors.
a, Case with glass doors for appara-
    tus.
c, Closet for Teacher.
g, Grate.
r, Hot air register.
v, Flues for ventilation.

PLAN OF THIRD FLOOR.

Figure 9   "A MODEL PLAN"

This floor plan of the new (1848) Bowdoin School, demonstrated the latest
thought about school design and ventilation. The schoolhouse and schoolyard
totaled an area of 75' by 68', bounded on all sides by city streets; the three
floors were to house 370 students.

SOURCE: Barnard, *Practical Illustrations*, p. 106.

perimented with two schools. One they left alone, while in the other they
installed a ventilating apparatus of their own design. Both schools were
tightly closed, although it was customary to leave windows open for
ventilation even in the frost of winter, a practice which often resulted
in colds and chills for many students. After two hours the air of the
school with the ventilating device remained "fresh and pure." But in the
school, left to the consequences of its own construction, "the air was
found intolerably foul and foetid—four children were asleep, two had gone
home sick, two were in the act of vomiting, and the master said he could
bear the experiment no longer."[50]

In its 1846 annual report the School Committee understated the obvious conclusions reached from using the students as guinea pigs. The construction of city schoolhouses in the past "have had little reference to the purposes of instruction." The Committee ordered that in the future no schoolhouse was to be built without contractors consulting the Committee on Building and Ventilation. Parents would not send children to school only to have their health destroyed.[51]

Despite the admonitions of the School Committee, few immediate changes were forthcoming. In 1852, Nathan Bishop, the first superintendent of the Public Schools, found it necessary to try to educate the public on the proper laws of health at home, elsewhere in society, and especially in the schools. In sentiments familiar to the times, Bishop affirmed the intimate connections among the physical, mental, and moral development of children. "It is manifestly *our* duty," he informed fellow members of the School Committee, "in the work of education to learn all we can in regard to the nature and offices of the various capabilities of children." After all, Bishop emphasized, "children, trained in accordance with the Creator's plan, thus developing all their powers in harmonious proportions, will be more likely to grow up into a willing obedience to all his laws regulating the duties of mankind." On a previous occasion Bishop had made clear his belief that the duties of mankind included respect for law and order in the city, "cordial obedience" to all established authorities, and the practice of such moral virtues as industry and sobriety. To inculcate an acceptance of these "duties of mankind" was the major purpose of public schools.

Bishop declared that to accomplish this goal educators and teachers had to study the laws of human physical growth. Only by providing adequate conditions for physical health, could schools also ensure the mental and moral health of children. If we measure current health practices in our schools against any knowledge of the laws of health, Bishop warned fellow Bostonians, we must realize that those laws are being violated and the duty of properly educating youth thus has been abandoned.

After a lengthy critique of the methods of heating and ventilating schools, Bishop concluded that nearly two hundred of the classrooms of the city in 1852 still transgressed the laws of human growth and health. Matters had to be changed. Children, he asserted, had to attend school because parents neglected their duties at home and "many a child must receive at school his first notions of his various duties as a social and an immortal being." In schools, physical health must be preserved if moral health was to be assured.[52]

The city attempted to heed its superintendent's urgings, but even the best new schools failed to measure up to his and others' standards. In 1856, for example, the new Lawrence School opened in South Boston.

Built at a cost between $60,000 and $70,000, citizens considered it one of the finest schoolhouses in the city. Four stories high, constructed of brick, the school had wide corridors, the latest innovations in steam heat, and even separate outhouses for students and teachers in the schoolyard. The model school nonetheless was badly ventilated. Windows were the chief source of fresh air, with all the problems that presented for ventilation in the dead of winter. There were flues in the walls of each classroom leading to an open attic, but the air in the attic was more dense than that in the classrooms. The flues therefore were of little utility.[53] Nor was the situation measurably different in other Boston schools.

By 1860, after more than thirty years of discussion and debate, some changes had occurred in the physical structure of Boston schoolhouses. If ventilation was not yet ideal, schoolmen and lay members of the School Committee (that is, men who were not professional educators) knew the problems and were introducing innovations to provide for the health of children. Buildings which had once been constructed exclusively of wood were now built of brick. More adequate sanitation facilities served many schools. While few schools were surrounded by grass and trees, many had small playgrounds in which children could romp without hazard from the street. Boston schools, in their methods of construction, provided models which other urban school systems copied.[54]

Yet critics still found much to condemn. And, as was true in the past, educational reformers persisted in judging the physical construction and locations of the city's schools, as well as the health of urban schoolchildren, against a rural ideal. In his annual report for 1860 John Philbrick, the new superintendent of Boston Public Schools, summarized the longstanding opinion that "of the persons born and educated in our cities within the last thirty or forty years, but a small proportion can be said with truth to possess a sound mind in a sound body." Under present conditions of city life at home and in school, Philbrick continued, a child stood a poor chance of beginning life in good health. "It is frequently observed that the city boy with all his knowledge and mental training, is outstripped in the race of life by the boy from the country, with little book-learning, but with a body invigorated and hardened by the gymnastics of the farm and by an unlimited supply of pure mountain air."[55] The pastoral ideal lived on.

In the construction of schools, Bostonians gradually had attempted to meet the challenges of urban conditions. If they did not believe they had always succeeded, it was because many still did not accept the city on its own terms. As long as friends and foes alike insisted on measuring urban life by idealized rural standards, the city would be found wanting.

III

THE MACHINERY OF PUBLIC EDUCATION

5

Neighborhoods and Graded Schools

In organizing a system of popular education, the same practical judgment is to be exercised in making special adaptations of means to ends, as in any manufacturing or other business enterprise.

Nathan Bishop (1852)[1]

Confronted by the challenges of establishing schools in the city, Boston educators responded by organizing—and reorganizing—a system of public instruction. Between 1820 and 1860, they attempted to flesh-out a loosely joined skeleton of public education into a well-rounded body. They sought to create a hierarchy of schools for children of all ages, a structure that might truly be called a "system," in the comprehensive meaning of the word. The schoolmen were fortunate in having at hand a successful model of organizational skill. For Boston was the New England capital of the "American System of Manufacturing"—the innovative combination of the separate processes of production with the use of interchangeable parts—that revolutionized American industry.

In 1813, Francis Cabot Lowell and other successful Boston merchants organized the Boston Manufacturing Company to experiment with new methods of textile production. The "Boston Associates," as Lowell and his partners became known, built a small factory in Waltham, Massachusetts, in which they introduced a power loom. Their method of organization was deceptively simple: first, the principal processes of cotton cloth production were gathered in one location under unified management; second, the managers were men noted for executive ability rather than for specialized knowledge of industrial techniques; and third, the factory produced a standardized cloth of a weave that required little skill on the part of the laborer.[2]

The American System (and its English counterpart) was at once a culmination of scientific thought and practice from the seventeenth century on, a predictable partner in the general processes of urbanization and industrialization, and a harbinger of nineteenth-century reorderings of social institutional arrangements. The desire and ability of men to impose order on social chaos and to find practical solutions to economic problems that so characterized the process of industrialization in the nineteenth century evolved directly from the seventeenth-century symbiosis of natural philosophy, scientific inquiry, and practical technology. Describe! Subdivide! Measure! Count! Weigh! Manipulate! Regiment!— these were the watchwords of seventeenth- and eighteenth-century scientists and social philosophers. These injunctions called forth the secular religion of the Machine, the worship of technological innovation and the God of material prosperity, that deeply troubled nineteenth-century social critics like Ralph Waldo Emerson, Thoreau, Hawthorne, and others. And, the commands became central tenets of the social and economic philosophy that spawned the Waltham System of factory manufacturing and paternalistic control of the working classes. The division of labor and the specialization of economic activities that marked industrial development could have arisen only within an intellectual framework that stressed the discovery and manipulation of the bits and pieces· which together made up both the physical universe and the foundations of human society.[3]

The industrial transformation of the economy which accelerated during the first half of the nineteenth century paralleled shifts in the social order. The intellectual concept of mechanistically organizing men and events into a productive system which would yield predictable and standardized results found fullest expression in urban social policies. In the professionalization of police forces and fire departments, in assertions of more vigorous public controls over matters like health, sanitation, and charitable activities, and in a host of reform movements which sought close public regulation of the moral lives of private citizens, the watchwords of mechanistic philosophy became translated into social policy.

Certainly the enormous success of the factory system was not lost on Boston educational reformers. What might be labeled, for shorthand purposes, the "factory mentality" sparked the common school movement in Boston and throughout New England. In the new methods of industrial organization the schoolmen saw the perfect model for retooling the schools to cope with such urban problems as population density, residential mobility, and the increasing numbers of rural native Americans and foreign immigrants whose arrival required innovative methods of assimilation to the routines of urban life. Educators consciously adopted and adapted the American System of Manufacturing to their own ends. Although they often clung emotionally to an outmoded rural ideal as the standard for city schools, the educators reorganized the system of schools along the lines of factory production.

A STANDARDIZED PRODUCT

Educators who undertook a reorganization of Boston schools in the 1820's found they first had to clear away the debris of the past. They had inherited a tradition of public education which was less glorious than it was cumbersome. Their first task was to gather under one roof children who were scattered in separate schools throughout the city for separate purposes.

Customarily, children attended two separate schools, often in different sections of the city. In what was called the "writing school" youth laboriously acquired the skills of penmanship and tried to perceive the mysteries of a rudimentary business education. In a city which, from its earliest days, had depended upon commercial trade for survival, men trained in the keeping of financial records performed invaluable services. Arithmetic, from simple addition to decimal fractions and principles of exchange, thus long formed part of the writing school curriculum. In the "reading school" (or grammar school) children learned to spell, to read prose and verse, and to untangle the intricacies of English grammar and composition. They also received some instruction in the classics of Greek and Latin literature.

The grammar schools had not developed as a result of carefully considered educational theory. Rather, they had arisen from expediency. The pressures of population growth and business expansion had required a broader course of study than that available in the writing schools. With proportionately fewer boys pursuing professional callings like the ministry and the law, and with growing commercial needs, late eighteenth-century Bostonians believed that young men must be prepared for mercantile and other branches of business activity. Formal education, community leaders urged, should train youth for the practical life of adulthood, ready to engage in any number of occupations. Since most writing school masters were incompetent to teach any skills save those of penmanship and simple ciphering, the city had to turn elsewhere to achieve its educational aims. The shallow preparation of the writing master, coupled with the educational requirements of a growing city, gradually brought about a loosely organized system of two schools, designed to accomplish different purposes. Finally, in 1789, the custom of separate reading and writing schools became official practice under the Boston Education Act.[4]

By locating a reading and writing school in each general section of the city, the School Committee responded to the wants of Boston parents and businessmen. But, at the same time, Committee members failed to establish school districts. No legal boundaries prevented children from attending the schools of their parents' choice. Although many children went to schools nearest their homes, others attended where and when their parents chose. This practice allowed parents full control over both their children and the local school. For if parents found fault with the schools or the masters in their neighborhood, they could protest simply by sending their children to another public school, to a private school— or to no school at all.

Although parents welcomed control over the schooling of their youth, the city did not. The lack of any centralized administration resulted in both an inequality of numbers in the various schools, and in an uneven balance in the quality of instruction. One master might be responsible for four hundred pupils while another had authority over only two hundred. Some children who attended a reading school never went to a writing school; the reverse was also common. Neither parents nor the School Committee could be certain that children even attended school regularly, let alone judge the nature of the children's education.[5]

In a small town or rural village this administrative anarchy was not important. There were only a few schools to worry about; distances among them were short; and children could not wander far from the watchful eyes of parents. Interested parents gained an accurate understanding of the quality of instruction owing to the practice of boarding the teacher in their homes as part of his salary. They also conveniently could and did visit the nearby school frequently.[6]

But in the city—with its large population, its greater number of schools, its longer distances between home and school, and its heavier demands of occupations and interests on the time of parents—the lack of effective administration meant chaos in the ordering of the educational system.

By 1819, the School Committee began to recognize the necessity of updating the organization of Boston schools. The Committee undertook to standardize the system of education and initiated a process which continued unabated for the remainder of the antebellum period, and beyond. Just as fellow New Englanders like the enterprising Lowell and Nathan Appleton were arranging new manufacturing processes through the standardization of parts and labor, so Boston educators came to believe that new and better methods of education would result from collecting and organizing youth under one unified system of schooling. If the desired product—the "educated child," however vaguely defined—was to be obtained, the schoolmen implied that the chief emphasis must be on the process of manufacture. Somehow, they assumed, the product and the process were equal and inseparable. They thus devoted far more attention to the mechanics of school organization than they did to the more difficulty defined quality of education.

Upon the recommendation of a special committee in 1819 the process of standardization began. Advising that the order of schools would be improved "if each should be considered as consisting of two divisions, one for writing and arithmetic, and the other for reading and the other branches of an English education," the committee proposed a new physical arrangement for the schools. The same building henceforth would house both a writing and a reading school, but in separate rooms. Each division would have a separate master, although both would have equal jurisdiction over all pupils in matters of instruction and discipline. This became known as the "double-headed system." Later reformers rightly criticized this division of authority, but, when introduced, it was a welcome act of standardization. The 1819 committee also suggested that any child who voluntarily entered one division of the school automatically become a member of the other branch, with attendance required at each. The plan took effect immediately with the building and opening of the new Boylston School, and became the standard of organization.[7]

By 1823 the School Committee had introduced the system into most of the schools. Bostonians subsequently referred to both the reading and the writing schools, now sharing the same building, as the grammar schools.

In each schoolhouse there were usually two large rooms of equal size, one above the other. Each room accommodated between three hundred and four hundred children. The reading school occupied the upper room, an appropriate location for its elevated curriculum. Being about equal in number, the students in each of the two departments usually found themselves divided into four large classes. The master, in turn, subdivided each class into whatever size grouping he thought best suited educational progress. Depending upon the total number of children in the school, the master, at his own discretion, might assign a child to any class from the first through the eighth. A child therefore might find himself placed in the eighth class in writing school among other youth of mixed ages, while in the reading school, under a different master, he might be assigned to the second class. Complicating the division of students into classes was an attempt to maintain moral purity by carefully segregating the girls from the boys. Further, the masters often personally taught only the first and second classes. Children in lower classes received instruction from young women—assistants or "ushers"—who were usually untrained for the task.[8]

This rudimentary classification of children was an attempt to achieve a more balanced system of instruction than the city had known in the past. In beginning to standardize the process of schooling, educators responded as much to economic and demographic conditions in the city as they did to pedagogical theory. The classification derived from such pragmatic considerations as: the size of the school building; the number of beginning students in the local area; the presence of enough female applicants for supervising the lower classes; the current city budget for education; and the hurried evaluations of student ability by harassed masters responsible for hundreds of children. Rather than a pursuit of intellectual excellence, the practice of public instruction was an exercise in the art of the possible.

That the possible was not often the desirable became quickly evident. The new system accommodated a large number in each school, but it thereby hindered the process of learning. Arbitrarily divided into classes of varying ages and abilities, many children suffered the boredom of performing mechanical tasks of penmanship or simple equation under the tutelage of instructors scarcely more capable than themselves. Proud observers might acclaim the Boston schools as the "richest jewel in New England's crown," but to an untold number of children attending them, monotony tarnished the luster. Of even the first-rate Latin School writer Edward Everett Hale recalled that "it was on the monotony of school life that my dislike of it was founded."[9]

Concerning his experiences in the public schools, another resident was more caustic. He remembered that at the age of nine, along with other youths seeking to enter the school, "we were examined, found generally to know nothing, and admitted." Arranged on a long bench, overlooked by the master for some days, the would-be scholars sat "thinking of the evils to come, nerving ourselves to meet them like youth of spirit, and trying in vain to get used to the odor of decayed pedagogism pervading the building " Finally, the master took note of them, and "suddenly incorporated" the boy and others into the eighth, or lowest, class. "An observing eye," noted the writer, "in passing from the eighth through the intermediate classes to the first, might have noticed a gradual improvement in appearance and habits, but not sufficiently marked to strike a casual visitor." For months, "in a state of light stupefaction," he remained in the eighth or seventh division. After spending five years in school, years devoted to boredom and rote training devoid of enlightenment, he finally graduated "depressed in spirits, and unfitted for active life." Not until later did he find that "school-days could be made the happiest portion of life, a sentiment seldom entertained by the students of the Boston Public Schools." Although the writer exaggerated for comic effect, his account was not far from the truth.[10]

Although the reorganization of the schools in the early 1820's failed to provide exciting intellectual fare for the children, it did accomplish the immediate goal of bringing a semblance of order to the chaos of school administration. Students traveled shorter distances than before to get to schools and no longer had to commute between two different locations during the day. The schools had become more equally governed with two co-equal masters heading each division. This standardization in turn had strengthened the control of the School Committee over the direction of public education. Bostonians appeared to have adapted well to the challenges of educating a growing populace. Yet, appearances were deceiving.

PATTERNS OF POPULATION

By the early 1820's Bostonians already faced the most pressing problem of city schools—overcrowding. As the city grew from a compact town of 43,298 people in 1820 to a metropolis of 177,840 by 1860, the number of children whom educators hoped to enroll in public schools naturally multiplied (see Table 3).[11] During the early years of reorganization (1820-26), enrollment nearly doubled.[12] From 1820 to 1860 both primary schools and grammar schools strained under the continually mounting pressures of population growth. In 1820, slightly over 1,600 pupils attended the newly formed primary schools. By 1840 the number had risen to just over 5,400. By the late 1850's over 12,000 children attended. In the grammar schools a similar increase in enrollment occurred. In the late 1820's some 2,900 boys and girls enrolled. By 1840 the number had grown to 5,500. By the late 1850's over 12,000 students went to the grammar schools. In 1855, out of a city population of 162,748, the School Committee estimated there were 29,092 children between the ages of five and fifteen who should be in school, of which some 23,500 actually attended at one time or another during the year.[13] Comparisons of these figures with those in Tables 3 and 14 illustrate both the magnitude of change and the relationships between age distribution and school attendance.

Adding to the problems of population increase was the density of settlement. In the late eighteenth century, Boston was a pleasant, uncrowded, compact city. Thomas Pemberton, whose *Topographical and Historical Description of Boston* (1794) was the first such account to be published, delighted in the fact that "the town is capable of great increase, as many large spaces of land still remain vacant." By the 1820's, however, Boston residents were complaining that vacant spaces had vanished under the pressures of population density. In 1826, for example, a leading newspaper editor cautioned that men of moderate means would have to retrench in their choice of homes. "There are not so many people in Boston, now," he observed, "as there were four years ago, who have

TABLE 3
DISTRIBUTION OF BOSTON YOUTH
BY AGES, 1810-1855*

Age	1810	1820	1830	1840	1855
Under 5			8,107	10,922	15,851
5-10			7,137	9,486	12,235
Under 10	9,075	11,068	15,244	20,408	28,086
10-15	4,092	5,577	6,875	8,824	11,063
TOTAL	13,167	16,645	22,119	29,232	39,149
Children, Per Cent of Total Population	38.97	38.44	36.02	31.30	24.39
Primary School Ages, 4-7	3,630	4,427	5,190	6,927	9,288
Grammar School Ages, 7-15	7,900	9,987	10,509	13,732	17,474
TOTAL	11,530	14,414	15,699	20,659	26,762
School-Age Children, Per Cent of Total Population	34.12	33.29	25.57	22.12	16.67

* Figures for the number of children of primary school age, 4-7, and of grammar school age, 7-15, do not exist as such in the various censuses used. They should be taken, then, as relatively accurate for the years given, but not as precise. To estimate these statistics, I assumed an equal distribution of children for each age group, by years. That is, I took the total number of children ages 0-10, divided by ten to obtain an average distribution, and then added for the number of children ages 4-7. I repeated the process for children ages 10-15. I then checked my estimates against the few reasonably accurate figures of school attendance and enrollment extant, and discovered significant correlations. I believe my estimates are accurate within the acceptable .05 per cent margin of error.

SOURCES: Derived from Lemuel Shattuck, *Letter to the Secretary of State on the Registration of Births, Marriages, and Deaths* (Boston, 1845); Francis DeWitt, *Abstract of the Census of Massachusetts . . . 1855* (Boston, 1857); Lemuel Shattuck, *Essay on the Vital Statistics of Boston* (Boston, 1893); Carroll D. Wright, *Analysis of the Population of the City of Boston . . . Census of May, 1885* (Boston, 1885).

houses by themselves: in many streets, where there was but one family in a house—two families upon an average, will be found at present." To add desperately needed acreage to the city, developers partially cut away the slope of Beacon Hill in the heart of old Boston, laid streets over the newly exposed surface, and carted the soil down to the Mill Pond, northwest of The Common, for land-fill. In the North End and around the Fort Hill area, both staging grounds for the entry of native and foreign newcomers, crowding continued unabated during the decade of the thirties; by the early 1840's nearly every room in the Fort Hill area was occupied by several families. By 1850 Boston remained a compact, "walking city"; the area of dense settlement barely exceeded a two-mile radius from City Hall. But residents who had lived in Boston for the previous thirty years had witnessed a tremendous growth and concentration of population within a relatively fixed geographical area.[14]

With increases in population density came changes in the residential character of neighborhoods throughout the city. The rural nature of many neighborhoods, the houses set in garden spots that had impressed Pemberton, underwent steady transformation into urban streets lacking greenery and a sense of spaciousness. By 1838, Philadelphia educator E. C. Wines, visiting Boston, could still observe that "another pleasant feature of Boston is the many green and shady front yards which relieve and refresh the eye. . . . More or less of these are met with in every part of the city; but Summer street, on both sides, is lined with them from one end to the other." But a decade later Summer Street (on the southeast side of The Common) ran like a plumb-line of urban growth, measuring the changes in neighborhood character. It began in an expanding warehouse district near the wharves and ended close to The Common in a residential district housing some of the city's wealthiest clans. Along the way, however, and even in the residentially elite section itself, Summer was a street pocketed and surrounded by enclaves of foreign immigrants and native laborers, a district whose "quiet, homelike atmosphere" of rural greenery had been disrupted by stores, other businesses, and the invasion of tenements. And Beacon Hill, another residential bastion of wealth and gentility, now overlooked the principal Black district of the city, an area of crowded alleys and dilapidated houses into which Negroes had concentrated steadily over past years.[15]

While a map of the social geography of Boston in the late 1840's might give the impression of a city divided into distinct residential sections (see Map 1), even those areas showing general patterns of residential similarity were not homogeneous in population make-up. During at least the first four decades of the nineteenth century people of different backgrounds and occupations tended to live intermingled in the various parts of the compact city. Streets of the poor, the foreign, the working classes, lay side-by-side and fed into streets occupied by the growing middle classes and the community's wealthier and more distinguished citizens. To be sure, there were districts that had a general reputation based upon the class character of the majority of inhabitants, but not until the early 1850's was there any clear-cut residential segregation along income, occupational, ethnic, or racial lines. Like that of other

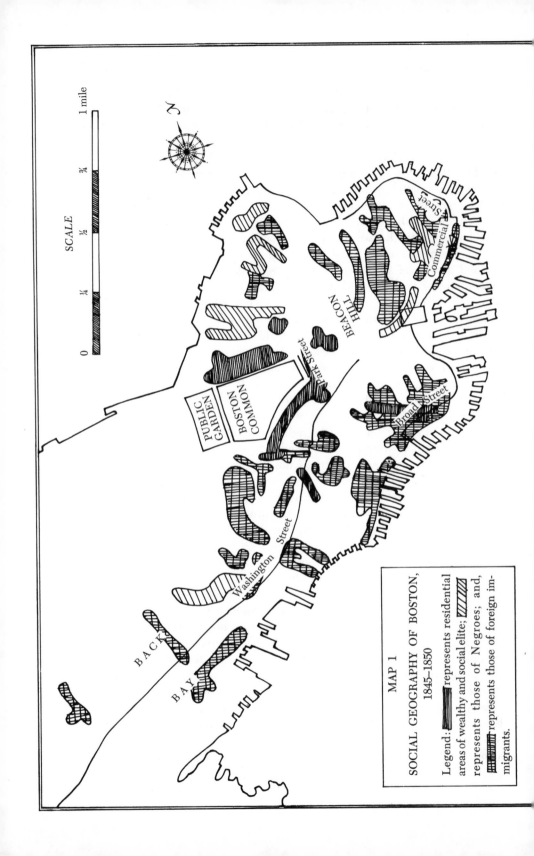

SCALE

0   ¼   ½   ¾   1 mile

N

BACK
BAY

PUBLIC
GARDEN

BOSTON
COMMON

Park Street

Washington Street

BEACON
HILL

Commercial Street

Broad Street

MAP 1

SOCIAL GEOGRAPHY OF BOSTON,
1845–1850

Legend: represents residential
areas of wealthy and social elite;
represents those of Negroes; and,
represents those of foreign immigrants.

large American cities, Boston's core remained a jumble of social classes, mixed residentially, with places of residence competing for land space with places of business and manufacturing.[16] Nonetheless, contemporaries often labeled certain neighborhoods as districts of "the poor," "the laborers," or the "distinguished families," and also complained about seemingly rapid changes in the residential character of various parts of the city.

Compounding the problems raised by population increase and density was the fact of residential mobility. As the city grew slowly in physical size and more rapidly in population, certain sections became more crowded than others. The most congested neighborhoods did not remain stable. There was a continual reshifting of population. Each year thousands of workers moved from one room or house to another within the same neighborhood, from one neighborhood to another, or entirely out of the city. Some tried to remain near or move nearer to their places of employment. Others sought cleaner surroundings or cheaper rents. Nor were residential changes exclusive with the working classes. By the late 1830's and throughout succeeding years, the middle classes and the wealthy flocked in increasing numbers to West Boston, South Boston, and the nearby suburbs of Cambridge, Roxbury, and Dorchester. Some sought better homes while others hoped to escape the conglomerations of working-class and immigrant families in the core of Boston. Between 1830 and 1860 the population as a whole underwent an astonishing turnover rate (movement into and out of the city, including births and deaths) of 30 to 40 per cent each year. Whatever the social class, the odds were two in five that a family might move somewhere in any given year, either from neighborhood to neighborhood, or completely out of the city. And the odds were about one in five that during any year a family might move about within a neighborhood, short moves that kept the family within the same ward even though they might involve uprooting from immediate friends and neighbors. Over the period foreign immigrants, who totaled an increasing number of the urban labor force, tended to change residence twice as often as native citizens, and, after about 1850, congregated in the core of the city while native citizens moved to the periphery and suburban areas at an accelerating pace.[17]

Increases in population density and residential mobility placed heavy burdens on city administrators charged with supplying adequate public services to local residents. While educators hoped to broaden the reach of public schools to include all classes of citizens, the lower income neighborhoods of the poor and the working classes especially challenged the ingenuity of school administrators. Both the density of population and the rapid rate of residential mobility among those groups demanded continual readjustments in the school system. Although the major difficulties came after 1840 with an influx of foreign immigrants, even before then schoolmen were hard-pressed to keep up with population changes. Whatever the reasons for movement into and around the city, educators found the task of providing adequate school facilities more difficult in the face of such residential mobility. Eventually they questioned the possibility of maintaining the traditional neighborhood control of schools while the neighbors kept moving away. Like their administrative counterparts in industry and manufacturing circles, the educators began to ponder the necessity of centralizing their activities instead of continuing an essentially home-craft operation. They began an attack on the principle of local control over the neighborhood school, an attack that would remain controversial in American cities long after the Boston schoolmen had gone to their just rewards.

THE NEIGHBORHOOD SCHOOL AND LOCAL CONTROL

The word "neighborhood," as used by nineteenth-century Americans, was ambiguous.[18] Deriving originally from Old English, the word literally meant near a farm or farmer and referred to persons living adjacent to one another on the countryside. In a rural context, then, the "neighborhood" was distinguished by: the relatively close physical proximity of dwellers; cooperation among them to accomplish set goals; intimate social contacts; and a strong feeling of social and group consciousness. When carried over into the commercial city, "neighborhood" bore slightly different connotations. The urban neighborhood was still distinguished by the close physical proximity of residents within limited geographical boundaries, but the spirit of self-sufficiency and disinterested group cooperation broke down. People tended to group themselves together along ethnic, income, and occupational lines, in homogeneous enclaves. For economic survival they depended as much on the wider opportunities offered by the city as on cooperation among themselves. Still, even in the city, "neighborhood" carried the traditional connotation of local political and social autonomy of citizens and of harmony among neighboring groups.[19]

When early nineteenth-century visitors arrived in Boston they found this latter meaning still characteristic of the Bay City. Timothy Dwight, Congregational minister and president of Yale College, for example, could observe that Boston was large enough "to ensure all the benefits of refined society, and yet so small, as to leave the character of every man open to the observation of every other. . . . His virtues, his vices, his wisdom and his folly, excite here much the same attention, and are examined in much the same manner, as in a country village."[20]

Within a few short years, however, as George Ticknor observed, the increase in population and business enterprise destroyed the "compact, united, and friendly community" in which citizens "felt involved in each other's welfare." As working-class, middle-class, and wealthy citizens gradually began to congregate in separate residential areas, they cooperated less with one another and began to depend more on city government to meet their demands for curbing disorder and promoting political and social harmony.[21] By the mid-1830's, the bastion of neighborhood sovereignty was the public school.

Boston educators and parents constantly gave allegiance to the principle of the neighborhood school. Nothing less than local control was acceptable—or so the argument went. Children should not have to travel far from home or have to cross heavily trafficked streets to attend school. Schools should be close to children's homes so that teachers might consult easily with parents; and especially so that parents could be intimately familiar with the daily operations of the schools.[22] This commitment to local control was a carry-over from Boston's younger days when the city was physically a village and when parents supposedly devoted more attention to local school matters than was true by the late 1820's. By then, the city was physically larger, the population greatly enlarged, and the affairs of business and labor more demanding on parents' time. More importantly, the social reach of schools was broader than in the eighteenth century when schools had enrolled mostly middle-class children. By the 1820's more and more children entering the schools came from working-class families whose parents either lacked the time, the interest, or both, to scrutinize the operations of public schools. The administration of schools appeared to require more centralized control than in the past, particularly in wards which held large numbers of working-class, poor, and immigrant families—or so many educators asserted. Whatever the current realities might seem to demand, rhetorical devotion to the principle of neighborhood schools and local control burned brightly. But, rhetoric and reality often conflict, and changing times brought changed needs in the location and administration of public schools.

During the 1820's and early 1830's schoolmen tried desperately to uphold the principle of neighborhood schools. Educators opened classrooms in warehouses and ward rooms, in church basements, stores, and rooms behind stables. By 1830 a number of schoolmen had realized that the school system of the past was collapsing. Some schools—for example, the Hancock School on Hanover Street that served the northern wards of the city—had to refuse admittance to new applicants because of overcrowded conditions. Other schools in other parts of the city were nearly deserted. If the schools were to achieve their social mission, and if the public tax monies of the city were to be spent efficiently, educators believed they had to offer new ways of shaping the school system.[23]

Between 1830 and 1860, the schoolmen considered a variety of plans to achieve an equitable and uniform distribution of the school population. Some plans they put into operation; many others went no further than items on a committee agenda. Whatever the specifics, most of the schemes arose from a common philosophical basis and intellectual orientation.

The educators assumed, without question or quibble, that schools could and should be patterned after the model of the factory. Time and again, schoolmen tried to draw up a blueprint of the ideal-size school which would house the maximum number of students compatible with efficient operation. Their public and private statements implied that "the educated child" was a product that could be manufactured quickly and inexpensively if only the school system were correctly organized. One educator, unconsciously mimicking the Coketown schoolmaster in Charles Dickens' *Hard Times* who saw children as nothing more than empty vessels waiting to be filled with "facts! facts! facts!," summed up Boston's past experience and present ambitions. Educators, he proudly stated, wanted to give "to every child in the city an education of *the best quality, in the shortest time, and at the smallest expense.*"[24] The desire was not ignoble, only the execution. When the School Committee took action on its plans it helped graft onto American educational thought an assembly-line approach that would confound future generations of school reformers. The Committee's use of the factory analogy also contained long-term implications for school administration and the future of local control.

When Boston schoolmen attempted to balance enrollment by arbitrarily redistributing students among various schools, they repeatedly found themselves checked by parental disapproval, hindered by a lack of legal tools of coercion, and bound by the principle of the neighborhood school. The educators thus faced the dilemma of trying to harmonize local control of schools with their need to centralize administration and to gain a uniformly populated system of schools. Like most men caught in a dilemma, the educators often became further ensnared as they tried to escape. Their words and actions frequently conflicted, or, at best, made their position appear ambiguous. Perhaps the most instructive illustration of the educators' difficulties was an attempt in 1837 to redistribute a large number of children throughout the Boston school system. The background of that effort and its immediate aftermath told volumes about the schoolmen's views on education and about the private and public limits of their autonomy.

In an 1837 *Report on the Distribution of Students* that became a cen-

ter of controversy, the School Committee promised to preserve the principle of neighborhood schools, and then set about its undermining. The
Committee claimed that redistribution could take place within existing
facilities, thereby saving money, so that "very few children, could they
go in a straight line to school, would have to travel as far as 160 rods."[25]
To ask a child to walk a straight line to school over the twisting streets
and back alleys of Boston was quite a request. Still, if existing schools
could accommodate all students within a given neighborhood, many parents wondered why overcrowding had occurred in the first place, and
why any shuffling around of their children was necessary. The answer
seemed apparent: the growth of population, its density, and residential
mobility accounted for imbalances in school attendance. If those were not
reasons enough, the School Committee reminded itself and parents about
one of the hallowed traditions of the city's educational practice.

Many Bostonians believed that public schools should be sexually segregated. Educational theories and moral persuasion had traditionally
called for separate schools for the sexes, although in practice the separation had not always been complete. In fact, the haphazard application of
the principle in the past had contributed to present overcrowded conditions in some of the schools, for expediency sometimes overruled moral
principle. Still, in resurrecting traditional attitudes on the subject, the
School Committee brought the past to bear on the present, thereby
erecting a totem that might justify whatever actions they undertook.

Bostonians had long questioned whether girls should attend the public schools at all. Although the city had provided schools for boys from
the earliest days of settlement, no like provisions had existed for girls
until the first reorganization of the schools in 1789. In that extension of
education, grammar schools admitted girls from the twentieth of April
to the twentieth of October each year. Girls had to leave the schools in
the middle of October to make room for boys returning from agricultural
and industrial pursuits. But at least, by the early years of the nineteenth
century, there was general agreement among Boston educators that girls
should receive some education. As John Lathrop, a noted Boston teacher,
argued in 1813, "when it is considered that there is an inseparable connection between domestic comfort and happiness, and feminine virtue
and knowledge, we cannot be too grateful to the institutors of the present enlarged and benevolent plan of instruction" that admitted girls to
school. The educated girl would become a good wife and mother who in
turn would make men "prudent, prosperous, and happy." While girls
attended schools with boys for part of the year, they usually gathered
in classrooms separate from boys, and sometimes attended school in separate buildings.[26]

Educators offered two reasons for segregating the sexes. Lathrop expressed the first when he observed that a girl's "tenderness of soul, and acuteness of sensibility require the guardian care of education in her early years." A good education for girls demanded a different course of studies from those suited for boys because girls had different emotional needs and were called to a different class of duties in later life. As wives, mothers, and arbiters of the home, women formed the future character of the nation. "Whatever concerns the culture of the female mind," William Russell, editor of the Boston *American Journal of Education* wrote in 1826, "extends ultimately to the formation of all minds, at that early and susceptible period, when maternal influence is forming those impressions which eventually terminate in mental and moral habits." Several years later Horace Mann echoed that sentiment: "the rulers of our country need knowledge (God only knows how much they need it!) but mothers need it more; for they determine, to a great extent, the very capacity of the rulers' minds to acquire knowledge and to apply it."[27]

New conceptions of children inherent in the discovery of the child required that women gain knowledge of domestic science, of the principles of health and nurture so that, as one writer put it, they may know "how to treat children, both as physical and mental beings."[28] But knowledge of these principles, many people argued, was unnecessary for boys who would become workers, merchants, ministers, and public officials in adult life. Girls therefore should pursue a different education than boys. This required separate classrooms, if not separate schools.

The comments by John Lathrop of the "tenderness of soul" and "acuteness of sensibility" hinted at a second reason for segregating children by sex in the classroom. Girls possessed a moral nature that required separate cultivation. Bostonians and other New Englanders claimed repeatedly that if girls were to become mothers and wives whose daily example and influence molded future generations, they themselves had to be morally pure. The 1837 *Report on Redistribution* put the matter plainly: "It has often been urged . . . that on moral grounds it is inexpedient for young persons of both sexes to go to school together." Intelligent citizens, alleged the *Report,* could not fail to perceive at once "the impropriety and danger of girls and boys, at an age approaching that of maturity, going every day, for years, to the same school." Certainly, the *Report* affirmed, not one thoughtful parent in a hundred would send his daughters to a mixed school "where they must be often liable to meet with at least some boys, not only rude in speech and manners, but of immoral dispositions and habits," if equal schools exclusively for girls were available. In separate schools girls could be trained to be elevated in their tastes, refined in their manners, and thoroughly imbued with moral principles.[29]

In the primary schools girls and boys usually mingled together in the same classrooms, "trained up together," as one educator noted, "in the same way as the boys and girls in any well regulated family." But as soon as children went on to grammar schools, their pathways usually separated. In some wards girls and boys attended grammar school together due to lack of separate facilities, but neither parents nor schoolmen were happy with the situation. Then, in 1828, matters were complicated further when the School Committee finally decided to allow girls to attend school throughout the year. This action, for all the approval registered by parents, promised even more overcrowding of many schools.[30]

To conform practice to theory and to give teachers a better opportunity to train each sex properly, the School Committee attempted to divide the schools completely on the basis of sex. In 1830 the Committee transferred all the girls in the seven grammar schools of the city to the Franklin, Bowdoin, and Hancock schools, located respectively in the southern, central, and northern sections of Boston. The four remaining schools—Adams, Boylston, Eliot, and Mayhew—admitted only boys. Temporarily the arrangement seemed satisfactory. On the whole, parents approved the scheme, and School Committee members enthusiastically endorsed it.[31]

But parents and schoolmen also wanted as much as possible to preserve the neighborhood school. Under the complete separation of the sexes too many girls had to travel too far to attend school. After a brief trial period, the School Committee partially abandoned the experiment of fully segregated schools and ordered boys and girls to resume joint attendance at four of the schools, although in separate classrooms.[32]

The experiment raised serious questions about the practicality of maintaining schools on a limited neighborhood basis and about the issue of local control. Parents had welcomed the School Committee's assertions of authority when it arbitrarily segregated the sexes. But they were less enthusiastic about relinquishing local control to the Committee when it chose to ignore parental preference. By 1837, then, when the Committee claimed authority to redistribute students among the schools as it saw fit,[33] there was a renewed effort by parents to keep control of neighborhood schools in their own hands and in the hands of locally elected ward representatives on the School Committee.

While the motivations of Committee members in responding to the issue of local control were unclear, their actions suggested a willingness to increase their own authority by any means possible. Certainly the Committee's arguments for redistribution brought together conflicting goals for the schools in a way that skirted the edges of honesty. The Committee contended that to reduce overcrowding and to uphold the principle of sexually segregated schools, redistribution of students was the only realistic solution. Given financial constraints during the depression of 1837, the Committee was probably offering the safest way of increasing the efficient operation of the schools, although Boston suffered less economically from the depression than did other large cities.[34] But the Committee did not plead economic circumstances; rather, it virtuously claimed to champion tradition. The neighborhood school, sexual segregation, local control—the Committee promised to preserve all of these traditions at the same time that its actions subverted them. Without directly stating it, the line of reasoning adopted by the Committee led to a modification of the neighborhood school concept, a reaffirmation of sexual segregation to a point of absurdity, and a tacit assertion of its own authority in the direction of more centralized administration of the school system. The Committee performed a juggling act with traditional principles in which the hand was indeed quicker than the eye.

The Committee's performance seemed forthright. A redistribution of students would preserve the neighborhood school by allowing more efficient use of physical facilities than was currently the case, and would reinstitute the practice of segregating the sexes. To achieve the desired uniformity of system, the Committee set about the task of moving over 4,000 students in ten grammar schools from one location to another. Having few ideas and even less agreement on what the ideal balance of student population might be, Committee members eventually compromised their differences by adopting the easiest and most mechanical method. They divided the number of students by the number of schools. This human arithmetic resulted in an average of 411 pupils for each school. Trying to apply that arbitrary formula, while also making full use of neighborhood school facilities and segregating the sexes, proved a more complicated business than the Committee anticipated. And, because the formula was arbitrary and the Committee insisted on its application regardless of parental wishes, challenges to the extent of local control had arisen without the Committee having given notice of its intentions.

Before implementing its formula, the Committee carefully drew up the battleplan. Four of the grammar schools—Wells, Adams, Franklin, and Boylston—enrolled both sexes due to neighborhood congestion and lack of alternate facilities. Schoolmen proposed to meet that situation by reorganizing Wells and Boylston as girls' schools and the other two for boys. On paper the Committee then shuttled about other children from neighborhood to neighborhood, dispersing them among the remaining schools according to the formula. There were difficulties in hewing precisely to the average, for several school buildings were simply not large enough to hold 411 children in anything better than sardine fashion (see Table 4). But when the paper game was completed, Committee members

TABLE 4

SEXUAL SEGREGATION AND REDISTRIBUTION
OF STUDENTS, 1837

Schools	No. of Boys	Schools	No. of Girls
Eliot	453	Hancock	520
Mayhew	482	Bowdoin	450
Adams	355	Johnson	488
Franklin	337	Boylston	330
Winthrop	375	Wells	332
TOTAL	2,002	TOTAL	2,120

Total No. of Students Involved: 4,122

SOURCE: Ms., School Committee Minutes, 1837-1841 (December 27, 1837), p. 67.

believed they had succeeded in establishing a satisfactory degree of uniformity among the schools.[35]

Many parents and taxpayers did not agree. Residents of all but four of Boston's twelve wards quickly filed petitions protesting the Committee's plans. Although the nature of the protests varied from petition to petition, generally all of the complaints touched upon the questions of sexual segregation and the sanctity of attendance at neighborhood schools. Surprisingly, none of the petitions struck directly at the heart of the redistribution effort, that is, the issue of local control versus centralized administration. Perhaps parents naïvely assumed that as long as their children attended school within the immediate neighborhood, control of the schools would remain in parental hands. If so, continued and ultimately successful efforts by the School Committee to arrogate power to itself over the next few years would dispel that illusion.[36]

Several of the petitions stated that parents did not want their children to attend sexually segregated schools. A resolution submitted by residents of Ward Five, for example, graciously asked the Committee to drop its plan to segregate the Wells School. The residents did not believe that joint attendance of the sexes was morally harmful or that educational requirements called for distinctly different educational experiences for boys and girls. The petition thus belied the Committee's allegations that all Bostonians demanded segregated schools and implicitly undercut one of the Committee's rationalizations for redistribution. Whether Committee members were surprised by this challenge to the doctrine of sexual segregation or whether they had known all along that their use of the doctrine was questionable went unrecorded. On a vote of 12 to 6, the Committee overruled the objection and ordered the reorganization of the Wells School according to the formula. In like manner the Committee voted down a motion by one of its members, sparked by the petitioners' response, to reconsider the entire matter of reorganizing the schools along sexual lines. It was determined to enforce its decision whether or not parents agreed.[37]

Other petitioners charged that the School Committee really was trying to cut across neighborhood boundaries, to ignore the residential mix throughout the community, and to divide the schools across class lines. According to these complainants, the schoolmen sought to produce conformity among children by gathering together in separate schools youngsters from like social, economic, and ethnic backgrounds. There was little truth to that charge. Most School Committee members apparently agreed with some parents that children benefited from contact with other students of different abilities and backgrounds. In fact, Committee efforts over past years to broaden the reach of public education in the city refuted the complaint. In spirit and practice Committee members shared Horace Mann's appraisal of the importance of a class mixture in the neighborhood school. In his *First Annual Report* for the same year (1837) Mann asserted of such schools that "it is on this common platform, that a general acquaintanceship should be formed between the children of the same neighborhood. It is here, that the affinities of a common nature should unite them together . . . against the alienating competitions of subsequent life."[38] The neighborhood school, in short, was to function as an incubator of social tolerance.

Still, these petitioners had a point, though not the one they emphasized. On whatever basis the schoolmen moved children outside their own neighborhoods and around the city, essentially they were denying the tradition that school attendance should be based upon residential location. If the Committee was not guilty of destroying the principle of the neighborhood school, it was responsible for violating the practice.

The last complaint levied by the petitioners dealt also with the neighborhood school principle, but this time on the issue of inconvenience and safety. Parents denounced the hardships caused children, especially younger ones, in having to travel from one section of the city to another. That grievance was accurate. Despite their best efforts, Committee members had not been able to segregate the sexes, balance the school population, and still allow children to attend the school closest to their homes.

To achieve uniformity, the Committee had to require a number of children to attend school in neighborhoods far removed from their own. Children living near Cambridge Bridge, for example, in the extreme west of the city, had to transfer from the Wells School to the Adams School on Mason Street. Daily those children had to walk past their neighborhood school, past the nearby Bowdoin School, and across The Common to reach their new school. Other youngsters, residing near the Charlestown Bridge in the extreme North End, had to bypass several schools enroute to their new assignment at the Wells School in the West End, or at the Boylston School at the easternmost limits of the city. Outraged at this uprooting, many parents threatened to keep their children home rather than force them to make such daily trips (see Map 2).

The distances which children had to walk were not too lengthy, perhaps a mile or a mile and a half in most cases. Yet parents were opposed to any plan that took children too far away from their homes to schools, too far away from watchful parental eyes. Parents demanded a return to the former scheme of neighborhood schools, even though such schools might be overcrowded. And some parents, disagreeing with the attitudes of Ward Five residents, also demanded that their neighborhood schools be sexually segregated. These parents argued that boys and girls did not necessarily have to attend different schools to enjoy different educational surroundings. The Committee, they suggested, had no business requiring long trips to and from school just to achieve segregation of the sexes. Neighborhood schools could have separate entrances for boys and for girls, separate playgrounds, and different teachers for each sex.[39]

The School Committee might turn down one specific request concerning the schools, but it could not afford to ignore the outpouring of public reaction to its schemes, which the petitions represented. Its initial response was to stall for time. In late December 1837 the Committee ordered the "proper" dissemination of information on the issues, hoping that parents throughout the city would agree to the reorganization program once they fully understood all the details. To its chagrin, the Committee's propaganda failed. Parents continued to denounce some or all parts of the scheme and tried to pressure the Committee into accepting organizational plans that embodied the wishes of the local community.[40]

The School Committee answered its critics by first admitting the legitimacy of many of the complaints and then re-emphasizing its general point that some kind of redistribution of students was necessary if all children were to receive an adequate education. But the defense proved futile and the basic scheme of reorganization abortive. The Committee had no legal authority to enforce its demands. The most it could do was to refuse admitttance to a child applying to his neighborhood schools in

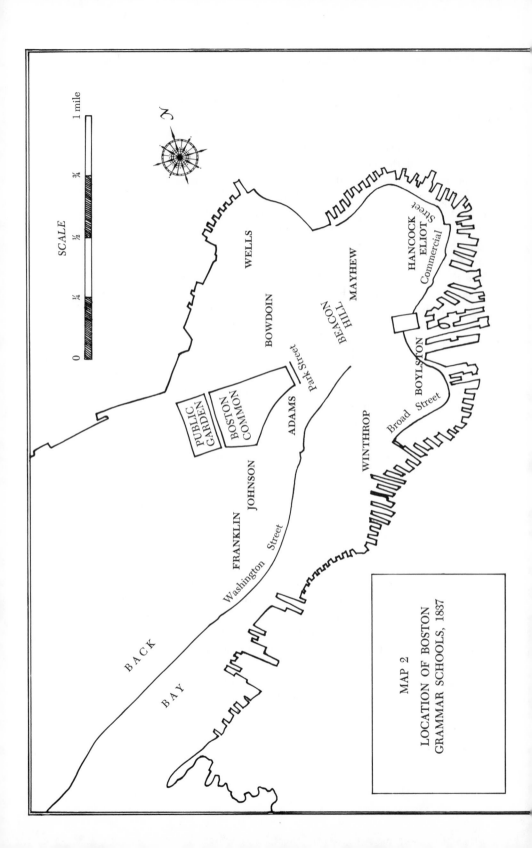

SCALE

0   ¼   ½   ¾   1 mile

N

BACK

BAY

PUBLIC
GARDEN

BOSTON
COMMON

FRANKLIN

JOHNSON

Washington   Street

ADAMS

Park Street

BOWDOIN

WELLS

BEACON
HILL

MAYHEW

WINTHROP

Broad   Street

BOYLSTON

HANCOCK

ELIOT

Commercial   Street

MAP 2

LOCATION OF BOSTON
GRAMMAR SCHOOLS, 1837

the hope that the parents would send the child to the school selected by the Committee. Parents in turn had the options of refusing to cooperate, of enrolling their child in a private school if they could afford the cost, or ultimately of keeping the child out of school entirely. As yet there was no law, state or local, that compelled school attendance. The Committee therefore had little choice but to modify its plans to allow parents the right of placing their children back into the neighborhood schools. Thus, early in 1838, the Committee voted to reinstitute four schools on a sexually integrated basis, and promised to seek funds for a new school in the congested wards of the North End.[41] To that extent at least, some parents had carried the day on the issue of local control.

From the educators' viewpoint, the task of accommodating public schools to a growing urban population became more difficult every year. Grand-scale redistribution of students and sweeping victories over the defenders of local control were not possible in the late 1830's or early 1840's. Yet, while the Committee failed to conquer a broad front, it established its claim to authority and control on a limited basis. It did not entirely abandon the reorganization plans. Occasionally over the next few years the Committee transferred a few children at a time from one school to another, from one neighborhood to another. Not until the 1850's, however, would the School Committee gain the legal tools necessary to refashion the imbalance of the school population.[42]

But educators did not abandon the hope of creating a uniform system of schools. After the effort toward massive redistribution of students had failed, school officials and educational reformers sought other means. If they could not ensure that all schools would contain an equal number of children, they could attempt to standardize the divisions of students within each school. By classifying children along lines other than sex, educators sought to reduce the overcrowding of classes, increase educational efficiency, and turn out a product of uniform excellence.

GRADED SCHOOLS FOR THE CITY

From the early 1820's students of approximately the same age and the same level of progress in the schools had been grouped together. But the classifications were vague and, in some schools, not practiced. In 1837 the *Report on Redistribution* urged that the classifications be made more rigid. "It is desirable," the educators stressed, "that the schools should be so nearly alike in respect to classification as well as numbers, that we may ascertain, with ease and accuracy, their comparative merits. At present, this is far from being the case."[43] School Committee members feared that without a uniform method of arranging the children for processing, the quality of their product surely would suffer.

The demands of educators for appropriate divisions of students within each school led to the creation of graded schools in Boston. The concept of the graded school was mechanistic. It assumed that children arrived at school in pre-packaged units according to age and intellectual abilities. Those units could be grouped together for convenience and efficiency, and run through the school as though on an assembly line. When the children completed the last grade, they graduated—finished products as far as the school was concerned. As introduced in Boston schools, the mechanical nature of the system became most evident in the primary schools. Children were expected to pass from one grade to the next each half-year, between the ages of four and seven, thereby graduating in three years.[44] This process of standardization also imbued the grammar schools; it was developed initially to solve the problems of overcrowding and inefficiency of instruction in the grammar schools. When educators first considered a widespread application of graded schools in the late 1830's, however, they failed to recognize its implications of regarding education (and the child) as a product rather than a process.

To bolster their arguments for the graded school, educators drew heavily upon European practice and experience. Paradoxically, those reformers most anxious to design an educational system for republican America borrowed elements from autocratic Prussia.

Americans had discovered value in the Prussian system of education as early as the 1820's. Among the first discussions was one by a New York physician and educator, John H. Griscom. In his book, *A Year in Europe, 1818-1819,* Griscom lauded the Prussian practice of state support for public schools, which all children had to attend, and also praised the principle of classifying children by ages in the schools. Shortly thereafter two Bostonians, George Bancroft and Joseph Cogswell, returned from study in Germany and in 1823 organized the Round Hill School in Northampton, Massachusetts. Impressed with the German Gymnasium, a school which united liberal education, physical exercise, and age classification, Bancroft and Cogswell added moral training to the combination. The result was an arrangement which visitors, like George Ticknor in 1824, applauded as "easy, cheap, and *practical.* . . . All was orderly, exact, useful"; in short, a perfect model for New England schools.[45]

Later travelers to Germany aroused so much excitement and enthusiasm for the Prussian model that by 1833 George P. McCulloch, a writer for the Boston *American Annals of Education,* warned that "the design of education in America is radically different than in Europe, and we can not hope to copy their practices and meet our needs in this country." But his appeal fell on deaf ears. In 1835 the Massachusetts legislature seriously considered emulating the fiscal policy of Prussian state aid to education and adopted a similar policy the following year. In 1836 Calvin Stowe, a transplanted Boston educator, undertook an investigation for the state of Ohio and published *The Prussian System of Public Instruction, and Its Applicability to the United States.* Stowe's panegyric of the Prussian system enjoyed a national readership of educators. When the Cincinnati reformer asked, "do not patriotism and the necessity of self-preservation, call upon us to do more and better for the education of our whole people, than any despotic sovereign can do for his?" he sparked enthusiasm in many Americans.[46]

While these and other accounts of Prussian schools informed Boston educators, many of their ideas about the application of Prussian principles derived from a comprehensive review by Horace Mann in his *Seventh Annual Report* to the Massachusetts legislature in 1843. Leading citizens, for instance Charles Sumner, had looked forward to Mann's report, anticipating that "great good" would come of it.[47] They were not disappointed.

In his report Mann approvingly described features of the Prussian school system which he believed to be pre-eminent among the "most highly civilized and conspicuous nations of Europe." To charges that borrowing from a monarchy inevitably meant introducing an alien spirit of despotism into American schools, Mann replied that educators like himself could easily separate evil from the good principles of education he had found. "If the Prussian schoolmaster has better methods of teaching reading, writing, grammar, geography, arithmetic, &c., so that, in half the time, he produces greater and better results, surely," Mann entreated, "we may copy his modes of teaching these elements, without adopting his notions of passive obedience to government, or of blind adherence to the articles of a church." Mann asked, "if a moral power be turned to evil, may it not also be employed for good?"

Among the most laudable methods of organization, teaching, and disciplining which he recounted, Mann declared that "the first element of superiority in a Prussian school, and one whose influence extends throughout the whole subsequent course of instruction, consists in the proper classification of the scholars." Wherever in Prussia the school population was large enough, children were divided according to age and attainment. Teachers had charge of only one class at a time, rather than five or six of different age groups as was common practice in Boston and throughout the rest of New England. Mann conceded that if the individual American teacher were brilliant, he or she might be able to accomplish something under such confusing conditions. But, he lamented, most teachers were not very capable, "hence the idleness and the disorder that reign in so many of our schools." But if schools copied the

Prussian system, and divided children properly into grades, placing one teacher in charge of each grade, even poor teachers might perform better. This innovation of the graded school, affirmed Mann, could be introduced at once "in all our large towns." No obstacle, save "that *vis inertia* of mind," prevented the graded school from solving the problems facing urban schools.[48]

Boston educational reformers seized upon Mann's remarks to use in their battle for the graded school. On this issue, as on so many other current questions of educational policy, the two most influential men were Samuel Gridley Howe and George B. Emerson. Both Howe, the physician turned reformer and educator of the blind, and Emerson, a successful teacher and a founder of the American Institute of Instruction, were close friends of Horace Mann. It was to Howe and Emerson that Mann most often turned for advice; to them also Mann owed thanks for their vigorous public defenses of his controversial policies.[49] In 1845 Howe authored a reform-minded annual report of the School Committee; Emerson echoed Howe's suggestions, adding some of his own, when he wrote the annual report for 1847. In both of these documents, the writers urged a unified system of schools organized on a graded basis.

Howe found that the number of classes and their size varied considerably from school to school. It was therefore impossible to derive any meaningful comparisons among individual schools. He charged that inefficient supervision, the large body of students, and the growing number of schools demonstrated the inability of the School Committee to ensure a uniform quality of education.

In an attempt to compare the schools, despite the difficulties involved, Howe and his committee introduced a new practice into American schools—written examinations for the students. Written examinations, they hoped, would yield more accurate information than the traditional oral form.[50] The committee tested all of the children involved in every school in the same subject on the same day. Since there were only three committeemen to examine nineteen grammar schools, only the first class in each school could be examined. Results of testing presumably the best students in each school discouraged Howe, and, he claimed, revealed the inadequacies of school organization. "If the children who have, during the year, enjoyed that special care and attention which our teachers give to the upper classes, go out unperfectly instructed," Howe pondered, "what must be the case with the hundreds and thousands of the children of our less-favored citizens, whom necessity forces to leave the schools without even reaching the first class!"

Even worse, thought Howe, was the fact the masters of the schools as currently organized, had little to do with the instruction or discipline of the lowest classes, "and in most cases positively nothing to do with their moral training." Howe and his committee concluded that the best answer to these problems was to introduce the graded school. With Mann, Howe believed that the graded school would make teachers more effective by allowing them to devote more time to children of equal ages and abilities, and would reduce the overcrowding of many classrooms. Mann heartily approved this and other suggestions of the Howe committee, widely publicizing them in his *Common School Journal*.[51]

George B. Emerson, in his 1847 report, carried on the campaign for the graded school. Of the various questions he raised concerning the schools, Emerson examined most carefully whether a proper distinction was made between the necessary kinds of education for boys and girls. "Are the boys formed to be good, virtuous and capable citizens," he asked, "and the girls prepared for the duties and requirements of women, who are to be the teachers of the coming generation?" The only way to ascertain the answer, he suggested, was to discover if the arrangement of the various grades of schools was all that it should be "for the thorough and economical instruction of all the children, of all classes, in the city." After personal investigation, Emerson reported that the schools were not properly ordered to accomplish their educational goals.

Emerson found deplorable overcrowding in many schools, but disagreed with those citizens and schoolmen who wanted to reduce overcrowding by building more and smaller schools. Emerson argued that whatever the system of internal organization, it was best for schools to remain large. "There would be very nearly the same diversity of capacity and attainment among one hundred children, within the school ages," he asserted, "as among six hundred." Whether there were 100 or 600 students, they should be "arranged in one descending line, to be divided into classes and sections, according to their progress. . . . There would thus be great economy of time, of explanation, and of study." Emerson called for a uniform system of grading children throughout the city schools to reduce overcrowding while also keeping the schools large enough in number to be "effective and economical." Only through such organizational changes, Emerson believed, could public schools accomplish their chief aim—"the management of the highest interest that belongs to human creatures —the formation of character."[52]

With the emphasis given the principle of graded schools by Mann, Howe, and Emerson, Boston educators set about the task of overhauling the entire school system on that model. Under the leadership of John D. Philbrick, Boston opened the first urban graded grammar school in the nation. By 1847, when the school began operations, Philbrick had already acquired the reputation of an able teacher; he later became superintendent of the Boston schools and a distinguished national authority on education. The Quincy School, or "the experiment" as it was then called, followed the Prussian model outlined by Mann, Howe, and Emerson. There was only one headmaster, rather than two as elsewhere in the city. There was one large assembly hall for all the students, and twelve separate classrooms, each with its own teacher, for the separate grades. Rather than sitting in the traditional parade fashion along a common bench, each student had his or her individual desk. The building was large enough to accommodate over six hundred pupils, so that effective classification of children was possible, while the city saved money at the same time. The Quincy experiment was completely successful. Other Boston schools soon followed its example; over the next fifty years school systems in other cities copied its method of organization.[53]

In arguing for the graded school, the reformers continued the drive toward standardization which had begun in the early 1820's, and they constantly invoked the metaphor of the factory. Their very language reflected an underlying assumption that children were a raw resource ready for the finishing. The educators were certain that children had plastic natures and could be molded into the desirable kind of adults. Public schools, organized like any efficient industry, could stamp out useful and moral citizens of the republic. The pragmatic and mechanistic attitudes of the schoolmen were revealed, for example, in the justification for reorganization of the schools advanced by Edmund G. Loring, author of the 1846 annual report of the School Committee. Loring emphasized that "our children are to be trained for this community in which most of them are to live and labor. It is said that the age is practical; if it is not, New England is, and so is its Capital. No where is intellect more precisely valued by its efficiency; no where is the mind itself more generally held to be, not a basket, but a machine, whose capacity is, not what it can hold, but what it can do." It was not surprising that educators should think and write in such terms. Contemporary New England literati like Ralph Waldo Emerson constantly used metaphors of the new industrialization to interpret daily life, even while they deplored the mechanistic social philosophy of their times.[54] Educational reformers were thus employing one of the literary commonplaces of the day.

By the 1850's public discussions about educational policy illustrated the complete acceptance of the industrial model by educators. In 1852, Nathan Bishop, the first superintendent of Boston schools, reaffirmed the principle of the graded school by explicitly drawing upon the example of the factory system. "The proper size of a School House in a large city, where the population is dense," Bishop stated, "must be determined by the number of pupils required in one building in order to make the *best classification.*" "The best classification," he continued, "is nothing more than a wise application of the principle of the division of labor, which has done so much to advance and to perfect the various branches of industry." Children, Bishop implied, were the interchangeable parts of a factory system of production, while schools were the factories themselves. Both educational policy and expediency required "organizing our System throughout on one uniform plan, thus bringing the whole into harmony with the great practical principles on which the best-managed business-enterprises are carried forward."

Just as the products of industrialization added to the comforts of life, so children, educated in uniform, graded schools, would contribute to the comfort and safety of American society. At a time when social instability and a lack of respect for authority seemed the hallmark of urban life and the leading characteristic of the younger generation, Bishop affirmed that the newly organized schools would "inspire the young with a sentiment of respect for law, and should teach them by precept to yield a cordial obedience to the regulations of Schools, the ordinances of the City, and the laws of the Commonwealth and of the Nation."[55] There was little doubt in the minds of educational reformers that the Uniformity System or the American System of Manufacturing could be adapted to the system of public education with the same beneficial results for citizenship as it had for material prosperity. The graded school was to be one of the chief tools used in the process of manufacturing good Americans. By 1860, all of Boston's primary and grammer schools operated on a graded system.[56]

The factory mentality shared by many educators had inspired a complete reorganization and systematization of the urban schools. The drive toward standardization had left some casualties along the way and had required some readjustments of traditional policies like sexual segregation, the neighborhood school, and the primacy of local control. To be sure, the schoolmen sometimes had tried to remain faithful to the principle of the neighborhood school. The introduction of graded divisions into the schools had facilitated the preservation of neighborhood schools in some sections of the city by reducing the overcrowding of some classrooms. Still, the reorganization efforts had smashed the traditional linkage between the neighborhood school and local control. The School Committee had increased its authority over the directions of public education in the city. The American System required unified management by men noted for executive ability rather than specialized knowledge, and in copying that system the educators inevitably became the power brokers of public education. Some of the managers would have had it no other way.

6

A Want of Symmetry:
The Beginnings of Bureaucracy

*Our school system is admirable, and beautiful in some parts,
but it is defective in others. It is a fabric, the elements of
which are perfect, but the beauty and design are marred
from a want of symmetry and proportion.*

George B. Emerson (1847)[1]

Throughout the years of struggle over neighborhood and graded schools,
Boston educators sought to tighten their reins of control over public education. As schools grew in number and the school-age population increased, educational reformers and members of the School Committee
found that they lacked the information necessary to readjust speedily
and sensibly the schools to changing conditions. When educators attempted to impose uniform standards of class size, instruction, and administration, they discovered how little authority over the schools or the
children they actually possessed. Schoolmen learned, to their discontent,
that traditional methods of organization and control had become outmoded when compared to the needs of public education in the city.

From the 1830's through the 1850's, a handful of Boston educational
reformers formulated new means of standardizing their system of education. Borrowing freely from innovations in the process of manufacturing,
they experimented with ways of reorganizing education and of strength-
ening their control of the school system.

If the schools were to be remodeled along the lines of the successful
factory, the industrial methods of management had to be employed.
Administration of schools had to become more impersonal than in the
past. The managers of the system—School Committeemen—had to be
more efficient in executive ability than they had been in the past. An
educational specialist had to be given authority to make decisions involving the increasingly complex system of public schools. In short, educational reformers argued that control over public education had to become less the private bailiwick of amateurs and more a public bureaucracy

132

of professionals. They demanded order in place of a "want of symmetry."

To call for such changes was easy, to institute them more difficult. Tradition, vested interests, public apathy, the growing complexity of coordinating public enterprises in an expanding city—all blocked the efforts of educational reformers. The customary composition of the School Committee itself reflected these obstacles and presented a difficult hurdle for the reformers. The difficulties were greater since both the reformers and their adversaries were members of the same social class.[2]

The intra-class struggles for centralized authority over the system were an integral part of the movement for common schools in Boston and other American cities.[3] The contests resulted not only in a reorganization of schools but also in the creation of an urban educational hierarchy. As the century wore on the governance of schools would rest less and less with an uneasy coalition of parents, other neighborhood residents, ward politicians, and distinguished citizens elected to the School Committee. In the pursuit of order and efficiency a new breed of professional educators began to emerge. Their surfacing promised a business-like approach to management of the schools, but also foreshadowed the entrenchment of an educational bureaucracy whose principal goal would be self-preservation.

AN ADMINISTRATIVE OLIGARCHY

The Boston Education Act of 1789 had provided for an elected School Committee representing city-wide interests. Citizens annually elected to the Committee one member from each of the city's twelve wards. With this provision, residents believed that they had served their personal interests in the schools and had established local control over the future of public education. Actually, they had done neither. The call for yearly elections clearly set up a mechanism for local control, but citizens rarely used that tool for effecting change. From year to year the same individuals served on the Committee, elected by their constituents. Perhaps by re-electing the same men Bostonians showed their satisfaction with a well-performed job; undoubtedly that was often true. But the more likely explanation was voter inertia. Neither in Massachusetts nor in its capital were there high voter turnouts before the 1840's.[4]

Voters tended either not to vote at all, or, in the absence of stirring issues, to re-elect current officeholders. Political apathy reflected a lack of serious tensions and cleavages in the community until the immigrant arrivals during the 1840's. And, in a city dominated by commercial and manufacturing interests, voters saw little purpose in turning out of power men whose personal success clearly demonstrated their ability to govern. Voters who saw their own social aspirations mirrored in the values and accomplishments of their leaders confirmed the worth of their judgments by continuing to vote for the same man.[5]

The social prestige of Boston School Committee members had long contributed to voter inertia. The first School Committee, elected in 1789, was composed of businessmen and professional men: doctors, merchants, ministers, and public servants. Men such as Judge Thomas Dawes, who served on the Supreme Court of the Commonwealth and the Boston Municipal Court for many years; George R. Minot, also a judge and an accomplished historian; Dr. James Freeman, one of the city's most respected clergymen; and the nationally famous architect Charles Bulfinch typified the kind of men elected and re-elected to the School Committee. Boston voters so trusted their prominent citizens that in 1821 a newspaper editor could observe that "it was a long established usage to elect on this important committee three gentlemen from each of the learned professions, and the other three from gentlemen in other employments." While occasional departures from the rule occurred, in 1821 there were three ministers, three physicians, and two lawyers among the twelve members of the School Committee.[6]

These men were not professional educators. Rather, they were men who served the community in a number of different capacities during their lifetimes. It was their undifferentiated success that commended such individuals to the electors. Men who performed ably in several endeavors showed themselves worthy to run the schools as well. In an age of self-help philosophy when the roads to economic success seemed open equally to all who would make an effort; at a time when social mobility was a favorite topic of public discussion, the election of successful men confirmed the voters' own hopes of personal achievement.[7]

For the most part those who served as School Committee members represented the ruling elite of Boston. In the late eighteenth and early nineteenth century this class of public men included: merchants of modest wealth, but of great social prestige; members of prominent families, brought to the fore either as patriots during the American Revolution, or of older, patrician origins; and ministers who still wore the mantles of public respect and authority first donned by their Puritan ancestors. They were men who shared the same religious attitudes, the same sense of decorum and manners, the same love of learning, the same devotion to the "republic," and the same suspicion of "democracy" that motivated the ill-starred Essex Junto. They were individuals who felt themselves to be the leaders of a "compact, united, and kindly community." They believed that they played a vital role in maintaining the structural continuity of society. Down through the 1830's such men continued to govern the community, serving as mayors, aldermen, and members of the Primary School Board and the School Committee.[8]

By the 1840's, however, long-time residents of the city and members of the ruling elite were complaining that the "compact" and "united" community was no more. Those who served in various city offices were no longer bound tightly by class and party. Men who were not merchants, doctors, lawyers, or other professional men began to enter government as mayors and councilmen. The hostilities directed toward the older elite by Wendell Phillips, whose father had been the first mayor of Boston in 1822, or by Charles Sumner, whose father had served as sheriff, revealed how thinly stretched the older bonds of community had become.[9]

Concerned educators, among other citizens, viewed the shifts in power as dangers to the stable life of the city. Reflected in the problems of education in Boston they saw at work the same disruptive forces which wracked the larger community. Too many citizens were ignorant and vicious, charged Horace Mann in an 1842 address on the perils of popular government, and those traits were responsible for immoral men coming to power, for election "days of turbulence, and bacchanalian riot, of insulting triumph or revengeful defeat." For the salvation of society men must be educated. As the *Common School Journal* put it, "the education of all classes of the community, in the same nurseries of mind, would produce the happiest social and moral effects." Or, as a speaker before the American Institute of Instruction proclaimed: "the most important interests of individuals and of society, the stability and permanency of our institutions," demanded the public education of all children.[10]

Faced with variations in the social climate of the city and believing strongly in the ameliorating power of schooling, some educators worked all the harder to ensure the election of the proper community leaders to the School Committee. They wanted to make certain that men of the traditional ruling elite continued to oversee the schools, regardless of any other changes in public leadership. The matter was all the more pressing for the state legislature in 1835 had passed an act doubling the size of the Committee. Now with two men to be elected from each city ward, educators believed it was vital to make certain that additional membership did not dilute the social composition of the Committee.[11]

The educators had little trouble convincing the voters to keep the traditional membership of the Committee intact. Although a disgruntled citizen might characterize committeemen as "physicians with limited practice, or preachers on small salaries waiting for a louder call—shallow adventurers in the fields of science and theology," men of social prominence usually predominated.[12]

The Committee for 1842 was typical. Edward Wigglesworth came from one of the oldest families in the city, dating back to his famous ancestor Michael Wigglesworth, author of the *Day of Doom*. Charles H. Stearns, like his father before him, was a successful merchant in shipping and family stores, and a leader of the city's best-known volunteer fire brigade. Benjamin A. Gould had started his career as a schoolmaster, later becoming principal of the Boston Latin School at the age of twenty-seven. By 1842 Gould had already served a number of years on the Committee. He was to end his days as a moderately wealthy merchant in the Calcutta trade. George H. Hillard was a scholar, frequent contributor to the *North American Review,* a member of the State House of Representatives, and the law partner of Charles Sumner. The Reverend Alexander Young, a Unitarian minister, served as an Overseer of Harvard College, as corresponding secretary of the Massachusetts Historical Society, and was one of the city's accomplished antiquarians. Other members of the Committee were also merchants and professional men.[13]

The presence of seven ministers on the Committee showed that electors still valued the learning and moral authority of clergymen. There was no doubt that the schools were under lay control. But there was also little doubt that educators prized a strong Christian influence in the schools. Horace Mann urged clergymen to run for office and to visit the schools regularly. Such visitation, Mann reminded ministers, was "among their parochial duties and part and parcel of the care of souls." And ministers, increasingly worried that their influence was waning, responded by participating enthusiastically in educational reform. "The pulpit, I say," boasted one clergyman, "has led this reform not only in self-defence, but as a means of moral progress and Christian enterprise. Every stroke that has been struck well, in this work of public education, has been so much done in building the great temple of salvation."[14]

Even a rapid extension of the suffrage, particularly for immigrant voters, had little effect on the type of men elected to the School Committee after the early 1840's.[15] Until the coming of the Civil War, Boston citizens continued to elect men of importance and social prestige in the community to govern their schools. Those men in turn appointed individuals of like beliefs and social class to the Primary School Board, until they finally abolished the sister organization in the interests of efficiency, thrift, and greater authority for themselves. While the Primary Board lasted, however, its composition mirrored that of the School Committee.[16]

Between the founding of primary schools in 1818 and the absorption of the Primary School Board by the general School Committee in 1855, a total of 742 men served on the Board. Each man received appointment from the School Committee; actually, recommendations for new members came from the Primary Board itself and rarely met opposition from the

Committee. The large number of appointees over the years was deceptive. The most influential members of the self-perpetuating Primary Board were its chairmen, secretaries, chairmen of Standing Committees, and secretaries of Standing Committees. During the life of the Board these positions, respectively, were filled by eleven, ten, twelve, and eight men. Often these same individuals served in more than one capacity in directing the activities of the Board, and most of them at one time or another were elected members of the general School Committee. The policy-making functions and the appointment of new members lay, then, in the hands of a very small group of men who held virtual autonomy over the control of primary schools.[17]

Voter inertia, manifested in a curious lack of interest in exerting local control over the schools through the ballot box, re-enforced the vigorous efforts of the educators to gain firm authority over the public schools. The result, though beneficial for the development and continuity of education in the city, was an administrative oligarchy.

By the mid-1840's, that oligarchy had exercised control over the schools for half a century. To be sure, the same individuals did not serve for forty or fifty years. But the same type of men, coming from similar social backgrounds and sharing, as Oliver Wendell Holmes put it, the tendency to "carry the Common in our heads as the unit of space, the State House as the standard of architecture, and measure off men in Edward Everetts as with a yardstick," dominated the schools as they generally dominated Boston society.[18]

From time to time, there were internal squabbles within the oligarchy. Schoolmen often argued about the rapidity of change within the school system and how to control it. Occasionally bitter political battles occurred over election to the School Committee. Yet even when one faction temporarily defeated another, individuals of the same social class succeeded each other. Conflicts ensued not along class lines, but over varying conceptions of reform and, indeed, over the necessity of reform at all. The absorption of the Primary School Board by the School Committee in 1855 was an example of one such tangle.

The dissolution of the Primary Board exemplified the centralization of educational authority in a small, administrative hierarchy. Shortly after taking office in 1837 as the first secretary of the Massachusetts Board of Education, Horace Mann criticized the shoddy administration of the Boston primary schools and called for supervision by a professional superintendent. Board members replied that through the diffusion of authority they remained closer to the people and to the concept of local control over the neighborhood school. During the following years the battle for centralization continued. By the early 1850's there were over

190 primary schools in the city, and an equal number of administrators on the Primary Board. This unwieldy group prevented unified administration of the school system. The debate became heated and in 1855 the Board finally merged, kicking and screaming as it were, into the School Committee, which then appointed a small group of men to oversee the primary schools.[19] While this struggle illustrated the kinds of infighting among members of the oligarchy, with different sides jockeying for power, far more significant for the direction of public education in the city was the earlier school election battle of 1845. The dissolution of the Primary Board, in fact, was the logical culmination of that earlier battle, the checkmate of the game.

IN SEARCH OF REFORM: THE ELECTION BATTLE OF 1845

The first important challenge to the composition and performance of the School Committee came in 1845 with the election of several reform-minded members. Like so many other controversies involving education in mid-nineteenth-century Massachusetts, this one had been instigated by the activities of Horace Mann.

The confrontation began with Mann's *Seventh Annual Report* in 1843. Mann had detailed the pedagogical advantages of the tightly controlled, centralized system of education in Prussia and had compared Prussian practices of teaching and discipline with current methods in Massachusetts schools. An "Association of Masters of the Boston Public Schools" vigorously attacked Mann for ridiculing them. The secretary had couched his criticisms in general terms, but the masters felt certain he meant to denegrate their efforts. "Who," they questioned, "at home or abroad, will not think of the metropolis, when they read the secretary's *reflections* upon the teachers and schools of Massachusetts?"[20] Mann did consider the masters inadequate, and especially as little more than barbarians in their exercise of corporal punishment.[21]

Close friends and other leading citizens of Boston jumped to Mann's defense. Mann himself launched caustic counter-attacks, in the vindictive hope that "thirty one of them hung on the same shaft would look like a string of onions." Following public and private charges and counter-charges, Mann and his friends decided to bore from within the system itself. In the fall of 1844 Mann encouraged his close friend Samuel Gridley Howe to seek the election of himself and others of like mind to the School Committee. In this way, they might gain the upper hand in properly administering the schools.[22]

The supporters of Mann—Howe, Charles Sumner, Edward G. Loring, George B. Emerson, and others—chose to work for school reform within the confines of the Whig party. In Boston, as throughout the state, the Whigs still represented the traditional leadership class of merchants and professional men. Party unity had crumbled slightly before the attacks of its more reform-minded members, especially on the issue of slavery. By the mid-1840's some dissident Whigs had even joined together in their own wing of the party as nativists, opposed principally to the Irish. For the most part, however, conservatives and reformers agreed to continue to work together. Until the mid-1850's, the political machinery of Boston avoided party issues as much as possible. Nonpartisanship, as an ideal, commanded the devotion of Whigs, Democrats, and a mélange of smaller factions. During the 1840's, then, reform Whigs still hoped that change could come within the party. That Howe, Sumner, and others considered themselves Whigs attested their affiliation with the customary ruling class of Boston, in spite of their reform intentions.[23]

At the December 1844 caucus of the Whig party, Mann's associates sought to take charge. They were aided by a heavy turnout. The public controversy surrounding Mann and the masters had aroused local residents from their usual torpor about School Committee elections. An observer reported that the meeting was unusually large, and that "little interest appeared to be felt in the nominations of candidates to any of the offices except that of School Committee —after that was made, a large portion of the persons present left the room." He added that in his opinion Howe had packed the hall with citizens friendly to Mann.[24] The large gathering, however, was due more to the spirited exchanges between the teachers and Mann and to the excitement caused by the entry of several anti-Catholic, anti-Irish Native American Party candidates, than to Howe's machinations alone.

Nonetheless, Howe had laid a careful groundwork for the meeting. He received the nomination for the School Committee from Ward Twelve, home base in South Boston. Despite heavy opposition, he also succeeded in securing the nomination from Ward Four for Charles Sumner. That ward included East Boston, a section of the city in which an island of native citizens were feeling the pressures of a sea of Irish immigrants. Residents of East Boston objected to Sumner's nomination, stating that he was unpopular with the people. The candidate whom the dissidents eventually ran against Sumner, however, showed their real concern. The Reverend H. A. Graves was a Baptist clergyman, vigorously anti-immigrant, and a member of the Native American Party. In addition to himself and Sumner, Howe secured the nominations of at least six other reform candidates.[25]

Election results justified the course of action chosen by Mann and Howe. Although Graves defeated Sumner, Howe himself won. From other wards such reform candidates as the Reverend James I. T. Coolidge, a liberal Unitarian; Rollin H. Neale, a Baptist minister; Theophilus Parsons, noted classical scholar and lawyer; and William Brigham, another lawyer; were also elected. Enough men took their places on the School Committee to promise that Horace Mann's demands for centralization of authority in overseeing the schools would have a sympathetic following.[26]

That the reformers' views on reorganization would receive serious public attention became evident when the newly elected School Committee appointed Howe, Parsons, and Neale to make the annual examination of the public schools. On August 7, 1845, after three months of labor, the examining committee presented its report, authored by Howe. Given the relationship among Mann, Howe, and other members of the committee, the results were a foregone conclusion.

The report indicted the organization and functioning of the School Committee. The reform committee was aware of two criticisms made in recent years and repeated these in its own report. Both charges concerned the prerogatives and thus the performance of the Committee. Despite the fact that the mayor and the president of the Common Council served as ex officio members, the School Committee was not legally required to report to either the Council or the mayor's office. It managed the schools entirely within its own body. Theoretically such autonomy was democratic; only the whims of the voters could circumscribe the actions of the Committee. But in practice, the election year after year of the same men, or of men similar in social outlook, meant that the Committee rarely had to feel itself accountable to anyone. This lack of responsibility in turn led, or might lead, to a casual approach to overseeing the schools. It was lamentable but true, Howe and the others charged, that in fact "no one man, and no Sub-Committee, is ever required or expected to know the actual condition of all the Grammar Schools of Boston."[27]

This lack of knowledge stemmed partly from the composition of the examining committee. Three years before the Howe Report, the Reverend Charles C. Shackford, chairman of the Annual Visiting Committee, had complained that only six hours could be spent in examining each of the various schools. His committee, he admitted, was painfully aware of how little time that was to evaluate any one school adequately. No definite judgments, therefore, could be made; the committee could give only vague impressions.[28] Howe and his fellow reformers took up that criticism and expanded it to a broader attack on the composition of the Committee.

In his comments about the School Committee, Howe emphasized that any understanding of the problems of administering the schools had to rely on an understanding of changes in the city itself. Over the past years, the city had grown rapidly both in population and in physical size, and also in the complexity of governing. Howe agreed with his friend Horace Mann, who had written a correspondent that "the increased means for education for the last sixty years, have not kept pace with the increasing obligations, duties, and temptations of the community."[29] The problems of administration of the city's school system had compounded with urban growth, Howe reported, but the means of administration had not.

Of the School Committee, Howe observed that "numerous, chosen without concert, in many different parts of the city, offering to those of its members who cannot turn it to their pecuniary benefit, no motive but the mere love of usefulness to induce them to remain long in office, it is, necessarily, an uncertain, fluctuating and inexperienced body." That Howe employed a phrase like "the mere love of usefulness" to describe the motives for service revealed both how far the Puritan ideal of public stewardship among community leaders had fallen and how much the profit motive had taken its place.[30] Life in the cities had expanded economic opportunities, while the demands of commerce and manufacturing had limited the time which enterprising men could give to civic duties. In administering the schools, Howe thus explained, "the duties which we do perform, though quite as much as can be expected or ought to be asked of men who give to these only their leisure, and give it without compensation, are but a very small part of those which lie upon us." In questioning the amount of time which busy men, who knew little of school affairs in the first place, could give to administering the schools, Howe raised an important reason for professionalism among schoolmen.[31]

THE PROMISE OF PROFESSIONALISM

The earliest English usage of "profess" was to declare a religious belief. But by the early seventeenth century the word had become secularized. "Profession" no longer meant faith in an external, spiritual being, but rather confidence in one's self. It was the fact or act of professing qualifications uniquely suited to certain tasks. By the time Samuel Gridley Howe and others began to use the word in relation to teaching and administering schools, in common usage "profession" had come to mean a vocation in which claimed knowledge of some branch of learning was applied to the affairs of others. Occupations such as the ministry, law, or medicine bore the status of professions.[32]

Inherent in this meaning of the word was the understanding that those who claimed the status of professionals professed to have specialized knowledge without which certain community affairs could not be managed effectively. The professional claimed indispensability. He also demanded a degree of authority, for if his knowledge was vital to the community, it was necessary that he possess control over the application of his skills. The aspiring professional further demanded permanancy, or at least some assurance of permanancy, in the exercise of his occupation. He required that his skillful performance become institutionalized in some lasting structure that would guarantee the exercise of his authority. Professionals sought clearly understood and carefully defined relationships between themselves and society for the performance of their tasks. They wanted an administrative bureaucracy which had, as its chief characteristic, the maintenance of accepted standards of judgment and behavior over time. Only in this manner could the best interests of both the community and themselves be served.[33] It was with these goals in mind— however hazily conceived—that Samuel Gridley Howe pressed the need for changes in the organization of the Boston School Committee.

Howe charged, correctly, that members of the School Committee were not professional men with a specialized knowledge of school matters. That the men lacked such knowledge was regrettable, but even worse was the fact that committeemen did not often possess even the executive ability necessary to administer the schools. In part, Howe believed, the men were at fault; in part the lack of organizational structure was to blame. To govern the schools, Committee members divided themselves into sub-committees, each consisting of three men. Because there were twenty-four men to handle the problems of nineteen grammar schools, each member had to serve on the sub-committee of two schools, and nine members served on three. The law required sub-committees to visit every school at least once a quarter. This meant that no sub-committee regularly visited all the schools.

When a sub-committee did visit a school and attempted to determine its quality and the abilities of its teachers and students, the methods of investigation were so haphazard that results were unreliable. Of these examinations Howe affirmed that "that which is made by the regular sub-committees, never, by any possibility, subjects all the schools to the same standard. It never ascertains their comparative merits." There was no bureaucratic structure ensuring common standards of administration or progress in this most vital of community endeavors. There were "no means by which improvements that are of great service in one school, may be adopted in another; none by which the example of one school may be made profitable to another; and the greatest and most unnecessary difference may remain for years, in schools almost in sight of each other."

There was no guarantee that this administrative vacuum left by sub-committees would be filled by the Annual Visiting Committees. In one day, or perhaps two, Howe criticized, the annual visitors were to ascer-

tain the whole condition of the school. They were to judge the profi-
ciency of all the students engaged in various studies; the methods of
instruction; the discipline and "motive-powers" relied upon; the character,
demeanor, and abilities of the masters, ushers, and assistants; the
physical condition of the schoolrooms; and they were to determine
whether defects and errors could be cured and the most effective means
for improvement. Obviously, Howe concluded, this was an impossible
task. A few men, unspecialized in educational matters, could hardly be
expected to carry out such a charge.[34]

Other barriers to efficiency blocked the reformers' efforts. Perceptive
men like Howe understood the difficulties in communicating among various parties interested in the governmental problems of an expanding
city. The word "government" is derived from a Greek root referring to
the steering or piloting of a ship. Steering a ship meant directing its
course from knowledge of the present position and from information
about its past performance. Presumably those in charge had a specific
destination in mind and all authority necessary to carry out their orders.
Certainly Howe, Mann, and other educational reformers viewed government in this manner, for they repeatedly used a ship and steersman analogy when referring to the social role of government.[35]

For government to function properly, it was vital that all the governors possess ample information on the state of public affairs and that they
have the power to enforce their decisions. Howe and others who believed
that the goal of public education was social stability and the proper
steering of the ship of state knew that having sufficient information for
the intelligent government of schools was essential to reaching that goal.

They also knew that the necessary information had not always been
available. Within the School Committee itself over the years, members
had not possessed adequate knowledge to formulate and apply common
standards in administering the schools. "The examiners are, by long
usage," Howe pointed out, "new men every year, which makes anything like systematic and continuous observation out of the question; and
the Reports of successive years show a discrepancy which we cannot
otherwise explain."[36]

Nor were the schoolmen themselves the only persons acting in the
dark. The citizens of Boston who presumably (and legally) controlled
the destinies of public education had rarely received enough information
to choose intelligently among prospective candidates for the School Committee or to make their views known to that body. Not until 1845, with
the Howe report, were the annual reports of the visiting committees
printed and distributed throughout the city. Only when newspapers or
periodicals published excerpts from the reports was much of the public

informed about conditions in the schools. When facts did become available, many citizens showed their desires to be informed by avidly reading any materials at hand. In 1851 a writer in the Boston periodical, the *Christian Review*, observed that the numerous reports on education "have of late years come to be regarded as among the most important and interesting public documents" published. He undoubtedly exaggerated when he claimed that the reports were read not only by professional men, but also by the humblest artisan, mechanic, or laborer who realized their importance to him. But with the numerous periodicals and public reports dealing with education that flourished after 1840, the writer's claims for widespread popularity of reading material about education was accurate.[37] Nevertheless, when Howe and others complained about the absence of adequate information in the past about the Boston schools, they hit upon a major problem affecting the administration of public education in the city.

"Our citizens seem to have built up an extensive establishment of Schools," Howe observed, "to tax themselves annually for their support to the amount of more than two hundred thousand dollars, and then to leave them without anything like adequate or appropriate supervision." Howe implied that had voters only possessed adequate information on school conditions, they might have elected men of new ideas to govern the schools, or might have shown more personal interest in overseeing education themselves. But School Committee members, misinformed themselves, in turn misled the public. Through public statements in the past, Committee members had lulled the public into complacency about the glories of the schools. The Committee "protects and perpetuates defects, by preventing that personal examination by parents, which might, in some degree at least, be given, if it were supposed to be needed;—thus verifying the saying of Jeremy Bentham, in his argument in favor of individual responsibility, that a 'Board' is but too apt to become a 'Screen.'" The problem, as Howe saw it, was twofold: first, how to facilitate communication between parents and school officials; and, second, how to increase the efficiency of school administration in a city which had grown too large to depend upon individual responsibility alone.

Some people had suggested a complete overhaul of the School Committee. Howe did not agree. For the most part he believed that School Committee members were decent men who had shown their abilities in numerous activities. If they were not professional educators, perhaps there was an advantage to that fact; perhaps because of their lack of specialized knowledge they would be more flexible in handling school affairs. There were also advantages in the system of representative government that regulated the educational affairs of the city. "Its members," Howe noted of the Committee, "come fresh from the people, every year; and being chosen from all the wards, they represent all the wants and interests which should be provided for."[38] Howe meant there were advantages to having men like himself, men of his social class and community standing, elected to govern the schools. This representative government and the unspecialized nature of most committeemen offered an opportunity, Howe believed, for professional educators to take control. The unknowledgeable committeemen and the uninformed citizens might be willing to have experts run their schools.

BEGINNING A BUREAUCRACY

Howe proposed to the people of Boston a new position, school commissioner, or superintendent of public schools. The individual chosen would be an officer of the city, appointed by the City Council, and subject to the dual authority of the Council and the School Committee. Through this appointment the city could gain the best of two worlds. The tradition of local control, exercised by citizens in each ward who voted representatives into office, would be continued, at least in theory. Of greater importance, the increasingly complex administration of the school system would be in the hands of an expert. Although he praised the "excellent elements for a Board of Education which we now possess," Howe knew that the old method of laymen governing the schools was outmoded. The position of superintendent would add badly needed qualities "which are wholly wanting" in administration. These were "permanence, personal responsibility, continued and systematic labor." Although chosen annually, if he performed satisfactorily, the new superintendent should enjoy a permanent tenure of office. Governing the schools "should be his business —his whole business; and he should be adequately paid."[39]

In short, Howe urged that the democratic practice of school administration be retained, but that it continue within a new, bureaucratic structure.[40] Professional expertise had to temper lay control. The proper training of citizens in an expanding and turbulent city was too important a task to be left to chance and to the private jealousies and ambitions of some parents and politicians. The current system stumbled under the burden of expecting twenty-four men, unpaid and sharing fragmented responsibility, to do a good job. Efficiency could not be expected when individuals were willing to serve on the School Committee "by every variety of motive, from the highest and purest love of usefulness, down to a mere personal purpose of coining its privileges and opportunities into dollars and cents." Howe knew that in recent years citizens had often registered complaints about some individuals using their positions on the School Committee as a stepping-stone to political advancement or personal profit.[41] Mentioning suspicions about the integrity of some of the School Committeemen was a clever propaganda ploy.

Howe stressed that private responsibility had to give way to public control. As an appointed official, the superintendent would link the School Committee and the city government. As a professional, "liable to lose his livelihood if he goes wrong," a superintendent of schools would bring administrative order out of chaos.[42] Howe therefore proposed a marriage of convenience between private and public control of the schools so that the legitimacy of the offspring might not be questionable.

Howe and his fellow reformers recognized a new truth about mid-nineteenth-century urban life. In Boston, as elsewhere, the needs of a growing population and a physical plant increasing in size could no longer be met by private enterprise alone. The city had become too complex a unit of interrelated parts to allow piecemeal control. By 1846 Boston was a city of over 115,000. Due to lack of information, a dearth of pooled financial resources, and citizen disinterest, it was impossible for all of the people to provide adequate services for themselves. Recognizing this fact, during years past conscientious citizens had placed greater authority in public agencies. To ensure quality services both city and state had licensed, as semi-monopolies, many occupations. Lawyers, doctors, owners of glass factories, auctioneers, shopkeepers, newsboys—the list had grown yearly.[43]

In the 1820's, Mayor Josiah Quincy had begun the reorganization of public services. Despite massive opposition from volunteer fire companies who rightfully feared losses of political power and loot which they often claimed as salvage from blazing buildings, Quincy had succeeded in putting the fire department on a professional course. Alarm over public health problems resulting from inadequate housing, overcrowding, unclean water supplies, and imperfect drainage had prompted official investigations. The terror of cholera epidemics had especially brought public action. By 1832 Boston had created a special Board of Health Commissioners which was short-lived but which continued past attempts at city-wide control and which set a precedent for similar public action in the future. In 1846, following the example of Philadelphia and New York City, Boston had broken ground for a public water system. In these and in other activities, the city had assumed responsibility for public services and safety in place of private enterprise. In calling for a centralization of authority and stronger professional control of the school system, Howe and others trod a well-worn path.[44]

Despite cogent reasons favoring the appointment of a superintendent,

Howe realized that some citizens would oppose the measure. Conservatives who always rejected any innovation would refuse this one. Some people would find it too expensive, although Howe argued effectively that having one man in a position of authority would eliminate wasted effort by many men and thereby save money for the city. He pointed out that other cities that had experimented with the office had effected savings.[45] If the suggested reforms met with public favor, Howe knew that many interests, personal and financial, would be threatened "and therefore much influence will be exerted against it." The recent experience of Horace Mann demonstrated the kind of opposition to centralization efforts he could expect.

The State Board of Education, with Mann as its Secretary, had been in existence less than two years when opponents of centralization came forward to challenge its authority. Among the first was Orestes A. Brownson, a Democrat and radical reformer, who feared that the country was headed toward absolute control by "associated wealth." That "Proteus of doctrine," as Mann aptly characterized Brownson, had previously championed the potential of public education for enlarging the morality of a community. But in the formation of the Board of Education he though he saw another attempt by the few to control the destinies of the many. Now he ridiculed the faith in universal education, arguing that children would grow up in the same way if all schoolhouses were closed immediately. Brownson charged that the Board was really a promotional bureau for Whig philosophy. Centralization of authority in educational matters, Brownson believed, would lead to a Prussian type of autocracy.[46]

Criticism similar to Brownson's came quickly from other quarters. Mann felt himself besieged by "political madmen . . . raising voice and arm against the Board." Marcus Morton, newly elected governor of the state, was a Jacksonian Democrat, and shared the Jacksonian persuasion that centralization of governmental power in expanding, bureaucratic agencies was dangerous to the public good. Morton attacked both the concept of centralization and the Board of Education. Then, in March 1840 members of the Committee on Education in the State Legislature launched a bitter attack on the Board, labeling it contrary to "the true spirit of our democratical institutions."[47]

Personal beliefs and jealousies motivated the two chief authors of the Committee *Report*. Allen W. Dodge, an orthodox Baptist minister, attacked Mann and the Board as the agents of Unitarianism. Frederick Emerson, a former Boston public school teacher, bore a personal grudge against Mann for having replaced him as an initial member of the Board of Education and later for refusing to recommend school usage of an arithmetic text which he had authored.[48] Though the movement to abolish the Board failed, the spirit of antagonism toward centralization lingered on.

When Samuel Gridley Howe feared that "much influence" would be exerted against his suggested reforms, he realistically read the political and personal pressures in the city. His apprehensions were probably strengthened when even Mann cautioned patience in the reform effort. "There is no man but yourself, who can carry it thro', *at this time*," Mann wrote, "but another year, if not now."[49] Events quickly confirmed the pessimism of both men about immediate success.

Editorial reactions to the Howe report varied, but the Democratic *Boston Times*, in labeling the report a "libel on our schools by its errors and mis-statements," spoke for many Bostonians who were outraged at criticisms of their educational system. Those citizens who for years had ignored the conditions of the schools did not wish to be reminded of their laxity. They had preferred to elect a friend or prominent citizen to the School Committee, rather than take an active part in exercising local control over neighborhood schools. It was a curious circumstance that such people now reacted against the appointment of a professional educator who, according to Howe, would "impart such information as shall bring all our schools to that degree of excellence which our citizens not only have a right to demand, but without which they have no right, in justice to themselves and to their children, to be satisfied."[50] Inefficiency and public indifference marred administration of the schools; to combat them Howe, Mann, and others demanded centralized, professional control.

Howe had correctly questioned the competence of some of the teachers in his report. Some of the masters lived out of the city, in suburban areas, and never saw their students except in the classrooms. Howe had suggested that those teachers could know very little of the daily influences that affected the lives of their pupils.

From a tactical standpoint, his criticism was an error. The same "Thirty-one," the masters who had condemned Mann after his *Seventh Annual Report*, felt their interests threatened by Howe. They responded with personal attacks on his character. As William B. Fowle, a Boston educator and compatriot of Mann and Howe, sarcastically observed, apparently "the greatest offence that any citizen can commit is to doubt the perfection of our schools, and any attempt to improve them, on the part of a committee man, is madness, and is instantly visited by official death."[51]

The storm of controversy raging over their proposals blew Howe and his fellow reformers off the Committee. In November 1845 Howe and all those who agreed with him, except Theophilus Parsons, were dropped from the slates of candidates for the upcoming election.[52]

The friends of Howe and of reform reacted quickly. The most blunt reply came from William B. Fowle, a man of social standing and reputation in the community. He had pioneered the public education of girls in Boston during the 1820's; had authored a number of textbooks as well as popular literature; in 1842 had joined Horace Mann in publishing the *Common School Journal;* and in 1843 had served in the state legislature. In expressing his social views Fowle often employed satire.[53] But in defense of Howe and the others he did not mince words. On no subject, he charged, were citizens so ignorant and so indifferent as on the schools. Yet, when a few committeemen dared to tell the truth "at a great sacrifice of ease, and time, and money, and health, . . . they are to be ungratefully set aside. Forbid it shame! Forbid it justice! Forbid it interest, if no higher motive can move us!"

Fowle declared that political trickery was at work. While the citizens had abandoned their faithful servants, the teachers and "those interested in the continuance of abuses" had gathered in their ward rooms and had substituted in their places reliable, acquiescent men. Teachers, some competent but many more incompetent, Fowle asserted, had ruled the School Committee for years with their threats and complaints. Fowle hinted that the teachers had been aided by unscrupulous men who had profited financially from alliances with teachers, bookmakers, and booksellers. To the ballot box, then, he urged. "The men proscribed by the masters and their friends have been nominated by higher authority than a packed caucus, *they have been nominated by their good works!*" Like most good democrats Fowle approved of men of "good works" packing caucuses for elections, as Howe had done, although he condemned such knavery on the part of others. His attack failed to secure the re-election of his friends; still, he continued to agitate on their behalf.[54]

Howe and the others now took up their own defense. Howe, William Brigham, and J. I. T. Coolidge tried to cut away the mountain of criticism and personal vilification that had descended upon them. R. H. Neale withdrew from the controversy, and Theophilus Parsons filed a separate defense of their 1845 report since he still served on the Committee. On their own behalf, Howe and the others appealed "To the Citizens of Boston."

Reviewing their previous findings, the reformers attempted to justify their attitudes from an angle well-calculated to soften the hearts of business-minded Bostonians—money. Perhaps, they ventured, the $100 plus spent per child for each of ten years in school was not money wisely spent. Perhaps there was a more efficient, and less expensive, way of organizing and controlling the schools. If Boston would appoint professional educators to direct public education, the city could save a good deal of money. The reformers also sought to blacken their opponents with the same financial soot stirred up by Fowle. Persons suggested that a good part of the reason for all the opposition "springs from the fact that our present school system is an engine for money-making of great power; a fact unknown to our citizens generally, but many years ago discovered by some of them."[55]

The pleas of Parsons, Howe, and the rest were to no avail at first. Horace Mann promised Howe that "you will hereafter be hailed as the regenerator of the Boston Schools," but Howe might be forgiven if he did not agree. Bitterly he responded to Mann that the faithful had deserted him. They had "thought it best to let the children suffer." Most of the teachers he had opposed still taught. There still was not a superintendent of public education. The cause of centralization appeared hopeless.[56]

The seeds of reform, sown in controversy, nevertheless soon bore fruit. In his inaugural address in 1846, Mayor Josiah Quincy, Jr., recommended that Bostonians seek the necessary power from the Legislature to appoint a "City Superintendent of Public Schools." Edmund G. Loring, chairman of the Visiting Committee in 1846, also lent his support. To administer the schools properly, Loring declared, required more time and exertion than laymen, pursuing their daily occupations, could give. Therefore, "after having served the shortest time that will satisfy their consciences," men who might have learned something about the mysterious operations of the schools left the Committee. Administration by a competent and permanent professional, however, would bring efficiency and leave to laymen, Loring affirmed, "the comparatively easy, and the positively delightful task, of sitting here, in well informed council, and supervising the schools committed to our charge."[57]

In the 1847 *Report* of the Visiting Committees, the prominent and influential George B. Emerson observed that "it is very generally conceded that the system is far from being perfect or complete." At the height of the controversy in 1845 few people had conceded imperfection, but in 1847 Emerson was more diplomatic in calling for reform than had been the obstreperous Howe. Of the school system Emerson explained that "it is a fabric, the elements of which are perfect, but the beauty and design are marred from a want of symmetry and proportion." Among other changes, he suggested that the appointment of a superintendent would order the elements of the fabric into whole cloth.[58] Under the guise of a simple rearrangement of current conditions, Emerson helped to forward a fundamental change in the administrative structure of the schools.

Finally, in January 1851 the School Committee yielded to the internal and external pressures of the previous few years and appointed a special committee to confer with the City Council about a superintendent of schools. A Joint Committee of Conference on the subject met at the close of February. In early March it issued an elaborate report, including all the past arguments in favor of centralized control and concluding with the unanimous opinion that the appointment of a superintendent "would add greatly to their [the schools] efficiency and usefulness, and ought not longer to be delayed." On March 31 the City Council appropriated $2,500 for the post and authorized the School Committee to choose a superintendent. On May 13 the Committee complied.[59] The long-fought battle was over.

The School Committee appointed Nathan Bishop the first superintendent. Bishop was a perfect example of a self-made man. He had worked his way through Brown University by school-keeping, private tutoring, acting as a bell-ringer, and milking the president's cows. Following graduation in 1837, he tutored mathematics at the university, where in 1842 he became a member of the Board of Trustees. Three years earlier he had received appointment as the first superintendent of public schools in Providence, Rhode Island. He had served so capably in the position that Boston could find no better qualified professional educator to fill its newly created post.[60]

Bishop soon justified the hopes of Boston reformers for efficient administration. Like them, he was devoted to intellectual discipline and moral culture in the schools. He believed that schools should be havens of stability in the stormy uncertainties of city life. Schools, he affirmed, should inculcate in children a sense of law and order, a "cordial obedience to established laws." The respect for authority, he said, was an essential element in the education of an American citizen.[61]

While he was passionately dedicated to public education as a tool for shaping the future course of society, Bishop was dispassionate in the daily administration of the school system. He had the makings of a good bureaucrat. He evinced a willingness to cooperate with and encourage advice from the School Committee and the teachers.[62] Such cooperation had been sadly lacking in the past.

Bishop knew that effective administration depended upon effective organization. Just as reformers and other educators had argued for the reorganization of schools on a factory model, so did Bishop. A school system could, and should, be rationalized along the lines of business experience. Bishop was certain that "in organizing a system of popular education, the same practical judgment is to be exercised in making special adaptations of means to ends, as in any manufacturing or other business enterprise."[63]

Under Bishop's superintendency, numerous changes occurred in the school system. A bureaucratic structure emerged, more rigid in its organization than the system had been in the past. In preparation for the abolishment of the Primary School Board and the assumption of its duties, in 1854 the city enlarged the School Committee from two to six men elected in each of the twelve wards. As before, these men were responsible for examining the schools and making recommendations for their improvement. For a body of this size to administer effectively over 190 primary schools, more than 20 grammar schools, and 2 high schools, proved nearly as difficult as had the previously slip-shod means of organization. But unity and centralization demanded unified control; thus the responsibilities and authority of the superintendent increased. His position as the head of an emerging hierarchy of administration took on greater importance. Once begun, the process of centralization became self-perpetuating.

In 1856 Bishop turned over the reigns of power to a new superintendent, John Philbrick, the same man who had inaugurated the process of grading in Boston schools. Under Philbrick's regime (1856-78) professional administration expanded. Grammar school masters became principals of the primary schools in their districts. Six paid, full-time supervisors joined the ranks of administration, with the superintendent acting as chairman of a Board of Supervisors. The School Committee itself moved further from the restraints of local, neighborhood control by the voters when, in 1875, a new law provided that it be composed of twenty-four men, elected at-large from the city.[64]

The process of centralization so long advocated by reformers led ultimately to the creation of a bureaucracy that proved unamenable to their control. By the late 1870's another generation of reformers could only lament that "the taxes of the people go to fatten 'organization' and the children suffer." John Philbrick responded to such charges that "the smooth and harmonious working of a great and complicated system, requires that all its parts should be properly adapted to each other," and urged still greater powers for the office of superintendent. In Boston, as elsewhere, the machinery of bureaucracy ground forward relentlessly.[65]

The reformers of the 1840's and 1850's had not foreseen such an outcome. As they envisioned it, the good of society demanded an end to waste and inefficiency in administering the schools. Educators concerned about the role of the schools in fostering social harmony had tried to consolidate their authority. To do so, of course, meant that the destinies of public schools could not be left to the whims and wishes of individual parents, or even of their locally elected representatives. The school system, educators knew, had grown too large, and the affairs of the city too complex, to allow such dispersal of control. Defenders of the diffusion of authority might cogently argue that "the large number of our citizens who, by this means, were brought into immediate contact with the schools, became thoroughly acquainted with our system of public education, . . . felt a higher degree of interest in its success, . . . and by this means strengthened and elevated our Public Schools in the estimation of the people at large."[66]

But other educators and reformers like Horace Mann, Samuel Gridley Howe, George B. Emerson, William B. Fowle, and Nathan Bishop could not agree. Over the years, they, and other men of like mind, had sought to reorganize and reform the school system in the hopes of thereby exercising stronger control over public education. Increased authority over public education, they believed, meant increased control over the future of urban society. That such men failed to appreciate the possible alternative courses that centralization might bring to public education was their misfortune. Unfortunately, it was a misfortune for which subsequent generations of urban dwellers would pay.

IV

SEGREGATION AND INTEGRATION: BLACKS IN PUBLIC SCHOOLS

7

Black Schools in White Boston

*I believe that education has made the distinctions from which
you suffer, and that to education you must look for a remedy.
The character of a race is altered by slow and insensible
degrees.*

Judge William Minot (1835)[1]

On Tuesday, December 4, 1849, lawyer Charles Sumner stepped before
the bench in the Massachusetts Supreme Judicial Court to begin arguments for the educational rights of Blacks in Boston public schools. In a
speech a year earlier Sumner had incurred the wrath of wealthy and conservative Boston "Cotton Whigs" when he had linked the "lords of the
lash and the lords of the loom." Now, before Chief Justice Lemuel Shaw,
Sumner endeared himself to the radical abolitionists by arguing against
racial segregation in the schools. Bostonians had proudly proclaimed to
the nation their leadership in the common school movement, but the
community had taken a back seat to other cities of the state, including
Salem, New Bedford, and Lowell, in abolishing separate schools for
Black children. In the case of *Roberts v. City of Boston* Sumner and
other abolitionists set out to test the legality of segregated schools in the
most educationally progressive city in the United States.[2]

Sumner, and other men of like mind, were certain that the cause of
humanity and the reputation of their city demanded an end to racial
segregation in the schools. Among the abolitionists joining the cause
was the fiery orator Wendell Phillips who three years earlier had railed
against the Boston "Caste System" of education. Deriding the members
of the School Committee, Phillips had charged that "it has long been one
of the avowed evils of our city and town organizations, that some important powers are necessarily committed, at times, to very small men."[3]
In the Roberts case, Phillips, Sumner, and their cohorts turned their
anger against the last state stronghold of educational discrimination, determined to make Boston once again a model of reform triumph.

They were joined by a small group of Black militants who for some

157

years had crusaded for equal rights with white Bostonians. Long before "Black Power" would become a rallying cry in the struggle for civil rights, the school desegregation battle had provided a vehicle for an emerging sense of group consciousness among some Boston Blacks. As the campaign developed, however, the same lack of unity that would foil later civil rights strategies became evident among members of the local Black community. From the beginnings the engine of equal rights bumped along on less than full power.

Similar internal misfirings were evident in the programs of white liberals involved in the desegregation cause. Despite the participants' humanitarian rhetoric, the whole affair smacked of opportunistic paternalism. In calling for the end of school segregation the white champions of Black rights were on the side of morality and racial justice. But their performance lent credence to the often-repeated charge that liberal paternalism generally masks a desire for social control. When Sumner presented the "cause of humanity" before the Court, he also implied the reformers' schemes for restructuring the social composition of American life along lines attractive only to men of their own liberal persuasion. The school desegregation campaign was a panorama in miniature not only of the impact of the common school movement but also of the foibles and fancies of social reform activity in antebellum America. By the time that Sumner was ready to argue his case, the patterns and policies of liberal reform were well set.

The system of separate instruction for Black children in Boston dated back to the late eighteenth century. When Sumner and his companions finally challenged the legality of segregated schools, they had to confront over fifty years of complacency. Leaders in the city and elsewhere had commended the benevolence of Bostonians in educating the Black population, even though the city maintained segregated schools. Certainly Boston educators had attempted to provide public schools to educate Black children well before other cities in the North. Still, occasionally, the separate schools had suffered attack by whites and Blacks alike in the past. Sumner, Phillips, William Lloyd Garrison, and other abolitionists might pride themselves on broadcasting the evils of school segregation, but their tirades were not the sole cause of discontent. Preceding the Roberts case was a half-century of discussion, debate, confusion, certainty, praise, disavowal, agreement, and disagreement about the place of Blacks in the public school system of the city—and in the society at large.

SEGREGATION BY CHOICE

During the years immediately following the Revolution, the Black population of Boston dwindled. In 1765, 848 Blacks resided in the city; by 1790, the number had fallen to 766 in a total population of 18,038. But even this handful was concerned about education for its children, recognizing that without sharing in the widespread enthusiasm for free schooling, Blacks would be doubly disadvantaged—first, by being black, and second, by remaining ignorant. Thus, in 1787, a group of Blacks petitioned the state legislature to furnish them schools of some sort, stating that they currently received "no benefit from the free schools" of Boston. The legislature did not grant the request.[4]

While a later generation accepted the charge that Black "children could not attend the public schools on account of the prejudice then existing against them," that claim was partly a product of abolitionists' imaginations. There was prejudice, but there was even more indifference. At the turn of the nineteenth century, there existed neither a written nor a tacitly accepted rule against Black children attending the public schools. Until the close of the first decade of the new century those Black children who wished attended the same schools as white youth. The parents of a few Black children could afford to send their youngsters to private schools and did so, while a slightly larger number went to the public schools. But, on the whole, very few Black children enrolled in public schools.[5] Although precise reasons for the scant attendance were not entirely clear, two facts of Black life in white Boston help explain the situation.

First, the economic conditions of the Black community worked against school attendance. In the 1790's only Boston, of the northern cities, held no slave population. Freedom, however, did not mean economic equality with white men. Blacks occupied the bottom of the occupational heap. Of the nearly 1,200 Blacks in Boston in 1800, apparently a large number was unemployed. Many employers seemed to prefer white laborers, and many white artisans refused to work with Blacks. Those Blacks who did find jobs worked chiefly in maritime trades as rope-makers, anchorsmiths, and ship carpenters. A few others found employment as day laborers, servants, waiters, and second-hand clothing dealers. A rising number of Blacks found themselves relegated to the pauper rolls, accepting whatever relief the city or private charity might offer. Like their lower-class white counterparts, many Black families could not afford to put their children in the public schools; their absence from the home meant the economic loss of whatever pittance the children might bring from street begging or odd jobs.[6]

Second, the prevalence of prejudice, sometimes passive and sometimes active, probably hurt Black attendance at the schools. The abolitionists' later claims of rampant prejudice preventing school attendance were partly true; if the law did not bar Black participation in the schools, perhaps social contempt did. Undoubtedly teachers often gave a hostile reception to Black children entering the schools, for teachers, along with many other Boston citizens, seemed to hold very low opinions of most Blacks. Boston social and religious leaders constantly characterized Blacks as "improvident and indolent, though a subsistence for laboring people is here very easily obtained." Men like the Congregationalist minister Jeremy Belknap, for example, expressed shock at the lack of family solidarity among Blacks. "Negro children were reckoned as an incumbrance in a family," declared Belknap in 1795, "and when weaned, were given away like puppies. They have been publicly advertised in the newspapers 'to be given away.'" Racial sentiment ran so high in the city at times that Black leaders could advise the Black community only to "bear up under the daily insults we meet on the streets of Boston."[7] Confronted in their daily lives by hostility, suspicion, and indifference, perhaps a number of Black parents hesitated to send their children to public schools in which the tradition was for some teachers to punish white children by sending them to sit in the "nigger-seat," the symbol of stupidity, the place of shame.[8]

Whatever the exact reasons for limited attendance in the schools, Boston Blacks became one of the first minority groups in any American city to request segregated schools. In 1798, a group of Black parents asked the city to create a system of separate schools for their children. The request came at a time when white citizens were starting to demand extension of the public school system to encompass the children of the working classes and the poor—presumably including Blacks as members of those groups. Whether fully justified, some Black parents appeared convinced that their children received unequal treatment in the public schools. Wanting to satisfy both their desires for their children's education and to shield them against the brunt of prejudice, those parents urged segregation. In separate schools, they reasoned, Black youth would not have to suffer embarrassments and still would be able to gain a rudimentary education. Apparently the parents did not consider the possible long-range effects of such schools. There, whether for good or ill, Black children would be reinforced in a self-consciousness of color distinction.[9]

The city fathers expressed reluctance to establish separate schools. Some Bostonians thought that to provide special schools would be unfair to other special interest groups in the city. If separate schools for Blacks, why not provide separate schools for the scattered French, Irish, Scotch-

Irish, and German children? Others questioned the propriety of discriminating in favor of Black youth at the possible expense of native, white children. Nor did the additional costs of a separate system of schools seem justified. Ample provisions, city fathers argued, had been made for the education of all children. If Black parents did not wish to seize the opportunities, the city was not at fault. In spirit the city leaders agreed with Congregational minister Jedidiah Morse who urged Blacks to "be contented in the humble station in which providence has placed you." The selectmen denied the request for segregated schools.[10]

The petitioners were determined to provide alternative opportunities for education to their children, and, when the city refused to cooperate, turned to other sources. Enlisting the aid of several well-to-do white citizens, Black parents obtained permission from the selectmen to start their own private school. They established it in the home of Primus Hall (sometimes called Prince Hall), a prominent Black citizen, veteran of the Revolution, and president of the African Grand Lodge of Masons. Most of the school's financial support came from white philanthropists, although a few Blacks also contributed. The first teacher was a white man, one Elisha Sylvester. The school struggled along for a few months, then closed down in the wake of a yellow-fever epidemic.[11]

Again, members of the Black community turned to the city for help. In 1800, sixty-six Black petitioners asked the School Committee to establish a separate school for their children. An appointed sub-committee, including the Reverend John T. Kirkland of Harvard College, the popular minister William Emerson, and the young Josiah Quincy, strongly recommended the school. But again the Committee, on behalf of the city, refused. Two years later, members of the sub-committee and other interested citizens revived the private school in the house of Primus Hall. Two young, white Harvard students named Brown and Williams taught the children.[12]

At some undetermined point within the next several years a majority of the School Committee members accepted the idea of segregated schools. The circumstances of the Black private school changed and accompanying that change was the new attitude of the School Committee. White contributors to the school demanded that Black leaders hire a classroom more appropriate than a room in Hall's home. Since the dames' schools and other private, white schools usually met at the teacher's residence, the demand was a curious one, but the Blacks complied. In 1806 a permanent school settled into the basement of the newly erected African Baptist Church in Belknap Street on the northwest side of "Nigger Hill," in the heart of the largest Black district in the city. White benefactors required the Black leaders to pay the rent, but contributed $1,000 to meet such other expenses as instructional materials and fuel for heat. For the first time, the School Committee tentatively agreed to support the separate facility through an annual contribution from public funds of $200. Final, definite commitment of public funds came six years later, when the School Committee voted that sum and stated that in return it claimed the right to assume all future control of the school and any other schools that might become desirable.[13]

By 1812, then, the loosely organized Black community of Boston had achieved its goal. The results were not wholly satisfactory; much remained to be done, but Blacks had succeeded in segregating their children into an all-Black school, one taught, since 1808, by Black instructors. To be sure, white help had proved necessary and was welcomed. Still, for whatever social reasons, separate schools had come about through the urgings and actions of Blacks themselves. Members of the School Committee, for unannounced reasons, had come to agree with Black leaders, and had officially adopted a policy of supporting separate schools. No legal actions were needed or taken. In fact, no law requiring segregated schools would ever be passed in the city. Just the same, *de facto* segregation divided the white and Black children of Boston in the public school system.

FROM PRIVATE TO PUBLIC SEGREGATION

During much of the nineteenth century, cities provided services for their citizens through a mixed investment base of private and public funds. Few municipal services—whether police protection, fire-fighting, public health, or sanitation—operated on a wholly public basis. For the most part, cities continued the eighteenth-century practice of providing certain municipal services for their residents and requiring those citizens to bear a portion or perhaps the entire cost of the services. Early nineteenth-century Bostonians departed from custom only in the case of public education, with school expenses coming completely from the public coffers. For more than a decade following the School Committee's decision to allot some tax funds for the support of the segregated, all-Black school, that institution struggled along on this mixed basis of private and public enterprise, with the private sector bearing the brunt of the costs. Gradually, however, the city fathers increased their financial support and administrative control over segregated education. As it unfolded, the process revealed a slow but steady shift from privately sought to publicly accepted segregation. At no time in their existence would the separate schools come to rely exclusively on public funds, but they would finally yield all private autonomy to public control.

In 1815, a bequest by one of Boston's wealthy and philanthropic "merchant princes" established the prime source of private income for Black schools in the years to follow. Abiel Smith died in 1815, leaving to the city a number of shares in New England turnpikes and bridges, as well as some United States bonds. His will directed representatives of the town to appropriate the whole income for the maintenance and support of a school or schools for people of color, "either colored or mixed," to be trained in reading, writing, and arithmetic. Smith had been one of the earliest contributors to the segregated school in the church basement. The benevolent thrust of his will resulted from the urgings of the current teacher of the Black school, a man named Prince Saunders.[14]

Saunders was a Black teacher of intelligence and sophistication who had settled in Boston principally because of the efforts of William Ellery Channing, an important figure in early nineteenth-century Boston intellectual circles. The teacher enlisted early in the ranks of Black abolitionists with the publication of *A Memoir . . . to the American Convention for Promoting the Abolition of Slavery* (1818). In later years Saunders became an intimate of the English abolitionist William Wilberforce and received a commission to establish an educational system in Haiti. When he died in 1839 Saunders was the attorney general of Haiti. Saunders' influence as a man of reason and dedication, and his ability to move with ease in both the white and Black social circles of Boston, so impressed Abiel Smith that he acceded to the teacher's request for a legacy to Black education.[15]

Boston selectmen voted in January 1811 to accept the terms of Abiel Smith's bequest. Perhaps the promised income was the clincher in debates about official recognition and support by the city for segregated schools. Perhaps the city fathers and the members of the School Committee agreed that the wisest and most equitable (as well as the most politically expedient) method of resolving the differences of opinion on separate schools for Black children was to become public trustees for a private fund, and to ante up just enough public funds to make their demands for final control of the school appear reasonable. On these points, the record is unclear. Ultimately, Smith's will yielded a principal of about $5,000, held in permanent trust by the city. In doling out the income of that trust, the selectmen promised that no exertions would be spared to carry out the intentions of the will.[16]

Ironically, Smith's legacy achieved an unforseen result. Black education gained support, but that financial support confirmed more strongly than ever the continuance of segregated schools. With the $200 annually contributed by the School Committee, plus the income from Smith's properties, the town leaders believed they had provided more than generously for the schooling of Black children. The fact that most Black parents apparently welcomed the largesse, and viewed the school in the Belknap Street African Church as a great privilege for their children, only served to underscore that belief.[17] The mixture of public and private funds for segregated education seemed to be satisfactory to everyone concerned.

Boston Blacks were not content, however, to rely solely on the public bounty. From time to time, some Black parents tried to begin other instructional classes for their children. Following the example, for instance, of the Society for the Moral and Religious Instruction of the Poor, in 1817 Black leaders started an African Sabbath School for their youngsters. Gradually the number of children attending increased. By the mid-twenties Black leaders were so heartened by the attendance of youth, that they initiated a separate Sunday school for adults. As in white Sunday schools, instruction was given in reading and writing since many Blacks were illiterate. The enthusiastic response necessitated yet another school. In 1825, in Southack Street, which was, according to one observor "the most wretched part of the city, where idleness and drunkenness abound," Blacks cooperated with members of the Society for the Moral and Religious Instruction of the Poor in beginning another Sunday school. More than two-thirds of the children attending this school could not read, and only a few of them attended the African school during the week.[18] The Sunday school nonetheless was evidence of Black interest in securing some kind of schooling for their children.

Despite these and other private efforts, for the most part Blacks had to rely upon provisions made by the city and the School Committee. By the end of the second decade of the nineteenth century the School Committee had taken over the directing of Black education in the city. In 1818 the Committee, without consulting Black parents, voted to dismiss the present master of the school and appointed another in his place. In 1819 Committee members requested the pastor of the African Baptist Church, the Reverend Thomas Paul, to report quarterly on the general condition of the Black school. In 1821, accompanying the election of a new master, the Committee appointed an Annual Sub-Committee for the African School which would have control over its future course.[19] Such actions left little doubt that segregated schooling had become a fixture of the public school system.

Whatever doubt might have existed was soon dispelled. During the early 1820's the Primary School Board sought to include Black children under its jurisdiction and to complete the segregated system of education by opening separate Black primary schools. But, because of Black efforts in providing private schools and Sunday schools, the Board only had vague information about which young Black children were or were not receiving instruction. In April 1821 therefore, it appointed a committee to investigate the situation and to consult with Black parents. The Board's interest encouraged Black parents and the following June they applied for a primary school in the northern section of the city. At this point, unsure of its own powers in relation to the parent School Committee, the Primary Board turned the request over to the Committee, noting that it was willing to "undertake the control of such African Primary Schools as the General School Committee may give them authority to institute." The Board recommended schools in both of the predominently Black sections of the city, in the North and West ends. Beyond providing elementary instruction for young Blacks, the proposed primary schools were intended to prepare them to enter the regular African grammar school.[20] Apparently the Board acted on the assumption that a completely segregated system of schools would best meet the needs of the Boston Black community.

On August 7, 1822, the first Black primary school opened in another room of the Belknap Street Church. As in similar white primary schools, the teacher was a young, educationally inexperienced single woman, in this case a Black, Miss Charlotte Foster. Initial enrollment was forty-seven students, both boys and girls, although attendance increased so quickly that within four months the Board opened another school a short distance away. There the enrollment was over thirty pupils. In addition, under its own temporary control, the School Committee established yet another school in the North End. In all of these schools the children came from poor families who had been unable to provide any kind of prior instruction for their children. Thus it was impossible to limit enrollment, as originally planned, to children between the ages of four and seven. Many of the students admitted to the Black primary schools were ten and twelve years old and completely illiterate. For similar age children of native white and of immigrant parents the School Committee and the Primary Board were establishing special intermediate schools, but no such alternative was given Black youth.

Educators granted equal financial support to the separate Black primary schools. The Board allotted $240 to each of the Black primary schools, an annual sum equivalent to that given white schools. That amount was to pay for rent, furniture, winter fuel, and the teacher's salary. The impoverished condition of the Black students required charitable relief, however, and some of the members of the Primary Board, out of generosity, bought books, shoes, and clothing for the students.[21]

Despite the Board's provisions and the initially enthusiastic response, attendance at the primary schools remained irregular and lower than anticipated. The reasons stemmed in part from the reticence of parents to send their children to school, either because of economic considerations or because of lack of interest. Many parents probably saw little utility in educating their children when, as adults, they could not profit from that education. Their sentiments probably paralleled those of a valedictorian of a Black school in New York City who asked: "What are my prospects? . . . Shall I be a mechanic? No one will employ me; white boys won't work with me. Shall I be a merchant? No one will have me in his office; white clerks won't associate with me. . . . Can you be surprised at my discouragement?" Like their brethren in other northern cities Boston Blacks worked largely as unskilled laborers, servants, porters, bootblacks, grocery clerks, seamen, waiters, and chimney sweeps. The only skilled profession traditionally open to Blacks was that of a barber. In none of these occupations would a rudimentary education offer any real advantage.[22]

Some Black parents also questioned the true quality of instruction in the separate primary schools. Black teachers of any experience were even more difficult to find than trained white teachers. Many of the teachers in white schools were either earning money while attending college, or were young college graduates who as yet had found no other occupation. But during the 1820's no Blacks attended or graduated from recognized colleges. Across the board, Boston primary school teachers were far from competent, but the young Black women whom the Primary Board hired to teach were usually more incompetent than most. Black parents doubted with reason the benefits to be derived from placing their children under such care. Due in part to their complaints and in part to the concern of the Board, the teacher of the second school established was fired and replaced by the wife of the Reverend Paul. The school in turn shifted location to the Paul's home. In that school lagging attendance soon picked up, although the number remained irregular, averaging between thirty and fifty.[23]

At the close of 1824, the School Committee decided to take stock of the educational situation of the city. They discovered that among themselves there was no person with sufficient knowledge to report on the Black schools. No one was certain of how many schools, public and private, existed. Further, Black parents had complained about the unsatisfactory conditions of the Black public schools. The parents charged that their children were only marking time in the classrooms, learning little of real value, a charge that might well have been hurled at the schools in general. A sub-committee set about to investigate the claims of the Blacks so that they might be "prudently and equitably answered."

The very fact that the Committee's knowledge of Black educational facilities was so vague revealed its lack of interest. Having made the original provisions, Committee members appeared content to let the Black schools function more or less on their own, as long as no problems arose.[24]

But, when the Annual Sub-Committee for the African School reported, the School Committee decided that too much public money was being spent on the Black schools. At the primary school established by the Committee in 1822, for example, attendance was too irregular to justify the expense. After suitable discussion, therefore, the Committee voted to discontinue Mrs. Parkman's African School in Robison's Alley in the North End. In another case, it expressed its satisfaction with William Bascom, the current master of the African (grammar) School by raising his salary to $300 a year. Although he received extra compensation from the Smith Fund, Bascom's income remained considerably less than the $1,200 a year paid to masters of the white grammar schools. In yet another instance, the Committee rejected the petition of Barney Smith, brother of the late Abiel Smith, and others for the establishment of a high school for Black children. The explanation was simple: Blacks did not need education beyond the grammar school level. Also, there had to be some economic limit to the extension of public educational facilities for the children of Boston's 1,800 Black residents. The Committee rejected the petition as "inexpedient." That euphemism would be used with increasing frequency in the years to come.[25]

By 1830, a completely segregated system of public education had developed to serve the Black community of Boston. Initially sought by members of the Black community, the segregated schools had been accepted and confirmed by city leaders. For almost twenty years the School Committee had expended public funds to support a separate grammar school. Under the aegis of the Committee and the Primary Board three primary schools had functioned to provide elementary instruction for Black youth. Both the Committee and the Board congratulated themselves at having tried to hire the best available teachers for the Black schools under admittedly trying circumstances. If Black parents were not always satisfied with the results, both groups of educators were equally dissatisfied with the slack attendance at the schools. The city, after all, had done all that it could to meet the educational wishes and needs of the Black community—or so the city fathers claimed. In future years, members of the School Committee and the Primary Board recalled with pride their efforts on behalf of the Black citizens of Boston. From a private school for Black children had grown a publicly supported system of segregated schools that attested the educational beneficence of the city.

INTEGRATION BY DEMAND: THE BEGINNINGS OF PROTEST

Complaints about the inferior quality of instruction and the generally shabby conditions of their separate schools marked only the beginnings of protest by Black parents and leaders of the Black community. By the late 1820's Blacks came increasingly to question the usefulness or desirability of segregated schools. They also raised complaints about their loss of local control to a School Committee bent on exercising authority over all the schools of the city, Black and white. At first only a trickle, their requests for rethinking the reasons underlying the separate schools eventually mounted to a torrent of demands for re-integrating the public schools. The School Committee and the Primary Board tried in numerous and ingenious ways to wall off those demands and to prevent the swamping of the school system. In the end, the educators failed. Still, for a time in the late twenties and early thirties, the schoolmen succeeded in countering Black demands for local control and reintegration. Educators became more solicitous than ever about the state of Black education in the city and more determined to improve its quality while keeping a tight grip on the center of power.

Some members of the School Committee sympathized with the Blacks' requests for better instruction, while others recognized at most a limited obligation to provide limited educational facilities for Black children. Occasionally the Committee abandoned its usual apathy and exerted itself on behalf of the Black population. Early in 1831, for example, after rejecting a similar proposal for the school system as a whole, the Committee voted to furnish free books to children of the African School who could not afford to purchase their own. The appropriated sum of $25, though hardly munificent, showed the concern of some Committee members. In light of the irregular and limited attendance at the school, perhaps the amount was adequate. A May 1832 report on the African School stated that the average attendance was only forty children. More students should have enrolled in the school, but far too many children over eight years of age remained in the three primary schools. Committee members posed two possible explanations for the low attendance figures: either instruction in the primary schools was so haphazard and inadequate that children could not advance to the grammar school; or, through lack of desire many young Blacks did not want to take advantage of further training opportunities. To discover which reason was correct, the School Committee asked the Sub-Committee on the African School to investigate.[26]

In October 1833 the Sub-Committee finally presented its long-awaited report. After reviewing the history of Black education in Boston since 1798, the report summarized the current status of both the intellectual and physical condition of educational facilities for Blacks. The Sub-Committee's principal conclusion was that the separate educational system was not equal to the other schools of the city. Not only was the quality of education inferior, but the physical accommodations were unhealthy and inadequate. Surely, protested Sub-Committee members, a classroom better than a basement room in the African Church could be found. After all, Black parents paid taxes which helped to support white schools. They deserved a more equal return on their share of the city's income. The authors of the report urged the City Council to furnish funds for a better school building. Finally, they attacked the system of segregated schools as being beneficial to neither race.[27] Other public officials chose to ignore the social policy conclusion of the Sub-Committee; they preferred to concentrate on the politically less explosive suggestion of a new school.

Over the next two years the City Council and the School Committee debated the issue of erecting a separate school building for Blacks. Largely through the efforts of Samuel A. Eliot, an alderman, and Frederick Emerson, for some years past a master in the grammar schools, the Council appropriated funds and erected a new building on Belnap Street, not far from the African Church. In February 1835 the School Committee voted to name the new school after the former benefactor of Black education, Abiel Smith. At the dedication ceremony a month later, the main address captured both the spirit and the letter of white Bostonians' beliefs about the past and future of Black education in the city.[28]

Judge William Minot, chairman of the Committee of the Smith School, displayed a cautious yet hopeful attitude about the betterment of the Black race. Some citizens of both Boston and the nation, Minot observed, had little faith in the intellectual and moral progress of Blacks. They believed that the Negro was not equal to the white man in having a power of "endless improvement." Other citizens, including himself, the judge continued, did not share that belief. Negroes could improve themselves; furthermore, whites could guide them onto a pathway of progress. The first step in the right direction was a decent education.

Judge Minot was certain that a good educational environment was vital for the solution of many social problems. Discussing the poor quality of instruction and guidance given Negroes in the past, Minot told his Black listeners that "I believe that education has made the distinctions from which you suffer, and that to education you must look for a remedy." Apparently the judge thought that the economic and social relationships of urban life had already become so complex that at least a minimum level of schooling was requisite for "getting ahead." Certainly among many of Minot's contemporaries there was a deepening faith in the power of formal education to alter the present habits and future lives of individuals. Identical claims about the role of public schools in transforming foreign immigrants into good Americans were being advanced by Boston educators. Why then not believe that for Blacks poor jobs, housing discrimination, and social prejudice might all be mitigated through rote learning and better grammar?[29]

Figure 10   "FOR ENDLESS IMPROVEMENT"

The corner building on Belknap Street (opposite the wooden structure) was the Smith School for Africans; erected in 1835, it remained a citadel of segregation for twenty years.

SOURCE: Brayley, *Schools and Schoolboys*, p. 48.

Blacks were to improve themselves through education, but were to remain segregated while doing so. The promise of future opportunities waiting somewhere beyond the educational horizon might cause Blacks to take greater advantage of present opportunities for schooling. More Black children therefore might be brought under the guiding influence of dominant white standards of conduct and morality. The process of improvement, moreover, was to be gradual. Minot emphasized that "truth is not entirely stationary; it moves a little, and it is in our power to accelerate its course." Negroes should not be impatient. "The character of a race," insisted the judge, "is altered by slow and insensible degrees."[30]

There was no reason to doubt the sincerity of Judge Minot or of other members of the School Committee. They believed that Blacks, although not equal to themselves in morality, in respect for law and order, or in intelligence, could be improved. They believed that through formal schooling the process of improvement could be accelerated. They affirmed and worked for that improvement, however gradual they thought it might be. By their own lights, they had shown concern for the situation of Blacks in the city. If Blacks were poor, so were many other residents. If Blacks were immoral and ignorant, so were most of the urban poor. Minot and other Bostonians were certain that public education could improve all members of the lower classes, Black and white alike.

Leaders of the Black community, and their followers, however, believed that they had good reasons to doubt the good intentions of the educators. Blacks agreed with white educators on the virtues of public education. But they could not agree that separate schools were the best means of training their children for entry into a society controlled by white leaders; they could not agree that their separate schools were equal to those enjoyed by white children, despite the new Smith schoolhouse. Over the past few years Black parents had witnessed an erosion of their own authority over the segregated schools. They had demanded that their voices be heard on the education of their youth—and time and again the School Committee had replied with assertions of its authority, or with silence.

An excellent example of Black impotence to effect change had come during the deliberations of the Sub-Committee on the African School. Black parents had repeatedly objected to William Bascom, the white master of the African School, as an incompetent teacher. Then, in the closing months of 1833 they charged Bascom with "improper familiarities" with female students. The School Committee launched an immediate inquiry. To agree that a master of a Boston school, even of the Black school, could have so offended the social sensibilities of Bostonians and could have so transgressed the boundaries of conventional morality was unthinkable. To admit the truth of the charges would have also been to admit faulty judgment by members of the Committee who had originally hired Bascom. Whatever the truth of the situation, the Committee could be expected to defend one of its own masters. Investigation revealed that the alleged "immoralities" had occurred two years earlier. Why hadn't the issue surfaced before? Perhaps, reasoned Committee members, because these were trumped-up charges. In any event, the Committee argued, the three girls leveling the accusations were known to be of "bad character." Since the girls themselves were immoral, obviously their statements were falsehoods, and Master Bascom was innocent. Therefore the Committee dismissed the charges.[31]

The dismissal brought yet another humiliation in a long line of defeats over issues of local control and further aroused Black discontent. Parents reasoned that their children not only attended inferior, segregated schools, but also had to contend with immoral teachers. Whether the charges against Bascom were true (and that question remained unanswered), Black parents realized that the School Committee placed little faith in their judgment, and heeded even less their complaints. Aware of the Blacks' rising anger, the Committee belatedly transferred Bascom the following year, and, without consulting Black parents, replaced him with another white master.[32] But the damage had been done; the breach between Blacks and whites had widened. Never mind the fact that, despite a clamor for local control throughout the city's neighborhoods, the School Committee was tightening its administrative grip on the public schools. Black leaders were coming to recognize their powerlessness.

They were not yet willing to challenge the entire structure of white society and the unequal relationships between the races. But as their frustrations mounted, they became more ready, by whatever means possible, to press their case for equal and integrated education. It was no accident of history that radical abolitionism centered first in Boston, nor was it coincidental that Black abolitionists gained some of their earliest victories in campaigns for equal schools. By the mid-1830's white intransigence on the public school question had fed Black hostilities for some years. Several Black leaders were quite ready to accept the radical critique of white society offered a few years before by a local Black polemist and to take up his challenge to the established order. The writings of David Walker helped to turn Boston into a center of abolitionism and to lay the groundwork for the test case that would ultimately determine the future of segregated schools.

David Walker was born in North Carolina in 1789, the year in which Boston citizens organized the first urban public school system in the nation. The son of a free mother and a slave father, under southern law Walker was a free man. Although little is known of his early life, he apparently traveled widely in both North and South. Somewhere he managed to acquire the rudiments of an education. Finding it impossible to live in the South where he found Blacks "degraded, wretched, abject," Walker journeyed north and settled in Boston some time during the early

1820's. By 1827 he had established a second-hand clothing business in a small shop on Brattle Street. Shortly thereafter he became the Boston agent for the country's first Black newspaper, the *Freedom's Journal*, begun in New York City in 1827 by John Russwurm, a former teacher in the Boston African School. Walker soon became a contributor to the Black abolitionist journal. By 1828 he was well known in Boston as a fiery writer and public speaker, a man dedicated to the extinction of slavery and racism.[33]

Four principal factors, according to Walker, accounted for the miserable conditions of Blacks in America. The most obvious, of course, was slavery. The second was the mask of religion donned by hypocritical preachers of the gospel of Jesus Christ. "Even here in Boston," Walker complained, "pride and prejudice have got to such a pitch, that in the very houses erected to the Lord, they have built little places for the reception of coloured people, . . . and the preachers say nothing about it." Third, there was the African colonization movement which operated under the guise of benevolence, but which in reality was "a plan got up, by a gang of slave-holders to select the free people of colour from among the slaves, that our more miserable brethern may be the better secured in ignorance and wretchedness." The fourth factor, in many ways, Walker viewed as the most degrading. In every manner possible, white Americans had tried to keep Blacks from acquiring any measure of education. In the southern states, through laws against teaching them to read and write, and in northern states by customs of segregation, Blacks had been kept in intellectual and moral darkness. "I must truly say," Walker charged, "that ignorance, the mother of treachery and deceit, gnaws into our very vitals. . . . We are an unlettered people, brought up in ignorance, not one in a hundred can read or write, not one in a thousand has a liberal education."

Walker had only harsh words for the city that took pride in its educational provisions for Black people. Repeatedly drawing on Boston for his examples, the journalist pointed out the total inadequacy of educational facilities in the North. He admitted that some attention had been given to educating Black children but regretted that his fellow Blacks were so ready to accept poor schools as their due. "Most of the coloured people," he lamented, "when they speak of the education of one among us who can write a neat hand, and who perhaps knows nothing but to scribble and puff pretty fair on a small scrap of paper, immaterial whether his words are grammatical, or spelt correctly, or not; if it only looks beautiful, they say he has as good an education as any white man." But, Walker protested, the children knew nothing of arithmetic, of accounting, of neat compositions in prose or verse, or of grammar. The "education" they received in the segregated Boston schools was really part of a conspiracy to keep Blacks in ignorance of any knowledge necessary for advancement. He cited the story of a young man who told him that he had attended school for nine years, under a white master, and knew "nearly" as much grammar as he had known the first day he entered the school. Why? Because, Walker explained, the School Committee forbade any but the white children to study grammar. While that particular statement was untrue, the point was not. Walker was correct; Blacks received inferior training in the schools.

Yet, so did many native white children. Apparently the journalist had not carefully investigated the general conditions of Boston schools. The kind of instruction given Black children differed little from that given most illiterate children of the poorer classes. In Black primary schools, as in the white, the basic textbook was the New Testament. Advanced students in both types of schools used the same elementary readers. Learning by rote was the standard method of instruction. Nor were there significant differences between the African Grammar School and the other poorly managed grammar schools in various parts of the city. In the late 1820's, despite the best efforts of reformers, instruction in Black and white schools alike was, by later standards, far from adequate.

David Walker, however, was interested only in the conditions of Black schools. Unaware of the poor quality of education in most white schools, he demanded that Blacks receive an education equal to that of whites.

Walker linked formal education, spiritual values, and race pride in a call for self-improvement. He foresaw a day when this trinity would govern Black people and when Black people would finally govern themselves. "Remember," he urged his readers, "to let the aim of your labours among your brethren, and particularly the youth, be the dissemination of education and religion." He prayed that his ignorant brethren might see the truth, might "throw away pretentions, and seek after the substance of learning, . . . for coloured people to acquire learning in this country, makes tyrants quake and tremble on their sandy foundations." Walker warned charitable Americans to change current conditions or to suffer the consequences. "Our sufferings will come to an *end*, in spite of all the Americans this side of *eternity*. Then we will want all the learning and talents among ourselves, and perhaps more, to govern ourselves.—'Every dog must have its day,' the American's is coming to an end."[34]

In 1829, these were bold words. As Walker's *Appeal* reached ever-widening audiences in the North and then infiltrated the South, reactions were not slow in coming. The antislavery publisher Benjamin Lundy condemned the work as a "daring, inflamatory publication." William Lloyd Garrison, not yet the radical publicist he would soon become, deplored the circulation of this "most injudicious publication," but admitted that it contained "many valuable truths and seasonable warnings." In the South, a group of Georgians offered $1,000 for Walker dead and $10,000 for him alive. The governors of Georgia and of North Carolina obtained immediate legislation of more severe restrictions on the activities of free Blacks within their states. Joined by the governors of Mississippi and Louisiana, they gained the passage of bills which bordered up their mails against such "seditious' propaganda. The mayor of Savannah heatedly wrote to Harrison Gray Otis, the mayor of Boston, requesting the arrest and punishment of the clothes dealer. Otis' reply revealed that some of the respectable citizens of Boston shared a disgust for Walker's tactics and a feeling of indignation at his criticism of Black schools. Nonetheless, Otis stated, Walker had broken no law and therefore could not be arrested.[35]

David Walker died under mysterious circumstances in 1830. His pamphlet had run through three editions. It continued to plague its opponents and to increase radical abolitionist sentiment during pre-Civil War years.[36] Walker's *Appeal to the Coloured Citizens of the World* was an initial declaration of abolitionist sentiment in Boston—and, though it was not intended as such, a summation of growing Black dissatisfaction with segregated schools in the city. Before its publication there were over a hundred antislavery societies more or less active throughout the United States, but not one in Boston. Within two years after its publication William Lloyd Garrison had set up shop and had begun to print literature more inflammatory than Walker at his best. To argue a direct cause-and-effect relationship between Walker's *Appeal* and Garrison's activities would be convenient, but probably untrue. Historical events rarely fall into so neat a pattern. But, it would not be far from the truth to argue that Walker's attitudes on education fed Garrison's own discontents. Nor would it be inaccurate to consider the *Appeal* one of the first salvos fired by Blacks in the city in their attack against the separate system of schools. In the years to follow, Garrison, with other white and Black abolitionists in Boston, took up and elaborated on Walker's demands for the equal education of white and Black children.

8

Separate-But-Equal Schools?
White Abolitionists and Black Education

Prejudice is the child of ignorance. It is sure to prevail where people do not know each other. . . . If the colored people are ignorant, degraded, and unhappy, they should be the especial objects of your care.

Charles Sumner (1849)[1]

By the early 1830's, the first phase of racially segregated public education in Boston was drawing to a close. A new day of militant attacks—by Blacks and whites—on the separate schools was beginning, and with it emerged a new coalition of reformers bent on shaking-up the institutional arrangements of American society. Black leaders whose forebears had requested segregated schools were now demanding integrated schools. They mounted a petition campaign and for nearly twenty years bombarded the School Committee, the Primary School Board, and the City Council with legal, moral, and emotional pleas. They briefly waged a school boycott in the hope of dramatizing their cause. They brought suit in the case of *Roberts v. the City of Boston*, pitting a five-year-old girl against the ruling elite of the community, and thereby raised a constitutional question of the regulation of race relations that would reverberate over the next hundred years. Finally, they succeeded in convincing a sympathetic state legislature of the rightness of their crusade and gained legislation that ended the half-century of segregated schools in the educational capital of the nation. In all of these efforts, white abolitionists joined, prodded, and, some said, manipulated members of the Black community.

The story of the drive for integrated schools, however, was not black and white, not a clear-cut one of untarnished virtue nor of unrelieved villainy. Like most socially troublesome issues, the school campaign combined diverse motivations, varying social aims, strong and weak personalities, political infighting ultimately unrelated to the moral problems at hand—the dash and fancies of some men driven by a desire for power

176

and the quiet certitudes of others whose self-interests seemed submerged beneath a committment to social justice.

As the decade of the thirties opened, "gradualism" in race relations had become a word despised by some Americans. More and more the word "immediate," observed poet and abolitionist John Greenleaf Whittier in 1833, cropped up "in contrast with that of gradual." Throughout the North a small but growing band of men and women began to agitate for immediate solutions to the social problems of Blacks, both slave and free. In newspapers and periodicals, from lyceum platforms and from pulpits, the abolitionists called for an end to slavery and for the extension of equal opportunities to free Blacks.[2]

By the 1830's the eastern seaboard of the United States was a hothouse of reform activity. National societies existed to promote a bewildering variety of reform interests. Among others, the American Bible Society, the American Tract Society, the American Sunday School Union, the American Education Society, the American Peace Society, and the American Society for the Promotion of Temperance all clamored for public support in their attempts to diagnose and cure the various ills of national life. Indeed, as Ralph Waldo Emerson later observed in his 1841 address "Man the Reformer," some Americans sought "to revise the whole of our social structure, the state, the school, religion, marriage, trade, science, and explore their foundations in our own nature; we are to see that the world not only fitted the former men, but fits us, and to clear ourselves of every usage which has not its roots in our own mind." In uprooting the evils of society, abolitionism eventually dominated the field of reform. But in the early 1830's the abolitionist urge was slow to develop into a program. Abolitionists recognized the need to gain widespread support. They began their campaigns in New York City and Boston, but Boston soon became the headquarters of those who demanded immediate solutions to the problems of Blacks.[3]

On January 1, 1831, Bostonians read the first issue of the *Liberator*, a new paper edited by the young abolitionist William Lloyd Garrison. From the outset, Garrison rejected any gradualist approach to the issue of slavery or to the social problems of free Blacks. "Tell a man whose house is on fire to give a moderate alarm," he wrote in a famous passage, "tell him to moderately rescue his wife from the hands of the ravisher, tell the mother to gradually extricate her babe from the fire into which it has fallen, but urge me not to use moderation in a cause like the present!" Garrison, and those of like spirit who gathered beneath his banner, thus began their long campaign for the abolition of slavery in the South. But they also turned to affairs closer to home. Both to recruit field hands for the crusade and to dramatize the plight of Black people in American society, the abolitionists attacked the legal and social segregation confronting free Blacks in the North. The most obvious case was the public schools. Like other reformers of the day, the abolitionists believed that ignorance and lack of formal education were among the chief reasons for the inferior social positions of some groups or classes within society. They wasted little time, therefore, in declaring their support of equal educational opportunities for the Black population.

ABOLITIONISTS JOIN THE BLACK CAUSE

In 1832, the first antislavery organization established in Boston by Garrison, Joshua Coffin, and others, passed resolutions to open a school for Black children and to found a Manual Labor System school for adult Blacks. In *The First Annual Report . . . . of the New-England Anti-Slavery Society* in 1833 Garrison reviewed and praised the efforts of Blacks to obtain equal education. The Society would do all it could, he vowed, to further that cause. Together with New York philanthropist Arthur Tappan, and Simeon S. Jocelyn, a white minister of a New Haven Negro church, Garrison proposed to a national convention of Blacks the establishment of their own college. Among other advantages, such a school would demonstrate the capability of Blacks to be educated and would further the abolitionist cause by producing a "band of educated men to take up the pen." Although the convention adopted the plan enthusiastically, the residents of the target city, New Haven, successfully fought against it. The attitude of a New York newspaper editor typified popular opinion about Black education and repeated what some Bostonians had been saying for many years. If a few elementary schools educated the Blacks, this was sufficient. As to any higher education, "what benefit can it be to a waiter or coachman to read Horace?"[4]

The school receiving the greatest national attention was the abolitionist-sponsored school for Black girls in Canterbury, Connecticut. In January 1833, Miss Prudence Crandall, a young school-mistress, had admitted into her private school for girls Miss Sarah Harris, daughter of a local Black family. Hostile reactions from white parents forced Miss Crandall to close the school. At the urging of Garrison and other Boston and New York abolitionists she proposed to reopen the school exclusively to Black girls, recruited from the best families in Boston, New York, Philadelphia, and Providence. Canterbury citizens threatened mob action and bitterly protested what they termed the abolitionist plot. Harassment by townsmen greeted the reopening of the school in April. In May, the legislature passed a law prohibiting any school for Black people not residents of the state. When Miss Crandall persisted, she was brought to trial. Although convicted of violating the law, an appellate court ultimately reversed her conviction on a technicality. The defense in the case presented the abolitionists' view, shared by many educators, that education was one of the fundamental legal rights of a citizen, "the first and fundamental pillar on which our free institutions rest—the last privilege we will give up."[5]

The prosecution's argument, however, more accurately reflected current popular attitudes toward Blacks and toward abolitionist attempts to foster Black education. Blacks attended segregated district schools; that was sufficient. Under the Federal Constitutional definition, Blacks were not citizens. Attempts by outside agitators to provide unnecessary educational facilities for Blacks in addition to those already established by local authorities demonstrated the existence of a dangerous conspiracy to destroy the American character. "The professed object," prosecutor Andrew T. Judson affirmed, "is to educate the blacks, but the real object is to make the people yield their assent by degrees, to this universal amalgamation of the two races, and have the African race placed on the footing of perfect equality with Americans." Here was the crux of the matter: Blacks were not equal to whites on either a social or moral level. If they received only a cursory education in their own schools, that was sufficient to prepare them for inferior roles in society.[6]

To their own educational efforts, Boston abolitionists experienced a similarly hostile response. For example, strong protests greeted an attempt by Bronson Alcott, teacher and later Transcendentalist sage, to admit a Black child to his private Temple School. Like most Americans, Bostonians had long been conditioned by training and experience to anti-Black prejudice. Most of the textbooks used in schools, when they mentioned Blacks at all, regarded them as a "brutish people, having little more of humanity but the form," not as a people destitute of education but a race "destitute of intelligence." Classroom experiences often reinforced the textbook tirades. Hosea Easton, a local Black minister, testified that disobedient white children suffered punishment by teachers who threatened to send unmanageable youth to a Negro school. Easton thought such training "most disastrous upon the mind of the community; having been instructed from youth to look upon a black man in no other light than a slave." Foreign visitors also noted the role of prejudice in maintaining segregated schools. In his personal notes the young Frenchman Alexis de Tocqueville observed that "in Massachusetts the blacks have the rights of citizenship, they may vote in elections. But the prejudice is so strong that it is impossible to receive their children in the schools."[7]

Opinion makers and civic leaders generally expressed their prejudices in genteel statements, when they chose at all to voice publicly their private fears. Conservative newspaper editorials often lamented the local attitudes but offered few, if any, solutions. In 1831, Mayor Harrison Gray Otis, a staunch Federalist of the old school, evaluated the Blacks as a "quiet, inoffensive, and in many respects a useful race," but concluded that the "repugnance to intimate social relations with them is insurmountable." Otis and other proper Bostonians feared that Blacks and white abolitionists hoped to integrate schools precisely because they desired intimate social relations between the races. As Frederick Douglass, the leading Black abolitionist, later told New York Blacks, "contact on equal terms is the best means to abolish caste. . . . With equal school rights, . . . colored children and youth come into contact on equal terms with white children and youth, three hundred days in the year, and from six to ten hours each day." Proper Bostonians were determined to avoid such contacts. Whatever the attacks of abolitionists and Black community leaders, the barriers of segregated schools would stand firm.[8]

But the abolitionists and their sympathizers were as unrelenting in their attacks as the Mayor Otises were in their defenses. Boring from within and shelling from without the educational system of the city, reformers demanded immediate changes in the nature of Black schooling. A dynamic young couple, David and Lydia Maria Child, spearheaded the first campaign.

David Child was both a lawyer and journalist, a member of the School Committee for some years, a one-time sub-master of the Boston Latin School, and, by the early 1830's, an abolitionist. He was in the original group of ten men who met with Garrison in December 1831 to found the New England Anti-Slavery Society. Although he had balked at Garrison's insistence on inserting the word "immediate" in the Society's constitution, he remained a follower. When he had married Lydia Maria Francis in 1828, she was already a popular novelist and editor of a successful children's magazine, *Juvenile Miscellany*. Like her new husband, she had formerly taught school and had become an early foe of slavery and an ardent Garrisonian. David Child set about using his position on the School Committee to improve Black educational opportunities; his wife employed her literary talents. Because of her writings, she quickly became one of the nationally best-known abolitionists. In the same vein mined by David Walker's *Appeal* a few years before, Mrs. Child challenged white Americans in her best known work, *An Appeal in Favor of That Class of Americans Called Africans*.[9]

The small volume, published in July 1833, hit the opposing camp like a literary bombshell. Hostile reaction to a lady of gentility publishing a frank statement alleging the equal humanity of Blacks and whites brought an immediate decline in her personal popularity and in the sale of her novels. As Wendell Phillips later observed, the response to the book was like "a thunderbolt from a summer sky." But if, as Mrs. Child later wrote to a friend, she "marched into the enemy's camp alone," her work also gathered converts to the abolitionist crusade. William Ellery Channing, the leading Boston religious liberal, and Charles Sumner, then a struggling young lawyer, both testified to the powerful impression the *Appeal* made upon them. While adding impact to the growing abolitionist sentiment in Boston, Mrs. Child's work also brought additional workers to the struggle for equal educational opportunities by emphasizing the poor quality of Black education in Boston and other cities.[10]

Remarking that in the North "our prejudices against colored people is even more inveterate than it is at the South," Mrs. Child pointed to the segregation of Black and white children in schools as the most successful of "unrelenting efforts to keep the colored population in the lowest state of degredation." Black children were not admitted to private schools. When their parents sent them to attend segregated public schools the children were subject to many discouragements and difficulties. Public opinion, she commented, not only made it difficult for Blacks to obtain schooling, "but it prevents them from making profitable use of what knowledge they have." If, in job opportunities, "their ignorance is an objection, let them be enlightened, as speedily as possible." If, she granted for the sake of discussion, a large proportion of Blacks were vicious, "is it not our duty, and of course our wisest policy, to try to make them otherwise?" Such reform could be effected only through education.

But, Mrs. Child asserted, white people should not expect Blacks to attend inferior schools. Of the grammar school in the basement of Boston's African Church, Mrs. Child noted that "the apartment is close and uncomfortable, and many pupils stay away who would gladly attend under more convenient circumstances. There ought likewise to be a colored teacher instead of a white one. Under the domain of existing prejudices, it is difficult to find a white man, well-qualified to teach such a school, who feels the interest he ought to feel, in these Pariahs of our republic." Mrs. Child demanded that the city at least provide better facilities and a new school for Black children at public expense. To repay the injustices of society against them, the city owed better schools to Blacks. For their sake and for the sake of public safety, better education was a practical investment. For, as she asked, "what will so effectually elevate their character and condition, as knowledge?"[11]

In taking a strong public stand on the unpopular issue of Black education, David Child followed the lead of his wife. His dual role of abolitionist and educator gave him a unique opportunity to act on his sentiments. For several years he urged his fellow members of the School Committee to improve the educational lot of Blacks. Then, in 1833, he seized a chance to spread his views before a wider public. He authored the controversial report to the School Committee on the condition of Black educational opportunities in the city, the report that prompted the eventual construction in 1835 of the new Smith School. The report was one of the first arguments made in the nation for special social privileges for a particular minority group.

Child argued that it was undesirable to separate the children of Black and white parents into segregated schools. Neither race benefited, he implied, and both perhaps suffered from a caste system of education. But, he continued, "if any distinction be made between them [the Blacks] and others, it ought to be in their favor." Through prejudice and custom, Black parents failed to gain the better jobs and higher wages that enabled white parents to be more "liberal and public spirited" regarding education. It was not surprising that attendance lagged in the Black schools. Some Black parents were not fully convinced that children would gain anything of value in segregated schools. Black children therefore deserved special treatment if they were to have any chance for success in future life. Child suggested that the School Committee should bend over backwards to aid the education of Black children, even if that meant taking away some of the funds allocated to the city's white schools. He concluded that if the community sentiment did not yet favor integration, surely the School Committee could build a modern and well-staffed grammar school for the Black children. Considering the social plight of Black people in white Boston, Child thought this was the least society could do.[12]

The city responded to the abolitionist appeals. The Smith School for Black children opened its doors in 1835. The combined efforts of abolitionists and other sympathizers had achieved results.[13] But the results were limited. Segregated education still ruled in Boston. The businessmen, ministers, and merchants who dominated the political, economic, and social life of the city tried to ignore the demands of abolitionists and of leading members of the Black community. In its very absence of reference to the problems of Black education in the city, the customary yearly address by the mayor to the City Council in 1835 was revealing. In his "State of the City" address, Mayor Theodore Lyman, Jr., reviewed, in greater detail than was usual for such speeches, every aspect of Boston's public obligations. Mayor Lyman praised the enlightened and comprehensive system of public schools. Despite his reputation as a benefactor of education, he completely ignored the Blacks of the city.[14]

In spite of the efforts of the abolitionists and others, or perhaps because of them, the decade of the 1830's closed with Blacks and whites still attending segregated schools. In Boston, as in other northern cities, abolitionists were not popular. When, on October 21, 1835, the famous Boston riot against local abolitionists occurred, it was a violent outburst of the inward opinions of many Bostonians. A mob broke up a scheduled meeting of the Boston Female Anti-Slavery Society. Mayor Lyman urged the women to leave, warning them it was dangerous to remain. One of the ladies retorted that "if this is the last bulwark of freedom, we may as well die here as anywhere." The ladies escaped death easily, but the mob led Garrison through the streets with a rope around his neck. Mayor Lyman finally rescued the editor and put him in jail for safekeeping. As Lydia Maria Child observed a month later, abolitionism was not acceptable to those whom she called the aristocrats of the city. The farmers and some of the merchants were sympathetic she said. "The majority of their voices would be on the right side if the question were fairly brought before them. . . . Withdraw the aristocratic influence, and I should be perfectly easy to trust the cause to the good feeling of the people."[15] But the "aristocrats" still ruled in Boston. Segregated schools remained.

Over the next twenty years, William Lloyd Garrison, David and Lydia Maria Child, and others pursued the goal of integrated education in Boston, but they were not consistent in their attacks. Their interest in the issue flagged and then revived again as other problems captured their attentions or declined in appeal. Like most reformers who have probed the many weak spots of the body politic, the abolitionists often flailed about indiscriminately. For them segregated schools was one issue among many.

The motives which led the abolitionists to engage in the struggle with the Boston School Committee were unclear. Given the attitude of many Bostonians toward the Blacks of the city, the fight seemed to be a losing cause. While some leaders of the Black community joined the fray, most of the common citizens remained apathetic. This issue was not like the attack on slavery in the South. When Garrison and others thundered against the immoralities of holding men, women, and children as chattel property, many other Americans—Black and white—added their protests against the obvious immorality. But when a handful of known agitators attacked the long-standing system of public education in a city proud of its efforts, and when they were not joined by an overwhelming majority of the people they were allegedly trying to help, they were denounced as trouble-makers.

Even the abolitionists' sense of the urgency of immediate reform was suspect. From the frequently equivocal statements made by many of the leading abolitionists, a hostile public might easily charge them with holding their own prejudices against Blacks. Anti-slavery societies throughout the North frequently debated such questions as "Is it expedient for

Abolitionists to encourage social intercourse between white and colored families?" answering at best that it was not their duty to encourage relations. Samuel J. May, a prominent Garrisonian, admitted in a *mea culpa* Boston speech as early as 1831 that "we are prejudiced against the blacks." As late as 1860 Theodore Parker affirmed that the Anglo-Saxon with common sense did not relish the Africanization of America. Referring to the physical appearance of Blacks, Garrison noted that "they are branded by the hand of nature with a perpetual mark of disgrace." At most, all that abolitionists demanded for Blacks was, as Samuel J. May later recalled, that they "shall be permitted, encouraged, assisted to become as wise, as virtuous, and as rich as they can, and be acknowledged to be just what they have become and be treated accordingly."[16]

In a society professing egalitarian virtues, this was a noble sentiment. But, the statement implied definite limits of the capabilities of Blacks to become citizens equal in every respect to whites. Abolitionists rarely argued for intimate or even casual social relationships between Blacks and whites. Neither the public at large nor many of the abolitionists themselves were without prejudice against the Black population. There was an ambivalence to antislavery sentiments which the unsympathetic could point to in defense of their own views.

Whatever their underlying motives, there was no doubt that in championing the cause of integrated public education in Boston, the abolitionists capitalized on existing Black discontent. Through the earlier years of the nineteenth century a few of Boston's Blacks had complained about the quality of education provided their children. Garrison, the Childs, and others inherited a ready-made disquietude. Whether through dedication to moral principle or a shrewd perception of the advantages offered for publicity, the abolitionists seized upon the situation of the Boston schools and challenged the status quo. Throughout the bitter debates, neither the alleged friends of the Blacks nor the members of the Boston School Committee covered themselves with honor.

THE CAUSE ACCELERATES

During the early 1840's both Blacks and abolitionists repeatedly petitioned the School Committee and the City Council to end separate educational facilities for Blacks and whites. In 1840, Garrison, Francis Jackson (who had opened his home to the abolitionists for their meetings after the 1835 riot), Henry W. Williams, and William C. Nell, a Black leader in the struggle, petitioned the City to grant equal school rights. Unsuccessful, the petitioners continued their complaints. "Appeals," "Remonstrances," and "Petitions" became standard orders of business at School Committee meetings.[17]

While most of the petitions concerned the fundamental issue of segregated schools, some spoke to the immediate practical problems of educational quality in the separate schools. Working toward the final goal of integration, Black leaders and their white allies still sought improvements in the Black schools. They were certain that, short of integration, the separate schools could offer sounder educational programs only if members of the Black community wielded most of the authority over their neighborhood schools. The issue of local control, of course, was not confined to the Black community, but, given the climate of opinion about race relations in the city, local control perhaps stirred up stronger political passions among the Black minority than among the white majority. In 1841, the case of Miss Woodson, a young Black teacher in one of the segregated primary schools, demonstrated to members of the Black community their lack of political muscle.

Five years earlier a vacancy had occurred in a Black primary school. Before appointing a replacement, the Primary Board asked parents whether they wanted a Black or a white teacher. The parents requested a Black instructress, and Miss Woodson got the job. She served without complaints being brought against her until 1841, when, for unexplained reasons, the Primary Board suddenly decided that she was inadequate. To cover their tracks, the Board explained that "at no time since her appointment, has Miss Woodson given satisfaction in the management and instruction of her school." The Board had condoned her lack of ability for so long only because members agreed that she had very poor students to work with and could hardly be expected to show much for her efforts. Also, benevolent members of the Board had agreed to retain her "partly to a wish to give the experiment of a colored teacher a long & fair trial, and a reluctance to wound the feelings of the colored people by her removal." Now, however, the Board had decided that the students' interests were paramount, and thus informed Miss Woodson that she could serve only three months longer. The Board chose a Miss Symmes, a white teacher, to replace her.

Black parents immediately protested, filed petitions demanding the reinstatement of Miss Woodson, and, when these failed, appealed to the School Committee to exercise jurisdiction over the Primary Board's decision. The School Committee's response left no room for doubt of its social and political stance. It rejected the principal of local control, especially by Black parents. Their vigorous self-interests, springing "from a proper pride, a desire to elevate their social position & a wish to gain every advantage within their reach," announced the Committee, disqualified Black parents from making the best educational choice for their children. The Committee sympathized with "colored parents," but decided to leave the final decision in the hands of intelligent, dispassionate gentlemen. Black leaders had lost another round.[18]

In 1844, Boston Blacks held public meetings at which they passed resolutions condemning separate schools and claimed the right of sending their children to white schools. Blacks and abolitionists presented another petition to the School Committee to abolish the special schools, and saw it rejected by a vote of seventeen to two. In the fall elections that year, Samuel Gridley Howe, who had already distinguished himself by pioneering the education of the blind and who was to take an active part in coming abolitionist campaigns, stood for election to the School Committee. To aid his old friend Horace Mann, who was in the midst of a flurry with the Association of Boston Schoolteachers, Howe sought to have other supporters of Mann elected to the committee. He induced Charles Sumner, a rising political star in Massachusetts politics, to run also. Sumner lost in his first reform fight. But his entry into the lists of educational controversy subsequently had an important effect on the struggle for integrated schools.[19]

The following year abolitionists and Blacks shifted their attack. Having vainly appealed to the School Committee, they decided to try again for results from the Primary School Board. That group controlled the destinies of far more children than did the School Committee. In the past the Board's actions had strengthened the system of segregation by establishing separate schools for the youngest children in the various predominately Black neighborhoods of the city. Blacks and their allies reasoned that if changes could be effected at the level of primary schools, no reasonable argument would remain against integration in the grammar schools of the city.[20]

Henry I. Bowditch presented the latest petition. A noted physician in the city, Bowditch had served on the Primary School Board since 1837. He had also earned a reputation as an ardent Garrisonian. Some people even believed that his efforts on behalf of George Latimer, the runaway slave whose illegal arrest in Boston in 1842 had incensed many citizens, had unbalanced Bowditch's mind. The Board received the petition asking for an end to segregation in the primary schools but failed to act on it before the close of their quarterly meeting. At the next meeting, a report signed by the majority recommended refusal. Bowditch read a vitriolic minority report denouncing the alleged prejudice of the Board. After long discussion, the Board, by a vote of fifty-five to twelve, adopted the vacillating resolution "that it is inexpedient, at the present time, for this Board to act upon the subject."[21]

By the mid-1840's, the stage was set for an all-out assault by abolitionists and Blacks on the Boston system of segregated schools. Years of frustration over abortive efforts had only increased determination to end the hated system. In social relationships other than schooling, Blacks throughout the state had achieved marked results. They had long enjoyed the right to vote and to hold office. In 1843, after much abolitionist campaigning, the state repealed a law against interracial marriage. Abolitionist rhetoric and public opinion forced the abandonment of Jim Crow railroad cars about the same time. To a greater extent than in any other northern state, Blacks had gained a measure of civil equality in Massachusetts. In addition, other Massachusetts towns and cities, including Lowell and Salem, had abandoned exclusive schools for Black children. Boston remained the citadel of segregated schools. The abolitionists determined to mount a concentrated attack.[22]

Again the target was the Primary School Board. In February 1846 George Putnam and eighty-five other Blacks presented yet another petition. They argued for the closing of separate schools on moral, financial, and legal grounds: segregated schools did great injury to Blacks by depriving them of equal rights due all citizens; they cost more and accomplished less than other schools; and they were believed to be illegal. The petition admitted that attendance of Black children at their own schools was at best irregular. It also confessed that Blacks probably constituted an inferior social class. But rather than blaming themselves for poor attendance and educational inferiority, Black leaders assigned guilt to members of the Board. The petitioners argued not on the basis of theory but, like other pragmatically minded Americans, from past experience. "Experience teaches," they affirmed, "that where a small and despised class are shut out from the common benefit of any public institutions of learning and confined to separate schools, few or none interest themselves about the schools,—neglect ensues, abuses creep in, the standard of scholarship degenerates, and the teachers and the scholars are soon considered and of course become an inferior class." Only the abolition of segregated schools could remedy this situation.

As might have been expected from past responses, the Primary Board reacted negatively. It disagreed with each of the charges and offered reasons for continuing the current system. As justification, it pleaded its duty to "be both just and kind to the colored people, and to act for the best good of all the schools under our charge."

Addressing itself first to the legality of separate schools, the Board correctly stated that no child, white or Black, had any "legal" right to attend the public school of his choice. Nor had scholars the right to attend the closest neighborhood school. If such schools were overcrowded, any child might be compelled to go elsewhere. Further, children of either race were not legally entitled to attend a school within their supposed "dis-

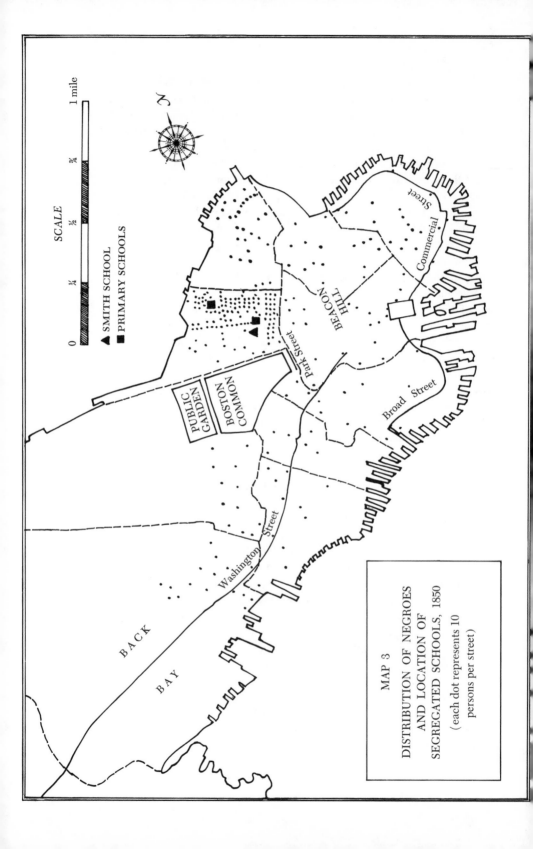

SCALE

0   ¼   ½   ¾   1 mile

▲ SMITH SCHOOL
■ PRIMARY SCHOOLS

N

PUBLIC
GARDEN

BOSTON
COMMON

Park Street

BEACON
HILL

Commercial Street

Broad Street

Washington Street

BACK
BAY

MAP 3

DISTRIBUTION OF NEGROES
AND LOCATION OF
SEGREGATED SCHOOLS, 1850

(each dot represents 10
persons per street)

trict" because Boston had never been officially divided into districts as allowed by state law. Legally the city of Boston was one district, with divisions for the sake of convenience being made at the discretion of the Board. Because of the compactness of the city, argued the Board, Black children actually benefited from this arrangement. Since there were no districts, Black youth might attend either of the two primary schools for their race without having to travel as far each day "as multitudes of children in country towns" did in order to conform to arbitrary school districts.

The question, of course, was not how far children in country towns had to travel but how far Black city youth had to walk each day to attend school. The heaviest concentration of Blacks in the city surrounded the separate schools provided for them. But the disbursement of the rest of the Black population throughout the city worked hardships for school attendance (see Map 3 and Table 5).

TABLE 5
NEGRO POPULATION OF BOSTON, 1800-1860[a]

Year	Total Negro Pop.	Per Cent Total Pop.	Under Age 10	Per Cent Negro Pop.
1800	1,174	4.70		
1810	1,468	4.34		
1820	1,690	3.90		
1830	1,875	3.05	372	19.84
1840	2,427	2.59	416	17.14
1850	2,085	1.50		
1855	2,160	1.34	461[b]	21.34[b]
1860	2,284	1.28	344	15.06

[a] By census definition, "Negro" included mulattoes and Indians.

[b] This is an estimate based on the assumption that the ratio of Negro youth, ages 0-10, to white youth, ages 0-10, was proportionate to the ratio between Negroes and whites in the whole population. The figures available for 1855 are for Suffolk County as a whole, but, as Boston's population accounted for 160,490 out of the 171,841 total population of the country, this estimate is reasonably accurate.

SOURCES: Jesse Chickering, A Statistical View of the Population of Massachusetts, from 1765 to 1840 (Boston, 1846), pp. 111-60; Report and Tabular Statement of the Censors . . . State Census of May 1, 1850 (Boston, 1850), "Table A," pp. 19-30; George Wingate Chase, Abstract of the Census of Massachusetts, 1860, from the Eighth U.S. Census, with Remarks on the Same (Boston, 1863), "Table II," pp. 106-9; Oliver Warner, Abstract of the Census of Massachusetts, 1865: with Remarks on the Same and Supplementary Tables (Boston, 1867), pp. 228-31.

It was true, the Board admitted, that in the past it had designated certain "districts" within the city. But, since these were not established by law, law could not compel the attendance of any child in any district. If law could not compel, however, the tradition of local control could. By custom the 150 primary schools of the city had been divided into districts governed arbitrarily by a local sub-committee of the Board. At their own discretion, the local groups admitted or refused to admit children into the schools. Shortly before receiving the petition of the Blacks, the Primary Board had acted on complaints from white parents about the arbitrary rule of the sub-committees. The Board had incorporated into its rules the provision that all children of suitable age and qualifications were entitled to enter the school nearest their residence. If the school was overcrowded and the local sub-committee wanted to refuse admission, the matter had to be taken before the executive committee of the Board for final action.[23]

The Primary Board denied this principle of local control over neighborhood schools to Black parents. "If it be said," the Board stated with curious logic, "that colored children are denied the privileges of the schools for white children nearest their residences, it may be replied, that the white children are in like manner excluded from the schools for colored children nearest their residences."[24]

With this in mind, one of the Board's justifications for continuing the segregated schools must have been difficult for Black parents to understand. The Board noted that in many small towns throughout the commonwealth there were few Black children. If those towns established separate schools for Black children, their actions could be viewed as illegal and undemocratic. To found special schools for the few rubbed against the grain of democracy. But in Boston, with its large Black population, to provide separate schools for the many was democratic and humanitarian. In the segregated schools, the Board argued, Black youth could receive special instruction tailored to their own needs—instruction they would not receive if integrated into white schools with common training for all. By a curious twist of logic the Board claimed that Black and white schools were equal and, at the same time, asserted that segregated schools offered unique instructional opportunities for Black children. In yet another sophistry, the Board declared that it was unreasonable for Black parents to maintain that separate schools harmed their children any more than did the separate schools for white children. In all decisions about school attendance in any area of the city, the Board claimed final jurisdiction.

The Board refused to accept the allegation that Blacks, in their own schools, did not receive instruction equal to that of white children. In one respect, the Board was accurate in evaluating the quality of education in the various schools. Teachers in the segregated schools were as competent as those in the regular schools; indeed, teachers had quite often taught in the white schools before arriving at the Black schools. In white and Black primary schools alike most teachers had no professional training, little acquaintance with the various textbooks available, and only a limited amount of previous teaching experience. Incompetency reigned throughout the primary school teaching ranks.

Nor were there differences in the instructional materials used in the various schools. Each year or two the Board voted on the textbooks and materials (maps, blackboards, picture cards, and other items) for classroom use. Once adopted, these materials had to be used in all the schools. To the best of its ability the Board prevented the introduction of new materials into any school without its approval. The use to which textbooks were put undoubtedly varied from classroom to classroom, but presumably all children began on an equal footing, with equal instructional materials.[25]

In reply, legal counsel for the petitioners admitted that the schools were of equal quality, but argued that separate schools prejudiced the social standing of Blacks. To provide equal schools was not enough. Black children had the right to mingle with the mass of society. Common schools would produce like men, men who shared the same social hopes and goals, whether white or Black. "It is," counsel maintained, "the humanizing, socializing influence of the school system, which is its most important feature."[26]

By emphasizing this role of the public schools, counsel snared the educators in a trap of their own making. Acceptance of the social purpose of public education rested on foundations laid during two decades of advertising by its proponents. A generation of Bostonians and New Englanders had asserted this goal in press and periodical. Horace Mann, George B. Emerson, Henry Barnard, and other champions of education had urged the legal extension of public schooling to ensure a sense of community among unlike men in society. The proponents of education had particularly stressed the role of the urban school in assimilating the large numbers of foreign immigrants to values of American society.[27]

But in relation to Blacks, the Board illogically rejected this traditional view of educational purpose. They claimed the laws on public education were not intended to regulate social customs, although law always functioned as a social regulator. There was no obligation for any children, "colored or white, to associate with, or be 'crumbled up' among, any class of people, except those to whom it may be mutually agreeable." As revealed in the words "mutually agreeable," the denial of integrated schools arose from prejudice alone.

But, protested the Board, color was not the grounds of distinction. In words similar to, if not often identical with, those uttered by southern defenders of slavery, the Board set down its reasons for maintaining segregated schools:

> But this is not the ground of distinction. It is one of races, not of colors, merely. The distinction is one which the All-wise Creator has seen fit to establish; and it is founded deep in the physical, mental, and moral values of the two races. No legislation, no social customs, can efface this distinction. . . .
>
> In reply to this question, we must say, that, in our opinion, the less the colored and white people become intermingled, the better it will be for both races. . . . We maintain, that the true interests of both races require, that they should be kept distinct. Amalgamation is degradation. We would urge on our brethren of the African race, the duty of cultivating the genuine virtues, peculiar to that race. Is it degrading to them to be unmingled with their pale-faced neighbors? Confound the tongue that would utter such slander upon them! . . . Let them not come to us with the humiliating confession, that they cannot make their separate schools as good as those for the white children; and tell us that their children, if put by themselves, even under the best instruction, must sink, unless they have white children to pull them up. We will not believe this, we pronounce it a slander on the colored people; but we do say that this course of policy will never elevate them, not cause them to be respected.[28]

One reason for maintaining segregated schools—a reason at which the Board only hinted—overrode all others. Members of the Primary School Board and the general School Committee feared that if Black children entered the regular public schools, white children would leave. The Board veiled this fear in three ways. First, it emphasied the irregular attendance of Black children at their own schools. Second, it asserted that Black truancy would set a bad example for white children if the races were integrated. Third, it claimed that constant quarrels and insults from white youth would greet the introduction of Black children into the general schools, and that therefore they enjoyed a better educational climate in their own schools. On face, each of the statements was reasonable, but none of them could hide the Board's anxiety over the possibility of wholesale white desertion of integrated schools. Whatever the personal opinions of its members, the Board knew that many white parents would not allow their children to associate daily with Black youth.

Refusal to mix the races came most strongly from lower-class and immigrant parents.

Immigrants, especially the Irish, and Blacks had long competed for the same jobs as day laborers and menials of various kinds. Also they had often vied for the limited housing available in the crowded city. Irish hostility to "Niggerology" (abolitionism) in Boston had deepened steadily during the 1840's. Irish leaders typically warned that

> . . . when the negroes shall be free
> To cut the throats of all they see,
> Then this dear land will come to be
> The den of foul rascality.

Some Irish sympathized with the "unfortunate" conditions of "the creature," but wondered "in the country of the whites where the labor of whites find it difficult to earn a subsistence, what right has the negro either to preference or to equality, or to admission?" Blacks, in turn, had denounced the Irish as riotous, drunken mob-makers—threats to law and order. Black leaders rebelled against these newcomers who drove the poor, Black American citizen out of places of business and labor.[29]

Recognizing the deep hostilities between immigrants and Blacks, the Primary School Board refused to desegregate the public schools. Since the chief reason behind the initial formation of primary schools had been to induce poor native and immigrant children into the schools, the Board would take no action that might jeopardize that goal. The children of these parents were "among the class who most need instruction." With unconscious irony the Board observed that "the prejudices against color are strongest among the most ignorant," implying that the best attack against the prejudices of the immigrant youth was to keep them separated from Black children in the public schools. Board members could make this statement about prejudice at the same time that other prominent Bostonians were agreeing that "the theory of a natural antagonism and insuperable prejudice on the part of the white man against the black is a pure fiction. Ignorant men are always full of prejudices and antagonisms; and color has nothing to do with it."[30]

Confronted with the choice of angering a relatively small segment of the city's population by continuing them in separate schools, or with alienating and failing to reach the growing and potentially dangerous foreign population of the city, the Board stood firm on the status quo. In their quest for integrated schools and a chance at social mobility, Blacks became hostages to the immigrant invasion.

The Board desired that everyone know "that our decision is not only *legal*, but RIGHT." But moral declarations alone were not strong enough

to withstand the mounting pressures of opposition. To shore up the uncertain platform of morality, Board members sought to erect legal girders.
They requested an opinion from the city solicitor, Pelig W. Chandler.
Chandler, the leading municipal law expert of the day, pointed out the
vagueness of state laws on common schools. He believed the legislative
intention was to leave internal policing to the various towns. If so,
school committees had the power to make all decisions in each town.
This legal right, Chandler observed, had never been questioned regarding
white children. This did not mean that unreasonable decisions were bind-
ing; a number of cases expressly recognized a rule of reason in certain
situations. In his opinion, School Committee members had acted both
reasonably and legally in establishing and maintaining separate schools
for Black and white children, "when in their judgment, the best interests
of such children will be promoted thereby." By an overwhelming vote of
fifty-nine to sixteen, the Board rejected the latest petition.[31]

The reformers reacted immediately. The two leading abolitionist members of the Board, Edmund Jackson and Henry I. Bowditch, filed a
lengthy minority report. While they alleged "gross and deliberate mis-
representation" of the facts by the majority, they advanced an essentially
moral and psychological argument for integrated schools. One of the
chief values of a system of public education was the "fusion of all
classes." Under a republican system of government every citizen presumably enjoyed civil equality and legal rights. Neither wealth, education, nor color should deny those rights. Keeping Blacks segregated injured white children by oppressing their sense of morals and humanity
and by fostering feelings of repugnancy and contempt for an apparently
inferior people. Further, separate schools strengthened the Blacks' own
sense of inferiority. "Shut out and separated, they are sure to be neglected
and to experience all the evils of an isolated and despised class." The
minority members appreciated the Board's desire to herd immigrant
children into schools, and to take no actions which might upset a delicate balance between the parents of native and immigrant children. But,
they responded, if Black children were integrated into public schools,
"no doubt some parents would feel aggrieved, and the delicate sensibilities of others might be moved—but we do doubt if we should meet as
much complaint upon the admission of colored children as we do now,
respecting the admission of Irish children, which in many schools are
sufficiently numerous to give tone and character to the school."[32]

The Liberator, as expected, supported the minority report and vigorously denounced the actions of the Board. It called for new petitions and
for a more concerted attack.[33] To that end, another abolitionist took up
the public fight.

Wendell Phillips first attracted public notice in the struggle against segregated schools. This orator of the abolitionists—Ralph Waldo Emerson once dismissed him as having only a "platform existence"—brought all of his critical skills and his venemous prose to bear on what he termed the "caste schools" of Boston.[34]

To the August 28, 1846, issue of *The Liberator*, Wendell Phillips contributed a long essay on the problem of separate schools. He directed most of his barbs at the unfortunate Pelig Chandler. While admiring the solicitor as a man of "unbending integrity," Phillips harshly criticized Chandler for "persecuting the colored children." It was grievous, Phillips complained, to see in office a man "so little imbued with a knowledge of our laws or the spirit of our institutions." But the attack on Chandler was a blind. Phillips' real target was America itself. Phillips observed that any time color entered the question, no confidence could be placed in any American civil or religious body of authority. He indicted not a man, but a society. If, he declared, the best interests of white and Black children could truthfully be served only through segregated schools, then "their best interests cannot be secured under any system of public State instruction."

From the standpoint of the abolitionists' emotional appeals, the 1846 decision of the Primary School Board appeared unreasonably and unabashedly prejudiced. But from their own vantage point, in light of racial attitudes shared by many Americans North and South alike, the Board's response was understandable. Its position faithfully reflected the opinions of many citizens of Boston. Had Blacks been admitted to white schools in the mid-1840's, the resulting uproar might well have seriously disrupted the education of both Black and white children. As elected representatives of the people of the entire city, the school officials were sincere in claiming their responsibilities to the best interests of all children, even though a later generation might view their stance as, at best, misguided.

THE SCHOOL COMMITTEE STANDS ITS GROUND

Neither the militant Blacks nor the abolitionists accepted defeat. A year after his initial outburst, Wendell Phillips returned to the fray, this time to attack Horace Mann. In his recently published *Eleventh Annual Report* Mann had praised the progress of popular education in the state as worthy of "devout gratitude to Heaven." How, Phillips demanded, could Mann speak of progress when the Black people of Boston suffered segregation? Phillips denounced Mann as one of those people who claimed to worship Truth but who willingly sacrificed their deity to expediency.

"He is a politic man and stands weighing out the blood and morals of a despised class, buying, by his indifference thereto, well-ventilated school houses! new school books! physiological seats! broad playgrounds! and philosophical apparatus!" Phillips's shafts were on target, but perhaps unfairly aimed. Mann was hardly a Garrisonian, but he was decidedly opposed to slavery and to anti-Black prejudice. Clearly, however, he believed that the cause of public school reform throughout the commonwealth should not be jeopardized by antagonizing potential supporters who might be prejudiced against Blacks. As he wrote his friend Samuel J. May, a leading Garrisonian, "the moment it is known or supposed that the cause is to be perverted to, or connected with, any of the exciting party questions of the day, I shall never get another cent." Such temporizing could never please a moral absolutist like Phillips. He professed moral outrage that an individual of Mann's reputation and authority, a man whose position and prestige could have accomplished much for Boston Blacks, should remain in "timid silence." For one of the few times in his controversy-filled career, Mann refused to rise to the bait.[35]

After the Phillips' attack, members of the School Committee finally realized that to stem the mounting tide of criticism they must demonstrate their genuine interest in the educational plight of Blacks. They decided, therefore, to undertake expensive alterations and repairs on the Smith School. For a number of years the masters of that school, as well as the annual visiting committeemen, had complained of the run-down condition of the building. In 1846, while the petition storm raged, the master of the school urged immediate repairs. School rooms were too small; paint was defaced; there were no recitation rooms; playgrounds were far too small and "only accessible through a dark, damp cellar. The apparatus has been so shattered and neglected, that it cannot be used until it has been thoroughly repaired." The complaints were familiar ones. Masters of all-white schools and a host of educational reformers had leveled the same charges for many years at all the Boston schools. Only the Blacks and the abolitionists believed they had discovered new evidence of discrimination in the run-down condition of Smith School.[36]

In 1848 the visiting committee to the Smith School again criticized the physical surroundings as "discreditable to the City." But the report also disparaged protests about the educational quality of the school and praised its intellectual achievements. To guard against further attacks on the school, the Committee requested funds from the city government, and in the early months of 1849 spent over $2,000 remodeling the building.[37]

Although it could not have been surprised, the Committee was offended in July 1849 when it received a new "Petition of the Colored

People" asking for the abolition of the Smith School. Why, the Committee questioned, had not Blacks come forward months earlier when the proposed repairs were under debate? Although their petition stressed the financial savings to the city to be gained by abolishing the school, the Committee noted that Blacks quite obviously were not concerned with economy. Rather, it implied, they were eager to stir up new trouble.

This time trouble came in larger quantities than before. In addition to the petition signed by Jonas W. Clark and 201 other Blacks, there was "An Appeal of the Colored People of the City of Boston" signed by three of the most vocal Black leaders and a paper with the names of thirty-eight colored children praying for the abolition of the Smith School and for free access to the other public schools of the city. Behind this formidable activity the Committee professed to see not only Black dissatisfaction but also a conspiracy. Joseph M. Wightman wrote that "it was well known at that time, that the effort to discontinue the colored schools originated and was fostered by the white-professed friends of the colored people, and not by the people themselves." As to Black efforts to abolish the Smith School, Wightman concluded that "they receive the countenance and favor of certain outsiders." The implication was clear; the white abolitionists were to blame.[38]

Either from ignorance or for tactical purposes Wightman's comments clearly underestimated the extent of Black discontent. Still, there were grounds for suspicion. The new petitions, like some of the previous ones, contained a number of false or duplicate signatures, as well as names of non-parents and non-residents of the city. The non-residents may have been former residents who had moved, as Black leader William Nell later explained, "to Cambridge, Charlestown, Roxbury, Salem, New Bedford, and elsewhere, where equal school privileges prevail, rather than submit to the fiat of colorphobia which school committees in the Athens of America yet ingloriously thrust upon colored tax-payers." Nonetheless, abolitionists, like other special interest groups, were not above exaggerating the strength of their ranks.[39]

The reaction of the Committee to the latest demands for desegregation was the same as in 1846. This time, however, the Committee specifically stated its opinion about what constituted equality of education. To ensure that all children of the city shared in "common school privileges," the Committee affirmed that care must be taken, "with due regard to situations and capacities, that like means and facilities of education be extended to all." Having judged the capacities and situations of Black children, the Committee claimed to have provided separate, but equal schools.

To support its contentions, the Committee solicited and published information about separate schools for Blacks in Providence, Rhode Island, in Nantucket and Worcester, Massachusetts, in Philadelphia, and in New York City. All the responses to its queries (at least those it published) emphasized that Blacks preferred separate schools. Even if this were not the case, wrote President Francis Wayland of Brown University, the hostility of local whites made it unwise, "for the sake of opposing a prejudice, to break up our schools altogether." Urban America, at least in the North, appeared solidly united on the social utility of segregated education.[40]

Disagreement among Boston's Black leaders further bolstered the School Committee's determination to reject school integration. For several years members of the Black community had wrangled over the best methods of obtaining a good education for their children. While Clark and his supporters chose to present their demands in the 1849 petitions, other Black leaders had attempted to dramatize their demands for integration by organizing a boycott of the segregated schools.

The leader of the effort had been William C. Nell, a Black writer and journalist and a former graduate of the separate schools. His father had been one of the initial members of the General Colored Association of Massachusetts in 1826. The son had carried on the family tradition of militancy by early becoming a Garrisonian abolitionist. In 1840 his name had headed the list of the first petition to the state legislature asking for an end to segregated schools.[41]

In 1844, Nell and a small group of Blacks had banded together to oppose segregation in the Boston schools by urging parents to withdraw their children from the Smith School. Some had responded to the call. The following year the *Liberator* had happily announced that "many parents" were keeping their children out of school, thereby condemning the practice of segregation. Over the next few years attendance continued to drop, but slowly. In 1848 the average attendance had been sixty-six students; by 1849 it had fallen to fifty-three. Writers in the *Liberator* complained that the Black clergy did not support the boycott effort. A few Black businessmen, fearful of losing profits and white customers, withheld support on the basis of "imprudence." While no one recorded any useful "head-count," apparently only a handful of Blacks followed Nell's lead. Unable to arouse widespread Black support for the boycott, Nell—and the other Black and white Garrisonians—made little impact upon the members of the School Committee or on other white Bostonians.[42]

Indeed, not all Black citizens supported school integration. Shortly after receiving the 1849 petitions for abolishing separate schools, the Committee accepted three counter-petitions from "Colored Citizens,"

"Colored Clergymen and Parents," and "Colored Children." These all urged a continuance of the current system, asking only that a Black teacher be substituted for the white master of the Smith School. In addition, two Black leaders publicly defended segregated schools. Thomas P. Smith, a graduate of the Black schools, claimed that they exerted "no baleful influences, no degradation, no oppression or prejudice," but rather offered the "greatest advantage to the colored people." John H. Roberts pointed out the disadvantages which Black children would suffer from competition with more advanced white children, to say nothing of the prejudice they would encounter. Neither the wishes of the whites, he asserted, nor the necessities of the Blacks demanded the abolition of separate schools.[43]

The School Committee was delighted to follow the letter, if not the spirit, of Roberts' remarks. It resolved that in future elections for master of the Smith School, competent colored applicants (graduates of an acceptable college) would receive preference. Against the wishes of the Garrisonians, who viewed the move as an attempt to undermine their position, the Committee appointed a Black master. The new master was Thomas Paul, son of the former minister of the African Baptist Church in whose home one of the first primary schools for Black children had met. The boycotters tried to discourage children from attending the Smith School under Paul's direction, but, following a disturbance on the first day, the School Committee kept the school open. Hoping to keep their drive alive, the boycotters promised to establish "temporary schools" of their own, but they succeeded in opening only one.[44] The boycott dramatization proved to be meager fare, drew a small audience, and closed after a short run.

Bolstered by that failure and encouraged by the support of separate schools from some other Blacks, the School Committee refused to honor the latest appeals. In denying the petition for integrated schools, the Committee referred to the "sense of the community" as determining its actions. "A state of feeling and opinion prevalent in the community" opposed any change. "The Committee lament that it is thus: quite as much so, probably, as the most ostentatious and patronizing friends of the colored people themselves, may do. But they cannot overlook nor ignore the fact." Correctly rejecting the assertion that integrated schools by themselves would crumble the walls of racial prejudice, the Committee mockingly summarized the arguments of the petitioners:

> The Ethiopian would be washed white: Social distinctions would be all done away: And with the opened portals of our other schools, the avenues would be unbarred to every place, and seat, and trust, now guarded and kept shut by hereditary

usages—to our jury boxes, our legislative halls, our fire companies, and the rank of our military; from none of which at the
present, by Law, (any law of our State,) is the colored man
excluded, but by custom more despotic, however to be depre-
cated, and which your Committee apprehend must long continue
to exist, and oppose its barrier of stern and jealous restrictions.
Compared with it—such massive wall of prejudice,—the destruction of the Smith School would be but the fall of the puniest
out-work.

As it had done in 1846, the Committee urged Black citizens to seek their
goal of integration through law. The School Committee had rejected
their "useless assaults" and would continue to do so. Only through the
courts could the system be changed.[45]

Nevertheless, a minority report from one of its members attacked the
decision of the Committee. Charles T. Russell rejected the concept of
Black inferiority but added that the question of capacities made little
difference to the concept of equality. Nor did the plea of "expediency"
justify maintaining segregated schools. "We have no moral or legal right
to exclude the colored children from the ordinary public schools of the
City," Russell declared. The design of the public schools and their whole
practical influence was to teach the great theoretical principle of American government, that all men are born free and equal. "Destroy this in
the free schools," he concluded, "and you not only destroy these schools,
but the government which rests upon them as one of its main supports."[46]

But Russell's arguments mattered little. The time of petitions and
appeals had come to an end. After almost five years of continuous agitation, Boston Black and white abolitionists had decided to test segregation
in the courts.

SEPARATE-BUT-EQUAL SCHOOLS: THE ROBERTS CASE

Benjamin Roberts was one of the three signers of the most recent "Appeal" by Blacks. He had worked for integration for a long time. His five-
year-old daughter Sarah now became a pawn in a legal match to end
segregation. Between her home and the primary school for Blacks in her
area, Sarah passed five other neighborhood primary schools, all for white
children only. On several occasions her father had tried to enroll Sarah
in any one of these schools. Each time the Primary Board had rejected
the application because of her race. Rather than have his daughter attend a segregated school, Roberts sued the city under a recent statute
providing recovery of damages for any child unlawfully excluded from
public school instruction. The case was already under way when the
School Committee on August 29, 1849, rendered its decision on the re-

cent petitions. In fact, the Committee had used the pending case as an excuse for not abolishing separate schools, claiming it would welcome a final decision by the court.[47]

Representing Roberts in his suit were Robert Morris, a lawyer "whose very presence as a colored member of the Massachusetts Bar, was a living protest against all colored institutions," and Charles Sumner. Pelig W. Chandler defended the city of Boston. Hearing the case in the Supreme Judicial Court was Lemuel Shaw, the most noted justice in Massachusetts history. A man of firm principle, Shaw dominated the Court for over three decades. In over 2,000 opinions during that time, he wrote only one dissent, and in only three of his constitutional opinions was the Court less than unanimous in concurring.[48] A stellar cast dramatized the issue of segregation.

Sumner began by briefly outlining the history of separate schools in Boston. Then he eloquently described the situation: "On the one side is the City of Boston, strong in its wealth, in its influence, in its character; on the other side is a little child, of a degraded color, of humble parents, still within the period of natural infancy, but strong from her very weakness, and from the irresponsible sympathies of good men." This little child, "asks at your hands her *personal rights.*" For the argument, Sumner claimed, hinged on a "single proposition—the equality of man before the law."

In the course of his statements, Sumner ran the gamut of historical attitudes toward equality. Beginning with Seneca and continuing with the ideas of Cromwell, Milton, and the French philosophes Diderot and Rousseau, the aims of the French Revolution, the principles of the American Declaration of Independence and John Adams' Massachusetts Constitution of 1789, he applauded the concept of "equality before the law." He then denounced the tirades of John C. Calhoun and other southerners against equality and likened decisions of the Boston School Committee to these sentiments. For northerners becoming increasingly hostile toward the South, the emotional appeal bore heavy weight. Boston's schools were caste institutions, Sumner charged, resting on the same foundations of prejudice as the caste system of India. Under Massachusetts law, he claimed, the power to segregate was illegal. The Committee had no legal right to "brand a whole race with the stigma of inferiority and degredation." The Committee had only the authority to allocate children to certain schools on the basis of age, sex, and moral and intellectual qualifications. Race could not enter in. The law required that the actions of municipal corporations be reasonable, he argued, and the *a priori* assumption of the inferiority of an entire race was unreasonable.

It was ludicrous, Sumner stated, to affirm as had the School Committee that separate schools for Blacks and whites were educationally equal.
He followed the lead of the abolitionist minority of the School Committee
in alluding to a recent decision by Justice Richard Fletcher involving
the School Committee of Salem. Fletcher had ruled that Black children
were "lawfully entitled to the benefits of the free schools" and were not
legally bound to accept an "equivalent." A separate school, Sumner declared, was not an "equivalent," nor a "public school," because of incon-
veniences and the stigma of caste. "The matters taught in the two schools
may be precisely the same, but a school devoted to one class must differ
essentially in spirit and character from that Common School known to
the law, where all classes meet in Equality.'

In the final analysis, Sumner's argument relied as much on a moral appeal as on an issue of law. In his summation, he acknowledged this himself. White people, he alleged, were injured by segregation for it taught
them to ignore the greatest principle of Christianity—the Brotherhood of
Man. Prejudice therefore worked moral havoc on both races. The school
was the little world in which morality must be taught if adults were ever
to behave as moral men.
He concluded:

> Prejudice is the child of ignorance. It is sure to prevail where
> people do not know each other. Society and intercourse are
> means established by Providence for human improvement. They
> remove antipathies, promote mutual adaptation and concillia-
> tion, and establish relations of reciprocal regard. . . . But this
> is not all. The vaunted superiority of the white race imposes
> upon it corresponding duties. The facilities with which they
> are endowed, and the advantages they possess, are to be exer-
> cised for the good of all. If the colored people are ignorant, de-
> graded, and unhappy, they should be the especial objects of
> your care. From the abundance of your possessions you must
> seek to remedy their lot.

A more lofty commitment to the moral power of public education could
scarcely be imagined.[49]

Chief Justice Shaw was familiar with the activities and men of the
Boston School Committee. In his youth he had taught school in Boston
and had served for a time on the School Committee. He knew that the
Committee believed it had tried to serve the best interests of the entire
community. In responding to Sumner's pleas, he showed his acceptance
of the Committee's self-evaluation.

If the Committee possessed legal authority, Shaw reasoned, then the
"expediency" of exercising that authority belonged to it exclusively. As a
broad principle, he agreed, equality before the law was sound:

But when this great principle comes to be applied to the actual and various conditions of persons within society, it will not warrant the assertion, that men and women are equally clothed with the same civil and political powers, and that children and adults are legally to have the same functions and be subject to the same treatment; but only that the rights of all, as they are settled and regulated by law, are equally entitled to the parental consideration and protection of the law, for their maintenance and security. What these rights are, to which individuals, in the infinite variety of circumstances by which they are surrounded in society, are entitled, must depend on laws adapted to their respective relations and conditions.

Shaw was satisfied that the School Committee had acted on just grounds of reason and experience. Ignoring the precedent set by Judge Fletcher (who, for some curious reason, did not participate in this decision), Shaw maintained that under the law the Committee had provided equal schools for Black children. Sarah Roberts had not been unlawfully excluded from public instruction. On April 8, 1850, the Court dismissed the suit. For the first time in American legal history, the doctrine of separate-but-equal facilities for different races was established.[50]

THE CAUSE TRIUMPHS

Although disheartened by the decision, Blacks and white abolitionists did not abandon the struggle. They formed an "Equal School Rights Committee" and resolved to carry the fight to the legislature. William Lloyd Garrison promised that the subject would be agitated throughout the state and that the "people (who are greater than the Court) will, we are confident, remedy this injustice." In 1850 William C. Nell asked the annual convention of the New England Anti-Slavery Society for its help in the campaign. The Society promised aid, but then had its attention diverted when Congress passed a new fugitive slave law. When, in 1851, a crowd of Blacks stormed a Boston courtroom to free an escaped slave arrested under the new law, local citizens became outraged. Their anger precluded any favorable response to the cause for desegregated schools.[51]

During 1851 and 1852 the School Committee resolutely stood its ground on the issue of integration. When abolitionists succeeded in introducing before the state legislature a bill that forbade the exclusion of any child from any public school on account of race, the Committee "*unanimously*" opposed it. Boston, the Committee argued, had provided equal opportunities for both races "without subjecting either to objectionable associations." The Committee warned that if the bill should become law, "it would greatly disturb and distract the present liberal and happy arrangement of our Schools." The pending bill died, at least for the current legislative session, and the Committee figuratively breathed a sigh of relief. The following year, to stave off integration, the Committee agreed to pay what in modern terms would be called busing charges. Mr. and Mrs. William Stith, a Black couple living across the harbor in East Boston, petitioned the Committee to transfer their children from the Smith School to nearby Chapman School. The Committee refused, citing its 1849 *Report,* and discounted the complaints about distance traveled, stating that some white children traveled just as far to attend school. But the Committee did agree to defray the expense of ferry tickets for the Black children, "rather than establish a precedent which they foresee, at no distant period, will prove very troublesome and dangerous."[52]

Then, in 1854, Blacks and white abolitionists received help from an unexpected source. School officials had excluded from the regular schools a young boy named Edward Pindall. Although he appeared to be white, the boy was of mixed white, Indian, and Negro heritage. On the grounds of race, officials ordered the boy to attend the Smith School. His father immediately lodged a complaint with the city. Where others had failed, this complaint brought action. A select Committee on Public Instruction investigated the Pindall case and the general situation of separate schools in the city. This committee concluded that racial segregation was doing more harm to the quality of the public schools "than any other influence." It recommended that segregation be ended, hopeful that Boston would become the first major American city to abolish separate schools for Black children.[53]

This seemingly sudden change of heart reflected changed political circumstances in the city. The elections of 1854 replaced some members of the Old Guard in public office with men of a new party, the Know-Nothings. Their election campaigns had played down the troublesome presence of militant Blacks and their white allies and instead had highlighted the dangers to social order from the multitudes of foreign immigrants entering the city. In general, Know-Nothing attitudes favored Blacks and stressed anti-slavery sentiments. Conservative members of the School Committee rightly feared challenges to their traditional independence in school affairs and thus were willing to compromise some of their rigid stands on administrative matters. With Know-Nothingism in the saddle, Committee members accepted the necessity of riding out the storm.[54]

In reaction to the Pindall case, the School Committee took a softer position on the segregation controversy. Under the pressure of events, the

Committee noted that no official regulation compelling attendance at the Smith School had ever existed, nor had any hard-and-fast rule prohibited attendance of Black children at white schools. Since 1849, the Committee had clearly changed its tune. Committee members also observed that it was "the practice of many of the Sub-Committees to allow colored children to attend the schools nearest their places of residence when the Smith School is inconveniently distant." Whether that statement was correct remained unclear. Certainly the Stith case of two years earlier showed no such practice. But the statement did reveal a new willingness of the Committee to wink at established custom and judicial decision. Apparently most Committee members believed that their benevolence should satisfy all critics. One committeeman, however, felt that the bow toward expediency was not enough. In a minority report that expressed his Know-Nothing bias as much as it demonstrated possible sympathy for Blacks, Dr. Luther Parks charged his fellows with focusing on the wrong issues. Distance from schools, he pointed out, was not the principal question; segregation was. Any arguments in favor of segregating Black children from white youth in schools, Parks asserted, should "apply with less force than in the case of a large class of children of foreign parentage." If there was to be segregation, he implied, let it involve the sorting-out of native children from those of the foreign intruders.[55]

While the School Committee temporized and debated, the opponents of segregation acted. Encouraged by the results of the Pindall case, Nell, Garrison, and others resumed their attack in earnest. Black leaders and white abolitionists circulated petitions throughout the state supporting desegregation. Finally, on April 28, 1855, the governor signed into law the provision that in determining the qualifications of any student in the public schools of the state, "no distinction shall be made on account of the race, color or religious opinions, of the applicant or scholar."[56]

After over half a century of separatism, the schools of Boston became integrated. In September 1855 Black students, accompanied by their mothers, peacefully entered the white schools. A few white parents withdrew their children, but no violent hostilities occurred. "And since the 3rd of September to the present time," a Black leader happily observed, "the sun, moon and stars are regular in their courses! No orb has proved so eccentric as to shoot madly from its sphere in consequence, and the State House on Beacon Hill, and old Faneuill Hall, remain as firm on their bases as ever."[57]

The reactions of white Bostonians were mixed. The Catholic *Boston Pilot* doubted that integration would succeed; the editor was certain that Black children would soon discover they could not compete with whites and would return to their own schools. But the *Pilot* was wrong.

Attendance at the formerly all-Black schools fell off so quickly that the School Committee closed them down altogether. The Committee itself responded ambivalently. On the one hand, after ordering that Black children be admitted to the regular public schools, the Committee organized several new schools to accommodate the influx of Black youth. On the other hand, the Committee spitefully refused to pay a portion of their salaries as recompense to those teachers unemployed by the closing of the Smith School. The Committee defended its decision by observing sourly that previous expenses "for a few colored children" had been "equal to that of educating the same number of students at Harvard University." Whatever the other reactions to the closing of the separate schools, the opponents of segregation were delighted. Black leaders and white abolitionists rejoiced together in a mass rally with Wendell Phillips and others drawing loud cheers.[58]

The "sense of the community" had changed. Any final evaluation of the reasons lay buried in the emotions and minds of many Bostonians. Some citizens undoubtedly had long supported the Black population. Others perhaps had developed sympathy as Boston became a main way-station of the famous Underground Railroad. Certainly the Compromise of 1850 had deepened sectional differences over the race issue and had perhaps convinced still more citizens not to share the same guilt of prejudice and racism as their southern countrymen And the Know-Nothing victories of 1854 brought into various positions of power some men who were determined to heighten tensions between natives and aliens by reducing the antagonisms between white and Black. Under the Know-Nothing administration came the successful proposals for eliminating segregation in the schools. The School Committee had fought a holding action for many years; it had won almost all of the battles, but, in the end, it had lost the war.

Over thirty years of agitation, first by a handful of militant Blacks and then by abolitionist sympathizers, brought to an end the system of segregated schools. The list of those active in the struggles was a "Who's Who" of northern abolitionists: William Lloyd Garrison, Wendell Phillips, Theodore Parker, Henry I. Bowditch, Francis and Edmund Jackson, Henry Wilson, William Nell, Thomas Dalton, and others. Whatever their ultimate motives, and however suspicious at times their methods, white and Black abolitionists had succeeded in lessening the traditional prejudices of citizens in the "Hub of the Universe." That Blacks and whites now attended the same schools and now grew up with the same formal education would not destroy the social barriers that remained. Still, at the time, the new order seemed like a good beginning.

V

POVERTY, IMMIGRATION, AND PUBLIC MORALITY

9

Poverty and the Urban Crisis

The poor, therefore, have lived and to a great extent are living as a caste, cut off from those in more favored circumstances; and doomed to find their pleasures, and sympathy in their sufferings alone among themselves.

Joseph Tuckerman (c. 1830)[1]

American social observers have long shared a taste for crisis. If we could recall a Cotton Mather, a Thomas Jefferson, a Thoreau, a Jane Addams from the past and place them on the couch, we might draw forth fascinating explanations of this phenomenon. With more certainty than we now enjoy we might be able to pinpoint the origins of the crisis syndrome in periods of substantial change in the tempo of social relations. We might be able to relate psychological perceptions to sudden shifts in the processes of urban expansion and commercial and industrial development. In the absence of psychoanalysis we are left with the impressionistic evidence more familiar in historical writings. From that evidence emerges one central fact: our social critics have displayed a lust for visions of disaster.

Certainly many American Cassandras during the first half of the nineteenth century reveled in predictions of human tragedies of city growth, or, as we rephrase today, the "urban crisis." Wherever nineteenth-century critics looked, they found cracks in what they conceived to be the traditional structure of urban social relationships. Never mind the accuracy of their assertions about tradition; the critics generally showed more interest in gloomy appraisals than in precise historical analysis. Their prime complaint was the galaxy of dangers to moral health, life, and limb presented by residence in large cities. To the doom-sayers the cities loomed as a universe of social disorder.

Of the various disorders in urban life, the most evident was poverty. While American cities had always known the poor, urban leaders of the past had believed in the transciency of poverty. In young and slowly expanding colonial cities, the economic horizons had appeared limitless;

the poor did not always have to remain poor. But during the late eighteenth and early nineteenth century, these attitudes altered dramatically. City officials and concerned private citizens began to suspect, perhaps already too late, that urban poverty was not a passing phenomenon but a permanent condition. In Philadelphia, New York, Baltimore, Boston, and elsewhere, the story was the same. A growing number of urban paupers presaged a day when cities might be divided sharply along class lines; when foreign indigents might threaten the hegemony of native Americans; and when public financial resources might be devoted more to charitable relief, to workhouses, and to prisons, than to other needed public services. A fear of poverty haunted the imaginations of social critics. That fear, and its ramifications for social policy, played a principal role in contemporary interpretations of an urban crisis.[2]

FEAR OF THE STRANGER

At the core of any sense of community among individuals or social groups lies a suspicion of outsiders. People who share a sense of community tend to view themselves bound together by commonly held values, standards of public and private behavior, and social goals. Outsiders are often seen as posing threats to the continued harmony of the community. The threats may be real or imagined, but to the threatened they take on an independent life of their own.[3] During the first half of the nineteenth century a growing number of American social critics focused public attention on threats to established order. They feared the periodic waves of native poor from rural pockets of poverty who swept into the cities in search of jobs and homes. They saw foreign migrants turning the centers of eastern cities into tenement ghettos. They beheld aliens depressing the living standards of native American workers through the lowering of wages. They assured themselves that Roman Catholic priests were directing their followers to subvert the political and religious foundations of society. The critics' fears of internal subversion by such invaders as Mormons and Freemasons led to powerful countermovements which attracted widespread public support. Above all, the critics feared the stranger in their midst.

Boston had no room for strangers. Socially, economically, politically, and psychologically, during the early decades of the nineteenth century, Boston was a closed community. A relatively small group of men yearly exchanged office-holding in a political round-robin. A handful controlled the economic destinies of the city. A coterie of intellectuals dominated cultural and social life. Residents of the city valued the homogeneity of the population and congratulated themselves when visitors exclaimed, "why all these people are of one race. They behave like members of one family."[4] Bostonians neither encouraged nor welcomed the prospect of a large number of newcomers in their midst—still, the strangers came.

Like other American cities during the first half of the nineteenth century, though not always at the same pace, Boston underwent commercial expansion and the beginnings of industrialization. In percentage growth of population, American cities experienced the most rapid rate of urbanization in the nation's history between 1820 and 1860, and Boston was no exception.[5] In the 1820's and early 1830's a large number of migrants

TABLE 6

POPULATION OF BOSTON AND ITS ANNEXES[a]

Year	Total Population	Native Population	Foreign Population	Foreign Per Cent of Total Population
1790	18,038			
1800	24,937			
1810	33,787			
1820	43,298	38,137	5,161[b]	11.9
1825	58,277			
1830	61,392	50,011	11,381[b]	18.5
1835	78,603	62,720	15,883[b]	20.2
1840	93,383	72,784	20,599[b]	22.1
1845	114,366	77,077	37,289[c]	32.6
1850	138,788	75,322	63,466[c]	45.7
1855	161,490	75,872	85,618[c]	53.3
1860	177,840	113,995	63,845	35.9

[a] Annexes include East Boston (1636); South Boston (1804); Washington Village (1855); and the Islands.

[b] These are estimates derived from Frederick A. Bushee, "The Growth of the Population of Boston," American Statistical Association *Publications*, VI (June 1899), 240ff.

[c] "Foreign" includes native-born of one or more foreign-born parents.

SOURCES: Lemuel Shattuck, *Report of the Committee of the City Council Appointed to Obtain the Census of Boston for the Year 1845* (Boston: J. H. Eastburn, 1846); Nathaniel B. Shurtleff, *Abstract of the Census of the Commonwealth of Massachusetts . . . June, 1855* (Boston: Moore & Crosby, 1856); *Report and Tabular Statement of the Censors . . . State Census of Boston, May 1, 1850* (Boston: City Printer, 1850), pp. 19-65; *Report of the Special Joint Committee on the Census of Boston, May, 1855* (Boston: Moore & Crosby, 1856); Carroll D. Wright, *Analysis of the Population of the City of Boston . . . Census of May, 1885* (Boston: City Printer, 1885).

entering the city came from the depressed rural areas of New England. In 1820, foreign residents comprised only 12 per cent of Boston's total population, but over the following forty years, the immigrant population increased from roughly 5,000 to over 60,000. Despite a rising tide of complaints against the aliens, during the 1820's and 1830's the city had been able to absorb the newcomers gradually and peacefully. But, in the single decade of the 1840's, the immigrant percentage of the entire population jumped from 22 to nearly 46 per cent, and the problems of adjustment and assimilation mounted correspondingly. Between 1845 and 1850 (the peak year of foreign immigration during the period), the foreign populace boomed by over 70 per cent, while the native population declined by over 2 per cent. By 1850, less than half the descendants of Bostonians alive in 1820 remained in the city. Throughout the thirty-year period, the natural increase of native American Bostonians accounted for only some 12 per cent of the total population growth.[6] The portents were clear: Due to native out-migration, alien immigration, and a much higher birth rate among foreign than among native residents, the population had become more mixed than ever in its history (see Tables 6, 7, and 8).

Ethnic group composition in Boston varied in nationality over the period. French immigrants arrived in small numbers during the early years, and again following the European revolutions of 1830 and 1848. Those political upheavals also swelled the ranks of German, Italian, Austro-Hungarian, and Polish migrants. Still, the extent of political emigration was not overly significant. As a Belgian observer commented in 1846, the immigrants "did not leave their native villages to seek political rights in another hemisphere. The time of the Puritans . . . is past." Even the familiar German "Forty-eighters" did not add measurably to the number of that nationality in Boston which totaled less than 2,000 by 1850. The handful of English, Welsh, and Scottish emigrants arriving in the 1820's had increased in the early 1830's, subsided, and then rapidly accelerated during the 1840's and early 1850's. Yet, by 1850, residents of these nationalities comprised only 4,000 of a total population over 136,000. The bulk of migrants from Germany, England, and the Scandinavian countries who disembarked in Boston port between 1820 and 1860 were of rural and agrarian origins and chose to remain in the city proper only a short while. Such travelers were usually financially able to leave the city for the west, where they often took over farms abandoned by restless native Americans. Only one group, migrating in substantial numbers, ultimately stayed in the city. Eventually the Irish concentrated more heavily in Boston and other cities than any other ethnic group. And it was to the Irish that native Bostonians chiefly reacted when they attempted to cope with immigration into their city.[7]

TABLE 7
PER CENT GAIN IN NATIVE AND FOREIGN POPULATION, 1820-1860

Year	Population (thousands)	Native Per Cent of Pop.	Foreign Per Cent of Pop.	Per Cent Gain in Population Over Past			Native Over Past		Foreign Over Past	
				5 yrs.	10 yrs.	Over 1820	5 yrs.	10 yrs.	5 yrs.	10 yrs.
1820	43.3	88	12	n.a.[a]	28		n.a.	n.a.	n.a.	n.a.
1825	58.3	n.a.	n.a.	5	n.a.	5	n.a.	n.a.	n.a.	n.a.
1830	61.4	81	19	5	42	42	n.a.	31	n.a.	121
1835	78.6	80	20	28	35	82	25	n.a.	40	n.a.
1840	93.4	78	22	18	52	116	16	45.5	30	81
1845	114.4	67	33	23	45	164	6	23	81	135
1850	136.9	54	46	21	49	221	-2	3.5	70	208
1855	161.4	47	53	16	41	273	.07	-2	35	130
1860[b]	177.8	64	36	10	28	311	50	51	-25	.006

[a] "N.a." means figures are not available.

[b] The apparent decline in foreign percentage of population between 1855 and 1860 is illusory; the only available figures for 1860 do not break down (as did figures for 1845-55) native-born children of foreign parents from all native-born children.

SOURCES: Lemuel Shattuck, *Report of the Committee of the City Council Appointed to Obtain the Census of Boston for the Year 1845* (Boston: J. H. Eastburn, 1846), "Appendices 12-17"; Nathaniel B. Shurtleff, *Abstract of the Census of the Commonwealth of Massachusetts . . . June, 1855* (Boston: Moore & Crosby, 1856); *Report and Tabular Statement of the Censors . . . State Census of Boston, May 1, 1850* (Boston: City Printer, 1850), pp. 19-65; *Report of the Joint Special Committee on the Census of Boston, May, 1855* (Boston: Moore & Crosby, 1856; U.S. Census Office. *Eighth Census* (1860); *Population of the United States in 1860 . . .* (Washington, D.C.: Government Printing Office, 1864); Carroll D. Wright, *Analysis of the Population of the City of Boston . . . Census of May, 1885* (Boston: City Printer, 1885).

Many Irish immigrants arriving in America prior to 1830 came from the ranks of substantial farmers and could afford to move beyond the Atlantic seaboard. Yet, as early as 1818, Boston businessmen recruited Irish laborers for the express purpose of constructing the Mill Dam, a project which enclosed a large part of the Back Bay area and provided considerable land space to the city. This job, and other public works during the early 1820's, added to the number of Irish workingmen entering the city. The stream of Irish immigration, however, remained a trickle until the early 1840's. Between 1840 and 1860 at least 169,000 Irish arrived in Boston. Not all of those remained. But by 1850, there were almost 54,000 Irish residents in the city. Except for spurts in 1853 and 1854, the number of Irish arrivals and departures leveled off about 1855, with the number residing in the city remaining fairly constant until the early 1860's (see Table 9).[8]

With the sudden, dramatic immigrant invasion between 1845 and 1855, Boston's political and social leadership underwent cultural shock at the prospect of absorbing the crowd of strangers. The immigrants—poor, uneducated, unfamiliar with republican institutions—appeared to threaten cultural homogeneity and the very safety of society. As one writer observed, "it is a fact not to be ignored, but admitted and met in advance, that in a nation increasing its population by immigration, . . . it is a delicate point to preserve the unity, continuity, and predominance of the native interests." Boston educators were more blunt. "A House divided against itself cannot stand," warned the School Committee in 1853. "Distrust, dissension and disunion would follow." The foreigners must be made to recognize and work toward, "the common interests of the whole body of the community." Although the leaders of the city in the 1850's evidenced dismay and anxiety over the presence of large numbers of strangers in their midst, they were not unprepared to take action. From the 1820's, the arrival of immigrants had tested the city's capacity to adjust to new and increasingly pressing social problems. By the 1850's the magnitude of the difficulties had grown, but the modes of response had been years in the making.[9]

WHO ARE THE POOR?

Boston had traditionally enjoyed a reputation of caring for its indigent. As early as 1732 a public agency, the Overseers of the Poor, had undertaken annual surveys to determine the condition of the poor. The city had provided tax funds and built work-houses for its own poor residents. It had been unwilling, however, to feed and clothe a host of newcomers. Boston had periodically legislated against granting relief to incoming in-

TABLE 8

NATIVE AND FOREIGN POPULATION OF BOSTON
BY PARENTAGE, 1840-1855 (PER CENT)

Year	Total Population	Native	Foreign*	Increase Over Past 5 Years Native	Foreign*
1845	114,366	67.4	32.6	6	81
1850	138,788	54.3	45.7	−2	70
1855	161,490	47.0	53.0	.07	35

* "Foreign" includes native-born children with foreign parents.

SOURCES: Lemuel Shattuck, *Report to the Committee of the City Council Appointed to Obtain the Census of Boston for the Year 1845* (Boston: J. H. Eastburn, 1846), "Appendix 20"; *Boston City Documents, 1850*, Doc. No. 42, p. 30; *Report of the Joint Special Committee on the Census of Boston, May, 1855* (Boston: Moore & Crosby, 1856), p. 21.

TABLE 9

NATIVITY OF BOSTONIANS, 1850-1855

National Origins	1850	1855
United States	88,948	98,018
England, Scotland, and Wales	4,110	5,241
Ireland	35,287	46,237
Germany	1,816[a]	3,376[b]
France	225	372
Italy	134	245
Spain	67	
British America		5,850
Others	5,038	1,032
Unknown	1,256	119
TOTAL	136,881	160,490

[a] This figure includes Prussia.

[b] This figure includes Holland.

SOURCES: Ephraim M. Wright, *Twelfth Registration Report, 1853* (Boston, 1854), p. 110; Nathaniel B. Shurtleff, *Abstract of the Census of the Commonwealth of Massachusetts Taken with Reference to Facts Existing on the First Day of June, 1855, with Remarks on the Same Prepared under the Direction of Francis DeWitt, Secretary of the Commonwealth* (Boston, 1857), pp. 98-132; *Report and Tabular Statement of the Censors . . . State Census of Boston, May 1, 1850. Also, A Letter from Jesse Chickering, M. D. in Reference to the Same* (Boston, 1850), pp. 19-65.

digent strangers. Many Bostonians, dependent on the Overseers to deal with the situation, had been able to ignore the poor or remain confident that they knew the dimensions of poverty within the city.[10]

"The poor were personally subjects of knowledge and cognizance to the more favored classes," reminisced a charity worker about the halcyon days of the 1820's. "Pauperism was a thing determinable in nature and quantity. . . . Every man was known by his neighbor, . . . none were overlooked, nor could escape in the crowd." Like many memories, the statement was partly romantic illusion. From the vantage point of the more troubled 1850's, the twenties looked like a time of close ties between the poor and the more favored classes. But it was not. Migrants to the city, whether rural native Americans or foreigners, swelled the ranks of Boston's poor. As the number of poor increased, so did the social distance between them and the better sort. The complacency of middle- and upper-class Bostonians gave way to apprehension as the poor became more visible threats to social order.[11]

Beginning in the early 1820's, crimes common to the lower classes— drunkenness, assault and battery, "lewd" behavior, and vagrancy—accounted for a growing number of court convictions. The better class might avoid Ann Street in the North End or similar streets and alleys in the West End frequented by the poor, by "highbinders, jailbirds, known thieves, and miscreants, with women of the worst description." But in an increasingly crowded city, the upper classes began to complain that even on The Common and in the business districts of the North End the indigent and the vicious were becoming more evident. After his election as mayor, in 1823, Josiah Quincy initiated a clean-up campaign of the city's most notorious districts. Closing down "houses of infamous characters," revoking liquor licenses, and calling for a physical cleaning of the streets, Quincy proceeded "upon the principle that if in great cities the existence of vice is inevitable, that its course should be in secret, . . . not obtrusive, not powerful, not prowling publicly in the streets."[12]

But what of the less visible poor, those who did not often appear in court or become identifiable public nuisances? Politicians, clergymen, charity workers, and educators felt a pressing need to identify these poor, to discover who they were, where they lived, what chances of success or failure they faced, and to evaluate their potential and real threat to community safety and stability. Periodically between the 1820's and the 1860's concerned citizens conducted a bewildering variety of investigations to find the answers to these questions. From their efforts emerged a composite picture of the poor.[13]

Identified by occupations and origins, the employed poor were white native-born, Black, and foreign laborers who worked at the most menial tasks as domestics and unskilled hands in factories and the building trades, or as semi-skilled and service workers, for example, waiters, cooks, seamstresses, barbers, and butchers. Contemporaries rarely, if ever, carefully defined "poor" in dollar values of income earned or property owned; they assumed that "the poor" owned little personal or real property or managed much in the way of savings. Fortunately, a recent study by historian Peter Knights sheds light on the matter. Sampling Boston's population between 1830 and 1860, Knights defined the lower class as those who paid only a poll tax and thus owned less than $200 in property. (He admitted, at least implicitly, that many of Boston's poorest residents could not be captured in this arbitrary classification.) The numbers of these poor rose steadily, and at times spectacularly, over the period. Unskilled and menial heads of households showed an increase of 85 per cent during the 1830's, 230 per cent in the 1840's, and 10 per cent in the 1850's. Nor were these poor likely to advance occupationally or financially (in property assessment). From 1830 to about 1850 the gap widened between the successful and the non-successful (those who advanced versus those whose position remained steady or even declined). The ratios of non-success changed most rapidly in the decade of the forties, with the odds for advancement running six to one against the unskilled and menial workers and two and one-half to one against the semi-skilled and service workers. By 1850, as shown in the Federal Census, unskilled laborers comprised almost 20 per cent of Boston's total work force, with the Irish and Black segments of the population respectively totalling 48 and 20 per cent of the laboring class. More than half the work force was unskilled or semi-skilled. From 1850 to 1860 disparities between the successful and the non-successful narrowed, but only slightly.[14] Bostonians who did not have these figures at their fingertips knew nonetheless that the numbers of poor in their midst were booming; they also believed that for every employed poor person, far more remained unemployed, either temporarily, or on a permanent basis.

While various groups within the population did not enjoy rapid occupational or economic mobility, the same could not be said for residential mobility. Like other American cities of the time, Boston held an astonishingly mobile population. Between 1830 and 1860, the rate of population turnover (moves into, around, and out of the city) averaged about 30 to 40 per cent. This implies that roughly one-half of the population vanished from place of residence and were replaced by newcomers every one or two years. Over the course of a decade the total turnover possibly reached several times the city's entire population. Mobility ratios were highest among the lower classes, with the ratios for foreign-born nearly twice those for native-born.[15] Within certain older areas of the

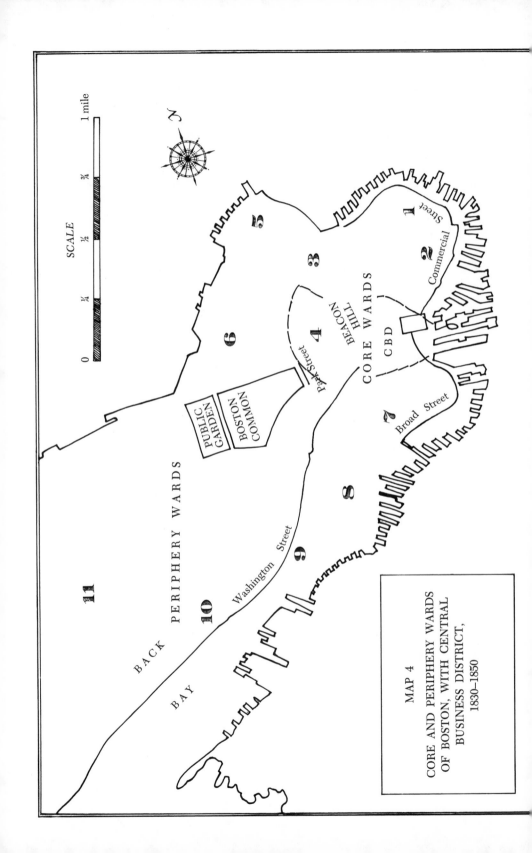

SCALE

0   ¼   ½   ¾   1 mile

N

PERIPHERY WARDS

BACK

BAY

11

10

Washington Street

9

PUBLIC
GARDEN

BOSTON
COMMON

8

6

Park Street

4

BEACON
HILL

CORE WARDS

CBD

7

Broad Street

3

5

1

Commercial
Street

2

MAP 4

CORE AND PERIPHERY WARDS
OF BOSTON, WITH CENTRAL
BUSINESS DISTRICT,
1830–1850

TABLE 10

POPULATION DISTRIBUTION IN CORE AND PERIPHERY WARDS OF NATIVES AND FOREIGNERS, 1825-1850

Year	Core	Periphery	Natives		Foreigners		Per Cent of Foreigners to Total Population	
			Core	Periphery	Core	Periphery	Core	Periphery
1825	25,101	33,176	n.a.		n.a.		n.a.	
1830	25,416	35,976	23,509	34,415	1907[a]	1561[a]	7.5[a]	4.3[a]
1837[c]	32,210 (46,221)	48,613 (34,602)	n.a.		n.a.		n.a.	
1845	57,481	56,885	42,903	44,359	14,578[b]	12,526[b]	25.4[b]	22.0[b]
1850[c]	60,647 (74,289)	78,141 (64,499)	32,835 (39,882)	42,487 (35,440)	27,812[b] (34,407)	35,654[b] (29,059)	45.9[b] (46.3)	45.6[b] (45)

[a] Defined as "aliens"; does not include native-born of foreign parents or naturalized citizens

[b] Defined as "foreign-born" which included native-born of foreign parents

[c] Figures in parentheses reflect population differences after redistricting of ward boundaries in 1837 and 1850.

SOURCES: U.S. Census Office. Fifth Census (1830), *Fifth Census; Or, Enumeration of the Inhabitants of the United States, as Corrected at the Department of State. 1830* (Washington, D.C.: Duff Green, 1832), 20-21; Lemuel Shattuck, *Report to the Committee of the City Council, 1837,* in, *Boston City Documents, 1838,* Doc. No. 20, pp. 5-10; Shattuck, *Report to the Committee of the City Council . . . Census of Boston for the Year 1845* (Boston: J. H. Eastburn, 1846), "Appendix 20"; *Boston City Documents, 1850,* Doc. No. 42, p. 30; *Report of the Joint Special Committee on the Census of Boston, May, 1855* (Boston: Moore & Crosby, 1856), p. 7.

city, especially the core wards (One, Two, Three, Four, Five, Seven—see Map 4 and Table 10), the poor were seemingly more migratory than the rest of the population—or so it appeared to contemporaries. Indigents and other members of the lower classes moved from street to court, from cellar to chamber to attic with a rapidity that defied the accurate keeping of records. Lemuel Shattuck, Boston's first demographer, noted that the "locomotive habits" of the population as a whole made record keeping far more difficult than among "the more stationary population of the country." And, with a note of despair, one of the city's missionaries to the poor complained of the fluctuating nature of his flock and lamented that "it is characteristic of the poor everywhere, to be continually shifting their places of abode."[16]

The social geography of Boston's poor population—the patterns of population distribution, spatial arrangement, and social class separation— typified that of other large American cities during the period.[17] The walls of residential segregation by occupation, income, and class began to rise in the 1850's (see Map 1). Until then commercial, industrial, and residential uses of land remained well-mixed, and Bostonians of various social classes often lived jumbled together in various sections of the community. Still, long before the 1850's Boston's poor found themselves increasingly crushed together in given neighborhoods within the city's oldest wards.

Physically Boston was a small city, completely waterlocked, laid out on a narrow peninsula about one mile wide and two miles long. For the poor the possibility of living in the environs—South Boston, West Boston, Charlestown, Cambridge, and elsewhere—was remote. To travel in any direction from the main part of the city was costly, for bridge tolls were too high for the average laborer to afford on a regular basis and public transportation costs (about twelve cents a day) were out of reach for the laborer earning about a dollar a day. The poor fortunate enough to obtain regular employment therefore had to live within walking distance of work, a fact noted by contemporaries who stated that "we cannot doubt, that a very large proportion of the day laborers, would pay almost any rents, near their work, rather than move."[18] For all of the first half of the nineteenth century the commercial and manufacturing establishments of Boston clustered in the core wards. The docks, markets, stores and shops, offices and counting-houses, banks and insurance companies—the central business district—remained in Ward Four over the period. Corridors of work shops, the garment district, tool shops, foundries, light industries such as sugar refining, and handicraft trades surrounded the central business district in adjacent wards. Laborers who had to live close to places of employment therefore crowded themselves together in boarding houses, flats, and tenements in the core wards. The lower classes, and especially the foreign poor, were centrally concentrated during the 1830's and the 1840's (see Table 10). With some alarm, Boston's better sort reacted to the shifting social geography of the city. A newspaper editor sounded the tocsin in 1837: "In some of the central Wards in the City there are, comparatively, but few houses which the extreme poor inhabit. In other wards—No. 2, for example—requires only to be perambulated by Inquirer, or anyone else, who will find the abodes of poverty, and the dwellings of the destitute, in every street." By 1852, a City Council committee summed up several decades of population movement by charging that "the great influx of foreigners is changing entirely the character of various portions of the City." "The older parts of the City are crowded," the committee observed, "rents are exhorbitant, and it is with extreme difficulty that a comfortable tenement can be obtained."[19]

For the native or the foreign poor to find any tenement fit to live in, let alone a "comfortable tenement," had been difficult in the 1820's; by the 1850's it was nearly impossible. The numbers of unskilled laborers and foreign indigents entering the city put heavy burdens on the supply of available housing. Real estate owners and speculators seized the opportunity to meet the housing needs of the newcomers and, at the same time, to fill their own pockets. They transformed former mansions, warehouses, and abandoned factories into crowded and unsanitary living quarters. Boardinghouse owners subdivided their buildings into immigrant flats rented by the week at costs far exceeding the quality of living quarters. In the alleyways formed by the irregular pattern of the streets, speculators erected new structures, three and four stories high, with twenty and thirty tiny apartments lining narrow, sunless passages. The foulest slums arose on whatever vacant spots remained behind or beside existent old buildings. Every inch of space was used in these tenements, sheds, and shanties. The immigrant poor squeezed into attics less than three feet high, and into cellar apartments lacking either light or fresh air.[20]

One of the worst sections was in the Fort Hill area where rising land values led speculators to carve out portions of the hill and to fill the niches with jerry-built wooden tenements. "Burgess' Alley," "Half-Moon Place," and "Jacob's Ladder" (all names of tenement districts in the Hill area) became synonymous with "filth," "degradation," and "poverty." The polluted waters from poorly constructed privies tumbled down the Hill from tenements above to shanties below. Fire was a constant threat. Investigators found living quarters littered with "putrefying vegetable matters" and "no small portion of substances still more loathsome." The tenements were breeding grounds of cholera, tuberculosis, and other diseases.

In a cellar room below "Jacob's Ladder" as many as thirty-nine men, women, and children huddled together in one room, a room often inundated by a flood tide that, as one physician reported, rose "so high that it was necessary to approach the bedside of a patient by means of a plank which was laid from one stool to another; while the dead body of an infant was actually sailing about the room in its coffin." The Broad Street-Fort Hill district "is a perfect hive of human beings, without comforts and mostly without common necessaries," investigators discovered in 1849.

Figure 11   "A NATURAL SETTING"

The Boylston School, erected on Fort Hill in 1819, with its spacious grassy schoolyard and trees, exemplified Bostonians' notions about the proper physical setting for a grammar school.

SOURCE: Brayley, *Schools and Schoolboys*, p. 90.

There, crammed together "like brutes, without regard to sex, or age, or sense of decency," investigators observed "grown men and women sleeping together in the same apartment, and sometimes wife and husband, brothers and sisters, in the same bed." Could there be any doubt, sympathetic Bostonians wondered, that "under such circumstances, self-respect, forethought, all high and noble virtues soon die out, and sullen indifference and despair, or disorder, intemperance and utter degradation reign supreme."[21] What was true of living conditions in the Fort Hill area was equally true of similarly squalid districts in the North End and West End.

As this portrait of the poor took shape in civic investigations and in the popular press, citizens began to notice a distinctively alien hue. Increasingly "the poor" and "foreign immigrants" became synonymous

Figure 12   "A PERFECT HIVE OF HUMAN BEINGS"
Burgess' Alley, built against the side of Fort Hill, was typical of the over-crowded, unsanitary, dilapidated housing occupied principally by foreigners. The sketch only suggests the narrow limits crammed by a booming immigrant population during the late 1840's.
SOURCE: *Report of a General Plan for the Promotion of Public and Personal Health . . . Relating to a Sanitary Survey of the State* (Boston: Dutton & Wentworth, 1850), p. 433, in Littauer Library; used by permission of Harvard University Libraries.

terms, used alike by those Bostonians who looked with compassion and those who viewed with contempt the growing numbers of indigents in their midst. Foreigners afforded the most visible examples of those dwelling in poverty. Their styles of dress, their culinary customs, their speech mannerisms (and, for some, their completely alien tongues), and their personal habits of behavior signaled their differences from the native poor. At the same time, their very distinctness made the immigrants appear to be the majority of the poor population of the city. The difficulties of converting the strangers into neighbors made the presence of poverty all the more unbearable. The mixed reactions of Boston's leading citizens toward the aliens during the period chronicled a growing awareness of poverty and a rising debate over the safety of the community. As public-spirited men who had gained the trust of their fellow citizens, the politicians, ministers, physicians, businessmen, and educators who manned the committees investigating poverty reflected the concern, faith, and hopes of the community. Concerned about the presence of the poor during the 1820's, public leaders became even more troubled in the 1830's. With the heavy influx of Irish immigrants in the 1840's, concern would give way to paranoia, faith to fear, hope to despair.

THE PERMANENCE OF URBAN POVERTY

The possible entrenchment of the native and immigrant poor as a permanent urban class did not bother many Bostonians during the 1820's. Mindful of Christ's dictum that "the poor always ye have with you," Bostonians were convinced that economic and social mobility opened the way for many of the city's poor to rise above poverty. Josiah Quincy, James Savage, and Henry J. Oliver, a lawyer and School Committee member, who in 1821 proposed a new public workhouse for the indigent, clearly displayed that faith. These men carefully distinguished those who were poor because of infancy, advanced age, or misfortune from those "who are degraded to the ranks of beggary, by vice, or idleness." Indigents orphaned in youth could be saved from a life of poverty through education and employment. Those who had suffered misfortune could be helped through charity until they were ready to provide for themselves. Even the "idle and vicious poor" might be reclaimed from poverty through a House of Industry. Such an institution, claimed its adherents, would save Boston money by confining all public nuisances to one location, and by ameliorating the condition and improving the morals of "that unhappy portion of the community." The proposed institution meant not punishment and disgrace but an opportunity for useful labor and moral uplift. Neither economically nor spiritually need the poor remain poor. Other citizens agreed; in 1822 the city opened its new House of Industry.[22]

In the years to come civic leaders continued to express faith in the openness of Boston's social ranks. In his inaugural address as mayor in 1830, Harrison Gray Otis noted of the city that "Many of those who are in its first ranks rose from humble beginnings." Mechanics, working men and the "middling class" enjoyed "more real equality and a more general acquaintance and intercourse among the different vocations than is elsewhere to be found in a populous city." Delivering the annual Fourth of July oration in 1838 the popular minister Hubbard Winslow reflected on the progress "in the scale of respectability and usefulness" made by the city's mechanics in recent years. Cautioning that these members of the lower classes still needed to be given a greater stake in society through home ownership or investments in banks, railroads, and manufactures, Winslow still congratulated his listeners on the opportunities they offered to the poor. Shortly thereafter, an editor of a Boston newspaper rejoiced that the profession of a mechanic was daily becoming more respectable. No longer could a man be reproached for being a "son of a mechanic."[23]

A Boston newspaper printed an account of a worker whose career was a model of the economic and social mobility that residents wanted to believe in. Although his case was exaggerated (and therefore newsworthy), it reflected the conditions of opportunity that Bostonians affirmed were open to all. This journeyman left home at the age of nine, become an apprentice at age thirteen, and began traveling shortly thereafter. He visited England, Ireland, Scotland, Wales, France, Canada, Nova Scotia, South America, the West Indies, and the entire Atlantic seaboard of the United States. At one time or another he served as a sailor, a soldier in the American army, a theological student for two years, a medical student for one year, and a temperance lecturer. As a journeyman printer he worked in New England, New York, New Jersey, Pennsylvania, and Virginia. In New Hampshire, Maine, and Massachusetts (Roxbury and Boston) at different times, he published his own newspaper. In the process he acquired a stake of $7,300 and two wives, not at the same time. When the article on his career appeared in the paper, the worker had not quite reached the age of twenty-six.[24]

With the spurt of growth in Boston's commercial and manufacturing enterprises during the 1840's, optimism for individual economic success remained high among the city's economic elite. Popular books like *The Rich Men of Massachusetts* (1851) listed numerous men who had started poor in life and had climbed the heights to wealth. Writing in *Hunt's Merchants' Magazine*, the leading business journal of the day, Elias H. Derby, a wealthy man himself, gave the secret to social and economic mobility in the community. "Here every artisan aspires to own his house," Derby commented, "and to leave a patrimony to his children. Having secured his dwelling (through great frugality), he buys a single share in a bank, railway, or factory, and gradually becomes a capitalist." Unfortunately for the dream, reality had a way of dispelling illusions. Those citizens who took the trouble to glance at the *Returns of the Overseers of the Poor in Massachusetts* noticed that the numbers of paupers on the state rolls increased yearly, and that Boston led the state. Local statisticians like Jesse Chickering labored under few illusions about the extent of mobility. In 1850 Chickering reported to the City Council that incoming foreigners had put a damper on the rate of mobility for natives and for themselves. "The increased competition for employment," he observed, "has diminished the facility for obtaining it, and reduced the compensation for labor." The following year Chickering warned that "of those who resort to cities to better their condition, but a very few succeed in obtaining wealth or other reputable distinction." Most, he concluded, "very soon sink down under the weight of care, labor and misfortune, and perish and are forgotten."[25]

If, by the 1850's, some citizens recognized that individual social mobility did not automatically result from urban economic progress, the discovery could not have been too shocking. Early spadework had revealed that behind the obvious expansion of population and commercial activity lurked the potential contraction of the poor into a permanent urban social class. Despite public rhetoric about an open and socially mobile city, astute observers suspected that all was not well. As early as the 1820's some Bostonians had begun to draw vague distinctions between "the poor" and "pauperism." In those distinctions lay their ultimate concern over the dangerous classes, the urban crisis, and the future of the city.

Josiah Quincy, mayor during most of the 1820's and nineteenth-century Boston's most vigorous leader, predicted that an inevitable result of the city's growth would be an increase in the number of those living in perpetual poverty. In two reports, issued in 1820 and 1821, Quincy noted differences between those he called the transient poor and paupers. The latter, he claimed, were addicted to intemperance and to a lasting dependence upon public and private charitable relief. Paupers somehow managed to remain poor in spite of opportunities for betterment. A major enterprise of the city, he urged, should be to prevent the temporary poor from falling into pauperism.[26]

Although Quincy's reports were illuminating, real enlightenment came through the efforts of a Unitarian clergyman, Joseph Tuckerman. Tuckerman had been born and raised in Boston, educated at the Boston Latin School, and graduated from Harvard. Although a minister, he cared little for theological doctrines; he preferred social action. In 1826 he left his pastorate at Chelsea, Massachusetts, to take a position tendered by William Ellery Channing and the American Unitarian Association as "Minister-at-Large" to the poor of Boston. During the ensuing decade his work and writings changed the attitudes of Bostonians and other Americans toward the urban poor.[27]

A disciple of the Scottish moral theologian and urban critic Thomas Chalmers, Tuckerman sharpened Chalmers' distinctions between the poor and the paupers. The poor were individuals in temporary need of adequate subsistence; paupers were permanent dependents upon the largesse of society. The poor required only a helping hand in times of strife, while the paupers—ignorant and debased as they were—expected and demanded permanent social welfare subsidies. Tuckerman knew that Boston contained both classes of the poor for "in all times cities have been the centers of the moral corruption of countries," and would so continue unless men found a scientific way to break the cycle of poverty.[28]

Following the leads of Josiah Quincy and investigators in other cities, Tuckerman sought to isolate the causes of urban poverty and pauperism; to classify scientifically the various poor of Boston; and to help those whom aid would uplift, while finding ways of rendering the dangerous poor less threatening.[29] Considering the scope of his ambition, it was not surprising that he succeeded, to his own satisfaction at least, in cataloging a rigid subdivision of the city's lower classes. Pauperism, or at least its chief cause, the minister found easy to explain and to solve. Intemperance, he declared, was the primary generator of pauperism and therefore of vice and crime as well. He must have been gratified that other reformers shared that interpretation.[30] In his hierarchy of the urban lower classes, Tuckerman located paupers and those facing pauperism at the bottom. He suggested that the able-bodied paupers be sent to workhouses to take them off the rolls of charity and to provide a useful work force for city projects. Manageable orphan children should be placed in male and female orphan asylums. "Vicious" children should be sent to reform schools. Rigorously enforced laws against intemperance should be passed. For those paupers or potential paupers that presently fitted none of his categories, the minister invoked the traditional Puritan doctrine of the stewardship of wealth. If the wealthier classes of the city would only carry out their God-given duty to improve the conditions and characters of the poor, he asserted, "an incalculable sum of vice and misery will be prevented."[31] Tuckerman found the causes of poverty somewhat harder to define. His investigations, however, drove him to one certain conclusion: Various circumstances in contemporary urban life had forged links in a chain of poverty that extended over generations.

In his analysis of the crisis indicators in city life Tuckerman labeled as villains the conditions of employment, the cost of living, a lack of moral leadership, and a growing sense of class consciousness. Certainly mechanical innovations in manufacturing had cost many laborers their jobs and driven them into the ranks of the temporary poor. For those who were employed, low wages and high rents were evident reasons for hardship. The failure of the city to provide moral and religious instruction contributed heavily to want and crime. The real causes of poverty, however, he identified as the "spirit of monopoly," the luxury and extravagance and "profligacy" of the "more favored classes," and the low estimation in which the more affluent held "the humbler of their fellow beings." The better classes of Boston society in the past had guaranteed the permanency of poverty by their refusal to recognize, as another contemporary put it, "how the other half lives." The result, as Tuckerman saw it and as he succeeded in bringing others to see, was that *the poor, therefore, have lived and to a great extent are living as a caste, cut off from those in more favored circumstances; and doomed to find their pleasures, and sympathy in their sufferings alone among themselves.*[32]

By the early 1830's Joseph Tuckerman and other perceptive Bostonians had become aware of what seemed to them to be a new social phenomenon. Twentieth-century social scientists would give the phenomenon a catchy name, and argue endlessly about the "culture of poverty" they had discovered.[33] Tuckerman and other social reformers did not use the term, nor did they measure its dimensions as "scientifically" as would later become fashionable. All the statistics they had to rely on were head-counts of individuals in correctional and rehabilitative institutions, numbers on the charity rolls, the figures of employment which they knew were often only guesses, and their own first-hand experiences of working with and walking among the poor. But terms are only handles attached to concepts, and there were striking similarities between the analyses of the poor made by Tuckerman and other nineteenth-century observers and the more elaborate investigations undertaken by twentieth-century social critics. Within their own intellectual frameworks, Tuckerman and others perceived a widening culture of urban poverty. Whatever the real facts and time might prove to the contrary, antebellum urban reformers believed that their generation was witnessing the formation and growth of a permanent class of poor in the cities.

In an expanding cash economy still largely dependent upon unskilled labor, both native and immigrant workers suffered from low wages, underemployment, and unemployment.[34] The poor were either ignored or else condemned by many in the city for personal immorality and for failing in a society which claimed opportunity for all. Except for a few ameliorative measures—the almshouse and the Houses of Industry and Correction, among others—Boston's leaders had failed to provide social, political, or economic organization for the poor. As Tuckerman, other charity workers, and members of the School Committee emphasized, the poor had become a permanent urban caste. They lived by their own values and standards of behavior rather than by those of the dominant middle and upper classes of Boston. The poor comprised a caste which promised to perpetuate itself over time as children trained in idleness, vagrancy, ignorance, and crime reached maturity. By 1849, Theodore Parker confirmed that the poor had become a permanent urban class which, despite all benevolent efforts, "will linger for some ages to come."[35]

The "permanent poor" that Bostonians had discovered were not necessarily always the same people over time. Between 1830 and 1860 the composition of Boston's poor population shifted dramatically. What some Bostonians did fear, and correctly so, was the probability of a lasting social class of poor people in the city, regardless of the transience of its individual members. No single group in Boston afforded more visible examples of that growing culture of poverty than foreign immigrants.

The stereotyped views of foreigners that filled the daily press and padded the sparse outlines of historical and geographical textbooks in the schools illustrated Bostonians' belief in the distinctiveness of the immigrants' culture. The Irish, in particular, were seen as "clannish," "deceitful," "licentious," "lazy," "riotous," and "hard-drinking." As early as 1835, before the mass tide of Irish immigration, at least one Boston newspaper confirmed the prevalence of the stereotypes by defending the Celtic strangers: "They are not the idle, sloth-loving, improvident, and intemperate people they are represented and too generally believed to be. They are as a class, industrious and hard-working. . . . There is an unkind, an unjustifiable prejudice, entertained by very many citizens, of which we are ashamed." Several years later a correspondent to Horace Mann's *Common School Journal* lamented that native citizens too often regarded the Irish as an inferior race. But, he suggested, they could be trained to take part in our institutions. The writer ventured that they "are as susceptible of intellectual and moral training as those [children] of any other people." Still, the stereotypes continued to capture the popular imagination, with even the conservative Irish press itself occasionally lending assent. To many Bostonians the Irish stereotype mirrored all immigrants, and immigrants were the dominant poor.[36]

The Commonwealth had long led the Union in legislating against incoming foreign paupers, yet their numbers seemed to increase almost daily. Some observers feared that their continuing arrival would affect not only the physical health but also the moral climate of the city. In 1833 the *American Annals of Education* printed a familiar complaint: "European immigration is not now, as formerly, from the best classes of the community. On the contrary, the government and individuals of foreign countries are employing our country as a convenient receptacle for the most ignorant, and too often the most vicious of their subjects and dependents." "No one doubts," continued the editor, "that most of these people come from an atmosphere of moral infection." Horace Mann later repeated that charge. "Everybody acknowledges the justness of the declaration," Mann wrote in his *Ninth Annual Report* (1845), "that a foreign people, born and bred and dwarfed under the despotisms of the Old World, cannot be transformed into full stature of American citizens, merely by a voyage across the Atlantic. . . . They remain unfitted, until they have become morally acclimated to our institutions."[37]

The political and social leaders of Boston, however, questioned whether the immigrants were becoming "morally acclimated" to American institutions quickly enough. By their measurement, to be an American meant to be at least a New Englander, and preferably, a Bostonian. Incoming strangers, to be fully accepted had to conform in all outward appearances to the Boston model of industriousness, political conservatism, and scrupulously moral behavior.[38] As early as 1820, John Quincy Adams had expressed succinctly what citizens of the "Hub of the Universe" expected of foreign immigrants:[39]

> They come to a life of independence, but to a life of labor— and, if they cannot accommodate themselves to the character, moral, political and physical, of this country with all its compensating balances of good and evil, the Atlantic is always open to them to return to the land of their fathers. To one thing they must make up their minds, or they will be disappointed in every expectation of happiness as Americans. They must cast off their European skin, never to resume it. They must look forward to their posterity rather than backward to their ancestors; they must be sure that whatever their own feelings may be, those of their children will cling to the prejudices of this country.

In later years, Bostonians remained firm in believing that foreigners had to be assimilated to American mores if the nation was to prosper. Occasionally, public spokesmen, like the popular minister Ezra S. Gannet, gave lip service to a notion of cultural pluralism, but never without reaffirming the primacy of American values. Speaking in 1840, Gannet commented on the stream of immigration: "We must expect an importation of the opinions and manners of the old countries. . . . All that we can do is, to form a national character *with the help of these influences.*" But he also qualified the nobility of sentiment by noting that "there is much in the opinions of the Old World, which is neither suited to our position, nor in harmony with truth; much in foreign manners, that is

condemned alike by sound principle and pure taste." "Alas for us!" he
concluded, "if the corrupt habits of older communities should be introduced into our young system. It would be like tainting the blood of
childhood, and so infusing the cause of subsequent debility and prema-
ture decay."[40]

Most skepticism about the ability of the immigrants to become morally
acclimated to the Puritan chill of Boston centered around three questions. First, what would be the effects of immigration on the political and
social structure of Boston? Second, could the ruling elite survive the possible challenges to power by the urban poor? Third, since most of the
incoming strangers came from religious backgrounds different from the
Puritanism of Boston, what potential threats did they present to Protestant orthodoxy—that "softened Puritanism," as Josiah Quincy, Jr., described it, with "so much of the old severity as remained [supporting]
the moral standards?"[41]

THE IMMIGRANT POOR AND COMMUNITY ORDER

Boston citizens had long feared that incoming aliens would topple the
experimental structure of republican government in America. A number
of Boston leaders in the 1820's and the 1830's had been active politically
in the early days of the Republic and kept alive their youthful antagonism toward foreigners. Shortly after state ratification of the national
Constitution, for example, Boston Federalists had urged that naturalized
citizens be kept from holding office for fear that foreigners might con-
taminate the purity of the national character. Boston's Harrison Gray Otis,
later a mayor of the city, declared that it was wrong "to invite hordes of
wild Irishmen, and the turbulent and disorderly of all parts of the
world, to come here with a view to distract our tranquility, after having
succeeded in the overthrow of their own governments." The support
given Thomas Jefferson throughout the East by urban lodges of United
Irishmen confirmed the Boston Federalists' fear of foreigners.[42]

The pathological suspicion of aliens burned unchanged through the
1820's. Subsequent political events added fresh cause for alarm. In 1828
and 1829 a grim winter of financial depression settled on Boston and
other cities. In the midst of national difficulties emerged a new hero—
Andrew Jackson—to rouse the hopes of some citizens. To the old Federalists and young Whigs of Boston, Jackson was a monster and his local
supporters irresponsible plotters. "Dreading all respectable competitors
in the expected distribution of offices," complained a contemporary of
Boston's Jacksonians, "they sought recruits only in the kennels and
gutters. Proclaiming Jackson an Irishman, they planted their flags in the

ménage of Broadstreet; and holding him up as the champion of the poor against the rich, they received, with 'hugs fraternal,' the tenants of poor-houses and penitentiaries." It was this fear of growing class consciousness and class warfare that haunted Boston's political leaders and educators, just as it troubled conservatives throughout New England and the nation.[43]

Public discussions about the potentiality of political and social class struggles between the poor and the rich in cities during the 1830's and 1840's revealed the extent of hostilities toward foreigners. Workingmen, educators, and reformers joined in bewailing the immigrant threat.

Native workingmen and their leaders saw increasing class divisions in urban society and, in part, held immigrants responsible.[44] The best-known and most influential labor spokesman in Boston—Seth Luther—was an itinerant carpenter and mill worker, self-educated, and, by contemporary standards, a radical social reformer. In 1832, in Boston, Luther delivered *An Address to the Workingmen of New England, on the State of Education, and on the Condition of the Producing Classes in Europe and America* that enjoyed wide distribution in the city and throughout New England. Discussing in lurid detail the abuses of the factory system—"a cruel system of exaction on the bodies and minds of the producing classes, destroying the energies of both"—Luther warned of the separation between the wealthy and the poor. "The *wives* and *daughters* of the rich manufacturers would no more associate with a '*factory girl*' than they would a *negro slave*. So much for equality in a republican country." The rich were fleecing the poor. They were cutting the wages of good American workers by importing cheap and degraded foreign labor. A social revolution was in the making.[45]

Responding to Luther's charges, the editor of the *American Annals of Education* spoke for conservative Bostonians in asserting that workers should not be pitied: they ate good food; they slept soundly; they pursued occupations that were favorable to their morals. Other writers in the *Annals* admitted that the working classes and the poor suffered from social inequalities. "And are we not preparing," questioned one author, "a new set of *white slaves* at the North, by our neglect of foreign emigrants, and native children, and by the too early and constant confinement of multitudes in our manufactories, who will be as ignorant and corrupt as those of a different color?" The only difference among northern and southern slaves, continued the writer, was that the working class and immigrant poor in the North "will have the power to be our masters." This class of people must somehow be taught to "look upon the distinctions of society without envy," or social revolution was probable.[46]

Horace Mann agreed with these prophecies of crisis. Society, he believed, faced the danger of continuous agitation and upheaval through entrenched divisions between the wealthy and the permanent poor. In republican America, Mann pointed out, popular opinion ruled through the political process. Either by controlling the ballot box or by violent rebellion, the self-interested immigrants and native poor could threaten the community. "He who has been a serf until the day before he is twenty-one years of age," Mann observed, "cannot be an independent citizen the day after; and it makes no difference whether he has been a serf in Austria or in America."[47]

Mann contended that both immigrants and the native poor remained serfs while living in urban slums. "In the byways and crowded streets of a city, where poverty casts its victims into heaps, and stows them away in cellars and garrets, . . . it often happens that the surface disease of coarse and untamed manners is aggravated and made virulent by moral distempers within," Mann noted in his *Tenth Annual Report* (1846). In urban society not even "the purest virtue can secure happiness," he wrote, "or an immunity from danger, to any class, while vice abounds in another. . . . The favored classes may think they occupy favored apartments in the ship but, if it does founder, the state will go down with the steerage."[48]

Other social leaders in Boston and the rest of the commonwealth shared this dread of cataclysm. Men as diverse in their political and social viewpoints as Josiah Quincy, William Ellery Channing, Edward Everett, Robert Rantoul, Theodore Parker, and Orestes Brownson all implied their belief in a separate culture of poverty among immigrants and native workers which threatened community order.

Quincy argued that a republic contained within itself the seeds of anarchy, despotism, and revolution, and that any one of these might result unless all children were taught to revere law and authority, to resist political demagogues, and to become responsible citizens. Channing hoped that society was not permanently and invidiously divided between the rich and the poor, but feared that "by their recklessness, their passionateness, their jealousies of the more prosperous and their subserviency to parties and political leaders," the poor and the working classes "may turn all their bright prospects into darkness, may blight the hopes which philanthropy now cherishes of a happier and holier social state." Everett stressed that free government could exist only on the basis of enlightened public opinion and that the working classes must be educated to keep them from acting viciously. Rantoul warned that without greater equality of condition and democratic education, class strife was inevitable. And, in separate addresses on the laboring population, both Theodore Parker and Orestes Brownson emphasized the dire plight of the permanently poor in Boston, and prophesized social chaos unless reme-dial measures were forthcoming.[49]

As subsequent events proved, there were few reasons to fear that the ignorant and vicious poorer classes might overwhelm the better sort at the polls. During the Jacksonian period "The Workingmen's Party" of Boston was an extremely weak political organization. Although party lines and votes shifted back and forth in the 1830's, Boston remained solidly Whig. Many of the candidates of the Workingmen's Party were Whigs and among the wealthiest men in the community. A political overturning of the ruling elite by the immigrant poor was hardly possi-ble. Few Irish or other immigrants were naturalized citizens with the right to vote. Even as late as 1845, less than one-sixth of the male adult foreigners were citizens. Not until the mid-1850's was there a significant increase in the number of naturalized voters.[50]

Nonetheless, many Bostonians remained fearful. Not reality itself, but imagined reality alarmed city leaders. The arrival of foreign strangers and their infusion with the poor and paupers of the city threatened the homogeneity of the population and therefore the safety of republican institutions—or, so many believed.

If possible class warfare, either by ballots or violent revolution, failed to undermine society, there remained yet another barrier to the moral acclimation of the immigrants. To Protestant Boston, steeped in a Puritan past, Roman Catholicism challenged every tenet of New England so-ciety. For in Boston, community order rested upon political, social, *and* religious orthodoxy.

Anti-Catholicism had been a tradition in New England since colonial days. A Boston festival day had been Pope Day, celebrated each No-vember 5, when rival lower-class groups from the North End and South End of the city had borne effigies of the Pope and the Devil through the streets, usually concluding the parades with a free-for-all. Although Pope Day celebrations were abandoned after the American Revolution, the hostile spirit pervading the celebrations was not. The first public debates in the nation over the possible evils of Catholicism occurred in Boston toward the close of the eighteenth century when the Reverend George Lesslie, a Protestant, and the Reverend John Thayer, Catholic mission-ary in the city, exchanged attacks in a series of newspaper articles. Al-though expressed antipathies toward Catholics tapered off during the early years of the nineteenth century, they flared anew following the War of 1812.[51]

After 1815, Evangelical Protestantism girded its loins for a fresh assault on the alleged immoralities of the day. Beginning in Boston in 1815 with the formation of the American Education Society to subsidize students for the ministry, Presbyterians and Congregationalists in several cities joined together in national societies dedicated to a rebirth of Protestant orthodoxy. In 1816, Congregationalists pioneered an evangelical weekly newspaper, the *Boston Recorder*. It was soon followed by the Baptist *Christian Watchman* (1819), the Unitarian *Christian Register* (1821), and the Methodist *Zion's Herald* (1823). While the Unitarians usually expressed tolerance toward Catholics, the newspapers of the other denominations launched attacks. Charges of "Popish intolerance," "idolatry of Popery," and "Romish deceptions" filled the pages of the weeklies. Orthodox ministers claimed that the Church of Rome had changed little from the Middle Ages when Popery enthralled the world in "ignorance, superstition, and delusion."[52]

The leader of anti-Catholic evangelicals was the Calvinist minister, Lyman Beecher. Fresh from religious triumphs in rural Connecticut, Beecher arrived in Boston in 1826 to war against Unitarians in their stronghold, but quickly discovered that Catholics posed an even greater threat to orthodoxy. From his Hanover Street church (called "Brimstone Corner" by contemporaries) he sparked a series of revivals during which he vigorously attacked the Catholic Church, affirming that Romanism and despotism went hand in hand and that both would destroy American republicanism. Other spokesmen for orthodoxy concurred. "Let Roman Catholicism march forward with the same rapid strides in our beloved country, as it has lately," editorialized the *Boston Recorder* in 1829, "and soon may we expect the establishment of the Inquisition and all its accompanying horrors."[53]

The rising tide of immigration brought many new Catholics, mostly Irish, into the city. Between 1820 and 1824 a marked increase of Catholic population occurred; from 1825 to 1828, a steady, moderate growth; and in 1829, a large influx.[54] In 1835, Bishop Benedict Fenwick, head of the diocese, could observe that "the faith is constantly spreading, and its progress has been so rapid, especially in the city of Boston, that all who have witnessed it are astonished." Ten years ago, noted the bishop, there were scarcely 10,000 Catholics in the city, now there were at least 20,000. Since the foreign population of Boston in 1835 was almost 16,000 out of a total population of 78,603, foreign immigration clearly accounted for the sudden rise in the number of Catholics. Within the next ten years, the Catholic Church became the largest single religious body in Boston, with adherents numbering over one fourth of the total city population.[55]

The most thorough and hysterical indictment of Roman Catholicism came from Samuel Finley Breese Morse, artist, inventor, and son of the Catholic-baiting, Calvinist minister of the heyday of Massachusetts Federalism, Jedidiah Morse. Of the ignorant immigrants daily flocking to our shores, Samuel F. B. Morse wrote in 1835, two-thirds were Catholic, and the Irish were the worst. European despots were forcing America to take the dregs of their societies, to support them, to keep their criminals, and to put up with "the expatriated turbulence of their cities." If these creatures, Morse affirmed, would renounce their native countries and adopt America, then the nation might ride out the storm of foreign, Popish ignorance sweeping its shores. But the immigrants would not, could not Americanize themselves while remaining slaves to religious despotism. "If we mean to keep our country, this life-boat of the world from floundering with all the crew," warned Morse, "we must take on board no more from the European wreck until we have safely landed and sheltered its present freight."

Morse charged that immigrants inevitably added to the class of permanent poor in the cities. They increased crime. Under Jesuit leaders they clanned together and intolerably demanded equal rights with Americans. Perhaps not all immigrants were of equal blame, Morse admitted, but "we must of necessity suspect them all." He little doubted that immigration would shatter the foundations of society in republican America. "It is impossible in the nature of things," he claimed, "that the moral character, and condition of this population, and its immense and alarming increase within a few years, should not have produced a counteracting effect on the benevolent operations of the day. . . . Can one throw mud into pure water and not disturb its clearness?" Foreign immigration would dilute the national character and upset the social stability of American cities. Boston's evangelical newspapers approved and widely reprinted Morse's allegations and rantings.[56]

The resurgence of religious orthodoxy and increase in the number of Catholic foreigners aggravated hostilities toward the immigrant poor in Boston and other cities throughout the commonwealth. A romantic visionary like Ralph Waldo Emerson might call for "a sermon on Blessed Poverty. Who have done all the good in the world? Poor men. 'Poverty is a good hated by all men.' " But most of those who wrote sermons and delivered addresses on the subject usually agreed with the sentiments expressed by Emory Washburn, lawyer, reformer, and one-time governor of Massachusetts. In 1848, speaking primarily of Boston, but also including other cities in the state, Washburn complained about the metropolis "gathering within its crowded masses those poisonous seeds of vice, which by some strange law of our nature, germinate most surely where men do most congregate; with hosts of foreigners crowding to our shores, and bringing with them the habits and associations of foreign lands; with intemperance, that great mother of poverty and vice, and crime, spreading out her lures on every side."[57] Urban society was a hotbed of permanent and vicious poverty that threatened the safety of citizens and the stability of social institutions.

THE IMMIGRANT POOR AND URBAN DISORDER

Between 1820 and 1860 Bostonians increasingly protested about criminal activity in the city. Almost any behavior which disturbed the peace or threatened the comfort of the respectable classes came under the heading of "crime" and often led to arrest. Behavior most commonly considered criminal included such offenses as drunkenness, beggary, vagabondage, "lewd" behavior, assault and battery. Prostitution, especially in the North End where many new migrants settled, increased as New England farm girls and, later, immigrant women moved into the city. Swearing, gambling, and violation of the Lord's Day brought the guilty before local courts. A host of misdemeanors including breaking glass, selling lottery tickets, extinguishing street lamps, keeping noisy houses, peddling without a license, and an occasional case of a woman dressing in men's clothing branded the perpetrators as criminals.[58]

Imprisonment for debt declined somewhat during the period as citizens recognized that jailing one man for a trifling sum might put those dependent on him onto the charity rolls. From 1820 to 1822 the city imprisoned some 3,500 people for debts; 2,000 of those were confined for owing less than $20. As a result, estimates indicated that an additional 10,000 people became charity recipients. With legislative redefinitions of "debt," the number imprisoned between 1835 and 1845 averaged approximately 470 individuals a year, still a fairly high figure.[59]

Considering the growth of population, the rate of homicides remained quite low. Some murders may have gone unreported; Boston recorded only thirty homicides between 1810 and 1850. The incidence of another capital crime, burglary, was low during the 1820's but rose during the 1830's and 1840's. While it was often difficult to distinguish accidental from deliberately ignited fires in a city whose buildings were constructed primarily of wood, arson appeared to be on the upswing during the period. There was relatively little professional crime by organized gangs.[60]

Yet, Bostonians feared that criminal activity threatened social safety more and more. Newspapers of the 1830's fostered concern as they devoted larger coverage to crime and the courtrooms. By the late 1830's Mayor Samuel Eliot expressed the fears of many of his fellow citizens when he charged that "the incendiary, burglar, and the lawlessly violent [were] increasing at a ratio faster than that of the population." Even the popular literature of the day reflected the belief that Boston and other cities were becoming breeding grounds of crime and that poverty and pauperism were the seedbeds of criminal activity. Whether the poor were actually "morally vicious," or turned to crime out of financial necessity, contemporaries viewed the increase in pauperism as a portent of an increase in crime.[61]

The "facts" of urban pauperism and poverty catalogued in numerous public and private reports reiterated the central position immigrants occupied among the poorer classes. The highest rates of unemployment and dependence on public aid seemed to be among the foreigners. They increasingly filled the almshouses, the Houses of Industry and Correction, and other local public institutions.[62] As immigration figures rose, so did the numbers on the pauper rolls and charitable relief. In 1830 Boston spent slightly over $37,000 for poor relief; in 1840, over $43,000; in 1848, over $52,000; in 1850, almost $80,000; in 1855, over $117,000; and in 1860, over $168,000. And, each year, the number of foreigners receiving relief mounted proportionately. In 1845, for example, the total number of applicants for aid from the Society for the Prevention of Pauperism was 4,531; foreigners accounted for 4,075 of the petitioners, Americans only 456. Boston mayors complained that immigrants, especially the Irish, were draining the public treasury. Moreover, whether in or out of pauper institutions, diseases like tuberculosis and cholera ran rampant among the immigrant classes. Some Bostonians, like Americans in other cities, were disposed to place the entire blame for epidemics on foreigners.[63]

As the pauper rolls increased and relief costs soared, crime appeared to increase as well. By the 1850's the Society for the Prevention of Pauperism could lament that "a vast influx of foreign pauperism, ready made and hatched abroad, combined of the worst and most intractable elements constituting such a social past . . . has been thrown upon us; and difficulties and embarrassments unknown to men of an earlier day . . . have multiplied apace." Even as benevolent a soul as Theodore Parker, who saw an intimate connection between poverty and crime, bemoaned that "we have not only our own native criminal class to deal with, but a great army of foreigners, many of whom are the off-scouring from the streets of a civilization filthier than ours." "The number of foreigners in Boston," Parker continued, "is quite large. . . . You trace this foreign stream in the annals of poverty and crime . . . Out of the 17,500 persons arrested by the Boston police last year [1856] 13,500 were foreigners!"[64]

Statistics of arrest and imprisonment attested the relationship between poverty, immigration, and crime. There had long been general agreement among city leaders that intemperance underlay almost all poverty and crime, so it was not surprising that a major index of criminal activity was drunkenness. Under codification of state law in 1835 the "crime of drunkenness by the voluntary use of intoxicating liquor" became a punishable moral offense. Of that crime the Irish were the most visibly guilty. Whether from homesickness, fatigue, or love of the drop, the Irish rejoiced, as one wrote home to his father, that "if he was here he could soon kill himself by drinking if he thought proper. . . . I can go into a store, and have as much brandy as I like to drink for three half-pence, and all other spirits in proportion." A certain area of the city, filled with groggeries and taverns, was known to local residents as "Dublin Row." By 1850 there were 1,500 stores in Boston that sold liquor; of these, Irishmen operated 900.[65]

Arrests for drunkenness more than doubled during the 1850's. For over twenty years the largest number of those arraigned for intemperance had been the immigrant poor, and during the 1850's the percentage of Irish arrested rose even higher than before. Boston newspapers, Catholic and Protestant, criticized intemperance among the Irish with one editor pointing out nonetheless that a poor Irishman was more likely to be arrested for drunkenness than was a poor or middle-class native, simply because of the foreigners' reputation for tippling. Aside from this offense, and except for prostitution, the police seldom arrested the Irish. Still, intemperance alone was enough to confirm the stereotyped image held by many Bostonians of the criminal strangers in the city.[66] Particularly troublesome was the fact that "drunken" and "mob" seemed to be inextricably linked terms. And of all the dangers of urban life, Bostonians feared the mob and mob riots most.

A certain amount of brawling and inter-group hostility was endemic to nineteenth-century cities.[67] Competition for employment, drunken arguments among lower-class riffraff, battling for loot following one of the many fires that continually broke out in narrow lanes and crowded alleys —all had been occasions for street fighting.[68] With a heterogeneous population competing daily for living space in the more congested city, such outbreaks of hostilities appeared inevitable. But public tolerance for fist fights among the lower classes and for looting battles between rival volunteer fire brigades began breaking down in the 1820's when the number of strangers entering the city had increased markedly.

Group conflicts involving native Bostonians and immigrants, Protestants versus Catholics, and whites versus Blacks, intensified. In 1823 the first serious Boston riot between natives and the Irish occurred when native citizens attacked the homes of the Irish population in Ann Street, destroying a considerable amount of property. Three years later un-

named individuals leveled several houses on "Nigger Hill." That same
year, in the heat of July, three days of rioting ensued when a labor controversy erupted into open war, sending throngs of natives through the
Irish districts of Broad, Merrimac, and Ann Streets. Old World hostilities
transferred to America also contributed to riots. In 1829, for example,
South Boston watched the English and Irish Protestants fight the Irish
Catholics for two days. In the same year white sailors attacked Negroes
in Ann Street, and native Protestants, enfevered by a revivalist preacher,
attacked and stoned Irish Catholics' homes in the city. By 1830, Boston
citizens realized that clashes between natives and strangers over racial
and religious issues would be a recurrent threat to civil order.[69]

Religious and nativist antipathies scaled new heights during the
1830's. In August 1834 anti-Catholic feelings brought on the first burn-
ing of a convent in the United States when the Ursuline convent at
Mount Benedict in Charlestown fell in ruins at the hands of a Boston mob.
More than a thousand men roamed the streets, eager to battle a band of
Irish laborers rumored to be descending on the city. Although well-
intentioned civic leaders tried to atone for the outrage through disclaim-
ers and charity, a well-spring of anti-Catholic and anti-immigrant feeling
remained.[70] In 1837, the most severe riot in antebellum Boston occurred.

On June 11, 1837, on a hot Sunday afternoon, Boston firemen returning from a blaze in Roxbury collided with an Irish funeral procession
in East Street in the heart of an Irish district. A fight started. Before its
conclusion, nearly all of the engine companies in the city had joined the
struggle as had most of the residents of the East Street and Broad
Street areas. Following a two-hour battle, the firemen had carried the
day, and joined by other citizens, had turned from pitched street fighting
to raiding and destroying Irish homes in the vicinity, robbing women
and children, and beating whatever men they could lay hands on.[71]

From his study not far away, Horace Mann heard the sounds of mar-
tial music in the streets. Jotting in his diary, Mann observed of the riot
that "it will, of course, be the subject of judicial investigation: but, I
have fears, that antipathies will pursue the foreigners, that sympathies
will protect the natives, and that justice will be administered with an
unequal hand." No one could know public opinion, Mann ventured, without "painful forbodings in regard to the future." If men of wealth, character, and influence had not openly encouraged nativist violence, they
had done nothing to discourage it. A reverence for law had not been
inculcated among either natives or foreigners. The spirit of insubordination had not been condemned. Hostilities were such that "an occasion
was only waiting for thoughts to become actions, for ideas to find arms,
for the impulse to take the weapon." Two days later Mann confided in

his diary that a meeting of citizens at the office of the Visitors of the Poor had confirmed that personal losses from the riot totaled about $3,000. "It all, I believe, falls upon the Irish. Many families are utterly despoiled. Very few, if any of them had any agency or concern with the riot. From all I can learn, I believe that Americans had about all the guilt and the Irish will suffer all the punishment."[72]

Horace Mann knew well the sentiments of his fellow citizens. Authorities immediately arrested thirty-four Irishmen, several of them seriously injured, and no natives. Eventually, officials did arrest eight Americans, finally indicting four of them along with fourteen Irishmen. Of those who appeared at the trial, the jury convicted three Irish but no native residents. Concluding that in a city and nation with high wages and a shortage of labor there was little cause for anti-immigrant feelings, the city's official report of the Broad Street Riot condemned the Irish for "retaining their national ways," and for not becoming quickly enough like native Americans in their social outlook and behavior.[73]

In coming years sporadic rioting between natives and immigrants continued, with Bostonians usually laying the blame on the immigrants. "Who are the political, street canal and railroad rioters?" questioned one newspaper editor. "Foreigners! Men always ready and prepared to enter into any fray, whose object may be to resist the authorities."[74]

While rioting impressed Boston leaders as the single most dangerous element of criminal activity in the city, they were equally dismayed by what they saw as the entire picture. They believed the rate of crime was rising to near crisis levels. They may have been wrong. It is possible that between 1830 and 1860 more arrests were made, especially of newly arrived immigrants, for offenses that in the quieter, smaller city of the 1820's would have gone unprosecuted. Social pressure and an occasional "example" made of drunkards, idlers, and prostitutes sufficed in the more compact and homogeneous city, while by the 1840's rigorous enforcement of law appeared more vital to urban order in a growing and increasingly heterogeneous city. Crime rates themselves may not have risen as sharply as did public awareness of the potential dangers of drunkenness, prostitution, and petty theft in a city where the older bonds of social control by the "better sort" no longer had strength. The impact of a large minority group whose habits of behavior looked completely unlike those of native Americans may have exaggerated the actual incidence of crime in the city.

But, as is often the case, the gap separating social reality and men's fears of crisis was shrouded by half-truths and anxieties over the unfamiliar. Few could pierce that veil to see the truth within. So, many apparently agreed with a Fourth of July orator in the 1850's who questioned:

"Have we not a right to protect ourselves against the ravenous dregs of anarchy and crime, the tainted swarms of pauperism and vice Europe shakes on our shores from her diseased robes?"[75] Rioting, disease, crime —these were the indictments leveled daily against the immigrant poor. And the most damning charge of all was that the poor threatened not just the city's present, but also its future. While many Bostonians worried over what they saw as a rising rate of adult crime, other men, with an eye to the future, worried about juvenile delinquency.

A CHILD'S GARDEN OF VICES

At a time when journalists, novelists, physicians, ministers, and educators were newly discovering the child—when as Ralph Waldo Emerson observed: "children had been repressed, and kept in the background; now they were considered, cosseted and pampered"—it was likely that men would focus attention on the children of poverty.[76] When they did, they saw tender reeds maturing into hardened criminals who one day would overrun the city as a garden is overtaken by weeds. And they were certain that however much of the fault lay within poor children themselves, nourishment toward a life of crime came principally from the city itself.

The old Puritan concept of innate depravity had given way to an environmental approach to human ills and evils. Whether discussing the insane, the infirm, or the criminal, practitioners of medicine and moral science (psychology) stressed that physical environment had a nearly determinative effect on human behavior. Reformers and educators implied that children began life essentially equal in their innate potential for good or evil. The environment in which they lived either encouraged moral behavior or brought forth immoral actions. "Why is it that so many children in a large city grow up in ignorance and vice?" asked William Ellery Channing. "Because that city abandons them to ruinous influences, from which it might and ought to rescue them." In the spirit of inverted Calvinism characteristic of Unitarianism Channing queried: "is it not an acknowledged moral truth, that we are answerable for all evil which we are able, but have failed, to prevent?"[77]

Environmentalists drew few careful distinctions among "pauperism," "poverty," and "crime." The three terms were interchangeable in relation to anti-social behavior. A tacit understanding existed among numerous social critics that children born and raised in an atmosphere of pauperism or poverty would most likely become criminals. A perceptive analysis of the problem of urban crime and juvenile delinquency came from Boston's contentious minister, Theodore Parker.

In an 1847 sermon entitled "The Dangerous Classes," Parker stated that individuals passed through distinct stages of growth and development—babies, children, youth, adulthood. Each new child, he claimed, "is born at the foot of the ladder, . . . with only desires and faculties." But this common start in life did not necessarily mean that all men were equal. Parker affirmed there were inferior peoples in the world: "some are inferior in nature, some perhaps only behind us in development; on a lower form in the great school of Providence—negroes, Indians, Mexicans, Irish, and the like." Nevertheless, "the same human nature is in us all, only there it is not so highly developed." As with races, so with individuals. While some men leaned toward evil by heredity, many others formed "a dangerous class" in society through no fault of their own. "There are the foes of society," Parker claimed, "men that are criminals in soul, born criminals, who have a bad nature." But also "there are the victims of society; men that become criminals by circumstances, made criminals, not born."

The minister hesitated to adopt a wholly environmental interpretation, "but all experience shows that circumstances, such as exposure in youth to good men or bad men, education, intellectual, moral, and religious, or neglect thereof, . . . have a vast influence in forming the character of men, especially of men not well endowed by nature." Those who became criminals, Parker continued, were men born of tenement life, sent into the streets early to earn their own way, and subjected to the vices of the city. "In the corruption of a city, in the midst of its intenser life, what wonder that they associate with crime." Add to that the fact that many of the poor were foreign immigrants not bred in the moral atmosphere of Christian America, and one could understand why most of the inmates of the House of Correction were aliens. Parker was sure that "the destruction of the poor is their poverty," and that poverty bred juvenile delinquency.[78]

Theodore Parker was not alone in his concern about juvenile delinquency, nor in his analysis of how the youthful poor became the criminal poor. For many years Boston had tried to protect itself and at the same time to reform young offenders of the law. As early as 1814 private citizens had founded the Boston Asylum for Indigent Boys which, though not strictly intended to reform boys convicted of crimes, still sought to prevent the youthful poor from becoming a criminal class. In following the example of New York City in investigating juvenile delinquency and establishing a Society for the Prevention of Pauperism, Boston, spurred by the leadership of Josiah Quincy and Joseph Tuckerman, had built the House of Reformation for Juvenile Offenders.[79]

The House of Reformation operated under the provisions of a statute in 1788—the "Vagabond Act"—and a statute of 1826—"An Act concerning Juvenile Offenders in the City of Boston." Its founders took as their models Houses of Refuge established in New York City in 1825 and Philadelphia in 1827. Stubborn servants or children, orphans without visible means of support, youthful idlers in the streets, pilferers, va-

TABLE 11

DAILY SCHEDULE FOR CHILDREN
IN HOUSE OF REFORMATION, 1838

Time	Activity—Monday through Saturday
A.M.	
4:30	Rising (May, June, July, August)
5:00	" (March, April, September, October)
6:00	" (January, February, November, December)
	From rising to breakfast there were 5 to 8 minutes of private devotions, assembly for scripture reading and prayer by chaplain, washing-up, cleaning of house, and recreation
7:00	Breakfast
7:30	School classes begin, continue to 9:30
9:30	Work shop, continuing to 12:30
P.M.	
12:30	Play, wash-up
1:00	Dinner
1:30	Work shop, continuing to 4:30
4:30	Exercise, wash-up
5:00	Supper
5:30	School classes, continue to 7:30
7:30	Discipline for misconduct during day (if any), scripture reading, hymn singing, 5 to 8 minutes for private devotions
8:00	To bed

Activity—Sunday

Entire day devoted to morning and afternoon chapel, Sunday School classes, and training in church music

On Christmas, Thanksgiving, and July 4 the schedule was abandoned, better food given, and children allowed to indulge in "innocent and agreeable recreations."

SOURCE: "House of Reformation," *Boston City Documents, 1838* (Boston: City Printer, 1838), Doc. No. 8, pp. 7-9.

grants, and children who could not or would not attend public schools —these were the juvenile offenders of the city. Directors of the House of Reformation unabashedly stated that the purposes of the institution were to remove "a moral pest from the community" and to reform the morals of the inmates. Under the law, females could be confined until the age of eighteen, males until twenty-one. To effect reformation, the directors followed a program of elementary instruction in reading, writing, and arithmetic, based on the plan of the common schools. They subjected the children to a daily regimen that would have exhausted a Spartan (see Table 11). The directors also offered limited manual training in crafts that would prove useful when boys and girls were contracted to tradesmen and merchants of the city.

This practice was common in the early 1830's. While "binding-out" children provided a source of cheap labor for local businessmen, supporters of the practice alleged benefits for the children's morals. A City Council Committee called for even more instruction in the "mechanic arts," inferring that such training would better adjust children to living in the city. The Committee argued that "boys might cultivate regular habits of industry, acquire a certain degree of manual dexterity, contribute more effectually to their own support, better prepare themselves for their future occupations, and thus lay the foundation of a more lasting reformation."

As its records demonstrated, the House of Reformation gathered together under one roof a motley collection of lower-class children:

> *Boy, 7 yrs. Vagrant*
> Admitted, April, 1827. Indented, Dec., 1829.
> Mother in House of Correction

> *Girl, 13 yrs. Wanton*
> No hopes entertained of this case from the beginning—no reformation.

> *Boy, 11 yrs. Pilferer*
> Admitted, March, 1831. Indented, May, 1832.
> No accounts—belonged to a gang of boys—family vicious.

> *Girl, 14 yrs. Dissolute*
> Admitted, July, 1828. Indented, Oct., 1828.
> Letter, April, 1832, she had absconded, taking more clothes than her own. Mother notoriously profligate. House one of ill fame.

> *Girl, 12 yrs. Idle and Dissolute*
> Admitted, May, 1831. Indented, Oct., 1831.
> The two last are sisters, their father dead, mother abandoned woman, in the House of Correction, and the children were of course vagrant.

Boy, 10 yrs. Disobedient
Admitted, July, 1829. Indented, Nov., 1830.
The parents of this boy are vicious and neglected him.

Boy, 15 yrs. Disobedient
Admitted, May, 1828. Indented, Jan., 1832.
Letter, Jan., 1832, states his conduct to be pretty regular, but refuses to attend the School of the district.

His previous character had been very bad—he was habitually intemperate, surly, and malignant—"the nuisance of Fort Hill."

And, perhaps most poignant of all:

Boy, 17 yrs. Vagrant
Admitted, April, 1827. Indented, May, 1829.
Died Aug. 1830—nothing remarkable about him—simple—no letters.

Children could be incarcerated in the House of Reformation on the best—and the flimsiest—of evidence. On application of the mayor, an alderman, any director of the House of Industry or the House of Reformation, or any Overseer of the Poor, any part-time Police Court judge had the power of sentence. In addition, teachers who could not control children, parents who did not wish to provide room and board, even strangers who discovered young idlers in the streets, could denounce children as vagrants and see them committed.[80]

Over the years Bostonians were diligent about committing children to the House of Reformation (see Tables 12 and 13). To be fair to the City Fathers and troubled citizens, one must admit that in many cases to send a child to the House was probably an act of benevolence. The child who might otherwise never learn the rudiments of reading and writing, nor have any chance to learn a skill might benefit from his time within the walls. More often than not, however, the scanty records present a picture of capriciousness in committing children for the vaguest of offenses. Running beneath the surface of the inspectors' and directors' reports was an indelible strain of nativist hostility. Given the deplorable conditions of poverty in the city, directors found it hardly surprising "that pauperism and crime increase, and that charitable and penal institutions are tenanted." Nor did they find surprising the fact that problems were compounded by population growth, "much of it coming direct from the dregs of pauperized European society." One almost has the feeling that children of foreign parents were often committed to the House primarily because they were immigrant children. Take the case of John Robinson, his wife Ann, and their fourteen-year-old son Edward, "plus another unnamed younger child." The couple had arrived from Halifax and had taken up residence on Ann Street in the heart of an Irish district. Fre-

TABLE 12

CHILDREN IN THE BOSTON HOUSE OF REFORMATION, 1826-1847[a]

Inmates	Total Committed	Total Discharged	Total Apprenticed	Total Died	Total Escaped	Total No. of Boys	Total No. of Girls
	981	314	539	11	51	843	138

Place of Birth[b]	Boston	Other Towns in Mass.	Elsewhere in New Eng.	South and West	British Dominions	Other Foreign Countries	Unknown
	431	127	80	46	223	38	37

Types of Sentencing[b]	Larceny, Theft and Petty Pilfering	Stubbornness and Disobedience	Vagrancy	Living an Idle and Dissolute Life	Other Offences[c]
	429	246	193	67	42

[a] Children were usually defined as between the ages of 0-15.

[b] The totals, which vary slightly from the total number of children committed during the period, probably reflect errors in the directors' bookkeeping.

[c] Other offences varied over the period and included: "common drunkard"; "passing counterfeit coins"; "arson"; "attempt to commit arson"; "cheating by false pretences"; "attempts at breaking in offices, stores, etc."; and "assault and stabbing." In no given year were there more than 1-3 commitments for the individual offence.

SOURCES: Derived from "Annual Report of the Directors of the Houses of Industry and Reformation," *Boston City Documents, 1848* (Boston: City Printer, 1848), Doc. No. 17, p. 20, and individual reports over the period.

quent cries of "murder" and disturbances had been reported coming from their rooms. A constable who investigated a complaint found the woman on the floor, unable to get up, with a young child beside her, "the man very drunk, and the boy very little better off." There was no bed in the room, and the only items of personal use were a teakettle and a mug. The father had pawned his son's jacket for "ninepence to get rum." The father and mother were sent to the House of Correction, Edward to the House of Reformation, and the young child, reported the newspaper, "will probably be carried to the House of Industry."[81] The point was clear: no real crime had been committed; certainly Edward had done nothing more than be unwise in his choice of parents. For that unalterable indiscretion he was taken from his parents and sent away to be "reformed." A spirit of benevolence and a fear for public safety demanded no less.

Yet, despite such charitable efforts, the rate of juvenile delinquency mounted steadily. With the influx of immigrant poor in the early 1840's Bostonians saw additional cause for alarm over both the incidence and nature of youthful crime. "During the year 1845," Judge S. D. Parker stated before a state legislative committee, "there has been a great and alarming increase of juvenile offenders, and the crimes these youths have committed were of a very aggravated nature, including arson, stabbing, shopbreaking, larcenies, etc." There was little doubt that responsibility for increased delinquency could be laid to the incoming strangers. "Our foreign population furnishes altogether, the largest proportion of children, left to the moral infection of the streets," commented lawyer and schoolman Edward G. Loring in 1847, "and those children, furnish five-sevenths of our juvenile convicts." Other educators, and writers in children's magazines made the same charge.[82]

Under the hardships of urban poverty children turned to crime. "They are the hawkers of papers, or sellers of matches," explained School Committeeman George B. Emerson in 1847, "most of the time occupied in quarreling and gambling. They are beggars, male and female, strolling from street to street, through lanes, byways and alleys, practicing the elementary lessons of pilfering, lying, deception and theft." "They are the loafers on wharves and in stables," he continued, "spending their time in idleness, profanity, and in all the modes of juvenile vice. Are these children in the way to become useful citizens or happy and respectable men? Are they not growing up to be the occupants of jails and almshouses? Are they not in a course of education for worthlessness and crime?"[83]

The statistics of juvenile delinquency in the city offered by Chief Marshall Francis Tukey in 1850 seemed to confirm the worst fears that

TABLE 13

SENTENCES OF CHILDREN IN THE
HOUSE OF REFORMATION, 1846-1850[a]

Year[b]	Larceny, Theft, and Petty Pilfering	Stubborn and Dis-obedient	Vagrant	Living an Idle and Dissolute Life	Other Offences[c]	Total
1846	50	32	3	13	6	104
1847	63	29		17	11	120
1848	80	27	1	18	8	134
1849	53	10	1	19	8	91
1850	73	16	1	29	16	135
TOTAL	319	114	6	96	49	584

[a] "Children" were usually defined as between ages 0 to 15. From 1850, a number of children who previously would have been incarcerated in the Boston House of Reformation were sent instead to the new State Reform School at Westborough.

[b] The year reported ran from March 31 of the previous year to March 31 of the year in which the report was issued; thus "1846" actually means March 31, 1845, to March 31, 1846.

[c] "Other Offences" included: "Common drunkard"; "passing counterfeit coins"; "arson"; "attempt to commit arson"; "cheating by false pretences"; "attempts at breaking into offices, stores, etc."; "assault and stabbing." In no given year were there more than 1-3 children committed for any one of these offences.

SOURCE: Derived from, "Annual Report of the Directors of the Houses of Industry and Reformation," *Boston City Documents, 1846-1851* (Boston: City Printer, 1846-51).

the children of the poor constituted a real "menace to community safety." Increases in the numbers of youthful offenders in the state reform school also showed that the children from the class of the permanent poor tended to form a lasting criminal class. Of 440 boys committed during 1850-51, 172 boys had been arrested previously, and 116 had been in prison or reform school before. In contemporary thought, juvenile delinquency and adult crime clearly signaled the existence of a "dangerous class" in urban society, a class largely composed of the immigrant poor.[84]

Among several alternative methods of dealing with the "dangerous class," social, political, and intellectual leaders of the city tended to endorse three solutions. One obvious answer to the problem of urban poverty and crime was to escape the city. Native residents, both the wealthy and the workingmen, who felt oppressed and endangered by the immigrant presence could flee Boston proper. By the late 1840's census takers recorded that

many whole streets have been abandoned by the American residents, and are now occupied exclusively by foreigners, mostly
Irish. . . . Many merchants and others doing business in the
City, have of late been induced to remove to the neighboring
towns whence they can go to the places of their employment as
quickly and as cheaply as if they had continued in their former
residences. . . . With the increase of foreign mechanics, the
encouragements have become less to the American mechanics
who have consequently gone elsewhere.[85]

For those who remained in the city, the solution was to remove the
poor themselves. Some reformers urged that the social threat posed by
the poor might be alleviated and the victims of poverty redeemed by
separating them from the temptations of the city and exposing them to
the morally healthy environment of the countryside. Children especially
might be saved in this manner. To that end Joseph Tuckerman, George
Ticknor, Judge Charles Jackson, and educator W. C. Woodbridge, among
others, had met in 1832 to establish a farm school "in the country,
where the idle and morally exposed children of the city may be rescued
from vice and danger." This school "would be not only a great benefit to
such children, but would greatly conduce to the peace and good order
of this community." The farm school began operations in 1833; united
with another institution in 1835 under the name of the Boston Asylum
and Farm School for Indigent Boys; paved the way for the later state
reform school at Westborough; and received the whole-hearted approval
of Boston's leaders.[86]

Taking the poor from the city to the country, however, was only a
superficial answer to the problem. With a growing class of permanent
poor, other remedies had to be employed. A third way to cure the ills
of urban poverty had been to measure out large doses of charitable
relief. Public and private, Protestant and Catholic, piecemeal attacks on
poverty came from such diverse groups as the Boston Dispensary (1801)
for medical relief; the Boston Female Asylum (1803) for orphaned girls;
the Charitable Irish Society (1809); the British Charitable Society
(1818); the City Missionary Society (1820) for the moral and religious
instruction of the poor; the Society for Employing the Female Poor
(1821); the Boston Children's Friend Society (1834); the Association
of Delegates from the Benevolent Societies of Boston (1834) to provide city-wide investigation of poverty and pooling of resources; the
Boston Society for the Prevention of Pauperism (1835, incorporated
1847), to investigate the causes and extent of pauperism; and the Benevolent Fraternity of Churches (1835).[87] These and other charitable
organizations hoped to relieve the distress and suffering of the poor
while also protecting society through identifying, confining, and con-

trolling those paupers and victims of poverty whose vice and immorality seemed so potentially dangerous.[88]

But some citizens remained unconvinced that charitable relief alone would dispel threats to social stability. Catholics often refused to cooperate with Protestant-run charities complaining, as did the Vicar General in 1847, that "God knows how many of these poor children are taken to Protestant asylums where they lose all remembrance of their religion." That attitude prompted responses such as Theodore Parker's in 1850. "Anglo-Saxon," Negro, and German pauperism in the city was trivial, Parker affirmed; the few Jews there were took care of themselves; but the Irish refused to become Americans, drained dry the wells of philanthropy, and represented an intolerable nuisance in the city.[89]

No matter how efficacious, benevolent institutions did not work a thorough cure. As the young lawyer Christopher C. Andrews reminded his fellow citizens: "while we furnish subsistence to those whom intemperance and idleness have brought to destitution—while we erect asylums where reason may be restored to the shattered mind—while we enlarge prisons in which to punish the violators of the law—we should remember that some endeavors should be made to prevent others from requiring the same charities, and incurring the same penalties." Prevention was as important as cure, Andrews stressed. "Instead of standing merely by the fatal shoal to rescue the sinking crew, we should raise a warning signal to avert further shipwrecks."[90]

Although the metaphor was strained, Andrews' warning reflected the prevailing attitudes of the day. For some years, political, social, and cultural leaders in Boston had agreed that the best way to break the cycle of poverty was to prevent its formation. Believing that a continuing culture of poverty existed and that the poor lived as a caste alone and apart among themselves, politicians and reformers urged that the cycle could be ended, or that at least the poor could be rendered harmless. During the antebellum years the means most favored by Boston leaders for that task of prevention was public education.

10

Education for the Lower Classes

Such a force is a policy of insurance for our republican and protestant institutions. . . . Open, free, universal, these schools draw in the children of alien parentage with others, and assimilate them to the native born.

New Englander (1855)[1]

Between 1815 and 1860, urban New Englanders became more aware than ever of poverty and its relation to social disorder. In the minds of many, poverty was linked inseparably to the growing numbers of foreign immigrants in the cities. Viewed as a cohesive and permanent social group, the immigrant poor threatened class divisions and class warfare dreaded by many New Englanders. In Boston the fears were strongest because the threat seemed most imminent. In response, some residents demanded restrictions on foreign immigration; others joined nativist organizations; still others hoped that the lower classes, given time and assistance, could become contributing members to a stable society.

These varied attitudes toward the immigrant and the native poor pervaded the ranks of those intellectuals, social reformers, and educators who worked for social stability to alleviate and to avert urban crisis. Those who sought the extension of public education reflected both their own anxieties and their willingness to turn the immigrant threat to their own advantage. They played upon the fears and hostilities of their contemporaries. The presence of the poor and immigrant classes offered a perfect opportunity to the prophets of chaos who argued that ignorance, vice, and crime would engulf the republic in waves of urban disorder.

To be sure, the critics advanced differing justifications for their demands of education. Many hoped that public education would check the onrush of social upheaval by teaching the lower classes the responsibilities of citizenship. Others stressed that schooling would elevate the masses from lives of squalor and poverty by widening their economic opportunities and by training them in proper social habits. Still others emphasized that education at least would instill in the lower classes a respect for law and authority.

But whether the reformers and schoolmen desired a vehicle for social improvement or an instrument for social engineering, they all agreed that the growing numbers of native and foreign paupers in Boston called for an extension of public education. Although arguments shifted in emphasis from decade to decade, throughout the antebellum years educators and reformers relied on the presence of the immigrant poor as one of their main advertising ploys.

EDUCATION AS SOCIAL INSURANCE

In 1819, lexicographer Noah Webster, in a letter to John Brooks, the last Federalist governor of Massachusetts, introduced the theme upon which later educators played endless variations. Webster felt alarm over the prospect of increasing numbers of the lower classes enjoying the franchise in Massachusetts. He shared the Federalist faith that only moral men should govern, men who were industrious and who owned property. In his letter Webster expressed agreement with the governor's views on early instruction and discipline. "To form plans for diffusing literary and moral improvement among the poorer classes of citizens, in connection with religious instruction," Webster observed, "will be no less our pleasure than it is our duty. To draw from the obscure retreats of poverty the miserable victims of ignorance and vice, to enlighten their minds and correct their evil habits, to raise them to the rank of intelligent, industrious, and useful members of society will never cease to be the object of deep solicitude with a wise legislature." This was, he added, "the most efficacious mode of preventing crimes."[2]

Through his numerous textbooks for school usage, Webster made his own modest contribution to elevating the poor while also attempting to influence their moral values. As early as 1816 he boasted that he had shaped the education of "at least four millions of the rising generation." His famous *Elementary Spelling Book* (the "Blue-Backed Speller") sold over 20 million copies between 1782 and 1847, copies which undoubtedly were used by many more children than the total number sold. Through its various editions, Webster paraded the virtues of industry, thrift, sobriety, piety, and submissiveness to authority. Poverty, he stressed, could be ennobling if the poor would only remain content with their lot while simultaneously attempting to climb the ladder of virtues to American respectability. Webster believed that with his textbooks and through the common schools a benevolent society could enlighten the lower classes—and render them harmless.[3]

Boston journalists and educators became wedded to sentiments like Webster's. In the late 1820's a Boston school committee could report that schools were performing their task of training the children of the lower classes. "Although the children in the vicinity of Broad-Street, of which the school is chiefly composed, do not present the best materials for instruction," the committee noted of an institution located in the heart of an immigrant district, "yet it is believed . . . scholars will compare in the several branches with those of any other school." But, at the same time, influential local journals such as the *American Journal of Education* and the *American Annals of Education* complained that educators had taken too little notice of the increase of population by "vicious" and "ignorant" foreign immigrants. Public feeling must be aroused, the editor of the *Annals* demanded. Schools must be established and sustained "to prevent us from descending to the grave of nations!" If immediate action regarding children was imperative, to provide schools for adults was equally important. The editor declared that evening and Sunday schools, offering training in the English language and in civic responsibility, must be organized. Too soon would immigrants become members of the elective body governing the country; education alone could "purify the thick atmosphere of moral pollution which they have always breathed, and which still envelopes them."[4]

Occasionally, educators conceded that the immigrants were not completely to blame for their hopeless condition. As the *American Journal of Education* admitted, the poor had "none of those means of elevating their conceptions above the spinning machine or the work bench" which the wealthy enjoyed. The poor were "doubly exposed to the torrents of corruption which flow through the streets, and to the exhalations of vice which arise from crowded shops and manufactories." Still, problems remained and had to be dealt with by every concerned citizen. "The question for *every individual*," wrote the editor of the *Annals* in 1833, "is whether he shall aim at the highest degree of security for his property and life, by educating every individual around him in such a manner that he may sustain himself, and be furnished with the knowledge necessary to guide him in the right way, and to guard him from seduction." A man could depend on bars and bolts, judges and sheriffs, prisons and executioners "for taking care of his neighbors, and securing his own safety," rather than support schools. But, the editor implied, public action was no substitute for private endeavor. To protect himself as well as to guard society, each individual had to become his brothers' keeper. An individual could best carry out this private responsibility by lending his financial and political support to public schools.

If the logic behind this proposed mixture of private and public cooperation appeared strained, the editor did not realize it. In a society in which the masses govern either for good or ill, he observed, "the simple question is, do the wealthy or well educated prefer to be ruled by ignorance, and the corruptions which follow in its train, rather than to pay the expense of universal education? Do they value a tithe of their income more than property and life?"[5]

Throughout the 1830's literate Bostonians became accustomed to reading and hearing demands for the use of public education as a measure of prevention against the evils of immigration and poverty. Joseph Tuckerman, the city's "Missionary to the Poor," repeatedly called upon his fellow citizens to broaden educational opportunities if for no reason other than self-protection. Lyman Beecher, minister to the middle and upper classes, pleaded for the expansion of Protestant public schools to offset the heresies of Catholicism and prepare the foreigners for an American way of life. Samuel F. B. Morse observed that unlettered Catholic immigrants who entered the country added to the abundant mass of ignorance. "Republican education," he stated, "were it allowed freely to come in contact with their minds, would doubtless soon furnish a remedy for an evil for which, in the existing state of things, we have no cure." It was the uneducated poor without intelligence or moral restraint, echoed educator Frederick A. Packard, who were found at the head of mobs, strikes, riotous assemblies, and trade unions. The only way of stopping their war upon the peace and order of communities and their plundering of the mansions of the rich was through the inculcation of proper social, civil, and moral principles in the common schools. Articles in educational magazines and even in agricultural journals emphasized the need to protect society by educating the urban poor.[6]

Although sentiments like these were commonplace by the early 1840's, the conception of public education as an instrument of social engineering received fullest exposition during and after those years. With inadequate physical resources at their command, with an economic system in transition from commercial to manufacturing interests, in a political climate dominated by conservative forces, and in an intellectual atmosphere distinctly hostile to foreigners, Boston leaders had to find ways of assimilating the sudden influx of immigrants. A few years earlier Mayor Theodore Lyman had feared that the incoming Irish were a "race that never will be infused into our own, but on the contrary will always remain distinct and hostile."[7]

By the early 1840's that fear seemed to have become a reality. Appalling slums dotted the urban landscape; foreign paupers and beggar children crowded the streets; aliens unfamiliar with the law and unaccustomed to city living lined the courtrooms and boosted the crime rate.

If the city were to survive, Boston leaders mused, the immigrants and the native poor must somehow be kept in check. Foreign and native members of the lower classes had to become better assimilated to American civic and moral standards of behavior. Many public spokesmen ardently desired at least one public institution that could create and sustain a sense of community and shared purpose among divergent classes of people in the city. Political leaders, ministers, educators, School Committee members, and journalists thus seized upon the changing composition of the urban population to propagandize for the further expansion of common schools.

In his inaugural address in 1840, Mayor Jonathan Chapman assured his worried fellow Bostonians that "every interest essential to her well being as a community has been liberally assumed and generously provided for at the public charge. Churches and school-houses are her most numerous and cherished monuments." But some citizens knew that Protestant churches no longer dominated the community. The Catholic immigrant population had so increased during the early 1840's that it accounted for nearly one-fourth of the total population. A typical Sunday morning, estimated the Catholic *Boston Pilot*, saw as many worshippers attending the four Catholic churches as all the Protestant churches together. While "the Church," in the Puritan capital, might remain an enduring monument, clearly the Protestant leadership could not depend upon it for rapid assimilation of the immigrants. As the local Baptist periodical the *Christian Watchman* put it in 1842, discussing the most recent census, "the apparent proportion of popular ignorance is materially increased . . . by the presence of large numbers of aliens. Thus New York and Massachusetts, second to none in the facilities for education, have in their large towns great numbers of foreigners, not yet assimilated to American institutions."[8] To hasten the social integration of immigrants, the second of Mayor Chapman's "cherished monuments"—the schools—appeared to be the answer.

Edmund G. Loring, chairman of the Visiting Committee of the School Committee in 1846, offered that body's opinions that "it is a matter of daily remark, that immigration is constantly countervailing the Puritan leaven of our people, and reducing the scale of public morality and public intelligence." Unless the ignorance, bad manners, and corrupted morals of the foreigners "are corrected by our schools," Loring queried, "what foundation is there for the hope of those who are hopeful of the final fortunes of the country?" The following year, George B. Emerson reported to the Committee that "some provision has been made for the vast accessions to our population by immigration from foreign countries of persons of every age, and of every condition of ignorance." But, Emerson pointed out, much remained to be done about those whom street life educated only to vice and crime. "Unless they are made inmates of our schools," he warned, "many of them will become inmates of our prisons."[9]

These two reports—for 1846 and 1847—set the tone for the response of Boston's educational leadership down to the eve of the Civil War. Educators, reformers, and politicians had long hoped to fashion public instruction into a tool capable of controlling the rate of social change, but the influx of immigrant and native poor demanded heightened efforts. Yearly, results of investigations into the conditions of poverty in Boston emphasized the necessity of action.[10]

With a zeal bordering on the religious, educators dedicated the public schools to the mission of transforming the aliens into responsible American citizens. The *School Report* for 1853, for example, announced democratically that the public schools were as free to the children of foreigners as to "those of our own citizens." "But," continued the authors of the *Report,* "the whole character of the instruction given, must be such and such only, as will tend to make the pupils thereof, American citizens, and ardent supporters of American institutions." The shared interests of the community would allow no other course.[11]

This conception of the school as the training ground of Americanism—however that vaguery was defined—captured the imaginations of schoolmen and laymen alike. Foreign visitors praised this view of the public schools. Isabella Lucy Bird, an English noblewoman visiting Massachusetts in the early 1850's, noted that the public school brought together children of different origins while their natures were yet pliant, "and besides diffusing knowledge among them, it softens the prejudices of race and party, and carries on a continual process of assimilation." In an 1853 article entitled "The Catholics and the School Question," Boston's *Christian Review* happily observed of the common schools that "the scrupulous attention to order, and the spirit of subordination, which are the essential ingredients of the system, tend to make the future man methodical in the pursuit of his calling, and loyal to constituted and rightful authority. Over such a people the despot can gain no substantial power, and the demagogue no lasting influence."[12]

In a similar vein, the prestigious *New Englander* devoted articles to the evils of immigration and the social role of the school. Some foreigners, admitted the periodical, arrived in America with a "tendency to assimilate." Far more did not. To preserve the unity, continuity, and predominance of the native interests was therefore a "delicate point." The *New Englander* pointed to the experience of Massachusetts in employing the schools as the balancing factor in America's favor. "Such a force is a

policy of insurance for our republican and protestant institutions. . . .
Open, free, universal, these schools draw in the children of alien parentage with others, and assimilate them to the native born." The immigrants,
concluded the writer, thus are "liberalized, Americanized, and with an
import far beyond its technical [meaning], naturalized. . . . So they
grow up with the state, of the state and for the state."[13] What more
could cities confronted with labor problems, religious disputes, and
general social unrest ask?

Bolstered by such praise of their educational goals, Boston leaders
remained steadfast. As Edward Everett Hale summarized the opinions
of his fellow citizens, "the stranger cannot serve the country while he is
a stranger. . . . His children must grow up in its institutions. . . . He
must plunge, or be plunged, into his new home." Boston educators relied on public schools as the most trustworthy mold by which to cast
immigrants into Americans. Schools alone, they conceded, might not
accomplish the task, but without formal education the problems of securing urban order and stability were insurmountable. Samuel Bates, chairman of School Visiting Committees during the early 1850's, explained
that "our Public School System is a branch of the Government itself; as
much so as are our courts, our police, criminal, and charitable regulations
for the poor." To be effective, Bates noted, governments had to be stable.
The chief aim of city government in establishing and maintaining
schools, therefore, "is its own preservation." In administering the school
system, Bates candidly admitted, the object of the city was "to train
up all the children, within its jurisdiction, to be intelligent, virtuous,
patriotic, American citizens."[14]

"To train up all the children"—the statement was a rare admission of
an oft-hidden truth. Propagandists for education wanted to lure, and if
necessary to force, all children of the city into the public schools. Foreign and native, poor as well as rich—all must be milled and honed in the
educational machinery. Certainly educators had not lied about their
goal, but they had dissembled. Whether consciously or not, the schoolmen had relied upon the spectres of poverty and foreign immigration
to convince the citizens of Boston that public education had to be extended to encompass the lower classes.

At the same time, however, educators had argued effectively that native children must also attend schools. They hoped that the integration
of different social and ethnic groups would prevent class warfare and
would promote urban stability. On the one hand, an educator like E. C.
Wines could assert that the only practical antidote to the ills of immigration "is in so thorough an education of all our own citizens as shall nullify
foreign influence, . . . and secure real personal independence in the

natives of the soil." On the other hand, Horace Mann could use the presence of the immigrants to further the cause of common schools by affirming that foreigners remained unfitted for America "until they have become morally acclimated to our institutions." But can it make any difference, Mann continued in his *Ninth Annual Report*, whether an individual secured American citizenship from the bondage of an Irish lord or from the equally rigorous bondage of an ignorant native parent or guardian? Mann answered that the person who was a serf up to the age of twenty-one, whether in Austria or America, could still not become a responsible citizen.[15]

The lesson was clear. To avert social upheaval the common school had to mold all children into virtuous, patriotic Americans. "The value of educational institutions and influences," declared an article in Mann's *Common School Journal*, "having this assimilating and uniting tendency, as have common schools eminently, cannot be easily exaggerated in their relation to our native population, and especially in their relation to our immigrant population." Educators reiterated the necessity of educating the children of the aliens and the poor to cement the support of middle-class and wealthy Bostonians for common schools.[16]

William B. Fowle, one of the city's most eminent teachers, illustrated the case. For years Fowle, a close friend of Horace Mann, had campaigned for public schools. In an 1857 essay on "Preventive Teaching" he admitted that schools were more numerous than a generation before, but also alleged that "they are less numerous in proportion to our population and our means." The census returns of immigrants, he went on, "show an adulteration of our population annually to an appalling extent, and yet we are boasting of our schools as if they were more than sufficient to remedy every evil that impends. . . . If you would save your institutions," Fowle urged his fellow citizens, "teach these children." Like other educators in the city, Fowle hoped to convince the public of the need for schools which would reach all children by emphasizing their usefulness in assimilating the immigrant youth.[17]

Even in the midst of the Civil War, when public attention was diverted from the common school crusade, Boston leaders drummed out the theme. In an 1863 address, Edward Everett, the grand old man of conservative Boston politics, expounded the crucial role of schools in maintaining a civilized community. In Boston, as in all large cities, Everett observed, there was a city within a city—a city of the ignorant, the wretched, the forlorn: In that city lived the children of poverty, those who grew up to become the pests and scourges of the community. But if those children, together with all the youth of the city, attended schools which their parents generously provided, the community might yet be secure. For the preservation of civil peace, Everett claimed, we are indebted in the last resort "to this peaceful army of twenty-seven thousand children . . . waging the great war against the legion hosts of ignorance, vice, and anarchy, not with cannons and Minie rifles, but with the spelling-book, the grammar, and the Bible!"[18]

Between the 1820's and the 1860's, the leadership of Boston articulated a philosophy about the role of public education in securing urban stability. Vague notions had sharpened into theories as the problems of poverty became more evident. Political leaders, School Committee members, and individual educators had agreed that the poor, especially the immigrant poor, represented the most visibly dangerous threat to social harmony. To secure property, to protect life, and to shield society from permanent class strife, immigrants had to be trained as American citizens and the cycle of poverty broken. At the same time, native children could also be molded into virtuous citizens.

Many thoughtful Bostonians apparently came to agree with the first Secretary of the Massachusetts Board of Education. "Other social organizations are curative and remedial," Horace Mann observed in 1841, but the common school "is a preventive and an antidote." Let it "be expanded to its capabilities, let it be worked with the efficiency of which it is susceptible, and nine-tenths of the crimes in the penal code would become obsolete; the long catalogue of human ills would be abridged; men would walk more safely by day; every pillow would be more inviolable by night; property, life and character held by a stronger tenure; all rational hopes respecting the future brightened."[19] This was a tall order for one social institution to fill, but there were still a host of believers.

Public education was to be a form of social insurance. Due to population trends, the theory of public education as a form of social insurance was most clearly (and publicly) articulated during the late 1840's and early 1850's. Yearly, almost daily it seemed to some, hundreds of children who were ignorant of American standards of behavior and unaccustomed to city life entered Boston. Roaming the streets and alleys, pilfering from shop stalls, loafing on the docks—these children were models of the "vicious" poor. Certainly, according to educators and city officials, these were not children who by themselves would become useful citizens of the city.[20] When schoolmen spoke about "assimilation" of these strangers they were discussing ways and means of instilling in them an appreciation of American social values. The educators were also debating methods of adjusting members of the lower classes to the pace and demands of urban life.

Only the sense of urgency in the debates was new. If educational theories of assimilation appeared more sharply focused by the 1850's, it was because educators had been working out the fundamental approaches, however vaguely conceived, for many years.

PUBLIC SCHOOLS FOR THE URBAN POOR

Had Boston following the War of 1812 not already contained a sizable lower-class population, the city would have made few provisions for the extension of public education. Certainly there were influential citizens who opposed any marked increase in spending public funds for schooling. Tuition schools and private academies met the needs of children of the more economically fortunate classes. The Boston Education Act of 1789 had established numerous free grammar schools. By the early 1820's, the city itself was spending nearly as much on public instruction as the rest of the state combined. This fact inspired educator James G. Carter to chide the state for too slight an expenditure while it led Boston conservatives to demand that the city either cut back on expenses or, at least, not increase them. Those who favored limited public expenditures could point to the fact that charitable enterprise had long provided instruction for the poorer classes. In vain, it seemed, educators pointed out that both Philadelphia and New York City had provided more extensively for the free instruction of the poor than Boston had.[21]

Between 1816 and 1820 both the Boston Society for the Moral and Religious Instruction of the Poor and several select committees of leading citizens urged the city to establish tuition-free public schools for the very young children of the poor. The petitioners stressed that few poor or immigrant children between the ages of four and seven attended the private dames' schools. Either the poor were ignorant of the opportunities open to them, or parents needed whatever financial assistance young working children could provide, or families were too proud to accept charity. Conservative members of the School Committee replied that to be of general utility public schools for "this class," must be very numerous. The proposal was too expensive. If such schools were few in number, attendance would be limited because respectable parents would not send their children to crowded and distant schools in which the multitudes mingled.

Proponents of public education for the lower classes persevered. Referring to children who were destined to remain vicious, wretched street-beggars unless educated, the authors of an 1820 educational report entreated the city that the poor had a right as Americans to "civil, religious, and social privileges" from which ignorance barred them. More important, "the public good, both in a moral and social view" required that lower-class children attend school. If they were not trained as citizens, "their ignorance, insubordination, and vicious habits" would remain serious threats to social stability.[22] During the 1820's, educators and concerned citizens kept up the pressure for a system of public primary schools. Their efforts met with success.

There was no doubt that the chief motive behind the extension of primary school education in Boston was to reach the children of the poor and immigrant classes. To such early leaders as Elisha Ticknor, a well-known teacher, and James Savage, prominent lawyer and historian, it was evident that without public primary schools a large number of lower-class children would never receive an education. Ticknor and Savage underscored the need for schools by pointing out that a constantly increasing foreign immigration was swelling the size of this class of children to an alarming state. Following the establishment of several primary schools in various sections of the city, the Primary School Board sought to encourage lower-class parents to send their children to school. Apparently the new public schools bore the stigma of the old "charity schools," for the first two reports of the Primary Board lamented that the pride of many parents "revolted from acknowledging that they needed assistance" and urged that more extensive efforts be made to encourage attendance.[23]

Primary school attendance increased slowly during the 1820's. In 1821 there were 36 schools providing elementary instruction for over 1,800 pupils. By 1826, when the city undertook the first complete survey of enrollment, the number of schools had grown to 51, with total attendance of more than 2,800. Early reports often failed to state either the financial or the ethnic composition of various student bodies. But implicit in the reports was the fact that most children came from families of the native and immigrant poor. Even though the schools were presumably tuition-free, many teachers charged a nominal sum of fifty cents a year to offset expenses for which they were responsible, especially the cost of textbooks and instructional materials. The reports indicated that a considerable number of students were so impoverished that they could not afford even this paltry sum and therefore did not attend the public schools. To enable the poor to attend the schools, members of the Primary School Board and generous townsmen often furnished clothing, shoes, and books for the many students requiring charitable relief.[24]

Because of inadequate public funding of primary schools for the poor, the extension of elementary education in the city thus had to rely upon a marriage of convenience between private and public enterprise—an arrangement during the twenties which also characterized such other urban services as fire brigades, the water supply, public health provisions, and an embryonic police force. As a transitional method this merging of private and public endeavor worked well. Educators succeeded in drawing larger numbers of poor and immigrant children into the schools. By the end of the decade over 3,500 students attended the schools; youth of foreign parentage accounted for more than half of the total enrollment. A contemporary observed that this was "a fact of infinite moment, clearly showing that the city, even at that early date, was educating a host of aliens in the principles of our Puritan ancestors."[25]

Despite the seeming success of the primary schools in one short decade, educators and reformers were not satisfied. Although precise figures were not available to them, educators knew that far too many children of the lower classes still did not enroll in school. They only had to glance at the annual reports of the House of Reformation for Juvenile Offenders to confirm their suspicions. And, since three of the six directors of the House—Moses Grant, Joseph Lewis, and Daniel Henchman—were also members of the Primary School Board, knowledgeable schoolmen could point to the growing numbers of juvenile delinquents as proof of the necessity of expanding the common school system.[26]

Clearly the beneficent reach of public education failed to touch these delinquent children of immigrant, native-poor, and working-class parents. Joseph Tuckerman, a member of the Primary School Board and Boston's "Minister-to-the-Poor," identified these as the neglected children of the city. In a series of impressive reports on the conditions of the poor, Tuckerman discussed both those children who wanted to attend school but could not, and those who could attend school but refused to. Some were too old to attend primary school but were barred from grammar schools because of illiteracy. Others could read but were not enrolled in schools because of the poverty, unconcern, or viciousness of their parents. If they somehow completed primary school, most youth did not continue on to grammar school, preferring instead the life of street beggars and idlers. Tuckerman was willing to see some of these children committed to the House of Reformation—those who were "vicious," who attended no school, who could hardly read and could not write, who were wholly beyond the authority of parents, or who contaminated other children by their association. But he believed that many of these children could be salvaged for society if the city would tailor appropriate public schools to their needs. Tuckerman therefore lent his influence to a movement for special schools that had been under way for several years.[27]

MONITORIAL SCHOOLS FOR THE POOR

As early as 1820 members of the Primary School Board, together with other concerned citizens, had become aware of a number of children who were "idlers, truants, and such as have no visible or known employment, and who do not habitually attend any school." These were children too old to be admitted to the primary schools, yet unqualified to enter the grammar schools. They came from families too poor to afford private instruction. If these immoral waifs remained unschooled, the educators prophesied that "they will not only go quickly to destruction themselves, but by their pernicious example and influence, they will draw many others after them to the same deplorable ruin." A select committee of the Primary School Board urged the city fathers to take action, both for the sake of the street urchins and for "the public good, both in a moral and social view." The School Committee presented to the town meeting the recommendation of the Primary Board for one or more schools for these children to be opened at a "trifling expense" to the city. On July 2, 1820, the town appropriated $1,000 to establish a "School for Mutual Instruction" for the over 300 children of the poor between the ages of seven and fourteen who did not attend public school. The Primary Board then organized the first of an anticipated system of such schools.[28]

The initial school opened in a basement room of the Boylston School House on Fort Hill, in the heart of the city's heaviest concentration of immigrant families. Under the direction of William B. Fowle, a twenty-six-year-old novice whose only educational training had been an apprenticeship in the bookstore of Caleb Bingham, a former Boston teacher of renown, the new school was the earliest example in the city of a recent innovation—the monitorial or Lancastrian school.[29]

The introduction of a monitorial system in Boston and other American cities was an initial response to the challenge of mass urban public instruction. The scheme was deceptively simple: a teacher would instruct older children in the first or second class of the school; in turn these children would repeat the lesson to younger pupils. Through such instruction a school could presumably accommodate a much larger than usual enrollment and one individual could teach far more children than was customary. This assembly-line technique, so similar in conception to the "New England Idea" of interchangeable parts to increase production, had originated in English cities.

The leading proponent of the system was an English Quaker schoolmaster, Joseph Lancaster, who had experimented with it early in the nineteenth century. The notion of mutual instruction quickly became attractive to educators and politicians in American cities who viewed it as an ideal solution for providing inexpensive instruction to the poor.[30]

The New York City Free School Society introduced the scheme into America in 1806, at the urging of its president (and later governor of New York), DeWitt Clinton. Clinton lauded Lancaster's system as "a blessing from heaven to redeem the poor and distressed of this world from the power and dominion of ignorance," adding that it "operates with the same efficiency in education as labour-saving machinery does in the useful arts." Other cities, including Philadelphia, Baltimore, Washington, and New Haven, followed New York City's example.[31]

In 1818 Lancaster himself arrived in America to promote his system. Touring through both the North and South, he advertised his plan of dividing a classroom into small groups of ten, each led by a monitor, so that one lad, "from fourteen to eighteen years of age, can be rendered competent to the government of a school containing from 200 to 1,000 scholars." Lancaster was not encouraged by his reception in Boston. Writing his daughter from Richmond, Virginia, in October 1819 he noted of his success in lecturing: *"The people here are not like the Bostonians;* they do not put in *buttons—*bad silver and copper—*forged* notes and *bits of tin;* but they pay their 50 *cents* each and *call* it *cheap."*[32] While the citizens of Boston may not have lined Lancaster's pockets in appreciation of his speeches, they paid him the compliment of adapting his system to meet the needs of their own poor population.

The initial attempt—Fowle's school on Fort Hill—lasted less than two years. The school won high praise from Mayor Josiah Quincy, but when Fowle resigned in 1823 to begin a private girl's school based on the monitorial plan, the School Committee unaccountably dropped the effort. Members of the Primary School Board, however, were unwilling to see immigrant and native poor children "abandoned to idleness, vagrancy, ignorance, and crime," and they supported the idea of mutual instruction. In 1824 they requested that the system be incorporated into the primary schools. Their petition resulted in an application to the City Council for funds, but in 1826 the Council refused to act. In true bureaucratic fashion, the Council referred the matter to a subcommittee for thorough study. While the monitorial system had the advantage of being inexpensive, it bore the disadvantage of being innovative.[33]

Mayor Josiah Quincy, as ex-officio chairman of the School Committee, headed the sub-committee. Quincy was in the midst of a campaign to increase efficiency in all public services while simultaneously cutting costs. He looked favorably upon the plan of educating more children at less expenditure. When the sub-committee submitted its report to the City Council in February 1828 its recommendations were a foregone conclusion.

The *Quincy Report*, as it was labeled by the press, urged the adoption of the monitorial system in grammar and writing schools. As recent precedents, the *Report* pointed to both the school kept by William B. Fowle and to experiments in the primary schools. Having failed to obtain funds from the Council in 1826, the Primary School had gone ahead on its own and had used its limited resources to introduce mutual instruction into one school in each of the eight districts in the city. The Board judged the results as favorable. Building upon this experience, Quincy offered various justifications for monitorial schools: learning was less irksome because it was simplified; student attention was enhanced because idleness was not possible; youthful character was enriched because the system disposed "their minds to industry, to readiness of attention, and to subordination, thereby creating in early life a love of order, preparation for business and acquaintance with the relative obligations and duties, both of pupil and instructor." He also implied that mutual instruction would inculcate the moral values of non-sectarian Christianity, a claim often made by Joseph Lancaster himself.[34] Why, then, Quincy asked, was there opposition? As he saw it, there were at least three reasons.

First, there was a naturally conservative bent to human nature which tended to reject any innovation. Second, the present grammar and writing teachers of the city expressed reluctance to accept a system which gave them new responsibilities. Teachers did not want to undergo the painful experience of disrupting their routines or of having to learn new methods of instruction. Finally, teachers feared that their ranks would be lessened and their influence undermined through a system that substituted student monitors for professional assistants. To counteract these alleged objections, Quincy suggested that the School Committee initiate the program immediately but carry it out gradually. In this way schools and schoolmasters throughout the city would have time for local accommodations.

The mayor proposed that the monitorial plan be introduced first in the Boylston and Bowdoin grammar schools. This suggestion revealed the main thrust behind the scheme—to save money for the city while also morally benefiting the poor and the immigrants by increasing their educational opportunities. Both schools served areas heavily populated with the lower classes. Without disrupting the general system of schools, Quincy argued, the city could provide instruction for those boys who passed the legal age of admission into primary school without being qualified to enter the grammar schools. Certainly the experience of New York City demonstrated the practicality of the plan.[35]

The city accepted the *Quincy Report* and authorized the School Committee to make the necessary arrangements. The Committee advanced limited funds to begin the experiment in both primary and grammar schools. By 1829 there were twelve primary schools operating on the monitorial system and an undetermined number of grammar schools. Results were mixed. The Primary School Board reported that none of the schools had deteriorated in quality, while several actually appeared to have improved. In the grammar schools, however, the system met with great opposition.[36]

In theory, the monitorial scheme not only had the advantage of economy but also offered a kind of apprentice, on-the-job training program for prospective teachers. But in practice, the plan became a method by which the inexperienced monitored the ignorant. As one schoolboy later reminisced, the system consisted of "having a girl sit at the end of the long rows of boys; and it seemed to be the chief business of the monitors to report any whispering or sly winks, which now and then might be seen." A writer in the Boston periodical *The New-England Magazine*, probably best summed up hostile reactions of respectable citizens who refused to send their children to a monitorial school. The Lancastrian plan, he wrote, had some value in providing cheap mass instruction for the poor, but by accepting it we "have set aside the old method of spontaneous effort and individual exertion, to throw our children into a sort of intellectual hopper, where they must be ground in a mill." This might be acceptable for producing sailors or soldiers who should be automatons, but it was intolerable for republican free men. "All self-exertion prevented; all responsibility lost; every generous feeling crushed; and the whole body taught to march on like a platoon of soldiers, as if they were moved by one spring and were parts of a single machine." The sole merit of the plan, the author argued, was that it saved money. It might be better to see children in such a school rather than on the streets, but monitorial schools were surely "worse than the worst plan of instruction that was ever before devised—

> With the same cement ever sure to bind,
> They bring to one dead level every mind."[37]

The writer failed to realize that any system of common schools which was designed to mingle different economic and social classes under the same lock step scheme of rote instruction would tend "to bring to one dead level every mind." Already by the 1830's it had become increasingly difficult to educate equally the heterogeneous urban masses.

In the face of such opposition the monitorial scheme fell from favor to disfavor to dissolution. While individual schools occasionally experimented with mutual instruction, by the early 1830's educators bowed to public pressure and to their own experience. They abandoned any notions about systematic monitorial instruction throughout the city. Like Boston, New York and Philadelphia also shelved their Lancastrian schools. Rows of orderly pauper children disciplined and instructed at the cheapest possible expense to the city appeared attractive to penny-pinching politicians and some schoolmen. But workingmen and middle-class reformers alike decried the inadequacies of such schooling. By the early 1840's Horace Mann could observe that "at least nine-tenths of all the monitorial schools I have seen, would suggest to me the idea that the name 'monitorial' had been given them, by way of admonishing the world to avoid their adoption." Mann held only contempt for the boast of monitorial school promoters, "Give me twenty-four pupils to-day, and I will give you back twenty-four teachers to-morrow." Cities would have to find some other way of mass public instruction.[38]

SEPARATE SCHOOLS FOR VAGRANT CHILDREN

Although mutual instruction as a method of accommodating the unschooled poor had failed in Boston by the early 1830's, educators pressed the need for intermediate schools of some nature.

But the effort proved unsuccessful. Worried about expense, the city fathers failed to share in the educators' enthusiasm for the proposed new schools. Scattered efforts over the next few years to establish other types of intermediate schools in various sections of the city met with little or no encouragement. In 1834 a group of citizens joined with several schoolmen to advocate another try at founding intermediate schools for the vagrant and idle children of the poor and the immigrants. Under pressure, the School Committee refused to open a separate school, but did agree to experiment by permitting unqualified children over the age of seven to enter already established schools. These children, however, had to be kept apart from the qualified youngsters. They were to be seated at separate desks on the opposite side of the classroom from those regularly enrolled in the school. So that the valuable time of the instructor might not be misspent, the segregated children were to be taught by boys of the highest rank in school for whatever period of time necessary to allow them to finally take their places with other children in the lowest class of the school. This was to be a kind of selective "mutual instruction."

For men who repeatedly stated the necessity of getting lower-class children into schools, this proposed procedure was curiously lacking in perspective. Children who did not want to attend school in the first place would hardly be induced to enter under circumstances of separation from their peers. Roman Catholic parents, by disposition suspicious of the good intentions of Protestant educators, could not be expected to approve this unequal treatment. The results of the experiment, therefore, should have surprised no one. Of some 300 "vagrant" children between the ages of twelve and fifteen, the Committee discovered, 125 preferred the truant and street life to attending school. Of the remaining number, about one-third were Catholic children whose parents and priests refused to enroll them in the public schools. So few children took advantage of the offer of a special permit to enter the schools that the experiment was dropped. Those citizens and educators who believed that vagrant children should attend some kind of school opened several private schools for the purpose.[39]

Another attempt to provide public schools for unprepared children came four years later. In 1838, after frequent appeals, the City Council authorized the Primary School Board to select one school in each of the primary districts for children not educationally prepared to enter the grammar schools. A sub-committee formed to make the arrangements responded that to start a school for special instruction in every district in the city was unnecessary. Since they were "only for the accommodation of those who, coming from abroad, or who, from misfortune or neglect, are excluded from the Grammar Schools on the ground of qualification, and from the Primary Schools on account of age," the sub-committee recommended that such schools be established only in areas containing the largest numbers of immigrant and lower-class native children. Accepting this recommendation, the Primary School Board established four intermediate schools which were so successful that by the end of the year they served almost 1,000 children, or, about 13 per cent of the total school population.[40]

Although the records were unclear, the special schools apparently continued in operation with mixed results over the next few years. For example, the Primary Board experienced some difficulty in finding qualified teachers willing to serve in the special schools, possibly because, as a contemporary observed, the pauper children for whom the schools were intended were lawless terrors to many citizens. Gang fights among children living on different blocks in the immigrant districts and their participation in riots like that on Broad Street in 1837, as well as other outbreaks involving "many idle and vicious" boys, alarmed Bostonians and probably drove away prospective teachers for the intermediate schools. In 1845, the Primary School Board considered offering higher wages to teachers of the "Schools for Special Instruction." How successful an inducement the "danger pay" proved to be remains unknown.[41]

In 1847 George B. Emerson, representing the School Committee, urged a further extension of the intermediate schools, especially into those population-swollen areas where new schools were needed. "Our system was contrived and adapted to a small city, peopled by persons born in New England," Emerson explained. But "now there are great masses coming in upon us who are not educated, except to vice and crime; the creatures or the victims of the justice or the oppression, or the overpopulation

of the old world." Unless the children of these foreigners "are made inmates of our schools, many of them will become inmates of our prisons."
Emerson reminded cost-conscious Bostonians that "it is vastly more
economical to educate them in the former than to support them in the
latter." Many of these children had been graduated from primary schools
"from the necessity of age or unmanageableness." Emerson feared that
their lack of ability and interest might infect other children in the grammar schools. To keep these ignorant children from monopolizing the
master's time or diluting the quality of instruction given brighter students,
Emerson suggested that the city build new intermediate schools to supplement the twenty-one special classes of instruction which met separately
in the classrooms of the regular schools.[42]

With all good intentions, Emerson was arguing for a system of segregated schools. He did not realize—or, at least, did not admit—that he was
advocating for poor and foreign children schools much like those for
Boston's Black population. In principle Emerson agreed with a correspondent of his close friend Horace Mann, who had written discussing the
separate schools for the Irish in nearby Lowell. The writer did not think
that in all cases segregated schools were advisable. But, if necessary "in
order to overcome the effects of prejudice," one could be comforted "to
think of these strangers on our shores, with this key to knowledge in their
hands, and with such habits as they must form under such teaching."
Although educators hoped to assimilate lower-class white children into
the mainstream of city life, Emerson and others implied that schools
specifically created for those children and separated from the regular
schools would best achieve that social goal.[43]

Neither by law nor by publicly announced design were the special
intermediate schools to enroll only the lower classes—educators could not
summarily deny almost half a century of propaganda for public schools
attended equally by all children of the city. But the natural process of
selection—by age, intelligence, and residential location—effectively re-
stricted enrollment to the native and foreign children of poverty. By the
mid-1850's, the special schools had become almost exclusively provinces
of the poor. The 1856 annual *School Report* testified that attendance had
boomed among those dull, misfortunate, wayward children deprived of
proper parental care "through the vices of their parents, and the continual
influx of strangers from foreign ports." For an undetermined number of
poor children in the city, the special schools had apparently proven useful.
Whether the schools had fostered harmonious relations between wealthy
and poor, foreign and native residents was a difficult question—one which
the schoolmen declined to answer. The logical contradictions of their
actions appeared not to trouble them. But such de facto segregation along

income, residential, and class lines did not bode well for the future stability of the city. Educators' beliefs that schooling per se would reduce class tensions and produce responsible citizens had fostered the special schools. But schools that became compounds for the poor could never create social harmony, as later generations of Bostonians would discover.[44]

While educators hoped to reach a certain number of lower-class youth through intermediate schools, they also wanted to be sure that other poor children did not escape the web of public instruction. During the years that schoolmen experimented with intermediate schools, they also searched for ways to educate lower-class children too young to enter even the primary schools.

THE ABORTIVE KINDERGARTEN

Eager to broaden the use of the public school as a means of socializing the poor, educators carefully examined a private innovation in the city— the infant school. This type of school was the forerunner of kindergartens which became widely popular in Boston and St. Louis after the Civil War. As introduced in Boston in the late 1820's, infant schools reflected the discovery of childhood as a separate stage of human development and demonstrated the growing awareness of the special needs of the impoverished classes. The influential *American Journal of Education* published article after article discussing the idea of the infant school and particularly stressed the importance of educating the infant poor.[45]

The chief intellectual sources of pre-school education were the writings of the Swiss educator Johann Heinrich Pestalozzi (1746-1827), and English examples of infant schools begun by such notable reformers as Henry Peter Brougham and Samuel Wilderspin, some of whose writings received wide circulation in America as *Infant Education; or Remarks on the Importance of Educating the Infant Poor, from the Age of Eighteen Months to Seven Years* (1827). Like their American counterparts, the European educators rejected any notion of the innate depravity of the infant. Rather, as the transcendentalist Bronson Alcott tried to demonstrate in his Temple School in Boston, Pestalozzi argued that children contained seeds of divinity which the proper educational processing could develop to maturity. Boston educators initially ignored Pestalozzi's insistence that infant education was only appropriate within the home and insisted instead on establishing formal schools. They were certain that infant schools could not only foster the natural process of human development, but could also help adjust the child to his or her urban environment.[46]

Infant schools enrolled the children of the poor, beginning at the age of eighteen months and continuing up to four or five years of age when they would presumably enter the primary schools. Proponents defended the importance of such schools by pointing out, as did one annual report of the "Infant School Society of the City of Boston," that "people seem to feel that because children are little things, they are of little consequence. They forget that the quarrelling and profane children of this generation, are to be the robbers and murderers of the next—that those who are now the distress of their parents, are hereafter the bane of society." Intellectual architects of the infant schools designed them in part to relieve the working-class mother of child-care responsibility during the day. But the innovators also determined to make infant schools the incubators of civic righteousness and Protestant morality.[47]

Officers of the Infant School Society believed that by reveling in ignorance and vice the parents of poor children set only bad examples for their offspring. "To counteract the bad influence of home," infant schools placed children under the care of a pious and intelligent teacher, "who from day to day, endeavors to instill into their tender minds the great truths and duties of religion." By blending amusement and instruction, by drawing children "to the love and practice of every virtue," the infant-school officers claimed that impoverished youth would grow up with correct moral principles, enlightened minds, and the strength of character to become respectable and useful adults. As a result these children would be far better citizens than their parents. "Perhaps, in the third generation," Society leaders mused, "the work of moral renovation will be complete. . . . What an interesting spectacle would a city present, where the meanest dwellings were the abodes of comfort, intelligence and virtue!" As adults the products of the infant schools might continue in the humbler walks of life, but they would never become very poor. It was clear in their reports that by "very poor" the officers referred to those who were dangerous to social order. "If we can succeed in preventing ignorance and vice," the Society predicted, "there will be none to cure."[48]

To convince skeptics of the worth of infant schools, proponents offered case examples. "I. & H.M.," respectively six years of age and twenty months old, "are the children of an intemperate mother, who . . . assured us that she gave liquor to these children that they might be inured to it early!" These youngsters could be saved from the demon rum. Another child, "M.F.," was the daughter of a Catholic working mother who was forced to leave home early in the morning "and to lock her poor child out, committing her to the mercy of Heaven." Although the mother had "natural fears" about entrusting her girl to a Protestant infant school, Society members prevailed and could proudly report that "now she labors with a grateful heart." As an example of one of their greatest triumphs, the Society offered "E.B. [who] came to us a month ago, covered with vermin, and the picture of all miserable passions." Love and kindness, however, "are humanizing the heart of this neglected child, and she can scarcely be forced to her home, where none await even for her food: she invariably remains with us until the school is closed for the night."

The Society noted that if critics of the schools could see with their own eyes the pit from which such children were extracted, they surely would not fail "to admire the progress which has been made toward their becoming polished stones." Admittedly the children were not far advanced in knowledge, "but they are taken up out of the streets, and placed for a great portion of their time under a happy moral influence, and the effect upon their tempers and habits is manifestly great and happy." Who could doubt that the infant schools provided a valuable service to the city?[49]

Members of the Primary School Board seriously considered adopting the infant schools as a permanent branch of the public school system. By the early 1830's, they had concluded reluctantly that infant schools accomplished as much harm as good. Although the schools helped poor parents by partially relieving them from the care of their little ones, the Board stated that the instruction given children proved detrimental once they entered the public primary schools.

The ultimate reasons behind the rejection of the infant schools were difficult to understand; perhaps professional jealousy explained some of the hostilities. Teachers complained to the Board that it was better to receive children into the primary schools who had no instruction whatever than to admit those who had graduated with the highest honors of the "Infant Seminaries." Teachers alleged that such children were "peculiarly restless in their habits," and were "thereby the cause of restlessness and disorder among the other children."[50] The instructors apparently wanted reeds that could be bent to their own whims rather than children already trained in a given direction.

In any case, Primary Board members protested, children of such a tender age could not properly be taught lessons in arithmetic, geography, and spelling. They learned only bad habits which then had to be unlearned in the primary schools. After extensive investigation the Standing Committee reported to the Board that "no good effect had resulted from the new and popular system of 'Infant School,' regarded as a means of discipline and instruction, preparatory to admission into the Primary Schools." Although other educators criticized the Primary School Board, it remained steadfast in its decision.[51]

Not until 1870, when Boston established the first public kindergarten in the nation, did the city return to the idea of incorporating infant schools into the public school system.[52] Yet even the willingness to consider grafting infant schools onto the public schools showed how eager some educators were to explore all opportunities for reaching the children of the poor.

Even before the heavy foreign immigration of the mid-1840's, the presence of large numbers of native and foreign poor had prompted Boston educators to educational experimentation. But the very concept of mass education for the urban poor limited the extent of innovation. The difficulties were best illustrated in what might be called the "textbook war."

PREVENTING INNOVATION: THE TEXTBOOK WAR

By the 1820's, educators in American cities had already begun to act like entreprenuers. With city councils yearly allocating more funds for educational expenses, the competition among educators to provide equipment and books for the schools became more intense. Changing theories of education over the next two decades brought demands for revisions of instructional materials. The heaviest in-fighting came in the textbook market, centered in Philadelphia and Boston. Presses in the two cities rolled out new texts literally by the ton. Between 1804 and 1832, the number of different textbooks in use throughout the nation increased from 93 to 407 as schoolmasters vied with one another for a share of the profits. Expenditures for all printed school materials rose from $2,500,000 in 1820 to over $16,000,000 by the 1850's, with school books the publishing mainstay.[53]

In Boston, Joseph E. Worcester, William B. Fowle, John Pierpont, Josiah Bumstead, and Josiah Holbrook all published competitive grammars and readers while outsiders like Samuel G. Goodrich ("Peter Parley"), Noah Webster, and John S. C. Abbott struggled to keep their works on the required reading lists in the schools. Yearly the School Committee and the Primary School Board re-evaluated the books to be used, often bending to whatever pressure individual authors could bring to bear on the choice. Despite the pressures, however, innovation in the selection of new materials was slow in coming. The city fathers, and occasionally the schoolmen themselves, were reluctant to pay all of the instructional costs for poor people who could not contribute their share of expenses—either directly or in tax dollars.[54]

During the 1820's both the primary and grammar schools charged a nominal sum, usually fifty cents a year per child, for textbooks. Often the sum was inadequate for the purchase of new books. The Primary School Board feared that very young children would destroy the few books that schools could afford to buy, yet regretted that some schools did not own enough books for proper instruction. The city would not allot any sum for the purchase of books; those poor children who could pay the annual sum could not afford any higher costs; thus there were not enough books to go around. The grammar schools faced the same predicament.[55]

In 1829, the School Committee appointed a group to determine whether books could be furnished at lower cost to the children of the poor and whether the Committee should apply to the City Council for specific book appropriations for indigent children. In a lengthy report the following year this sub-committee concluded that because of public hostility to increased expenditures for schools, "it is inexpedient to take any further measures for the subject of a supply of books for the schools, at the public expense."[56] "Public hostility" probably meant hostility toward providing for the poor—the parents of other children could afford the textbook fee or could provide additional materials for their own children.

Conscientious teachers found the lack of adequate materials detrimental to instruction and often solicited or accepted new supplies from parents and groups of citizens. The most glaring example of this practice, in the eyes of the Primary School Board, involved Josiah Holbrook, promoter of the Lyceum Movement in New England and a member of the Primary School Board. In 1832, to promote his own merchandise, Holbrook presented to several primary schools in his district some of the "Peter Parley" books, maps, and a few globes. The Primary Board reacted quickly, dropped Holbrook from its membership, and stated that such innovations destroyed the uniformity of the system and introduced inequalities in instruction. "The Primary Schools were established for *elementary* instruction," proclaimed their chronicler Joseph Wightman, "and particularly for the benefit of the poorer classes." The friends of education wanted to make schooling as inexpensive as possible for both the community and for the poor parents. Holbrook had attempted to introduce new materials in selected schools without due regard for the consequences. Apparently the children of the poor had to accept uniformly inadequate instruction.[57]

The controversy over the book fee became more heated as foreign immigration increased the ranks of poor children. In 1844 and 1845 a power struggle between Horace Mann and the Association of Boston Schoolmasters touched on the question of the textbook war. In his *Seventh Annual Report* (1843), Mann called for publicly supported school libraries throughout the state so that areas too poor to acquire needed materials might be better equipped. He also commented on the superiority of European textbooks and instructional apparatus to most of those in use in America. Among other complaints, the Boston school teachers denounced Mann for his alleged slur on their books and their teaching methods. No innovations were necessary, they argued. Hastening to

Mann's defense (as well as revealing his pique at the teachers' failure to use books he had authored), William B. Fowle noted that "to the poor, nothing is cheap. No matter how inexpensive the price of required books in schools, the poor cannot afford them. The city should finance school books for the poor."[58]

The *Annual Report of the School Committee* for 1846 echoed Fowle's statement. Any charge inflicted a burden where it was hardest to be borne—on the very poor. "Our schools," the *Report* continued, "are attended by many children whose impoverished and struggling parents, by their utmost exertions and extremist self-denial, are unable to supply *all* their children with the decent clothing and the books, which attendance at school requires." The School Committee contended that it was precisely the children of poor parents "whose attendance at school is most important for themselves and society." Publicly supplied school libraries, like Mann had suggested, should be provided for all schools.[59]

The gravest concern of the School Committee during the 1840's was not educational innovation—it was to increase attendance of the poor and immigrant children in school. According to the educators, the city's failure to provide free books kept too many such children from going to school. In 1847, Edward G. Loring, chairman of the Committee, stated the case in a special report to the City Council. Noting that the annual cost of school books per child appeared low at $2.00, Loring explained that there were scores of poor families who could not afford that price. Most of the children not attending school were foreigners. The City of Boston differed from the rest of the commonwealth in its extremes of wealth and poverty, he continued, and in the numbers of immigrants arriving daily. If the schools were to fulfill their purpose as a "public defence" against the moral infection of the streets, the immigrant children must be induced to attend. The city, Loring therefore urged, had to underwrite the cost of textbooks for all children so that the foreign poor could go to school. Appealing to economic motives, Loring added that such an action would eventually save the city money, both through the purchase of textbooks at wholesale prices, and in later criminal costs. The educated poor were the safe poor.[60]

While schoolmen urged, the city delayed. By 1852, however, the Council had provided funds so that every grammar school had one or two globes, sets of outline maps, a large map of Massachusetts and of the United States. But there were still no school libraries nor any uniform sets of textbooks. If a particular school had superior instructional materials, it was because the parents of its children could afford additional costs above the standard fee annually charged each child. If working-class parents, either native or foreign, wanted to send their children to school, they had to "wring from their scanty savings the price of new books, or must proclaim their poverty, and ask the City to lend their children the books required."[61] Nor did matters change over the years before the Civil War.

The very presence of the poor in large numbers had ensnared the educators and politicians in a dilemma: on the one side they affirmed the need to induce foreign and native lower-class children into attending the schools; on the other, they were unable or unwilling to make special financial arrangements to meet the educational needs of the poor. Educators repeatedly asserted that mass education was vital to the safety of urban society. Yet, they lamented, it was too expensive. In the textbook war there were few winners and too many losers.

During the antebellum years, Bostonians thus tried various means to encompass the lower classes with public education. Believing in education as a form of social insurance, schoolmen and political leaders tried to create schools that would enroll the poor, assimilate them into the mainstream of Boston society, and render them harmless as threats to urban order. In some instances the schoolmen failed, and their frustrations often led them to blame the poor for the failure, rather than themselves. But in other cases, considering the unwillingness of some citizens to spend additional tax dollars on the poor, the educators succeeded too well.

11

The Pitfalls of Coercion:
The State Versus the Children of Poverty

*We shall have little to fear from the much talked of dangers
of immigration, if the rising generation of immigrants can thus
be brought practically to understand . . . that the State will
take equal care of them, as of the children of the soil.*
                                        Boston School Committee (1848)[1]

In 1861 John D. Philbrick, superintendent of Boston Public Schools,
urged segregated schools for the city. Having examined the population
and evaluated its potential, he concluded that "there is in every large
city, a class of children, more or less numerous, which is too low down in
the depths of vice, crime, and poverty, to be reached by the benefits
of a system of public education." He did not suggest that these children
could not improve by schooling; that suggestion would have violated every
canon of faith held dear by nineteenth-century educators. He did believe
that such children harmed the general process of education when mixed
among their social betters in common classrooms, so he called for schools
that would segregate the native and foreign children of poverty. Philbrick piously intoned that the hand of "Christian love" still had to be
extended to the unfortunates, and asserted that the most useful means
would be to establish special industrial schools wherein children could
learn work skills as well as how to read and write. Within a few years
educators in other cities would agree, and a manual-labor school movement directed primarily at lower-class children would become popular.
But Philbrick was concerned less with industrial benevolence and Christian love toward the poor than with severing their associations with native
children "to purify and elevate the character of the public schools."[2]

The superintendent's lambast against lower-class children in the public
schools fell on receptive ears. His cynicism was becoming the dominant
viewpoint. Nonetheless, Philbrick's attitude directly contradicted the
hopes of those schoolmen who for many years had worked to extend the
reach of the schools to the children of poverty. By hook-and-by-crook, by

278

public propaganda and private persuasion, by overriding local control with administrative authority, the schoolmen had tried to tighten the net of public education to pull in the children of the dangerous classes. In 1850 Boston educators had managed to push through the state legislature the nation's first sweeping compulsory attendance law. Determined to use public education to assimilate the native and foreign poor into mainstream Boston (and American) society, the schoolmen ultimately came to despair of success. Why? Why were schoolmen, administrators, and even once idealistic reformers ready by the 1860's to abandon their hopes, or, at the very least, to confess feelings of ambivalence where they had once professed certainty? Why were they now willing to recognize the pitfalls of coercion when previously they had seen attendance at school as a bridge to social harmony and community stability? Much of the story of the public school movement during the nineteenth century lay in the answers to these questions. For the manner in which educators had responded to the challenges of assimilating the native and especially the foreign poor revealed the possibilities and the limitations of public education as an urban social institution.

PATTERNS OF IMMIGRANT ATTENDANCE

Determined to "domesticate them, and to give them American feelings, and identify them with ourselves as one people, with common interests," Boston educators, politicians, and reformers had worked diligently to increase immigrant attendance in the public schools. For two decades leaders had employed various means—public persuasion; private charity; infant, primary, evening, and monitorial schools—with mixed results. By the mid-1840's the long years of labor seemed to be over; success appeared imminent. Educators welcomed the growing numbers of foreign children in the schools. Reporting for the School Committee in 1847, George B. Emerson happily estimated that out of a total school-age population (four to sixteen years old) of 25,731, no more than 1,600 failed to attend the schools. To those critics who demeaned the provisions for lower-class youth, Emerson responded that the Committee had established facilities for most immigrant and native poor children. Those not in school "seem to be far more numerous than they are, because," Emerson explained, "as they are wandering from place to place, we see the same in many different places, and because, from their noisy and disorderly conduct, they attract far more notice than the same number of quiet, well-mannered children would do." Emerson's estimates of attendance were probably exaggerated; few reliable records were available to him. But if he erred, it was on the side of optimism, a wise advertising ploy by a man eager to boost the attendance of lower-class children, and hopeful for greater financial support from the city.[3]

Within the husk of every success, however, lie the seeds of failure; the methods of harvesting ultimately influence future growth. Emerson and other Boston educators had successfully advertised the schools and had drawn many children into classrooms. But, at the same time, they had failed to devote attention to providing enough new classrooms and new school buildings to meet the city's needs. The decade of the 1840's, with its inpouring of foreign population, was the critical decade for the common school experiment in Boston (see Table 14). During that decade,

TABLE 14

ENROLLMENT IN BOSTON PUBLIC PRIMARY
AND GRAMMAR SCHOOLS, 1840-1860

Year	Primary	Grammar	Total	Per Cent Growth Over 1841
1841	5,968	6,433	12,401	
1843	7,540	7,533	15,073	22
1845	8,599	8,511	17,110	38
1847	10,060	8,836	18,896	52
1849	11,257	9,332	20,589	66
1851	11,970	9,981	21,951	77
1853*	12,002	10,337	22,339	80
1855	12,580	11,188	23,768	92
1857	12,834	12,154	24,988	101.5
1859	13,077	12,238	25,315	104.0

* figures available for school year 1852-53, rather than 1853-54

SOURCES: Derived from Nathan Bishop, First Semi-Annual Report of the Superintendent of Public Schools of the City of Boston (Boston: City Printer, 1852), pp. 45-48; Bishop, Third Annual Report . . . 1853, pp. 78-79; John D. Philbrick, Second Semi-Annual Report of the Superintendent of Public Schools of the City of Boston (Boston: City Printer, 1861), pp. 17-20.

over fifty years of boosterism growth psychology collided head-on with demographic realities—and the city's educational system would henceforth bear the scars.

Had the city started building new schools at the outset of heavy immigration, it probably still would not have been able to provide sufficient schools to accommodate the incoming masses. Their sheer numbers were too many. But, at least schools would not have become as overcrowded as they did by 1850. Planning could have relieved some of the pressures of population. The sad fact remained, however, that few educational or political leaders saw the need for new institutions. The long years of mixed success in trying to encourage greater attendance among the native and foreign poor had convinced schoolmen that only a limited number of those children would ever reach the grammar schools. This belief accounted for the emphasis on primary schools as the educational mainstay for the poor. Schoolmen continued to hope that lower-class youth would enter the advanced schools, but their hope was edged with doubt. Given their reading of the situation, many educators remained certain that existing facilities could accommodate all the children of the city. The sudden rush of events proved them wrong.

Boston educators and political leaders had no way of foreseeing the mass influx of Irish immigrants. Past experience had demonstrated only that schools in various sections would become overcrowded as an increasingly mobile population entered the city. Educators had tried to cope with that problem through the redistribution of students during the late 1830's. But no information was available which would have allowed schoolmen to predict the sudden congestion of schools from foreign immigration after the mid-1840's. This lack of information compounded the task of readjusting the schools to the population, or of redistributing students among the various schools. In providing for education, as with other public services for a growing urban population, the tendency had been to rely on existent facilities until events demonstrated the need for catch-up measures. Opposition to building new schools was less a conservative reaction (as a contemporary approvingly noted) against suggestions "incompatible with the general system which long experience had shown to be well adapted to its end," than a reluctance to overextend the system to meet possible future challenges.[4] By the time that educators became aware of the magnitude of the problems facing them, events had nearly outrun the possibility of solution.

By the mid-1840's the dimensions of demographic change could be ignored no longer. On the outskirts of the city the increase of native and foreign poor and working-class families demanded attention. In 1847 the School Committee surveyed the situation of South Boston where industrialists were building new manufacturing plants. Recognizing that the foreigners who lived in South Boston were "of that better class who will not live in cellars or congregate together closely," the Committee nevertheless realized that industrialization would draw more Irish laborers into the area. The Mather and Hawes schools, the only two grammar schools in South Boston, were already overcrowded. The Committee urged the city to build another school, cautioning against "proving recreant to the best interests of the rising generation." By 1850 the new Bigelow School, named for the current mayor of Boston, opened its doors, dedicated by seventeen young ladies singing praises to Heaven:

> For the intellectual wealth,
> Which exalts the present age:—
> Social culture—moral health,—
> Which the *master minds* engage!

Whether the girls were of the Irish working class was not recorded.[5]

While the periphery of the city suffered population pressures, matters were far worse in the core. Most schools were in danger of severe overcrowding by foreign children. Yearly, during the forties, various sections of the city had grown in immigrant density. Except for Wards Five and Six (in northwest and west Boston), every ward in the city contained as foreign at least 36 per cent of its school-age population between the ages of five to fifteen (see Table 15). Six wards—One, Three, Four, Seven, Eight, and Twelve—counted over half their children as immigrants,

TABLE 15

BOSTON CHILDREN BY WARDS, 1850

Ward	Under Five Years	Native Five to Fifteen Years	Foreign* Five to Fifteen Years	Total Number of Children	Foreign* Per Cent Five to Fifteen Years
One	2,302	1,223	1,689	5,214	58.0
Two	1,166	1,150	766	3,082	39.9
Three	1,323	809	942	3,074	53.8
Four	640	521	609	1,770	53.9
Five	1,058	1,142	427	2,627	27.2
Six	1,013	1,427	256	2,696	15.2
Seven	2,289	675	2,283	5,247	77.2
Eight	1,299	740	1,203	3,242	61.9
Nine	1,143	1,059	597	2,799	36.1
Ten	1,373	958	932	3,263	49.3
Eleven	1,589	1,159	1,036	3,784	47.2
Twelve	1,889	1,280	1,392	4,561	52.1
TOTAL	17,084	12,143	12,132	41,359	47.65 (average per ward)

* "Foreign" includes native-born of one or both foreign-born parents.

SOURCE: Derived from *Report and Tabular Statement of the Censors . . . State Census of Boston, May 1, 1850* (Boston: City Printer, 1850), "Table A," pp. 19-30.

and the figures were almost that high in Wards Ten and Eleven. Ward Seven, the Broad Street and Fort Hill areas with the foulest tenements of the city, numbered more than three-fourths of its children as foreign. Citywide, the average of foreign children per ward was 47.65 per cent which meant that the representation of immigrant children in the school-age population more than doubled the percentage of school-age children in the city's total population (compare with Table 3). Not all immigrant children, by any means, attended the public schools, but those who did seemed to increase in number with each passing year.

Few schools kept accurate records. While individual members of the School Committee and the Primary Board were responsible for oversee-ing attendance at schools in their residential areas, they usually reported only yearly figures, and rarely delineated the number of foreign and native children. At best the figures offered only "snapshots" of attend-ance on the semi-annual and annual days of visitation by school officials. For the School Commmittee to know precisely how many children, and of what nationality, were in attendance at any given time was almost im-possible. When the Englishman Edward Twisleton arrived in Boston in the early 1850's on an inspection tour, for example, he experienced great difficulty in learning the exact number of Roman Catholic children attending the public schools. To furnish such information, he noted, "was evidently not within the line of the ordinary duties of the School Com-mittees, or of the General Board of Education." The only knowledge he could glean was that in 1852, with some 22,000 students in Boston schools, "more than one-third of them were from Roman Catholic families."[6]

Although citywide statistics were not always reliable, Bostonians were aware of the crowded and crowding conditions of some schools. In 1849 there were 168 primary schools throughout the city, enrolling over 10,000 students. Almost half of these were foreign children. The following year 11,376 children were enrolled, with an average attendance of 77 per cent, or 8,683; of these, 6,130 children were of foreign parentage. In 1852, as a result of attempting to keep pace with population growth, there were 190 schools, with over 6,600 of the 11,800 pupils the children of immigrant parents. Faced with the wave of immigrant population some educators were not yet prepared to abandon their goals for the schools.[7]

Alvan Simonds, for some years secretary of the Primary School Board, resigned his influential position in 1852. In carrying out his duties, Simonds had visited every school, and was optimistic about the progress of primary education. "Here are one hundred and ninety teachers in daily intercourse with eleven thousand pupils," he noted. "More than half of these children are of foreign origin." Despite the overburdening ratio of one teacher for every fifty-eight students, Simonds was "persuaded that our Primary Schools are doing more to *Americanize* that class of our population than all other classes combined." Certainly that was the purpose of the schools. As Samuel W. Bates, a member of the School Committee, observed the following year of the 195 primary schools: "While they are attended by the children of our most respectable citizens, [they] are also designed to provide a place for those thousands of children in this city, whose parents, engaged in manual labor, would often otherwise be obliged to leave them to wander the streets, acquiring habits of vagrancy, idleness and vice. . . . These Schools . . . are about equally attended by the children of the poorest of our foreign population, and those of our richest citizens and most honored statesmen."[8]

The accounts of Simonds and Bates showed the impact of foreign immigration on primary school conditions and hinted at the effect of those schools on foreign children. If the children were learning any lesson about America, it was that Americans believed in packaged education. The ruling philosophy seemed to find value in crowding as many young children as possible into one classroom with one teacher to enlighten, invigorate, and ennoble their young minds. Though the school might keep immigrant children off the streets, unanswered questions remained about the educational value of such congested conditions and such burdensome ratios of teachers and students.

In several grammar schools, matters were little better. "There is an immense difference in the materials of the different Schools," the School Committee reported in 1849. "Some of the Schools are filled with children, mostly of the native population, whose parents are of respectable standing in the community." These were intelligent youngsters, displaying self-respect and "propriety of conduct." But there were other schools accommodating ill dressed and ragged students, "not overclean in their persons." These were institutions "composed in a great measure of foreigners, in the most humble and destitute circumstances." To its consternation, the Committee discovered one school in which a class of fifty girls contained but one "American." In 1850 the Committee reported that the second class (a year away from graduation) of the Endicott School had an enrollment of fifty-eight boys, forty-five of whom were Irish. The first class of the Boylston School included a mixture of native and immigrant children, while the second class contained only six Americans in the total of fifty-two boys and girls.[9]

Both the Boylston and Endicott schools were located in districts heavily populated by foreigners (see Maps 5 and 6). The Boylston School was the only grammar school in Ward Seven, the most immigrant-congested ward in the city. The Fort Hill district of this ward had long been infamous for miserable housing conditions, its crime rate, and as a breeding-

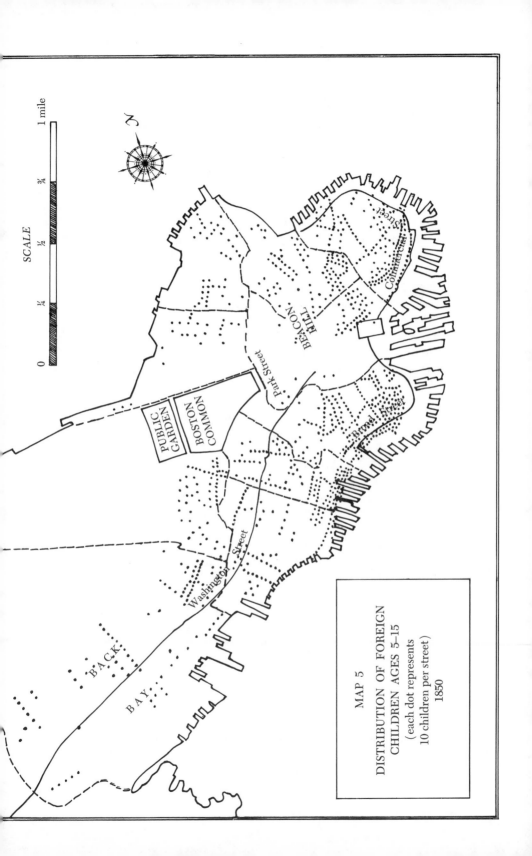

SCALE

0   ¼   ½   ¾   1 mile

N

PUBLIC
GARDEN

BOSTON
COMMON

Park Street

BEACON
HILL

Commercial Street

Broad Street

Washington Street

BACK

BAY

MAP 5

DISTRIBUTION OF FOREIGN
CHILDREN AGES 5–15
(each dot represents
10 children per street)
1850

ground of cholera and other diseases. There was a curious inconsistency, then, between the professed goal of schools as instruments of assimilation and a failure to provide additional educational facilities in a district over-flowing with foreign population.

The case of the Endicott School was slightly different. In Ward One, the old North End of Boston—also long notorious as a foreign and lower-class section of the city, teeming with the houses of prostitution on Ann Street, local grogshops, and gambling dens—there were two other schools to accommodate the immigrant children in addition to Endicott. The Hancock and Eliot schools, in fact, appeared so adequate to the task that in 1852, in an effort at consolidation, the School Committee closed down the Endicott School.[10] Still, there were large pockets of foreign popula-tion in Wards Three and Four, adjacent to the Endicott and Hancock schools, that were left with no educational institution in the immediate vicinity.

Elsewhere in the city the Winthrop and Adams schools (Ward Eight), Johnson (Ward Nine), Brimmer (Ward Ten), and the Otis School (Ward Three) were all surrounded by enclaves of foreign immigrants (see Maps 5 and 6). Of these, only Otis and Brimmer had been built within the previ-ous ten years. Despite ambitious hopes for the social role of public educa-tion, a time-lag had occurred between the ability of the City Council and the School Committee to build new schools and the population influx that cre-ated the demand for new schools. By 1850, Bostonians were still trying to overhaul their public facilities to meet the needs of those thousands of migrants fleeing the "great hunger" in Ireland. In 1847 the *Boston Tran-script* had reported on "groups of poor wretches [who] were to be seen in every part of the city, resting their weary and emaciated limbs at the corners of the streets and in the doorways of both private and public houses." Within that single year, the city of some 114,000 had witnessed the arrival of over 37,000 Irish immigrants.[11] By 1850 the foreign per-centage of the total population had jumped from 32.6 per cent in 1845 to almost 46 per cent.

As late as 1848 the School Committee proudly expressed its satisfaction with current conditions. "We have been much pleased," stated the *An-nual Report,* "to find that our Irish population avail themselves largely of the benefit of our Schools, and that many of the Irish children have at-tained a high rank in scholarship, and are in other respects among the best children in attendance." "We shall have little to fear," the Committee asserted, "from the much talked of dangers of immigration, if the rising generation of immigrants can thus be brought practically to understand that a common career is open to them with the native population, and that the State will take equal care of them, as of the children of the

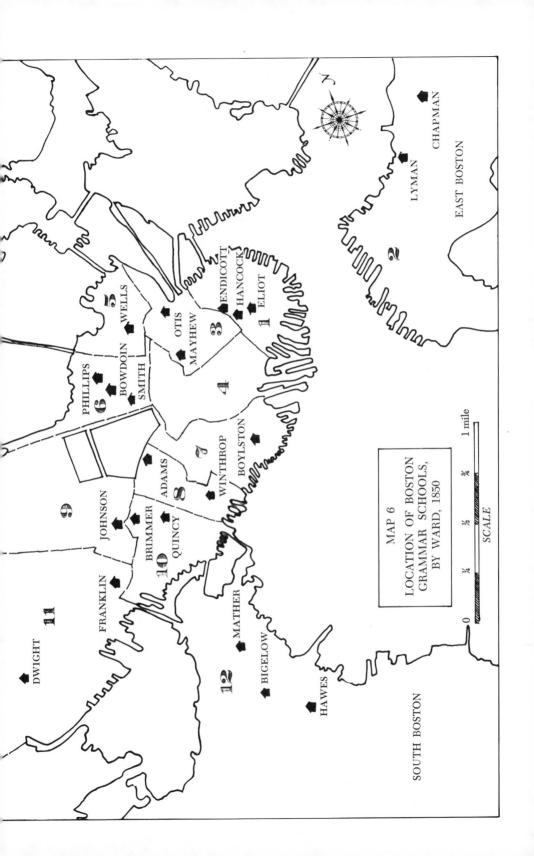

MAP 6

LOCATION OF BOSTON
GRAMMAR SCHOOLS,
BY WARD, 1850

SCALE

0   ¼   ½   ¾   1 mile

soil."[12] But in view of population pressures which rendered grammar schools in different sections of the city inadequate as useful centers of assimilation, this was an empty boast.

By the late 1840's, however, first-hand experience and the scattered available records of enrollment convinced Boston schoolmen that their attempts to induce immigrant and poor children into the public schools had succeeded—and succeeded too well. In various wards of the city, the grammar schools had to refuse admittance to many students due to overcrowding. In other schools the rapid increases in foreign enrollment threatened to upset the whole ethnic and social class balance of the school population. As a result, some educators' attitudes about the schools during the course of the forties took on previously unknown tones of ambivalence. Educators still believed in the capacity of schools to assimilate the strangers into American patterns of thought and behavior. But their assertions about the social role of the schools became tinged with fears about the effect of too many alien youth in the classrooms on native children.

The *Annual Report* for 1846, reflecting anxiety over the year of increased immigration just concluded, warned that the dangers of ignorant and immoral immigrants were nowhere as momentous "as in our common schools. In the first place, the ratio of increase is far greater among the children of our foreign population, than among those of our native population—in the district most purely native, the increase is one to every fifty only, while in the Broad Street district [Ward Seven], so called, it is one to every fifteen."[13]

The School Committee had discovered the bane of birth rates that allegedly poisoned their educational mixture—a bane which other Bostonians in subsequent years would use to justify their conceptions of Anglo-Saxon racial superiority.[14] Statistics soon confirmed the fears of the School Committee. The City Census of 1850 proved a tacitly accepted fact: mortality figures were higher for immigrants than for native Americans. But it also revealed that the natural increase of the foreign population (the excess of births over deaths), was greater than that of the American population. To the School Committee in 1846, who suspected the fact, higher foreign birth rates ominously portended a loss of educational effectiveness. The Committee cautioned that "a bad man, at the polls or in society, is a much less dangerous and harmful person than a bad boy at school." Adults could resist the dangers of immoral men, but "the bad boy at school acts on other boys susceptible of evil, and prompt to propagate it."[15]

If the higher birth rates of immigrants meant that many schools would experience an inrush of foreign children, the locations of various schools also promised an imbalance of immigrant over native students. "Already whole districts are becoming depopulated of the native inhabitants," complained the School Committee in 1849. A "tide of pauper immigration" was pushing native Bostonians out of the heart of the city. The Committee, of course, was correct. The residential mix in former years of native and foreign lower- and middle-income groups had given way to increasing separation of middle-class Bostonians into suburbs and neighboring towns and of immigrants into their own enclaves in the city proper. By 1850, whole streets, entire districts within Boston had been taken over by immigrants. Among the poor and foreign groups there was also considerable change of residence as people moved from neighborhood to neighborhood in search of better living conditions and better economic opportunities.[16]

The composition of the school population by the late 1840's and early 1850's inevitably reflected this residential mobility. In part, neighborhood instability accounted for the reticence of schoolmen to provide more schools in the areas of the city which most needed new facilities. Referring to the Boylston School on Fort Hill, the School Committee in 1850 observed that "this School is situated on an airy and commanding eminence, but it is surrounded by a population chiefly foreign. The pupils do not exhibit the same neatness of personal appearance which is constantly noticed in Schools more favored, and they are so constantly changing, that the condition of the School is necessarily disturbed." Of the Endicott School the Committee noted that "the locality of this school is very unfavorable to conspicuous eminence, and interferes with its regular progress; many of the pupils being Irish, their attendance is irregular and not long enough for much improvement. They receive little or no attention at home, and are often kept from School, as well by the requirements of the church, as by parental command for household purposes."[17]

Those Bostonians still living in areas undergoing transition from native to foreign population concentration voiced alarm over the increasing immigrant flavor of local schools. Many native parents applied for permits to transfer their children to schools which they hoped would provide better associations with other American youth. Parents did not want their children attending schools such as that recalled by one schoolboy as "mostly composed of lads of Irish birth or descent. . . . These boys emitted a pungent odor, fearfully suggestive of cholera, and, at times, young as all of them were, an odor more pungent still, of a flavor strange to me then, which experience has since taught me was the fumes of New-England rum and molasses." Though some transfers were granted, members of the School Committee tried to discourage the practice, explaining that "it has the effect of still further depressing the Schools which are thus avoided, by taking from them the children whose domestic training is such as would enable them to exert the best influence in reclaiming their less favored fellows." To further concentrate one ethnic and income group in individual schools appeared educationally unsound and morally unwise.[18]

Other schoolmen professed understanding of the "misgivings and complaint with many," but hoped that citizens would put up with an admitted evil. "We are all of foreign parentage and but a short distance removed from such an origin," stressed the Primary School Board in 1850. "Alike true is it, that the children alluded to, will soon be found of us and with us, as thoroughly americanized as we are or ever can be—alike lovers of American soil and sustainers of American institutions." Only with education "a quickening impulse may be given to all the industrial movements of the day; without it, the future is full of doubt and danger."[19] But this plea for tolerance and patience went unheeded.

The schoolmen were snared in a trap of their own making. They wanted to bring all children of all classes in the city into the schools, but that looked increasingly difficult, if not impossible. The parents of many native children apparently did not want to send their offspring to school with the children of poverty, and, in turn, some immigrant parents were beginning to demand separate schools for their children. The School Committee would not agree to the immigrant requests. Reacting to a petition from German parents who requested a branch school for their children, the Committee refused on several grounds: it had no legal authorization to establish such schools; there were many groups in the community who would like separate schools, and the Committee could not honor one request without honoring all; and, most important, German children should go to school with native Americans to learn "as early as possible" their national characteristics. The public schools were designed to produce American citizens, to be a "powerful instrument in support of the political institutions of our government," explained the Committee. The only circumstance under which the Committee would consider establishing schools in which two languages were taught would be where it was "necessary in Americanizing foreigners." This presently did not seem to be such a circumstance.[20]

The educators stuck firmly to their goals for socially and ethnically integrated schools, even as they expressed doubts that such schools were always desirable or even possible. Too many alien children in a given school might cause an exodus of native American youth; but the failure to bring poor native and immigrant children into the schools, thought the schoolmen, would probably result in social chaos. Fearing the results

of too heavy an immigrant enrollment, they feared even more the consequences of failing to educate such children. "If we let them run wild,"
stressed the School Committee in 1850, "we shall feel the effects ten
years hence, in the insecurity of property, in the records of our criminal
courts, in the expenses of our houses of punishment, and in our taxes
for pauperism. . . . We must open the doors of our school houses and
invite and compel them to come in. There is no other hope for them or
for us. . . . In our Schools they must receive moral and religious teaching, powerful enough if possible to keep them in the right path amid the
moral darkness which is their daily and domestic walk." If there was
more than a trace of the patronizing in the attitude of the Committee,
there was an even clearer tone of social anxiety. The Committee was
convinced that "unless we can reclaim this population in their childhood
by moral means, we must control them by force, or support them as
paupers, at a maturer period of life."[21]

The educators had no ready-made solutions for overcrowding or for
preventing the imbalance of native and foreign children in some of the
schools. But of one fact they were certain. The School Committee could
accomplish nothing without stronger legal controls over the children
than those it currently possessed. Unless the Committee could force children to go to school, and to attend whatever school it selected, the difficulties would mount.

The lack of authority was hardly a new complaint. By 1850 the
schoolmen had spent three decades trying to increase their power. The
central issue of their power struggles with parents, city, and state had
been whether society had the right to compel children to attend school.
Until that issue was resolved, all other questions about the extension of
public education were academic. Until society (embodied here by the
School Committee) possessed the legal right of coercion, rising tax levies
or new buildings for public education seemed relatively unimportant.
The press of immigrant children into the schools made the resolution of
that issue imperative. By 1850 the schoolmen felt compelled to secure
the legal right of compulsion.

THE TRIALS OF TRUANCY

While educators struggled with the difficulties of increased immigrant
enrollment in the schools, they also wrestled with the problem of truancy.
Concern over non-attendance appeared paradoxical when expressed by
the same men who decried the immigrant imbalance of some schools. If
schools were already overcrowded, how could the educators and political

leaders of Boston deplore the number of children not in school? The answer lay buried deep within the excuses, justifications, stated motives, and implicitly held fears of men who believed that the present and future stability of urban society rested on their actions. By the late 1840's educators had not yet accustomed themselves to their success in enlarging the school population. They had not yet fully plumbed the implications of that success. The quixotic twists of educational thought nowhere revealed themselves more completely than in the drive to end truancy in the late 1840's and early 1850's. Like most men overtaken by sudden and unexpected success, the educators remained intellectually in hostage to the past.

In earlier decades, when the principal task had been to induce greater numbers of the poor and immigrant classes into the schools, local politicians and schoolmen had identified truancy as their primary concern. One of the first actions of the new Primary School Board in 1819 was to appoint a group in each ward to ascertain the number of "idlers, truants, and such as have no visible or known employment, and who do not habitually attend any school." Discovering a large number of truants, the Board sought to remedy the situation over the next few years by sending its members throughout the wards to admonish parents and students.[22]

The effort proved only temporarily successful. When the Reverend Joseph Tuckerman arrived in Boston in 1826, he was astonished at the extent of truancy. After visiting the homes of the poor to encourage them to send their children back to school, Tuckerman came to believe that "no boy becomes at once an obdurate truant or in any respect obdurately vicious." But he also agreed with the schoolmen that truancy led to depravity, and that a boy who had become a truant if "left uncared for, will probably sink into the corruption of those with whom he seeks his pleasures and becomes a vagrant." The minister advised the city to appoint a special officer to oversee the "idle, vagrant, and vicious children of the city." This specialist would roam the streets, round up the truants, and either return them to school, find employment for them if they were over twelve years of age, or admit them to the House of Reformation for Juvenile Offenders if the children were too immoral to re-enter the schools.[23]

In general, the city fathers followed Tuckerman's advice. In addition to myriad other duties, Constable George Reed took on the responsibility of part-time truant officer. Reed found many truants loitering in the streets or idling away hours on the wharves, and returned them to school or to the police courts, depending on his own judgment of their character. Unfortunately, Reed's judgment and integrity were questionable—he built his reputation as the greatest "thief-taker" of the period by coercing petty criminals into becoming informants. That many of the children he placed in the House of Reformation were there on the flimsiest of reasons was evident in that institution's *Reports*.[24]

But schoolmasters were delighted with Reed's performance; he rid them of many troublesome youths and reduced the amount of time they had to spend in tracking down wayward students. In 1831 the School Committee recommended that all schools follow the course taken by the Boylston School in calling on Constable Reed to remove legally children of incorrigible character to the House of Reformation. Charles Fox, master of the school, so faithfully had discharged this "duty" that he could report that "truantship is of very rare occurrence in this school." Apparently it never occurred to Master Fox that such prompt action on incarcerating children explained the lack of truancy—faced by the prospect, undoubtedly many children never entered the school in the first place. But if Fox was untroubled by truancy, he was "exceedingly annoyed by a set of miserable, dirty, ragged boys, of wretched parents, who generally are about our streets and wharves. . . . The fact is," Fox wrote Mayor Otis, "that some parents will not send their children to any school: they want their services to procure chips, to beg, or steal—in fine, *to get anything in any way they can.*" It was partly to reach this class of children that the School Committee had attempted to establish the system of intermediate schools. Fox, however, was suspicious of this action. "If a school were established for them" he charged, "it would require fifty constables, possessing the vigilance of Reed, to catch them every morning and bring them to school. They will not attend school, unless deprived of their liberty." Fortunately, other schoolmen in the city were less certain than Fox of the innate depravity of the children of the poor.[25]

Throughout the 1830's educators sought reliable information on the number of truant and vagrant children. In 1834 a part-time truant officer reported on the names, ages, and character of three hundred idle youth to the School Committee, though the Committee itself recognized that his estimate was probably too low. In 1836 the Committee appointed former mayor Josiah Quincy and five others to confer with a like group empowered by the City Council to investigate and adopt more effective measures of getting "vagrant" and "idle" children into the schools. The following year, as a result of the investigation, the Council authorized the mayor and alderman to employ a suitable person as truant officer. If parents would not comply with the officer's demands to enroll their children in school, he was to report their names to the mayor who would aid in all legal steps toward placing the children in the House of Reformation. To that end the Council also resolved to seek modifications of state law so that councilmen could commit children to the House without going through the "formality" of a trial before a Police Court justice. In this endeavor the Council was not successful; the law continued to require the "formality." But the appointment of the truant officer was gratifying to Council members. By 1839, over a thousand truant children were assigned to various schools through his efforts. Both politicians and educators agreed that schooling for the poor was so vital that any means of persuasion and intimidation were not only necessary but also defensible.[26]

The commonwealth had also undertaken certain coercive measures for education. In 1836, in his first annual message, Governor Edward Everett commented that Massachusetts was a society composed of individuals whose happiness was "the great design of the association." But he added that "almost the only compulsion exercised toward the citizen, in his private affairs, by the State, is that which compels him to provide the means of educating his children."[27] To merely require tax support of education, however, did not assure that children would attend school. Many people had come to believe that the State had to compel more. State action had to encompass the children of poor and working-class families. In Boston, and throughout the state, people recognized that a major cause of truancy was child labor.

Urban and small town manufacturing establishments had sprung up almost overnight. In most cases the manufactories employed large numbers of young children as cheap labor. In 1832 the New England Association of Farmers, Mechanics, and Other Working Men emphasized this evil of industrialization in much the same language as that of an earlier legislative commission in the mid-1820's. The Association reported that two-fifths of all workers in New England factories were children aged seven to sixteen; that children labored from daylight to eight in the evening; that parents could not remove their children to enroll them in school on penalty of losing their own jobs; and that children could attend school only after work in the evening or on Sunday. That few working-class youth attended schools under such circumstances was obvious.[28]

By modern standards the conditions of child labor during the period seem incredibly harsh. To shut up young children in cotton mills, in printing, dyeing, shoe, and iron manufactories for ten to fourteen hours a day at wages ranging from twenty-five to fifty cents, to deny them the privileges of common schooling, affronts twentieth-century notions of child-rearing. But to nineteenth-century observers and participants the sense of injustice was not always as clear. To men and women reared on faith in the gospel of work, to individuals who believed that honest labor, even for the young, built character and moral responsibility, child labor was not an unmitigated evil. In the best of establishments children were not driven unmercifully at their tasks. Harriet Robinson, for example, a young Boston girl who started work in the famous Lowell mills at the age of ten, recalled that the greatest hardship was having to be on duty "nearly fourteen hours a day. . . . But in every other respect it was a pleasant life. We were not hurried any more than was for our good, and no more work was required of us than we were able easily to do." She viewed the cotton factory as a good "school" for life for many young people like herself. "For, without this incentive to labor, this chance to earn extra money and to use it in their own way, their influence on the times, and also, to a certain extent, on modern civilization, would certainly have been lost."[29] Still, the Lowell mills in their early days represented the most attractive working conditions for children. Elsewhere, matters were far worse, as investigators discovered.

The generation that "discovered the child" was the same generation that experienced the beginnings of the factory system of labor. The impact of industrialization—the division and specialization of labor in manufacturing processes—fell most heavily on child labor. By the early 1830's (if not before) children who ten or twenty years previous would have been apprenticed to a journeyman carpenter, printer, or mechanic now found themselves hired out indiscriminately to a factory operator or mill owner. In essence, child labor was the initial form of assembly-line machinery, performing many of the routine, unskilled tasks that mechanical inventions later would accomplish. It was precisely this kind of dehumanizing labor that drew the fire of opponents of child labor. One of the best summary statements about the situation came from an 1836 legislative commission on education, chaired by James G. Carter, a long-standing friend of schooling for the children of poverty:

> The sons and daughters of New England are presented . . . with the alternative of becoming essentially a manufacturing people, or of bidding adieu to their native hills, the land, the home, and the graves of their forefathers, and following the rising glories of the west.
> . . . Nor is it difficult to understand that a change in occupation, from those diversified employments which characterize a sparse and agricultural population, to the simple operations consequent upon that minute subdivision of labor, upon which the success of manufacturing depends, is not a circumstance favorable to intellectual development. By the former, the ingenuity and inventive powers are called into action, in the combination and adaptation of means to ends, and thereby they are developed and strengthened. By the latter employment, the invention having been made by some master spirit, the operative is reduced, in some degree, to the humble sphere of a part of the machinery.

Certain that the conditions of labor deprived children of essential opportunities of "mental and moral development and cultivation," Carter's
committee recommended a bill which provided that no child under
fifteen could be employed in any manufactory unless he or she had attended either private or public school for at least three months during
the previous year. As enacted, the new law also established a fine of $50
for any employer who failed to respect the law. Thus Massachusetts
passed the first type of compulsory school-attendance bill in the nation.
Unfortunately, the legislature did not provide any means of enforcement.
On the whole, apparently the law was observed more carefully by large
enterprises in Boston and other towns than it was by less successful and
smaller independent manufacturers.[30]

Still, this bold legislative venture proved inadequate to affect measurably truancy from school. Within a few years newspaper editors were
complaining that "this law is evaded by the cruel and mercenary owners
of the children, who keep them nine months in one factory, and then
take them directly to another, with the lie in their mouths, that the children have had three months schooling." And, in 1839, Horace Mann
observed harshly that "there are many parents, not only of our immigrant, but of our native population, so lost to the sacred nature of the
relation they sustain towards the children . . . that they go from town
to town, seeking opportunities to consign them to unbroken, bodily toil;
. . . thus pandering to their own vicious appetites by adopting the most
efficient measures to make their offspring as vicious as themselves." The
following year Mann intensified his attack on the conditions of corrupted
family life and child labor. He demonstrated that the law of 1836 was
simply not being obeyed. As a result, in 1842 the legislature amended the
earlier law so that no manufacturer could employ a child under twelve
for more than ten hours a day. Mann welcomed the change, slight
though it was. He estimated that approximately 60 per cent of children
between the ages of four and sixteen attended some school, at some time,
during the year. Yet he deplored the fact that almost 40 per cent of
working-class children received no schooling. To combat the "epidemic"
of parental indifference, Mann urged a new law requiring parents either
to send their children to school regularly, or not at all.[31]

In Boston, citizens and schoolmen alike were not yet prepared to accept such rigorous state control, nor were they ready to abandon hope
of enrolling all children in the public schools by adopting such an either-
or proposition. By the mid-1840's, however, truancy in the city had become so troublesome that educators determined to eliminate it.

In 1845, the initial year of heavy immigration, newly elected Mayor
Josiah Quincy, Jr., promised the School Committee full cooperation in a

drive to end truancy. Quincy created a committee of the City Council to investigate the extent of the problem. In 1846 that committee reported that "the mischief caused by habits of truancy, which prevail in many of our schools can hardly be overrated. No valuable or permanent reform will ever be carried into full effect until this obstacle is removed." Quincy found intolerable the fact that "hundreds of children of both sexes, are daily kept from school to support their parents, often in idleness and drunkenness, by pilfering about our wharves, or by some other profitable form of vice, and are regularly educated for the brothel and the dram-shop, for the poorhouse and the jail."[32]

Sharing the mayor's concern, the School Committee responded that existing law, if enforced, could correct the evil, but it also offered a new plan which became part of the "School Regulations." Under the new rules, police officers spent part of their time tracking down children who had failed to enter their names at the appropriate neighborhood school and determining whether that failure was due to regular employment, other legitimate excuses, or sheer parental neglect. The Committee also ordered school masters to report monthly any "incorrigibly stubborn" or "habitually truant" youth.[33] While the new procedures helped, they did not solve the problem. Persuasion and limited threats of sending children to the Houses of Reformation and of Correction were not sufficient whips to force poor and immigrant parents into line, especially when they remained suspicious of public schools and needed the financial aid of working children.

Members of the School Committee and the legislature recognized that among the poorer classes "the services or daily earnings of their children are the primary matter." But they also believed that financial need, real as it might be, was secondary to the formation of character that only schooling could provide. Truancy was an intolerable evil to the righteous cause of improving urban schools. Horace Mann did not exaggerate when he wrote Mayor Quincy in January 1848 that "if the evil can be grappled with in this city, the difficulties presented by any other place in the State may be laughed at."[34]

The influx of immigration during the previous two years had swelled the ranks of the truant to an alarming size. Schoolmen were encouraged "to find that a large proportion of foreign parents are very desirous to place their children under our care, immediately on their arrival on our shores," but they were equally disturbed to discover that many more immigrant parents did not send their children to school. "The offence occurs principally among the Irish. We daily see great numbers of boys and girls who are hanging round places where the demolition or erection of buildings, is going on, to gather chips from among the rubbish for fire wood." The Committee speculated that many of these children probably had their names on some school roster, but never attended. "All these children ought to be in the Schools," the Committee concluded.[35]

In demanding that all immigrant and poor children attend school, the Committee displayed its confusion over means and ends. Its own statistics revealed that many city classrooms had already become overburdened from the increased enrollment of such children. Masters did not have enough time to teach effectively the students they had; parents of native children did not want to send their offspring to schools overpopulated by the immigrant poor. The city was reluctant to situate new schools in immigrant districts "where there is a population turnover of three of four hundred every year with great irregularity of attendance."[36] Under such circumstances neither native nor foreign youth could benefit measurably from forced attendance at school. Yet the schoolmen remained so convinced that the common education of rich and poor, native and foreign children alike was the only bedrock for urban stability, that they overlooked the practical obstacles in their way. They had worked so long to end truancy in the city, they felt so strongly the need to gain legal authority over the fate of school-age children, that they could not comprehend the complications involved in compelling school attendance. As the figures of overcrowding and truancy mounted, educators largely ignored the implications of the former and stressed the dangers of the latter.

Mayor Quincy kept his promise and asked the City Council to take more effective measures in dealing with truants. Quincy agreed with Horace Mann and other educators that truancy should be made a criminal offence, but in 1848 he could not convince the City Council to take such drastic action. In November of that year, the School Committee appointed another in its long line of sub-committees to investigate truancy. The following months the sub-committee reported back with a list of vagrant and truant children throughout the city. Mayor Quincy in turn had not been idle; to supplement the findings of the School Committee he had ordered Francis Tukey, the city marshal, to obtain statistics on the number of truants and vagrants.[37] In February 1849 Tukey submitted his findings to John P. Bigelow, the new mayor (see Table 16).

Marshal Tukey confirmed the assertions of the School Committee on wide-spread truancy, especially among the immigrant classes. While he did not claim complete accuracy, he estimated that about 1,500 children (in an average-attendance school-age population of approximately 12,-000) between the ages of six and sixteen were either vagrants or truants. He actually counted 1,066 in those categories. The means Tukey employed to gather the statistics provided an instructive commentary on police methods and on the determination of the city to coerce lower-class children into attending school.

The marshal appointed one of his officers, Oliver H. Spurr, to take charge of truants. As there was no official city policy on the treatment of truants, Spurr improvised. He called upon parents to learn about a

TABLE 16
VAGRANT AND TRUANT CHILDREN IN BOSTON, 1849

Whole number, ages 6-16	1,066
Male	882
Female	184
Children of American parents	103
Children of Foreign parents	963
Children belonging to some school, but truant	106
Boys regularly employed in bowling saloons	139
Children not attending any school nor lawfully employed	821
Children not attending school for want of clothing, books, etc.	129
Children of widows	238
Children with fathers, but no mothers	29
Orphans	54

SOURCE: Derived from "Truants From School," *Boston City Documents, 1849,* Doc. No. 9, p. 2.

boy's character, then found the boy and returned him to the proper school. In some cases, that was sufficient. If he called again for the same boy, Spurr first asked the consent of the parents, then locked-up the youth for several hours to teach him a lesson. If the "police-man's badge and staff" held no terrors for an incorrigible, Spurr explained that "the only course left for us after this, was to watch the boy until we could arrest him for some trifling offence *known to the law,* and have him punished, which seemed to be necessary for the good of the boy, as well as the School."[38] The city never reprimanded either Spurr or Tukey for this procedure. As long as there was no law against truancy, politicians and educators condoned any action that would remove troublesome children from the streets—either to enroll them in school or to place them in correctional institutions.

Marshal Tukey thought not as an educational reformer but as a policeman. That he wanted nuisances off the streets was understandable;

vagrant and truant children, idlers on the docks, petty criminal offenders in the congested immigrant districts all demanded too much attention from him and from his limited force. The significance of his arguments against truancy lay in their similarity to those by educational reformers. Using language that might have been copied directly from School Committee reports Tukey stated that "I am satisfied that it will cost the State and City more for Police, Courts, and Prisons, if they are suffered to go at large, than it would, to take them now, maintain them and make them useful citizens." Both the marshal and the schoolmen envisioned education of the lower classes as the best means of securing urban order. If the educators refused to accept Tukey's extremist recommendation that offensive children be bound out as domestics or apprentices until the age of twenty-one, they concurred in the marshal's demand for a law against truancy.[39]

In March 1849 the School Committee requested Mayor Bigelow and the Council to pass a law compelling all children to attend school; at the same time friendly lawmakers introduced a similar proposal in the legislature. Several councilmen and state legislators demurred, affirming that a compulsory law threatened parental rights over the child. Educators had anticipated such a response; in 1848 the School Committee had admitted of truancy that "the only effectual remedy lies with the parents and the influences they bring to bear at home." But, along with other social observers who bewailed the decline in family solidarity, Committee members had declared that "such influences are not properly exerted, especially among the poorer classes." Now, in 1849, the schoolmen mounted a propaganda campaign in favor of compulsory attendance in the press and at the November convention of the State Teachers' Association. Under public pressure, on May 3, 1850, the legislature passed a bill authorizing the towns and cities to make any needed provisions for habitual and unemployed truants, and to establish penalties for those parents who profited from "their wretched gains or . . . dishonest pursuits."[40]

Boston educators and city officials were delighted at their success. Their cooperation in the name of public safety marked a turning-point in community relations. The police force added a full-time truant officer, the first in any American city.[41] The arm of public control had reached further into the private domain. Those who favored the new law now set about sharpening its teeth, for the law was permissive, not restrictive, and did not contain precise means of enforcement.

In 1852, the efforts of Bostonians resulted in the first statewide compulsory school law in the United States. The new act required every child between the ages of eight and fourteen to attend public school for at least three months every year; six of those weeks had to be consecutive. Any parents who kept their children from attending school were subject to a fine. School Committees were required to keep accurate accounts of truancy and to report violations to the city. The act, however, did not go as far as some Boston educators would have liked. A child could be exempted from the law: if physical or mental ill-health kept him from school; if evidence demonstrated that he had received equivalent education by some other means; or if parents were so impoverished that they could not furnish a child with the means of education.[42] Still, Boston officials had triumphed in their battle against truancy.

In October 1850 Boston had enacted its own ordinance based on the recent state statute. To guarantee its effectiveness, the City Council empowered the local courts to confine any habitual truants to the House of Reformation for Juvenile Offenders. In 1853, and again in 1854, Boston supplemented its own ordinance of 1850 under the new state provisions of 1852. The police courts of the city obtained full jurisdiction for enforcement of the law against truancy. While those courts were enmeshed in local politics, educators had good cause to believe that jurists would rule favorably in their behalf on cases involving immigrant and poor parents; the number of arrests and convictions of Irish for other offences had mounted steadily in recent years.[43]

In Boston and throughout the state the effects of the laws of 1850 and 1852 became quickly apparent. Of children committed to the state reform school at Worcester 367 of 440 boys had been truants from school, a "crime" exceeded in villainy only by the number who had been addicted to lying, and closely followed by those who used profane language. In 1852 Boston truant officer William F. Reed reported that only a few incorrigibles remained among the 36 native and 211 foreign truants he had dealt with during a three-month period. These were all poor children lacking clothing and shoes. Most preferred school to the life of the streets but might have to stay at home unless private charity would clothe them properly. For the year ending June 30, 1853, Reed reported a total of 98 American and 559 foreign truants and reiterated his belief that few habitual truants remained. Not all working-class children, of course, remained in school for lengthy periods. Many, perhaps 1,000 by the early 1860's, left school by age ten or twelve to be apprenticed to various trades or to assist their parents in some industrial occupation. But under the law, these were not truants. On the whole, Boston officials could be satisfied that compulsory education was achieving the minimum goal of ensuring some school experience for the mass of immigrant and poor children in the city.[44]

One fact was clear throughout the campaign for effective control of truancy—educators and local officials had been determined to exalt public over private interests. Urban life had become too complex, the relationships of individuals too interdependent, the stability of society too tenuous, to allow private citizens complete freedom in the daily exercise of their lives. Population increase among both the urban poor and the immigrant classes had only aggravated an already difficult situation. Schoolmen and politicians had long agreed that the school was the one reliable public institution that could render the poor harmless and assimilate the stranger. Having accepted that unproven fact as faith, it was inevitable that Boston leaders would use any coercive means to assure the triumph of public education. It was only a matter of time.

In their trials against truancy, Boston educators raised and confronted the fundamental question facing an allegedly democratic society—how deeply could the state impinge upon the rights of individuals? How narrowly could society limit individual freedom of choice in the name of social necessity? To be sure, the question was not new; Americans had debated it in myriad ways for many years. But in the context of urban public education the query took on added meaning, for it struck at the core of society's most hallowed institution—the family. The movement for compulsory education was nothing less than a debate over who owned the child.

WHO OWNS THE CHILD?

That the debate took place during a period of years when Americans "discovered the child" and believed they had "lost the family" as a stable social institution was not coincidental. The rise of the common school movement in the cities was partly a reaction to those broader social concerns. Perceiving particular stresses on urban family life in a competitive economy and on the child maturing in the city, educators had long asserted a public responsibility for the welfare of individual citizens. As early as 1830 Joseph Tuckerman, referring to orphaned children of the poor, had affirmed that "the city to which they belong should become their parent and, as far as possible, should discharge a parent's duty towards them." Civic and commonwealth institutions such as the House of Reformation and the State Manual Labor School considered inmates adopted children until they had been thoroughly instructed, "mentally and morally."[45]

Intellectual formulations such as these seemed curiously contradictory to the new concept of the child as an independent entity with a life and needs of its own. This new view of childhood appeared a confirmation of the prevalent Jeffersonian belief in the sovereignty of the living, an evidence of the vitality of the present over dead yesterdays and unborn tomorrows. "Every child begins the world again," explained Henry David Thoreau; future generations thus had no claim on the present. Philosophical sophistries of such Boston transcendentalists as Ralph Waldo Emerson, Thoreau, and Bronson Alcott advised contemporaries that their only responsibility, as Alcott put it, was to "self-culture, self-exultation: you may not violate this high trust." With the others, Alcott denied the rights of society over the individual. The times, he ventured, had called forth a new man who "washes away the ancient boundaries, and sets afloat institutions, creeds, usages, which clog the ever-flowing Present, stranding them on the shores of the Past." Alcott professed to find the new man of tomorrow in the children of today.[46]

Against such glorifications of the individual, Boston educators extolled the primacy of social order. The cooperation which urban life demanded of individuals for daily survival elevated social needs over individual caprice. Educators and politicians, from necessity if not from deeply held philosophical convictions, celebrated an organic conception of society. The present generation was the child of the past and the father of the future.

The most thorough philosophical exposition of this attitude came, appropriately enough, from the widest-ranging educational "post-rider" of the period—Horace Mann. Throughout his career as a missionary of the common schools, Mann evinced a Burkean conviction that individuals were entities not of self-creation but of historical experience. Taken collectively, the successive generations of men constituted one great commonwealth. Materially successful men in each generation thus owed a debt to the past and to the future. As the trustees of social wealth (a conception Mann shared with certain other contemporary reformers) such individuals were duty-bound to pay that debt by supporting public education. If they did not, they were guilty of "embezzlement and pillage from children and descendants."[47]

The primary responsibility of an individual in society, in turn, was not "self-culture" or "self-exultation," but "self-government." The political institutions of America, Mann observed, rested upon the "great idea of the capacity of man for self-government." But Mann believed it was obvious that the institutional permissiveness of American society and the flow of foreigners bred under the despotisms of Europe had threatened that human capacity. "The freedom of our institutions," he charged, "gives full play to all the passions of the human heart."[48] Mann believed that public education alone could check uncontrolled passions, thereby reinvigorating the practice of self-government. Only the man who governed himself could be at once an individual and a socially responsible citizen. By accepting self-imposed limitations, such a person would accept more willingly the few limitations which society had to impose on all men for the sake of social order. If circumstances or human foibles hindered men in developing the capacity for self-government, the state had to prepare an environment for nurturing that precious ability. In Mann's view, the appropriate environment was the public school.

In his *First Annual Report* (1837) Mann attacked the apathy of many individuals about education, stating that "the maintenance of free schools rests wholly upon the social principle. It is emphatically a case where men, individually powerless, are collectively strong." American society, he argued, had an educational duty to itself, for "above all others must the children of a Republic be fitted for society, as well as for themselves." A self-governed nation required self-governed men. No one could doubt that "in a government like ours, each individual must think of the welfare of his own family; and therefore, of the children of others as well as of his own." But if individuals failed in this responsibility, the State, as the collective agency of the governed, must take control. "Every child should be educated," Mann confided in his diary, and "if not educated by its own father, then the State should appoint a father to it." That father was to be the common school. Employing a familiar phrase of the day Mann observed that "as 'the child is father to the man,' so may the training of the schoolroom expand into the institutions and fortunes of the State." For self-protection, society had to take charge of its youth, instilling in them a "regard to the great social duties and prerogatives that await them in after-life."[49]

Mann conjectured that government, by enforcing the principle of common education, could make 80, 90, or 99 per cent of all children temperate, frugal, industrious, public-spirited, financially honest, and philanthropic. Even if that high goal could not be attained, if "any other given per-centage of all children can be rescued from vice and crime, and can be so educated and trained as to become valuable citizens," the state still had a responsibility to demand the education of all children and to provide the necessary means.[50]

Mann's logic was tenuous and his aspirations utopian. But his conception of society as an organism, headed by a benevolent government that forced men to become "valuable citizens," appealed to other men beset by the problems of urban disorder, poverty, and mass immigration. His evangelism for public education aroused others and firmly implanted in their minds a faith in the state ownership of the child—for educational purposes, at least. In 1838, at the beginning of his career as an educational reformer, Mann could assert that "Society, in its collective capacity, is a real, not a nominal sponsor and godfather for all its children." In 1846, near the close of that career, Mann could note, with a measure of self-pride in his own work, that "Massachusetts is *parental* in her government. More and more, as the years roll by, she seeks to substitute prevention for remedy."[51]

State political leaders, as evidenced by their support of compulsory attendance laws, agreed with Mann's views about parental government. In his annual message to the state legislature in 1848, for example, Governor Briggs chastized those parents who committed a flagrant wrong against the community and the state by refusing to send their children to school. Briggs conceded that citizens might allow their homes to be dark abodes of ignorance and stupidity for their offspring, but also asserted that parents had no right "to send them forth into society vicious men and women, to corrupt it by their example, or disturb its peace by their crimes." The interests of the individual and of the public demanded that every child "receive the priceless blessings of a Common School education."[52]

Leading Protestant ministers, alarmed by an alleged Catholic challenge to orthodoxy, pointed to the presence of ignorant foreigners as reason enough for society's claim on the lives of children. In 1849 the Unitarian clergyman Charles Brooks, a close friend of Horace Mann's and a tireless advocate of public schools, addressed the American Institute of Instruction on the duties of legislatures in relation to the public schools in the United States. A "paternal and Christian legislature," Brooks stressed, could disarm the "animal ferocity" of the ignorant only "by the implantation of moral principle." The state should compel every child to receive some intellectual and moral culture. Whether or not parents approved, the law compelling attendance at school "is a law of political economy and comprehensive love." And if benevolent paternalism did not justify an infringement on family rights, immigration did. "In the present state of our mixed population," Brooks concluded, "this law is called for as our defence." If society had the undeniable right to protect itself against crime, it had an equal right to defend itself against the cause of crime—ignorance. Several years later the influential Congregationalist periodical the *New Englander* lent the prestige of the Divinity to compulsory education. Estimating that 72 per cent of all children between the ages of five and fifteen, especially those of aliens, came under "this efficient regimen to make good citizens," the magazine asked: "Against such an annual array of mental forces, . . . what can the Jesuit or hostile foreigner do the injury of the State?" There was no doubt that "the state, as the will of the mass impersonated, may, as a divine agent, go by all parents and guardians, over all obstacles . . . till it find the child."[53] Apparently God Himself approved this form of democratic coercion.

The clearest evidence that laws for compulsory attendance were aimed directly at the children of poverty appeared in the reports of the Boston School Committee. Throughout the 1850's schoolmen justified legal coercion on those grounds, but the most dogmatic assertions came in the report for 1853. Some parents disregarded the welfare of their children, explained the Committee, while others remained ignorant of their own true interests in sending children to school. In either case, government had the right to compel attendance:

> The parent is not the absolute owner of the child. The child is a member of the community, has certain rights, and is bound to perform certain duties, and so far as these relate to the public, Government has the same right of control over the child, that it has over the parent.
> It furnishes those means of education, which are calculated to prevent the child from becoming a burden to society and a pest to his fellow citizens.

And taxpaying residents of the city, the Committee continued, also have a right to demand that "those children should be brought within the jurisdiction of the Public Schools, from whom, through their vagrant habits, our property is most in danger, and who, of all others, most need the protecting power of the State."[54]

Some Irish immigrants did not want to accept the "protecting power of the State." They correctly saw that the compulsory attendance laws asserted "that the education of children is *not* the work of the Church, or of the Family, but that it is the work of the State." When the state adopted the child, it weakened "the ties which bind it to the parent." With the State claiming all authority, "it can and does exclude from the schools religious instruction." Irish Catholics feared that Boston leaders sought to reduce the influence of the Catholic Church. The *Boston Pilot* charged that all the public institutions of Boston were establishments for the perversion of Catholic children. In 1849 a prominent priest bemoaned the loss of faith among the 3,000 Catholic children attending the public schools. Another priest, Father G. F. Haskins, who prior to his conversion from Episcopalianism had worked as a Protestant chaplin, testified that "I heard a distinguished philanthropist of Boston, and a member of the City Government say, that the only way to elevate the foreign population was to make Protestants of their children."[55]

Catholics saw the use of the Protestant Bible in the public schools as the most glaring evidence of this desire to proselytize their children.[56] The Bible had been required reading in Boston schools since 1789. But in recent years Boston Catholics, like their fellow churchmen in Philadelphia and in New York City, had begun to question the propriety of required reading from the Scriptures. Indeed, heavy attacks on Bible reading had come from numerous sectarians during the 1840's. Neither the Protestant sectarians nor the Catholics hoped to strike a blow for separation of church and state. Rather they sought to defend their own religious interests and interpretations.[57]

To that end, Boston Catholics hoped to establish their own parochial school system. By the early 1850's they had met with indifferent success.[58] And in the public schools Catholic children were still required to read from the Bible and recite Protestant prayers; if they did not comply they were often punished or expelled from school. In 1851 a group of parents warned the city of an impending court case if matters were not changed. The following year the editor of the *Boston Pilot* demanded that the "bigots" on the School Committee cease their enforcement of Protestant theology in the schools. In 1853 the annual report of the School Committee clearly stated its position. "Moral and religious instruction is necessary to sound education," the Committee asserted. "Our schools will fail of producing the results expected of them, unless such instruction is there given." The Committee boldly confirmed the worst suspicions of the Catholics. "The ends of government therefore require that religious instruction should be given in our Public Schools. . . . The whole character of the instruction given, must be such and such only, as will tend to make the pupils thereof, American citizens, and ardent supporters of American institutions."[59] The right of the School Committee to require Protestant instruction was upheld several years later in a controversial trial—the Eliot School case.

While the social and theological implications of the case were far-reaching, the facts themselves were mundane. On March 14, 1859, an open rebellion occurred in the Eliot School which resulted in dismissals for over 300 students. All of the Catholic children, some 900 apparently, had refused to recite the Ten Commandments and to read the opening scripture passages for the day. On Wednesday, March 16, William Wall, on behalf of his son Thomas, filed a complaint in Police Court against McLaurin F. Cooke, the sub-master of the school, alleging assault-and-battery upon the boy for his refusal to obey instructions about Bible reading. At the trial, the Court accepted as fact the assertions offered by the School Committee (in defense of Mr. Cooke). Apparently Father Wiget, of St. Mary's Church on Endicott Street, had instructed young Wall and others to refuse to participate in Protestant religious activities at the school. The boy's father had ordered his son to take part in the religious exercises and had come to the Eliot School to ask the head-master to keep his boy in school and to punish him if he did not participate. But the boy had listened to his priest, and had refused to obey his teacher. According to testimony, young Thomas was heard to say to friends on the streets, "Faith and I wan't agoin to repate thim damned Yankee prayers."

Lawyer Henry C. Durant, representing the School Committee, argued that the boys (and their priest) had no reason to rebel. According to Durant, the "Saxon Bible" was non-sectarian. He appealed to the legislative tradition that required prayer and scripture reading in the public schools, and charged that a foreign priest was attempting to undermine American liberty, which had always seen religion and government co-joined. Speaking of the Bible, Durant claimed that "it has been the household god of the school-room from the infancy of the country. The schools which made us free, which will make worthy and true citizens of your children, have grown up under its influences. And will you take it from us now?" Durant concluded his presentation by demanding: "Banish the vain delusion forever that our Saxon Bible can be taken away; neither foreign tyrants or foreign priests will ever have that power." The Court concluded that he was correct. It ordered the rebellious youth to return to school and to follow all orders there, and dropped the charges against sub-master Cooke.[60]

The Eliot School case came at the end of a decade of growing dissatisfaction with the public schools among Catholic parents and represented their last attempt to work within the established system of public instruction. Previously, and despite the use of the Protestant Bible and similar methods of proselytizing in the schools, Irish children continued to attend public schools throughout the 1850's. The compulsory-attendance law forced some into schools, while others came because their church had not yet established enough parochial schools to accommodate all who might wish to attend. Not until 1861 did the School Committee find it necessary to report that Irish attendance had fallen off slightly during the previous year, "due in part, probably, to the establishment of Catholic schools."[61] Until that time, at least, piety, not popery, reigned in Puritan Boston. And, for better or worse, society had staked out its claim in ownership of the child.

By the mid-1850's, Boston educators had come full circle in their campaign to reach the immigrant and native poor of the city. In earlier decades they had tried to induce children to enter the schools. Like other social reformers, when moral suasion had failed, the educators had turned to legal compulsion. Even when they had succeeded too well, when some schools had become overcrowded with immigrant children, the educators had continued to bemoan the incidence of truancy. Certainly there was widespread truancy among immigrant children, but there were also too many children attending too few schools to accommodate the growing population. But the educators could not tolerate the thought of even one foreign child escaping their grasp. Boston schoolmen could not succeed without failing, yet they could not accept intellectually the failure to succeed.

The problem appeared nearly insurmountable to educators of the 1850's. So their responses to the changing conditions of the school population were necessarily ambivalent. Schools had to reach children of all social classes and ethnic groups if they were to fulfill their function as mediating forces of urban disorder. If too many foreign children crowded native American youth out of the schools, if schools became the exclusive province of the poor, education could not create shared patterns of social behavior. It could neither offer social insurance nor could it foster any sense of community among diverse city dwellers. But if mass education failed to include the poor and the strangers, it would also fail to accomplish its social goal.

Had Bostonians foreseen the ultimate outcome of their years of propaganda, possibly they would have urged less vigorously the extension of public education. But, like most men, the educators and the politicians rarely questioned tomorrow—they were too concerned with today. Indeed, they were too concerned with yesterday, with the small New England city that had grown haphazardly to a bursting metropolis in a few short years. Not willing to come to terms with the present, educators sought refuge in the past. But the sanctuary of yesterday, with schools enough and time to mold the stranger into friend, was no more. The tragedy was that Bostonians never understood the folly of marking time against the inexorable flow of urban growth. The past had caught up with them, and though they dimly perceived the event, educators felt helpless to challenge the present.

List of Abbreviations Used in Notes

AAE	*American Annals of Education and Instruction*
AHR	*American Historical Review*
AJE	*American Journal of Education*
AQ	*American Quarterly*
BAJE	*Barnard's American Journal of Education*
BCD	*Boston City Documents*
BPL	Boston Public Library
BSR	*Boston School Reports;* usually given first by proper title such as *Reports of the Annual Visiting Committee . . . 1845*
CSJ	*Common School Journal*
DAB	*Dictionary of American Biography*
JAH	*Journal of American History*
JEH	*Journal of Economic History*
LAII . . .	*Lectures before the American Institute of Instruction*
MHS	Massachusetts Historical Society
MSA	Massachusetts State Archives, State House, Boston
NAR	*North American Review*
NEM	*The New England Magazine*
RRC	*Reports of the Record Commissioners, Boston*
SCM	*School Committee Minutes;* Ms. minutes of the Boston School Committee, bound in volumes, Rare Book Room, Boston Public Library

Each of the above is cited in full the first time used in each chapter.

Notes

CHAPTER 1

1. Fisher Ames to George Richards Minot, New York, September 3, 1789, in Seth Ames, ed., *Works of Fisher Ames* (2 vols., Boston, 1854), I, 69.

2. *Twentieth Annual Report of the Massachusetts Board of Education together with the Twentieth Annual Report of the Secretary of the Board* (Boston, 1857), pp. 5-6.

3. W. K. Jordan, *Philanthropy in England, 1480-1660* (London, 1959), pp. 282-83; Wallace Notestein, *The English People on the Eve of Colonization, 1603-1630* (New York, 1954), pp. 116-17, and 116-29, *passim;* Lawrence A. Cremin, *American Education: The Colonial Experience, 1607-1783* (New York, 1970), pp. 167-76. Cf. Fritz Caspari, *Humanism and the Social Order in Tudor England* (Chicago, 1954), and A. L. Rowse, *The England of Elizabeth: The Structure of Society* (London, 1950).

4. "Boston Town Records [1634-1660/61]," in City of Boston, *Reports of the Record Commissioners,* II (Boston, 1877), 5, 17, 65, 82, 86, 92-95, 97-99, 109, 160; Nathaniel B. Shurtleff, ed., *Records of the Governor and Company of the Massachusetts Bay in New England* (5 vols., Boston, 1853-54), II, 203; Darrett B. Rutman, *Winthrop's Boston: A Portrait of a Puritan Town, 1630-1649* (Chapel Hill, 1965), pp. 72-75, 220-22; Geraldine Joanne Murphy, "Massachusetts Bay Colony: The Role of Government in Education" (unpublished Ph.D. dissertation, Radcliffe College, 1960), Chapter 3.

5. *RRC,* VIII, 90-91, 110; Cremin, *American Education,* pp. 400-401; Carl Bridenbaugh, *Cities in the Wilderness: The First Century of Urban Life in America, 1675-1742* (New York, 1955), pp. 121-22, 281.

6. Murphy, "Massachusetts Bay Colony"; Pauline Holmes, *A Tercentenary History of the Boston Public Latin School, 1635-1935* (Cambridge, Mass., 1935), p. 28; Edward Eggleston, *The Transit of Civilization from England to America in the Seventeenth Century* (1900; reprinted, Boston, 1959), pp. 214-215, 226-27, 230-32; Walter H. Small, *Early New England Schools* (Boston, 1914), *passim;* Samuel Eliot Morison, *The Intellectual Life of Colonial New England* (2nd ed., New York, 1956), pp. 105-6.

7. *RRC,* XIII, 153; Robert Middlekauff, *Ancients and Axioms: Secondary Education in Eighteenth-Century New England* (New Haven, 1963), pp. 54-56.

8. *RRC,* XIV, 177, and XVIII, 26; Middlekauff, *Ancients and Axioms,*

p. 57; Charles S. Grant, *Democracy in the Connecticut Frontier Town of Kent* (New York, 1961); G. B. Warden, *Boston, 1689-1776* (Boston, 1970), pp. 67-69; Bridenbaugh, *Cities in the Wilderness*, pp. 130, 444.

9. *RRC*, XIV, 197; Middlekauff, *Ancients and Axioms*, p. 56.

10. Carl Bridenbaugh, *Cities in Revolt: Urban Life in America, 1743-1776* (New York, 1955), p. 376. Figures giving the percentage of school-age children in the total population are not available.

11. H. F. Jenks, *Catalogue of the Boston Public Latin School Established in 1635. With a Historical Sketch* (Boston, 1886), "Historical Sketch," pp. 35-36; Robert F. Seybolt, *The Public Schools of Colonial Boston, 1635-1775* (Cambridge, Mass., 1935), p. 74; Samuel Eliot Morison, "Harrison Gray Otis," in Allen Johnson and Dumas Malone, eds., *Dictionary of American Biography* (11 vols.; Subscription ed., New York, 1958), VII, Part II, 98; Morison, *The Life and Letters of Harrison Gray Otis, Federalist, 1765-1848* (2 vols., Boston, 1913).

12. Middlekauff, *Ancients and Axioms*, p. 128; Mary Ann Connolly, "Boston Schools in the New Republic" (unpublished Ph.D. dissertation, Harvard University, Graduate School of Education, 1963), pp. 24-25.

13. George B. Emerson, "Education in Massachusetts, Early Legislation and History," in *Early History of Massachusetts, Lowell Institute Lectures* (Boston, 1869), p. 25.

14. Francis N. Thorpe, ed., *Federal and State Constitutions, Colonial Charters, and Other Organic Laws of the States* (7 vols., Washington, D.C., 1909), II, 1068-69; Cotton reprinted in Perry Miller and Thomas H. Johnson, eds., *The Puritans: A Sourcebook of Their Writings* (2 vols., rev. ed., New York, 1963), I, 319-27. The first reliable population figures appeared in the Federal Census of 1790. In a total state population of 378,787, more than 104,500 people (approximately 28 per cent) lived in towns of 2,500 and above. By census definitions in usage since 1940, such areas are considered "urban." See Bureau of the Census, *Current Population Reports*, "The Development of the Urban-Rural Classification in the United States: 1874-1949," Series P-23, No. 1.

15. John Adams to Abigail Adams, August 28, 1774; October 29, 1775, in L. H. Butterfield, ed., *Adams Family Correspondence* (2 vols.; *The Adams Papers*, Series II; Cambridge, Mass., 1963), I, 145, 316-17. Cf. Middlekauff, *Ancients and Axioms*, p. 123.

16. Abigail Adams to John Adams, August 14, 1776, *ibid.*, II, 94.

17. L. H. Butterfield, ed., *Diary & Autobiography of John Adams* (4 vols.; *The Adams Papers*, Series I; Cambridge, Mass., 1961), *Diaries, I*, March 18, 1759; August 19, 1760; January 1761; February 1763; February 1765; March 10, 1766; pp. 80-81, 152-53, 190-91, 196-97, 242-43, 257, 304; III, July 21, 1786, p. 195. Quotations respectively from I, 80-81, 190-91, and III, 195.

18. Thorpe, *Federal and State Constitutions*, "The Massachusetts Bill of Rights"; and for a perceptive account of social structure in Boston, see James A. Henretta, "Economic Development and Social Structure in Colonial Boston," *William and Mary Quarterly*, XXII (January 1965), 75-92.

19. *RRC*, XXXI, 16. For adherence to the principle of "free schools" open to all voted on in the Town Meeting, see, for example, *RRC*, VII (1683), 158, 161, 171; XI (1711), 137; XIV (1751), 199. On finances, see Seybolt, *Public Schools*, pp. 32-42; and Charles P. Huse, *The Financial History of Boston: From May 1, 1822, to January 31, 1909* (vol. 15, *Harvard Economic Studies;* Cambridge, Mass., 1916), p. 4. Contrary to assertions by Mary Ann Connolly, "Boston Schools," p. 23, the principle and practice of free schools open to all residents was not a direct outgrowth of any equalitarian spirit fostered by the Revolution.

20. Thorpe, *Federal and State Constitutions*, II, 957 ff.; "Constitutional Provisions in Regard to Education in the Several States of the American Union," *Circulars of Information of the Bureau of Education, 1875* (Washington, D.C., 1875), No. 7; Allen O. Hansen, *Liberalism and American Education in the Eighteenth Century* (New York, 1926).

21. Noah Webster, "On the Education of Youth," reprinted in Frederick Rudolph, ed., *Essays on Education in the Early Republic* (Cambridge, Mass., 1965), pp. 43, 45, 47, 53-55, 59, 61-64, 65-68. This collection provides an excellent introduction to contemporary educational thought during the 1780's and 1790's.

22. *Acts and Laws of the Commonwealth of Massachusetts, 1780-1808* (13 vols., Boston, 1890-98), V, 416-20.

23. Daniel Cony to George Thatcher, Boston, January 28, 1789, in George Thatcher *Papers*, Maine Historical Society. For this reference I am indebted to Professor Kenneth Bolling of the University of Wisconsin.

24. Fisher Ames to George Richards Minot, *Works*, I, 69; Henry Adams, *The United States in 1800* (Ithaca, 1955), p. 54.

25. "Discourses on Davila" (1790), in Charles F. Adams, ed., *Works of John Adams* (10 vols., Boston, 1850-56), VI, 232, 234, 249-57; "Letters to John Taylor of Caroline, Virginia in Reply to his strictures on some Parts of the Defence of the American Constitutions," *Works*, VI, Letters XVIII and XXXI, 484, 517.

26. Connolly, "Boston Schools," pp. 40-41; *RRC* (1789), p. 285; George H. Martin, *The Evolution of the Massachusetts Public School System: A Historical Sketch* (New York, 1923), p. 128; Douglass Adair and John A. Schutz, eds., *Peter Oliver's Origin and Progress of the American Rebellion: A Tory's View* (San Marino, Calif., 1961), pp. 39-40; Ames to Minot, September 3, 1789, *Works*, I, 68. Adams was uncommonly adept at raising a "public clamor" as Ames had good cause to know. Less than a year before, Ames had defeated Adams for Congress in a bitterly fought election. For perceptive insights into Adams' personality, see Ralph V. Harlow, *Samuel Adams, Promoter of the American Revolution: A Study in Psychology and Politics* (New York, 1923).

27. *The Independent Chronicle*, October 1, 1789. In contemporary usage "Cato" was shorthand for rebellion against autocracy in favor of democratic control. See Bernard Bailyn, *The Ideological Origins of the American Revolution* (Cambridge, Mass., 1967), pp. 43-44. For other letters to newspapers, see Connolly, "Boston Schools," pp. 40-44.

28. For these and other provisions, see *RRC* (1789), "Education Act of 1789."

29. It is a moot point as to whether some girls received instruction at public expense. Some private schools for girls probably obtained support from the town (Small, *Early New England Schools,* p. 14). The first formal action, however, appears to have been the Education Act of 1789. See also Joseph M. Wightman, comp., *Annals of the Boston Primary School Committee, From Its First Establishment in 1818, to Its Dissolution in 1855* (Boston, 1860), p. 7; Robert F. Seybolt, *The Private Schools of Colonial Boston* (Cambridge, Mass., 1935); Benjamin Rush, *Thoughts upon Female Education, Accommodated to the Present State of Society, Manners, and Government in the United States of America* (Boston, 1787), reprinted in Rudolph, *Essays of Education,* pp. 27-28.

30. Connolly, "Boston Schools," pp. 40-42.

31. Henry K. Oliver, "Schools As They Were in the United States Seventy Years Ago in Boston, Mass.," *Barnard's American Journal of Education,* XXVI (April 1876), 210, 215; William B. Fowle, "Memoir of Caleb Bingham. With Notices of the Public Schools of Boston, Prior to 1800," in Henry Barnard, ed., *Memoirs of Teachers, Educators, and Promoters and Benefactors of Education* (New York, 1859), pp. 57-58.

32. James W. Hale, *Old Boston Town . . . by an 1801-er* (New York, 1880), pp. 28-30; Walter Muir Whitehill, *Boston: A Topographical History* (Cambridge, Mass., 1963), pp. 47-72, gave me many bibliographic leads. Even though children of differing backgrounds attended schools, Fowle, "Memoir of Caleb Bingham," could note (p. 58) that "those who went only to public school were considered a somewhat inferior caste."

33. Clifton Johnson, *Old-Time Schools and School-books* (New York, 1904), pp. 69-99; Paul Leicester Ford, ed., *The New England Primer* (New York, 1899); Monica Kiefer, *American Children Through Their Books, 1700-1835* (Philadelphia, 1948), pp. 139-40.

34. *The System of Public Education Adoped by the Town of Boston, 15ᵗʰ October, 1789,* in *American Antiquarian Society Pamphlets,* X, in Widener Library, Harvard University; Caleb Bingham, *American Preceptor* (Boston, 1794), "preface," quoted in Johnson, *Old-Time Schools,* p. 276; Noah Webster, *An American Selection of Lessons in Reading and Speaking* (Salem, Mass., 1805), p. 147.

35. Arthur Wellington Brayley, *Schools and Schoolboys of Old Boston* (Boston, 1894), pp. 36-37; *System of Public Education Adopted . . . 15ᵗʰ October, 1789;* Fowle, "Memoir of Caleb Bingham," p. 61.

36. See the perceptive work by sociologist Gideon Sjoberg, *The Preindustrial City: Past and Present* (New York, 1960), pp. 8-11, 33, 286-300.

37. Louis C. Karpinski, "Nicholas Pike," *DAB,* VII, Part II, 597-98; Oliver, "Schools As They Were," p. 211; Fowle, "Memoir of Caleb Bingham," p. 62; Brayley, *Schools and Schoolboys,* pp. 37-38.

38. *Laws of Massachusetts, 1788-89; Acts, 1789,* Chapter 19, p. 417. Similar provisions for moral and religious education occurred elsewhere during the same period. See William Lailer Dunn, *What Happened to Religious Educa-*

tion? The Decline of Religious Teaching in the Public Elementary School, 1776-1861 (Baltimore, 1958), pp. 62-72.

39. Quoted in G. H. Martin, "Boston Schools 100 Years Ago," *New England Magazine,* XXVI (1902), 628.

40. *The Constitution of the School in Federal-Street by the Proprietors* (Boston, 1797). Copy in Rare-Book Room, Watkins Library, University of Chicago.

41. This marked the appearance in Boston of what modern sociologists refer to as a "strategic elite"—a small group of individuals designated to serve a collectivity in a socially valued way. See Suzanne Keller, *Beyond the Ruling Class: Strategic Elites in Modern Society* (New York, 1963), p. 4 and *passim.* This specialization of leadership became much more important during the first half of the nineteenth century when an influx of population and increasing commercial and industrial activity placed added burdens on the political ability of the city to govern itself. See Chapter 6, *infra.*

42. George Silsbee Hale, "The Charities of Boston," Justin Winsor, ed., *The Memorial History of Boston* (4 vols., Boston, 1881), IV, 646; Josiah Qunicy, *A Municipal History of the Town and City of Boston* (Boston, 1852), pp. 419-20.

43. Fowle, "Memoir of Caleb Bingham," pp. 59-60. Biographical information on several members may be found in the appropriate volumes of the *DAB* and in James G. Loring, *The Hundred Boston Orators* (Boston, 1876); on Bulfinch, see Fiske Kimball, "Charles Bulfinch," *DAB,* II, Part II, 245-47; and C. A. Place, *Charles Bulfinch* (Boston, 1925), pp. 38-39, 95, 114, 199-200; Connolly, "Boston Schools," pp. 58-61, briefly discusses the composition of this first Committee.

44. *RRC* (1789), p. 215.

CHAPTER 2

1. Warren Burton, "On the Best Mode of Fixing the Attention of the Young," *Introductory Discourse and the Lectures Delivered before the American Institute of Instruction, in Boston, August, 1834. Including the Journal of Proceedings, and a List of the Officers* (Boston, 1835), p. 57.

2. Ms. minutes of the Boston School Committee, bound in volumes in Rare Book Room, BPL, I (1815-36); Joseph M. Wightman, comp., *Annals of the Boston Primary School Committee, From Its Establishment in 1818, to Its Dissolution in 1855* (Boston, 1860), p. 9; William B. Fowle, "Memoir of Caleb Bingham. With Notices of the Public Schools of Boston, Prior to 1800," in Henry Barnard, ed., *Memoirs of Teachers, Educators, and Promoters and Benefactors of Education* (New York, 1859), pp. 63-64 and *passim.*

3. *Boston Columbian Centinel,* August 16, 1806.

4. "School-age population" refers to children ages four to fifteen. In 1800 there were apparently 7,582 such children. About 900 children attended the public reading and writing schools, 160 the Latin School, and some 500 the private schools, as estimated in *SCM,* I.

5. As an educational training ground, the apprenticeship system was falling into disrepair. See, for example, Robert F. Seybolt, *Apprenticeship and Apprenticeship Education in Colonial New England and New York* (New York, 1917); Paul H. Douglas, *American Apprenticeship and Industrial Education* (New York, 1921), pp. 25-52; and Forest C. Ensign, *Compulsory School Attendance and Child Labor* (Iowa City, 1921), pp. 30-45.

6. *Massachusetts Centinel*, September 19, 1789; Wightman, *Annals*, p. 7; *Report of the School Committee of the City of Boston on the State of the Schools. May, 1826* (Boston, 1826); Arthur Wellington Brayley, *Schools and Schoolboys of Old Boston* (Boston, 1894), pp. 35-36, 49; "Subjects and Courses of Instruction in City Public Schools," *Barnard's American Journal of Education*, XIX (1870), 469.

7. R. S. Longley, "Mob Activities in Revolutionary Massachusetts," *New England Quarterly*, VI (1933), 108-11; Jesse Lemisch, "Jack Tar in the Streets: Merchant Seamen in the Politics of Revolutionary America," *William and Mary Quarterly*, XXV (1968), 387-93; and James A. Henretta, "Economic Development and Social Structure in Colonial Boston," *W&MQ*, XXII (1965), 75-92.

8. Lemuel Shattuck, *Report to the Committee of the City Council Appointed to Obtain the Census of Boston for the Year 1845* (Boston, 1846), p. 54.

9. Josiah Quincy, Jr., "Social Life in Boston," in Justin Winsor, ed., *The Memorial History of Boston* (4 vols., Boston, 1881), IV, 13; Charles Phillips Huse, *The Financial History of Boston: From May 1, 1822, to January 31, 1909*, vol. 15, *Harvard Economic Studies* (Cambridge, Mass., 1916), Appendix I, pp. 348, 358; and Boston Committee of Finance, *Auditor's Reports, 1815-1867*.

10. Charles K. Dillaway, "Education Past and Present: The Rise of Free Education and Educational Institutions," in Winsor, *Memorial History*, IV, 245; George H. Martin, *The Evolution of the Massachusetts Public School System: An Historical Sketch* (New York, 1923), pp. 142-44; "To the Public. Address of the Trustees of the 'Society for Establishing a Free School in the City of New York, for the Education of such Poor Children as do not Belong to or are not Provided for by, any Religious Society, May, 1805,'" reprinted in Edgar W. Knight and Clifton L. Hall, eds., *Readings in American Educational History* (New York, 1951), pp. 319-20.

11. Hamilton Andrews Hill, *History of the Old South Church* (2 vols., Boston, 1889), II, 419.

12. Guy Kendall, *Robert Raikes: A Critical Study* (London, 1939); Richard D. Altick, *The English Common Reader: A Social History of the Mass Reading Public, 1800-1900* (Chicago, 1957), p. 67; M. G. Jones, *The Charity School Movement: A Study of Eighteenth-Century Puritanism in Action* (Cambridge, Mass., 1938), p. 153.

13. Edwin W. Rice, *The Sunday-School Movement, 1780-1917, and the American Sunday-School Union, 1817-1917* (Philadelphia, 1917), pp. 55-58; Nathan Goodman, *Benjamin Rush: Physician and Citizen, 1746-1813* (Philadelphia, 1934), p. 319.

14. *Collections* of the Massachusetts Historical Society, ser. 1, III, 266-67.

15. Frederick T. Gray, "The Origin of the Ministry at Large, and Its Free Chapels," *Sixteenth Annul Report of the Executive Committee of the Benevolent Fraternity of Churches*, reviewed and discussed in the *Christian Examiner*, XLIX (1850), 204-14; Asa Bullard, *Fifty Years with the Sabbath Schools* (Boston, 1876), pp. 38-39, 206-8. The organization later (1820) changed its name to the City Missionary Society. I have profited from bibliographical guides given by J. Leslie Dunstan in *A Light to the City: 150 Years of the City Missionary Society of Boston, 1816-1966* (Boston, 1966).

16. *Boston Recorder*, October 15, 1841; Dunstan, *Light to the City*, pp. 14-15.

17. *A Brief Account of the Origin and Progress of the Boston Female Society for Missionary Purposes, with Extracts from the Reports of the Society in May, 1817 and 1818* (Boston, n.d.), pp. 7-8; *Annual Report of the Boston City Missionary Society, 1818* (Boston, 1818), pp. 3-4; Josiah Quincy, *A Municipal History of the Town and City of Boston* (Boston, 1852), pp. 101-4; Edward H. Savage, *Police Records and Recollections; Or, Boston by Daylight and Gaslight for Two Hundred and Forty Years* (Boston, 1872), pp. 57, 63, 107-12; *Columbian Centinel*, July 3, 1825.

18. *Annual Report . . . 1818*, p. 4; Wightman, *Annals*, p. 12; Josiah Quincy, *Remarks on Some of the Provisions of the Laws of Massachusetts Affecting Poverty, Vice, and Crime* (Cambridge, Mass., 1822).

19. *Annual Reports of the Boston City Missionary Society, 1817-1820*. Boston editions of the *Childs First Book* appeared in 1810 and 1816, see Sherman M. Smith, *The Relation of the State to Religious Education in Massachusetts* (Syracuse, 1926), p. 90. *Annual Report . . . 1819*, pp. 6, 35.

20. *Boston City Directory, 1813*, pp. 272-76.

21. For example, see *The Report of the Annual Examination of the Public Schools of the City of Boston, 1849* (Boston, 1849). The argument of children reclaiming their parents through moral example implicitly underlay all the claims for the schools as the agents of domesticating and assimilating immigrant children. See Chapter 10, *infra*, and *Boston Pilot*, April 24, October 9, 1852.

22. William Thurston to Turner Phillips, Esq., Chairman of the Honorable Board of Selectmen, Boston, March 18, 1818, reproduced in Wightman, *Annals*, p. 13.

23. *Annual Report . . . City Missionary Society, 1818*; Wightman, *Annals*, p. 14; Brayley, *Schools and Schoolboys*, p. 49.

24. Wightman, *Annals*, pp. 19-20.

25. Quincy, *Municipal History*, pp. 101-5; quotation from Mark A. DeWolfe Howe, *Boston Landmarks* (New York 1946), mentioned in Walter Muir Whitehill, *Boston: A Topographical History* (Cambridge, Mass., 1963), p. 113. Whitehill discussed physical and population changes in the area, pp. 12, 15, 27-29, 84, 88, 112-14.

26. It has been a continuing phenomenon in the process of urbanization that residents in a "zone of emergence" or a "zone of transition" have turned to public education as one means of stemming the tides of change. For a discus-

sion of this phenomenon, as well as the pioneer attempt to classify changing residential areas of the city, see Robert A. Woods and Albert J. Kennedy, *The Zone of Emergence,* abridged and ed. by Sam B. Warner, Jr. (Cambridge, Mass., 1962), "Preface," pp. 1, 23, and "Introduction," p. 37.

27. Wightman, *Annals,* pp. 20-21. Committeemen for Wards One through Twelve respectively were: Henry J. Oliver, Redford Webster, Jacob Hall, James W. Burditt, Jona P. Hall, Isaac Winslow, Gideon Snow, John Dorr, Samuel May, David W. Child, Isaac Stevens, and Joseph Field. Bibliographical data on Bulfinch may be found in Fiske Kimball, "Charles Bulfinch," Allen Johnson and Dumas Malone, eds., *Dictionary of American Biography* (11 vols., Subscription ed., New York, 1958), II, Part I, 245-47; and C. A. Place, *Charles Bulfinch* (Boston, 1925). Thatcher was discussed in James G. Loring, *The Hundred Boston Orators* (Boston, 1876), pp. 323-24. *SCM,* I (1815-36), November 2, 1817.

28. The most convenient source for this survey is Wightman, *Annals,* pp. 21-28. The body of the survey gave $18,911 as the total, but ward-by-ward breakdowns totalled $19,911. The first reliable figure for student population in the grammar schools dates from 1820-21. As the student population grew by only 100 students in the intervening three years, it is reasonable to estimate the costs in 1820-21 as not significantly higher than in 1817. In 1820-21 expenditures for public grammar schools were $28,430.55 as stated by Shattuck, *Census of Boston . . . 1845,* "Appendix T," p. 31. See also "Subjects and Courses of Instruction in City Public Schools," *BAJE,* XIX (1870), 469-70.

29. Wightman, *Annals,* pp. 23-24.

30. See George Ticknor, "Memoirs of the Buckminsters," *Christian Examiner,* XLVII (1849), 169-95; Van Wyck Brooks, *The Flowering of New England* (New York, 1936), pp. 1-20; James Walker, "Memoir of Josiah Quincy," Massachusetts Historical Society *Proceedings,* IX (1866-67), 83-166; Paul Goodman, "Ethics and Enterprise: The Values of a Boston Elite, 1800-1860," *American Quarterly,* XVIII (Fall 1966), 437-51.

31. Wightman, *Annals,* pp. 23-25.

32. *The Statistical History of the United States from Colonial Times to the Present* (Stamford, Conn., 1965), Chapter H, Series 223-233, p. 207.

33. Wightman, *Annals,* pp. 24-26.

34. Huse, *Financial History of Boston,* p. 4; Carroll D. Wright and Horace G. Wadlin, "The Industries of the Last Hundred Years," Winsor, *Memorial History,* IV, 8; Henry P. Kiddler and Francis H. Peabody, "Finance in Boston," *ibid.,* IV, 160; Hamilton Andrews Hill, "The Trade, Commerce and Navigation of Boston, 1780-1880," *ibid.,* IV, 221-22. For an excellent brief discussion of the ice trade, see Daniel J. Boorstin, *The Americans: The National Experience* (New York, 1965), pp. 10-15. The best history of Boston commerce during the periods remains Samuel Eliot Morison, *The Maritime History of Massachusetts, 1783-1860* (Boston, 1921).

35. Wightman, *Annals,* 26.

36. *SCM,* I (1815-36), October 30, 1817.

37. Wightman, *Annals,* p. 29.

38. See Sidney Gunn, "James Savage," *DAB*, VIII, Part II, 387-88; Loring, *Hundred Boston Orators*, p. 356.

39. Wightman, *Annals*, p. 30, stated that the original paper in the town files was in the handwriting of Ticknor, with interlineations by Savage. Cf. *Boston Columbian Centinel*, May 27, 1818.

40. Armistead Churchill Gorden, Jr., "Elisha Ticknor," *DAB*, IX, Part II, 524-25; petition and list of signers reproduced in Wightman, *Annals*, pp. 30-32.

41. *Ibid.*, pp. 33-35.

42. Samuel Eliot Morison, "Harrison Gray Otis," *DAB*, VII, Part II, 98-100; Morison, *The Life and Letters of Harrison Gray Otis, Federalist, 1765-1848* (2 vols., Boston, 1913).

43. Letter of James Savage, February, 1841, to Joseph Wightman, quoted in Wightman, *Annals*, p. 65. Letter of Harrison Gray Otis, read at Centennial Celebration of Harvard University, September 8, 1836, quoted in Loring, *Hundred Boston Orators*, pp. 196-97.

44. *Diary of Charles Francis Adams*, Ser. I, *The Adams Papers*, Aida DiPace Donald and David Donald, eds. (2 vols., Cambridge, Mass., 1964), II, April 31, 1829, p. 361.

45. Wightman, *Annals*, p. 34. *SCM*, I (1815-36), June 16, 1818; *Boston Daily Advertiser*, March 13, 1821.

46. "Report of James Savage to Ward Committees, July 20, 1818," in Wightman, *Annals*, pp. 36-38; "First Annual Report of the Primary School Board, May 31, 1819," *ibid.*, pp. 40-43.

47. Nathan Bishop, *Third Annual Report of the Superintendent of Public Schools of the City of Boston* (Boston, 1853), pp. 35-36; "First Annual Report . . . 1819," Wightman, *Annals*, p. 43.

48. Cited by Wightman, *Annals*, pp. 44, 60-61, from the reports of committees during 1820.

49. Anonymous letter to John Codman, August 2, 1849, printed in *BSR, 1849*.

50. "Final and Seventh Annual Report of the School of Industry, No. 1 . . . Boston, November, 1819," printed in "Appendix," Wightman, *Annals*, p. 280.

51. *Rules and Regulations Adopted by the Primary School Committee, Boston, July, 1820* (Boston, 1820).

52. *Report of the Standing Committee to the Primary School Board, April 25, 1820* (Boston, 1820); Table 3, Chapter 5, *infra*, p. 110; *Boston Daily Advertiser*, August 25, 1820.

53. "Inaugural Address of Josiah Quincy, Mayor of Boston, May 1, 1823," in *The Inaugural addresses of the Mayors of Boston* (2 vols., Boston, 1894), I, 13.

CHAPTER 3

1. *Reports of the Annual Visiting Committees of the Public Schools of the City of Boston, 1847* (Boston, 1847), p. 31, hereafter such reports are cited as BSR (*Boston School Reports*) plus year.

2. Philippe Ariès, *Centuries of Childhood: A Social History of Family Life*, trans. Robert Baldick (New York, 1965), pp. 137-336; J. W. Hudson, *The History of Adult Education* (London, 1851), pp. 5-6; Frank Thistlewaite, *America and the Atlantic Community: Anglo-American Aspects, 1790-1850* (New York, 1963), p. 137; Richard Johnson, "Educational Policy and Social Control in Early Victorian England," *Past & Present*, No. 49 (November 1970), pp. 96-119.

3. Marcus W. Jernegan, *Laboring and Dependent Classes in Colonial America, 1607-1783* (Chicago, 1931); Robert F. Seybolt, *Apprenticeship and Apprenticeship Education in Colonial New England and New York* (New York, 1917); Forest C. Ensign, *Compulsory School Attendance and Child Labor* (Iowa City, 1921), pp. 30-45. The history of apprenticeship has been neglected and calls for intensive research. A helpful starting point is Lawrence W. Towner, "A Good Master Well Served: A Social History of Servitude in Massachusetts, 1620-1750" (unpublished Ph.D. dissertation, Northwestern University, 1955). On the family, see Edmund S. Morgan, *The Puritan Family: Religion and Domestic Relations in Seventeenth-Century New England* (rev. ed., New York, 1966); Arthur W. Calhoun, *A Social History of the American Family* (3 vols., 1917; reprinted, New York, 1960), I, 51-151. For additional references, see note 27, below. On the church, see Sidney E. Mead, "Denominationalism: The Shape of Protestantism in America," *Church History*, XXIII (1954), 291-320; Mead, "From Coercion to Persuasion: Another Look at the Rise of Religious Liberty and the Emergence of Denominationalism," *ibid.*, XXV (1956), 317-37; Winthrop S. Hudson, *American Protestantism* (Chicago, 1961), pp. 49-96; H. Richard Niebuhr, *The Social Sources of Denominationalism* (New York, 1929); Robert Baird, *Religion in America* (New York, 1856).

4. Benjamin Wadsworth, "The Nature of Early Piety," *A Course of Sermons on Early Piety* (Boston, 1721), p. 10; Edward Eggleston, *The Transit of Civilization from England to America in the Seventeenth Century* (1900; reprinted, Boston, 1959), pp. 174-77; Morgan, *Puritan Family*, pp. 65-108.

5. Review of a work entitled *A General View of the Doctrines of Christianity, designed more especially for the Edification and Instruction of the Family* (Boston, 1809), in *The Works of William E. Channing, D.D.* (Boston, 1891), pp. 459-68; *Christian Disciple*, II (August 1814), p. 248. The implications of this piece and others are discussed in an important although forgotten book, Anne L. Kuhn, *The Mother's Role in Childhood Education: New England Concepts, 1830-1860* (vol. XIX, *Yale Studies in Religious Education*, New Haven, 1947), pp. 17-19; see also "Future Punishment of Infants not a Doctrine of Calvinism," *Spirit of the Pilgrims*, I (January 1828), 42-52, a piece by Lyman

Beecher; and Barbara Cross, ed., *The Autobiography of Lyman Beecher* (2 vols., Cambridge, Mass., 1961), II, Chapter 16.

6. *The Father's Book, or Suggestions for the Government and Instruction of Young Children on Principles Appropriate to a Christian Country* (Springfield, Mass., 1834), p. 31; Heman Humphrey, *Domestic Education* (Amherst, 1840), pp. 118-19, 139. Cf., James K. Morse, *Jedidiah Morse: A Champion of New England Orthodoxy* (New York, 1939), p. 76; Rev. Alvan Hyde, *Essay on the State of Infants* (New York, 1830), pp. 3-12.

7. Horace Bushnell, *Christian Nurture* (1861; reprinted, New Haven, 1947), esp. pp. 3-51, 54, 198-99. This material first appeared in 1846. On Bushnell, see Sanford Fleming, *Children and Puritanism* (New Haven, 1933), pp. 195-207; and Barbara M. Cross, *Horace Bushnell: Minister to a Changing America* (Chicago, 1958). Horace Mann had anticipated Bushnell's views in his "Value and Necessity of Education," *Common School Journal*, I (November 1838), 4, and in a series of letters written in 1843 but published in 1863, Mary Peabody Mann, an influential educator in her own right, strongly recommended Bushnell's views; see Mrs. Horace Mann and Elizabeth P. Peabody, *Moral Culture of Infancy and Kindergarten Guide* (Boston, 1863).

8. Noah Webster, *The First Part of a Grammatical Institute of the English Language* (1783) on the five stages of human life—"infancy, childhood, youth, manhood, and old age"—quoted in Clifton Johnson, *Old-Time Schools and School-books* (New York, 1904), p. 177; Samuel G. Goodrich, *Fireside Education* (New York, 1838), p. 65; Henry Barnard, reviewing Bushnell's work commented on his emphasis on children as independent creatures rather than miniature adults as the most important aspect of that work, see *Barnard's American Journal of Education*, XIII (1867), 79-80, 93-102. This new view of childhood revealed the influence in America of the educational theories of the Swiss writer Johann Heinrich Pestalozzi. See Joseph Neef, *Sketch of a Plan and a Method of Education Founded on an Analysis of Human Faculties and Natural Reason: Suitable for the Offspring of a Free People, and for all Rational Beings* (Philadelphia, 1808); James Simpson, *Necessity of Popular Education,* a book which heavily influenced Horace Mann as discussed in Mary Mann, *Life of Horace Mann* (1867), vol. I of *Life and Works of Horace Mann* (5 vols., Boston, 1891), p. 85. Cf. Will S. Monroe, *History of the Pestalozzian Movement in the United States* (Syracuse, 1907), and Chapter 5, *infra.*

9. "Nursery Maxims," *CSJ*, VIII (January 15, 1846), 31; Samuel R. Hall, *Hall's Lectures on School-keeping*, Arthur D. Wright and George E. Gardner, eds. (1829; reprinted, Hanover, N.H., 1929), p. 45.

10. Information may be pieced together from Calhoun, *Social History of the American Family*, II, 51-77, 131-48; Fleming, *Children and Puritanism;* Kuhn, *The Mother's Role;* Monica Keifer, *American Children Through Their Books* (Philadelphia, 1948); Robert Sunley, "Early Nineteenth-Century American Literature on Child Rearing," in Margaret Mead and Martha Wolfenstein, eds., *Childhood in Contemporary Cultures* (Chicago, 1955), pp. 150-67; Charles Strickland, "A Transcendentalist Father: The Child-Rearing Practices

of Bronson Alcott," *Perspectives in American History,* III (1969), 5-73; and Bernard Wishy, *The Child and the Republic: The Dawn of Modern American Child Nurture* (Philadelphia, 1968), Part I, although his discussion adds nothing to that by Anne Kuhn; indeed, while not acknowledging the debt, Wishy has done little more than reproduce Miss Kuhn's work.

11. Ariès, *Centuries of Childhood,* pp. 15-133; Bernard Bailyn, *Education in the Forming of American Society* (Chapel Hill, 1960), pp. 15-28, 75-78; Ihab H. Hassan, "The Idea of Adolescence in American Fiction," *American Quarterly,* X (Fall 1958), 312-24. The most useful introductions to a vast recent literature on the nature of children are Robin M. Williams, Jr., *American Society: A Sociological Interpretation* (2nd ed., New York, 1966), pp, 39-86; and Erik H. Erikson, *Childhood and Society* (2nd ed., New York, 1963), pp. 247-74.

12. For example, see H. Rood, "The Government of Children"; "Management of Infants"; Willis G. Clark, "Education of Young Ladies," *Parent's Magazine,* I, II (January, September 1841; March 1842), 105-7, 3-4, 149-51; Mrs. L. Pillsbury, "How To Train Your Children Aright," *Mother's Assistant,* VIII (January 1846), 1-6; Catherine Sedgwick, "A Plea for Children," *Ladies' Magazine,* VIII (February 1835), 93-99; "Clothing of Children," *Family Magazine,* IV (1837), 461-62. For other citations, see dissertation copy, Chapter 3, pp. 89-90. Cf. E. Douglas Branch, *The Sentimental Years, 1836-1860* (New York, 1934), pp. 291-318.

13. William M. Thayer, "The Era for Mothers," *Mother's Assistant* (May 1851), pp. 129-46; "Religion is the Strength of Women," *Ladies' Magazine,* VII (May 1834), 226; "The Mother of Washington," *ibid.,* IV (September 1831), 385-94; Kuhn, *The Mother's Role,* pp. 51-52; Wesley Frank Craven, *The Legend of the Founding Fathers* (New York, 1956), pp. 66-101.

14. Representative selections of this literature are John S. C. Abbott, *The Mother at Home* (2nd ed., Boston, 1833); Jacob Abbott, *Gentle Measures in the Management of the Young* (New York, 1872), a compendium of advice from the 1830's on; Lydia Maria Child, *The Mother's Book* (2nd ed., Boston, 1831). See also Jabez Burns, *Mothers of the Wise and Good* (Boston, 1851), "Preface"; John Hall, *On the Education of Children* (2nd ed., Hartford, 1836), p. 41; *American Annals of Education,* III (1833), 16-19.

15. *A Treatise on Domestic Economy for the Use of Young Ladies at Home and at School* (rev. ed., Boston, 1842), p. 37; Beecher, *Suggestions Respecting Improvements in Education* (Hartford, 1829), p. 54. On Catherine Beecher, see William James Cunningham, "Catherine Esther Beecher," Allen Johnson and Dumas Malone, eds., *Dictionary of American Biography* (11 vols., Subscription Ed., New York, 1959), I, Part II, 125-26; and Mae Elizabeth Harveson, *Catherine Esther Beecher: Pioneer Educator* (Philadelphia, 1932).

16. F. J. Darton, *Children's Books in England* (Cambridge, Eng., 1932). See also John Curtis Crandall, Jr., "Images and Ideals for Young Americans: A Study of American Juvenile Literature, 1825-1860" (unpublished Ph.D. dissertation, University of Rochester, 1957), p. 14. I have profited from and been guided by this excellent work.

17. Crandall, "Images and Ideals," pp. 16, 53-54; Kenneth L. Daughrity, "Nathaniel Parker Willis," *DAB*, X, Part II, 306-9; Frank Luther Mott, *A History of American Magazines* (4 vols., Cambridge, Mass., 1938-57), I, on Willis; and appropriate entries in the *DAB* for the others.

18. William B. Cairns, "Samuel Griswold Goodrich," *DAB*, IV, Part I, 402-3; Goodrich, *Recollections of a Lifetime* (2 vols., New York, 1856), II, 537; Peter Parley, *Manners and Customs of the Principal Nations of the World* (Boston, 1845), pp. 20-25.

19. Humphrey, *Domestic Education*, p. 103.

20. John R. Betts, "Mind and Body in Early American Thought," *Journal of American History*, LIV (March 1968), 787-805; Elizabeth A. Wilson, "Hygienic Care and Management of the Child in the American Family Prior to 1860" (unpublished M.S. thesis, Duke University, 1940); *Bowen's Boston News-Letter and City Record*, II (July 8, 1826), 11; William A. Alcott, *The Library of Health* (5 vols., Boston, 1837-41), I; Abel L. Peirson, *On Physical Education* (Boston, 1840); Paton Stewart, Jr., *Warren's Recommendation of Gymnastics* (Boston, 1856); *American Journal of Education*, I (January 1826), 19-23; II (May, August 1827), 289-92, 466-67.

21. Orson S. Fowler, *Education and Self-Improvement* (2nd ed., New York, 1844), p. 48; George Combe, *Lectures on Popular Education* (Boston, 1834); Andrew Combe, *A Treatise on the Physiological and Moral Management of Infancy* (2nd ed., Edinburgh, 1841).

22. *Sixth Annual Report of the Board of Education, Together with the Sixth Annual Report of the Secretary of the Board* (Boston, 1843), pp. 64, 65, and 56-160, *passim*. See also Horace Mann to Lydia Mann, November 9, 1838, in *Mann Papers*, MHS; *CSJ*, V (November 1, 1843), 323; Mann, *A Few Thoughts for a Young Man* (Boston, 1850), p. 83; William B. Fowle, "On the Best Method of Exercising the Different Faculties of the Mind," *Lectures Delivered Before the American Institute of Instruction . . . Boston, August, 1841* (Boston, 1842), pp. 45-46.

23. Gideon F. Thayer, "On Courtesy: A Lecture Delivered in Boston, Before An Audience of Female Teachers Engaged in Elementary Instruction, on Wednesday, January 23, 1839," *CSJ*, II (December 15, 1840), 378; A. Bronson Alcott, "Infant Instruction," reprinted in his *Essays on Education*, Walter Harding, ed. (Gainsville, Florida, 1960), pp. 4, 13, 19-20, 27, and on Alcott's Temple School experiment, Elizabeth Peabody, *Record of a School: Exemplifying the General Principles of Spiritual Culture* (Boston, 1836); Mann, *Life*, p. 83; and Mann, "Value and Necessity of Education," p. 4.

24. John D. Philbrick, *Quarterly Reports of the Superintendent of Public Schools of the City of Boston. For the Year 1857* (Boston, 1858), p. 12; Horace Mann, "Prospectus," *CSJ*, I (November 1838), 14; and numerous other citations in dissertation copy, Chapter 3, p. 99.

25. "End of Insubordination," *Parent's Magazine*, II (January 1842), 105-6; Mann, *Eighth Annual Report* (Boston, 1845), pp. 134-36.

26. Horace Mann to Elizabeth Peabody, two undated letters, 1836 File, *Mann Papers*, MHS.

27. There are conflicting interpretations of the nature of the family in colonial America, some writers viewing the family as nuclear, others as extended, and still others as a modified kinship system. See, respectively, Morgan, *Puritan* Family; Bailyn, *Education in the Forming of American Society*; John Demos, *A Little Commonwealth: Family Life in Plymouth Colony* (New York, 1970); Philip J. Greven, Jr., *Four Generations: Population, Land, and Family in Colonial Andover, Massachusetts* (Ithaca, 1970); David J. Rothman, "A Note on the Study of the Colonial Family," *William and Mary Quarterly*, XXIII (October 1966), 627-34. See also Philip J. Greven, Jr., and Edward N. Saveth, "The Problem of American Family History," *AQ*, XXI (1969), 311-29; John J. Waters, "Hingham, Massachusetts, 1631-1661: An East Anglican Oligarchy in the New World," *Journal of Social History*, I (1968), 351-70; and Kenneth A. Lockridge, *A New England Town: The First Hundred Years* (New York, 1970). On the European background, see Ariès, *Centuries of Childhood*; David Hunt, *Parents and Children in History: The Psychology of Family Life in Early Modern France* (New York, 1970); Lawrence Stone, *The Crisis of the Aristocracy, 1558-1641* (Oxford, 1965), pp. 589-671; Peter Laslett, "The Gentry of Kent in 1640," *Cambridge Historical Journal*, IX (1948), 148-64. Useful sociological literature includes Talcott Parsons and Robert F. Bales, *Family Socialization and Interaction Process* (Glencoe, Ill., 1955); Williams, *American Society*, pp. 39-44, 45-77; and the standard work by Willystine Goodsell, *A History of the Family as a Social and Educational Institution* (New York, 1924).

28. Horace Mann to Mary Messer, October 2, 1836, *Mann Papers*, MHS; Catherine Sedgwick, *Home* (New York, 1835), esp. Chapter 2, "A Glimpse at Family Government"; Mann to Lydia Mann, November 20, 1835, *Mann Papers*, MHS; Jonathan C. Messerli, "Horace Mann: The Early Years, 1796-1837" (unpublished Ph.D. dissertation, Department of Education, Harvard University, 1963), pp. 456-57; Goodrich, *Fireside Education*, p. 106; Terence Martin, "Social Institutions in the Early American Novel," *AQ*, IX (Spring 1957), p. 75, and 72-84, *passim*.

29. Noah Webster to John Brooks, May-June 1819, in Harry R. Warfel, ed., *Letters of Noah Webster* (New York, 1953), p. 398. For magazine pieces, see, for example, "Hints to Young Mothers," *Ladies' Magazine*, VII (February 1834), 52; Harvey Newcomb, "Rules for Family Government," *Parent's Magazine*, II (December 1841), 96; William A. Alcott, "There is No School Like the Family School," *Mother's Assistant*, III (January 1843), 1-3. Quotation on "God's primary school" from Charles Brooks, "Moral Education," *BAJE*, I (March 1856), 337. Cf. Rev. Nathan Colver, "Extent and Design of Parental Authority," *Christian Review*, XII (March 1847), 30; Warren Burton, "Home Education," *BAJE*, II (1856), 333; Gideon F. Thayer, "Letters to a Young Teacher," *ibid.*, p. 336; Henry Barnard, "Homes and Schools As They Were," *BAJE*, XVI (1870), 331-36; and William A. Alcott, *The Young Mother* (Boston, 1836).

30. Robinson, "Moral Culture Essential to Intellectual Education," *LAII . . . August, 1841* (Boston, 1842), pp. 131-32.

31. Francis J. Grund, *Aristocracy in America* (1839; first American ed., New York, 1959), p. 145. Cf. Seth Ames, ed., *Works of Fisher Ames* (2 vols., Boston, 1854), I, 440; George S. Hilliard, *The Dangers and Duties of the Mercantile Profession* (Boston, 1850), pp. 40-42; Calhoun, *Social History of the American Family*, II, 131-48.

32. For example, Jacob Abbott, *New England and Her Institutions* (Boston, 1835), p. 201; Harriet Martineau, *Society in America* (2 vols., London, 1837), I, 269-70. Cf. Warren Burton, *The District School As It Was* (1833; reprinted, New York, 1928).

33. "The Moral Significance of the City," in his *Moral Aspects of City Life* (New York, 1856), pp. 17-18, 19-21; Caleb Cushing, "Introductory Lecture," *LAII . . . August, 1834* (Boston, 1835), pp. 27-28.

34. John S. C. Abbott, "Parental Neglect," *Parent's Magazine*, II (March 1842), 148. Cf. George B. Emerson, "Address on Education," *CSJ*, X (October 15, 1848), 308-10; *LAII . . . 1841* (Boston, 1842), pp. 155-56; *Boston Daily Evening Transcript*, October 19, 1837; Willystine Goodsell, "The American Family in the Nineteenth Century," *The Annals of the American Academy of Political and Social Science*, CLX (March 1932), 13-15, 19-21.

35. William Russell, "On the Infant School System," *LAII . . . August, 1830* (Boston, 1831), p. 106; "Dr. Gregory," *AAE*, VII (July 1837), 229; William B. Fowle, "Preventive Teaching," ms. in *Fowle Papers*, MHS, dated August 1857. For a quixotic discussion by Horace Mann on polluted air and lack of space for exercising in the city, see "Physical Exercise," *CSJ*, VII (June 16, 1845), 177-78, and I (February 1, 1839), 40-41.

36. "Richard Rover," in *Parley's Magazine*, IV (1836), 318-19; *American Journal of Education*, II (August 1828), 510.

37. "Report of the Boston Infant School Society . . . 1833," quoted in "Infant Schools," *AAE*, III (July 1833), 300; *The Boston Common, or Rural Walks in Cities. By a Friend of Improvement* (Boston, 1838), pp. 22, 27-28, 32; Mann and Peabody, *Moral Culture*, pp. 107-8; Edward G. Loring, "School Books," *Boston City Documents, 1847*, Doc. No. 38, pp. 9-15; "Statistics of Public Instruction in Cities and Large Towns: Boston," *BAJE*, I (May 1856), 464-65. The term "moral jungles" was apparently in wide usage; see Henry Barnard, "Gradation of Public Schools. With Special Reference to Cities and Large Villages," *BAJE*, II (December 1856), 464. Mann, *Journal*, May 27, 1837, in *Mann Papers*, MHS.

38. Emerson, "Moral Education," *CSJ*, IV (September 15, 1842), 278, 280-81; Emerson, "Address on Education," p. 310; *Christian Watchman*, XXIV (January 27, 1843), 1; *CSJ*, VIII (September 1, 1846), 265.

39. Mann, *Eleventh Annual Report* (Boston, 1848), p. 57, and pp. 58-85 for replies from John Griscom, Catherine Beecher, and others; Colver, "Extent and Design of Parental Authority," pp. 36-38. On Colver, see Harris E. Starr, "Nathaniel Colver," *DAB*, II, Part II, 324.

40. H.R., "Duty of Children to Parents," *Mother's Magazine* (1840), pp. 135-36; Christopher C. Andrews, *Reflections on the Operation of the Present System of Education* (Boston, 1853), pp. 18-19; *BSR, 1849*, pp. 28-29; Fowle,

"Preventive Teaching," p. 1; *Remarks on the Seventh Annual Report of the Hon. Horace Mann, Secretary of the Massachusetts Board of Education* (Boston, 1844), p. 128; Alcott quoted in Octavius Brooks Frothingham, *Transcendentalism in New England: A History* (1876; reprinted, New York, 1959), pp. 280-81.

41. John H. Hopkins, D.D., "The Defect of the Principle of Religious Authority in Modern Education," *LAII . . . August, 1849* (Boston, 1850), pp. 9, 4-5, 8, 10-11, 25-26. For modern historiography on family stability during the period, see Paul Goodman, "Ethics and Enterprise: The Values of a Boston Elite, 1800-1860," *AQ*, XVIII (Fall 1966), 437-51; and William E. Bridges, "Family Patterns and Social Values in America," *AQ*, XVII (Spring 1965), 3-11. Before reaching any solid conclusions about family stability or instability during the period, however, other studies, such as those involving "career-line analyses" will be needed, similar to those by Greven, *Four Generations*, and Stephan Thernstrom, *Poverty and Progress: Social Mobility in a Nineteenth Century City* (Cambridge, Mass., 1964).

42. "The Education Demanded by the Peculiar Character of Our Civil Institutions," *LAII . . . August, 1849* (Boston, 1850), pp. 5-6.

43. Darrett B. Rutman, *Winthrop's Boston: A Portrait of a Puritan Town, 1630-1649* (Chapel Hill, 1965), pp. 3-22, 98-134; Perry Miller, "The Marrow of Puritan Divinity," in his *Errand Into the Wilderness* (Cambridge, Mass., 1956), pp. 48-98.

44. Dwight, quoted in Hudson, *American Protestantism*, p. 50; Alice M. Baldwin, *The New England Clergy and the American Revolution* (Durham, 1928), pp. 134-53; "Massachusetts Bill of Rights, 1780," in B. P. Poore, ed., *Federal and State Constitutions, Colonial Characters, and Other Organic Laws of the United States* (2 vols., rev. ed., Washington, D.C., 1878), I, 956ff., Articles II & III. A convenient summary of arguments pro and con during the 1820 Constitutional Convention appeared in Merrill D. Peterson, ed., *Democracy, Liberty, and Property: The State Constitutional Conventions of the 1820's* (Indianapolis, 1966), "I: The Massachusetts Convention of 1820-1821," pp. 8-11, 15-16, 19-53; and statistics of the vote on religious issues, "Table 1.2, B," p. 121.

45. William H. Channing, *The Life of William Ellery Channing, D.D.* (Boston, 1880), pp. 346-48; "On the Elevation of the Laboring Classes," and "Remarks on National Literature," in *Works of William E. Channing*, pp. 36-66, 124-38. State law upheld this belief in Christian order. See *Acts and Laws of Massachusetts*, June 25, 1789, Chapter XIX; *Laws of Massachusetts*, March 10, 1827, Chapter CXLIII, Sec. 3, and discussion of this law in *The Common School Controversy; consisting of Three Letters of the Secretary of the Board of Education, of the State of Massachusetts, . . . to which are added Extracts from the Daily Press, in regard to the Controversy* (Boston, 1844), pp. 22, 27, 48-50.

46. *American Unitarianism; or, a Brief History of "The Progress and Present State of the Unitarian Churches in America* (Boston, 1815); Joseph S. Clark, *A Historical Sketch of the Congregational Churches in Massachusetts from*

1620 to 1858 (Boston, 1858), pp. 269-72; Cooke, *Unitarianism*, pp. 130-33; Baker v. Fales, 16 Mass. 146, 487, 505 (1820); Dudley Atkins Tyng, *Reports of Cases, argued and determined in the Supreme Judicial Court of the Commonwealth of Massachusetts* (Boston, 1857), XVI; "The Exiled Churches of Massachusetts," *Congregational Quarterly*, V (July 1863), 216-40.

47. Beecher, *Autobiography*, I, 517-18; Samuel Eliot Morison, *Life and Letters of Harrison Gray Otis, Federalist, 1765-1848* (2 vols., Boston, 1913), II, 241-43; Arthur Burr Darling, *Political Changes in Massachusetts, 1824-1848* (New Haven, 1925), pp. 24-25; Charles Beecher, ed., *Autobiography, Correspondence, etc., of Lyman Beecher, D.D.* (2 vols., New York, 1871), II, 110.

48. *Ibid.*, I, 271.

49. Alexis de Tocqueville, diary entry, October 2, 1831, quoted in George Wilson Pierson, *Tocqueville in America* (abridged ed., Garden City, N.Y., 1959), p. 286; Grund, *Aristocracy in America*, pp. 202-3; Rev. Parson Cooke, *Remonstrance Against an Established Religion in Massachusetts* (Boston, 1831), esp. pp. 23-24; Article XI, "Constitution of Massachusetts," *The General Laws of the Commonwealth of Massachusetts* (Boston, 1921), I, xc.

50. Among these were two Unitarian publications, the *Christian Examiner* and the *Christian Register*; two Baptist periodicals, the *Christian Review* and the *Christian Watchman*; the Congregational newspaper, the *Boston Recorder*; and the Calvinist *American Quarterly Register*. See also Hudson, *American Protestantism*, p. 98; Clarke, *A Historical Sketch*, pp. 7-10; William Ellery Channing, "Remarks on Associations," *Works*, pp. 138-58; Edward Beecher, "The Nature, Importance, and Means of Eminent Holiness Throughout the Church," *The American National Preacher*, X (1835), 193-94; and Timothy L. Smith, *Revivalism and Social Reform: American Protestantism on the Eve of the Civil War* (1957; reprinted, New York, 1965).

51. *The First Annual Report of the Association of Delegates from the Benevolent Societies of Boston, October 12, 1835* (Boston, 1835); Baird, *Religion in America*, pp. 265-67, 348-50; Emerson Davis, *The Half Century: Or, A History of Changes that Have Taken Place, and Events that Have Transpired Chiefly in the United States, Between 1800 and 1850* (Boston, 1851); "The Last Fifty Years," *Christian Review*, XVI (January 1851), 11; *Society in America*, II, 290.

52. Francis J. Grund, *The Americans in Their Moral, Social, and Political Relations* (2 vols., Boston, 1837), I, 164-65. Cf. Josiah Quincy, Jr., *Figures of the Past* (Boston, 1883), pp. 302-3; Philip Schaff, *America: A Sketch of the Political, Social, and Religious Character of the United States of North America, in Two Lectures* (1855; reprinted, Cambridge, Mass., 1961), pp. 47, 53, 76, 117.

53. Robert H. Lord, et al., *History of the Archdiocese of Boston in the Various Stages of Its Development, 1604 to 1943* (3 vols., New York, 1944), II, 126, 179-204; Bishop Fenwick to the Society for the Propagation of the Faith, August 28, 1835, quoted, *ibid.*, p. 141.

54. John Barton Derby, *Political Reminiscences, Including a Sketch of the Origin and History of the "Statesman Party" of Boston* (Boston, 1835), pp.

143-44; Samuel Gridley Howe, "Atheism in New England," *The New England Magazine*, VII-VIII (December 1834; January 1835), 500-509, 53-62; *Massachusetts Senate Documents, 1838*, No. 22, pp. 53-54; Henry Steele Commager, "The Blasphemy of Abner Kneeland," *New England Quarterly*, VIII (March 1935), 29-41; and Arthur M. Schlesinger, Jr., *The Age of Jackson* (Boston, 1945), pp. 350-60; and the case itself, Commonwealth v. Kneeland, 20 Pick. 206 (1838).

55. "Semi-Annual Report of the Standing Committee, 1829," in Joseph M. Wightman, *Annals of the Boston Primary School Committee, From Its First Establishment in 1818, to Its Dissolution in 1855* (Boston, 1860), p. 119; Mann, *Seventh Annual Report* (Boston, 1844), p. 183; Labaree, "Education Now Demanded," pp. 49, 56; and Rev. Charles Brooks, "The Duties of Legislatures in Relation to the Public Schools in the United States," *LAII . . . August, 1849* (Boston, 1850), pp. 175-92, quotation on p. 182.

56. *CSJ*, VIII (August 15, 1846), 243-44; Hopkins, "Religious Authority in Modern Education," pp. 5-7, 10; *Christian Watchman*, XXIV (January 27, 1843), 1; Rev. E. H. Chapin, "The Three Social Forces," *Moral Aspects of City Life*, pp. 135, 136-39; Emerson, "Address on Education," pp. 310-11, 308-10. As chairman of the annual visiting committee of the Boston schools, Emerson stressed that moral training no longer occurred in the home, in church, or anywhere else in society. See *BSR, 1847*, pp. 39-41.

57. Emerson, "Address on Education," pp. 308-10.

58. "Speech on the Disposal of the State Fund of 2 Million Dollars" (February 1837), ms. in *Mann Papers*, MHS.

59. For example, "P," "Description of a Good School," *CSJ*, VIII (November 16, 1846), 345.

60. *Ninth Annual Report* (Boston, 1846), p. 64; *CSJ*, II (January 1, 1840), 5.

61. *CSJ*, III (January 1, 1841), 15; "Memorial of the Bristol Co. Education Convention," *Massachusetts Senate Documents, 1837*, No. 44; "W.A.A.," "Our Common Schools," *CSJ*, II (November 2, 1840), 337; "P," "Description of a Good School," p. 345; *BSR, 1853*, p. 18; "The Common School System of Massachusetts," *New Englander*, XIII (February 1855), 43.

62. "Duty of Parents to Cooperate with Teachers," *CSJ*, VIII (August 1, 1846), 226; *BSR, 1845*, p. 36; *CSJ*, VII (October 15, 1845), 312.

63. "To the Citizens of Boston" (May 23, 1836), p. 8, pamphlet in *Boston Public Schools File*, MHS. See also, for example, David P. Page, *Theory and Practice of Teaching: Or, The Motives and Methods of Good School-Keeping* (Syracuse, 1847), pp. 19-20; Warren Burton, "On The Best Mode of Fixing the Attention of the Young," *LAII . . . 1834* (Boston, 1835), p. 57; Brooks, "Duties of Legislatures," pp. 181-82; Jacob Abbott, "The Duties of Parents in Regard to the Schools Where Their Children Are Instructed," *LAII . . . 1834* (Boston, 1835), pp. 81-98; D. Bethune Duffield, "Education—A State Duty," *BAJE*, III (March 1857), 95-98; "Memorial of the American Institute of Instruction to the Massachusetts Legislature" (1836), reprinted in George B. Emerson, *Reminiscences of an Old Teacher* (Boston, 1878), pp. 77-95;

Thomas H. Palmer, "The Teacher's Manual," Prize Essay of the American Institute of Instruction for 1840, in *CSJ*, II (September 1, 15; October 1, 15; November 2, 16, 1840), 265-72, 281-87, 297-302, 313-18, 329-32; Mann, *Ninth Annual Report*, pp. 98-99; *CSJ*, VIII (June 1, 1846), 169. Mann's *Ninth Report* was largely a glossary on the social and moral role of teachers, reflecting a long-held belief that if children were not educated by their parents the state had the right to appoint parents in the form of schools; see his *Journal*, May 27, 1837, *Mann Papers*, MHS.

64. "Moral Education," pp. 280-81; "Address on Education," pp. 310-11; Mann, *CSJ*, VII (November 15, 1845), 350; *BSR, 1845*, pp. 49-51; Hopkins, "The Defect of the Principle of Religious Authority," p. 14; Mann, "Editor's Address," *CSJ*, VIII (January 1, 1846), 14; "The Last Fifty Years," *Christian Review*, p. 34; *BSR, 1854*, p. 24; *Quarterly Reports of the Superintendent of Public Schools, of the City of Boston. For the Year 1857* (Boston, 1858), pp. 30-31, 44-45.

65. *CSJ*, I (November 1838), 14-15, and IV (April 1, 1842), 99. Cf. Mann's address as President of the National Association of the Friends of Education, Philadelphia, October 17-19, 1849, in *BAJE*, XXIV (June 15, 1873), 330-36; *City of Boston. Primary Schools. Quarterly Report, June 4, 1850*, in *BCD, 1850*, Doc. No. 15, pp. 6-7.

CHAPTER 4

1. "Schools As They Were in the United States: Seventy Years Ago in Boston, Mass.," *Barnard's American Journal of Education*, XXVI (April 1876), 212.

2. George B. Emerson and Alonzo Potter, *The School and the Schoolmaster* (New York, 1842), pp. 79-90, 128-40, 350-51.

3. *Report of the School Committee of the City of Boston on the State of the Schools. May, 1826* (Boston, 1826), pp. 8-9. Excluding expenditures for primary schools, the city spent $45,193.56 on all schools during 1826. See Charles Phillips Huse, *The Financial History of Boston: From May 1, 1822, to January 31, 1909* (vol. XV, *Harvard Economic Studies*, Cambridge, Mass., 1916), Appendix I, "Schools, 1818-1859," p. 364.

4. Anne Royall, *Sketches of History, Life, and Manners in the United States* (New Haven, 1826), p. 324; James G. Carter, *Letters to the Hon. William Prescott, LL.D., on the Free Schools of New England, with Remarks upon the Principles of Instruction* (Boston, 1824), p. 34; George S. Hillard, Mrs. Anna E. Ticknor, and Miss Anna E. Ticknor, eds., *Life, Letters and Journals of George Ticknor* (2 vols., Boston, 1877), II, 188; George Ticknor, "Free Schools of New England," *North American Review*, XIX (1824), 448-57; *Bowen's Boston News-Letter*, I (1825), 224.

5. Enrollment figure an educated guess, derived from 1826 *BSR* attendance of 7,044 and school-age population figures for 1830—see Table 3, Chapter 5, p. 110, *infra*. See also *Bowen's Boston News-Letter*, I (1825), 168, 270, and II (1826), 211; Joseph M. Wightman, comp., *Annals of the Boston Primary School*

Committee, From Its First Establishment in 1818, to Its Dissolution in 1855
(Boston, 1860), p. 153; James G. Carter, *Essays upon Popular Education,
Containing a Particular Examination of the Schools of Massachusetts, and an
Outline of an Institution for the Education of Teachers* (Boston, 1826), p. 41.

6. "Actions of Boston School Committee of 1820-1821," in BSR, *1864*
(Boston, 1864), pp. 153-55; 1824 quotation in Wightman, *Annals*, p. 91.

7. Carter quoted in Henry Barnard, ed., "James G. Carter," *Educational
Biography: Teachers and Educators* (2nd ed., New York, 1859), pp. 185-86.

8. Stephen Farley, "On the Improvement Which May Be Made in the Condition of the Common Schools," *Introductory Discourse and Lectures . . .
American Institute of Instruction . . . Boston, August, 1834* (Boston, 1835),
p. 70; *BSR, 1845* (Boston, 1845), p. 30; *BSR, 1846* (Boston, 1846), p. 160.

9. Edward Everett, "The Boston Schools," *BAJE*, I (May 1856), 643;
Bowen, quoted *ibid.*, IV (September 1857), 14; I am indebted to Richard
Hofstadter for pointing out that "the educational jeremiad is as much a feature
of our literature as the jeremiad in the Puritan sermons," *Anti-Intellectualism
in American Life* (New York, 1963), p. 301.

10. *The Statistical History of the United States from Colonial Times to the
Present* (Stamford, Conn., 1965), Chapter A, Series A 181-94 and 195-209,
p. 14; Jeffrey G. Williamson, "Antebellum Urbanization in the American Northeast," *Journal of Economic History*, XXV (December 1965), 597-98 and
passim.

11. For interpreting the intellectual currents of the period I have relied upon
the perceptive discussions in Leo Marx, *The Machine in the Garden: Technology and the Pastoral Ideal in America* (New York, 1964); R. W. B. Lewis,
*The American Adam: Innocence, Tragedy, and Tradition in the Nineteenth
Century* (Chicago, 1955); Marvin Meyers, *The Jacksonian Persuasion: Politics
and Belief* (Vintage ed., New York, 1960); John William Ward, *Andrew Jackson: Symbol for an Age* (New York, 1955); Constance Rourke, *American
Humor: A Study of the National Character* (New York, 1931); Timothy L.
Smith, *Revivalism and Social Reform: American Protestantism on the Eve of
the Civil War* (1957; reprinted, New York, 1965); Louis B. Salomon, "The
Straight-Cut Ditch: Thoreau on Education," *American Quarterly*, XIV (Spring
1962), 19-36; Octavius Brooks Frothingham, *Transcendentalism in New England: A History* (1876; reprinted, New York, 1959).

12. William B. Fowle, *The Companion to Spelling Books* (Boston, 1843),
p. 17; Bliss Perry, ed., *The Heart of Emerson's Journals* (New York, 1958),
entries for October 17, 1840, and March 1844, pp. 157, 208; George Ticknor,
"Memoirs of the Buckminsters," *Christian Examiner*, XLVII (1849), 171-73.

13. Washington Irving, "The Legend of Sleepy Hollow," *Sketch-Book* (New
York, 1820), p. 253. On schoolbooks, see the brilliant discussion by Ruth Miller
Elson, *Guardians of Tradition: American Schoolbooks of the Nineteenth Century* (Lincoln, Neb., 1964), pp. 25-35. A starting point for comparison of the
portrayal of schoolhouse and teacher in nineteenth-century fiction and poetry
with actual physical and social conditions includes Arthur Foff, "Teacher
Stereotypes in the American Novel" (unpublished Ph.D. dissertation, School of

Education, Stanford University, 1953); Richard Allan Foster, *The School in American Literature* (Baltimore, 1930); and Maxine Greene, *The Public School & the Private Vision: A Search for America in Education and Literature* (New York, 1965). For a typical idealization of American education employing the rural symbol, see A. H. Nelson, "The Little Red Schoolhouse," *Educational Review*, XXIII (March 1901), 304-15.

14. Farley, "On the Improvement of Schools," p. 70; "Boston Public Schools," *North American Review*, LXVI (April 1848), 447-48.

15. Theodore Edson, *Memoir of Warren Colburn, Written for the American Journal of Education* (Boston, 1856); Walter Scott Monroe, "Development of Arithmetic As a School Subject," U.S. Bureau of Education *Bulletin, 1917*, No. 10 (Washington, D.C., 1917); "James G. Carter," in Barnard, ed., *Educational Biography*, pp. 182-94; "William A. Alcott," *ibid.*, pp. 249-67; "George B. Emerson," *ibid.*, pp. 333-43; Robert C. Waterson, *Memoir of Geo. Barrell Emerson* (Boston, 1884), reprinted from the *Proceedings* of the Massachusetts Historical Society, XX (Boston, 1882-83); "Boston Public Schools," *NAR*, p. 453; Samuel G. Goodrich, *Recollections of a Lifetime* (2 vols., New York, 1856); William B. Cairns, "Samuel Griswold Goodrich," Allen Johnson and Dumas Malone, eds., *Dictionary of American Biography* (11 vols., Subscription ed., New York, 1959), IV, Part I, 402-3.

16. This account of Mann, including excerpts from a letter describing his early experiences, appeared in Barnard, ed., *Educational Biography*, pp. 365-68. Cf. Jonathan C. Messerli, "Horace Mann: The Early Years, 1796-1837" (unpublished Ph.D. dissertation, Department of Education, Harvard University, 1963).

17. *Society in America* (2 vols., London, 1837), II, 163.

18. Carter, *Letters . . . on the Free Schools*, p. 55; "The Common School System of Massachusetts," *New Englander*, XIII (February 1855), 55; *Reports of the Connecticut Board of Education, 1847* (New Haven, 1847), p. 48; Mann, *Common School Journal*, IX (1847), p. 48. There was a plethora of literature on the inadequacies of teachers and teacher-training during the period. For examples, see William A. Alcott, *Confessions of a Schoolmaster* (Boston, 1839), pp. 13, 17, 136-38; Rev. Samuel Read Hall, "On the Necessity of Educating Teachers," *LAII . . . 1834* (Boston, 1835), pp. 257ff.; David Mack, "The Claims of Our Age and Country Upon Teachers," *LAII . . . 1839* (Boston, 1840), pp. 137-54; and, "P," "Definition of a Good School," *CSJ*, VIII (January 15, February 2, March 2, November 2, 16, December 1, 1846), 17-20, 42-47, 71-76, 329-31, 344-49, 353-58.

19. *Fireside Education* (New York, 1838), pp. 338-39.

20. This characterization derived from a number of sources. The best starting point is Warren Burton, *The District School as It Was* (1833; reprinted, New York, 1928). Cf. Orville J. Taylor, *The District School; Or, National Education* (Philadelphia, 1835); *American Annals of Education*, II (August, October 1831), 380-83, 468-72; Thomas H. Palmer, "The Teacher's Manual," prize essay in an 1838 contest sponsored by the American Institute of Instruction, printed in Boston, 1840, and reprinted in *CSJ*, II (September 1,

15; October 1, 15; November 2, 16, 1840), 265-72, 281-87, 297-302, 303-18, 329-32; and Clifton Johnston, *Old-Time Schools and School-books* (New York, 1904), pp. 100-34. The 1838 Massachusetts Report quotation came from Johnson, pp. 130-31; Horace Mann quoted by Palmer (September 15, 1840), p. 282.

21. Whittier, *The Complete and Poetical Works* (Cambridge, Mass., 1848), reprinted in Carl H. Gross and Charles C. Chandler, eds., *The History of American Education Through Readings* (Boston, 1964), pp. 127-28.

22. Carter, *Letters . . . on the Free Schools,* pp. 34-35: *Laws and Acts of Massachusetts, 1834* (March 31, 1834), Chapter 169; *ibid., 1841,* Chapter 17; *ibid., 1854,* Chapter 300; Josiah Quincy, "Taking Leave of Office, January 3, 1829," in *The Inaugural Addresses of the Mayors of Boston* (2 vols., Boston, 1894), I, 103-4; Theodore Lyman, "Inaugural Address," in *ibid.,* I, 183.

23. "Boston Grammar and Writing Schools," *CSJ,* VII (November 15, 1845), 344-45; *CSJ,* VIII (September 1, 1846), 270. Cf. *BSR, 1856* (Boston, 1856), Table I.

24. Oscar Handlin, *Boston's Immigrants: A Study in Acculturation* (rev. ed., Cambridge, Mass., 1959), pp. 14-15.

25. Edward Stanwood, "Topography and Landmarks of the Last Hundred Years," in Justin Winsor, ed., *The Memorial History* of Boston (4 vols., Boston, 1881), IV, 25-65; Alex C. Porter, "Changes in the Value of Real Estate in Boston: The Past One Hundred Years," Bostonian Society *Collections,* I (1880), 57-74; Walter Muir Whitehill, *Boston: A Topographical History* (Cambridge, Mass., 1959), pp. 73-140; David Ward, "The Industrial Revolution and the Emergence of Boston's Central Business District," *Economic Geography* (1966), pp. 152-71; Sam Bass Warner, Jr., *Streetcar Suburbs: The Process of Growth in Boston, 1870-1900* (Cambridge, Mass., 1962), pp. 1-34; Walter Firey, *Land Use in Central Boston* (Cambridge, Mass., 1947), pp. 44-55.

26. Rev. Edward Everett Hale, D.D., "School Street in 1830," *Proceedings of the Bostonian Society,* VIII (1923), 35-37.

27. Hale, *A New England Boyhood* (1893; new ed., Boston, 1964), p. 38. Cf. "Edward Everett Among the School Children of Boston," *BAJE,* I (May 1856), 642-43.

28. *Report of the Committee of Conference with the Committee of Primary Schools,* City of Boston, City Doc. No. 13 (1843), bound in *School Reports* (1842-43), III, Suffolk, Essex, Middlesex Counties, MSA.

29. "First Report of Primary School Board, May 31, 1819," In Wightman, *Annals,* p. 42; "Report of the Primary School Board to the Sub-Committee of the Boston School Committee, March 11, 1828," *ibid.,* p. 109; Nathan Bishop, *Third Annual Report of the Superintendent of Public Schools of the City of Boston* (Boston, 1853), pp. 35-36.

30. *Report of the Primary School Committee on Improvements* (Boston, 1833), quoted extensively in "Primary Schools of Boston," *AAE* (December 1833), pp. 584-87; John Odin, Jr., *Report of the Committee of Conference; Thirty-Fifth Annual Report of the Executive Committee of the Primary Schools, City of Boston, 1853* (Boston, 1853), pp. 37-38.

31. "Resolution of a Committee of the City Council, July 14, 1828," reprinted in Wightman, *Annals*, pp. 110-11.

32. *Ibid.*, p. 153; "Report of a Special Committee . . . 1838," reprinted in *ibid.*, pp. 181-83; Ms. School Census Schedule, bound in *School Reports* (1842-43), III, Suffolk, Essex, Middlesex Counties, MSA. Each group of children under one teacher was called a "school" by the Primary Board. It was not uncommon by the 1850's for six or more independent "schools" to be located in the same building; see Bishop, *Third Annual Report*, p. 36.

33. For example, Theodore Lyman, Jr., *Communication to the City Council on the Subject of Introducing Water into the City* (Boston, 1834); "Annual Appropriations, 1846-47," *Boston City Documents, 1846*, Doc. No. 15.

34. Arthur Wellington Brayley, *Schools and Schoolboys of Old Boston* (Boston, 1894), esp. pp. 101, 104-5.

35. For the history of the Franklin-Brimmer Schools, see Brayley, *Schools and Schoolboys*, pp. 87-89, 91; and Charles J. Prescott, "The Brimmer School, 1844-1911," *Proceedings* of the Bostonian Society, VII (1919), 31-46. For similar developments in other schools, see Thomas C. Simonds, *History of South Boston* (Boston, 1857), pp. 111-53; Leah L. Wellington, *History of the Bowdoin School, 1821-1907* (Boston, 1912); Amos M. Leonard, "History of the Lawrence and Mather Schools, South Boston," *Proceedings* of the Bostonian Society, VIII (1922), 24-45. An excellent brief description of the physical facilities of the schools may be found in *Report of the Committee on Public Instruction Respecting the Consolidation of Grammar Schools, BCD, 1852,* Doc. No. 27. On the Back Bay during the period, see Whitehill, *Boston*, pp. 120-29. The quotation comes from the *Minutes* of the School Committee of Boston, ms. bound in separate volumes in Rare-Book Room, Boston Public Library, IV, August 2, 1848, 215; hereafter cited as *SCM*.

36. "Semi-Annual Report of the Standing Committee, April 21, 1829," Wightman, *Annals*, p. 116; "Report . . . March 11, 1828," *ibid.*, p. 109.

37. *Report of the Primary School Committee on Improvements*, p. 583.

38. *Essay on the Construction of School-Houses, to Which Was Awarded the Prize Offered by the American Institute of Instruction, August, 1831* (Boston, 1832); *Report of the Primary School Committee on Improvements*, p. 586.

39. "Report of a Special Committee . . . 1838," Wightman, *Annals*, p. 181; "Health in Common Schools," *CSJ*, II (November 2, 1840), 343, and 337-43, *passim*.

40. See reports in Wightman, *Annals*, pp. 224, 225, 241.

41. *Inaugural Addresses of the Mayors of Boston* (2 vols., Boston, 1894), I (January 7, 1839), 237-39. See Horace Mann's comments, *CSJ*, I (February 1, 1839), 39, 40-41.

42. "Physical Exercise," *CSJ*, VII (June 16, 1845), 177-78.

43. For example, see John H. Griscom, *The Sanitary Condition of the Laboring Population of New York with Suggestions for Its Improvement* (New York, 1845); *Report of the Committee of Internal Health on the Asiatic Cholera, Together with a Report of the City Physician on the Cholera Hospital* (Boston,

1849). For general discussion, see Charles H. Rosenberg, *The Cholera Years: The United States in 1832, 1849, and 1866* (Chicago, 1962), pp. 75-81, 133-50; Richard H. Shryock, "The Medical History of the American People," *Medicine in America* (Baltimore, 1966), pp. 12-16; Mann in *CSJ*, I (February 1, 1839), 15.

44. For an excellent brief discussion, see E. Douglas Branch, *The Sentimental Years, 1836-1860* (New York, 1934), pp. 144-53. See also Marx, *The Machine in the Garden*, pp. 145-226; and Greene, *The Public School*, pp. 59-84. Editorial from *Boston Evening Transcript*, October 28, 1845.

45. *The Boston Common, or Rural Walks in Cities. By a Friend of Improvement* (Boston, 1838), p. 24. Cf. Mary Peabody Mann and Elizabeth Peabody, *Moral Culture of Infancy and Kindergarten Guide* (Boston, 1863), pp. 107-8; William Russell, "On the Infant School System," *LAII . . . August, 1830* (Boston, 1831), pp. 106-8; and the demand in 1838 by the Essex County Teachers Association for a quarter-acre playground for each schoolhouse in "Supplement," *Report of the Board of Education on the Subject of School Houses* (Boston, 1838), p. 35 and *passim*.

46. On Fort Hill and the Boylston School, see Brayley, *Schools and Schoolboys*, pp. 89-90; Josiah Quincy, *A Memorial History of the Town and City of Boston* (Boston, 1852), p. 148; *Report of the Committee of Internal Health*; Whitehill, *Boston*, pp. 114-18; and, Handlin, *Boston's Immigrants*, pp. 13, 15, 93, 107-9.

47. *Rules, Regulations and Orders of the Boston Board of Health Relative to the Police of the Town* (Boston, 1821); John P. Sullivan, "Health and Safety Regulations, 1634-1905, from the Boston Town Records and Various School Committee Records" (Boston, 1938) in Boston School Administration Library; John B. Blake, *Public Health in the Town of Boston, 1630-1822* (Cambridge, Mass., 1959), pp. 162-72, 190-206; *Report of the Committee of Internal Health*; Lemuel Shattuck, *Letter to the Secretary of State on the Registration of Births, Marriages, and Deaths* (Boston, 1845), pp. 19, 23; Josiah Curtis, "Boston Hygiene," American Medical Association *Transactions*, II (Philadelphia, 1849). Quotation from *Boston Almanac, 1850* (Boston, 1850), p. 169.

48. "School Architecture," *BAJE*, XXIII (December 1860), 488. This article (pp. 487-568) provides the best summary of opinions and designs for the perfect school characteristic of the first half of the nineteenth century. See also Emerson, *School and Schoolmaster*, Part II, "The School House."

49. On Brooks, see Wayland J. Chase, "Charles Brooks," *DAB*, II, Part I, 74-75. The Clark Report, in part, was reprinted as "Methods of Ventilation and Warming Recently Introduced into the School-Houses of Boston," *BAJE*, XLI (December 1865), 787-90. See also *BSR, 1846* (Boston, 1846), p. 38.

50. *Ibid.*, pp. 38-39.

51. *Ibid.*, pp. 35-36, 39.

52. Nathan Bishop, *Second Annual Report of the Superintendent of Public Schools of the City of Boston* (Boston, 1852), pp. 8-9, 12-13, *passim*.; Bishop, *First Semi-Annual Report* (Boston, 1851), p. 44. For a perceptive brief discussion of the connections among the physical, mental, and moral development

of children, see John R. Betts, "Mind and Body in Early American Thought," *Journal of American History*, LIV (March 1968), 787-805.

53. Leonard, "History of the Lawrence and Mather Schools," pp. 28-29.

54. "School Architecture," p. 488.

55. John D. Philbrick, *Semi-Annual Report of the Superintendent of Public Schools of the City of Boston* (Boston, 1860), pp. 6-7.

CHAPTER 5

1. Nathan Bishop, *First Semi-Annual Report of the Superintendent of Public Schools of the City of Boston* (Boston, 1852), p. 6.

2. Useful accounts of the "Uniformity" or "American System of Manufacturing" include Carroll D. Wright, "Report on the Factory System of the United States," and Charles H. Fitch, "Report on the Manufactures of Interchangeable Mechanism," in *Report on the Manufactures of the United States at the Tenth Census*, U.S. Census Bureau, *Tenth Census* (Washington, D.C., 1880), II, 527-606, and 611ff; Nathan Appleton, *The Introduction of the Power Loom* (Lowell, Mass., 1858); Caroline Ware, *The Early New England Cotton Manufacture, a Study in Industrial Beginnings* (Boston, 1931); Victor S. Clark, *History of Manufactures in the United States* (3 vols., New York, 1929), I; John E. Sawyer, "The Social Basis of the American System of Manufacturing," *Journal of Economic History*, XIV (1954), 361-79; George Rogers Taylor, *The Transportation Revolution, 1815-1860* (New York, 1951), pp. 229-49; Constance McL. Green, *Eli Whitney and the Birth of American Technology* (Boston, 1956); and on the relationship between popular thought and technological innovation, Daniel J. Boorstin, *The Americans: The National Experience* (New York, 1965), pp. 20-34.

3. See, for example, Lewis Mumford, *Technics and Civilization* (New York, 1934; new ed., 1963), *passim*, esp. pp. 31-59, 196-99; and Thomas S. Kuhn, *The Structure of Scientific Revolutions* (Chicago, 1962).

4. Nathan Bishop, *Third Annual Report of the Superintendent of Public Schools of the City of Boston* (Boston, 1853), pp. 7-8, and Chapter 1, *supra*; *Report of the Record Commissioners of the City of Boston* (1789), "Education Act of 1789."

5. Arthur Wellington Brayley, *Schools and Schoolboys of Old Boston* (Boston, 1894), pp. 51-52. Unlike other Massachusetts towns and cities Boston was not divided into separate school districts. For a discussion, see *Report to the Primary School Committee, June 15, 1846, on the Petition of Sundry Colored Persons, for the Abolition of the Schools for Colored Children. With the City Solicitor's Opinion* (Boston, 1846), pp. 3-7.

6. For example, see *American Annals of Education*, II (August 1831), 382-83; Henry Barnard, *Second Annual Report of the Secretary of the Board of Commissioners of Common Schools of Connecticut* (New Haven, 1840), pp. 26-27; and, Clifton Johnson, *Old-Time Schools and School-books* (New York, 1904), pp. 127-28.

7. "Report of a Special Committee, 1819," in Ms. minutes of the Boston

School Committee bound in volumes in the Rare Book Room of BPL, I (1815-36). The opening attack on the "double-headed system" came from Samuel Gridley Howe and other reform-minded members of the School Committee in 1845. See *Reports of the Annual Visiting Committees of the Grammar and Writing Schools of Boston for 1845* (Boston, 1845), pp. 34-42. Cf. Brayley, *Schools and Schoolboys*, p. 52.

8. Bishop, *Third Annual Report*, p. 9; *BSR, 1847* (Boston, 1847), p. 50. The author of this report was George B. Emerson. Neither Emerson nor other reformers objected to women teaching; indeed, the educators often praised female superiority in "moral power" as an example to children. See Horace Mann, *Eighth Annual Report of the Board of Education, Together with the Eighth Annual Report of the Secretary of the Board* (Boston, 1845), pp. 60-62.

9. The phrase came from *BSR, 1846* (Boston, 1846), p. 160. Edward Everett Hale, *A New England Boyhood* (1893; reprinted, Boston, 1964), p. 26.

10. Anonymous, "A Boston Public School Twenty Years Ago," *The Knickerbocker, or New-York Monthly Magazine*, LI (April 1858), 396-97, 98, 400. To support the generalization I have relied upon the semi-reliable reminiscences of older men, established citizens in the Boston community near the close of the nineteenth century. These can be found, accompanied by useful if often honorific biographical sketches in Brayley, *Schools and Schoolboys*, pp. 175-479, *passim*.

11. For population growth, see Table 6, Chapter 9, p. 211, *infra*.

12. This statement is based on the only reliable figures readily available, and may be somewhat deceptive as the rate of growth comes from figures for 1817 (two years before the beginning of reorganization) and for 1826. In 1817, exclusive of the public charity school in the Alms House, 2,298 pupils attended schools in the North, Center, West, and South Ends of Boston. In 1826, with reading and writing schools united under one roof, 4,156 students attended. Part of the increase was natural growth, but reorganization and more central location of schools appear to have been the primary factor. See "Report of a Sub-Committee on the State of Education, 1817," reprinted in, Joseph M. Wightman, comp., *The Annals of the Boston Primary School Committee, From Its First Establishment in 1818, to Its Dissolution in 1855* (Boston, 1860), p. 22; and, *Report of the School Committee of the City of Boston on the State of the Schools, May, 1826* (Boston, 1826), p. 8.

13. Figures derived from Wightman, *Annals*, "Appendix," p. 303; Josiah Quincy, *Report of a Sub-Committee of the School Committee Recommending Various Improvements in the System of Instruction in the Grammar and Writing Schools of this City* (Boston, 1828), p. 19; "Account of the Schools in Boston," *Common School Journal*, II (February 1, 1840), p. 37; Ms. *Schedules* in *Massachusetts School Reports*, III, Suffolk, Essex, Middlesex Counties (1842-43; 1846-47; 1850-51), MSA; "Statistics of Public Instruction in Cities and Large Towns: Boston," *Barnard's American Journal of Education*, I (May 1856), 458; and, *BSR, 1856* (Boston, 1856), p. 34.

14. Thomas Pemberton, *Topographical and Historical Description of Boston*, in Massachusetts Historical Society *Collections*, III (1794), 249; Edward Stan-

wood, "Topography and Landmarks of the Last Hundred Years," in Justin
Winsor, ed., *The Memorial History of Boston* (4 vols., Boston, 1881), IV, 29;
Bowen's Boston News-Letter and City Record, II, October 28, 1826, 199-200;
*Report of the Committee of Internal Health on the Asiatic Cholera, Together
with a Report of the City Physician on the Cholera Hospital* (Boston, 1849),
p. 14; *Report of the Committee on the Expediency of Providing Better Tenements for the Poor* (Boston, 1846); *Report and Tabular Statement of the Censors . . . State Census of Boston, May 1, 1850, in Boston City Documents,
1850, Doc. No. 42.* See also Walter Muir Whitehill, *Boston: A Topographical
History* (Cambridge, Mass., 1963), pp. 73-94; Sam B. Warner, *Streetcar Suburbs: The Process of Growth in Boston, 1870-1900* (Cambridge, Mass., 1962),
pp. 15-17; David Ward, "The Industrial Revolution and the Emergence of
Boston's Central Business District," *Economic Geography*, LXII (June 1966),
152-71.

15. E. C. Wines, *A Trip to Boston* (Boston, 1838), pp. 207-8; Abner Forbes
and J. W. Greene, *The Rich Men of Massachusetts: Containing a Statement of
the Reputed Wealth of About Fifteen Hundred Persons, with Brief Sketches
of More than One Thousand Characters* (Boston, 1851), forty-one of these
men, each worth over a half-million dollars, lived in the vicinity of Summer
Street, as did some of the oldest established families. Cf. Caroline G. Curtis,
Memories of Fifty Years in the Last Century (Boston, 1947), pp. 5-6, 11-12;
and Whitehill, *Boston*, pp. 106, 111, 120, 125, 136-37.

16. In addition to contemporary references given in note 14, for patterns of
population, see Lemuel Shattuck, *Report to the Committee of the City Council
Appointed to Obtain the Census of Boston for the Year 1845* (Boston, 1846);
Josiah Curtis, *Report of the Joint Special Committee on the Census of Boston,
May, 1855, Including the Report of the Censors, With Analytical and Sanitary
Observations* (Boston, 1856); Jesse Chickering, *Report of the Committee Ap-
pointed by the City Council; and also a Comparative View of the Population
of Boston in 1850, with the Births, Marriages, and Deaths in 1849 and 1850*
(Boston, 1851) in *BCD, 1851, Doc. No. 60;* Massachusetts Sanitary Commis-
sioners. *Report of a General Plan for the Promotion of Public and Personal
Health . . . Relating to a Sanitary Survey of the State. Presented April 25,
1850* (Boston, 1850); Elias H. Derby, "Commercial Cities and Towns of the
United States. Number XXII. City of Boston," *Hunt's Merchants' Magazine*,
XVII (November 1850), 483-97. See also David Ward, "Nineteenth Century
Boston: A Study in the Role of Antecedent and Adjacent Conditions in the
Spatial Aspects of Urban Growth" (unpublished Ph.D. dissertation, University
of Wisconsin, 1963), "The Emergence of Central Immigrant Ghettoes in Amer-
ican Cities: 1840-1920," *Annals of the Association of American Geographers*,
LVIII (June 1968), 343-59, and the same author's *Cities and Immigrants: A
Geography of Change in Nineteenth Century America* (New York, 1971);
W. I. Firey, *Land Use in Central Boston* (Cambridge, Mass., 1948); and, Oscar
Handlin, *Boston's Immigrants: A Study in Acculturation* (rev. ed., Cambridge,
Mass., 1959), pp. 88-123; cf. Peter R. Knights, *The Plain People of Boston,
1830-1860: A Study in City Growth* (New York, 1971).

17. Knights, *Plain People of Boston,* pp. 19-32, 48-77; Henry Marcus Schreiber, "The Working People of Boston in the Middle of the Nineteenth Century" (unpublished Ph.D. dissertation, Boston University, 1950), esp. pp. 290-92; primary materials in notes 14 and 16, *supra,* and, Massachusetts Bureau of Statistics of Labor, *Report of the Bureau . . . 1870,* in *Massachusetts Senate Documents, 1870,* Doc. No. 120; *Benevolent Fraternity of Churches of Boston, Eleventh Annual Report of the Executive Committee . . . 1845* (Boston, 1845).

18. The word has lost little of its early ambiguity. Its derivation may best be traced in *The Oxford English Dictionary on Historical Principles.* See also Wendell Bell, "Social Areas: Typology of Urban Neighborhoods," in Marvin B. Sussman, ed., *Community Structure and Analysis* (New York, 1959), pp. 61-92; Suzanne Keller, *The Urban Neighborhood: A Sociological Perspective* (New York, 1967), pp. 9-12, 87-123.

19. For discussion about literature on urban neighborhoods, see dissertation copy, Chapter 5, note 29. For introduction to literature, see Thomas Jesse Jones, *The Sociology of a New York City Block* (New York, 1904); Ernest W. Burgess, "Can Neighborhood Work Have a Scientific Basis?" in Robert E. Park and Ernest W. Burgess, eds., *The City* (Chicago, 1925), pp. 142-55; Herbert J. Gans, *The Urban Villagers: Group and Class in the Life of Italian-Americans* (New York, 1962), pp. 3-16 and *passim.*

20. Dwight, *Travels in New-England and New-York* (4 vols., New Haven, 1821-22), IV, 449-52, 466-69. By the 1830's a perceptive observer, Francis Grund, could write that "there are no better policemen than the ordinary run of Bostonians. . . . This is by some called the wholesome restraint of public opinion." See his *Aristocracy in America* (1839; first American ed., New York, 1959), p. 162.

21. George Ticknor, "Memoir of the Buckminsters," *Christian Examiner,* XLVII (1849), 171. The clearest evidence of increased dependence on city and state government for the promotion of civil order and harmony came in the resurgence of public licensing for an amazingly inclusive number of activities. See *The Charter of the City of Boston, and Ordinances Made and Established by the Mayor, Aldermen, and Common Council, with Such Acts of the Legislature as Relate to the Government of Said City* (Boston, 1827) and the similar volume for 1850. See also Oscar and Mary Flug Handlin, *Commonwealth: Massachusetts, 1774-1861: A Study of the Role of Government in the American Economy* (New York, 1947), pp. 72-80, 223-25, 253-55.

22. See, for example: "Report of a Special Committee of the Primary Board, July 3, 1838," reprinted in Wightman, *Annals,* pp. 186-87.

23. Brayley, *Schools and Schoolboys,* p. 108.

24. Bishop, *First Semi-Annual Report,* pp. 8-9. The remainder of the report discussed past practices and present needs, elaborating on these sentiments. Dickens' novel is available in a variety of editions.

25. *School Committee Report on the Distribution of the Pupils in the Grammar Schools of the City of Boston* (Boston, 1837), pp. 2-3.

26. Wightman, *Annals,* p. 7; *Reports of the Record Commissioners of Boston (1789),* "Education Act of 1789" (September 25, 1789); Bishop, *Third An-*

nual Report, p. 10; John Lathrop, Jr., "Address on the First Anniversary of the Boston Associated Instructors of Youth," reprinted in *BAJE*, XL (September 1865), 532.

27. William Russell, "Prospectus," *American Journal of Education*, I (January 1826), 3, and III (January 1828), 53-58; Horace Mann, "A Few Thoughts on the Powers and Duties of Women" (1853), in his *Lectures on Various Subjects* (New York, 1859), p. 65. See also William Woodbridge, *AAE*, I (August, September 1830), 329, 421-23; Catherine E. Beecher, *A Treatise on Domestic Economy* (rev. ed., Boston, 1842), p. 37; Bronson Alcott, "Maternal Influence," *AAE*, III (January 1833), 16-24.

28. *Ladies' Magazine*, VII (August 1834), 377; Catherine E. Beecher, *Suggestions Respecting Improvements in Education* (Hartford, 1829), p. 8.

29. For an excellent survey of pertinent literature, see Anne L. Kuhn, *The Mother's Role in Childhood Education: New England Concepts, 1830-1860* (New Haven, 1947), pp. 71-97. *Report on the Distribution of Pupils (1837)*, pp. 7-8. Nathan Bishop attested to this long-held belief among Bostonians in his *Fifth Annual Report (1855)*, quoted in *BAJE*, I (May 1856), 462.

30. *Ibid.*, 461; Report of the School Committee . . . May, 1826, "Schedule B"; Bishop, *Third Annual Report*, p. 11.

31. *SCM*, I (1815-36), November, 1830. The report urging the moral benefits of separating the sexes was prepared by Lemuel Shaw, then a member of the School Committee and shortly thereafter the Chief Justice of the Commonwealth.

32. Brayley, *Schools and Schoolboys*, p. 163.

33. School Committeemen had agreed upon the needed changes and had advertised them to parents the year before. See "To the Citizens of Boston" (May 23, 1836), a pamphlet at MHS.

34. See Charles P. Huse, *The Financial History of Boston From May 1, 1822 to January 31, 1909*, vol. 15, *Harvard Economic Studies* (Cambridge, Mass., 1916).

35. *SCM*, II (1837-41), May 23, December 27, 1837; *Boston Daily Evening Transcript*, November 25, December 9, 1837; *Report on the Distribution of Pupils (1837)*, pp. 2-3, 7-8, and *passim*.

36. For discussion, see Chapter 6, *infra*.

37. *SCM*, II (1837-41), November 22, December 6, 1837; *Boston Daily Evening Transcript*, December 16, 1837.

38. Horace Mann, *First Annual Report of the Board of Education, Together with First Annual Report of the Secretary of the Board* (Boston, 1838), pp. 55-56.

39. *Report of the Committee to Whom Were Referred the Petitions from Wards 1, 2, 3, 4, 5, 6, 10 and 12, Respecting the Late Changes in the Distribution of the Scholars Attending Several of the City Schools, . . . Together With a Minority Report* (Boston, 1838).

40. *SCM*, II (1837-41), December 13, 1837.

41. *Ibid.*, February 2, 1838.

42. See, for example, *SCM*, II, May 14, 1839; III (1842-45), May 3, 1842,

November 7, 1843. See Chapter 11, *infra,* for discussion of legal tools of compulsory attendance.

43. *Report on the Distribution of Pupils* (*1837*), p. 7.

44. John D. Philbrick, *Second Semi-Annual Report of the Superintendent of the Boston Public Schools, March, 1861* (Boston, 1861), pp. 5-7.

45. John H. Griscom, *A Year in Europe, 1818-1819* (2 vols., New York, 1823); Joseph G. Cogswell and George Bancroft, *Prospectus of a School to be Established at Round Hill, Northampton, Massachusetts* (Cambridge, Mass., 1823), p. 17, and *passim;* Ticknor to Jared Sparks, August 7, 1824, quoted in, David B. Tyack, *George Ticknor and the Boston Brahmins* (Cambridge, Mass., 1967), p. 102.

46. Stowe, "Report on Elementary Public Instruction in Europe" (1837), reprinted in Edgar W. Knight, ed., *Reports on European Education: John Griscom, Victor Cousin, and Calvin E. Stowe* (New York, 1930), p. 256. Not only was Stowe's report placed in every school district of Ohio by the state legislature, but also the legislatures of Massachusetts, Pennsylvania, Michigan, and elsewhere reprinted it for distribution. See Edward Dwight Eaton, "Calvin Ellis Stowe," in Allen Johnson and Dumas Malone, eds., *Dictionary of American Biography* (11 vols., Subscription ed., New York, 1958), IX, Part I, 115. In 1855, Philip Schaff, the perceptive German-American church historian observed that "all New England, New York, Pennsylvania, Ohio, and other States, have adopted a general free-school system, partly after the much admired Prussian model." See his *America: A Sketch of the Political, Social, and Religious Character of the United States of North America, in Two Lectures* (New York, 1855), p. 58.

47. Charles Sumner to Dr. Samuel G. Howe, Boston, December 31, 1843, in Edward L. Pierce, *Memoirs and Letters of Charles Sumner* (2 vols., Boston, 1877), II, 277. After Mann made public his report, Sumner endorsed it enthusiastically in the *Boston Advertiser,* March 12, 21, 1844.

48. Horace Mann, *Seventh Annual Report, 1843* (Boston, 1844), pp. 21-23. Mann testified to the reports of Stowe and others as influencing him. See pp. 69, 84, 85, *ibid.*

49. For examples, see Horace Mann to Samuel G. Howe, June 20, 1845, *Mann Papers,* MHS. Here Mann asked Howe's advice on the question of requiring teachers to conduct written examinations of the schools and to report on various faults and advantages in each school. Emerson defended Mann's remarks on the excellence of Prussian schools in his *Observations on a Pamphlet, Entitled "Remarks on the Seventh Annual Report of the Hon. Horace Mann, Secretary of the Massachusetts Board of Education"* (Boston, 1844).

50. Howe and his fellow committeemen were innovators; in 1845 Boston schools became the first in America to employ written examinations for testing students, although the practice was common in Europe. See *CSJ*, VII (October 1, 1845), 289; and, O. W. Caldwell and S. A. Courtis, *Then and Now in Education, 1845-1923* (Yonkers, N.Y., 1924).

51. *BSR, 1845,* pp. 17-18, 19, 30, 38-40; "Boston Grammar and Writing

Schools," *CSJ*, VII (October 1, 15; November 1, 15; December 1, 1845), 289-368. This marked the first extensive publication of any Boston school reports. Nor was Mann tardy in his efforts to give the Howe report wide circulation. The report itself first was read before the full School Committee on August 7, 1845. See *Boston Atlas*, August 9, 1845. The *Atlas* was the newspaper which most often reported and supported the efforts of the reformers.

52. *BSR, 1847*, pp. 3, 46-47, 52. This theme—the formation of character and the education of conscience—was Emerson's favorite, as it was with most other educators of the period. See Emerson, *An Address Delivered at the Opening of the Boston Mechanics' Institution, February 7, 1827* (Boston, 1827), pp. 11-13; Emerson, *Reminiscences of an Old Teacher* (Boston, 1878), p. 55. Cf. "Extracts from the Charlestown School Committee," *CSJ*, III (June 15, 1841), 186; "Annual Election Sermon by Rev. E. H. Chapin," *CSJ*, VI (February 15, 1844), 54.

53. Brayley, *Schools and Schoolboys*, pp. 115-16; Willard E. Elsbree, *The American Teacher: Evolution of a Profession in a Democracy* (New York, 1939), pp. 195-96. Henry Barnard pointed out that the need for graded schools was one of the most obvious educational changes in response to urban problems of overcrowding and a heterogeneous population. See "Gradation of Public Schools. With Special Reference to Cities and Large Villages," *BAJE*, II (December 1856), 455-64. There is no adequate history of the evolution of graded schools.

54. *BSR, 1846*, p. 3. The following year George B. Emerson employed similar language in describing "practical education." See *BSR, 1847*, pp. 44-45. For a persuasive discussion of the tension and interplay between the new techniques of industrialization and intellectual responses to American society, see Leo Marx, *The Machine in the Garden: Technology and the Pastoral Ideal in America* (New York, 1964), esp. pp. 1-33.

55. Bishop, *First Semi-Annual Report*, with quotations on pages 10-11, 42, 44, respectively. In light of Marx's identification of the railroad as the principle symbol of industrialization employed by New England authors, it was suggestive that Bishop's first report stressed that "the same practical judgment is to be exercised in making special adaptations of means to ends, as in any manufacturing or other business enterprise" (p. 6), on the heels of having devoted much of his first year in office "showing our Public Schools to strangers, who visited the City, either to witness, or to participate in, the festivities of 'the grand Railroad Celebration'" (p. 5).

56. "Report of the Committee on Public Instruction on the Present Organization of the Grammar and Primary School Committees," *BCD, 1852*, I, Doc. No. 22; Bishop, *Second Annual Report* (Boston, 1852), esp. pp. 27-35, 48; Wightman, *Annals*, pp. 266-67; Philbrick, *Second Semi-Annual Report*, pp. 5-7. The high schools long had been more or less graded on the basis of subject matter. See "Actions of the Boston School Committee of 1820-1821," in *BSR, 1864* (Boston, 1864), pp. 156-57.

CHAPTER 6

1. *Reports of the Annual Visiting Committee of the Grammar and Writing Schools of the City of Boston for 1847* (Boston, 1847), p. 9.

2. Few terms offer more leeway in preciseness and nuance than "social class." For lengthier discussion of this problem, see dissertation copy, Chapter 6, note 2. I believe it is useful to consider "social class" as referring to both economic position and qualitative judgments of merit within a society composed of heterogeneous individuals and groups. Thus I use the term to mean a body of persons who occupy a position in a social hierarchy because they demonstrate similarly valued objective criteria such as lineage; possessions; personal achievements; personal qualities; authority; and power. This usage follows Talcott Parsons, for example, "An Analytical Approach to the Theory of Social Stratification," *American Journal of Sociology*, XLV (May 1940), 841-62; "A Revised Analytical Approach to the Theory of Social Stratification," in Reinhard Bendix and Seymour Martin Lipset, eds., *Class, Status and Power* (Glencoe, Ill., 1953), pp. 92-128; and his *Essays in Sociological Theory* (Glencoe, Ill., 1949), pp. 171-72. For another work relying upon Parson's works in this manner, see Gideon Sjoberg, *The Preindustrial City, Past and Present* (New York, 1960), pp. 108-44.

3. See, for example, the excellent discussion in Carl F. Kaestle, *The Evolution of an Urban School System: New York City, 1750-1850* (Cambridge, Mass., 1973).

4. James McKellar Bugbee, "Boston Under the Mayors, 1822-1880," in Justin Winsor, ed., *The Memorial History of Boston* (4 vols., Boston, 1881), III, Chapter 2; Arthur Burr Darling, *Political Changes in Massachusetts, 1824-1848* (New Haven, 1925); and, Richard P. McCormick, *The Second American Party System: Party Formation in the Jacksonian Era* (Chapel Hill, 1966), pp. 36-49.

5. This explanation of voter apathy draws upon recent theories of voting behavior. Among others, see Samuel J. Eldersveld, *Theory and Method in Voting Behavior* (Glencoe, Ill., 1956), p. 268; Paul F. Lazarsfeld, Bernard Berelson, and Hazel Gaudet, *The People's Choice* (2d ed., New York, 1948); by Berelson, Lazarsfeld, and William McPhee, *Voting: A Study of Opinion Formation in a Presidential Campaign* (Chicago, 1954), pp. 333-47; E. H. Litchfield, *Voting Behavior in a Metropolitan Area* (Ann Arbor, 1941); V. O. Key, *Politics, Parties, and Pressure Groups* (New York, 1942); Seymour Martin Lipset, "Political Sociology," in Robert K. Merton, Leonard Broom, and Leonard S. Cottrell, Jr., eds., *Sociology Today* (New York, 1959), pp. 93-95. The concept that individuals may vote for and identify with men whose behavior and values they strive to emulate has been labeled by sociologists as "reference-group theory." See, among others, Robert K. Merton, *Social Theory and Social Structure* (rev. ed., Glencoe, Ill., 1957), pp. 234, 305-6, and 225-386, *passim*. The most persuasive attempt to understand voting behavior in a large, antebellum city was by Lee Benson in his *The Concept of Jacksonian Democracy: New*

York as a Test Case (Princeton, 1961). For ideals of personal success during the period, see John G. Cawelti, *Apostles of the Self-Made Man: Changing Concepts of Success in America* (Chicago, 1965), pp. 1-98.

6. *Boston Daily Advertiser,* March 13, 1821.

7. See, for example, Harrison Gray Otis, who affirmed on September 17, 1830, on taking office as mayor that many city leaders rose from humble beginnings and that "there is so far as I can judge, more real equality and a more general intercourse among the different vocations than is elsewhere to be found in a populous city," in *The Inaugural Addresses of the Mayors of Boston* (2 vols., Boston, 1894), I, 152. Cf. Frederick Robinson, *An Oration Delivered before the Trades' Union of Boston and Vicinity, July 4, 1834* (Boston, 1834); T. S. Arthur, *Advice to Young Men on Their Duties and Conduct in Life* (Boston, 1849); Abner Forbes and J. W. Greene, *The Rich Men of Massachusetts* (Boston, 1852).

8. George Ticknor, "Memoir of the Buckminsters," *Christian Examiner,* XLVII (1849), 169-95, quotation on sense of community on p. 173; Josiah Quincy, Jr., "Social Life in Boston: From the Adoption of the Federal Constitution to the Granting of the City Charter," in Winsor, *Memorial History,* IV; Van Wyck Brooks, *The Flowering of New England* (1936; reprinted, New York, 1952), pp. 1-20; Samuel Eliot Morison, *The Maritime History of Massachusetts, 1783-1860* (Boston, 1921), pp. 119-33; and, Paul Goodman, "Ethics and Enterprise: The Values of a Boston Elite, 1800-1860," *American Quarterly,* XVIII (Fall 1966), 437-51. For lengthier discussion of the use of the term "elite," see dissertation copy, Chapter 6, notes 9, 11. I have followed the definition—an elite is "a minority of individuals designated to serve a collectivity in a socially valued way"—given by Suzanne Keller in her provocative work, *Beyond the Ruling Class: Strategic Elites in Modern Society* (New York, 1963), p. 4. Cf. Talcott Parsons, *Structure and Process in Modern Societies* (New York, 1960), p. 183; and, Sjoberg, *Preindustrial City,* pp. 110-21; and the "structure-function" analysis developed by Robert K. Merton in *On Theoretical Sociology: Five Essays, Old and New* (New York, 1967), pp. 73-138.

9. Bugbee, "Boston Under the Mayors," pp. 247-51; *Members of the Common Council of the City of Boston for 1845, with Their Place of Birth, Occupation, Condition in Life, etc.* (Boston, 1845); see city directories from 1830 to 1850 for information on occupations of men elected to office. See also Thomas L. Wilson, *The Aristocracy of Boston . . . for the Last Forty Years* (Boston, 1848); *Mayors of Boston* (Boston: State Street Trust Company, 1910); Josiah Quincy, *A Municipal History of the Town and City of Boston* (Boston, 1852); Henry H. Sprague, *City Government in Boston, Its Rise and Development* (Boston, 1890); and, William Travis Davis, *Professional and Industrial History of Suffolk County, Massachusetts* (3 vols., Boston, 1894). For suggestive discussions of social class shifts in loyalty, see David B. Tyack, *George Ticknor and the Boston Brahmins* (Cambridge, Mass., 1967), pp. 193-241; and, Richard Hofstadter, "Wendell Phillips: The Patrician as Agitator," in his *The American Political Tradition* (New York, 1948), pp. 137-63.

10. "The Perils of Popular Government," in Mary Mann and George Mann,

Life and Works of Horace Mann (5 vols., Boston, 1891), IV, 364-65. Mann repeated this theme throughout his *Annual Reports* as Secretary of the Board of Education. See also *Common School Journal*, I (February 15, 1839), 60; Benjamin Labaree, "The Education Demanded by the Peculiar Character of Our Civil Institutions," *Lectures . . . before the American Institute of Instruction, August, 1849* (Boston, 1850), p. 56.

11. *Reports of the School Committees of the City of Boston*, City Doc. No. 21, in *School Reports* (1841-42), II, Suffolk, Essex, Middlesex Counties, MSA; *Rules of the School Committee, and Regulations of the Public Schools of the City of Boston* (Boston, 1841), p. 3.

12. "A Boston Public School: Twenty Years Ago," *The Knickerbocker, or New-York Monthly Magazine*, LI (April 1958), 398.

13. For members, see *Reports of the School Committees*, Doc. No. 21, *School Reports* (1841-42); see Stimpson's *Boston Directory* (1842) for occupational listings. For brief biographies of these men respectively, see Allen Johnson and Dumas Malone, eds., *Dictionary of American Biography* (11 vols., Subscription ed., New York, 1958), X, Part II, 192-93; Arthur Wellington Brayley, *Schools and Schoolboys of Old Boston* (Boston, 1894), p. 307; *DAB*, IV, Part I, 447; V, Part I, 49-50; X, Part II, 618-19.

14. "Duty of Clergymen to Visit Schools," *CSJ*, VIII (1846), 241-42; Rev. W. Warren, "School and Schoolmaster," *Mother's Assistant* (1856), p. 61.

15. The number of qualified voters increased almost 50 per cent between 1841 and 1845, remained largely the same until 1852, and then grew again by some 15 per cent between 1852 and 1855. See *Report and Tabular Statement of the Censors . . . State Census of Boston, May 1, 1850*, in *Boston City Documents, 1850*, Doc. No. 42, p. 12; and Josiah Curtis, *Report of the Joint Special Committee on the Census of Boston, May, 1855* (Boston, 1856), p. 11.

16. "Report of the Committee on Public Instruction on the Present Organization of the Grammar and Primary School Committees," *BCD, 1852*, I, Doc. No. 22. A convenient listing of members of the School Committee and the number of years each member served between 1835 and 1858 appeared in *BCD, 1858*, I, Doc. No. 11.

17. For a listing of these men and their years of service, see Joseph M. Wightman, comp., *The Annals of the Boston Primary School Committee, From Its First Establishment in 1818, to Its Dissolution in 1855* (Boston, 1860), pp. 293-302.

18. John T. Morse, Jr., *Life and Letters of Oliver Wendell Holmes* (2 vols., Cambridge, Mass., 1896), II, 157. See also Henry Adams, *The Education of Henry Adams* (New York, 1946), pp. 33-34; Josiah Quincy, Jr., *Figures of the Past from the Leaves of Old Journals* (Boston, 1883); and, Daniel Calhoun, *Professional Lives in America: Structure and Aspiration, 1750-1850* (Cambridge, Mass., 1965), pp. 178-95.

19. *Laws of the Commonwealth of Massachusetts, 1837*, Chapter CCXLI, "An Act Relating to the Common Schools"; Wightman, *Annals*, pp. 176-88, 266-67; Mayor John P. Bigelow, "Inaugural Address, 1850," *Inaugural Addresses*, I; Nathan Bishop, *Second* and *Third Annual Report of the Superin-*

tendent of Public Schools of the City of Boston (Boston, 1852, 1853), pp. 27-35, 48; 30-33; "Report of the Committee on Public Instruction" (1852).

20. *Seventh Annual Report of the Board of Education, Together with the Seventh Annual Report of the Secretary of the Board* (Boston, 1844), pp. 24, 47, 91, 105-6, 124-36; *Remarks on the Seventh Annual Report of the Honorable Horace Mann, Secretary of the Massachusetts Board of Education. Prepared by a Committee of the "Association of Masters of Boston Public Schools"* (Boston, 1844), p. 29.

21. A good portion of the controversy revolved about this question of corporal punishment and its debatable moral and religious efficacy. Referring to criticism of the system of corporal punishment in the *Annual Reports of the Boston School Committee for 1845*, Mann wrote a Dr. G. M. Brewer that "I am ashamed to send that Report *out of the State*, describing as it so justly does the degraded condition into which those schools have fallen—more, as I am constrained to believe, from the practices of the Masters in regard to corporal punishment than from all other causes." Mann to Dr. G. M. Brewer, Concord, September 21, 1845, in *Agnes C. Storer Collection*, MHS. For the religious aspects of the controversy, see Raymond B. Culver, *Horace Mann and Religion in the Massachusetts Public Schools* (New Haven, 1929), pp. 189-204.

22. Quotation from Mann to Samuel Gridley Howe, September 25, 1844, *Mann Papers*, MHS. See also Mann to Howe, October 8, 1844. Included among the circle of close advisers who regularly met with Mann and to whom he turned in this situation were Charles Sumner, George S. Hillard, Edward G. Loring, and George B. Emerson. See Edward L. Pierce, *Memoir and Letters of Charles Sumner* (2 vols., Boston, 1877), II, 324.

23. On party structure, see Bugbee, "Boston Under the Mayors," pp. 247-50; *Boston Daily Mail*, December 16, 1840, December 4, 1852; Samuel Eliot Morison, *History of the Constitution of Massachusetts* (Boston, 1917), pp. 41-42; Darling, *Political Changes in Massachusetts*, pp. 245ff., 312-17, 326-29, 334, 340-54.

24. *Boston Times*, September 1, 1845.

25. *Boston Advertiser*, December 12, 1844; Pierce, *Memoir and Letters of Charles Sumner*, II, 324-25; David Donald, *Charles Sumner and the Coming of the Civil War* (New York, 1961), pp. 101-3; Harold Schwartz, *Samuel Gridley Howe: Social Reformer, 1801-1876* (Cambridge, Mass., 1956), pp. 128-29, and 120-36, *passim*. Cf. the exchange of letters about the controversy and the school election between Howe and Horace Mann, reprinted in Laura E. Richards, ed., *Letters and Journals of Samuel Gridley Howe* (2 vols., Boston, 1909), II, 171-87.

26. Schwartz, *Samuel Gridley Howe*, pp. 128-30.

27. *Boston Atlas*, August 9, 1845; "Organization of the Boston School Committee," ms. report by Mayor Jonathan Chapman, in *School Reports* (1840-41), II, Suffolk, Essex, Middlesex Counties, MSA; *BSR, 1845* (Boston, 1845), p. 31, and on p. 34 the statement deploring the absence of any link between the School Committee and the City Government. For earlier statements about the autonomy of the Committee, see *Opinion of the City Solicitor to the Com-*

mon *Council of the City of Boston on the Rights and Powers of the School Committee, April 19, 1830,* included in *BCD, 1830,* Doc. No. 9; and Ms. minutes of the Boston School Committee, bound in volumes in Rare Book Room, BPL, II (1837-41), pp. 9-15.

28. See his ms. report for 1842 in *School Reports* (1842-43), III, Suffolk, Essex, Middlesex Counties, MSA.

29. Mann to J. A. Shaw, March 7, 1840, *Mann Papers,* MHS.

30. For contemporary criticism of the profit motive, see Francis J. Grund, *Aristocracy in America* (1839; first American ed., New York, 1959), p. 145; George S. Hillard, *The Dangers and Duties of the Mercantile Profession* (Boston, 1850), pp. 40-42. For a contrary view which saw the "almighty dollar" as "comparatively insignificant amidst a whole Pantheon of better gods," see Charles Dickens, *American Notes and Pic-nic Papers* (Philadelphia, n.d.), p. 26, reprinted in various editions.

31. *BSR, 1845,* p. 30. For earlier comments by Howe on the need for professionalization, see *CSJ,* III (November 1, 1841), 328. For the attitudes of other educators, see "The Profession of a Teacher, and the Conduct and Discipline of a School," in *Remarks on the Classical Education of Boys, by a Teacher* (Boston, 1834), pp. 107-14; "Professional Education of Teachers," *American Annals of Education,* III (October 1833), 455-57; John S. Hart, "Schools for Professional Education of Teachers," in Henry Barnard, ed., *Education, The School, and the Teacher, in American Literature* (2nd ed., Hartford, 1876), pp. 401-24; and a fuller treatment of the subject in, Paul H. Mattingly, "Professional Strategies and New England Educators, 1825-1860" (unpublished Ph.D. dissertation, University of Wisconsin, 1968).

32. The derivation of the word is best followed in the *Oxford English Dictionary on Historical Principles.* There is a large amount of literature on the formation and social functions of professions. Among the more useful introductory works are Everett C. Hughes, "Professions," and Bernard Barber, "Some Problems in the Sociology of Professions," in Kenneth S. Lynn, ed., *The Professions in America* (Boston, 1967), pp. 1-15, 16-35; Talcott Parsons, "The Professions and Social Structure" (1939) reprinted in his *Essays in Sociological Theory;* Howard S. Becker and James W. Carper, "The Elements of Identification with an Occupation," *American Sociological Review,* XXI (1956), 341-48, and "The Development of Identification with an Occupation," *American Journal of Sociology,* LXI (1956), 289-98; and Morris L. Cogan, "Toward a Definition of Profession," *Harvard Educational Review,* XXIII (1953), 33-50.

33. I have relied primarily on the description of bureaucracy advanced by Max Weber for my comments. See his discussion in Hans Gerth and C. Wright Mills, trans. & eds., *From Max Weber: Essays in Sociology* (New York, 1946), pp. 196-244. Also useful are Everett C. Hughes, "Institutional Office and the Person," *AJS,* XLIII (1937), 404-13; Israel Gerver and Joseph Bensman, "Toward a Sociology of Expertness," *Social Forces,* XXXII (1954), 226-35; and, Robert K. Merton, et al., *Reader in Bureaucracy* (Glencoe, Ill., 1952).

34. *BSR, 1845,* pp. 30-32.

35. *Oxford English Dictionary.* See, for example, Horace Mann, *Tenth An-*

nual Report, 1846 (Boston, 1847), p. 69; Mann, *Two Lectures on Intemperance* (New York, 1859), p. 100; Christopher C. Andrews, *Reflections on the Operation of the Present System of Education* (Boston, 1853), pp. 12-13. The concept of government as a process of steering by means of feedback, goals, and purposes is analyzed in Karl W. Deutsch, *The Nerves of Government: Models of Political Communication and Control* (rev. ed., New York, 1966), pp. 182-99. See also David Easton, *A Systems Analysis of Political Life* (New York, 1964); Richard L. Meier, *A Communication Theory of Urban Growth* (Cambridge, Mass., 1962); and the partly successful attempt to wed communications theory and historical narrative in Seymour J. Mandelbaum, *Boss Tweed's New York* (New York, 1965).

36. *BSR, 1845,* p. 32.

37. *City of Boston, Report of Superintendent of Public Schools* (March 1851), in *BCD, 1851* (Boston, 1851), Doc. No. 16, p. 11; "Moral and Religious Training of the People," *Christian Review,* XVI (April 1851), 280. For a list of the influential periodicals concerned with education published in Boston, see *Barnard's American Journal of Education,* XXXIX (June 1865), 383-84; and, Sheldon E. Davis, *Educational Periodicals During the Nineteenth Century* (Washington, D.C., 1919). In the early 1830's new technology made possible a cheap "penny press" and Boston newspapers began to carry more articles on education, as well as sensational accounts of crime, insanity, and prostitution. For an account of these changes, see Priscilla Hawthorne Fowle, "Boston Daily Newspapers: 1830-1850" (unpublished Ph.D. dissertation, Radcliffe College Archives, 1920), pp. 72ff. and *passim.*

38. *BSR, 1845,* pp. 32-33.

39. *Ibid.,* pp. 33-34.

40. Howe's demands for "permanence," "personal responsibility," and "continued and systematic labor" for effective administration, as well as his claims for the desirability of having a qualified professional serve as superintendent, strikingly presaged later scholarly descriptions of the nature of bureaucracy. See Weber and other sources cited above, and, Carl J. Friedrich, *Constitutional Government and Democracy* (rev. ed., Boston, 1950), pp. 44-57. See also Peter M. Blau, *The Dynamics of Bureaucracy* (Chicago, 1955). I am indebted to an article by Michael B. Katz, "The Emergence of Bureaucracy in Urban Education: The Boston Case, 1850-1884," *History of Education Quarterly,* VIII (Summer 1968), 157, for suggesting Friedrich. I have revised Katz's claim that the process of bureaucratization began only in the 1850's with the first appointment of a superintendent. Katz's concentration on the problems of bureaucracy in school supervision in the 1870's probably accounted for his failure to take note of the earlier unfolding of an embryonic bureaucratic organization.

41. *BSR, 1845,* p. 34. An excellent example of pressure to use certain texts from an insider of the school system involved Josiah F. Bumstead who served on the Primary School Board in various capacities from 1826 to 1855. See "Report of the Primary Board, 1843," Wightman, *Annals,* pp. 201-3, and Bumstead's own defense and comments on school books in general in a brief file,

"Letters about School Book Publications, 1841-1846," in *Josiah Bumstead Papers*, MHS.

42. *BSR, 1845*, p. 34.

43. *The Charter of the City of Boston, and Ordinances* (Boston, 1827), pp. 12, 35, 61-62, 134, 213-16; *Charter and Ordinances of the City of Boston* (Boston, 1850), pp. 175-80.

44. Quincy, *A Municipal History*, pp. 154-63; *Rules, Regulations, and Orders of the Boston Board of Health Relative to the Police of the Town* (Boston, 1821); *Regulations of the Boston Relief Association, with a List of Members* (Boston, 1832); *Boston City Council, Ordered . . . June 20, 1832* (Boston, 1832), on the Special Board of Health. Other investigations prompting action included Lemuel Shattuck, *Letter to the Secretary of State on the Registration of Births, Marriages, and Deaths* (Boston, 1845); *Report of the Committee of Internal Health on the Asiatic Cholera* (Boston, 1849); and Josiah Curtis, "Boston Hygiene," American Medical Association *Transactions*, II (Philadelphia, 1849). See also Charles P. Huse, *The Financial History of Boston from May 1, 1822 to January 31, 1909*, vol. 15, *Harvard Economic Studies* (Cambridge, Mass., 1916), p. 82; and, Nelson M. Blake, *Water for the Cities* (Syracuse, 1956).

45. *BSR, 1845*, pp. 34, 33-34. Earlier superintendents had been appointed in Buffalo (1837), Providence (1839), Utica (1840), and Springfield, Mass. (1840), among others. See Arthur C. Boyden, "Development of Education in Massachusetts," Commonwealth of Massachusetts, *Annual Report of the Department of Education for the Year Ending November 30, 1929*, Part I (Boston, 1930), p. 37; Walter J. Gifford, *Historical Development of the New York State High School System* (Albany, 1922), pp. 48-49.

46. Orestes Brownson, "Popular Government," *Democratic Review*, XII (May 1843), reprinted in Henry F. Brownson, ed., *The Works of Orestes A. Brownson* (20 vols., Detroit, 1882-1887), XV, 285; and a useful discussion of Brownson's views in Arthur M. Schlesinger, Jr., *A Pilgrim's Progress: Orestes A. Brownson* (Boston, 1939), pp. 61-111. See also Horace Mann to Samuel Gridley Howe, July 21, 1839, in *Mann Papers*, MHS; Orestes A. Brownson, "Education of the People," *Christian Examiner*, II (June 1836); Brownson in the *Boston Quarterly Review*, II (October 1839), 383.

47. Mann, *Journal*, January 5, 1840, *Mann Papers*, MHS. "Address of His Excellency Marcus Morton, to the Two Branches of the Legislature, on the Organization of the Government, for the Political Year Commencing Jan. 1, 1840," *Documents Printed by Order of the House of Representatives of the Commonwealth of Massachusetts, 1840*, No. 9 (Boston, 1840), pp. 29-30. "Majority Report of the Committee on Education, March 7, 1840," reprinted in the *CSJ*, II (August 1, 1840), 227. A "Minority Report," together with letters from Samuel Gridley Howe and George B. Emerson, supporting Mann and the Board, and later remarks by Allen Dodge, Chairman of the Committee and major author of the "Majority Report," appeared in that same issue, pp. 230-40, and in a subsequent *Extra* of the *Journal* (August 1, 1840), pp. 241-46.

48. Cyrus Pierce to Horace Mann, September 18, 1840, *Mann Papers*, MHS; Mann, *Journal*, March 21, 22, 1840, *ibid*. *SCM*, I (1815-36), July 18, 1823; Brayley, *Schools and Schoolboys*, p. 89; Marsh, Capen, Lyon, and Webb Publishers to Horace Mann, October 6, 1841, reprinted in *CSJ*, III (October 1841), 330; Culver, *Horace Mann and Religion*, pp. 127-48.

49. Mann to Samuel Gridley Howe, August 18, 1845, *Mann Papers*, MHS.

50. *Boston Times*, September 1, 1845. For an opposite reaction to Howe's report, see *Boston Atlas*, August 11, 1845. See also *BSR, 1845*, p. 33.

51. *Boston Times*, August 14, September 1, 1845; ms. entitled "The Public Schools!" in *Fowle Letters*, MHS. This piece was written for a handbill previous to the elections for school office in November 1845. In his papers Fowle noted that "it was altered" but there is no evidence as to the extent of the alteration.

52. *Boston Atlas*, December 8, 1845. William B. Fowle, *The Scholiast Schooled. An Examination of the Review of the Reports of the Annual Visiting Committees of the Public Schools of the City of Boston, for 1845* (Cambridge, Mass., 1846).

53. Scott H. Paradise, "William Bentley Fowle," *DAB*, III, Part II, 561-62; *Boston Daily Advertiser*, February 9, 1865. See also, as an example of Fowle's satire, "The School Committee," in his *Familiar Dialogues and Popular Discussions* (Boston, 1841), pp. 7-14.

54. "The Public Schools!" (1845); and Fowle's rigorous if sometimes overgenerous appraisal in *The Scholiast Schooled*.

55. "To the Citizens of Boston" (1846), p. 10, pamphlet in collection marked *Boston School Committee*, MHS.

56. Mann to Howe, August 29, 1845, *Mann Papers*, MHS; Howe to Mann, September 3, 1845, *Howe Papers*, Houghton Library, Harvard University, quoted in Schwartz, *Samuel Gridley Howe*, p. 135.

57. Quincy, quoted in *CSJ*, VIII (February 16, 1846), 56; *BSR, 1846* (Boston, 1846), p. 41.

58. *BSR, 1847* (Boston, 1847), pp. 8-9, 62-63.

59. *City of Boston. Report on Superintendent of Public Schools* (March 1851) in *BCD, 1851*, Doc. No. 16. See also Nathan Bishop, *First Semi-Annual Report of the Superintendent of Public Schools of the City of Boston* (Boston, 1862), description of events leading to his appointment as superintendent, pp. 1-4.

60. Thomas Woody, "Nathan Bishop," *DAB*, I, Part II, 296-97.

61. Bishop, *First Semi-Annual Report*, p. 44.

62. In each of his first three reports (1852-53) Bishop affirmed his desire to work closely with teachers and with members of the School Committee. Max Weber suggested that one index of the extent of bureaucracy in any given field was the degree of dispassion in administering the mechanism, and the degree of close-knit cooperation among bureaucratic functionaries.

63. Bishop, *First Semi-Annual Report*, p. 6.

64. To conveniently follow these and related developments, see Boyden,

"Development of Education in Massachusetts," pp. 35-39; and, "A Chronology of the Boston Public Schools," *Annual Report of the Superintendent of Public Schools of the City of Boston* (Boston, 1930), pp. 91-126.

65. Gail Hamilton, *Our Common-School System* (Boston, 1880), pp. 204-5, quoted in Katz, "The Emergence of Bureaucracy in Urban Education," p. 172. Weber suggested, and more recent studies confirmed, that once the machinery of bureaucracy was set in motion, further bureaucratization inevitably followed. Certainly that was true in the professionalization of Boston's police force. See Roger Lane, *Policing the City: Boston, 1822-1885* (Cambridge, Mass., 1967), pp. 157-219.

66. Wightman, *Annals*, p. 266.

CHAPTER 7

1. *Mr. Minot's Address . . . At the Dedication of the Smith School, March 3, 1835* (Boston, 1835), pp. 5-6.

2. Roberts v. City of Boston, 5 Cush. 198-210 (1849); Sumner speech, June 28, 1848, in *The Works of Charles Sumner* (15 vols., Boston, 1870-83), II, 81; Charles Sumner, *Argument of Charles Sumner, Esq., Against the Constitutionality of Separate Colored Schools, in the Case of Sarah C. Roberts vs. the City of Boston. Before the Supreme Court of Mass., Dec. 4, 1849* (Boston, 1849), hereafter cited as *Sumner's Argument*. For letters from various other Massachusetts School Committees on the subject of segregated schools, see *Report of the Minority of the Committee of the Primary School Board, on the Caste Schools of the City of Boston: With Some Remarks on the City Solicitor's Opinion* (Boston, 1846), "Appendix," pp. 21-27; *Boston City Documents, 1846* Doc. No. 40.

3. *The Liberator*, August 28, 1846.

4. Oliver Warner, *Abstract of the Census of Massachusetts, 1865: With Remarks on the Same and Supplementary Tables* (Boston, 1867), pp. 228-31. Herbert Aptheker, ed., *A Documentary History of the Negro People in the United States* (New York, 1951), pp. 19-20.

5. *Sumner's Argument*, pp. 27-28; *Report to the Primary School Committee, June 15, 1846, on the Petition of Sundry Colored Persons, for the Abolition of the Schools for Colored Children. With the City Solicitor's Opinion* (Boston, 1846), pp. 15-16; *BCD, 1846*, Doc. No. 23. No precise figures of attendance are available.

6. Jesse Chickering, *A Statistical View of the Population of Massachusetts, from 1765-1840* (Boston, 1846), pp. 111-60; the Reverend Jeremy Belknap, "Answers to 'Queries Respecting the Slavery and Emancipation of Negroes in Massachusetts,'" *Collections* of the Massachusetts Historical Society, Ser. 1, IV (Boston, 1795), 197-200; Jacques P. Brissot de Warville, *New Travels in the United States of America* (Dublin, Ireland, 1792), pp. 282-83; Helen T. Catterall, *Judicial Cases concerning American Slavery and the Negro* (5 vols., Washington, D.C., 1926-37), IV, 481; John Cummings, *Negro Population in the United States, 1790-1915* (Washington, D.C., 1918); Charles H. Wesley,

Negro Labor in the United States, 1850-1925 (New York, 1927), pp. 30-50; Sterling D. Spero and Abram L. Harris, *The Black Worker: The Negro and the Labor Movement* (New York, 1931), pp. 3-15; John Hope Franklin, *From Slavery to Freedom: A History of Negro Americans* (3rd ed., New York, 1967), pp. 146, 145-65; Leon F. Litwack, *North of Slavery: The Negro in the Free States, 1790-1860* (Chicago, 1961), pp. 153-55; and, *Free Negroes and Mulattoes. House of Representatives, January 16, 1822* (Boston, 1822).

7. Belknap, "Answers to 'Queries,'" pp. 200, 206; Prince Hall, "Extract from a Charge Delivered to the African Lodge, June 24th, 1797, at Menotomy, Massachusetts," in Benjamin Brawley, ed., *Early Negro American Writers* (Chapel Hill, 1935), p. 99.

8. Hosea Easton, *A Treatise on the Intellectual Character, and Civil and Political Condition of the Colored People of the United States; and Prejudice Exercised Towards Them* (Boston, 1837), p. 41.

9. *Report of a Special Committee of the Grammar School Board, Presented August 29, 1849, on the Petition of Sundry Colored Persons, Praying for the Abolition of the Smith School. With an Appendix* (Boston, 1849), p. 18. Cf. Carter G. Woodson, *The Education of the Negro Prior to 1861* (2nd ed., Washington, D.C., 1919), pp. 95-96; and Franklin, *From Slavery to Freedom*, p. 160.

10. *Report of a Special Committee . . . 1849*, p. 18; Morse, *A Discourse, Delivered at the African Meeting-House, in Boston, July 14, 1808, in Grateful Celebration of the Abolition of the African Slave-Trade, by the Governments of the United States, Great Britain, and Denmark* (Boston, 1808), p. 18.

11. David L. Child, et al., "Report on African Schools," Ms. *Minutes* of the School Committee of Boston, bound in separate vols., Rare Book Room, Boston Public Library, I, October 15, 1833, cited hereafter as *SCM*. See also *Report to the Primary School Committee . . . 1846*, pp. 15-16; *Report of a Special Committee . . . 1849;* Arthur Wellington Brayley, *Schools and Schoolboys of Old Boston* (Boston, 1894), p. 48. Primus Hall, see George W. Crawford, *Prince Hall and His Followers* (New York, 1914); Benjamin Brawley, ed., *A Social History of the American Negro* (New York, 1921), pp. 71-72; and, Harry E. Davis, ed., "Documents Relating to Negro Masonry in America," *Journal of Negro History*, XXI (1936).

12. *SCM*, I, March 20, 1800; *Report to the Primary School Committee . . . 1846*, p. 16; *Report of a Special Committee . . . 1849*, p. 19.

13. Existent records conflict on whether the school began in 1806 or 1808. Brayley, *Schools and Schoolboys*, p. 48, and Child, "Report on African Schools" (1833) give 1808, while *Report to the Primary School Committee . . . 1846*, p. 16, and *Report of a Special Committee . . . 1849*, p. 19, give the date as 1806. As these reports relied upon extensive investigation of then-available records I have accepted their dating. There is similar debate on the first year in which the School Committee voted funds, 1806 or 1812. The *Report of a Special Committee . . . 1849* gave the year as 1806 in the body of the report but changed the date to 1812 after further study of Town Records. See "Appendix," p. 68. At any rate, Boston clearly gave public support to segregated

schools by 1812, considerably before 1820, the date commonly accepted by historians. See, for example, James Truslow Adams, "Disfranchisement of Negroes in New England," *American Historical Review*, XXX (1925), 546; Franklin, *From Slavery to Freedom*, p. 160; Dwight Lowell Dumond, *Antislavery: The Crusade for Freedom in America* (Ann Arbor, 1961), p. 121.

14. For Smith's will, see *Report to a Special Committee . . . 1849*, pp. 20-21.

15. On Saunders, see Mary B. Slade, "Prince Saunders," Allen Johnson and Dumas Malone, eds., *Dictionary of American Biography* (11 vols., subscription ed., New York, 1958), VIII, Part II, 382.

16. *Report of a Special Committee . . . 1849*, "Appendix," p. 68.

17. *Report to the Primary School Committee . . . 1846*, pp. 15-20; *Report of a Special Committee . . . 1849*, pp. 21-23. Since both reports came at a time when the issue of segregated schools was being hotly debated, their assertions that Negroes during the early years of the century saw separate schools as a privilege might be suspect. But it seems reasonable to assume that in the absence of other educational facilities, Black parents, who had called for separate schools in the first place were happy to have them.

18. *Boston Columbian Centinel*, December 17, 1817; *Annual Report of the Boston Society for the Religious and Moral Instruction of the Poor* (Boston, 1826), p. 13. See also J. Leslie Duncan, *A Light to the City: 150 Years of the City Missionary Society of Boston, 1816-1966* (Boston, 1966), pp. 60-61.

19. *Report to the Primary School Committee . . . 1846*, p. 17.

20. Joseph M. Wightman, *Annals of the Boston Primary School Committee, From Its First Establishment in 1818, to Its Dissolution in 1855* (Boston, 1860), p. 61; *ibid.*, p. 69.

21. *Ibid.*, p. 69.

22. Speech given in 1819, quoted in Charles C. Andrews, *The History of the New-York African Free-Schools* (New York, 1830), p. 132. See also Wesley, *Negro Labor*, pp. 42-50; *Stimpson's Boston Directory, 1840*, pp. 445-51; Litwack, *North of Slavery*, p. 155; Handlin, *Boston's Immigrants*, pp. 59-60, 63, 65, 68-70.

23. Wightman, *Annals*, p. 94. Charles S. Johnson, *The Negro College Graduate* (Chapel Hill, 1938), p. 7; Willar S. Elsbree, *The American Teacher: Evolution of a Profession in a Democracy* (New York, 1939), pp. 209-12. Some of the teachers in the grammar school were more capable than others. John B. Russwurm, for instance, eventually became the first Negro college graduate in the United States. See William M. Brewer, "John B. Russwurm," *JNH*, XIII (1928), 413-22; Woodson, *Education of the Negro*, pp. 95-96.

24. *SCM*, I, December 30, 1824.

25. *SCM*, I, July 5, November 22, 1825, November 17, 1826; Wightman, *Annals*, pp. 68-69; *Bowen's Boston News-Letter*, II (November 11, 1826), 220. The School Committee prided itself for its provisions for Negroes "who are participating in the advantages of *each branch* of instruction enjoyed at our public schools." See *Report of the School Committee . . . May, 1826* (Boston, 1826), p. 4.

26. *SCM*, I, May 10, 1831, May 8, 1832.

27. Child, "Report on African Schools" (1833).

28. *SCM*, I, February 10, 1835; *Mr. Minot's Address*, "Introduction"; and, *Report to the Primary School Committee . . . 1846*, p. 18.

29. *Mr. Minot's Address*, pp. 5-6. For claims about immigrant assimilation, see Chapter 10, *infra*.

30. *Mr. Minot's Address*, p. 6.

31. *SCM*, I, November 12, 1833.

32. *Ibid.*, March 27, 1834.

33. Martha Gruening, "David Walker," *DAB*, X, Part I, 340; Charles Wiltse, "Introduction," *David Walker's Appeal, in Four Articles; Together with a Preamble to the Coloured Citizens of the World, But in Particular, and Very Expressly, to those of the United States of America* (rev. ed., 1830; reprinted, New York, 1965), p. viii; Litwack, *North of Slavery*, p. 232.

34. *Walker's Appeal*, pp. 12, 15, and *passim*.

35. Lundy, quoted in Litwack, *North of Slavery*, pp. 234-35; Garrison, *The Liberator*, January 29, 1831; Dumond, *Antislavery*, p. 115; Clement Eaton, "A Dangerous Pamphlet in the Old South," *Journal of Southern History*, II (August 1936), pp. 1-12; and the same author's excellent *The Freedom-of-Thought Struggle in the Old South* (rev. ed., New York, 1964), pp. 121-26; *Niles' Weekly Register*, XXXVIII (March 27, 1830), 87; Samuel Eliot Morison, *The Life and Letters of Harrison Gray Otis: Federalist* (2 vols., Boston, 1913), II, 262.

36. For example, see Henry Highland Garnet, *Walker's Appeal, With a Brief Sketch of his Life. By Henry Highland Garnet, and also Garnet's Address to the Slaves of the United States of America* (New York, 1848).

CHAPTER 8

1. Charles Sumner, *Argument of Charles Sumner, Esq., Against the Constitutionality of Separate Colored Schools, in the Case of Sarah C. Roberts vs. the City of Boston. Before the Supreme Court of Mass., Dec. 4, 1849* (Boston, 1849), p. 32. Hereafter cited as *Sumner's Argument*.

2. Whittier, "Justice and Expediency" (1833), in *The Prose Works of John Greenleaf Whittier* (Boston, 1892), III, 9-57, excerpted in Louis Ruchames, ed., *The Abolitionists: A Collection of Their Writings* (New York, 1964), p. 49. See also David Brion Davis, "The Emergence of Immediatism in British and American Antislavery Thought," *Mississippi Valley Historical Review*, XLIX (September 1962), 209-30; and Gilbert H. Barnes, *The Anti-Slavery Impulse, 1830-1844* (new ed., New York, 1964), pp. 48-50, 101-3, 138-39.

3. Clifford S. Griffin, *Their Brothers' Keepers: Moral Stewardship in the United States, 1800-1860* (New Brunswick, 1960); John R. Bodo, *The Protestant Clergy and Public Issues, 1812-1848* (Princeton, 1954); Emerson quote from Mark Van Doren, ed., *The Portable Emerson* (New York, 1946), p. 83.

4. *The Massachusetts Spy*, October 25, 1832; *The First Annual Report of the Board of Managers of the New-England Anti-Slavery Society* (Boston, 1833),

pp. 7-8; *Minutes and Proceedings of the First Annual Convention of the People of Colour* (Philadelphia, 1831), pp. 5-7; Robert A. Warner, *New Haven Negroes* (New Haven, 1940), pp. 55-56; *Boston Courier*, September 20, 1831; *New York Courier & Enquirer*, quoted in *The Liberator*, December 3, 1831.

5. *The Liberator*, March 2, 1833; *A Statement of Facts, Respecting the School for Colored Females, in Canterbury, Ct.* (Brooklyn, Conn., 1833); *The Liberator*, April 6, 1833; Helen T. Catterall, ed., *Judicial Cases Concerning American Slavery and the Negro* (5 vols., Washington, D.C., 1926-37), IV, 415-16, 430-33; *Report of the Argument of Counsel, in the Case of Prudence Crandall, Pltf. in Error vs. State of Connecticut, Before the Supreme Court of Errors, at Their Session at Brooklyn, July Term, 1834* (Boston, 1834), pp. 24-25.

6. *Andrew T. Judson's Remarks to the Jury on the Trial of the Case: State v. P. Crandall, Superior Court, October Term, 1833, Windham County Court* (Hartford, 1833), pp. 21-22. More detailed discussion of the case appeared in Leon F. Litwack, *North of Slavery: The Negro in the Free States, 1790-1860* (Chicago, 1961), pp. 126-31; Dwight Lowell Dumond, *Antislavery: The Crusade for Freedom in America* (Ann Arbor, 1961), pp. 211-17.

7. Odell Shepard, ed., *Journals of Bronson Alcott* (Boston, 1938), p. 110; Elizabeth Peabody, *Record of a School: Exemplifying the General Principles of Spiritual Culture* (Boston, 1836). On schoolbooks, see the thoughtful discussion by Ruth Miller Elson, *Guardians of Tradition: American Schoolbooks of the Nineteenth Century* (Lincoln, Neb., 1964), pp. 87-100. See also Hosea Easton, *A Treatise on the Intellectual Character, and Civil and Political Condition of the Colored People of the United States; and Prejudice Exercised Towards Them* (Boston, 1837), pp. 41, 43; Tocqueville quoted by George Wilson Pierson, *Tocqueville in America* (abridged ed., Garden City N.Y., 1959), p. 262.

8. See the lengthy editorial on the condition of Negroes in the *Boston Daily Evening Transcript*, September 28, 1830. Otis quoted in *Niles' Weekly Register*, XLV (September 14, 1833), 43. *Douglass' Monthly*, March 1859, quoted in Litwack, *North of Slavery*, p. 143.

9. Muriel Shaver, "David Lee Child," Allen Johnson and Dumas Malone, eds., *Dictionary of American Biography* (11 vols., Subscription ed., New York, 1959), II, Part II, 65-66; Walter C. Bronson, "Lydia Maria Child," *ibid.*, pp. 67-69; Lydia Maria Child, *Letters of Lydia Maria Child; With a Biographical Introduction by John G. Whittier and an Appendix by Wendell Phillips* (Boston, 1883), pp. v-xxv; Oliver Johnson, *William Lloyd Garrison and His Times* (Boston, 1880), pp. 83-84.

10. "Appendix," *Letters of Lydia Maria Child*, p. 264; Lydia Maria Child to Miss Lucy Osgood, May 11, 1856, *ibid.*, p. 77.

11. Lydia Maria Child, *An Appeal in Favor of That Class of Americans Called Africans* (Boston, 1833), pp. 208-32.

12. David L. Child, et al., "Report on African Schools," Ms. *Minutes* of the Boston School Committee, bound in volumes in Rare Book Room, Boston Public Library, I (October 15, 1833).

13. Joseph Tuckerman, Boston's Minister-at-Large to the poor, collected data on the Black population, visited the Belknap Street School, and met with numerous prominent citizens to encourage better means of "improvement among the colored population." He also opened a sewing school for Negro women, believing "that their want of skill in the use of the needle is one of the causes of their poverty, and of the filth, improvidence and suffering in which many are living." Garrison visited Tuckerman's school, and praised it warmly in *The Liberator*. See Daniel T. McColgan, *Joseph Tuckerman: Pioneer in American Social Work* (Washington, D.C., 1940), pp. 258-59.

14. For a fascinating account of the elite, see *The Aristocracy of Boston: Who They Are, and, What They Were; Being a History of the Business and Business Men of Boston, for the Last Forty Years. By One Who Knows Them* (Boston, 1848). See Lyman, "Address Made to the City Council of Boston, January 5, 1835," in *The Inaugural Addresses of the Mayors of Boston* (2 vols., Boston, 1894), I, 183-84; and, on Lyman's reputation as reformer and benefactor of education, see James McKellar Bugbee, "Boston Under the Mayors, 1822-1880," in Justin Winsor, ed., *The Memorial History of Boston* (4 vols., Boston, 1881), III, 251. See also Francis J. Grund, *Aristocracy in America: From the Sketch-Book of a German Nobleman* (1839; first American ed., New York, 1959), pp. 139-213; and, Douglas T. Miller, *Jacksonian Aristocracy: Class and Democracy in New York, 1830-1860* (New York, 1967), esp. Chapter 3, "Manners and Counting Houses," pp. 56-80. Miller's observations about the social pretensions and influence of business "aristocracies" applied generally to other large Eastern cities, including Boston.

15. Wendell P. and Francis J. Garrison, *William Lloyd Garrison, the Story of His Life Told by His Children, 1805-79* (4 vols., New York, 1885-1889), II, 15; Theodore Lyman III, ed., *Papers Relating to the Garrison Mob* (Cambridge, Mass., 1870), pp. 14-24; *Boston Recorder*, October 30, 1835; Lydia Maria Child to Rev. Convers Francis, December 19, 1835, *Letters of Lydia Maria Child*, p. 18.

16. See Litwack, *North of Slavery*, pp. 218, 214-46; Louis Filler, *The Crusade Against Slavery, 1830-1860* (New York, 1960), pp. 142-45; Stanley M. Elkins, *Slavery: A Problem in American Institutional and Intellectual Life* (Chicago, 1959), pp. 191-92; May sermon given May 29, 1831, printed in *The Liberator*, July 23, 1831; Samuel J. May, *Some Recollections of Our Anti-Slavery Conflict* (Boston, 1869), p. 29; Parker, quoted in William H. Pease and Jane H. Pease, "Antislavery Ambivalence," *American Quarterly*, XVII (Winter 1965), 686, see also 682-95, *passim*; Garrison in *The Liberator*, January 22, 1831.

17. *Proceedings of a Meeting of Colored Citizens . . . Testimonial to Wm. C. Nell, Dec. 17, 1855*, in box labeled "Boston, Negroes," MHS. Not coincidentally, these were the years of the abolitionists' warfare by petition. See Barnes, *The Anti-Slavery Impulse*, pp. 109-45.

18. *SCM*, II (1837-41), March 9, 1841.

19. *Niles' National Register*, LXVI (July 13, 1844), 320; *Boston Atlas*, June 28, 1844, included in *Boston Public School for Colored Children*, clippings

scrapbook, BPL, and other clippings, pp. 1-8; *SCM*, III (1842-45), May 7, June 12, 1844; *Report to the Primary School Committee, June 15, 1846, on the Petition of Sundry Colored Persons, for the Abolition of the Schools for Colored Children. With the City Solicitor's Opinion* (Boston, 1846), p. 20; Edward L. Pierce, *Memoir and Letters of Charles Sumner* (2 vols., Boston, 1877), II, 324-25; David Donald, *Charles Sumner and the Coming of the Civil War* (New York, 1961), p. 101.

20. At the request of the School Committee, the Board had established a new Black primary school as recently as 1842. See *SCM*, III (1842-45), December 27, 1842; Joseph M. Wightman, comp., *Annals of the Boston Primary School Committee, From Its First Establishment in 1818, to Its Dissolution in 1855* (Boston, 1860), p. 198.

21. John F. Fulton, "Henry Ingersol Bowditch," *DAB*, I, Part II, 492-94. On the Latimer affair and other similar experiences, see Commonwealth v. Tracy, 5 Metcalf 536 ff. (1843); James Freeman Clarke, "The Anti-Slavery Movement in Boston," Winsor, ed., *Memorial History*, III, Chapter VI; and, Lawrence Lader, *The Bold Brahmins: New England's War Against Slavery: 1831-1865* (New York, 1961), pp. 113-17, 161-67. See also Wightman, *Annals*, p. 209.

22. *Report of the Minority of the Committee of the Primary School Board, on the Caste Schools of the City of Boston; With Some Remarks on the City Solicitor's Opinion* (Boston, 1846), "Appendix: Letters to Edmund Jackson," pp. 21-27. For a general survey of conditions in other cities and states, see Henry W. Farnham, *Chapters in the History of Social Legislation in the United States to 1860* (Washington, D.C., 1938), pp. 211-24; U.S. Commissioner of Education, *Special Report of the Commissioner of Education on the Condition and Improvement of Public Schools in the District of Columbia, Submitted to the Senate, June, 1868, and to the House, with Additions, June 13, 1870* (Washington, D.C., 1871), Part II, *Legal Status of the Colored Population in Respect to Schools and Education in the Different States*, pp. 301-400.

23. Petition reproduced in *Report to the Primary School Committee . . . 1846*, pp. 3-7; Wightman, *Annals*, pp. 213-14.

24. *Report to the Primary School Committee . . . 1846*, pp. 3-6, 7-12, 23.

25. Wightman, *Annals*, p. 141.

26. *Report to the Primary School Committee . . . 1846*, pp. 7-12, 23, 10.

27. See Chapters 2-3, *supra*, and Chapter 10, *infra*.

28. *Report to the Primary School Committee . . . 1846*, pp. 7, 13.

29. *Boston Pilot*, December 31, 1859; Edward S. Abdy, *Journal of a Residence and Tour in the United States* (3 vols., London, 1835), I, 158-60; John R. Commons, et al., eds., *A Documentary History of American Industrial Society* (10 vols., Cleveland, 1910-11), VII, 60; Jesse Chickering, "The Colored Population," in his *A Statistical View of the Population of Massachusetts, from 1765 to 1840* (Boston, 1846), pp. 137, 156-57; *Boston Pilot*, January 22, 1853; June 17, 1854; March 3, 1855; October 18, 1856; and, John C. Murphy, *An Analysis of the Attitudes of American Catholics toward the Immigrant and the*

Negro, 1825-1925 (Catholic University of America *Studies in Sociology,* vol. I; Washington, D.C., 1940), pp. 31-79; *Boston Pilot,* August 16, 1862; Litwack, *North of Slavery,* pp. 162-66.

30. *Report to the Primary School Committee . . . 1846,* p. 14; *Massachusetts House Documents, 1841,* No. 17, quoted in Oscar Handlin, *Boston's Immigrants: A Study in Acculturation* (rev. ed., Cambridge, Mass., 1959), p. 180.

31. *Report to the Primary School Committee . . . 1846,* p. 12. Chandler's opinion reproduced in the same work, pp. 31-38; cf. *The Liberator,* June 27, 1845, August 28, 1846. On Chandler, see Howard Knott, "Pelig Whitman Chandler," *DAB,* II, Part I, 615.

32. *Report of the Minority . . . 1846,* pp. 4, 12-13, 15-16, 19.

33. *The Liberator,* August 21, 1846.

34. Phillips's remarks in *The Liberator,* August 28, 1846, and in the minority report of Jackson and Bowditch in 1846. See also Irving H. Bartlett, *Wendell Phillips: Brahmin* (Boston, 1961), pp. 87-91.

35. *Eleventh Annual Report of the Board of Education, Together with the Eleventh Annual Report of the Secretary of the Board* (Boston, 1848), p. 39; *The Liberator,* December 24, 1847; September 11, 1846; Horace Mann to Theodore Parker, April 15, 1853, *Theodore Parker Letterbooks,* No. 11, pp. 107-8, MHS; May, *Some Recollections,* p. 313; Mary and George Mann, *Life and Works of Horace Mann* (5 vols., Boston, 1891), I, 172.

36. *Reports of the Annual Visiting Committee of the Grammar and Writing Schools of the City of Boston for 1846* (Boston, 1846), pp. 150-52; and Chapter 4, *supra.*

37. *BSR, 1848* (Boston, 1848), p. 57; *Report of a Special Committee of the Grammar School Board, Presented August 29, 1849, on the Petition of Sundry Colored Persons, Praying for the Abolition of the Smith School. With an Appendix* (Boston, 1849), pp. 13-14.

38. *Ibid.,* pp. 7, 14; Joseph M. Wightman to Rev. Dr. Bigelow, August 6, 1849, *ibid.,* "Appendix," pp. 66-67.

39. *Report to the Primary School Committee . . . 1846,* pp. 21-22; *Report of a Special Committee . . . 1849,* pp. 8-10. Nell quoted in *The Liberator,* April 7, 1854.

40. *Report of a Special Committee . . . 1849,* p. 36. *Ibid.,* p. 40, for Wayland's letter; other letters expressing similar sentiments appeared on pages 37-42, 57-62, 65-66.

41. Harold G. Villard, "William Cooper Nell," *DAB,* VII, Part I, 413; *The Liberator,* December 18, 1846.

42. *The Liberator,* November 9, 1849; February 8, 1850. See also Carelton Mabee, "A Negro Boycott to Integrate Boston Schools," *New England Quarterly,* XLI (September 1968), 341-61. Mabee's article examines the boycott issue in greater depth than I have here, although I would not credit the boycott with the effectiveness he ascribes to it.

43. The petitions are reprinted in *Report of a Special Committee . . . 1849,*

pp. 7-8, discussed 8-13; see also pp. 48, 54, 55. Cf. Thomas P. Smith, *An Address Before the Colored Citizens of Boston in Opposition to the Abolition of Colored Schools* (Boston, 1850).

44. *SCM*, IV (1846-49), August 29, 1849; Wightman, *Annals*, p. 94; *The Liberator*, August 18, 1848; October 5, 12, 1849; John Daniels, *In Freedom's Birthplace: A Study of the Boston Negroes* (Boston, 1914), p. 448.

45. *Report of a Special Committee . . . 1849*, pp. 54, 24-25, 14-16, 43; *Report to the Primary School Committee . . . 1846*, pp. 12, 27, 29-30.

46. Russell, "Minority Report," in a second issue of the *Report of a Special Committee . . . 1849*, p. 45 and *passim*.

47. *SCM*, IV (1846-49), September 6, November 3, 1847; Roberts v. City of Boston, 5 Cush. 198, 200-1, 198-210, *passim* (1849); *Acts and Resolves of 1845*, Chapter 214; *Report of a Special Committee . . . 1849*, pp. 14-16.

48. This evaluation of Morris came later from William C. Nell. See *Proceedings of a Meeting of Colored Citizens*, p. 7. See also Leonard Levy, *The Law of the Commonwealth and Chief Justice Shaw* (Cambridge, Mass., 1957), pp. 25-26.

49. *Sumner's Argument*, pp. 3, 31, 6-31, *passim*, 24-25, 28-32. For Fletcher's opinion, see *Report of the Minority . . . 1846*, pp. 6-7.

50. 5 Cush. 198, 205-10. More extensive discussions of this vitally important case may be found in Levy, *Law of the Commonwealth*, pp. 109-17; Leonard Levy and Harlan B. Phillips, "The Roberts Case: Source of the 'Separate But Equal' Doctrine," *American Historical Review*, LVI (1951), 510-18; and Arthur Burr Darling, "Prior to Little Rock in American Education: The *Roberts* Case of 1849-1850," *Proceedings* of the Massachusetts Historical Society, LXXII (1963), 126-42.

51. *Report of the Colored People of the City of Boston on the Subject of Exclusive Schools, Submitted by Benjamin F. Roberts, to the Boston Equal School Rights Committee* (Boston, 1850); *The Liberator*, April 26, 1850; June 14, 21, 1850. See also Jonas W. Clark, et al., "Equal Schools for All Without Regard to Color or Race," printed letter of May 21, 1851, in BPL. The best account of the escaped slave incident appeared in Lader, *The Bold Brahmins*, pp. 161-67.

52. *SCM*, V (1850-54), May 13, 1851; March 23, 1852.

53. "Report of the Committee on Public Instruction, on the Case of a Child Excluded from a Public School of this City," *Boston City Documents, 1854*, vol. II, Doc. No. 54.

54. *The Liberator*, June 1, 1855; Handlin, *Boston's Immigrants*, pp. 201-4; and, George H. Haynes, "A Know Nothing Legislature," *American Historical Association Report for 1896*, I, 178-82.

55. *SCM*, V (1850-54), August 15, 1854.

56. *The Liberator*, February 9, 1855; *Proceedings of a Meeting of Colored Citizens*, p. 6; Henry Wilson, *History of the Rise and Fall of the Slave Power in America* (3 vols., Boston, 1872-77), II, 640; *Acts and Resolves of 1855*, Chapter 256; Litwack, *North of Slavery*, p. 149.

57. *Proceedings of a Meeting of Colored Citizens*, p. 9; *The Liberator*, Au-

gust 17, 31, 1855; *Boston Mail,* September 5, 1855, in *Boston Public School for Colored Children,* p. 26; Louis Ruchames, "Race and Education in Massachusetts," *Negro History Bulletin,* XIII (December 1949), 71; Litwack, *North of Slavery,* p. 150.

58. *Boston Pilot,* October 6, 1855, and, September 15, 1855; *SCM,* VI (1855-59), September 11, November 6, 1855; January 12, 1856; *The Liberator,* September 14, 1855; "Report of the State Board of Education," *Massachusetts Public Documents, 1860,* Doc. No. 2, p. 134; "Report of the School Committee, 1866," *BCD, 1866,* Doc. No. 137, pp. 187-88; *Triumph of Equal School Rights in Boston, Proceedings of the Presentation Meeting Held in Boston, December 17, 1855* (Boston, 1856).

CHAPTER 9

1. Edward Everett Hale, ed., *Joseph Tuckerman on the Elevation of the Poor* (Boston, 1874), p. 103.

2. Carl Bridenbaugh, *Cities in the Wilderness: The First Century of Urban Life in America, 1625-1742* (2nd ed., New York, 1955); John K. Alexander, "The City of Brotherly Fear: The Poor in Late-Eighteenth Century Philadelphia," in Kenneth T. Jackson and Stanley K. Schultz, eds., *Cities in American History* (New York, 1972), pp. 79-97; Raymond A. Mohl, *Poverty in New York, 1783-1825* (New York, 1971), pp. 14-65 and *passim;* Benjamin J. Klebaner, "Public Poor Relief in America, 1790-1860" (unpublished Ph.D. dissertation, Columbia University, 1952), and the same author's "Poverty and Its Relief in American Thought, 1815-61," *Social Service Review,* XXXVIII (December 1963), 382-99; and, Blanche D. Coll, "The Baltimore Society for the Prevention of Pauperism, 1820-1822," *American Historical Review,* LVI (October 1955), 77-87.

3. For discussion of this phenomenon in available social science literature, see Gordon W. Allport, *The Nature of Prejudice* (abridged ed., Garden City, N.Y., 1958), pp. 3-65; M. and Carolyn Sherif, *Groups in Harmony and Tension* (New York, 1953); Bruno Bettelheim and Morris Janowitz, *Social Change and Prejudice* (New York, 1964), pp. 178-97; Hadley Cantril, *The Psychology of Social Movements* (new ed., New York, 1963); and, Milton M. Gordon, *Assimilation in American Life: The Role of Race, Religion, and National Origins* (New York, 1964), pp. 84-114. For additional references and discussions, see dissertation copy, Chapter 9, note 14.

4. Quoted in Van Wyck Brooks, *The Flowering of New England* (New York, 1936), p. 6. Cf. Francis J. Grund, *Aristocracy in America* (1839; first American ed., New York, 1959), pp. 139-224; William Tudor, *Letters on the Eastern States* (2nd ed., Boston, 1821), p. 361; Henry Adams, *The United States in 1800* (Ithaca, 1955), p. 54.

5. Adna F. Weber, *The Growth of Cities in the Nineteenth Century: A Study in Statistics* (1899; reprinted, Ithaca, 1963); Jeffrey G. Williamson, "Antebellum Urbanization in the American Northeast," *Journal of Economic History,* XXV (December 1965), 592-608; and George Rogers Taylor, "Ameri-

can Urban Growth Preceding the Railway Age," *JEH*, XXVII (September 1967), 309-39. On Boston itself, indispensable general works are Walter Muir Whitehill, *Boston: A Topographical History* (Cambridge, Mass., 1959); and Oscar Handlin, *Boston's Immigrants: A Study in Acculturation* (rev. ed., Cambridge, Mass., 1959).

6. Jesse Chickering, *A Statistical View of the Population of Massachusetts from 1765 to 1840* (Boston, 1846), pp. 41-44; "Dr. Chickering's Report," in *Report and Tabular Statement of the Censors Appointed . . . to Obtain the State Census of Boston, May 1, 1850* (Boston, 1850), pp. 33-34, in *Boston City Documents, 1850,* Doc. No. 42; and the same author's *Report of the Committee . . . and A Comparative View of the Population of Boston in 1850, with the Births, Marriages, and Deaths in 1849 and 1850* (Boston, 1851), pp. 14-26; Percy Wells Bidwell, "Rural Economy in New England at the Beginning of the Nineteenth Century," *Transactions of the Connecticut Academy of Arts and Sciences,* XX (1916), 383-91; and, Frederick A. Bushée, "The Growth of the Population of Boston," *American Statistical Association Publications,* VI (June 1899), 245-50.

7. Quotation of the Belgian observer in Maldwyn Jones, *American Immigration* (Chicago, 1960), p. 98, cf. pp. 64-176 for general process of arrival. For general statistics on immigration into Boston (and other cities), see Jesse Chickering, *Immigration into the United States* (Boston, 1848); William J. Bromwell, *History of Immigration to the United States* (New York, 1856); George Wingate Chase, *Abstract of the Census of Massachusetts, 1860, from the Eighth U.S. Census . . . Prepared under the Direction of Oliver Warner* (Boston, 1863); Frederick A. Bushée, *Ethnic Factors in the Population of Boston* (New York, 1903); and, *Statistical Review of Immigration, 1820-1910,* U.S. Immigration Commission *Reports* (41 vols., Washington, D.C., 1911), III. For the Irish, see Thomas D. McGee, *History of the Irish Settlers in North America* (Boston, 1851); and, William F. Adams, *Ireland and Irish Emigration to the New World from 1815 to the Famine* (New Haven, 1932). The best brief account of the Boston experience is Handlin, *Boston's Immigrants,* pp. 25-53. For other references on immigration, see dissertation copy, Chapter 9, note 8.

8. Adams, *Ireland and Irish Emigration,* Chapter I; Justin Winsor, ed., *The Memorial History of Boston* (4 vols., Boston, 1881), III, 575; Anne Royall, *Sketches of History, Life and Manners in the United States* (New Haven, 1826). Jesse Chickering estimated that arrivals during the period should be raised by anywhere from 33 to 50 per cent to account for travelers overland to the city in addition to those arriving by sea. See *Report and Tabular Statement of the Censors . . . 1850,* p. 47. See also Robert H. Lord, et al., *History of the Archdiocese of Boston in the Various Stages of Its Development, 1604 to 1943* (3 vols., New York, 1944), II, 133; Chickering, *Report of the Committee . . . and Comparative View of the Population of Boston in 1850,* p. 9; Josiah Curtis, *Report of the Joint Special Committee on the Census of Boston, May, 1855* (Boston, 1856), p. 19 and *passim.*

9. "Immigration; Its Evils and Their Tendencies," *The New Englander,*

XIII (May 1855), 274; *The Report of the Annual Examination of the Public Schools of the City of Boston, 1853* (Boston, 1853), p. 21.

10. Bridenbaugh, *Cities in the Wilderness*, pp. 81-83, 233-35, 392-94. Cf. George S. Hale, "The Charities of Boston," in Winsor, ed., *Memorial History*, IV, 641-72.

11. Society for the Prevention of Pauperism, *Annual Reports*, XXIII (Boston, 1858), 6. The concept of social distance was first advanced by E. S. Bogardus in his book, *Immigration and Race Attitudes* (New York, 1928). By "visible threats" I mean both the outward actions of the poor and immigrant classes—that is, criminal behavior, intemperance, rioting, squalid living—and prejudicial responses by the better sort based on their readiness to perceive differences between themselves and the lower classes. Visibility generally has been discussed in relation to pathological social behavior and identifiable racial characteristics, such as color of skin, but dress, mannerisms, religious practices, food habits, vocabulary, names, and places of residence also act as visible cues to trigger prejudicial reactions. For a summary of literature, see Allport, *Nature of Prejudice*, pp. 127-37.

12. Massachusetts Temperance Society, *Plain Facts Addressed to the Inhabitants of Boston on the City Expenses for the Support of Pauperism, Vice, and Crime* (Boston, 1834); Josiah Quincy, *Remarks on Some of the Provisions of the Laws of Massachusetts Affecting Poverty, Vice, and Crime* (Cambridge, Mass., 1822); Quincy, *A Municipal History of the Town and City of Boston During Two Centuries* (Boston, 1852), pp. 104-10, quotation appearing on p. 102.

13. The pattern of investigation and conclusions about the poor was established in early nineteenth-century Boston with the formation (1816) of the "Boston Society for the Moral and Religious Instruction of the Poor." See the *Annual Report of the Boston City Missionary Society, 1818* (Boston, 1818), pp. 3-4; and, Frederick T. Gray, "The Origin of the Ministry at Large, and Its Free Chapels," *Sixteenth Annual Report of the Executive Committee of the Benevolent Fraternity of Churches* (Boston, 1850), and discussed in the *Christian Examiner*, XLIX (1850), 204-14. See also Charles Bulfinch, "Report on Boston Primary Schools, 1817," printed in Joseph M. Wightman, comp. *The Annals of the Boston Primary School Committee, From Its First Establishment in 1818, to Its Dissolution in 1855* (Boston, 1860), pp. 22-24; Joseph Tuckerman, *First Semi-Annual Report of the Second Year, May 5, 1828* (Boston, 1828); Tuckerman, *The Principles and Results of the Ministry-at-Large in Boston* (Boston, 1838), and the same author's *9th Semi-Annual Report, June, 1832* (Boston, 1832); William Ellery Channing, "On the Elevation of the Laboring Classes," sermon delivered February 1840, in *The Works of William Ellery Channing, D.D. With an Introduction. To Which is Added THE PERFECT LIFE* (Boston, 1891), pp. 36-66; *Report of the Committee of Internal Health on Asiatic Cholera* (Boston, 1849); Dr. Josiah Curtis, "Brief Remarks on the Hygiene of Massachusetts, more particularly on the Cities of Boston and Lowell," *Transactions* of the American Medical Association (Philadelphia, 1849), II; *Report of the Committee on the Expediency of Providing Better Tenements for the Poor*

(Boston, 1846); *Report and Tabular Statement of the Censors . . . 1850,* pp. 38-65; and, for a convenient secondary summary, see Handlin, *Boston's Immigrants,* pp. 54-87.

14. Peter R. Knights, *The Plain People of Boston, 1830-1860: A Study in City Growth* (New York, 1971), Chapter V, pp. 78-102; Handlin, *Boston's Immigrants,* Table XV, p. 253.

15. Knights, *Plain People of Boston,* pp. 58-65.

16. Lemuel Shattuck, *Report to the Committee of the City Council Appointed . . . to Obtain the Census of Boston for the Year 1845* (Boston, 1846), p. 26; Rev. Samuel B. Cruft, *Seventeenth Annual Report of the Executive Committee of the Benevolent Fraternity of Churches* (Boston, 1851), pp. 5-6.

17. See, for example, Sam Bass Warner, Jr., *The Private City: Philadelphia in Three Periods of Its Growth* (Philadelphia, 1968), pp. 49-62; David Ward, *Cities and Immigrants: A Geography of Change in Nineteenth Century America* (New York, 1971).

18. *Report . . . on Providing Better Tenements for the Poor,* pp. 4-5, 13-15, 16; George R. Taylor, "The Beginnings of Mass Transportation in Urban America," *Smithsonian Journal of History,* I (Summer and Autumn 1966), 35-50, 31-54; C. G. Kennedy, "Commuter Services in the Boston Area, 1835 to 1860," *Business History Review,* XXVI (Summer 1962), 153-70.

19. *Boston Daily Evening Transcript,* January 13, 1837; "City Council Committee on Public Lands," *BCD, 1852,* Doc. No. 11, p. 3.

20. Massachusetts State Bureau of Labor, *Report of the Bureau of Statistics of Labor . . . 1871,* in *Massachusetts Senate Documents, 1871,* Doc. No. 150; *Third Annual Report of the Bureau of Statistics of Labor . . . 1872,* in *Massachusetts Senate Documents, 1872,* Doc. No. 180; *Report of the Committee of Internal Health; Report . . . on the Expediency of Providing Better Tenements; Twelfth Report . . . Benevolent Fraternity of Churches* (1846).

21. Quotation on "Jacob's Ladder" by Dr. Henry Clark from *Report of the Committee on Internal Health,* and quoted in Norman Ware, *The Industrial Worker, 1840-1860* (Boston, 1924), p. 13; *Report of the Committee of Internal Health,* pp. 13-14.

22. *Report of the Committee for Erecting a House of Industry, October 22, 1821* (Boston, 1821), pp. 4, 13-15, and *passim;* C. W. Ernst, *Constitutional History of Boston, Massachusetts* (Boston, 1894), pp. 19-20.

23. Otis, September 17, 1830, in *The Inaugural Addresses of the Mayors of Boston* (2 vols., Boston, 1894), I, 152; Winslow's oration in *BCD, 1838,* Doc. No. 35, pp. 26-27; *Boston Bee,* March 7, 1843. For sentiments on the economic and moral mobility of the poor, see, for example, William Ellery Channing, "Ministry for the Poor," April 9, 1835, in *Works,* pp. 73-87. For references on who the mechanics were and how others viewed them in the social order, see dissertation copy, Chapter 9, note 26.

24. *Boston Post,* January 2, 1848.

25. "Commercial Cities and Towns of the United States. Number XXII. City of Boston," *Hunt's Merchants' Magazine,* XXIII (November 1850), 485; Jesse

Chickering, *Report of the Committee* . . . *1850*, pp. 49-50, and quotation from *BCD, 1851*, Doc. No. 60, pp. 57-58.

26. Quincy, *Remarks on . . . Poverty, Vice, and Crime* (1822), p. 3. See also *"Quincy" Report on the Pauper Laws. Report to the General Court of the Commonwealth of Massachusetts by the Committee to whom was referred the consideration of the Pauper Laws of the Commonwealth* (Boston, 1821); Massachusetts Citizens' Committee, Josiah Quincy, Chairman, *Report of the Committee on the Subject of Pauperism and a House of Industry in the Town of Boston, March 13, 1821* (Boston, 1821), MSA; and *Massachusetts House Documents, 1820*, Doc. No. 46.

27. Ethel Stanwood Bolton, "Joseph Tuckerman," in Allen Johnson and Dumas Malone, eds., *Dictionary of American Biography* (11 vols., Subscription ed., 1958), X, Part L, 46; Daniel T. McColgan, *Joseph Tuckerman: Pioneer in American Social Work* (Washington, D.C., 1940), pp. 63-68, 117-33. Reformers toward the close of the century attested Tuckerman's influence on their own investigations of poverty. See Francis G. Peabody, "Unitarianism and Philanthropy," *The Charities Review*, V (1895-96), 26-28; and, Frank D. Watson, *The Charity Organization Movement in the United States. A Study in American Philanthropy* (New York, 1922), pp. 70-76.

28. Thomas Chalmers, *The Christian and Civic Economy of Large Towns* (3 vols., Glasgow, 1821-26), II, 51, 55-61, 89-95; Tuckerman, *Elevation of the Poor*, pp. 89-90, 153; *Principles and Results of the Ministry-at-Large*, pp. 278-79, 286, 290-92; McColgan, *Joseph Tuckerman*, pp. 93-116; Tuckerman to Dr. Bowring, Secretary to the British and Foreign Unitarian Association, Boston, 1830, quoted in McColgan, *Joseph Tuckerman*, p. 186; Tuckerman, *First Annual Report, Association of the Delegates from the Benevolent Societies of Boston* (Boston, 1835).

29. For example, see Society for the Prevention of Pauperism in the City of New York, *First Annual Report of the Managers* (New York, 1818), pp. 14-20.

30. Tuckerman, *Principles and Results of the Ministry-at-Large*, p. 166; Quincy, *Municipal History*, p. 36; Horace Mann to Charles Sumner, February 1837, *Mann Papers*, MHS; Mann, *Two Lectures on Intemperance* (New York, 1859), pp. 21-22 summarized Mann's opinions over the previous three decades; Theodore Parker, "Moral Conditions," a sermon preached February 11, 1849, in Samuel A. Eliot, ed., Theodore Parker, *Social Classes in a Republic* (Boston, 1907), pp. 264-70.

31. Joseph Tuckerman, *Prize Essay on the Wages Paid to Females* (Philadelphia, 1830), pp. 40-54.

32. Tuckerman, *Elevation of the Poor*, p. 102; John H. Griscom, *The Sanitary Condition of the Laboring Population of New York with Suggestions for its Improvement* (New York, 1845), pp. 5, 9; *Elevation of the Poor*, p. 103.

33. For literature on the culture of poverty theme, see Oscar Lewis, *La Vida: A Puerto Rican Family in the Culture of Poverty—San Juan and New York* (New York, 1966), pp. xlii-lii and *passim;* and earlier works by Lewis including *The Children of Sanchez* (New York, 1961), and *Pedro Martinez* (New York, 1964). For debates between Lewis and his critics, see Oscar Lewis, et al.

"The Children of Sanchez, Pedro Martinez, and La Vida: A CA Book Review," *Current Anthropology*, VIII (1967), 480-500. For serious criticisms, see Charles A. Valentine, *Culture and Poverty: Critique and Counter-Proposals* (Chicago, 1968), pp. 48-77. See also the article by S. M. Miller, in Nona Y. Glazer and Carol F. Creedon, eds., *Children and Poverty: Some Sociological and Psychological Perspectives* (Chicago, 1968), and dissertation copy, Chapter 9, note 40.

34. With only slight modifications, the conditions laid down by Oscar Lewis as necessary for a "culture of poverty" to grow and flourish might have been modeled after circumstances in Boston between 1830 and 1860. Useful data appeared in L. McLane, *Report on Manufactures* (Washington, D.C., 1833), *House Document No. 308*, 22nd Congress, First Session, 1833, I, 432-71; *Report and Tabular Statement of the Censors . . . 1850;* Edith Abbott, "Wages of Unskilled Labor in the United States, 1850-1900," *Journal of Political Economy*, XIII (June 1905), 321ff.; Charles Phillips Huse, *The Financial History of Boston: From May 1, 1822, to January 31, 1909* (Cambridge, Mass., 1916), pp. 11-109.

35. William Ellery Channing, D.D., *Memoir, with Extracts from His Correspondence and Manuscripts* (3 vols., 2nd ed., Boston, 1848), III, 39-42; Channing, "On Preaching the Gospel to the Poor," *Works*, pp. 88-92; *The Boston Society for the Prevention of Pauperism, Constitution of the Boston Society for the Prevention of Pauperism, Nov. 5, 1835* (Boston, 1835); Tuckerman, *First Annual Report . . . Benevolent Societies of Boston*, pp. 28-41; R. C. Waterson, *Address on Pauperism: Its Extent, Causes and the Best Means of Prevention* (Boston, 1844); "Poverty," *Boston Daily Chronotype*, January 26, 1849, reprinted in Samuel B. Stewart, ed., Theodore Parker, *Sins and Safeguards of Society* (Boston, 1907) pp. 280, 263-87. See also *Boston Bee*, April 12, 1847; Edward S. Abdy, *Journal of a Residence and Tour in the United States* (3 vols., London, 1835), III, 263-64; *Massachusetts Senate Documents, 1847*, Doc. No. 109; *Annual Reports of the Benevolent Fraternity of Churches, 1858-59* (Boston, 1859), pp. 1-6. A major reason for the Special Censuses of Boston in 1850 and 1855 was to gather information about the foreign population in order to determine the "amount and growth of this element in the population of Boston during this period of time." See Curtis, *Report . . . Census of Boston, May, 1855*, p. 2.

36. *Boston Evening Transcript*, March 20, 1835; *Boston Pilot*, July 1, August 26, 1854; "Anonymous," *Common School Journal*, I (May 1, 1839), 151. For stereotypes in texts, see for example, Samuel G. Goodrich, *Peter Parley's Method of Telling Geography* (Boston, 1829); *Peter Parley's Common School History* (9th ed., Philadelphia, 1841), p. 312; Samuel Willard, *The Popular Reader, or Complete Scholar* (Greenfield, Mass., 1834), pp. 36-37. See also John Curtis Crandall, Jr., "Images and Ideals for Young Americans: A Study of American Juvenile Literature, 1825-1860" (unpublished Ph.D. dissertation, University of Rochester, 1957), pp. 409-15; and Ruth Miller Elson, *Guardians of Tradition: American Schoolbooks of the Nineteenth Century* (Lincoln, Neb., 1964), pp. 101-85.

37. "An Act Providing for the Relief and Support, Employment and Removal of the Poor, February 26, 1794," *Laws of Massachusetts, 1780 to 1800,* II, 628-29; "An Act to Prevent the Introduction of Paupers from Foreign Ports or Places, February 25, 1820," *Massachusetts Laws, 1820,* Chapter 290; "The Introduction into the United States of Paupers from Foreign Countries, April 18, 1836," *Massachusetts House of Representatives;* all reprinted in, Edith Abbott, *Immigration: Select Documents and Case Records* (Chicago, 1924), pp. 105-6, 108, 112-14; *American Annals of Education,* III (September 1833), 412, 413; Mann, *Ninth Annual Report of the Board of Education, Together with the Ninth Annual Report of the Secretary of the Board* (Boston, 1846), p. 95, and *CSJ,* VIII (June 1, 1846), 166-67. For comments on the proposal of many that immigrants be subjected to a period of "moral quarantine" (lengthier residence in the United States before gaining citizenship status), see "Immigration," *North American Review,* XL (April 1835), 457-76.

38. There is a large literature on the concept of conformation to the "host society" or "reference group" by newcomers—for example, Gordon, *Assimilation in American Life,* pp. 84-114; and, Jones, *American Immigration,* pp. 117-56. For other references and discussion, see dissertation copy, Chapter 9, note 54.

39. Letter from John Quincy Adams to Baron von Fürstenwarther, June 4, 1818, published in *Niles' Weekly Register,* XVIII (April 29, 1820), pp 157-58; approvingly quoted by Chickering, *Immigration into the United States,* pp. 79-80.

40. Ezra S. Gannet, *A Sermon Delivered in the Federal Street Meeting-House, in Boston, July 19, 1840* (Boston, 1840), pp. 17, 18, and *passim.*

41. Josiah Quincy, Jr., "Social Life in Boston: From the Adoption of the Federal Constitution to the Granting of the City Charter," in Winsor, *Memorial History,* IV, pp. 1-24.

42. For example, see Otis, quoted in John C. Miller, *The Federalist Era, 1789-1801* (New York, 1960), p. 230; and discussions of the Alien Act and the United Irishmen in Marcus Lee Hansen, *The Atlantic Migration, 1607-1860* (Cambridge, Mass., 1940), pp. 66-67; and, Jones, *American Immigration,* pp. 74, 82-91.

43. Josiah Quincy, Jr., *Figures of the Past* (Boston, 1883), p. 363; John Barton Derby, *Political Reminiscences, Including a Sketch of the Origin and History of the "Statesman Party"* (Boston, 1835), p. 27; See also Orville Dewey, "Popular Education," *NAR,* XXXVI (January 1833), 81; Quincy, *Municipal History,* 26-27, 115; William W. Story, *Life and Letters of Joseph Story* (2 vols., Boston, 1851), II, 154; Joseph Story, "Statesmen: Their Rareness and Importance," *New England Magazine,* VII (1834), 89-104; Samuel G. Howe, "Atheism in New-England," *NEM,* VII (1834), 500; and, Frederick A. Packard, *Thoughts on the Condition and Prospects of Popular Education in the United States* (Philadelphia, 1836), pp. 36-37.

44. For representative comments, see: "Inaugural Address of Mayor Theodore Lyman, 1835," *Inaugural Addresses,* I, 195; *Massachusetts Senate Documents, 1847,* Doc. No. 109; John R. Commons, et al., eds., *A Documentary*

History of American Industrial Society (10 vols., Cleveland, 1910-11), VIII, 133-51.

45. Percy H. Bidwell, "Seth Luther," *DAB*, VI, Part I, 511. Luther's address was published in New York City in 1833. On its and his importance, see Louis Hartz, "Seth Luther: The Story of a Working-Class Rebel," *New England Quarterly*, XIII (September 1940), 401-18; Luther, *Address to the Workingmen*, pp. 18-24.

46. *American Annals of Education*, III (June 1833), 255, 258-59. Cf. "The Necessity of Educating the Poor," *ibid.*, VI (April 1836), 163-64, and articles in III (November 1833), 501, and II (April 1832), 192.

47. *Ninth Annual Report, 1845*, p. 95. This was a persistent theme throughout Mann's career. For example, see *Eighth Annual Report, 1844* (Boston, 1845), pp. 134-36; *Twelfth Annual Report, 1848* (Boston, 1849), pp. 57, 59, 78-89; "Means and Objects of Common School Education," in Mary Mann and George Mann, *Life and Works of Horace Mann* (5 vols., Boston, 1891), II, 41.

48. *CSJ*, II (February 15, 1840), 50-51; Mann, "On the Perils of Popular Government" (1842) in *Life and Works*, IV, 345-65; a circular he sent to various leading educators soliciting their comments on the social necessity of common schools, reprinted in his *Eleventh Annual Report, 1847* (Boston, 1848), pp. 49-58; *The Massachusetts System of Common Schools; Being an Enlarged and Revised Edition of the Tenth Annual Report of the First Secretary of the Massachusetts Board of Education* (Boston, 1849), pp. 85-86; *Two Lectures on Intemperance*, p. 100.

49. Quincy quoted in *CSJ*, X (August 1, 1848), 233; "On the Elevation of the Laboring Classes," *Works*, p. 64; Everett, *Importance of Practical Education and Useful Knowledge* (Boston, 1840), pp. 83, 337-38; Luther Hamilton, ed., Robert Rantoul, *Memoirs, Speeches and Writings of Robert Rantoul* (Boston, 1854), "The Education of a Free People," p. 119; Theodore Parker, "On the Education of the Laboring Class," *Lectures Delivered before the American Institute of Instruction . . . Boston, August, 1841* (Boston, 1842), pp. 65-90; Orestes A. Brownson, "The Laboring Classes," *Brownson's Quarterly Review*, III (July, October 1840), 358-95, 473-74.

50. Edward Pessen, "Did Labor Support Jackson? The Boston Story," *Political Science Quarterly*, LXIV (June 1949), 262-74; cf. Robert T. Bower, "Note on 'Did Labor Support Jackson? The Boston Story,'" *ibid.*, LXV (September 1950), 441-44; Arthur Burr Darling, "The Working Men's Party in Massachusetts, 1833-1834," *AHR*, XXIX (October 1923), 81-86; George H. Haynes, "Causes of Know-Nothing Success in Massachusetts," *AHR*, III (1897), 74. On the increase in voters, see Curtis, *Report of the Special Joint Committee . . . 1855*, p. 11; *Report and Tabular Statement of the Censors . . . 1850*, p. 12.

51. Lord, et al., *History of the Archdiocese*, I; Ray Allen Billington, *The Protestant Crusade, 1800-1860: A Study of the Origins of American Nativism* (1938; reprinted, Chicago, 1964), pp. 5-7, 9, 14-18, 21-24. The newspaper debates, appearing originally in the *Boston Gazette*, were gathered together in

John Thayer, *Controversy between the Rev. John Thayer, Catholic Missionary, of Boston, and the Rev. George Lesslie, pastor of a Church in Washington, New Hampshire* (Boston, 1793).

52. For example, see *Boston Recorder*, January 1, 1820, October 6, 1826; *Christian Watchman*, January 22, 1820; Rev. Daniel Dunn, *The Importance of the Christian Ministry: A Sermon Preached before the American Society for Educating Pious Youth for the Gospel Ministry, at their Third Anniversary, Boston, Sept. 30, 1818* (Andover, 1818); discussion in Lord, et al., *History of the Archdiocese*, II, 184-87; and the best discussion of the national societies in Clifford S. Griffin, *Their Brothers' Keepers: Moral Stewardship in the United States, 1800-1865* (New Brunswick, 1960).

53. Charles Allen Dinsmore, "Lyman Beecher," *DAB*, I, Part II, 135-36; Lyman Beecher, *Autobiography, Correspondence of the Rev. Lyman Beecher, D.D.* (2 vols., New York, 1864), I, 438-39, 449; identification of "Brimstone Corner" in, Thomas Nichols, *Forty Years of American Life* (2 vols., London, 1864), II, 89. For Beecher's sermons, see, for example, Rev. Lyman Beecher, *Resources of the Adversary and Means of Their Destruction: A Sermon Preached Oct. 12, 1827, before the American Board of Missions at New York* (Boston, 1827). These and other sermons received wide distribution in evangelical periodicals and newspapers. See Billington, *Protestant Crusade*, pp. 70, 72-73, 81; *Boston Recorder*, November 18, 1829.

54. Figures compiled by Lord, et al., *History of the Archdiocese*, II, 126, probably err on the side of conservatism and should be viewed as relatively, not absolutely, accurate:

Year	Boston Catholic Pop.
1820	2120
1825	5000
1829	7040
1835	20,900
1843	30,000 (approx.)
1845	30,000
1846	32,000 (at least)

55. Bishop Fenwick to the Society for the Propagation of the Faith, Aug. 28, 1835, quoted in Lord, et al., *History of the Archdiocese*, II, 141. See also Shattuck, *Report to the Committee . . . 1845*, p. 125; Edward Everett Hale, *Letters on Irish Emigration* (Boston, 1852), p. 23.

56. George Harvey Genzmer, "Samuel Finley Breese Morse," *DAB*, VII, Part I, 247-51; Samuel F. B. Morse, *Foreign Conspiracy Against the Liberties of the United States* (New York, 1835), pp. xxvi, 62-63, 113, 156-57, 178; Morse, *Imminent Dangers to the Free Institutions of the United States Through Foreign Immigration and the Present State of the Naturalization Laws. . . . By an American* (New York, 1835), pp. iv, 12-13, 24, 25, and *passim*. His chosen weapons for ideological war were also those advocated by Boston educators: "The Bible, the Tract, the Infant School, the Sunday School, the Common School for all classes, the academy for all classes, the college and uni-

versity for all classes, a free press for the discussion of all questions." *Foreign Conspiracy,* p. 132. Cf. Billington, *Protestant Crusade,* pp. 123-25.

57. Emerson, *Journals,* May 12, 1832, quoted in Robert Bremner, *From the Depths: The Discovery of Poverty in the United States* (New York, 1956), p. 16; Emory Washburn, *An Address at the Dedication of the State Reform School at Westborough, December 7, 1848* (Boston, 1849), p. 102; Zechariah Chafee, Jr., "Emory Washburn," *DAB,* X, Part I, 499-500.

58. See the listing of criminal convictions in Massachusetts Temperance Society, *Plain Facts,* p. 15. For new laws, see *The Revised Statutes of the Commonwealth of Massachusetts, Passed November 4, 1835* (Boston, 1836), Chapter 15. For attitudes about increased criminal activity, see Quincy, *Municipal History,* pp. 102-4; *Columbian Centinel,* December 24, 1825; *Boston Daily Evening Transcript,* August 9, 1831; Joseph Tuckerman, *Third Quarterly Report of the Minister-at-Large* (Boston, 1827); Tuckerman, *A Letter to the Mechanics of Boston Regarding the Formation of a City Temperance Society* (Boston, 1831); *Fifteenth Annual Report of the Executive Committee, Benevolent Fraternity of Churches* (Boston, 1849); Parker, "Moral Conditions," pp. 264-85. For accounts of prostitution and various misdemeanors, see Edward H. Savage, *Police Records and Recollections: Or, Boston by Daylight and Gaslight* (Boston, 1873), p. 182; *Boston Daily Evening Transcript,* August 9, 1831; *Twelfth Annual Report of the Executive Committee of the Benevolent Fraternity of Churches* (Boston, 1846), pp. 30-31; *Boston Advertiser,* April 17, 1855; Roger Lane, *Policing the City: Boston, 1822-1885* (Cambridge, Mass., 1967), "Appendix I, Table I-A," pp. 230-31.

59. *Records of the Boston Society for the Relief of the Distressed, 1820-1822,* quoted in Alice Felt Tyler, *Freedom's Ferment: Phases of American Social History from the Colonial Period to the Outbreak of the Civil War* (Minneapolis, 1944), p. 284. See also Handlin, *Boston's Immigrants,* "Appendix, Table IV, Prison Commitments," p. 241.

60. Lemuel Shattuck, *Bills of Mortality, 1810-1849* (Boston, 1893), pp. 3-79 for information on homicides. Cf. Lane, *Policing the City,* pp. 54, 56.

61. See the discussion in, Priscilla Hawthorne Fowle, "Boston Daily Newspapers: 1830-1850" (unpublished Ph.D. dissertation, Radcliffe College Archives, 1920), pp. 172-73. Eliot, "Address to the City Council, September 18, 1837," quoted in Lane, *Policing the City,* p. 34. See also the excellent discussion on literature in David Brion Davis, *Homicide in American Fiction, 1798-1865: A Study in Social Values* (Ithaca, 1957), pp. 259-60 and *passim.*

62. See, for example, *Annual Reports of the Directors of the House of Industry* (Boston, 1824-40), esp., *Seventh Annual Report* (1830), *Sentences of the Police Court to the Institution* (1835), *Seventeenth Annual Report* (1840), all in MSA; *Report of the Commissioners on the Pauper Surplus of Massachusetts* (Boston, 1833); *Massachusetts House Documents, 1833,* Doc. No. 6; *Massachusetts Senate Documents, 1839,* Doc. No. 47; *ibid.,* 1844, Doc. No. 44; *ibid.,* 1852, Doc. No. 127; *Massachusetts House Documents, 1851,* Doc. No. 152. A convenient summary of Boston expenditures appeared in Huse, *Financial History of Boston,* pp. 66-70, and "Appendix I," p. 358. See also "Public

and Private Charities in Boston," *NAR*, CXXVIII (July 1845), 135-59; and, Joseph T. Buckingham, comp., *Annals of the Massachusetts Charitable Mechanic Association, and the Supplement, 1852 to 1860* (Boston, 1863).

63. Huse, *Financial History of Boston*, "Appendix I," p. 358; Handlin, *Boston's Immigrants*, "Appendix, Table III," p. 240; Theodore Parker, "Poverty," pp. 274, 278; *Boston Evening Transcript*, October 14, 1845; *Inaugural Addresses of the Mayors*, I, 363, 385; Shattuck, *Report to the Committee . . . 1845*, pp. 144-46; *Report of the Committee of Internal Health*, pp. 8-9, 13-14, 57-160; Massachusetts Sanitary Commissioners, *Report of a General Plan for the Promotion of Public and Personal Health* (Boston, 1850), pp. 69-71, 90-92; Charles E. Buckingham, et al., *Sanitary Condition of Boston* (Boston, 1875), pp. 64-84. For similar reactions in other cities, see Charles Rosenberg, *The Cholera Years: The United States in 1832, 1849, and 1866* (Chicago, 1962), pp. 61-63, 136-42, 175, 181-83, 230-31.

64. *Twenty Third Annual Report* (Boston, 1855), p. 7; "Crime and Its Punishment," in Stewart, ed., *Sins and Safeguards*, pp. 337-38.

65. Massachusetts Temperance Society, *Plain Facts; Twelfth Annual Report . . . Benevolent Fraternity of Churches* (1846); *Reports and Bills Relating to the Sale of Spiritous Liquors*, in *Massachusetts House Documents, 1839*, Doc. No. 37; Lane, *Policing the City*, p. 49; G. P. Scrope, ed., *Extracts of Letters from Poor Persons Who Emigrated Last Year to Canada and the United States* (London, 1831), p. 23; *The Boston Traveler*, January 12, 1857; *Annual Report of the Police Department of the City of Boston by the City Marshal* (Boston, 1852), pp. 11-13.

66. *Boston Herald*, January 25, 1853; Shattuck, *Report on the Census of Boston . . . 1845*, p. 126; *Annual Police Report, 1857*, pp. 17-19; *Boston Pilot*, March 3, 1855, and for the charge about discriminatory treatment, May 12, 1849. When they made arrests, however, the police made large hauls. In the famed Ann Street Descent in 1851, police arrested 51 young ladies of the night in a matter of minutes. See Savage, *Police Records*, pp. 259-62.

67. Richard C. Wade, "Violence in the Cities: An Historical View," Charles U. Daly, ed., *Urban Violence* (Chicago, 1969), pp. 7-26; Roger Lane, "Crime and Criminal Statistics in Nineteenth Century Massachusetts," *Journal of Social History*, II (December 1968), and a revised version, "Urbanization and Criminal Violence in the 19th Century: Massachusetts as a Test Case," in Hugh Davis Graham and Ted Robert Gurr, eds., *The History of Violence in America* (New York, 1969), pp. 468-84; Richard Maxwell Brown, "Historical Patterns of Violence in America," *ibid.*, pp. 53-55; Warner, *The Private City*, pp. 125-57.

68. Volunteer fire companies competing for goods recovered from fires were a major source of urban rioting during the period. Boston's experience may be traced in Arthur Wellington Brayley, *A Complete History of the Boston Fire Department* (Boston, 1889).

69. *Columbian Centinel*, June 21, 1823; Edward H. Savage, comp., *Boston Events. A Brief Mention and the Date of More Than 5,000 Events* (Boston, 1884), p. 131, with listings of other riots, pp. 131-32; *Boston Advertiser*, July

372 notes to pages 240-248

18, 1826, January 29, 1829; William Leahy, *The Catholic Church in New England* (2 vols., Boston, 1899), I, 53.

70. *Report of the Committee, Relating to the Destruction of the Ursuline Convent, August 11, 1834* (Boston, 1834). The event is fully described in Lord, et al., *History of the Archdiocese*, II, 205-39; and, Billington, *Protestant Crusade*, pp. 53-84.

71. Brayley, *Boston Fire Department*, pp. 197-99; Bugbee, "Boston Under the Mayors," pp. 243-46; Lord, et al., *History of the Archdiocese*, II, 243-51; *Boston Daily Advocate*, June 13, 1837.

72. Horace Mann, *Journal*, June 11, 13, 1837, *Mann Papers*, MHS.

73. Lord, et al., *History of the Archdiocese*, II, 250-51; *Records of the City of Boston: Mayor and Aldermen*, XV (June 22, 1837), 212-20. Beginning in 1822, these records are on microfilm, BPL.

74. *Native American*, September 17, 1844, quoted in Fowle, "Boston Newspapers," p. 256.

75. W. R. Alger, *An Oration Delivered before the Citizens of Boston, July 4, 1857* (Boston, 1857), p. 28.

76. "Historic Notes of Life and Letters in New England" (1867), in Mark Van Doren, ed., *The Portable Emerson* (New York, 1946), p. 513.

77. Norman Dain, *Concepts of Insanity in the United States, 1789-1865* (New Brunswick, 1964), pp. 85-90; Mark D. Altschule, *Roots of Modern Psychiatry* (New York, 1957), pp. 119-39; and the interesting discussion on various theories in Gerald N. Grob, *The State and the Mentally Ill: A History of Worcester State Hospital in Massachusetts, 1830-1920* (Chapel Hill, 1966), pp. 43-79; "A Discourse on the Life and Character of the Rev. Joseph Tuckerman, D.D." (1841), in Channing, *Works*, pp. 581, 578-97, *passim.*

78. "The Dangerous Classes" (1847), in Eliot, ed., *Social Classes in a Republic*, pp. 137, 143, 151, 158, 159-60, 166.

79. *An Account of the Boston Asylum for Indigent Boys. The Act of Incorporation, By-Laws, Rules and Regulations* (Boston, 1814); *Secretary's Report to the Board of State Charities, 1865* (Boston, 1865), pp. 97-100; Tuckerman, *Elevation of the Poor*, pp. 129ff.; "Inaugural Address of Mayor Josiah Quincy, 1829," *Inaugural Addresses of the Mayors*, I, 103-4.

80. *Report of the Standing Committee of the Common Council on the Subject of the House of Reformation for Juvenile Offenders* (Boston, 1832), p. 74 and *passim*. See also Wightman, *Annals*, pp. 297-98.

81. *Annual Report of the Directors of the Houses of Industry and Reformation, 1846*, in BCD, 1846, Doc. No. 19, pp. 10-11; *Boston Daily Evening Transcript*, February 6, 1837.

82. *Massachusetts Senate Documents, 1846*, Doc. No. 86, p. 16; "School Books," BCD, 1847, Doc. No. 38, pp. 9-10; *Reports of the Annual Visiting Committee of the Grammar and Writing Schools of Boston for 1847* (Boston, 1847), pp. 53-57; *The Youth's Companion*, XXXI (February 26, 1857), p. 36.

83. BSR, 1847, pp. 54-55. On youth gangs, see also *Annual Report of the Directors of the Houses of Industry and Reformation, 1846*, pp. 10-11; "Reports of the Inspectors of Prisons, for the County of Suffolk, on the House of In-

dustry—Boston Lunatic Hospital, House of Reformation, Gaol—and House of Correction," *BCD, 1843,* Doc. No. 21, p. 11.

84. *Annual Police Report, 1851,* pp. 26-31; *Massachusetts House Documents, 1851,* Doc. No. 14, pp. 24-25.

85. Chickering, *Census of 1850,* pp. 39, 38-40.

86. *First Report on the Establishment of a Farm School* (Boston, 1832); Percy H. Bidwell, "Theodore Lyman," *DAB,* VI, Part II, 518; *American Annals of Education,* IV (1834), 288; V (1835), 330, 461; VI (1836), 375. Nor were such attempts confined to Boston. In New York City, Robert M. Hartley, secretary and founder of the Association for Improving the Condition of the Poor advised the poor to "escape then from the city—for escape is your only recourse against the terrible ills of beggary; and the further you go, the better." *The Mistake* (New York, 1856), p. 4. See also Miriam Z. Langsam, *Children West: A History of the Placing-Out System of the New York Children's Aid Society, 1853-1890* (Madison, 1964).

87. For a convenient listing of these organizations, see McColgan, *Joseph Tuckerman,* "Appendix 4," pp. 434-39.

88. For example, see *The First Annual Report of the Association of Delegates from the Benevolent Societies of Boston* (Boston, 1835).

89. *Annals of the Propagation of the Faith,* VIII (London, 1847), pp. 353-54, quoted in Francis E. Lane, *American Charities and the Child of the Immigrant: A Study of Typical Child Caring Institutions in New York and Massachusetts Between the Years 1845 and 1880* (Washington, D.C., 1932), pp. 110-11. Parker quoted in, E. Douglas Branch, *The Sentimental Years, 1836-1860* (New York, 1934), p. 197.

90. *Reflections on the Operation of the Present System of Education* (Boston, 1853), pp. 12-13.

CHAPTER 10

1. "Immigration: Its Evils and Their Remedies," *New Englander,* XIII (May 1855), 275.

2. Noah Webster to John Brooks, Boston, May-June 1819, in Harry R. Warfel, ed., *Letters of Noah Webster* (New York, 1953), pp. 398-99. See also Emily E. F. Ford, *Notes on the Life of Noah Webster* (2 vols., New York, 1912), II, 458-59.

3. Webster to John Pickering, Amherst, December, 1816, *Letters,* p. 394. See also Merle Curti, *The Social Ideas of American Educators* (1935; reprinted, Paterson, N.J., 1959), pp. 32-34; "Noah Webster and his Spelling-books," in Clifton Johnson, *Old-Time Schools and School-books* (New York, 1904), pp. 167-84.

4. *Report of a Sub-Committee of the School Committee Recommending Various Improvements in the System of Instruction in the Grammar and Writing Schools of this City* (Boston, 1828), pp. 25-26; *American Annals of Education,* III (September 1833), 412-13.

5. *American Journal of Education*, II (August 1828), 510; *AAE*, III (November 1833), 495.

6. Edward Everett Hale, ed., *Joseph Tuckerman on the Elevation of the Poor* (Boston, 1874), pp. 112-39; *Seventh Semi-Annual Report of his Service as a Minister-at-Large in Boston* (Boston, May 5, 1831), pp. 10-16; Lyman Beecher, *Plea for the West* (2nd ed., Cincinnati, 1835), pp. 52-55, 117-30, 182; Samuel F. B. Morse, *Foreign Conspiracy Against the Liberties of the United States* (New York, 1835), p. 66; Frederick A. Packard, *Thoughts on the Condition and Prospects of Popular Education in the United States* (Philadelphia, 1836), pp. 6-7, 30-31, 32, 36; *AJE*, I, III (1826, 1828), 148, 158; 346-48; *AAE*, VI (1836), 163ff.; *Common School Journal*, I (February 15, 1839), 60; Robert Hall, "Opinion Upon Educating the Lower Classes," *New England Farmer* (February 13, 1833), 245.

7. "Inaugural Address of Mayor Theodore Lyman, January 1, 1836," in *The Inaugural Addresses of the Mayors of Boston* (2 vols., Boston, 1894), I, 195.

8. January 6, 1840, *ibid.*, I, 244; Lemuel Shattuck, *Report to the Committee of the City Council Appointed to Obtain the Census of Boston for the Year 1845* (Boston, 1846), 125; *Boston Pilot*, February 25, 1843; *Christian Watchman*, XXIII (January 21, 1842), 4.

9. *Report of the Annual Visiting Committee of the Grammar and Writing Schools of Boston for 1846* (Boston, 1846), p. 34; *BSR, 1847* (Boston, 1847), pp. 55-56.

10. For example, see Boston Common Council, "Committee Report on Foreign Paupers," *Boston City Documents, 1852*, Doc. No. 30.

11. *BSR, 1853* (Boston, 1853), pp. 20-21.

12. Isabella Lucy Bird, *The Englishwoman in America* (1856; reprinted, Madison, 1966), p. 436; *Christian Review*, XVIII (July 1853), 457.

13. "Immigration: Its Evils and Their Remedies," pp. 264, 268, 274-76; "The Morals of Statistics," *New Englander*, XIII (May 1855), 189-91. For a similar view about schools in New York City, see George B. Cheever, *Right of the Bible in Our Public Schools* (New York, 1854), pp. 111-13, 225.

14. Edward Everett Hale, *Letters on Irish Emigration* (Boston, 1852), p. 57; *BSR, 1853*, pp. 13-15.

15. E. C. Wines, *Hints on a System of Popular Education* (Philadelphia, 1838), p. 92; Mann, quoting from his *Ninth Annual Report* in his *CSJ*, VIII (June 1, 1846), 166-67.

16. "The Proposed Substitution of Sectarian for Public Schools, *CSJ*, X (June 1, 1848), 168; Horace Mann, *Fifth Annual Report of the Board of Education, Together with the Fifth Annual Report of the Secretary of the Board* (Boston, 1842), pp. 78-120.

17. William B. Fowle, "Preventive Teaching," ms. in *Fowle Papers*, MHS, dated August, 1857. Whether the paper in the ms. form was ever published is not certain, but it did contain sentiments which Fowle stated in public on numerous occasions.

18. Edward Everett, "Boston Public Schools," *Eclectic Magazine*, LX (September 1863), 68-70; reprinted from *Boston Daily Advertiser*.

19. *CSJ*, III (January 1841), 248; cf. Mann on education as "the balance-wheel of the social machinery," *Twelfth Annual Report, 1848* (Boston, 1849), p. 59.

20. *BSR, 1847,* pp. 54-55; *Officer's Report in Relation to Truant Children,* in *BCD, 1852,* Doc. No. 58.

21. James G. Carter, *Letters to the Hon. William Prescott, LL.D. on the Free Schools of New England, with Remarks upon the Principles of Instruction* (Boston, 1824), pp. 32-47; Theodore Edson, "On the Comparative Merits of Private and Public Schools," American Institute of Instruction *Proceedings, 1857* (Boston, 1824), pp. 93-107; Theodore R. Sizer, ed., *The Age of the Academies,* No. 22, *Classics in Education* (New York, 1964), pp. 1-49; Charles Bulfinch, "Report to the School Committee," October, 1817, printed in Joseph M. Wightman, comp., *Annals of the Boston Primary School Committee, From Its First Establishment in 1818, to Its Dissolution in 1855* (Boston, 1860), pp. 23-26; George H. Martin, *The Evolution of the Massachusetts Public School System: An Historical Sketch* (New York, 1923), p. 28; J. P. Wickersham, *A History of Education in Pennsylvania* (Lancaster, Pa., 1886), pp. 263-64; W. O. Bourne, *History of the Public School Society of the City of New York* (New York, 1870), from an 1805 "Address of the Trustees of the 'Society for Establishing a Free School in the City of New York, for the Education of such Poor Children as do not Belong to, or are not Provided for by, any Religious Society.'"

22. Printed in Wightman, *Annals,* p. 26.

23. See reports, *ibid.,* pp. 44, 60-61, 143, 18-19, 53-54.

24. *Ibid.,* p. 67; *Report of the School Committee of the City of Boston on the State of the Schools. May, 1826* (Boston, 1826), "Schedule B."

25. Arthur Wellington Brayley, *Schools and Schoolboys of Old Boston* (Boston, 1894), p. 51.

26. Wightman, *Annals,* pp. 74, 297-98.

27. Joseph Tuckerman, *The Principles and Results of the Ministry-at-Large in Boston* (Boston, 1838), pp. 98-100, 151-57; *Elevation of the Poor,* pp. 111-39; *Seventh Semi-Annual* (1831), pp. 10-15; *First Annual Report of the Minister-at-Large* (Boston, 1827), pp. 13-14; *Prize Essay on the Wages Paid to Females* (Philadelphia, 1830), pp. 43-45, 47-49. As a member of the Primary School Board in the late 1820's Tuckerman pressed the need for special schools adapted to the educational requirements of children of the poor and immigrant classes. See Wightman, *Annals,* pp. 22-27, 102-3.

28. "Report of the Sub-Committee to the Primary School Board, April 25, 1820," printed in Wightman, *Annals,* pp. 53-54, 55.

29. On Fowle, see Scott H. Paradise, "William Bentley Fowle," in Allen Johnson and Dumas Malone, eds., *Dictionary of American Biography* (11 vols., Subscription ed., New York, 1959), III, Part II, 561-62; *Barnard's American Journal of Education,* XXIV (June 1861).

30. Joseph Lancaster, *The Lancastrian System of Education, with Improvements* (Baltimore, 1821); William Russell, *Manual of Mutual Instruction* (Boston, 1826); "Memoir of Joseph Lancaster," *BAJE,* XXIV (June 1861),

355-62; David Salmon, *Joseph Lancaster* (London, 1904), pp. 7-19, the only "recent" biography of this influential man.

31. Clinton quoted in "Memoir of Joseph Lancaster." See also *Journal of the New York Senate and Assembly*, II (Albany, 1819), 903; Edward A. Fitzpatrick, *The Educational Views and Influence of DeWitt Clinton*, No. 44, *Teachers College Contributions to Education* (New York, 1911); Salmon, *Joseph Lancaster*, pp. 46-65; Joseph J. McCadden, "Joseph Lancaster and the Philadelphia Schools," *Pennsylvania History*, III (October 1936), 225-39; John S. Brubacher, "John Epy Lovell," *DAB*, VI, Part I, 440, for experiments in New Haven.

32. Lancaster, quoted in Edgar W. Knight and Clifton L. Hall, eds., *Readings in American Educational History* (New York, 1951), p. 134; Lancaster to his Daughter Elizabeth, Richmond, Virginia, 10 mo 28—1819, reprinted, *ibid.*, p. 140.

33. "Semi-Annual Report of the Standing Committee to the Primary School Committee, April 20, 1824," reprinted in Wightman, *Annals*, p. 91; *ibid.*, pp. 89, 95.

34. *Ibid.*, pp. 103-4; *BAJE*, XXIV (June 1861), 716; *Report of a Sub-Committee* (1828), pp. 20-21; Timothy L. Smith, "Protestant Schooling and American Nationality, 1800-1850," *Journal of American History*, LIII (March 1967), 683-87.

35. *Report of a Sub-Committee* (1828), pp. 21, 22-25, 30-32.

36. Ms. minutes of the Boston School Committee, bound in volumes in Rare Book Room, BPL, I (1815-36), February 21, 1828. See also "Semi-Annual Report of the Standing Committee to the Primary School Committee, April 21, 1829," in Wightman, *Annals*, p. 116; Brayley, *Schools and Schoolboys*, pp. 101-2; Josiah Quincy, *Farewell Address to the Common Council* (Boston, 1828); Ebenezer Bailey, *Review of the Mayor's Report* (Boston, 1828).

37. Memoir of William Winchester Hubbard, quoted in Brayley, *Schools and Schoolboys*, p. 216; "Common Schools," *NEM*, III (September 1832), 197-98.

38. *Free Enquirer*, May 22, 1829; Joseph J. McCadden, "Joseph Lancaster and Philadelphia," *PH*, IV (January 1937), 6-20; Mann, *Seventh Annual Report, 1843* (Boston, 1844), p. 60, quoting the boast of Dr. Andrew Bell, chief English rival of Lancaster in promotion of monitorial schools.

39. "Report of the Common Council, December 8, 1837," *BCD, 1837*, Doc. No. 17; Brayley, *Schools and Schoolboys*, pp. 108-9.

40. "Report of the Sub-Committee on Intermediate Schools, 1838," reprinted in Wightman, *Annals*, pp. 173-74.

41. Brayley, *Schools and Schoolboys*, pp. 110-11, Wightman, *Annals*, p. 210.

42. *BSR, 1847*, pp. 53-62.

43. "O.H.W.," "Report on Lowell Schools," *CSJ*, III (December 15, 1841), 375-76. See also Samuel Dickinson, *Boston Almanac for 1841* (Boston, 1841), pp. 116-17, on Catholic-staffed and attended public schools.

44. *BSR, 1856* (Boston, 1856), p. 8.

45. There had been several private infant schools in Boston as early as 1816. See Elwood P. Cubberly, *Public Education in the United States* (rev. ed., Cam-

bridge, Mass., 1934), pp. 137-41. See also Laura Fisher, "The Kindergarten," *U.S. Bureau of Education, Report of the Commissioner, 1903* (Washington, D.C., 1905); C. P. Dozier, "History of the Kindergarten Movement in the United States," *Education Bi-Monthly* (April 1908); Douglas E. Lawson, "Corrective Note on the Early History of the American Kindergarten," *Educational Administration and Supervision, Including Teacher Training,* XXV (1939), 699-703; *AJE,* III (1828), 346, 454, 572, 689; IV (1829), 8. Cf. *AAE,* I (1831), 582; IV (1834), 402; VI (1836), 170; VII (1837), 258, 281.

46. Will S. Monroe, *History of the Pestalozzian Movement in the United States* (Syracuse, 1907); Maris A. Vinovskis and Dean May, "A Ray of Millennial Light: Early Education and Social Reform in the Infant School Movement in Massachusetts, 1826-1840," unpublished paper in author's possession.

47. "Report of the Boston Infant School Society, by the Committee of Arrangements," and "Fifth Annual Report of the Infant School Society of the City of Boston. Instituted April 8th, 1828," both lengthily excerpted in *AAE,* III (July 1833), 300-303; quotation from the latter report, p. 303. See also *AJE,* III (1828), 346-48; Wightman, *Annals,* p. 124.

48. "Fifth Annual Report of the Infant School Society," pp. 302-3.

49. "Report of the Boston Infant School Society," pp. 302, 300.

50. "Report," in Wightman, *Annals,* p. 125.

51. *Ibid.,* p. 126. For criticism, see *AAE,* III (July 1833), 298-304. Cf. appeals for infant schools for the poor in *Ladies' Magazine,* III (November 1830), 224, and V (April 1832), 182.

52. Lawson, "Corrective Note on . . . American Kindergarten," 699-703.

53. Monica Kiefer, *American Children Through Their Books, 1700-1835* (Philadelphia, 1948), p. 139. Cf. Johnson, *Old-Time Schools;* John A. Nietz, *Our Textbooks* (Pittsburgh, 1961); Ruth Miller Elson, *Guardians of Tradition: American Schoolbooks of the Nineteenth Century* (Lincoln, Neb., 1964); Samuel G. Goodrich, *Recollections of a Lifetime* (2 vols., New York, 1856), II, 380-89; E. Douglas Branch, *The Sentimental Years, 1836-1860* (New York, 1934), pp. 109-11.

54. For brief biographies of Worcester, Fowle, and Pierpont, see the *DAB;* for Bumstead, see his *Papers,* MHS; for Holbrook, see the *DAB,* the *AJE,* III (1828), 753-58, and Cecil B. Hayes, *The American Lyceum; Its History and Contribution to Education,* U.S. Office of Education *Bulletin,* No. 12 (Washington, D.C., 1932); on Abbott, especially the use of his book *The Child at Home,* see Horace Mann to Frederick A. Packard, Boston, March 18, 1838, *Mann Papers,* MHS. For discussion of school texts to be used, see, for example, "Semi-Annual Report . . . Primary School Committee . . . 1824," in Wightman, *Annals,* p. 86; "Report of the Standing Committee of Primary Schools, January 10, 1833," *ibid.,* pp. 138-40; "Report on Books," *BCD, 1847,* Doc. No. 21.

55. *Report of the School Committee . . . May, 1826,* p. 9; see annual and semi-annual reports reprinted in Wightman, *Annals* (1820, 1824, 1828), pp. 57, 86-87, 113.

56. *SCM,* I (1815-36), December 1, 1829, December 7, 1830.

57. Willard S. Elsbree, *The American Teacher: Evolution of a Profession in*

a Democracy (New York, 1939), p. 224; "Report of the Primary School Board, January 18, 1833," reprinted in Wightman, *Annals*, pp. 137-40; and, *ibid.*, pp. 143-44.

58. *Remarks on the Seventh Annual Report of the Hon. Horace Mann, Secretary of the Massachusetts Board of Education* (Boston, 1844); "Mr. Mann and the Teachers of the Boston Schools," *North American Review*, LX (January 1845), 224-46; William B. Fowle, *The Scholiast Schooled. An Examination of the Review of the Reports of the Annual Visiting Committees of the Public Schools of the City of Boston, for 1845* (Cambridge, Mass., 1846), p. 31.

59. *BSR, 1846*, pp. 30-32.

60. "School Books," *BCD, 1847*, Doc. No. 38, pp. 6-7, 9-15. Cf. George B. Emerson, "Report on Books," *ibid.*, Doc. No. 21.

61. *BSR, 1848* (Boston, 1848), p. 22.

CHAPTER 11

1. *The Report of the Annual Examination of the Public Schools of the City of Boston, 1848* (Boston, 1848), p. 22.

2. John D. Philbrick, *Second Semi-Annual Report of the Superintendent of Public Schools of the City of Boston* (Boston, 1861), pp. 27-28. The best account of the beginnings of the manual labor school movement is still Charles A. Bennett, *History of Manual and Industrial Education up to 1870* (Peoria, Ill., 1926).

3. *BSR, 1848*, p. 22; *BSR, 1847* (Boston, 1847), pp. 53-55. Emerson's explanation relied upon the subjective evaluations by himself and fellow townsmen of the "visibility" of the strangers in their midst. The anxiety felt by many Boston leaders about the increase in foreign immigration spilled over into the issue of school attendance and made the problem appear even worse than it was. For comments on "visibility," see Chapter 9, *supra*.

4. Joseph M. Wightman, *Annals of the Boston Primary School Committee, From Its First Establishment in 1818, to Its Dissolution in 1855* (Boston, 1860), pp. 175-76.

5. The claim about the quality of residents came from Samuel Gridley Howe in "South Boston Memorial," *Boston City Documents, 1847*, Doc. No. 18, p. 11. See also "New School at South Boston," *BCD, 1847*, Doc. No. 32; and poem quoted in Thomas C. Simonds, *History of South Boston; Formerly Dorchester Neck, Now Ward XII of the City of Boston* (Boston, 1857), pp. 145, 145-47.

6. Edward Twisleton, *Evidence as to the Religious Working of the Common Schools of the State of Massachusetts, with a Preface* (London, 1855), p. 9.

7. "Semi-Annual Report of the Executive Committee of the Primary School Board, March 6, 1849"; *ibid.*, "1852"; and, "Thirty-Fifth Annual Report of the Executive Committee of the Primary Schools, City of Boston, 1853," in *School Reports* (1848-49; 1852-53), III, Suffolk, Essex, Middlesex Counties, MSA.

8. "Resignation Letter of Alvan Simonds, March 2d, 1852," in Wightman, *Annals*, p. 247, also pp. 232, 249; *BSR, 1853*, p. 9.

9. *BSR, 1849* (Boston, 1849), pp. 27-28; *BSR, 1850* (Boston, 1859), pp. 32, 36-37.

10. *BSR, 1852* (Boston, 1852), p. 26; *Report of the Committee on Public Instruction Respecting the Consolidation of Grammar Schools* (May 1852), in *BCD, 1852*, Doc. No. 27.

11. The best description of the Irish famine and of its results for America is, Cecil Woodham-Smith, *The Great Hunger: Ireland 1845-1849* (New York, 1962). The quotation from the *Boston Transcript* appeared on p. 242.

12. *BSR, 1848*, p. 22. See also Roger Lane, *Policing the City: Boston, 1822-1885* (Cambridge, Mass., 1967), pp. 3-117 *passim*.

13. *BSR, 1846* (Boston, 1846), p. 34.

14. For a perceptive discussion of this, see Barbara M. Solomon, *Ancestors and Immigrants: A Changing New England Tradition* (Cambridge, Mass., 1956), esp. pp. 43-81.

15. Jesse Chickering, *Report of the Committee . . . and A Comparative View of the Population of Boston in 1850, with the Births, Marriages, and Deaths, in 1849 and 1850* (Boston, 1851), pp. 14-15; *BSR, 1846*, p. 34.

16. *BSR, 1849*, p. 29; *Report and Tabular Statement of the Censors . . . State Census of Boston, May 1, 1850. Also, a Letter from Jesse Chickering, M.D. in Reference to the Same*, in *BCD, 1850*, Doc. No. 42, pp. 39-40. The problem of keeping up with residential mobility, particularly that of the foreign and poor populations, drew the attention of School Committee members in 1846, see *BSR, 1846* pp. 125-26.

17. *BSR, 1850*, pp. 32, 36-37.

18. "A Boston Public School Twenty Years Ago," *The Knickerbocker, or New-York Monthly Magazine*, LI (April 1858), 397; *BSR, 1849*, p. 28.

19. *Primary Schools. Quarterly Report, June 4, 1850*, in *BCD, 1850*, Doc. No. 15, pp. 7-8.

20. Ms. minutes of the Boston School Committee, bound in volumes in Rare Book Room, BPL, V (1850-54), October 21, 1851.

21. *BSR, 1850*, pp. 29-30.

22. "Minutes of the Board, July 16, 1819," in Wightman, *Annals*, p. 53; "Semi-Annual Report . . . 1824," *ibid.*, 83-85.

23. Joseph Tuckerman, *First Annual Report of the Minister-at-Large* (Boston, 1827), pp. 12-13; Tuckerman, *The Elevation of the Poor* (Boston, 1874), pp. 127-29; *Proceedings of the Boston School Committee, 1831* (Boston, 1831).

24. *Boston Herald*, March 13, 1887, quoted in Lane, *Policing the City*, p. 10; *Report of the Standing Committee of the Common Council on the Subject of the House of Reformation for Juvenile Offenders* (Boston, 1832).

25. Arthur Wellington Brayley, *Schools and Schoolboys of Old Boston* (Boston, 1894), p. 109; Charles Fox to Hon. H. G. Otis, October 7, 1831, reprinted, *ibid.*, p. 110.

26. *Boston Daily Evening Transcript*, December 15, 1837; Brayley, *Schools and Schoolboys*, p. 109; *SCM*, I (1815-36), March 8, 1836.

27. Edward Everett, "Address of His Excellency, 1836," *Massachusetts House Documents, 1836*, Doc. No. 6, pp. 5-6.

28. *Massachusetts Senate Archives*, No. 8074, reprinted in John R. Commons, et al., eds., *A Documentary History of American Industrial Society* (10 vols., Cleveland, 1910-11), V, 57; *Boston Evening Transcript*, March 24, 1832; *Boston Free Enquirer*, June 14, 1832, in Commons, *Documentary History*, V, 195-99.

29. Harriet Robinson, *Loom and Spindle, or Life Among the Early Mill Girls* (Boston, 1898), pp. 25-37, 40. Cf. Lucy Larcom, *A New England Girlhood, Outlined from Memory* (Boston, 1889), pp. 153-59.

30. *Massachusetts House Documents, May 17, 1836*, "Committee Report on the Education of Working Children, 1836," Doc. No. 49, pp. 5-14; *Acts and Resolves of the General Court of Massachusetts, 1836*, Chapter 245. See also Charles Persons, "The Early History of Factory Legislation in Massachusetts," in Susan M. Kingsbury, ed., *Labor Laws and Their Enforcement* (New York, 1911), pp. 1-129. Similar debates on child labor and similar legislation occurred at the same time in New York City and state. See Jay Marvin Pawa, "The Attitude of Labor Organizations in New York State Toward Public Education, 1829-1890" (unpublished Ed.D. dissertation, Teachers College, Columbia University, 1964). For general discussion, see Forest C. Ensign, *Compulsory School Attendance and Child Labor* (Iowa City, 1921), pp. 30-45. On obedience to the law, see Horace Mann, *Third Annual Report of the Board of Education. Together with the Third Annual Report of the Secretary of the Board* (Boston, 1840), pp. 41-42. Educational journals welcomed the new law as a step in the right direction. For example, see *American Annals of Education*, VI (May 1836), 222-23.

31. *Boston Daily Times*, July 16, 1839; Mann, *Third Annual Report*, p. 43; *Massachusetts House Documents, 1840*, Doc. No. 21, pp. 41-42; Mann, *Sixth Annual Report, 1842* (Boston, 1843), pp. 20-23; Frederick A. Packard, *Thoughts on the Condition and Prospects of Popular Education in the United States* (Philadelphia, 1836), pp. 15-16.

32. "Report on Truancy," *BCD, 1846*, Doc. No. 18, pp. 2-3, and *passim*; an address by Quincy, quoted in *Common School Journal*, X (June 15, 1848), 178. Quincy believed that "the State has a right to compel parents to take advantage of the means of educating their children."

33. John D. Philbrick, "Supplementary Report on Truancy and Compulsory Education," *BSR, 1861* (Boston, 1861), pp. 213-14.

34. *BSR, 1848*, p. 23; Horace Mann to the Honorable Josiah Quincy, Jr., January 31, 1848, printed in *CSJ*, X (June 15, 1848), 179.

35. *Primary Schools. Quarterly Report . . . 1850*, p. 8; *BSR, 1849*, pp. 31-32.

36. *BSR, 1846*, pp. 125-26.

37. Philbrick, "Supplementary Report on Truancy," pp. 221-22; *SCM*, IV (1846-49), November 15, December 20, 1848.

38. "Truants from School," *BCD, 1849*, Doc. No. 9, pp. 7-8.

39. Lane, *Policing the City*, p. 69; "Truants from School," p. 3; *Annual Report of the Police Department of the City of Boston by the City Marshal*, in *BCD, 1851*, Doc. No. 5, pp. 26-31.

40. Philbrick, "Supplementary Report on Truancy," p. 224; *BSR, 1848*, p. 23; *Acts and Resolves . . . 1850*, Chapter 294.

41. Lane, *Policing the City*, p. 62.

42. *Acts and Resolves . . . 1852*, pp. 170-71. Other states followed suit during the 1860's and 1870's. See *Report of the U.S. Commissioner of Education, 1888-1889* (2 vols., Washington, D.C., 1889), I, 471.

43. Accounts of Boston legislation appeared in Nathan Bishop, *Third Annual Report of the Superintendent of Public Schools of the City of Boston* (Boston, 1853), pp. 71-73; and, *BSR, 1853*, pp. 22-25. Trends in arrests and convictions are best followed in "Report of the Common Council," *BCD, 1834*, Doc. No. 9; "Reports of the Inspectors of the State Prison" (1830-45) in yearly volumes of the *Massachusetts Senate Documents*; and beginning in 1851 the *Annual Report of the Police Department of the City of Boston*, printed in BCD.

44. *Massachusetts House Documents, 1851*, Doc. No. 14, pp. 24-25; "Officers' Reports in Relation to Truant Children," *BCD, 1852*, Doc. No. 58; "Reports of Truant Officers, July, 1853," *BCD, 1853*, Doc. No. 55, p. 5; Philbrick, *Second Semi-Annual Report*, p. 27. The imprecision of records does not allow school-by-school comparisons of changes in attendance, so that the effect of the new laws on immigrant attendance is difficult to measure. Still, the reports of truant officers and the few scant figures for particular schools announced from time to time by the School Committee appear to indicate that the laws did have an initial impact of increasing immigrant attendance. One historian of compulsory attendance throughout the state estimated that the laws remained ineffective until after revision in 1873, but he clearly knew little of the Boston experience. See John William Perrin, *The History of Compulsory Education in New England* (Meadville, Pa., 1896), pp. 54-55, 57-71.

45. Joseph Tuckerman, *Prize Essay on the Wages Paid to Females* (Philadelphia, 1830), pp. 44-45; "Report of the Commissioners of the State Manual Labor School," *Massachusetts Legislative Documents, Senate, 1847*, Doc. No. 10, pp. 39, 42, 55, an important source for the special problems of delinquents in towns and cities of the state.

46. Daniel J. Boorstin, *The Lost World of Thomas Jefferson* (1948; reprinted, Boston, 1960), pp. 204-12; R. W. B. Lewis, *The American Adam: Innocence, Tragedy, and Tradition in the Nineteenth Century* (Chicago, 1955), pp. 13-27. Thoreau, quoted in Lewis, p. 26. For Alcott, see his "Orphic Sayings," *The Dial* (July 1840), nos. V, XXI; and, Charles Strickland, "A Transcendentalist Father: The Child-Rearing Practices of Bronson Alcott," *Perspectives in American History*, III (1969), 5-73, esp. 20-29.

47. Mann characterized himself, with his usual lack of humility, as an evangelist of common education, "a postrider from county to county looking after the welfare of children"; Horace Mann to Lydia Mann, July 16, 1837, *Mann Papers*, MHS. See also Mann, *Tenth Annual Report, 1846* (Boston, 1847), pp. 126-29. Mann direly predicted that "they who refuse to train up children in the way they should go, are training up incendiaries and madmen to destroy property and life, and to invade and pollute the sanctuaries of society." He was equally convinced that public education was "one of the steps in the transfer of prop-

erty from a present to a succeeding generation." See *The Massachusetts System of Common Schools; Being an Enlarged and Revised Edition of the Tenth Annual Report of the First Secretary of the Massachusetts Board of Education* (Boston, 1849), p. 32, and pp. 16-32, *passim*. For a cogent summary of Mann's views on stewardship, see Horace Mann to Honorable Josiah Quincy, Jr., Mayor of Boston, West Newton, January 31st, 1848, in *CSJ*, X (June 15, 1848), 178-82. For general discussion of the current attitudes on stewardship, see Clifford S. Griffin, *Their Brothers' Keepers: Moral Stewardship in the United States, 1800-1865* (New Brunswick, 1960).

48. *Ninth Annual Report, 1845* (Boston, 1846), pp. 68, 94-96.

49. Mann, *First Annual Report, 1837* (Boston, 1838), p. 49; *Ninth Annual Report*, p. 64; Mann, *Journal*, May 27, 1837, *Mann Papers*, MHS; *Twelfth Annual Report, 1848* (Boston, 1849), p. 43; *Ninth Annual Report*, p. 68, and pp. 64-70, *passim*.

50. Mann's estimates came in a circular he sent to other prominent educators, seeking their approbation of his views. The answers which he received demonstrated how widely held were his views, or, perhaps, how carefully he selected his sample. See *Eleventh Annual Report, 1847* (Boston, 1848), p. 56, and pp. 49-70, *passim*, for replies.

51. "Special Preparation a Prerequisite to Teaching," a lecture delivered in 1838, reprinted in Mary Mann and George Mann, *Life and Works of Horace Mann* (5 vols., Boston, 1891), II, 96; *Tenth Annual Report*, p. 232.

52. "Gov. Brigg's Annual Message to the Massachusetts State Legislature," quoted in *CSJ*, X (February 1, 1848), 40.

53. *Lectures Delivered Before the American Institute of Instruction . . . Montpelier, Vt., August, 1849* (Boston, 1850), pp. 184-85; cf. Brooks, "Moral Education, the Best Methods of Teaching Morals in Common Schools," *Barnard's American Journal of Education*, I (March 1856), 336, 336-44, *passim*. Brooks had held these views at least since the 1830's. See Brooks, *Elementary Instruction. An Address Delivered Before the Schools and the Citizens of the Town of Quincy, July 4, 1837* (Quincy, 1837), p. 11, and *passim*. See also "Immigration: Its Evils and Their Remedies," *New Englander*, XIII (May 1855), 275; *ibid.*, XVI (1858), 854. An excellent general account of religious support for common schools is Francis X. Curran. S. J., *The Churches and the Schools: American Protestantism and Popular Elementary Education* (Chicago, 1954).

54. *BSR, 1853*, pp. 21, 22, 22-25.

55. *Boston Pilot*, April 24, 1852, January 1, 1853; Sister M. Agnes McCann, *The History of Mother Seton's Daughters* (2 vols., New York, 1917), II, 73-75; G. F. Haskins, *Reports, Historical, Statistical, and Financial of the House of the Angel Guardian* (Boston, 1864), pp. 4-5.

56. In 1854 Horace Mann's successor, Barneas Sears, asserted that more Catholic parents would send their children to public schools if the Protestant Bible was not in use. See *Eighteenth Annual Report of the Board of Education, with the Eighteenth Annual Report of the Secretary of the Board of Education* (Boston, 1854), p. 66.

57. *Reports of the Record Commissioners of Boston* (1789), "Education Act of 1789"; see Chapter 1, *supra*. See also Hugh J. Nolan, *The Most Reverend Francis Patrick Kenrick, Third Bishop of Philadelphia, 1830-1851* (Philadelphia, 1948), pp. 294-311; *Address of the Roman Catholics to Their Fellow Citizens of the City and State of New York* (New York, 1840); *Boston Pilot*, February 12, April 23, 1853. Arguments pro and con on Bible reading in the schools are dealt with in William Kailer Dunn, *What Happened to Religious Education? The Decline of Religious Teaching in the Public Elementary School, 1776-1861* (Baltimore, 1958), esp. pp. 117-303.

58. McCann, *Mother Seton's Daughters*, II, 75; Richard J. Quinlan, "Growth and Development of Catholic Education in the Archdiocese of Boston," *Catholic Historical Review*, XXII (April 1936), pp. 28-34; *Boston Pilot*, November 16, 1839; January 27, 1849; April 16, 1853; July 30, 1853; November 18, 1854.

59. *Boston Pilot*, December 13, 1851; November 26, 1852; *BSR, 1853*, pp. 19-20; cf. "The Catholics and the School Question," *Christian Review*, XVIII (July 1853).

60. Henry F. Durant, *Defence of the Use of the Bible in the Public Schools. Arguments of Henry F. Durant, Esq. in the Eliot School Case* (Boston 1859), quotes from pp. 25, 43; and, an excellent summary of the Eliot School Case in Robert H. Lord, et al., *History of the Archdiocese of Boston in the Various Stages of Its Development, 1604 to 1943* (3 vols., New York, 1944), II, 587-601.

61. Philbrick, *Second Semi-Annual Report*, p. 21.

Index

Abbott, John S. C., 58, 274
Abolitionism, 41, 83, 157, 163, 172, 175, 176, 178, 180-84, 186-87, 194-95, 198, 200, 202-6
Adams, Abigail, 8
Adams, Charles Francis, 40
Adams, Henry, 12
Adams, John, 8, 9, 12, 13-14, 201
Adams, John Quincy, on assimilation, 230
Adams, Sam, on education in Boston, 12-13, 40
Addams, Jane, 209
Address to the Workingmen of New England, on the State of Education, and on the Condition of the Producing Classes in Europe and America, An, 232; *see also* Luther, Seth
African Baptist Church, 161, 164, 199
African Grand Lodge of Masons, 161
African Sabbath School, 164
Agnosticism, in Boston, 63-64
Alcott, Bronson, 60, 64, 179, 271, 303
Alcott, William A., 52, 74, 75, 91; *Essay on the Construction of Schoolhouses,* 90
Alden, Joseph, 52
Almshouse, 24, 25, 228, 238
American Annals of Education, 85, 90, 126, 229, 232, 254
American Institute of Instruction, 58, 64, 74, 128
American Journal of Education, 53, 118, 254, 271
"American System of Manufacturing," 103-4, 131
Americanization of immigrants, 170, 230, 236, 257-77, 279, 284, 288, 290; *see also* Education, formal; Immigrants; Irish
Ames, Fisher, 3, 11, 12, 13

Andrews, Christopher C., 251
Annual Reports of the Boston School Committee, 47, 67, 68, 71, 116, 118, 140, 214, 256-57, 276, 278, 286, 288, 306
Appeal in Favor of That Class of Americans Called Africans, An, 180-81; *see also* Child, Lydia Maria
Appeal to the Coloured Citizens of the World, 174-75; *see also* Walker, David
Appleton, Nathan, 106
Apprenticeship, educational importance of, 23, 31, 47; decline of, 47
Armstrong, Samuel, 27, 39
Assimilation, *see* Americanization; Education, formal; Immigrants; Irish
Association of Boston Schoolmasters, 138, 275-76
Austro-Hungarians, 212, 259

Baltimore, 210, 265
Bancroft, George, 73, 126
Baptists, 62, 139, 235, 256
Barnard, Henry, 191
Barrett, Samuel, 75
Bascom, William, 167, 171, 172
Bates, Samuel, 258, 284
Beecher, Catherine, 51
Beecher, Lyman, 51, 61, 62, 235, 255
Belknap, Jeremy, 160
Bellow, Hosea, 83
Benjamin (3), xiii
Bentham, Jeremy, 144
Bigelow, John P., 64, 298, 300
Bingham, Caleb, 16, 264
Bird, Isabella Lucy, 257
Bishop, Nathan, 99, 103, 130, 131, 151-53; reports by, as first Superintendent of Boston Public Schools, 81, 280

"Black Power," 158

Blacks, 157-206, 251; attendance at school of, 165-66, 168; boycott of public schools by, 198-99; complaints by, about educational opportunities, 159, 166, 168, 184; drive for integrated schools by, 176-206; education to improve condition of, 169-71, 191; educational desires of, 159-60; enrollment of, in schools, 159, 160; Equal School Rights Committee formed by, 203; fear of racial amalgamation with, 179, 192; integration of, in schools, 205-6; militants, 157-58, 172, 176, 195, 206; no legal segregation of, 159, 162, 187, 189, 201, 205; occupations and employment of, 159, 166, 181; petitions by, for school integration, 184-87, 191, 194, 197-200; poor relief for, 159; population size of, in Boston, 159, 167, 189; primary schools for, 164-65; private and public funds support school segregation of, 162-64; private schools organized by, 161-62, 164; relations between immigrants and, 193-94, 205-6; request by, for segregated schools, 160-61; residential location of, 29, 161, 188; segregated schools for, 32, 69, 158, 161-62, 165, 189-90; stereotype of, 179; teachers in schools of, 162, 164-67, 172, 185-86, 191; white teachers reactions to, 160; see also Abolitionism; Jim Crowism; Know-Nothings; Pindall, Edward; Prejudice, racial; Segregation, in schools, racial; Smith School

Boston Associates, 103

Boston Asylum for Indigent Boys, 243, 250

Boston Board of Health Commissioners, 146

Boston Caucus, 6

Boston City Council, reports by on poverty, juvenile delinquency, and public schools, 221, 245, 265-66, 269, 275-76, 286, 293-94, 297-98, 301

Boston Columbian Centinel, 36

Boston Daily Advertiser, 38

Boston, Federalists in, 11, 12, 33, 40, 180, 231, 253

Boston Female Anti-Slavery Society, 183

Boston Female Society for Missionary Purposes, 27

Boston Investigator, 63

Boston Pilot, 205, 206, 256, 306, 307

Boston Recorder, 235

Boston School Committee, 39, 47, 67, 68, 70, 80, 89, 97, 143, 166, 214, 229, 256, 260, 278, 284, 286, 288, 296, 300, 307-8; authority of, 19, 37, 41, 105-7, 109, 116-25, 132, 140-41, 145, 148, 152, 162-68, 171-72, 185-86, 283, 297-98, 300-302; early prototype of, 6; issue of local control and, 20, 36, 40, 116, 119-28, 131, 137, 144, 145, 148-53, 172, 279, 291, 300; organization of, 19-20, 32, 40-41, 138, 140, 142, 145, 152; social composition of, 20-21, 40, 96, 133-36, 139, 140

Boston Society for the Moral and Religious Instruction of the Poor, 27-30, 33, 164, 261

Boston Times, 148

Boston Transcript, 286

Bowditch, Henry I., 186, 194, 206

Bowen, Francis, 72

Briggs, Governor, 305

Brigham, William, 140, 149

British America, 215

Broad Street Riot, 240-41

Brooks, Charles, 64, 96, 305

Brooks, John, 56

Brougham, Henry Peter, 271

Brownson, Orestes A., 147, 233

Bulfinch, Charles, 21, 32-36, 38, 41, 134

Bumstead, Josiah, 274

Bureaucratization of school system, 133, 145-53; see also Public schools, organization of

Burton, Warren, 22

Bushee, Frederick A., 211

Bushnell, Horace, 49, 52; Christian Nurture, author of, 49, 50

Byrd, William, 6

Calhoun, John C., 201

Calvinism, 39, 48, 49, 61, 63

Cambridge (Mass.), 82, 113, 197, 220

Canterbury (Conn.), 178

Carey, Mathew, 26

Carter, James G., 70, 71, 74, 76, 80, 261, 295; Essays Upon Popular Education, 75

Catholic Church, 47, 63, 235, 256; hostility toward, in Boston, 210, 234-36, 240-41, 251, 255; immigrants in, 235, 256; Irish in, 63, 235-36, 306; public school attendance of children in, 268-69, 283, 306-8; see also Eliot School Case

Chalmers, Thomas, 227
Chandler, Pelig W., 194, 201
Channing, William Ellery, 39, 48, 62, 64, 163, 181, 226, 233, 242
Chapin, Edwin H., 57, 58
Chapman, Jonathan, 256
Charitable societies, 31, 43, 62-63, 243; listing of, in Boston, 250
Charity schools, 7, 25-26, 31, 33, 37, 39, 43, 279
Charlestown (Mass.), 5, 197, 220, 240
Chase, George Wingate, 189
Chelsea (Mass.), 82, 226
Chickering, Jesse, 189, 226
Child, David, 180-82, 184
Child, discovery of the, 48-55, 118, 242, 295, 302
Child, Lydia Maria, 180, 181, 183, 184
Child labor, problems of in city, 3, 27, 117, 159, 245, 248; increase of in factories, 232, 294-96
Child-rearing, 51-53
Children, age distribution of in city, 23, 32-33, 42, 43, 110, 189, 282, 298-99; "binding-out" of, 245-46; health of, 92-100; impact of city life upon, 10, 54, 58-59, 74, 92-94, 242-43, 250; juvenile delinquency among, 242-48; literature for, 51-52; numbers of immigrant, in schools, 282-89; ownership of, 302-9; see also House of Reformation
Christian Nurture, 49-50
Christian Register, 235
Christian Review, 144, 257
Christian Watchman, 59, 235, 256
Christopher (5), xiii
Civil Rights, for Blacks, 158, 194, 201, 203
Clark, Dr. Henry G., 96, 97
Clark, Jonas W., 197, 198
Clergy, 6, 51, 64-65, 136, 256, 305
Cleveland, Charles, 27
Clinton, DeWitt, 264
Cobb, Lyman, 52
Coffin, Joshua, 178
Cogswell, Joseph, 126
Colburn, Warren, 74, 75
Colver, Rev. Nathaniel, 59
Combe, George, 53
Common School Journal, 67, 68, 129, 135, 149, 229, 259
Community, sense of, in Boston, 73-74, 114-15, 135, 206, 210-11, 234, 309
Companion to Spelling Books, The, 73
Compulsory attendance, 291, 296-302;

legislation for, 279, 300-301, 305, 308
Congregationalists, 48, 62, 235
Connecticut, 6, 178
Cony, Daniel, 11
Cooke, McLaurin F., 307
Cooke, Rev. Parsons, 62
Coolidge, Rev. James I. T., 140, 149
Cooper, James Fenimore, 73
Cotton, John, 8
Crandall, Prudence, 178
Crane, Ichabod, 74
Crime, in Boston, 216, 237-39, 241-42, 248, 255, 301
Crisis, perceptions of, 209, 224, 226, 227, 232-33, 241; see also Urban crisis
Crockett, Davy, 73
Cultural pluralism, 230
Cutural shock, 214
Cushing, Caleb, 58
Cutler, Pliny, 27

Dalton, Thomas, 206
Dames' schools, 24, 32, 161, 261
Davis, Rev. James, 27
Dawes, Thomas, 20, 39, 134
Dedham (Mass.), 5, 61
Derby, Elias H., 225
DeWitt, Francis, 110
Dickens, Charles, 116
Diderot, Denis, 201
Disease, in city, 94-95, 146, 161, 221, 242, 286, 289
District schools, 75-79, 82, 90
Dodge, Allen W., 147
Dorchester (Mass.), 5, 113
"Double-headed system," 107
Douglass, Frederick, 180
Downing, Colonel Jack, 73
Durant, Henry C., 308; see also Eliot School Case
Dwight, Theodore, 49
Dwight, Timothy, 61, 114

Easton, Hosea, 179
Education, formal, moral goals of, 4, 8-10, 13-14, 20-21, 22, 29-30, 44, 99, 108, 253-54, 291, 307; social insurance offered by, 253-61, 309;; use of, to assimilate immigrants, 29, 113-14, 251, 252-53, 261-77, 279, 284, 288, 290, 309; see also Social institutions; Social order
Education, informal in city, 59, 74, 92-93

Education Act of 1789, in Boston, 11, 14-24, 105, 133, 261
Edwards, Jonathan, 61
Eliot, Samuel A., 92, 169, 237
Eliot School Case, 307-8
Emerson, Frederick, 147, 169
Emerson, George B., 59, 65, 67, 74, 128, 129, 130, 132, 138, 150, 153, 191, 248, 256, 269, 270, 279, 280; *The School and the Schoolmaster* co-authored by, 75, 96
Emerson, Ralph Waldo, 64, 73, 104, 130, 177, 195, 236, 242, 303
Emerson, William, 161
England, 4, 47, 81, 212, 215, 225
English (people), 212, 215
Environmentalism, attitudes of as explanation of social pathology, 28, 242-43; assumptions of, about ideal physical settings, 55, 82; *see also* Rural ideal
Essay on the Construction of Schoolhouses, 90
Ethnic groups, in Boston, 212, 215; *see also* Immigrants; Population
Everett, Edward, 72, 137, 233, 259, 260, 294

Factory, child labor in, 294-96; model for school organization, 103-6, 116, 125-26, 130-31, 132, 151; organization of, 103
"Factory mentality," 104, 116, 130-31
Family, the, 55-60; centrality of, in society, 55-56; changes in role of as social institution, 47, 56-57, 65-66; educational role of, 3, 6, 56-67; impact of city life upon, 57-59;; public school replaces, 66-68, 69
Farley, Stephen, 71, 74
Farm School, 250
Fenwick, Bishop Benedict, 235
Fertility rates, in city, 288-89
Fink, Mike, 73
Finney, Charles G., 62
Fisher, John D., 85, 90
Fletcher, Justice Richard, 202-3
Fort Hill area, 221-22, 264, 284, 289
Foster, Charlotte, 165
Fowle, William B., 53, 58, 60, 148, 149, 150, 259, 264, 265, 274, 276; *The Companion to Spelling Books*, 73; "Preventive Teaching," 259
Fowler, Orson S., 53
Fox, Charles, 293
France, 215, 225

Francis, Lydia Maria, *see* Child, Lydia Maria
Franklin, Benjamin, 51, 88
Franklin (Mass.), 75
Freedom's Journal, 173
Freeman, Dr. James, 21, 134
French (people), 160, 212, 215

Gannet, Ezra S., 230
Garrison, William Lloyd, 158, 174, 175, 177, 178, 180, 183, 184, 203, 205, 206; *see also* Abolitionism
General Colored Association of Massachusetts, 198
Georgia, state of, 175
Germans (people), 212, 215, 251, 290
Germany, 126, 212, 215
Girls, attendance of at Boston schools, 14-15, 117-19; attitudes about education of, 14-15, 25, 117-18
Gloucester Journal, 26
Godey's Lady's Book, 50
Goodrich, Samuel G., 52, 74-76, 274; *see also* "Peter Parley"
Gould, Benjamin A., 136
Graded school, the, arguments in favor of, 127-29; early types of classification, 107-9, 125; intellectual origins of, 126-28; introduction of, in Boston, 129-31; *see also* Prussia
Graham, Sylvester, 55
Grammar schools, changed definition of in 1820's, 107; curricula of, 5, 105; *see also* Public schools
Grant, Moses, 85, 263
Graves, Rev. H. A., 139
Great Britain, *see* England
Griscom, John H., 126
Gymnasium, 126

Hale, Edward Everett, 83, 108, 258
Hall, John, 51
Hall, Primus, 161
Hall, Samuel R., 52
Happy Home, 50
Harris, Sarah, 178
Haskins, Father G. F., 306
Haven, Rev. Samuel, 6
Hawthorne, Nathaniel, 104
Henchman, Daniel, 263
Hillard, George H., 136
Holbrook, Josiah, 52, 274, 275
Holland, 215
Holmes, Oliver Wendell, 137
Home (popular novel), 56
Home economics, 51

Homes, Henry, 27
Hopkins, Rev. John D., 68
House of Correction, 243, 248, 297
House of Industry, 224, 228, 237-38, 248
House of Reformation, 227, 243-49, 263, 292, 293, 297, 301, 302
Howe, Samuel Gridley, 63, 71, 128-30, 138-50, 186
Humphrey, Heman, 49, 52
Hunt's Merchants' Magazine, 225
Huse, Charles Phillips, 80

Illiteracy, 23, 25, 28, 30, 42; *see also* Literacy
Immigrants, assimilation of, 230-31, 256; attendance at public schools of, 254, 279, 282-91, 301, 306, 308; numbers of, in Boston, 3, 212-15; rise in city's crime rate attributed to, 237-39, 241-42, 248, 255; *see also* Children; Poor, the; Population; Social order
India, Boston schools like caste system of, 157, 201
Indigence, *see* Poor, the
Individualism, social perceptions of, 65-66, 302-4
Industrialization, 3, 104, 131, 211, 281
Industry, in Boston, 220, 228; *see also* Manufacturing
Infant Education; or Remarks on the Importance of Educating the Infant Poor, from the Age of Eighteen Months to Seven Years, 271
Infant schools, 271-74, 279
Intemperance, as indicator of poverty, 223, 226-27, 236-37, 239
Intermediate schools, 165, 268-71, 279, 293
Ipswich (Mass.), 5
Irish (people), arrests and convictions of, 301; attendance of, in public schools, 283, 284, 286, 289, 297-98, 308; burden of, on poor relief, 238; drunkenness of, 229, 239, 289; economic conditions of, 214; group conflict and, 239-41; numbers of, in city, 212, 214-15, 224, 281, 286; opposition among, to public schools, 306-8; political opposition to, 139, 231-32; refusal of, to Americanize alleged, 241, 251, 255; relations between Blacks and, 193, 194, 205-6, 239-40; segregated schools for, 268-71; settlement patterns of, in city, 32, 217-23,

250; stereotype of, 229, 243; *see also* Catholic Church; Eliot School Case; Immigrants; Intemperance; Poor, the; Riots
Italians (people), 212, 215

Jackson, Andrew, 63, 73, 231
Jackson, Charles, 250
Jackson, Edmund, 194, 206
Jackson, Francis, 184, 206
Jackson, Thomas, 39
Jacksonian Democrats, 139, 147, 149, 231
Jefferson, Thomas, 209, 231
Jews, in city, 251
Jim Crowism, 187
Jocelyn, Simeon S., 178
Jones, John Coffin, 21
Judson, Andrew T., 179
Juvenile delinquency, *see* Children
Juvenile Miscellany, 52, 180

Kent (Conn.), 6
Kindergarten, *see* Infant schools
Kirkland, Rev. John T., 161
Kneeland, Abner, 63-64
Knights, Peter, 217
Know-Nothings, 204-6

Labaree, Benjamin, 60, 64
Labor force, in city, 3, 113, 159, 214, 217, 220, 226, 228, 232, 241, 281, 284; *see also* Child labor
Ladd, William, 39
Ladies' Magazine, 50
Lancaster, Joseph, 264-66
Lathrop, Dr. John, 117-18, 121
Latimer, George, as runaway slave in Boston, 186
Lesslie, Rev. George, 234
Lewis, Joseph, 263
Liberator, The, 177, 194, 195, 198; *see also* Garrison, William Lloyd
Literacy, need for and training of in the city, 7, 10, 15, 18-19, 23-24, 26, 35, 42, 105, 173; *see also* Illiteracy
Local control, issue of relating to public schools, 106, 114-25, 131, 133, 168, 185, 190, 279; *see also* Boston School Committee; Primary School Board
London (England), 5, 7
Loring, Edmund G., 96, 130, 138, 150, 248, 256, 276
Lowell, Francis Cabot, 103, 106
Lowell (Mass.), 157, 187, 270, 295
Lundy, Benjamin, 174

Luther, Seth, 232
Lyman, Theodore, Jr., 182, 183, 255

McCulloch, George P., 126
Maine, state of, 225
Mann, Horace, 50, 53, 54, 55, 56, 60, 63-68, 74-76, 78, 90, 92-94, 96, 118, 128-30, 135-41, 143, 147-50, 153, 186, 191, 195-96, 229-33, 240, 241, 259, 260, 268, 270, 275-76, 296, 297, 298, 303-4; *Annual Reports* as first Secretary of the Massachusetts Board of Education, quoted, 53, 54, 122, 127, 138, 195, 233, 259, 275, 304; *Report on Schoolhouses*, 96; see also Teachers, criticism of; Association of Boston Schoolmasters
Manual training, see Public schools
Manufacturing, in city, 24, 35, 47, 113, 281; see also Industry
Martineau, Harriet, 63, 75
Massachusetts Board of Education, 54, 96, 137, 147-48; issue of centralization and, 147-48
Massachusetts constitutions, constitution of 1780, 8, 9, 61, 201; constitution of 1820, 61
Massachusetts, state of, 4, 7, 8, 10, 12, 64, 96, 103, 126, 133, 138, 179, 187, 198, 201, 225, 235, 236, 247, 253, 257, 276, 294, 296, 305
Mathematics, need for training in commercial city, 15, 16, 18, 19, 22, 35
Mather, Cotton, 6, 209
May, Samuel J., 39, 184, 196
Mechanics, as social class, 225; see also Social classes
Mechanistic philosophy, 103-4
Melville, Herman, 73
Memoir . . . to the American Convention for Promoting the Abolition of Slavery, A, 163
Methodists, 62, 235
Ministers, see Clergy
Minot, George R., 13, 21, 134
Minot, William, 157, 169, 171
"Mob," see Riots
Monitorial schools (Lancastrian), 264-68, 279
Morris, Robert, 201
Morse, Jedidiah, 161, 236
Morse, Samuel Finley Breese, 235, 236, 255
Mortality rates, in city, 288-89
Morton, Marcus, 147
Mother's Assistant, 50

Nantucket (Mass.), 198
Native American Party, 139; *see also* Know-Nothings
Neale, Rollin H., 140, 149
Negroes, *see* Blacks
Neighborhood schools, principle of, 35, 42, 114-17, 119-25, 131, 132; *see also* Boston School Committee; Local control; Primary School Board
Nell, William C., 184, 197, 203, 205, 206
New Bedford (Mass.), 157, 197
New England, 5, 26, 48, 51, 56, 58, 60, 61, 68, 71, 73, 75, 76, 79, 96, 104, 127, 130, 212, 225, 232, 234, 247, 269, 275, 295, 309
New England Anti-Slavery Society, 178, 203
New England Association of Farmers, Mechanics, and Other Working Men, 294
New-England Magazine, 267
New England Primer, 16-17
New Englander, The, 257, 305
New Hampshire, 225
New Haven (Conn.), 74, 178, 265
New Jersey, 225
New York, state of, 225, 264
New York City, 5, 6, 57, 146, 166, 173, 177, 178, 198, 210, 243, 244, 261, 265, 266, 267, 306
New York City Free School Society, 264-65
Newburyport (Mass.), 18, 39
"Nigger Hill," 161
"Nigger seat," 160
"Niggerology" (abolitionism), 193
North American Review, 74, 136
North Carolina, state of, 172, 175
North End, of Boston, as zone of transition, 31-32
Northampton (Mass.), 126

Ohio, state of, 127
Oliver, Henry J., 32, 224
Oliver, Henry K., 69
Oliver, Peter, 13
Original Sin, doctrine of, 28, 48-49, 242
Otis, Harrison Gray, 7, 8, 33, 40, 41, 61, 175, 180, 231, 293
Overseers of the Poor, in Boston, 20, 23, 24, 34, 37, 39, 214, 216, 226, 246

Packard, Frederick A., 255
Parents, change in social performance

of, 27, 38, 58-60, 67, 296; duties of, 35, 50; ownership of the child by, 36, 106, 304-6

Parent's Magazine, 50

Parker, S. D., 248

Parker, Theodore, 64, 184, 206, 229, 233, 238, 242, 243, 251

Parks, Dr. Luther, 205

Parlor Magazine, 50

Parsons, Theophilus, 140, 148, 150

Paul, Rev. Thomas, 164

Paul, Thomas (son of Rev. Thomas Paul), 199

Pauperism, in city, 24, 36, 216, 229, 238, 246, 253, 255, 291; definitions of, 226-29, 242; increase in ranks of, 226; Society for the Prevention of, 238, 243; urban, and class structure, 210; *see also* Poor, the; Poverty; Social classes

Peabody, Elizabeth, 55

Pemberton, Thomas, 109, 111

Pennsylvania, 225

Pestalozzi, Johan Heinrich, 271

"Peter Parley" (Samuel G. Goodrich), stories by, 52

Philadelphia, 5, 6, 14, 26, 79, 146, 178, 198, 210, 244, 261, 265, 267, 274, 306

Philbrick, John D., 54, 100, 129, 152, 278, 280

Phillips, Caleb, 7

Phillips, Wendell, 135, 157, 158, 180, 195, 196, 206

Phrenology, 53-54

Physical education, 53

Physiology, 53

Pierpont, John, 274

Piety, teaching of in schools, 4, 6, 9, 22, 65

Pike, Nicholas, 18

Pindall, Edward, 204

Playgrounds, 53, 83, 94, 100

Polish (people), 212

Political parties, in Boston, 6, 139, 147, 149, 157, 204-6, 231, 234; *see also* individual party names

Poor, the, as urban caste, 209, 228, 229, 251; attitudes about as threat to society, 25, 27-28, 37, 214, 216, 231-42, 254; concern about education of, 25, 28, 113-14, 261-77, 294; identification of, 24, 216-17; immigrants as part of, 24, 214, 223-24, 229-31, 238, 253; increase in numbers of, in city, 24, 212-15; investigations of, 27, 32,

37, 216, 222, 227, 257; public responsibility for, 214-15, 254, 292, 302-6; residential location of, 220-23; residential mobility of, 217-18, 220, 250, 289; social mobility of, 217, 224-26; *see also* Education, Formal; Segregation, residential; Social order

Poor relief, 24, 34, 224, 227, 238, 250

Pope Day, in Boston, 234

Popery, assailed in Boston, 235, 307-8

Population, changes in composition of the, as related to school attendance, 256-57, 279-91; immigration and changes in composition of the, 212-13, 215, 217-20, 259; size of, in Boston, 211, 215; *see also* Blacks; Ethnic groups; Immigrants; nationality groups by name

Portland (Mass.), 39

Poverty, 24, 236, 238, 246, 256; culture of, 228, 251; definitions of, 209-10, 224, 226-29, 242; fear of, 210, 224, 252; possible permanence of, in city, 210, 224-31, 237; *see also* Pauperism; Poor, the; Social classes

Prejudice, racial, 159-60, 179-82, 192, 196, 199-200, 202

Presbyterians, 62, 235

Primary School Board, of Boston, 90, 152, 176, 274, 290; authority and responsibilities of, 41, 42, 43, 83, 85, 86, 91, 137, 164-65, 200, 262, 264-66, 269, 273, 275, 283, 292, 293; local control issue and, 41, 42, 167, 168, 185-95; organization of, 41, 136, 137, 138; social composition of, 41, 85, 136, 263, 283

Prince, James, 39

Private schools, 5, 14, 15, 23-24, 33, 34, 42, 69, 164, 261

Privatism, conflicting interpretations of public duty vs., 20-21, 30-31, 33, 35-36, 43, 116, 146, 162, 254, 263, 302-9

Professionalization; general movement toward, 141-45; urban municipal services and, 104, 146

Prostitution, 28, 216, 241, 286

Protestantism, in Boston, decline in institutional strength of, 47, 48, 63-66, 234-36; public schools as inculcators of, 255, 305, 307-8; *see also* individual denominations

Providence (Rhode Island), 79, 151, 178, 198

Prussia, 215; educational influence of, 126, 138

Prussian System of Public Instruction and Its Applicability to the United States, The, 127

Psychology, 242

Public schools, in Boston, attendance figures for, 7, 23, 32-33, 34, 70, 81, 109, 120-21, 279-80, 284, 286, 288, 296; class hours in, 16; community reflected in, 66-69, 72; concern over non-attendance of youth at, 24, 33, 291-300; contribution of State School Fund to, 80; districts of, 105-6; early definitions of, 5-6; financial profiteering in, 145-46; introduction of written examinations in, 128; manual training in, 42-43, 245, 278; Massachusetts law on, 4, 8-9, 10, 11; number of, in city, 5, 7, 32, 43, 69, 86, 152, 262, 264-65, 269, 283-84, 287; primary schools, 42, 43, 70, 81, 86, 109, 262-63, 279-80, 283-84; religious instruction in, 16-17, 43, 291, 306-8; replacement of family and church by, 66-68, 69; tax support for, 5, 6, 7, 8, 11, 23, 42, 44, 69-70, 79-81, 82, 86, 162, 165, 167-69, 261, 264-65, 269, 276, 294; use of Protestant Bible in, 17, 43, 260, 306-8; *see also* Blacks; Boston School Committee; Education Act of 1789; Education, Formal; Graded school; Immigrants; Irish; Poor, the; Population; Primary School Board; Social institutions; Social order

Public schools, list of, in Boston; Adams, 119-20, 123, 286; Bigelow, 281; Boston Latin School, 15, 16, 22, 32, 69, 83; Bowdoin, 119, 123, 266; Boylston, 94, 119, 120, 123, 266, 284, 289, 293; Brimmer, 286; Chapman, 204; Eliot, 119, 286, 307, 308; Endicott, 284, 286, 289; English High School, 69; Franklin, 88-89, 119-20; Hancock, 88, 119, 286; Hawes, 281; Johnson, 87, 88, 286; Lawrence, 99; Mather, 281; Mayhew, 119; Otis, 89, 286; Quincy, 130; Smith, 171, 182, 196-99, 204-6; Wells, 120, 121, 122, 123; Winthrop, 286

Public schools, organization of, in Boston, 106, 115; appointment of superintendent, 145-53; arguments against centralization in, 147-48; arguments for centralization in, 116, 119-20; oligarchy controls, 133-38; political struggles about, 139-41, 148-50; standardization in, 132-33; systematization, debates about in, 4, 12, 19, 33-36, 40, 44, 103, 105-53, 261, 281; *see also* Bureaucratization; Factory, model for school organization; Graded school

Puritanism, 8, 55, 212, 242; Boston as capital of, 5, 256, 308

Putnam, George, 187

Quincy, Josiah (Jr.), 150, 161, 231, 233, 296, 297, 298; (Sr.), 44, 146, 216, 224, 226, 227, 243, 265, 266, 293

Quincy Report, monitorial schools discussed in the, 265-66

Raikes, Robert, 26

Rantoul, Robert, 233

Reed, George, 292-93

Reed, William F., 301

Reform schools, 250, 301; *see also* House of Reformation

Religious press, in Boston, 59, 144, 235-36, 256-57

Report on the Distribution of Students (1837), 116-25

Residential patterns, changes in Boston's, 31-32, 82, 94, 109-13, 221, 250

Returns of the Overseers of the Poor in Massachusetts, see Overseers of the Poor

Rhode Island, state of, 79, 151, 198

Rich Men of Massachusetts, The, 225

Richmond (Va.), 265

Riots, in city, 8, 239-41

Roberts, Benjamin, 200, 201

Roberts, John H., 199

Roberts, Sarah, 200, 203

Roberts v. City of Boston, 157-58, 176, 200-203

Robinson, Ann, 246

Robinson, Edward, 246, 248

Robinson, E. W., 56

Robinson, Harriet, 295

Robinson, John, 246

Roman Catholicism, *see* Catholic Church

Round Hill School, 126

Rousseau, Jean Jacques, 94, 201

Roxbury (Mass.), 5, 82, 113, 197, 225, 240

Royall, Anne, 70

Rural ideal, nineteenth-century social thought about, 58, 72-75, 92-95, 100, 104, 250; *see also* Environmentalism

Rush, Benjamin, 14, 26
Russell, Charles T., 200
Russell, William, 118
Russwurm, John, 173

St. Louis, city of, 271
Salem (Mass.), 5, 39, 157, 187, 197, 202
Saunders, Prince, 163
Savage, James, 38, 39, 40, 41, 224, 262
Scandinavians (people), 212
School and the Schoolmaster, The, 75, 96
School Committee, see Boston School Committee
Schoolhouses and schoolrooms, description of rural, 76-77, 106; location of urban, 82-87, 94, 117, 123, 281-87; non-educational uses of, 87-90; size of urban, 83, 90, 96, 107; ventilation and construction of, 85, 88-92, 93, 95-100
Schools, see separate headings for dames'; infant; intermediate; monitorial; private; public; public schools, list of
Scotch (people), 161, 212, 215, 225
Sedgwick, Catherine, 56
Segregation, residential, 111-13, 220, 221-23, 281, 283-91
Segregation, in schools, ethnic, 268-71, 278, 281-91, 309; racial, 157-206; sexual, 117-25
Sewall, Samuel, 6
Shackford, Rev. Charles C., 140
Shattuck, Lemuel, 110, 211, 213, 219, 220
Shaw, Lemuel, 157, 201-3
Shurtleff, Nathaniel B., 211, 213, 215
Simonds, Alvan, 283, 284
Slums, 221-23, 255; see also Tenements
Smith, Abiel, 163, 169
Smith, Barney, 167
Smith, Thomas P., 199
Social classes, in Boston, consciousness of divisions among, 232-34, 243, 249, 252, 258-59, 271; structure of, 20-21, 24, 134-36, 216-17, 220-21, 225, 227, 233, 288, 289
Social control, 158
Social engineering, 255
Social geography, of Boston, 219-20, 221
Social institutions, perceptions of the changing nature of traditional, 55, 57-59, 62, 64-66, 303; public schools

and the preservation of, 4, 8, 66-68, 257-61; urban impact upon traditional, 55, 65
Social mobility, belief in, 224-26
Social order, city life and threats to, 209, 210, 216; immigrants as threat to, 210, 214, 224, 230-42; public schooling as a means to achieving, 3-4, 8, 9, 12, 25, 151, 252-53, 254-77, 290-91, 300, 303, 309; see also Blacks; Crisis, perceptions of; Education, formal; Irish; Pauperism; Poor, the; Poverty; Urban crisis, the
Society for the Prevention of Pauperism, in Boston, 238, 243
South America, 225
Southworth, Eden, 55
Spanish (people), 215
Spurr, Oliver H., 299
State Manual Labor School, 302
Stearns, Charles H., 136
Stewardship of wealth, concept of, 227, 303
Stith, William, 204
Stowe, Calvin, 127
Suburbanization, 82, 197, 289
Success, philosophy of, 133-34, 225
Sumner, Charles, 127, 135, 136, 138, 139, 157, 158, 176, 181, 186, 201, 202
Sunday schools, 26-30, 36, 43, 65, 164; relationship of, to public schools, 29-30
Superintendent of Public Schools, see Public schools, organization of
Sylvester, Elisha, 161

Tappan, Arthur, 178
Tappan, Lewis, 41
Tax Support for Education, see Public schools
Teachers, 76; criticisms of, 127-29, 138, 148-49, 275-76; duties of, as surrogate ministers, 9, 67-68, 69; general responsibilities of, 41, 106-7; hiring of, 5, 41; in loco parentis, 67, 69; private school, 7, 42; salaries of, 42, 165, 167; see also Association of Boston Schoolmasters; Blacks
Temple School, 179, 271
Tenements, 221, 243, 283; see also Slums
Textbooks, 16, 18, 253; moral and religious values in, 16-17, 43, 253; providing of, in schools, 262, 274; stereo-

types of Blacks and immigrants in, 179, 229; struggles over use of particular, 274-77; use of Protestant Bible as, 17, 43, 260, 307-8
Thatcher, George, 11
Thatcher, Peter O., 32, 40
Thayer, Gideon F., 54
Thayer, Rev. John, 234
Thoreau, Henry David, 73, 104, 209, 303
Thurston, William, 27
Ticknor, Elisha, 39, 41, 262
Ticknor, George, 53, 70, 73, 115, 126
Tileston, John, 22
Tocqueville, Alexis de, 179
Topographical and Historical Description of Boston, 109
Transcendentalism, 73, 179, 303
Truancy, attempts to combat in city, 291-302
Truant officers, 292, 293, 299, 300
Tuckerman, Joseph, 85, 209, 226-28, 243, 250, 255, 263, 292, 302; see also Poor, the, as urban caste; Poverty, possible permanence of, in city; Unitarians, ministry to the poor by
Tukey, Francis, 248, 298, 299
Twisleton, Edward, 283

Underground Railroad, Boston as way-station of, 206
Unitarians, 96, 235; growth of denomination in Boston, 48, 61-63; importance of the Dedham decision to, 61; ministry to the poor by, 85, 226-28, 263; see also Channing, William E.; Tuckerman, Joseph
Urban crisis, the, 209-10, 226, 227; see also Crisis, perceptions of
Urbanization, 3, 4, 21, 24, 73, 211
Ursuline Convent Riot, 240
Usher, John, 7

Ventilation, of schools, see Schoolhouses and schoolrooms
Virginia, state of, 225, 265
Voting, patterns of in city, 133-37, 231-32, 234, 253

Wait, Thomas B., 41
Wales (Great Britain), 215, 225

Walker, David, 172-75, 180, 181
Wall, Thomas, 307-8
Wall, William, 307
Waltham (Mass.), 103
Warner, Oliver, 189
Washburn, Emory, 236
Washington, George, 51
Washington, D. C., 265
Wayland, Francis, 198
Webster, Daniel, 40
Webster, Noah, 16, 56, 253; educational views of, 10-11, 14, 253; Elementary Spelling Book, 253
Wells, Thomas, 85
Welsh (people), 212, 215
West, Benjamin, 39
West, Rev. Samuel, 21
West Indies, 225
Westborough (Mass.), 250
Whig party, in Boston, 139, 147, 157, 231, 234
Whitney, Asa, 39
Whittier, John Greenleaf, 78, 177
Wiget, Father, 307
Wigglesworth, Edward, 135
Wigglesworth, Michael, 136
Wightman, Joseph, 197, 275
Wilberforce, William, 163
Wilderspin, Samuel, 271
William, Nathaniel, 52
Williams, Henry W., 184
Williams, John D., 39
Wilson, Henry, 206
Wines, E. C., 111, 258
Winslow, Hubbard, 225
Winthrop, John, 41
Winthrop, Thomas L., 41
Woodbridge, W. C., 85, 90, 250
Woodson, Miss, case of as teacher in Black schools, 185
Worcester, Joseph E., 274
Worcester (Mass.), 198, 301
Workingmen's party, in Boston, 234
Wright, Carroll D., 110, 211, 213
Wright, Ephraim M., 215
Writing schools, curricula of, 5, 105; see also Public schools

Year in Europe, 1818-1819, A, 126
Young, Rev. Alexander, 136
Youth's Companion, The, 52

Zion's Herald, 235